OXFORD**READERS**

The Oxford Readers series represents a unique interdisciplinary resource, offering authoritative collections of primary and secondary sources on the core issues which have shaped history and continue to affect current events.

Class
Edited by Patrick Joyce

Ethics
Edited by Peter Singer

Fascism
Edited by Roger Griffin

Nationalism
Edited by John Hutchinson and Anthony D. Smith

War
Edited by Lawrence Freedman

Forthcoming:

Aesthetics
Edited by Patrick Maynard and Susan Feagin

Anti-Semitism
Edited by Paul Lawrence Rose

Classical Thought
Edited by Terence Irwin

Feminism
Edited by Sandra Kemp and Judith Squires

Political Thought
Edited by Jonathan Wolff and Michael Rosen

Sexuality
Edited by Robert Nye

OXFORD **READERS**

Ethnicity

John Hutchinson is an Associate Professor in the Faculty of Humanities at Griffith University, Brisbane, where he teaches modern European history. He has specialized in the cultural and political history of Britain and Ireland, but his most recent book, *Modern Nationalism* (1994), explores a wide range of issues in the field of ethnicity and nationalism. He is also the author of *The Dynamics of Cultural Nationalism* (1987).

Anthony D. Smith is Professor of Sociology at the London School of Economics. He has specialized in the study of ethnicity and nationalism, especially the theory of the nation. His work has focused particularly on the historical and social origins of nations; he is the author of *Theories of Nationalism* (1971), *The Ethnic Revival* (1981), *The Ethnic Origins of Nations* (1986), *National Identity* (1991), and *Nations and Nationalism in a Global Era* (1995).

John Hutchinson and Anthony D. Smith have also edited the Oxford Reader on *Nationalism* (1994).

Advance praise for *Ethnicity*: 'a most worthy companion to their well-received and broadly adopted reader of nationalism . . . no major aspect of the subject has been overlooked.'

Walker Connor, author of *The National Question in Marxist–Leninist Theory and Strategy.*

OXFORD**READERS**

Ethnicity

Edited by

John Hutchinson *and* Anthony D. Smith

Oxford · New York

OXFORD UNIVERSITY PRESS

1996

Oxford University Press, Great Clarendon Street, Oxford OX2 6DP

Oxford New York
Athens Auckland Bangkok Bogota Bombay Buenos Aires
Calcutta Cape Town Dar es Salaam Delhi
Florence Hong Kong Istanbul Karachi
Kuala Lumpur Madras Madrid Melbourne
Mexico City Nairobi Paris Singapore
Taipei Tokyo Toronto

and associated companies in
Berlin Ibadan

Oxford is a trade mark of Oxford University Press

First published as an Oxford University Press paperback 1996

British Library Cataloguing in Publication Data
Data available

Library of Congress Cataloging in Publication Data
Ethnicity / edited by John Hutchinson and Anthony D. Smith.
p. cm. — (Oxford readers)
1. Ethnicity. 2. Ethnic relations—Political aspects. 3. Nationalism.
I. Hutchinson, John, 1949– . II. Smith, Anthony D. III. Series.
GN495.6.E8845 305.8–dc20 96–2791
ISBN 0–19–289274–6

10 9 8 7 6 5 4 3 2 1

Typeset by Pure Tech India Ltd, Pondicherry
Printed in Great Britain
on acid-free paper by
Bookcraft (Bath) Ltd.
Midsomer Norton
Avon

Preface

Ethnicity as a term and a subject of study is very recent. For at least 150 years liberals and socialists confidently expected the demise of ethnic, racial, and national ties and the unification of the world through international trade and mass communications. These expectations have not been realized. Instead, we are witnessing a series of explosive ethnic revivals across the globe. In Europe and the Americas ethnic movements unexpectedly surfaced from the 1960s and 1970s, in Africa and Asia they have been gaining force since the 1950s, and the demise of the former Soviet Union has encouraged ethnic conflicts and national movements to flourish throughout its territory. Since 1990 twenty new states based largely upon dominant ethnic communities have been recognized. Clearly, ethnicity, far from fading away, has now become a central issue in the social and political life of every continent. The 'end of history', it seems, turns out to have ushered in the era of ethnicity.

Since the 1960s scholars have increasingly come to appreciate the centrality of ethnic cleavages in the operation of states, but they have tended to underestimate the role of ethnicity as a regulative cultural and political principle in world affairs. There has also been a relative neglect of the deeper historical roots of ethnicity. A longer-term perspective reveals the significance of ethnic ties and sentiments in every period of recorded history, even when there are problems in interpreting their meaning and diffusion in our often-fragmentary records. It is these historical and comparative dimensions, and the shared memories and symbols through which they are activated, that lend to modern ethnic identities and antagonisms their peculiar passion and intensity, raising questions about the degree to which modernity, as is so often assumed, constitutes a radical break with the past.

These are some of the considerations that have led us to compile a Reader on Ethnicity, as a companion to our earlier volume on *Nationalism*. In fact, the present Reader should be seen as a sequel to the earlier volume, in so far as it focuses on the wider ethnic dimensions of societies and states that form the background to a world of nations and politics. The present Reader, while cross-cultural in range and extensive in scope, is not intended to cover every aspect of ethnic behaviour. We have deliberately excluded the influence of ethnicity on social policy and vice-versa, in such fields as education, employment, mobility, housing, and welfare, and have concentrated instead on the interrelationships of ethnicity, culture, and politics in the broadest sense. Neither have we included the vast sociological literature on the economic and cultural performance of selected ethnic communities, nor the many anthropological studies of the social and cultural features of ethnic groups in simpler societies. For the same reasons, and given the constraints of space, we have had to curtail severely the section on race and ethnicity, which has generated a huge literature and which clearly deserves a volume to itself.

The field of ethnicity is far more diffuse and ramified than that of nationalism, which has made the selection of contributions a far more complex and hazardous undertaking, given the inevitable limits to any scholar's acquaintance with so immense a field of enquiry. We apologize to the many scholars whose fine contributions we were unable to include, and we refer our readers to the Select Bibliography for each section. Even here we have been unable to acknowledge the many important works of scholarship in the field. The field of ethnic phenomena, like that of nationalism, is rapidly expanding and diversifying, and it is impossible to keep up with the vast literature on every aspect of ethnicity.

One of our concerns has been to keep some balance between the various geographical and cultural areas of the world, despite the heavy preponderance of scholarly literature on Europe and North America. We are conscious of this imbalance within certain sections, but have attempted to rectify it by including more work on ethnicity and politics in non-Western societies in the sections on religion and language, and on ethnic conflict and nationalism. We have tried to include many of the different concepts, approaches, and interpretations that divide scholars of ethnicity. As the reader will see, these are every bit as pervasive as in the study of nationalism. We have also followed a similar sequence of sections to that of *Nationalism*, modified to take account of the greater variety of the field of ethnic phenomena, so as to enable some measure of comparison between the contributions in the two volumes.

We would like to record our thanks to Diana Solano for helping to assemble the texts of the readings, and to Amor Vieira for handling the correspondence. We are also grateful to the readers for their initial comments on our draft. We are especially appreciative of the support and encouragement of George Miller and Rebecca Hunt of Oxford University Press.

John Hutchinson
Anthony D. Smith

London, February 1996

Contents

IV. Ethnicity in the Modern World

V. Ethnicity, Religion, and Language

VI. Race and Ethnicity

VII. Ethnic Conflict and Nationalism

List of Maps

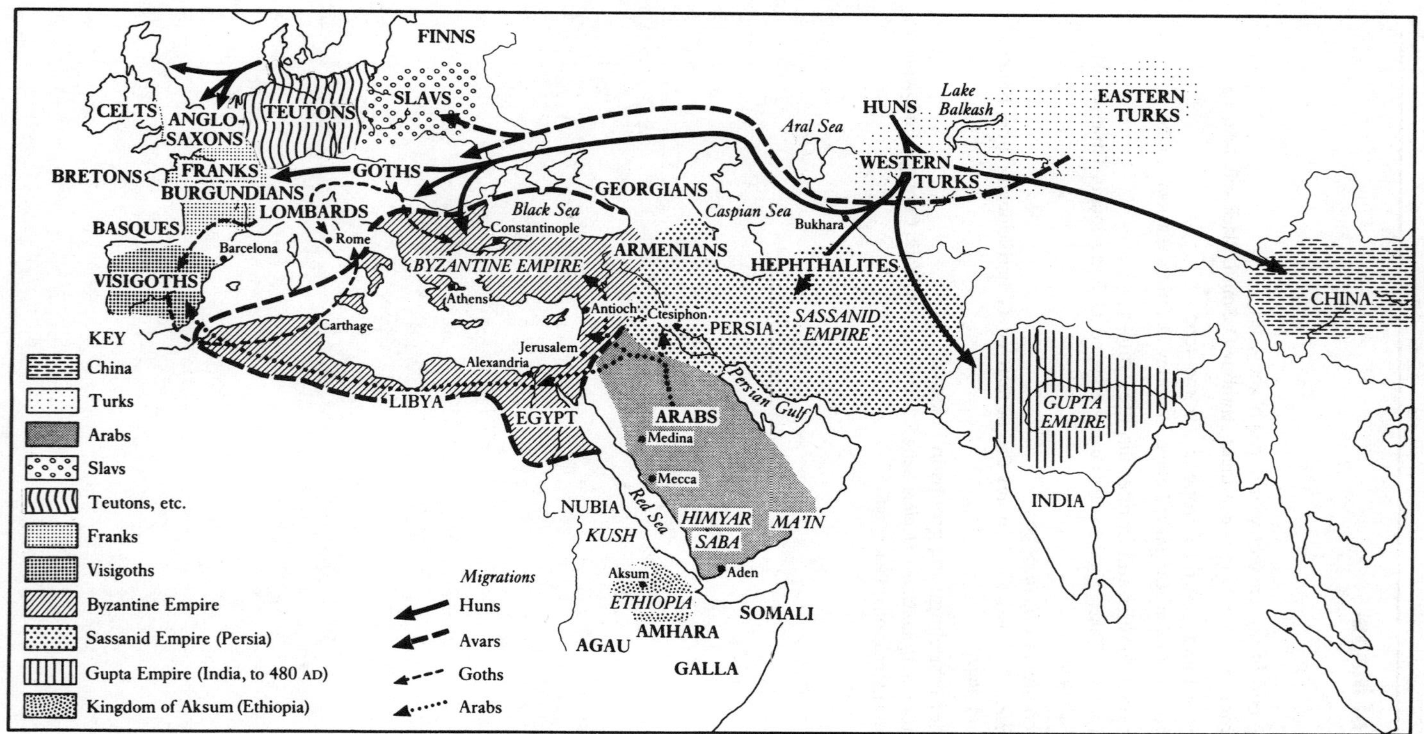

Map 1 The end of the ancient world, *c.*400–700 AD: empires, ethnic communities, and ethnic invasions

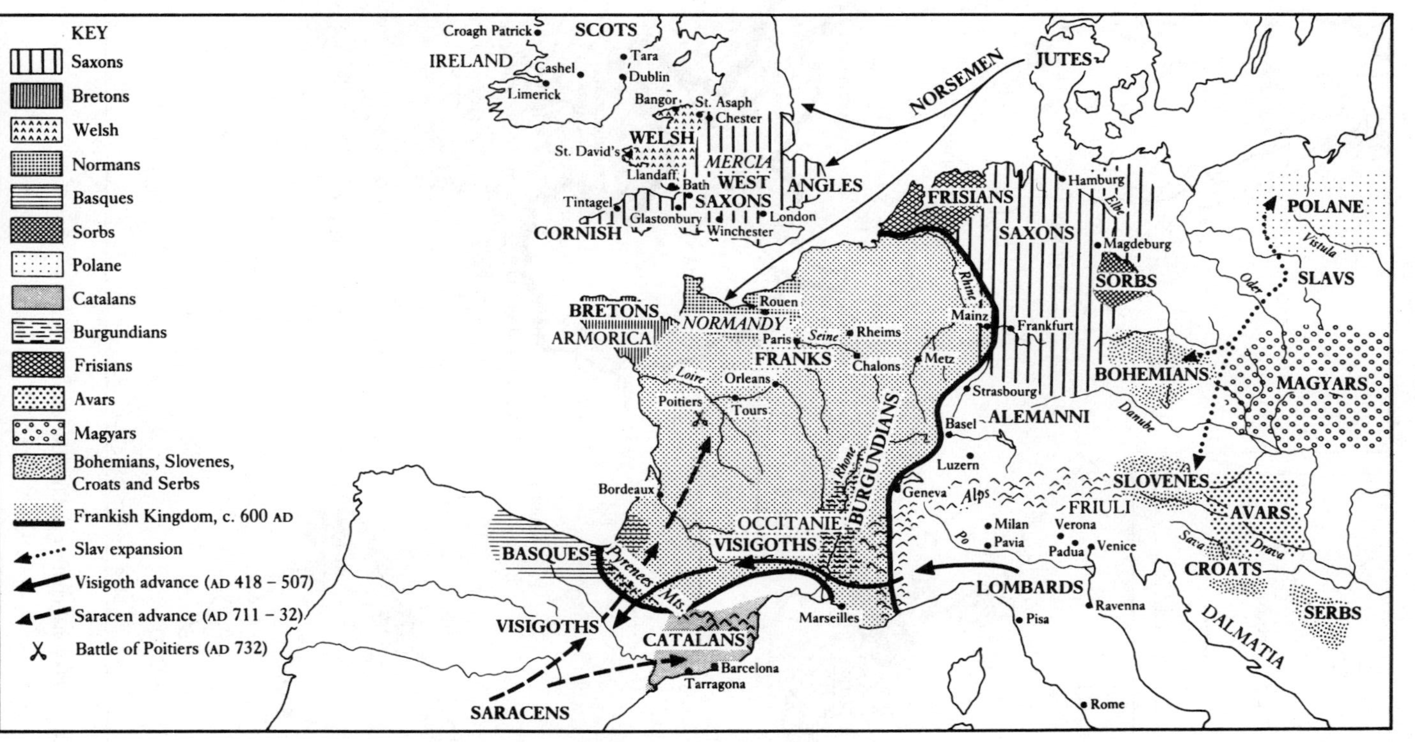

Map 2 Western and Central Europe, *c.*400–1000 AD: ethnic kingdoms and migrations

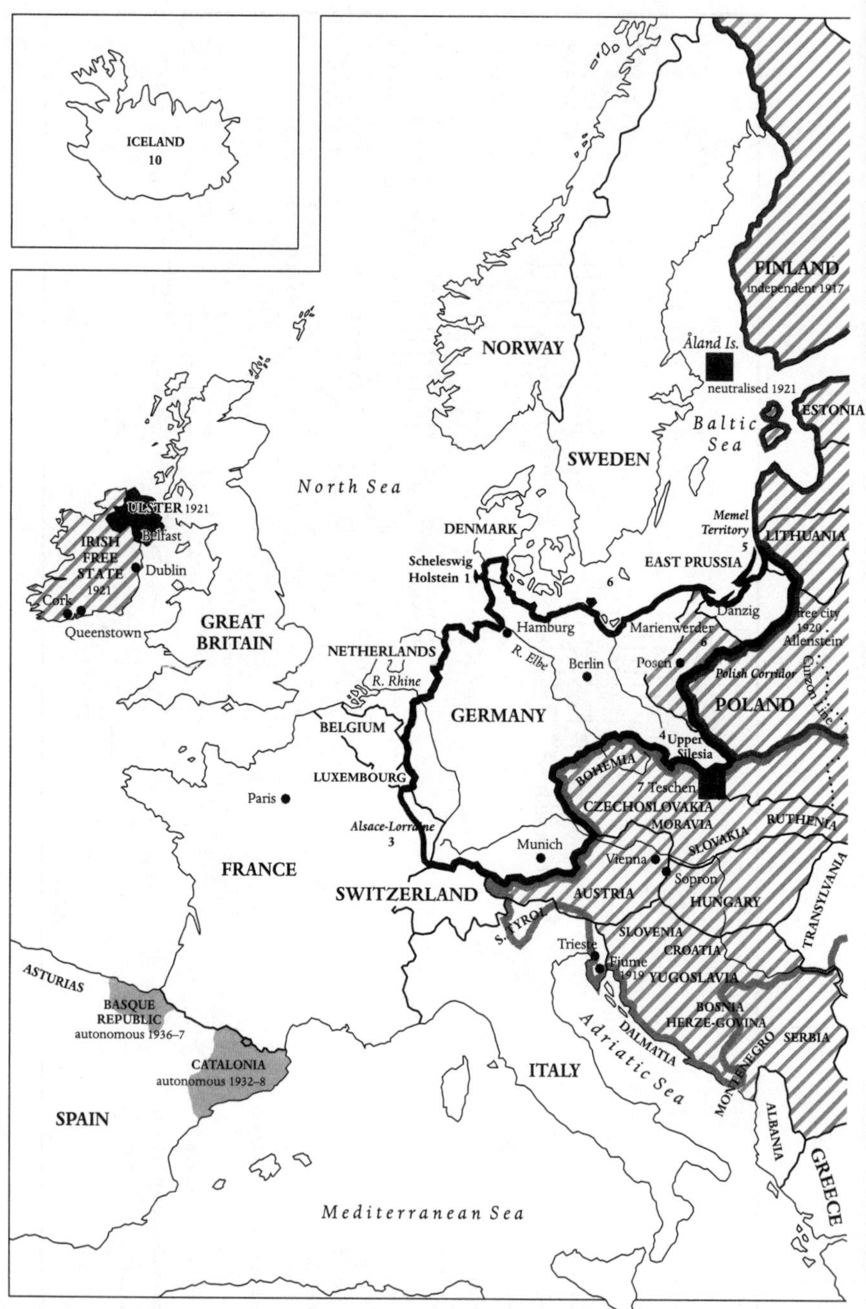

Map 3 National conflict and frontier disputes, 1919–34

Frontier of German Empire in 1914
Frontier of Austrian-Hungarian Empire in 1914
Frontier of Russian Empire in 1914
Post-settlement frontiers
New States
Areas of dispute
Areas temporarily autonomous or independent
1 Plebiscite Feb. 1920 divided between Denmark and Germany
2 League of Nations Mandate, by plebiscite to Germany 1935
3 To France 1919
4 Divided between Germany and Poland, plebiscite March 1921
5 Allied occupation 1920–3, annexed by Lithuania 1923, autonomous 1924
6 Marienwerder and Allenstein plebiscite for Germany July 1920
7 Partitioned between Czechoslovakia and Poland 1920
8 Annexed by Poland 1920, plebiscite for Poland 1922
9 To Greece from Bulgaria 1919
10 Independent, Personal Union with Denmark, 1918
LATVIA
Wilno (Vilna)
8
WHITE RUSSIA
independent 1919–21
UKRAINE
independent 1917–20
Caucasus Mts
Caspian Sea
BESSARABIA
ROMANIA
GEORGIA
independent 1918–21
AZERBAIJAN
independent 1918–20
DOBRUJA
R. Danube
Black Sea
ARMENIA
independent 1918–21
BULGARIA
Sofia
Adrianople
Greek occupied 1920–2
Macedonia
TURKEY
W. Thrace
9
Dodecanese
to Italy 1912
Alexandretta
to Syria 1920,
to Turkey 1939

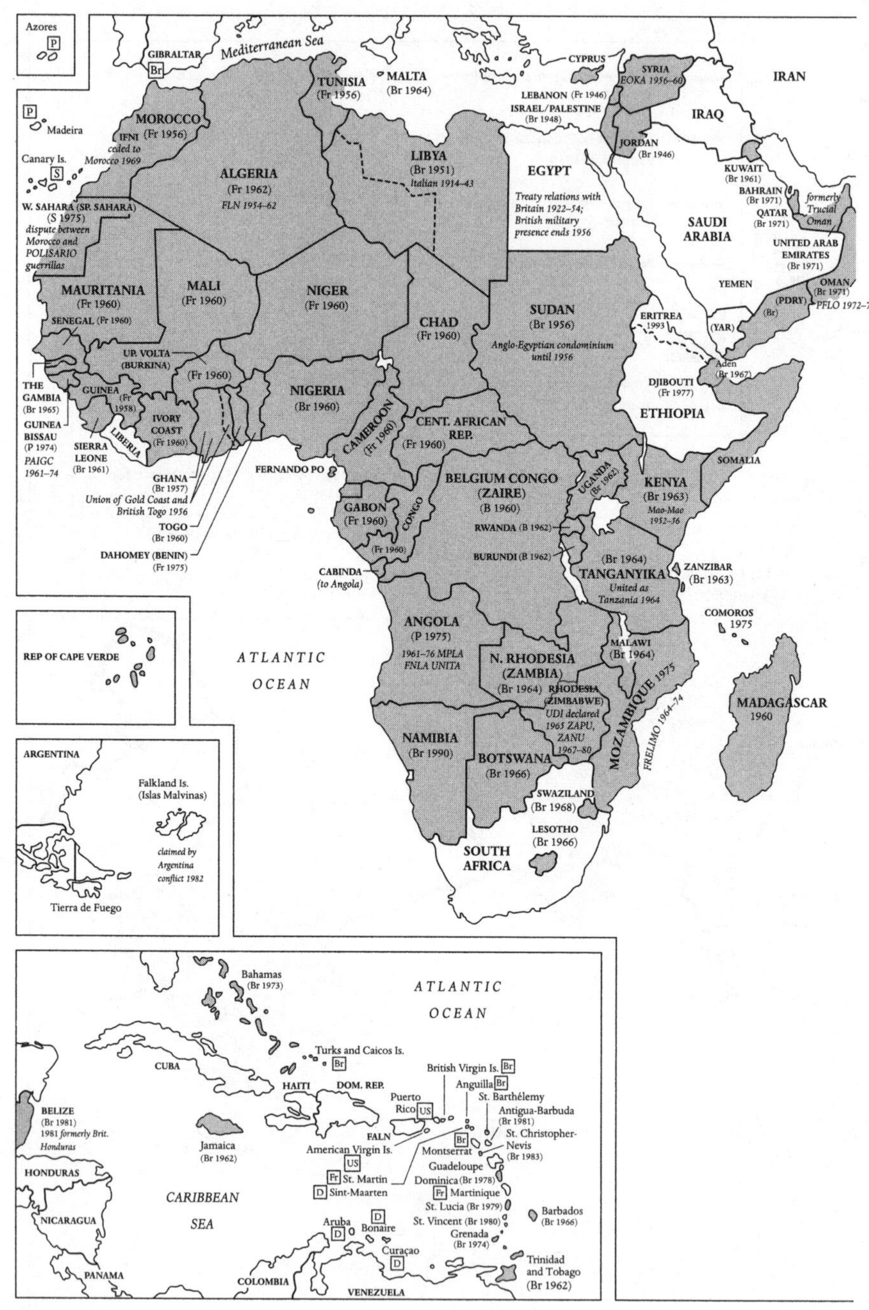

Map 4 Decolonisation, 1947–90

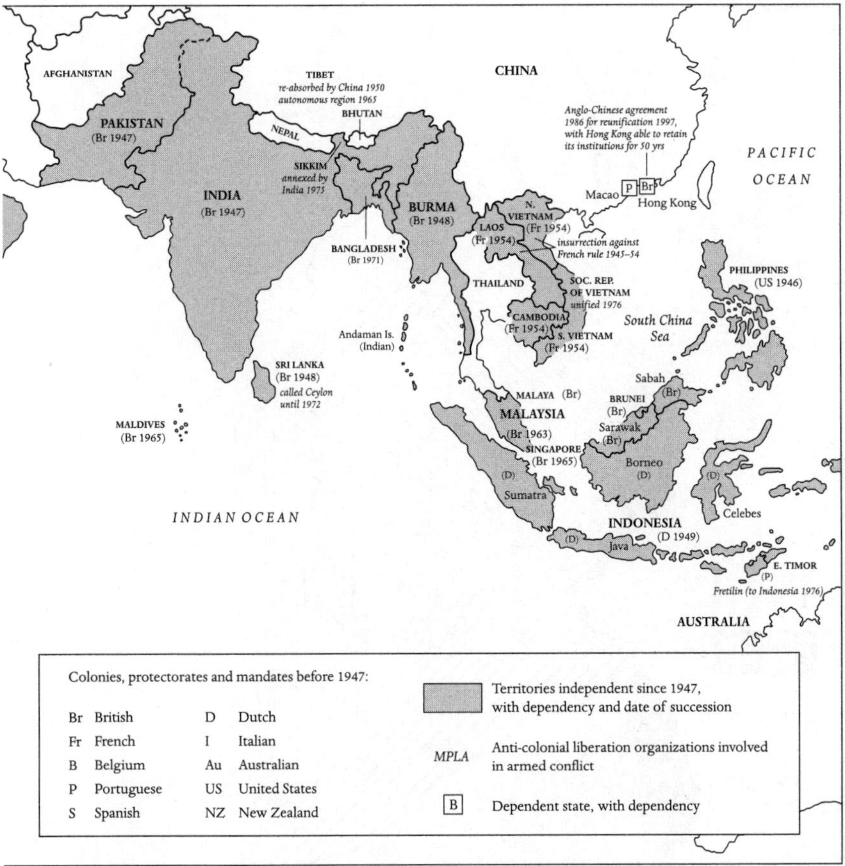

AFGHANISTAN
PAKISTAN
(Br 1947)
INDIA
(Br 1947)
TIBET
re-absorbed by China 1950
autonomous region 1965
NEPAL
BHUTAN
SIKKIM
annexed by
India 1975
BANGLADESH
(Br 1971)
CHINA
Anglo-Chinese agreement
1986 for reunification 1997,
with Hong Kong able to retain
its institutions for 50 yrs
P
Br
Macao
Hong Kong
PACIFIC
OCEAN
BURMA
(Br 1948)
N.
VIETNAM
(Fr 1954)
LAOS
(Fr 1954)
insurrection against
French rule 1945–54
THAILAND
SOC. REP.
OF VIETNAM
unified 1976
CAMBODIA
(Fr 1954)
S. VIETNAM
(Fr 1954)
PHILIPPINES
(US 1946)
South China
Sea
Andaman Is.
(Indian)
SRI LANKA
(Br 1948)
called Ceylon
until 1972
MALDIVES
(Br 1965)
Sabah
(Br)
BRUNEI
(Br)
Sarawak
(Br)
MALAYA (Br)
MALAYSIA
(Br 1963)
SINGAPORE
(Br 1965)
Borneo
(D)
(D)
Sumatra
(D)
Celebes
INDIAN OCEAN
INDONESIA
(D 1949)
(D)
Java
E. TIMOR
(P)
Fretilin (to Indonesia 1976)
AUSTRALIA
Colonies, protectorates and mandates before 1947:
Br British
Fr French
B Belgium
P Portuguese
S Spanish
D Dutch
I Italian
Au Australian
US United States
NZ New Zealand
Territories independent since 1947, with dependency and date of succession
MPLA Anti-colonial liberation organizations involved in armed conflict
B Dependent state, with dependency

W. NEW GUINEA
to Indonesia 1963
(D 1963)
PAPUA NEW
GUINEA
(Au 1975)
New Ireland
(Au 1975)
New
Britain
(Au 1975)
Solomon Is.
(Br 1978)
Nauru
(Br 1968)
Kiribati (Br 1979)
formerly Gilbert Is.
(Br)
Jarvis I.
US
Tuvalu
formerly Ellice Is.
PACIFIC
OCEAN
Marquesas Is.
Fr
Wallis and
Futuna Is.
Fr
Western Samoa
(NZ 1962)
American Samoa
US
Vanuatu
formerly New Hebrides
(Br/Fr 1980)
Fiji
(Br 1970)
Tonga
(Br 1970)
Society Is.
Fr
Tahiti Is.
Fr
New Caledonia
Fr
Cook Is.
NZ
Gambier Is.
Fr
Pitcairn I.
Br
AUSTRALIA
Norfolk I.
Au
Kermadec Is.
NZ
Lord Howe I.
Au
NEW ZEALAND

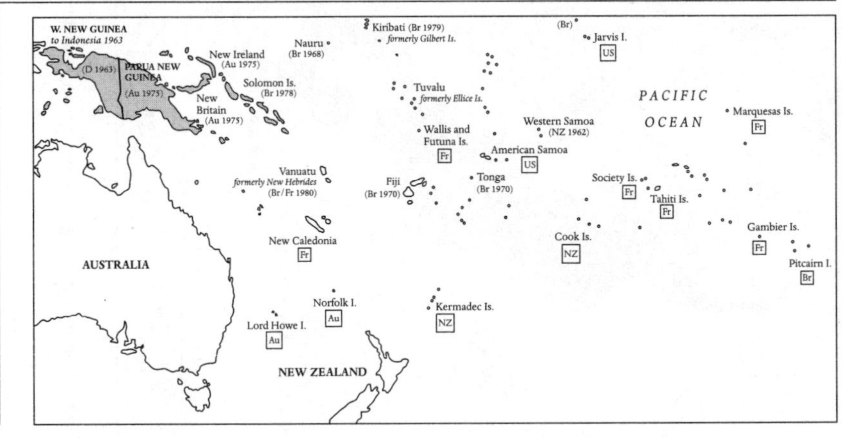

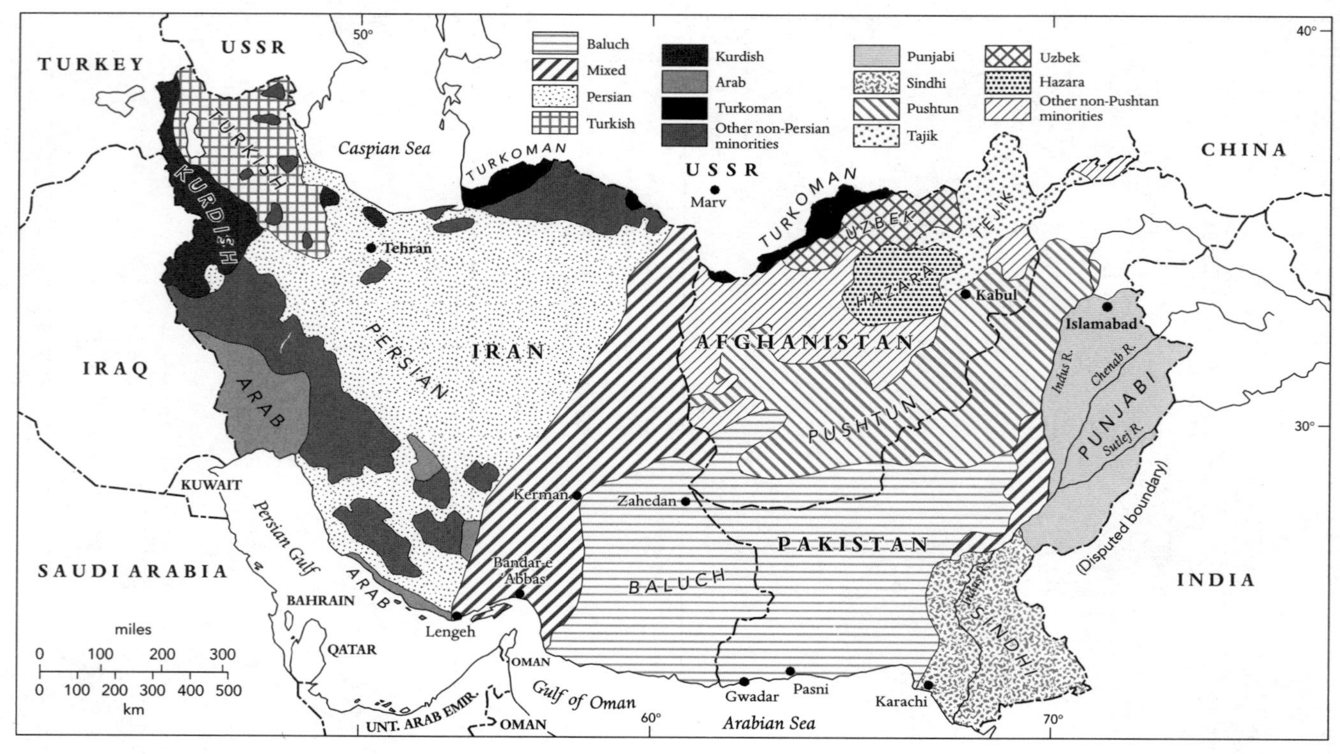

Map 5 Major ethnolinguistic groups in Pakistan

Ethnicity

Introduction

Though the term 'ethnicity' is recent, the sense of kinship, group solidarity, and common culture to which it refers is as old as the historical record. Ethnic communities have been present in every period and continent and have played an important role in all societies. Though their salience and impact have varied considerably, they have always constituted one of the basic modes of human association and community. The same is true of the sense of ethnic identity. Though more elusive, the sense of a common ethnicity has remained to this day a major focus of identification by individuals.

Ethnic community and identity are often associated with conflict, and more particularly political struggles in various parts of the world. We should observe, however, that there is no necessary connection between ethnicity and conflict. Quite apart from isolated examples, relations between ethnic communities and categories may be, and frequently are, peaceful and co-operative. That is indeed the image and ideal for which many in contemporary Europe have been striving under the slogan, *l'Europe des ethnies* (Heraud, 1963). At the same time, as Horowitz (1985) suggests, the basis for conflict exists in the inclusion of two or more ethnic communities within a territorial state. In what follows, the conflict potential of ethnicity will be highlighted. At the same time, the functions performed by ethnic community and identification for social integration and individual adaptation should not be overlooked.

Ethnic conflict can be considered under several headings. Here we are mainly concerned with the political impact of ethnicity, and conversely, the impact of political conflicts on ethnic community and identity. There are, of course, many other forms and sources of ethnic conflict. Economic inequalities and transformations are particularly important. Quite obviously, the perennial struggle for scarce resources exacerbates cultural differences; when economic inequalities are superimposed on ranked ethnic groups, severe conflict often results, especially when societies are undergoing rapid industrialization.

There are, however, other major sources of ethnic conflict. One is associated with cultural, notably linguistic and religious, differences. A second is concerned with the distribution of political rewards within polyethnic states; these often give rise to particularly bitter conflicts. Closely linked to such conflicts are those associated with the creation and maintenance of nations and national states in the modern world; here the influence of nationalist ideology is paramount. Finally, there are international conflicts triggered by ethnic differences: conflicts between national states which are caused or exacerbated by ethnic movements of secession and irredentism. These are the dimensions of ethnicity and ethnic conflict that our readings attempt to illuminate.

Ethnicity and ethnic identity

The term 'ethnicity' first appeared in the 1950s in the English language. It is first recorded in a dictionary in the *Oxford English Dictionary* of 1953, and one of the earliest compilations of articles under that heading states: 'Ethnicity seems to be a new term' (Glazer and Moynihan, 1975: 1). The meaning of the term is equally uncertain. It can mean 'the essence of an ethnic group' or 'the quality of belonging to an ethnic community or group', or 'what it is you have if you are an "ethnic group"' (Chapman *et al.*, 1989: 15), generally in the context of (opposed) other ethnic groups. Alternatively, it may refer to a field of study: the classification of peoples and the relations between groups, in a context of 'self–other' distinctions (Eriksen, 1993: 4).

The term 'ethnicity' is, quite clearly, a derivative of the much older term and more commonly used adjective 'ethnic', which in the English language goes back to the Middle Ages. The English adjective 'ethnic' in turn derives from the ancient Greek term *ethnos*; it was used as a synonym of *gentile*, that is, non-Christian and non-Jewish pagan (itself a rendering of the Hebrew *goy*) in New Testament Greek. In French, for example, the Greek noun survives as *ethnie*, with an associated adjective *ethnique*. As the English language has no concrete noun for *ethnos* or *ethnie*, the French term is used here to denote an 'ethnic community' or 'ethnic group'.

The ancient Greeks used the term *ethnos* in a variety of ways. In Homer we hear of *ethnos hetairon*, a band of friends, *ethnos Lukion*, a tribe of Lycians, and *ethnos melisson* or *ornithon*, a swarm of bees or birds. Aeschylus calls the Persians an *ethnos*, Pindar speaks of the *ethnos aneron* or *gunaikon*, a race of men or women, Herodotus of *to Medikon ethnos*, the Median people, and Plato of *ethnos kerukikon*, a caste of heralds. All this became, in the New Testament writers and Church Fathers, *ta ethne*, the gentile peoples. (Liddell and Scott, 1869; see A. D. Smith, 1986: ch. 2; Tonkin *et al.*, 1989: Introduction).

What these usages have in common is the idea of a number of people or animals who share some cultural or biological characteristics and who live and act in concert. But these usages refer to *other* peoples who, like animals, belong to some group unlike one's own. Hence, the tendency to characterize non-Greeks—peripheral, foreign barbarians—as *ethnea*; Greeks tended to refer to themselves as *genos Hellenon*.

This dichotomy between a non-ethnic 'us' and ethnic 'others' has continued to dog the concepts in the fields of ethnicity and nationalism. We find it reproduced in the ways in which the Latin *natio* was applied to distant, barbarian peoples, whereas the Roman term for themselves was *populus*.

We find it also in the English and American (White Anglo-Saxon Protestant) tendency to reserve the term 'nation' for themselves and 'ethnic' for immigrant peoples, as in the frequently used term 'ethnic minorities'. However, in what follows the terms *ethnie* and 'ethnic' will be applied to majorities and minorities, host and immigrant communities, alike.

From these terms certain key concepts for a study of ethnicity (conceived as a field of social phenomena) emerge. Apart from *ethnie* (described more fully below), we have such concepts as 'ethnic identity', 'ethnic origin', 'ethnocentrism', and 'ethnicism'. 'Ethnic identity' and 'ethnic origin' refer to the individual level of identification with a culturally defined collectivity, the sense on the part of the individual that she or he belongs to a particular cultural community. 'Ethnic origin' likewise refers to a sense of ancestry and nativity on the part of the individual through his or her parents and grandparents; although the concept may also have an even more problematic collective dimension, referring to the (usually diverse) cultural groups and migration origins of *ethnies*.

'Ethnocentrism' is often used in social psychology on an individual or interpersonal level as a synonym for disdain of the stranger. But it can also have a collective historical referent, as the sense of uniqueness, centrality, and virtue of an *ethnie* in its relations with other *ethnies*. This has been an important feature of most *ethnies* in history, helping to sustain their members in times of adversity. The term 'ethnicism' is more rarely used. It refers to movements of protest and resistance by and on behalf of *ethnies* against oppressive or exploitative outsiders; and again such movements have frequently punctuated the historical record (De Vos and Romanucci-Rossi, 1974; A. D. Smith 1986; chs. 2–3).

While each of these concepts may be used on both individual and collective levels, it is important to bear the distinction between them in mind and avoid the problems of attempting to read off individual ethnic behaviour from the collective character or trajectory of *ethnies*, and vice versa. This is very clearly illustrated by the fate of diaspora groups such as the Armenians, Greeks, Jews, and overseas Chinese. It is, after all, quite possible for large numbers of individuals of a diaspora *ethnie* to assimilate to their host societies, and yet leave the *ethnie* in question intact. Conversely, the *ethnie* may experience political destruction and cultural marginalization, yet, as occurred with so many minorities like the Frisians, Wends, and Huguenots, individuals bearing the culture may persist for many generations (Armstrong, 1982: ch. 7; Sheffer, 1986).

The concept of ethnie

The key term in the field is that of 'ethnic group' or 'ethnic community', but it is one for which there is no agreed stipulative or ostensive definition. The issue is complicated by the levels of incorporation which named human culture communities display. Handelman has distinguished four such levels: that of *ethnic category*, the loosest level of incorporation, where there is simply a perceived cultural difference between the group and outsiders, and a sense of the boundary between them. In the next stage, that of *ethnic network*, there is regular interaction between ethnic members such that the network can distribute resources among its members. In the *ethnic association* the members develop common interests and political organizations to express these at a collective, corporate level. Finally, we have the *ethnic community*, which possesses a permanent, physically bounded territory, over and above its political organizations; an example would be an *ethnie* in command of a national state (Handelman, 1977).

In fact, most people would tend to equate the latter with what are termed 'nations', and to simplify these levels by opposing the *ethnic category* to the *ethnic community*. The former is much as Handelman describes, but the latter conflates the *ethnic network* and the *ethnic association*. An *ethnic community* or *ethnie*, then, is one where the members interact regularly and have common interests and organizations at a collective level.

Handelman's typology is useful, but it fails to capture the specifically 'ethnic' content of an 'ethnic community' or *ethnie*. We need to consider other elements, and Schermerhorn's well-known definition points us in the right direction:

> An ethnic group is defined here as a collectivity within a larger society having real or putative common ancestry, memories of a shared historical past, and a cultural focus on one or more symbolic elements defined as the epitome of their peoplehood. Examples of such symbolic elements are: kinship patterns, physical contiguity (as in localism or sectionalism), religious affiliation, language or dialect forms, tribal affiliation, nationality, phenotypical features, or any combination of these. A necessary accompaniment is some consciousness of kind among members of the group. (Schermerhorn, 1978: 12)

If we drop Schermerhorn's insistence that ethnic groups are only to be construed as 'parts of a larger society', and exchange his long list of symbolic elements for 'elements of common culture', we arrive at the following definition of the term *ethnie*: 'a named human population with myths of common ancestry, shared historical memories, one or more elements of common culture, a link with a homeland and a sense of solidarity among at least some of its members.'

In other words, *ethnies* habitually exhibit, albeit in varying degrees, six main features:

1. a common *proper name*, to identify and express the 'essence' of the community;

2. a myth of *common ancestry*, a myth rather than a fact, a myth that includes the idea of a common origin in time and place and that gives an *ethnie* a sense of fictive kinship, what Horowitz terms a 'super-family' (Horowitz, 1985: ch. 2);
3. shared *historical memories*, or better, shared memories of a common past or pasts, including heroes, events, and their commemoration;
4. one or more *elements of common culture*, which need not be specified but normally include religion, customs, or language;
5. a *link* with a *homeland*, not necessarily its physical occupation by the *ethnie*, only its symbolic attachment to the ancestral land, as with diaspora peoples;
6. a *sense of solidarity* on the part of at least some sections of the *ethnie*'s population (A. D. Smith, 1986: ch. 2).

This brings out the importance of shared myths and memories in the definition of *ethnies*, and the subjective identification of individuals with the community; without the shared myths and memories, including myths of origin and election, and the sense of solidarity they engender, we would be speaking of an ethnic category rather than a community. The second key element is the orientation to the past: to the origins and ancestors of the community and to its historical formation, including its 'golden ages', the periods of its political, artistic, or spiritual greatness. The destiny of the community is bound up with its ethno-history, with its own understanding of a unique, shared past.

Approaches to ethnicity

The phenomena of 'ethnicity' are not only empirically very varied, they are characterized by paradox. On the one hand, we encounter highly durable *ethnies*, some of them indeed tracing their origins over several centuries, even millennia. On the other hand, we observe the rise of new *ethnies* and the dissolution of older ones, as well as the many transformations of culture that existing *ethnies* have undergone. Moreover, as we come closer to the object of investigation, we discern the many fissures in *ethnies* and shifts in ethnic identification; the literature is full of examples of 'multiple identity', which include not only the many different affiliations of individuals with other kinds of grouping such as gender, region, class, religion, and the like, but also the many shifting identifications between different *ethnies* or ethnic categories. In ancient Greece, for example, one could identify with one's *polis* (city-state), with one's ethno-linguistic group (Ionian, Boeotian, Dorian, Aeolian), or with one's *ethnie* (all Hellas). In modern Nigeria, one can identify with one's clan, one's *ethnie* (Ibo, Yoruba, Tiv, Hausa, etc.), one's religious community (Christianity, Islam), and with the national state of Nigeria, not to mention with

African culture. (See Alty, 1982; Coleman, 1958: Appendix.) It is no wonder, then, that we find such conflicting approaches to the study of so kaleidoscopic and seemingly paradoxical a set of phenomena.

For convenience, we can divide the existing approaches to 'ethnicity' into two broad camps, and a number of alternative approaches.

First come the so-called 'primordialists'. This is a term that was first used by Edward Shils (1957), who was influenced by his readings in the sociology of religion. He sought to distinguish certain kinds of social bond—personal, primordial, sacred, and civil ties—and to show how even in modern, civic societies the other kinds of social bonding persisted. It was an idea taken up by Clifford Geertz (1963), who spoke of the 'overpowering' and 'ineffable quality' attaching to certain kinds of tie, which the participants tended to see as exterior, coercive, and 'given'. It is important to note here that 'primordiality' is attributed by individuals to the ties of religion, blood, race, language, region, and custom; it does not inhere in these bonds. Geertz suggests that the drive for an efficient, dynamic modern state interacts with the other great drive for personal identity, which is based on the 'primordial ties'. This is not so far from Weber's belief that political action is the single most effective source of a 'belief in blood relationship, unless gross differences of anthropological type impede it' (Weber, 1978: 393).

'Primordialism' as such has come in for a good deal of criticism for presenting a static and naturalistic view of ethnicity and for lacking explanatory power (Eller and Coughlan, 1993). Scholars frequently point to the malleability of ethnic identity, its overlapping with other kinds of social identity, and people's capacity to assume various identities in different situations. Frequent migration, colonization, and intermarriage, particularly in the modern world, have undermined the view of ethnic communities as immemorial, discrete, persisting units.

Recently, however, sociobiologists have proposed a more radical primordialism, which regards genetic reproductive capacity as the basis, not only of families and clans, but of wider kinship-based groupings like *ethnies*. They suggest that these groups are bonded through mechanisms of 'nepotism' and 'inclusive fitness', and that the myths of descent which underpin *ethnies* correspond with such nepotistic reproductive strategies. This line of argument has been attacked for reducing cultural and social behaviour to biological drives, and for failing to account, except rather speculatively, for the bonding of large *ethnies* and nations (Reynolds, 1980; but cf. van den Berghe, 1986).

In stark contrast to 'primordialists', the 'instrumentalists' treat ethnicity as a social, political, and cultural resource for different interest- and status-groups. One version focuses on élite competition for resources and suggests that the manipulation of symbols is vital for gaining the support of the masses and achieving political goals (Brass, 1991; Cohen, 1974). Another version examines élite strategies of maximizing preferences in terms of individual 'rational choices' in given situations; here it is assumed that actors generally desire goods measured in terms of wealth, power, and status, and that joining ethnic or national communities helps to secure these ends either by influencing the state or, in certain situations, through secession (Banton, 1983 and 1994; Hechter, 1986 and 1992).

One of the central ideas of 'instrumentalists' is the socially constructed nature of ethnicity, and the ability of individuals to 'cut and mix' from a variety of ethnic heritages and cultures to forge their own individual or group identities (A. Cohen, 1969; Bhabha, 1990; Hall, 1993; R. Cohen, 1994). This risks divorcing the quest for individual cultural identity from its institutional bases. There is also the danger, common to instrumentalist approaches, of neglecting the wider cultural environment in which élite competition and rational preference maximization take place.

Instrumentalists can also be criticized for defining interests largely in material terms, for failing to take seriously the participants' sense of the permanence of their *ethnies* (which might be termed 'participant's primordialism'), and, above all, for underplaying the affective dimensions of ethnicity. This is well brought out by Connor's subjectivist and Fishman's historical critiques. Throughout history *ethnies* and nations have clearly aroused collective passions of a quasi-physical kind in ways that even classes failed to do. (Fishman, 1980; Connor, 1993).

Few scholars in practice adhere to either the primordialist or the instrumentalist pole *tout court*. But there have been few systematic attempts to synthesize the two types of approach. Both McKay and Scott have demonstrated that this can be done on a theoretical level; the question is rather how far such syntheses can be empirically helpful (McKay, 1982; Scott, 1990).

Three alternative traditions of enquiry into ethnicity are Barth's 'transactionalist', Horowitz's 'social psychological', and Armstrong's and Smith's 'ethno-symbolic' approaches. For Barth, ethnic groups must be treated as units of ascription, where the social boundaries ensure the persistence of the group. It is not the cultural content enclosed by the boundary, but the boundary itself and the symbolic 'border guards' (language, dress, food, etc.) that perpetuate the community and require intensive anthropological study. Nevertheless, Barth regards the boundary as permeable; indeed, transactions across the boundary help to render the boundary more durable. Barth has been criticized for assuming the fixity of bounded ethnic identities and failing to differentiate types of ethnic allegiance, the resources open to various ethnic groups, and their individual subjective dimensions (Francis, 1976; Wallman, 1986; Epstein, 1978).

Horowitz (1985), by contrast, uses the group psychology of Henri Tajfel and focuses on differential estimations of group worth, and on their collective stereotypes. Arguing that ethnic groups in Africa and Asia, included in modern territorial states, have different cultural and economic resources, he suggests that we can explain their strategies, including secession and irredentism, in terms of the 'backward' or 'advanced' nature of the group's resources and of the region they inhabit. Underlying his approach is the assumption that ethnic affiliation is ultimately based on kinship myths and on a sense of group honour in relation to other groups. Horowitz's account provides a welcome antidote to reductionist approaches. It can be supplemented by a historical perspective, particularly in non-colonial contexts, that includes other factors like the role of the intelligentsia, collective memories, and pre-existing group antagonisms.

The main concern of 'ethno-symbolists' is with the persistence, change, and resurgence of *ethnies*, and with the role of the ethnic past or pasts in shaping present cultural communities. Armstrong (1982) applies Barth's general approach to pre-modern ethnic communities, notably in medieval Christendom and Islam, but infuses it with a concern for the cultural forms that Barth had discounted. For Armstrong, as for A. D. Smith (1986), myths and symbols play a vital role in unifying populations and ensuring their continuity over many generations. Armstrong considers a range of factors, like nostalgia for past life-styles, religious civilizations and organizations, imperial *mythomoteurs*, and language fissures, in creating shifting ethnic identities. Smith examines some of the causes of ethno-genesis, distinguishes between 'horizontal' (aristocratic) and 'vertical' (demotic) *ethnies*, and traces the patterns by which they give rise to modern nations. He also emphasizes the cultural contents of myths, memories, and symbols, notably myths of origin and ethnic election, and memories of the golden age. There has, he argues, been a resurgence of ethnicity in the modern world, as intelligentsias have rediscovered ethnic roots as an antidote to the impersonality of bureaucratic rationalism (Smith, 1981; and 1991). Though clearly differing from 'primordialist' accounts, ethno-symbolism has been criticized for failing to identify sufficiently the mass bases of ethnic phenomena, relegating their material aspects, and privileging the contents of myths and memories.

Ethnicity in history

Ethnic phenomena have varied in importance and salience throughout history. We find records of 'tribes' and ethnic groups in the Middle East in the third millennium BC, with the advent of the ancient Egyptians, Sumerians, and Elamites. The subsequent history of inter-state conflict in the area is interwoven with ethnic migrations, invasions, and conflicts, as Indo-European groups came into contact with native Semitic-speaking groups. The Babylonian, Assyrian, and Persian empires dominated large numbers of *ethnies*, who were accorded varying degrees of autonomy but who intermarried and mingled freely. Certain ethnic groups stand out in the ancient world, notably the ancient Greeks and Jews, who have left copious historical records. Under the Hellenistic and Roman empires, ethnic élites were encouraged to adopt Greek and Roman mores and to participate in the social and political institutions, though ethnic prejudice remained widespread (Sherwin-White, 1952; Balsdon, 1979; Finley, 1986; Mendels, 1992).

In the Far East we can discern the outlines of ethnic states in China, Japan, and Korea, despite considerable internal disunity. In south and south-east Asia the ethnic components of social life and political order are less visible, given the frequent intermingling of peoples and cultures. However, in medieval Java, Kandy (Sri Lanka), Burma, Thailand, and Vietnam a sense of common ethnicity based on Buddhist, Hindu, and Muslim cultures emerged over long periods. In ancient and medieval India Hindu diversity and the segmentation of the caste system diluted a sense of common ethnicity; but in the Middle East Islam helped to give the Arabs a sense of ethnic unity, despite the early fragmentation of the Caliphates. In medieval Africa and Latin America the fluidity of ethnic affiliations and the fragility of empires largely prevented the emergence of ethnically based polities, and make it difficult to discern the impact of ethnicity on social life (Oliver and Atmore, 1981; Lehmann, 1982; Dikötter, 1992; Lapidus, 1988).

With the renewed migrations of Indo-European peoples into Europe under the late Roman empire, ethnically based kingdoms (*regna*) emerged in what is now France (Franks), Spain (Visigoths), Italy (Lombards), Germany (Saxons), and England (Anglo-Saxons), and later Scandinavia (Viking kingdoms) and Hungary (Magyars). Arguably, these became the prototypes and frameworks for the medieval kingdoms of France, Spain, England, Denmark, Sweden, and Hungary which formed the cultural basis of subsequent modern nations. In Eastern Europe Slavic-speaking peoples settled and became differentiated in the early medieval period into the familiar ethnic communities and states (Croatia, Poland, Serbia, Bulgaria, Kiev, Muscovy) that subsequently formed the basis of modern nations (Seton-Watson, 1977; Pearson, 1983; Reynolds, 1984, ch. 8; Llobera, 1994; Portal, 1969).

Ethnicity in the modern world

With the appearance of the modern bureaucratic state and capitalism, ethnic communities take on a new political importance. In the older empires *ethnies* remained passive, but recognized communities, like the *millets* of the Ottoman empire. In the modern rational state there was no room for an ethnic autonomy that conflicted with the requirement for all citizens to integrate into the new national state. The new ideologies of political nationalism required all the members of a 'nation-state' to be united and homogenous, and this produced quite new conflicts in most states which were, after all, composed of several ethnic communities (McNeill, 1986, ch. 2).

This can be most strikingly illustrated in the attitude of the French revolutionaries to minorities within the borders of the new nation of 'France'. In their view, France constituted an homogenous cultural nation, a 'republic one and indivisible'; minorities, therefore, though they might practise their customs and religion in private, had to assimilate *as individuals* into the French body politic and become equal citizens. Unlike the German ethnic conception, as Brubaker describes, the French embraced a 'civic' nationalism; as Clermont-Tonnerre put it in the French assembly in 1791: 'To the Jews as a nation we give nothing; to the Jews as individuals we give everything'. This 'civic' ideal has become the source of a vigorous debate about different bases of citizenship, with 'ethnic' and genealogical sources being treated as illiberal and anti-democratic (Brubaker, 1992; Breton, 1988; A. D. Smith, 1995, ch. 4).

From this debate there has emerged a wider concern for the elements of both ethnic and national identities. For many, the influx of immigrants, *Gastarbeiter*, asylum-seekers, and ex-colonials has decomposed received narratives of 'national identity' into their 'hybridized' cultural components. Multi-culturalism has become the political expression of a more pluralistic approach to nationhood in Western polyethnic states, though such tendencies have also generated nationalist reactions to ethnic minorities (Hammar, 1990; Husbands, 1991; Rex, 1995). At the same time, anti-essentialist anthropologists and others have sought to deconstruct ethnicity itself, suggesting not only that all ethnic communities are deeply divided, but also that ethnicity itself is an optional identity and is often overshadowed by other (gender, class, regional) identities. The role of women, in particular, in ethnic and national reproduction has in the last decade begun to attract considerable scholarly attention (see the essays in Tonkin *et al.*, 1989; Yuval-Davis and Anthias, 1989; Balibar, 1991; Hall, 1992; Walby, 1992; also Eriksen, 1993).

These approaches have received support, not only from liberal reactions to the exclusive and destructive tendencies of some expressions of ethnic conflict, such as those in Bosnia, the Caucasus, and the Indian subcontinent, but also from the expectation of cultural assimilation of smaller *ethnies* into wider national communities. This is especially marked in North America, where observers like Glazer and Moynihan (1963 and 1975), Bell (1975), Gans (1979 and 1994), and others have engaged in strenuous debate about the long-term prospects for minority ethnic communities in a melting-pot culture. For some, ethnicity has become largely 'symbolic' in modern societies, whereas others regard the wider 'ethnic revival' in both the West and the former Soviet Union as demonstrating the economic and political modernizing potential of ethnic loyalties, as, for example, in the case of 'middlemen minorities' (Stone, 1979; A. D. Smith, 1981; Taras and Bremmer, 1993). This also ties in with the recent politicization of diaspora communities who engage in an overseas 'vicarious nationalism', such as the Greeks, Irish, Jews,

Poles, and others in North America and Australia (Landau and Esman, in Sheffer, 1986; Zenner, 1991).

In non-Western societies ethnicity has a much more direct influence on the creation of nations and the distribution of resources in post-colonial states. Imperialism and colonialism drew the boundaries of new states in Africa and Asia without much regard for ethnic identities, yet also encouraged the ethnic classification of populations and required some ethnic communities to play special roles in the colonial polity, such as, for example, the 'martial races' (Enloe, 1980*a*). The new, urbanized, indigenous élites soon found it necessary to compete for power using ethnic constituencies and symbols as their bases of mass support (Horowitz, 1985; Brass, 1991). In Africa and Asia, as well as in parts of Europe, ethnicity continues to deeply divide the national state, with or without a return to 'fundamentalist' religion, or alternatively through the modernization of languages and language rivalries (Enloe, 1978; Edwards, 1985; Landau, 1986).

Ethnicity has also become allied to issues of 'race' especially in so-called 'plural societies' (Furnivall, 1948; M. G. Smith, 1969). Some states and regimes have gone even further, and employed racist ideologies to harden cultural cleavages so as to exclude and dehumanize minorities on the basis of colour, culture, and physical stereotypes. This has brought about a century of forced population transfers, mass murder, and genocide (Poliakov, 1974; Kuper, 1981; Fein, 1993). Even without racist categorization, ethnicity in the context of the modern state frequently provides the basis for conflicts over the distribution of resources, with grave regional and geopolitical consequences. This helps to account for the periodic recourse to ethnic secession and irredentism on the part of marginalized ethnic minorities. This is a phenomenon that has encouraged scholars and statesmen to examine various strategies for ethnic conflict regulation from partition to consociationalism and federalism, in the hope of peaceful accommodation of the different demands of *ethnies* and national states (McGarry and O'Leary, 1993; Smooha and Hanf, 1992).

Transcending ethnicity?

As we move into the third millennium, the prospects for ethnicity are uncertain. On the one hand, as Gellner (1983) and others suggest, the homogenizing tendencies of advanced industrialism and nationalism leave little space for 'sub-national' ethnic identities. Globalization, economic and cultural, tends to reduce ethnicity to the folkloristic margins of society; neither the multinationals nor mass electronic communications have any regard for ethnic or national boundaries (Featherstone, 1990). In many ways, ethnicity has become a residual category for people to fall back on when other projects and loyalties are found wanting (Hobsbawm, 1990; cf. Giddens, 1991). There is the parallel argument that post-industrial, polyethnic states, particularly in immigrant societies, must forge purely civic identities and symbols if they are to remain democratic and secure the loyal participation of all their members (Miller, 1995; Breton, 1988; Castles *et al.*, 1992; cf. Hutchinson, 1994).

On the other hand, recent advances in electronic communications and information technology provide 'sub-national' groups with dense cultural networks in 'post-industrial' societies (Richmond, 1984). This parallels the argument of Melucci (1989) about the uses of revitalized ethnic ties in sustaining interaction networks in the face of the depersonalizing, bureaucratic structures of late modernity, and the need for distinctive cultural and psychological ethno-national conceptions by economic élites in advanced industrial societies like Japan (Yoshino, 1992). For McNeill (1986), Connor (1993), and A. D. Smith (1995), ethnic differences and ethnic nationalism are unlikely to be eroded both because of the economic and political needs of modern, industrial societies and because of the constantly renewed impact of ethnic myths of descent and ethnic heritages on modern nations.

Given the longevity and ubiquity of ethnic ties and sentiments throughout history, it would be rash to make predictions about the early transcendence of ethnicity or to imagine that a world of so many overlapping but intense affiliations and loyalties is likely to be able to abolish ethnic conflicts.

Section I

Concepts of Ethnicity

INTRODUCTION

A major element in the confusion and conflict surrounding the field of 'ethnic phenomena' has been the failure to find any measure of agreement about what the central concepts of ethnicity signify or how they should be used.

There are several elements that contribute to this confusion. One is the widespread assumption that ethnic groups or communities are necessarily 'parts of a larger society'. This is very much the American sociological tradition that Richard Schermerhorn's definition and approach exemplify. It is a tradition that does not question the relationship between ethnic groups and nations, but assumes rather that ethnic groups are always minorities within a nation or national state. Thomas Eriksen, too, has pointed to the confusions arising over the move in anthropology away from the concept of 'tribe' to that of 'ethnicity', while retaining the sense of sub-national or minority status. Eriksen also highlights the links between concepts of ethnicity and class, race, and 'communalism', and later considers the issue of majority *ethnies* which may become nations, a problem raised by Walker Connor's well-known definition (Connor 1978, see Companion Reader on *Nationalism* (1994)). Altogether, this remains an under-explored area of research.

Further difficulties are caused by changes in the etymology of the key terms, 'ethnic' and 'ethnic community' (or *ethnie*) and the novelty of the term 'ethnicity'. Both Eriksen and Elisabeth Tonkin, Maryon McDonald, and Malcolm Chapman underline the problematic meanings and status of all these terms, and the fact that the English language has no equivalent proper noun for the Greek *ethnos*—unlike French, which retains the noun *ethnie*. Like Eriksen, Tonkin, McDonald, and Chapman are in the main anti-essentialist tradition of anthropology which aims to reveal the relational and subjective nature of ethnicity. Unlike the older 'objective' approaches that singled out cultural traits like language, religion, customs, and pigmentation, this subjectivist approach emphasizes the fluid and contextual meaning of 'ethnic phenomena'.

Manning Nash, on the other hand, while accepting much of the subjectivist position, proposes a set of building-blocks for the concept of an ethnic group—notably presumed kinship, commensality, and a common cult, which, along with a proper name and reverence for the past, maintain the group boundary. This is close to the historical subjectivism of Connor and Joshua Fishman as well as A. D. Smith (1986), who emphasize the emotional intensity and historical heritage of *ethnies*.

RICHARD SCHERMERHORN

1 Ethnicity and Minority Groups

Each society in the modern world contains subsections or sub-systems more or less distinct from the rest of the population. The most fitting generic term to designate this fraction of the whole is 'ethnic group.' An ethnic group is defined here as a collectivity within a larger society having real or putative common ancestry, memories of a shared historical past, and a cultural focus on one or more symbolic elements defined as the epitome of their peoplehood. Examples of such symbolic elements are: kinship patterns, physical contiguity (as in localism or sectionalism), religious affiliation, language or dialect forms, tribal affiliation, nationality, phenotypical features, or any combination of these. A necessary accompaniment is some consciousness of kind among members of the group. This would place it in Bierstedt's category of 'societal group'.[1]

A second term requiring definition is the expression, 'dominant group.' As used throughout this discussion, dominant group signifies that collectivity within a society which has preeminent authority to function both as guardians and sustainers of the controlling value system, and as prime allocators of rewards in the society. It may be a group of greater or lesser extensity, i.e., a restricted elite, incumbents of a governmental apparatus, an ethnic group, a temporary or permanent coalition of interest groups, or a majority.

In the third place, it is imperative to circumscribe the meaning of the term 'minority group.' In order to do this, however, we must look at the two dimensions of size and power as characteristics of groups in a larger society. This gives us the following paradigm:

FIG. I

	Size	Power	
Dominant Groups			
Group A	+	+	Majority Group
Group B	–	+	Elite
Subordinate Groups			
Group C	+	–	Mass subjects
Group D	–	–	Minority Group

AD and BC = typical intergroup configurations

It is quite possible, of course, to employ the term 'minority' for group B, though it would then be necessary to add the adjective 'dominant.' In order to avoid confusion, the constant use of qualifiers, and continual departure from common usage, I prefer to restrict the term 'minority' to groups of the D type rather than the B type, and the term 'majority' to the A type rather than the C type. The designation 'mass subjects' is a bit awkward, but clear in terms of the table.

As for ethnic groups, they may be either dominant or subordinate; in strict terms they run the whole gamut from A to D in the figure. However, since each society can, by our definition, have only one dominant group but a plurality of subordinate groups, it follows that an overwhelming preponderance of ethnic groups are in subordinate rather than dominant positions; it therefore seems justifiable to drop the adjective 'subordinate' as pragmatically unnecessary instead of adding it over and over again. There are times, of course, when the use of the adjective is necessary for purposes of clarity in a given context. But on the whole I will employ the term 'ethnic' without a qualifier for those in C and D groupings and add the word 'dominant' in those cases where it does apply.

Combining the characteristics of size, power, and ethnicity, we then use 'minority group' to signify any ethnic group in category D; this implies that it forms less than half the population of a given society, but is an appreciable subsystem with limited access to roles and activities central to the economic and political institutions of the society. When ethnics form an actual majority of the population but are in a status of subordination (Group C) they will be designated as mass ethnics.

Finally, a word about the term 'society.' For the purposes at hand, I am deliberately excluding the broader, generic meaning for a more limited one. Instead of orienting the choice to the whole evolutionary panorama of societies, the meaning is narrowed here to a much more limited sphere. In terms of Parsons' three-fold typology of societies as primitive, intermediate, and modern,[2] attention is centered wholly on his third category, and the definition that follows denotes that type alone. Thus in the modern world, it seems most appropriate to define a society as a nation-state, i.e., a social unit territorially distinguished from other such units, having a set of governmental institutions of a central character preeminent over local political controls, and empowered to act for the entire unit in external relations.[3]

[*Comparative Ethnic Relations* (New York: Random House, 1970), 12–14.]

ELISABETH TONKIN, MARYON MCDONALD, AND MALCOLM CHAPMAN

History and Ethnicity

Ethnicity permits us as anthropologists to come close to home, as it is both cheap and fashionable to do. It also allows us, however, having come close to home, to retain that grip on significant difference from ourselves (whoever *we* might be), that has been the moral and intellectual motor of the anthropological enterprise from the very first.[1] It also takes us quickly into many politically contentious areas, where intellectual interests can find themselves readily congruent with media and political concerns.

Ethnicity, however, is a term still obscure to the great majority of ordinary native speakers of English, and either justification or apology for its use is therefore suggested. It is also a term that invites endless and fruitless definitional argument among those professional intellectuals who think that they know, or ought to know, what it means. No attempt will be made here to provide the *right* definition, for such would be far from the spirit of this volume. Nevertheless, some consideration of the term may be useful.

As a term, ethnicity is a product of a long-standing feature of English sociolinguistics—the tendency to look to Greek, Latin, French, or more generally, Romance models, when a new word is needed to fancify a plain idea or expression. It comes from the Greek term *ethnos*, and survives as a fairly common intellectual's word in modern French, *ethnie*, with the associated adjective *ethnique*. The possible noun expressing what it is you have to have to be *ethnique, ethnicité*, is still not common in modern French. The adjective exists in modern English as 'ethnic' (cf. ethnic group, ethnic clothing), with a suffix added to give *ethnicity*. Neither the adjective nor the suffixation are particularly self-evident in vernacular English, and the result is an arguable and murky intellectual term. One of the problems for English speakers is that the concrete noun from which it is derived does not exist in our language. We have no *ethnos*, no *ethnie*.

It is worth looking at the etymology of this term, not for any essential meaning, but because it provides an interesting commentary on the fate of any term that tries to delimit human groups. In the earliest recorded uses, as *ethnos* in Homer, it was not a word used for familiar groups of people sharing a culture, an origin, or a language. It was used, rather, to describe large, undifferentiated groups of either animals or warriors. Frequently, *ethnos* is used for an animal multitude (bees, birds, or flies), which is then used as a simile for a like multitude of warriors, where great size, amorphous structure, and threatening mobility are the qualities to which attention is being drawn (e.g. *Iliad* 2.87 and 2.91; 4.59–69; 12.330). We might gloss it as 'throng' or 'swarm', both of which terms have ambiguously animal and human possibilities. Aeschylus uses *ethnos* to describe the Furies (*Eumenides* 366), and also the Persians (*Persai* 43, 56; see also *Herodotus* 1.101). Sophocles uses it for wild animals (*Philoctetes* 1147; *Antigone* 344). Pindar, again in very early recorded use, employs the term to describe groups of like people, but again people whose location or conduct put them in some way outside the sphere of Greek social normality (the husband-killing women of Lemnos, for example; Pythian Odes 4.448). Aristotle uses it for foreign or barbarous nations, as opposed to 'Hellenes' (*Politics*, 1324.b.10). When Herodotus describes the Greeks in his famous passage (8.144[2]), *ethnos* is not a term he employs. Romans, writing in Greek under the Empire, use the term to describe a province, or the provinces in general—areas that were, that is, *not* Rome (see *Appian Bella Civilia* 2.13; *Herodianus* 1.2.1; *Dion Chrysostom* 4.3.11).

We might perhaps compare early Greek use of *ethnos* to modern English 'tribe'—a term still used by many educated people to describe all political units that are not of the familiar nation and nation–state kind. Aspects of naturality, of non-legitimate social organization, of disorganization, and of animality, are strong in *ethnos*, and we might well remember 'the tribesmen swarming like ants over the rocks' in an account of some British Imperial campaign. It is characteristic of this area of vocabulary, perhaps in all languages, that any term for 'people' in a general sense, has the potential for being taken up into a duality of 'us' and 'them', and from early use this has been the fate of *ethnos*. The term co-existed with *genos*, more commonly used by Greeks of Greeks themselves, in a more-or-less restricted kinship sense. In later uses, in New Testament Greek, *ethnos* comes to be used, as we might expect, to mean non-Christian and non-Jewish, in an attempt to render the Hebrew *goyim*. The derived adjective *ethnikos*, at this stage, is very nearly synonymous with *barbaros*, with all its moral, social, and linguistic content—the barbarians were those who spoke unintelligible languages, and wanted for civilization, who were beyond the bounds of meaning, order and decency.

The term *ethnos*, of course, took its meaning in a vocabulary of related terms, most of which have come down to us in some form or another—*genos* (Gr.), *gens* and *genus* (L.); *populus* (L.); *tribus* (L.); *natio* (L.); *polis* (Gr.); *barbaros* (Gr.) and *barbarus* (L.); *civis* and *civitas* (L.), and so on (to cite only a few of many possibilities). There is no space for a thorough study of these, but it is important to notice that the legacy of these words in the modern Romance languages, and in English, is a rich and complex moral vocabulary, laid out along dimensions of inclusion and exclusion, dignity and disdain, familiarity and strangeness—gentle, Gentile; popular; tribe; nation, national; polite; barbarous; civil, civilized; and so on.[3]

The immediate successor to terms related to *ethnos* was, in an important sense, *gentile*, which, as *gentilis*, was how the Greek term was rendered in the Vulgate version of the Bible.[4] It was Church Latin that dominated literacy in Europe throughout the middle ages, and terms related to *ethnos* had no place in this. After the Reformation, and the English vernacular rendering of the Bible, it was as 'gentile', not 'ethnic', that the term appeared.

Just shows, in his discussion of the use of *ethnos* in modern Greek, that the term can now be used within a discussion of what is essentially Greek. This is a rather remarkable change from classical usage, and merits comment. Just comments upon the use of *ethnos* for 'non-structured', 'tribal', peripheral peoples in classical Greek, but remarks that the term has, in some sense at least, been 'transmitted unchanged (except phonetically) from classical antiquity' into Modern Greek.[5] An inversion of meaning has clearly occurred, however, and we are grateful to Dr Just for the subsequent (tentative) suggestion that this probably occurred during the Ottoman period. In the Byzantine and Mediaeval period, the term continued to be used for the 'gentiles'—a grouping of religious 'otherness'. Within the Ottoman empire, however, the Orthodox Christians themselves were the most prominent religious 'other', defined as such by the majority Muslim definition of the Empire. The various religious communities of the empire were termed 'millets', and it seems probable that *ethnos* was the term used to translate the Turkish term *millet*, as it applied to Orthodox Christians. The already existing sense of 'ethnos', a term suggesting both a religious grouping and 'otherness', would have made such a solution plausible. The Greeks may, then, have been referring to themselves as the *ethnos* (that is, the Orthodox millet) from the fifteenth century onwards. When Greece became a kind of experimental laboratory for modern nationalism, in the early nineteenth century,[6] the Greek *ethnos*, in both semantic and political opposition to the crumbling Ottoman Empire, came to be seen as a quintessentially self-realizing, self-defining entity; as such, the idea would have been generalized throughout classically educated intellectual Europe.

The term 'ethnic', along with various derived forms, has long been used in English in its Greek New Testament sense, as an unusual intellectual synonym for 'gentile', denoting 'pagan' or 'non-Christian', and it retained this sense until well into the nineteenth century (see the *Oxford English Dictionary*, 1971). From about the mid-nineteenth century, however, scholarship has made of *ethnos* a word meaning something like 'group of people of shared characteristics'. The term *ethnos* itself has not passed into common Anglophone intellectual discourse, but a variety of compound and derived terms have been formed, which are now in common academic use—ethnology, ethnography, ethnocentric, ethnic, ethnicity, and others. The term *ethnos* itself was not needed, in a sense, since all these terms relate to the discourse built around the idea of 'race', for which 'ethnos' would have been no more than a redundant synonym. Ethnology was 'the study of races'.

This is not a book about 'race', but the discourse of race is an essential background to any concern with ethnicity today. We now tend to regard 'race' as a concept primarily concerned with biology, but in nineteenth-century usage this biological component was only a part of a complex use. The term was frequently used to express commonalities of various kinds, and although the echo of biology was always there, many uses of the term could have been substituted by, for example, 'nation', 'society', 'culture', 'language', or 'tribe'. The interweaving of biology, culture, and language in the concept had itself a very simple basis in experience—in many societies, then as now, social and linguistic recruitment were often entirely congruent with biological recruitment. A child was born into the society of which it was to become a part, whose language and manners it would learn. In such a context, a concept which did not distinguish very clearly between social, cultural, linguistic, and biological classifications of people, and which tended to make a unity of all these, was very much at home.

Just says, in the context of discussion of ethnicity and ethnic identity, that 'there is, however, a Joker in the pack (and it seems to be a Joker studiously avoided by the academic proponents of ethnicity): namely, "race"'.[7] There can be little doubt that the reason for this studious avoidance is a sense of revulsion and shame at the events that racial doctrines, and specifically Nazi racial doctrines, brought about in Europe in the 1930s and 1940s. It was in the post-war period that the term 'ethnic' came into widespread employment in its modern sense. As Just observes, 'ethnic group' is very like 'race' without the biology (and with the biological implications always tending to creep back in).[8] In Africa it has come to replace 'tribe', which latter has come to be considered pejorative (and as will, perhaps, 'ethnic group' in its turn). The extent to which 'race', as a concept tying linguistic, cultural, and biological descent into the same thread, is still popularly accepted, is shown by a variety of the papers in this volume, and what Just says for the Greek case could be generalized for many other examples: 'Outside of a (growing) intellectual minority, one is Greek because one has . . . "Greek blood"'.[9]

'Ethnicity', as an abstract noun meaning what it is you have if you are an 'ethnic group', followed on behind the adjective 'ethnic'. The *Oxford English Dictionary* gives a first recorded usage in 1953, and an early compilation discussing the concept begins 'Ethnicity seems to be a new term'.[10] A variety of dictionary citations follows, dating from the 1960s and 1970s. What is immediately interesting is that the terms seem to have rediscovered, even without intention, the 'us and them' duality that related terms have had through most of recorded history. 'Race' as a term did not, so to speak, discriminate. Within the discourse of race, everybody had one, everybody belonged to one. In actual use, however, not everybody belongs to an 'ethnic group', or has an 'ethnicity'. In their common employment, the terms have a strong and familiar bias towards 'difference' and 'otherness'. It is, incidentally, not surprising that social anthropology should have found 'ethnicity' consonant with its ambitions and wishes, since an appetite for significant difference has always been present in the anthropological project, even when this has been disavowed.

The adjective 'ethnic', in common usage within say, England, has no obvious point of application within the indigenous patterns of social structure, or of geographical subordination and superordination, inclusion and exclusion. The adjective, however, is readily applied to groups of relatively recent immigrants who are perceived to be sufficiently different, and indeed one measure of perceived difference would be the ease with which the adjective 'ethnic' could be employed. These reflections relate, it must be stressed, to how the terms are used in practice, and not to how they ought to be used, supposing anybody to be competent to judge the matter. It might well be felt that 'ethnicity' is something that inheres in every group that is self-identifying—or at least that it ought to be considered as such. It was very much in this spirit that the conference topic that led to this volume was conceived, since we explicitly invited contributions dealing with 'majority' as well as 'minority' experience. Modern social anthropology, in dealing with 'ethnic' or 'race' relations, or with popular classification of populations, would recognize without difficulty that minimal significance required some kind of dyadic situation. In some situation in which two distinct groups meet, where it is generally accepted that 'ethnic group' might be a suitable description of one and not of the other, it is clear that the definition of the populations involves them both, in some kind of conceptual and practical collusion—the 'opposition' involves them both. New and acute problems of understanding and self-understanding are posed to both parties, in a manner that is in many respects reciprocal. It would seem appropriate, therefore, that the term we use for the kind of grouping created by such a situation should be readily applicable to all groups involved. 'Ethnicity', however, has so far refused to be socially neutral in this way. The problem is neatly presented, albeit inadvertently, by an article in the journal *Ethnicity*, in which the author begins by making fun of those who: 'somehow regard all newcomers to our country as ethnics but, simultaneously, in some vague way, regard themselves as non-ethnic. A false premise if there ever was one. Everett C. Hughes is entirely correct when he declares that "we are all ethnic".'[11] By the time, however, that we have been given a definition of ethnicity,[12] and been given a few examples ('Japanese Americans, the French in Canada, the Flemish in Belgium'), we have been talked into a blunt denial of the first formulation: 'In nearly all cases, however, ethnic groups are a minority of the population.'[13]

Ethnicity, and ethnic group, like so many less scholarly terms of human identification, occupy one side of a duality, tacit or otherwise, of familiarity and strangeness. It is, therefore, unsurprising that their appropriate application would vary very much from one context to another. Even given an agreement about the meaning of the adjective (which is not to be taken for granted), those groupings that look 'ethnic' from south-east England are not those that look 'ethnic' from California, Moscow, or Peking.

'Ethnicity', then, is an abstract noun, derived by non-vernacular morphological processes from a substantive that does not exist. 'Ethnic group' is a collocation often used in covert synonymy for another term, 'race', which has been morally and politically disallowed in many areas. 'Ethnicity' is a term that only makes sense in a context of relativities, of processes of identification, and that nevertheless aspires to concrete and positive status both as an attribute and as an analytical 'concept'. It is a term that half-heartedly aspires to describe phenomena that involve everybody, and that nevertheless has settled in the vocabulary as a marker of strangeness and unfamiliarity. No surprise, then, that the question 'What is ethnicity?' might often be asked, and that the answers should be less than lucid. Given this, it is easy to agree with Just's contention that it is 'a somewhat retrograde step that "ethnicity" should ever have entered into the *analytic* vocabulary of the social sciences'.[14]

Is the term 'identity' any better? It is certainly in common use, in senses that often overlap with those pertaining to ethnicity. It has been argued that difficulties arising from the term 'ethnicity' are not properly specific to the term, or to its etymology, but rather are the result of systematic features of human naming, and of attempts to delineate types of human group. If this is so, then no terminological innovation is going to solve these problems, which we might expect 'identity' to share.

We can, perhaps, contrast two notions of the term 'identity': one more-or-less essentialist notion, with identity as something (an attribute, entity, thing, whatever) which an individual or a group has in and of itself, an 'identity' that is subject to growth and decline, to health and sickness; and another much like that of ethnicity as already discussed—a notion only existing in a context of oppositions and relativities. This latter is no radically novel idea, but it is far from being well understood outside social anthropology, and it coexists uneasily with the discourse of identity as an essential and unitary entity. Social anthropologists have discussed in some detail what we might call, in this context, and in the search of neutral terminology, the 'classification of peoples', and some of this work is now quite old.[15] Within this discussion, a group or an individual has no *one* identity, but a variety (a potentially very large variety) of possibilities, that only incompletely or partially overlap in social time and social space.

[*History and Ethnicity* (London: Routledge, 1989), 11–17.]

MANNING NASH

3 The Core Elements of Ethnicity

Cultural categories with social and group referents are the focus of ethnic inquiry. Where there is a group, there is some sort of boundary, and where there are boundaries, there are mechanisms to maintain them. These boundary mechanisms are cultural markers of difference. The differences among groups are index features. The index features must be easily seen, grasped, understood, and reacted to in social situations. The index features implicate or summarize less visible, less socially apparent aspects of the group. These boundary-marking features say who is a member of what group and what minimal cultural items are involved in membership. Like all things at boundaries, these index features must be visible to members of the group as well as to nonmembers. The meanings associated with the boundary differences among groups need not be, and most frequently are not, isomorphic. Valued insider aspects of culture may be comic or derided by outsiders, and caricature and exaggeration frequently mark outsiders' depiction of boundary mechanisms. Stereotyping is a form of caricature of cultural, index features of group differentiation; an emphasis and ranking of features that in itself helps mark the boundaries among different groups.

The most common ethnic boundary markers, in the ethnographic record, and the most pervasive, in any system of ethnic differentiation, are *kinship*, that is, the presumed biological and descent unity of the group implying a stuff or substance continuity each group member has and outsiders do not; *commensality*, the propriety of eating together indicating a kind of equality, peership, and the promise of further kinship links stemming from the intimate acts of dining together, only one step removed from the intimacy of bedding together; and a *common cult*, implicating a value system beyond time and empirical circumstance, sacred symbols and attachments coming from *illo tempore*.

These cultural markers of kinship, commensuality, and religious cult are, from the point of view of the analyst, a *single recursive metaphor*. This metaphor of blood, substance, and deity symbolize the existence of the group while at the same time they constitute the group. If these boundary mechanisms were breached with regularity, the group as a differentiated entity would also cease to exist. And, indeed, history is littered with group names for which there are no contemporary groups, or even claimants to affiliation to vanished entities. Both the durability and the ephemerality of ethnic groups are cultural and social enigmas of the first magnitude.

This trinity of boundary markers and mechanisms is the deep or basic structure of ethnic group differentiation. It is the presence of cultural markers of blood, substance, and cult that separates ethnic groupings from other kinds of social aggregates, groups, and entities. But sometimes the members' basic symbols of ethnicity are not visible, graspable, or available in social interaction, and hence other surface features stand for the index features. These are, more or less, secondary to the basic recursive metaphor of ethnicity, and hence more mutable over time and less psychologically central to group identity.

These surface pointers make recognition at a distance, or in a fleeting instance, possible, and as such are in themselves often barriers to more intimate contact in much the same way as the core trinity of ethnicity.

The frequent surface pointers include dress, language, and (culturally denoted) physical features. To this secondary trinity a host of subsidiary indices of separateness can be layered on: house architecture and interior arrangements, ritual calenders, specific taboos in joint social participation, special medical practices, special economic practices, and a host of other secondary and tertiary markers of differentiation. All of them take their force of separating groups and persons only if they are linked to the core features of differences. Differences in dress, from whole costumes to single items of apparel, serve as surface markers of group differences. These items of apparel best serve when visible and public, but items of dress may reinforce group boundaries even if not visible, like the underwear of Sikhs, or the under-garment of pious Jews. The meaning of dress codes in ethnic boundary identification is a branch of semiotics until it is tied to the core elements of social differentiation.

Language is a marker akin to dress. A different language, or a series of public utterances far from the norms of communication, may mark off an ethnic group as does dress. And some language usage is akin to Sikh or Jewish hidden apparel; it serves an internal reminder of difference. Language as group marker has more social and psychological weight than dress does. Successful mastery of language implies learning it from birth, in the context of the kinship or primary group. Learning a language as an adult or as a later-in-life accomplishment is not the same as being a 'native' speaker of the language. I leave the problem of 'true' bilingualism to the linguists and the psychologists, while noting that culturally such a speaker is an ethnic anomaly.

Physical features are also secondary cultural markers, because what is relevant for social differentiation is not given in the body form of persons but in the cultural attention and stipulation of aspects of that body form. Again, body form has the Möbius band dimensions of inside and outside which form a continuous surface. Physical elements may include skin color, hair form, height, density, eye shape, or whatever superficial things the culture stipulates as making for essential difference. But it must also include the less visible physical features, some of which are internal to the group, like body mutilation (circumcision, scarification, or tattooing).

All of the secondary surface and tertiary indices of group differences must be related in determinate ways to the basic or core elements of ethnic group formation. Physical features, language, dress, and the others must stand for and imply differences in blood, substance, and cult and hence to the building blocks of ethnicity. If the social markers do not relate to the structure of the building blocks, they are forms of social differentiation of the sort that mark off lodges like the Elks from Masons, boy scouts from sea scouts, or other superficial and transient social identities. These transient social identities are often voluntary, in that they can be volitionally assumed or cast off. Some aspects of ethnicity are also voluntary in that sense, and the balance between voluntary social groups and involuntary elements in social groups is of foremost interest in the study of ethnic groups in modern societies. The ideas of assimilation, integration, fusion, and pluralism have in large measure to do with the mix of voluntary-involuntary aspects of ethnicity as that is defined by the social system and internally in the groups constituting that social and cultural system. The choice of 'cauldron' in the title of this work indicates my conviction that assimilation or total erasure of ethnic groups and differences is less likely than a pluralism resembling a sometimes calm, sometimes boiling pot more than it does either a melting pot or a pressure cooker, to borrow common images.

While ethnic differences and group identities have a history and a historical dimension, as noted in restricting the use of ethnicity *sensu stricto* to the historical time of the rise and spread of nation-states and to kinds of social and cultural orders called modern, there is a kind of time, or most exactly temporality, that is a cultural construct rather than a chronological record of time and events as they actually passed—if that sequence could be recovered and its facticity agreed upon. This temporal aspect of culture is grasped in the concept of 'tradition.'

Tradition is the past of a culture, as that past is thought to have continuity, a presence, and a future. These features of tradition bestow upon the past a weight of authority; the very fact of survival, pastness, and continuity give an aura of authority, legitimacy, and rightness to cultural beliefs and practices. The phrases common to most cultures—such as 'time honored,' 'the way of the elders,' 'in the eyes of the ancestors,' 'as our fathers before us,' and 'the way it was always done'—indicate the reverence and authority for the pastness of things. That things and practices have traditional warrant makes for a linkage over generations, thus bestowing upon even the most humble member of the group a pedigree, allowing him to identify with heroic times, great deeds, and a genealogy to the beginning of things human, cultural, and spiritual. Max Weber has written extensively on some of these aspects of tradition as has E. A. Shils, but since they were chiefly concerned with tradition as a form of authority neither did much to tie tradition to the pedigree of the dispossessed, the formerly 'historyless' and the newly arrived on the world scene.

Tradition, while chiefly concerned with the past and hence backward looking, has a forward, future dimension. The preservation and the continuity of tradition is enjoined on its carriers. The social-psychological meaning of this forward orientation binds the individual fate of group members to the fate of the future of the group. This set of attitudes tries to merge the life trajectory of persons with the trajectory of the group, positing the two as indissoluble. The group has strengths from the evident fact of its survival, and that strength is augmented if individual survival is but a link in group survival. In the forward motion of tradition the elements of blood, commensality, and cult are those most emphasized through their symbolic markers. In brief, an identity is fashioned by name and symbol. A recursive metaphor of social differentiation is constituted, and tradition is enshrined. Group and individual survival meld into a personal identity. These are the basic features when the differences between groups are of the sort called 'ethnic' and when this ethnicity takes place in a system of such differences in the political organization of a nation-state.

[*The Cauldron of Ethnicity in the Modern World* (Chicago and London: University of Chicago Press, 1989), 10–15.]

THOMAS H. ERIKSEN

4 Ethnicity, Race, Class and Nation

The term itself

'Ethnicity seems to be a new term', state Nathan Glazer and Daniel Moynihan,[1] who point to the fact that the word's earliest dictionary appearance is in the *Oxford English Dictionary* in 1972. Its first usage is attributed to the American sociologist David Reisman in 1953. The word 'ethnic', however, is much older. It is derived from the Greek *ethnos* (which in turn derived from the word *ethnikos*), which originally meant heathen or pagan.[2] It was used in this sense in English from the mid-fourteenth century until the mid-nineteenth century, when it gradually began to refer to 'racial' characteristics. In the United States, 'ethnics' came to be used around the Second World War as a polite term referring to Jews, Italians, Irish and other people considered inferior to the dominant group of largely British descent. None of the founding fathers of sociology and social anthropology—with the partial exception of Max Weber—granted ethnicity much attention.

Since the 1960s, ethnic groups and ethnicity have become household words in Anglophone social anthropology, although, as Ronald Cohen has remarked,[3] few of those who use the terms bother to define them. In the course of this book, I shall examine a number of approaches to ethnicity. Most of them are closely related, although they may serve different analytical purposes. All of the approaches agree that ethnicity has something to do with the *classification of people* and *group relationships*.

In everyday language the word ethnicity still has a ring of 'minority issues' and 'race relations', but in social anthropology it refers to aspects of relationships between groups which consider themselves, and are regarded by others, as being culturally distinctive. Although it is true that 'the discourse concerning ethnicity tends to concern itself with subnational units, or minorities of some kind or another',[4] majorities and dominant peoples are no less 'ethnic' than minorities. This will be particularly evident in chapters 6 and 7, which discuss nationalism and minority–majority relationships.

Ethnicity, race and nation

A few words must be said initially about the relationship between ethnicity and 'race'. The term race has deliberately been placed within inverted commas in order to stress that it has dubious descriptive value. Whereas it was for some time common to divide humanity into four main races, modern genetics tends not to speak of races. There are two principal reasons for this. First, there has always been so much interbreeding between human populations that it would be meaningless to talk of fixed boundaries between races. Second, the distribution of hereditary physical traits does not follow clear boundaries. In other words, there is often greater variation within a 'racial' group than there is systematic variation between two groups.

Concepts of race can nevertheless be important to the extent that they inform people's actions; at this level, race exists as a cultural construct, whether it has a 'biological' reality or not. Racism, obviously, builds on the assumption that personality is somehow linked with hereditary characteristics which differ systematically between 'races', and in this way race may assume sociological importance even if it has no 'objective' existence. Social scientists who study race relations in Great Britain and the United States need not themselves believe in the existence of race, since their object of study is the social and cultural relevance of the *notion* that race exists. If influential people in a society had developed a similar theory about the hereditary personality traits of red-haired people, and if that theory gained social and cultural significance, 'redhead studies' would for similar reasons have become a field of academic research, even if the researchers themselves did not agree that redheads were different from others in a relevant way. In societies where ideas of race are important, they may therefore be studied as part of local discourses on ethnicity.

Should the study of race relations, in this meaning of the word, be distinguished from the study of ethnicity or ethnic relations? Pierre van den Berghe does not think so,[5] but would rather regard 'race' relations as a special case of ethnicity. Others, among them Michael Banton,[6] have argued the need to distinguish between race and ethnicity. In Banton's view, race refers to the categorisation of people, while ethnicity has to do with group identification. He argues that ethnicity is generally more concerned with the identification of 'us', while racism is more oriented to the categorisation of 'them'.[7] However, ethnicity can assume many forms, and since ethnic ideologies tend to stress common descent among their members, the distinction between race and ethnicity is a problematic one, even if Banton's distinction between groups and categories can be useful. I shall not, therefore, distinguish between race relations and ethnicity. Ideas of 'race' may or may not form part of ethnic ideologies, and their presence or absence does not seem to be a decisive factor in interethnic relations.

Discrimination on ethnic grounds is spoken of as 'racism' in Trinidad and as 'communalism' in Mauritius,[8] but the forms of imputed discrimination referred to can be nearly identical. On the other hand, it is doubtless true that groups who 'look different' from majorities or dominating groups may be less liable to become assimilated into the majority than others, and that it can be difficult for them to escape from their ethnic identity if they wish to. However, this may also hold good for minority groups with, say, an inadequate command of the dominant language. In both cases, their ethnic identity becomes an imperative status, an ascribed aspect of their personhood from which they cannot escape entirely. Race or skin colour as such is not the decisive variable in every society.

The relationship between the terms ethnicity and nationality is nearly as complex as that between ethnicity and race. Like the words ethnic and race, the word nation has a long history[9] and has been used with a variety of different meanings in English. We shall refrain from discussing these meanings here, and will concentrate on the sense in which nation and nationalism are used analytically in academic discourse. Like ethnic ideologies, nationalism stresses the cultural similarity of its adherents and, by implication, it draws boundaries vis-à-vis others, who thereby become outsiders. The distinguishing mark of nationalism is by definition its relationship to the state. A nationalist holds that political boundaries should be coterminous with cultural boundaries, whereas many ethnic groups do not demand command over a state. When the political leaders of an ethnic movement make demands to this effect, the ethnic movement therefore by definition becomes a nationalist movement. Although nationalisms tend to be ethnic in character, this is not necessarily the case, and we shall look more carefully into the relationship between ethnicity and nationalism in chapters 6 and 7.

Ethnicity and class

The term ethnicity refers to relationships between groups whose members consider themselves distinctive, and these groups may be ranked hierarchically within a society. It is therefore necessary to distinguish clearly between ethnicity and social class. [...]

Theories of social class always refer to systems of social ranking and distribution of power. Ethnicity, on the contrary, does not necessarily refer to rank; ethnic relations may well be egalitarian in this regard. Still, many polyethnic societies are ranked according to ethnic membership. The criteria for such ranking are nevertheless different from class ranking: they refer to imputed cultural differences or 'races', not to property or archieved statuses.

There may be a high *correlation* between ethnicity and class, which means that there is a high likelihood that persons belonging to specific ethnic groups also belong to specific social classes. There can be a significant interrelationship between class and ethnicity, both class and ethnicity can be criteria for rank, and ethnic membership can be an important factor in class membership. Both class differences and ethnic differences can be pervasive features of societies, but they are not one and the same thing and must be distinguished from one another analytically.

[*Ethnicity and Nationalism* (London: Pluto Press, 1993), 3–7.]

Section II

Theories of Ethnicity

INTRODUCTION

The serious study of ethnicity, like so much else, owes much to the insights of Max Weber, whose reflections highlight the definition of ethnic groups as mass status groups (*Stände*). Weber is concerned to combine their subjective and objective aspects, and balance their cultural and political bases. In fact, he oscillates between according primacy to political factors and historical memories in the shaping of a sense of common ethnicity, and the prevailing preoccupation with cultural and biological differences in limiting ethnic affiliations.

We can detect the sources of the vigorous current debates on ethnicity in Weber's reflections. Clifford Geertz, following the pioneering distinctions made by Edward Shils, has emphasized the importance of cultural 'givens', like religion, language, race, nationality, and customs to which people attach a 'primordial' quality, at once overpowering and ineffable. This so-called 'primordialist' position has been severely criticized by Jack Eller and Reed Coughlan as aprioristic and asociological, reducing social phenomena to inherent bonds and thereby precluding the possibility of explaining collective passions. In his reply, Steven Grosby argues that mass emotion is not at issue. What we have to explain is why so many people attribute 'primordial' qualities to their relationships with vital sources of life, such as origin, descent, and ancestral territory. For Pierre van den Berghe, these sources lie even deeper, in the genetic reproductive drives of individuals and their propensity to favour close kin groups ('nepotism') and extend their range of relationships to wider groups like *ethnies* and races ('inclusive fitness' strategies). All these 'primordialist' accounts have been criticized for their relative failure to account for ethnic change and dissolution, as well as the effects of immigration and intermarriage in the modern world. (See the essays by Paul Brass and Francis Robinson in *Nationalism* (1994).)

While they do not share van den Berghe's sociobiological position, Joshua Fishman and Walker Connor are well aware of the intense passion aroused by ethnic bonds. Fishman examines the historical origins of these bonds in Hebraic and Hellenic cultures, and shows how, contrary to the liberal and materialist assumptions of Western intellectuals, ethnic bonds of 'being', 'knowing', and 'doing' are given concrete bodily expression in kinship, language, and religion. Connor too emphasizes the physical roots of mass ethnic psychology, which depends on presumed 'blood relationships', something that is only too clearly understood by ethno-nationalist leaders as they seek to whip up and manipulate the emotions of the masses. Questions that have been raised in relation to these accounts are how far kinship elements in mass ethnic appeals have any basis in fact, and how such elements emerge and influence ethnic groups.

Unlike these approaches, the transactionalist and instrumentalist perspectives of anthropology emphasize the malleability of ethnic ties. In fact, Fredrik Barth's seminal studies of the Swat Pathans of north-west India led him to emphasize the strength of the social boundary of ethnic groups at the expense of the changing cultural contents which it at any one time enclosed. Barth stressed the interplay between ethnic groups and the ways in which transactions across the boundary served merely to strengthen it. Nevertheless, Barth has been criticized for treating ethnic groups as fixed ascriptive categories, with borders permanently guarded by linguistic and cultural symbols (such as dress, food, and architecture).

With Abner Cohen's analysis of the Hausa traders we encounter a much more 'instrumentalist' approach to ethnicity. Cohen argues that ethnicity should be regarded as a type of political resource for competing interest groups, and therefore, unlike Barth, he refuses to take the ethnic boundary for granted. Cohen's analysis is one of many that stresses the ways in which ethnic groups and ties are useful and effective for the attainment of individual and collective goals. Brass takes this 'instrumental' political approach further, suggesting that in India the competition of élites for resources requires the manipulation of different sets of symbols (mainly linguistic and religious) to appeal to varying constituencies. This is especially true where societies undergo uneven rates of social change and mobilization. Brass accepts the cultural limits implied by the mass resonance of certain symbols, but focuses on the political sources and effects of such symbolic appeals.

Even further removed from any hint of 'primordialism' is the rational choice approach adopted, above all, by Michael Hechter and Michael Banton. Rejecting earlier normative and structuralist explanations, because both ignore the role of individual preferences, Hechter and Banton build models of group solidarity on the basis of individual pursuit of public goods. For Hechter, individuals, to secure their goals of wealth, prestige, and power, agree to give up certain freedoms to organizations. Ethnic organizations play a key role in monitoring and controlling information to their members, who will join them as long as they appear to deliver individual benefits. With examples drawn from Malaysia and Catalonia, Banton argues that ethnicity is defined at the micro-level by the methods we use to study it. He therefore explores individual ethnic preferences and uses a version of game theory, the prisoner's dilemma, to determine the circumstances in which individuals choose whether to align themselves with their ethnic kin rather than on the basis of class, religious, or gender identities.

Such 'instrumentalist' models can be criticized for taking the ethnic nature of organizations for granted, and more generally for failing to account for the mass passions evoked by ethnic ties and cultural symbols. Moreover, if the 'primordialists' fail to account for ethnic change, 'instrumentalists' seem unable to cope with ethnic durability. Neither type of approach, it could be argued, has much place for the vicissitudes of ethnic community and identity over the *longue durée*.

MAX WEBER

5 The Origins of Ethnic Groups

The belief in group affinity, regardless of whether it has any objective foundation, can have important consequences especially for the formation of a political community. We shall call 'ethnic groups' those human groups that entertain a subjective belief in their common descent because of similarities of physical type or of customs or both, or because of memories of colonization and migration; this belief must be important for the propagation of group formation; conversely, it does not matter whether or not an objective blood relationship exists. Ethnic membership (*Gemeinsamkeit*) differs from the kinship group precisely by being a presumed identity, not a group with concrete social action, like the latter. In our sense, ethnic membership does not constitute a group; it only facilitates group formation of any kind, particularly in the political sphere. On the other hand, it is primarily the political community, no matter how artificially organized, that inspires the belief in common ethnicity. This belief tends to persist even after the disintegration of the political community, unless drastic differences in the custom, physical type, or, above all, language exist among its members.

This artificial origin of the belief in common ethnicity follows the previously described pattern of rational association turning into personal relationships. If rationally regulated action is not widespread, almost any association, even the most rational one, creates in overarching communal consciousness; this takes the form of a brotherhood on the basis of the belief in common ethnicity. As late as the Greek city state, even the most arbitrary division of the polis became for the member an association with at least a common cult and often a common fictitious ancestor. The twelve tribes of Israel were subdivisions of a political community, and they alternated in performing certain functions on a monthly basis. The same holds for the Greek tribes (*phylai*) and their subdivisions; the latter, too, were regarded as units of common ethnic descent. It is true that the original division may have been induced by political or actual ethnic differences, but the effect was the same when such a division was made quite rationally and schematically, after the break-up of old groups and relinquishment of local cohesion, as it was done by Cleisthenes. It does not follow, therefore, that the Greek polis was actually or originally a tribal or lineage state, but that ethnic fictions were a sign of the rather low degree of rationalization of Greek political life. Conversely, it is a symptom of the greater rationalization of Rome that its old schematic subdivisions (*curiae*) took on religious importance, with a pretense to ethnic origin, to only a small degree.

The belief in common ethnicity often delimits 'social circles,' which in turn are not always identical with endogamous connubial groups, for greatly varying numbers of persons may be encompassed by both. Their similarity rests on the belief in a specific 'honor' of their members, not shared by the outsiders, that is, the sense of 'ethnic honor' (a phenomenon closely related to status honor, which will be discussed later). These few remarks must suffice at this point. A specialized sociological study of ethnicity would have to make a finer distinction between these concepts than we have done for our limited purposes.

Groups, in turn, can engender sentiments of likeness which will persist even after their demise and will have an 'ethnic' connotation. The political community in particular can produce such an effect. But most directly, such an effect is created by the *language group*, which is the bearer of a specific 'cultural possession of the masses' (*Massenkulturgut*) and makes mutual understanding (*Verstehen*) possible or easier.

Wherever the memory of the origin of a community by peaceful secession or emigration ('colony,' *ver sacrum*, and the like) from a mother community remains for some reason alive, there undoubtedly exists a very specific and often extremely powerful sense of ethnic identity, which is determined by several factors: shared political memories or, even more importantly in early times, persistent ties with the old cult, or the strengthening of kinship and other groups, both in the old and the new community, or other persistent relationships. Where these ties are lacking, or once they cease to exist, the sense of ethnic group membership is absent, regardless of how close the kinship may be.

Apart from the community of language, which may or may not coincide with objective, or subjectively believed, consanguinity, and apart from common religious belief, which is also independent of consanguinity, the ethnic differences that remain are, on the one hand, esthetically conspicuous differences of the physical appearance (as mentioned before) and, on the other hand and of equal weight, the perceptible differences in the *conduct of everyday life*. Of special importance are precisely those items which may otherwise seem to be of small social relevance, since when ethnic differentiation is concerned it is always the conspicuous differences that come into play.

Common language and the ritual regulation of life, as determined by shared religious beliefs, everywhere are conducive to feelings of ethnic affinity, especially since the intelligibility of the behavior of others is the most fundamental presupposition of group formation. But since we shall not consider these two elements in the present context, we ask: what is it that remains? It must be admitted that palpable differences in dialect and differences of religion in themselves do not exclude sentiments of common ethnicity. Next to pronounced differences in the economic way of life, the belief in ethnic affinity has at all times been affected by outward differences in clothes, in the style of housing, food and eating habits, the division of labor between the sexes and between the free and the unfree. That is to say, these things concern one's conception of what is correct and proper and, above all, of what affects the individual's sense of honor and dignity. All those things we shall find later on as objects of specific differences between status groups. The conviction of the excellence of one's own customs and the inferiority of alien ones, a conviction which sustains the sense of ethnic honor, is actually quite analogous to the sense of honor of distinctive status groups.

The sense of ethnic honor is a specific honor of the masses (*Massenehre*), for it is accessible to anybody who belongs to the subjectively believed community of descent. The 'poor white trash,' i.e., the propertyless and, in the absence of job opportunities, very often destitute white inhabitants of the southern states of the United States of America in the period of slavery, were the actual bearers of racial antipathy, which was quite foreign to the planters. This was so because the social honor of the 'poor whites' was dependent upon the social *déclassement* of the Negroes.

And behind all ethnic diversities there is somehow naturally the notion of the 'chosen people,' which is merely a counterpart of status differentiation translated into the plane of horizontal co-existence. The idea of a chosen people derives its popularity from the fact that it can be claimed to an equal degree by any and every member of the mutually despising groups, in contrast to status differentiation which always rests on subordination. Consequently, ethnic repulsion may take hold of all conceivable differences among the notions of propriety and transform them into 'ethnic conventions.'

Besides the previously mentioned elements, which were still more or less closely related to the economic order, conventionalization (a term expounded elsewhere) may take hold of such things as a hairdo or style of beard and the like. The differences thereof have an 'ethnically' repulsive effect, because they are thought of as symbols of ethnic membership. Of course, the repulsion is not always based merely on the 'symbolic' character of the distinguishing traits. The fact that the Scythian women oiled their hair with butter, which then gave off a rancid odor, while Greek women used perfumed oil to achieve the same purpose, thwarted—according to an ancient report—all attempts at social intercourse between the aristocratic ladies of these two groups. The smell of butter certainly had a more compelling effect than even the most prominent racial differences, or—as far as I could see—the 'Negro odor,' of which so many fables are told. In general, racial qualities are effective only as limiting factors with regard to the belief in common ethnicity, such as in case of an excessively heterogeneous and esthetically unaccepted physical type; they are not positively group-forming.

Pronounced differences of custom, which play a role equal to that of inherited physical type in the creation of feelings of common ethnicity and notions of kinship, are usually caused, in addition to linguistic and religious differences, by the diverse economic and political conditions of various social groups. If we ignore cases of clear-cut linguistic boundaries and sharply demarcated political or religious communities as a basis of differences of custom—and these in fact are lacking in wide areas of the African and South American continents—then there are only gradual transitions of custom and no immutable ethnic frontiers, except those due to gross geographical differences. The sharp demarcations of areas wherein ethnically relevant customs predominate, which were not conditioned either by political or economic or religious factors, usually came into existence by way of migration or expansion, when groups of people that had previously lived in complete or partial isolation from each other and became accommodated to heterogeneous conditions of existence came to live side by side. As a result, the obvious contrast usually evokes, on both sides, the idea of blood disaffinity (*Blutsfremdheit*), regardless of the objective state of affairs.

It is understandably difficult to determine in general—and even in a concrete individual case—what influence specific ethnic factors (i.e., the belief in a blood relationship, or its opposite, which rests on similarities, or differences, of a person's physical appearance and style of life) have on the formation of a group.

There is no difference between the ethnically relevant customs and customs in general, as far as their effect is concerned. The belief in common descent, in combination with a similarity of customs, is likely to promote the spread of the activities of one part of an ethnic group among the rest, since the awareness of ethnic identity furthers imitation. This is especially true of the propaganda of religious groups.

It is not feasible to go beyond these vague generalizations. The content of joint activities that are possible on an ethnic basis remains indefinite. There is a corresponding ambiguity of concepts denoting ethnically determined action, that means, determined by the belief in blood relationship. Such concepts are *Völkerschaft*, *Stamm* (tribe), *Volk* (people), each of which is ordinarily used in the sense of an ethnic subdivision of the following one (although the first two may be used in reversed order). Using such terms, one usually implies either the existence of a contemporary political community, no matter how loosely organized, or memories of an extinct political community, such as they are preserved in epic tales and legends; or the existence of a linguistic or dialect group; or, finally, of a religious group. In the past, cults in particular were the typical concomitant of a tribal or *Volk* consciousness. But in the absence of the political community, contemporary or past, the external delimitation of the group was usually indistinct. The cult communities of Germanic tribes, as late as the Burgundian period [6th century AD], were probably rudiments of political communities and therefore pretty well defined. By contrast, the Delphian oracle, the undoubted cultic symbol of Hellenism, also revealed information to the barbarians and accepted their veneration, and it was an organized cult only among some Greek segments, excluding the most powerful cities. The cult as an exponent of ethnic identity is thus generally either a remnant of a largely political community which once existed but was destroyed by disunion and colonization, or it is—as in the case of the Delphian Apollo—a product of a *Kulturgemeinschaft* brought about by other than purely ethnic conditions, but which in turn gives rise to the belief in blood relationship. All history shows how easily political action can give rise to the belief in blood relationship, unless gross differences of anthropological type impede it.

Tribe and political community: the disutility of the notion of 'ethnic group'

The tribe is clearly delimited when it is a subdivision of a polity, which, in fact, often establishes it. In this case, the artificial origin is revealed by the round numbers in which tribes usually appear, for example, the previously mentioned division of the people of Israel into twelve tribes, the three Doric *phylai* and the various *phylai* of the other Hellenes. When a political community was newly established or reorganized, the population was newly divided. Hence the tribe is here a political artifact, even though it soon adopts the whole symbolism of blood-relationship and particularly a tribal cult. Even today it is not rare that political artifacts develop a sense of affinity akin to that of blood relationship. Very schematic constructs such as those states of the United States that were made into squares according to their latitude have a strong sense of identity; it is also not rare that families travel from New York to Richmond to make an expected child a 'Virginian.'

Such artificiality does not preclude the possibility that the Hellenic *phylai*, for example, were at one time independent and that the polis used them schematically when they were merged into a political association. However, tribes that existed before the *polis* were either identical with the corresponding political groups which were subsequently associated into a *polis*, and in this case they were called *ethnos*, not *phyle*; or, as it probably happened many times, the politically unorganized tribe, as a presumed 'blood community,' lived from the memory that it once engaged in joint political action, typically a single conquest or defense, and then such political memories constituted the tribe. Thus, the fact that tribal consciousness was primarily formed by common political experiences and not by common descent appears to have been a frequent source of the belief in common ethnicity.

Of course, this was not the only source: Common customs may have diverse origins. Ultimately, they derive largely from adaptation to natural conditions and the imitation of neighbors. In practice, however, tribal consciousness usually has a political meaning: in case of military danger or opportunity, it easily provides the basis for joint political action on the part of tribal members or *Volksgenossen* who consider one another as blood relatives. The eruption of a drive to political action is thus one of the major potentialities inherent in the rather ambiguous notions of tribe and people. Such intermittent political action may easily develop into the moral duty of all members of tribe or people (*Volk*) to support one another in case of a military attack, even if there is no corresponding political association; violators of this solidarity may suffer the fate of the [Germanic, pro-Roman] sibs of Segestes and Inguiomer—expulsion from the tribal territory—, even if the tribe has no organized government. If the tribe has reached this stage, it has indeed become a continuous political community, no matter how inactive in peacetime, and hence unstable, it may be. However, even under favorable conditions the transition from the habitual to the customary and therefore obligatory is very fluid. All in all, the notion of 'ethnically' determined social action subsumes phenomena that a rigorous sociological analysis—as we do not attempt it here—would have to distinguish carefully: the actual subjective effect of those customs conditioned by heredity and those determined by tradition; the differential impact of the varying content of custom; the influence of common language, religion and political action, past and present, upon the formation of customs; the extent to which such factors create attraction and repulsion, and especially the belief in affinity or disaffinity of blood; the consequences of this belief for social action in general, and specifically for action on the basis of shared custom or blood relationship, for diverse sexual relations, etc.—all of this would have to be studied in detail. It is certain that in this process the collective term 'ethnic' would be abandoned, for it is unsuitable for a really rigorous analysis. However, we do not pursue sociology for its own sake and therefore limit ourselves to showing briefly the diverse factors that are hidden behind this seemingly uniform phenomenon.

The concept of the 'ethnic' group, which dissolves if we define our terms exactly, corresponds in this regard to one of the most vexing, since emotionally charged concepts: the *nation*, as soon as we attempt a sociological definition.

['Ethnic groups', in G. Roth and C. Wittich (eds.), *Economy and Society*, Vol. 1 (Berkeley and Los Angeles: University of California Press, 1978), 389–95.]

CLIFFORD GEERTZ

6 Primordial Ties

Some of this conceptual haze is burned away, however, if it is realized that the peoples of the new states are simultaneously animated by two powerful, thoroughly interdependent, yet distinct and often actually opposed motives—the desire to be recognized as responsible agents whose wishes, acts, hopes, and opinions 'matter,' and the desire to build an efficient, dynamic modern state. The one aim is to be noticed: it is a search for an identity, and a demand that that identity be publicly acknowledged as having import, a social assertion of the self as 'being somebody in the world.'[1] The other aim is practical: it is a demand for progress, for a rising standard of living, more effective political order, greater social justice and beyond that of 'playing a part in the larger arena of world politics,' of 'exercising influence among the nations.'[2] The two motives are, again, most intimately related, because citizenship in a truly modern state has more and more become the most broadly negotiable claim to personal significance, and because what Mazzini called the demand to exist and have a name is to such a great extent fired by a humiliating sense of exclusion from the important centers of power in world society. But they are not the same thing. They stem from different sources and respond to different pressures. It is, in fact, the tension between them that is one of the central driving forces in the national evolution of the new states; as it is, at the same time, one of the greatest obstacles to such evolution.

This tension takes a peculiarly severe and chronic form in the new states, both because of the great extent to which their peoples' sense of self remains bound up in the gross actualities of blood, race, language, locality, religion, or tradition, and because of the steadily accelerating importance in this century of the sovereign state as a positive instrument for the realization of collective aims. Multiethnic, usually multilinguistic, and sometimes multiracial, the populations of the new states tend to regard the immediate, concrete, and to them inherently meaningful sorting implicit in such 'natural' diversity as the substantial content of their individuality. To subordinate these specific and familiar identifications in favor of a generalized commitment to an overarching and somewhat alien civil order is to risk a loss of definition as an autonomous person, either through absorption into a culturally undifferentiated mass or, what is even worse, through domination by some other rival ethnic, racial, or linguistic community that is able to imbue that order with the temper of its own personality. But at the same time, all but the most unenlightened members of such societies are at least dimly aware—and their leaders are acutely aware—that the possibilities for social reform and material progress they so intensely desire and are so determined to achieve rest with increasing weight on their being enclosed in a reasonably large, independent, powerful, well-ordered polity. The insistence on recognition as someone who is visible and matters and the will to be modern and dynamic thus tend to diverge, and much of the political process in the new states pivots around an heroic effort to keep them aligned.

A more exact phrasing of the nature of the problem involved here is that, considered as societies, the new states are abnormally susceptible to serious disaffection based on primordial attachments.[3] By a primordial attachment is meant one that stems from the 'givens'—or, more precisely, as culture is inevitably involved in such matters, the assumed 'givens'—of social existence:

immediate contiguity and kin connection mainly, but beyond them the givenness that stems from being born into a particular religious community, speaking a particular language, or even a dialect of a language, and following particular social practices. These congruities of blood, speech, custom, and so on, are seen to have an ineffable, and at times overpowering, coerciveness in and of themselves. One is bound to one's kinsman, one's neighbor, one's fellow believer, *ipso facto*; as the result not merely of personal affection, practical necessity, common interest, or incurred obligation, but at least in great part by virtue of some unaccountable absolute import attributed to the very tie itself. The general strength of such primordial bonds, and the types of them that are important, differ from person to person, from society to society, and from time to time. But for virtually every person, in every society, at almost all times, some attachments seem to flow more from a sense of natural—some would say spiritual—affinity than from social interaction.

In modern societies the lifting of such ties to the level of political supremacy—though it has, of course, occurred and may again occur—has more and more come to be deplored as pathological. To an increasing degree national unity is maintained not by calls to blood and land but by a vague, intermittent, and routine allegiance to a civil state, supplemented to a greater or lesser extent by governmental use of police powers and ideological exhortation. The havoc wreaked, both upon themselves and others, by those modern (or semimodern) states that did passionately seek to become primordial rather than civil political communities, as well as a growing realization of the practical advantages of a wider-ranging pattern of social integration than primordial ties can usually produce or even permit, have only strengthened the reluctance publicly to advance race, language, religion, and the like as bases for the definition of a terminal community. But in modernizing societies, where the tradition of civil politics is weak and where the technical requirements for an effective welfare government are poorly understood, primordial attachments tend, as Nehru discovered, to be repeatedly, in some cases almost continually, proposed and widely acclaimed as preferred bases for the demarcation of autonomous political units. And the thesis that truly legitimate authority flows only from the inherent coerciveness such attachments are conceived somehow to possess is frankly, energetically, and artlessly defended:

> The reasons why a unilingual state is stable and a multilingual state unstable are quite obvious. A state is built on fellow feeling. What is this fellow feeling? To state briefly it is a feeling of a corporate sentiment of oneness which makes those who are charged with it feel that they are kith and kin. This feeling is a double-edged feeling. It is at once a feeling of 'consciousness of kind' which, on the one hand, binds together those who have it so strongly that it overrides all differences arising out of economic conflicts or social gradations and, on the other, severs them from those who are not of their kind. It is a longing not to belong to any other group. The existence of this fellow feeling is the foundation of a stable and democratic state.[4]

It is this crystallization of a direct conflict between primordial and civil sentiments—this 'longing not to belong to any other group'—that gives to the problem variously called tribalism, parochialism, communalism, and so on, a more ominous and deeply threatening quality than most of the other, also very serious and intractable problems the new states face. Here we have not just competing loyalties, but competing loyalties of the same general order, on the same level of integration. There are many other competing loyalties in the new states, as in any state—ties to class, party, business, union, profession, or whatever. But groups formed of such ties are virtually never considered as possible self-standing, maximal social units, as candidates for nationhood. Conflicts among them occur only within a more or less fully accepted terminal community whose political integrity they do not, as a rule, put into question. No matter how severe they become they do not threaten, at least not intentionally, its existence as such. They threaten governments, or even forms of government, but they rarely at best—and then usually when they have become infused with primordial sentiments—threaten to undermine the nation itself, because they do not involve alternative definitions of what the nation is, of what its scope of reference is. Economic or class or intellectual disaffection threatens revolution, but disaffection based on race, language, or culture threatens partition, irredentism, or merger, a redrawing of the very limits of the state, a new definition of its domain. Civil discontent finds its natural outlet in the seizing, legally or illegally, of the state apparatus. Primordial discontent strives more deeply and is satisfied less easily. If severe enough, it wants not just Sukarno's or Nehru's or Moulay Hasan's head it wants Indonesia's or India's or Morocco's.

The actual foci around which such discontent tends to crystallize are various, and in any given case several are usually involved concurrently, sometimes at cross-purposes with one another. On a merely descriptive level they are, nevertheless, fairly readily enumerable:

1. *Assumed Blood Ties*. Here the defining element in quasi-kinship. 'Quasi' because kin units formed around known biological relationship (extended families, lineages, and so on) are too small for even the most tradition-bound to regard them as having more than limited significance, and the referent is, consequently, to a notion of untraceable but yet sociologically real kinship, as in a tribe. Nigeria, the Congo, and the greater part of sub-Saharan Africa are characterized by a prominence of this sort of primordialism. But so also are the nomads or seminomads of the Middle East—the Kurds, Baluchis, Pathans, and so on; the Nagas, Mundas, Santals, and so on, of India; and most of the so-called 'hill tribes' of Southeast Asia.

2. *Race*. Clearly, race is similar to assumed kinship, in that it involves an ethnobiological theory. But it is not quite the same thing. Here, the reference is to phenotypical physical features—especially, of course, skin color, but also facial form, stature, hair type, and so on—rather than any very definite sense

of common descent as such. The communal problems of Malaya in large part focus around these sorts of differences, between, in fact, two phenotypically very similar Mongoloid peoples. 'Negritude' clearly draws much, though perhaps not all, of its force from the notion of race as a significant primordial property, and the pariah commercial minorities—like the Chinese in Southeast Asia or the Indians and Lebanese in Africa—are similarly demarcated.

3. *Language*. Linguism—for some yet to be adequately explained reasons—is particularly intense in the Indian subcontinent, has been something of an issue in Malaya, and has appeared sporadically elsewhere. But as language has sometimes been held to be the altogether essential axis of nationality conflicts, it is worth stressing that linguism is not an inevitable outcome of linguistic diversity. As indeed kinship, race, and the other factors to be listed below, language differences need not in themselves be particularly divisive: they have not been so for the most part in Tanganyika, Iran (not a new state in the strict sense, perhaps), the Philippines, or even in Indonesia, where despite a great confusion of tongues linguistic conflict seems to be the one social problem the country has somehow omitted to demonstrate in extreme form. Furthermore, primordial conflicts can occur where no marked linguistic differences are involved as in Lebanon, among the various sorts of Batak-speakers in Indonesia, and to a lesser extent perhaps between the Fulani and Hausa in northern Nigeria.

4. *Region*. Although a factor nearly everywhere, regionalism naturally tends to be especially troublesome in geographically heterogeneous areas. Tonkin, Annam, and Cochin in prepartitioned Vietnam, the two baskets on the long pole, were opposed almost purely in regional terms, sharing language, culture, race, etc. The tension between East and West Pakistan involves differences in language and culture too, but the geographic element is of great prominence owing to the territorial discontinuity of the country. Java versus the Outer Islands in archipelagic Indonesia; the Northeast versus the West Coast in mountain-bisected Malaya, are perhaps other examples in which regionalism has been an important primordial factor in national politics.

5. *Religion*. Indian partition is the outstanding case of the operation of this type of attachment. But Lebanon, the Karens and the Moslem Arakenese in Burma, the Toba Bataks, Ambonese, and Minahassans in Indonesia, the Moros in the Philippines, the Sikhs in Indian Punjab and the Ahmadiyas in Pakistani, and the Hausa in Nigeria are other well-known examples of its force in undermining or inhibiting a comprehensive civil sense.

6. *Custom*. Again, differences in custom form a basis for a certain amount of national disunity almost everywhere, and are of especial prominence in those cases in which an intellectually and/or artistically rather sophisticated group sees itself as the bearer of a 'civilization' amid a largely barbarian population that would be well advised to model itself upon it: the Bengalis in

India, the Javanese in Indonesia, the Arabs (as against the Berbers) in Morocco, the Amhara in—another 'old' new state—Ethiopia, etc. But it is important also to point out that even vitally opposed groups may differ rather little in their general style of life: Hindu Gujeratis and Maharashtrians in India; Baganda and Bunyoro in Uganda; Javanese and Sundanese in Indonesia. And the reverse holds also: the Balinese have far and away the most divergent pattern of customs in Indonesia, but they have been, so far, notable for the absence of any sense of primordial discontent at all.

['The integrative revolution', in C. Geertz (ed.), *Old Societies and New States* (New York: Free Press, 1963), 108–13.]

JACK ELLER AND REED COUGHLAN

7 The Poverty of Primordialism

The concept of primordialism, as used by Geertz and most of those who followed him, thus seems to contain three distinct ideas:

(1) Primordial identities or attachments are 'given', *a priori*, underived, prior to all experience or interaction—in fact, all interaction is carried out *within* the primordial realities. Primordial attachments are 'natural', even 'spiritual', rather than sociological. Primordial attachments are *ab origine* and *causa sui*: they have no social source. Accordingly, those things called primordial presumably have long histories. This is the aspect of primordialism which we call *apriority*.

(2) Primordial sentiments are 'ineffable', overpowering, and coercive. They cannot be analysed in relation to social interaction. If an individual is a member of a group, he or she *necessarily* feels certain attachments to that group and its practices (especially language and culture). The primordial realities are binding 'in and of themselves . . . by virtue of some unaccountable absolute import attributed to the very tie itself'. Geertz allows that the strength and type of bond may vary but offers no notion of how such a natural and underived phenomenon *could* vary nor any language to describe such variation. This aspect of primordialism is its *ineffability*.

(3) Primordialism is essentially a question of emotion or affect. Geertz speaks of primordial 'attachments', 'sentiments', and 'bonds'. Although some expositors of the concept have used it otherwise (say, as primordial identities or groups), the concept has most often to do with feelings. These feelings make primordialism more than a mere interest theory, and primordial identities are qualitatively different from other kinds of identities (e.g., class identities). This third aspect of primordialism we shall call its *affectivity*.

Thus, primordialism presents us with a picture of underived and socially-unconstructed emotions that are unanalysable and overpowering and coercive yet varying. A more unintelligible and unsociological concept would be hard to imagine, and furthermore, from a variety of sources—including sociology, anthropology, and psychology—material has emerged in recent years that renders the concept theoretically vacuous and empirically indefensible. If we look at primordialism more deeply in the light of its three aspects and of recent scholarship, we should find sufficient cause to discard the concept, at least in this primitive sense, permanently.

Apriority

Primordialism, as we saw, tends to refer to those social realities and personal attachments to them that are underived. The realities (language, culture, etc.) and the attachments exist prior to all interaction; rather, interaction is carried out in terms of them. They are ascriptive and therefore inflexible. However, investigations of recent ethnic phenomena around the world suggest that this is simply inaccurate. Ethnic identities, which ought to be in this view 'given' and long-established, are seen at the very least to be 'renewed, modified and remade in each generation. Far from being self-perpetuating, they require creative effort and investment'.[1] The literature burgeons with examples. Mary Waters for example,[2] has demonstrated the role of individual choice in the selection of ethnic identity in the United States. Joane Nagel has developed a thorough analysis of recent literature that stresses the volitional and fluid character of ethnic identity.[3] These studies provide a compelling case for seeing ethnicity as 'a socially constructed, variable definition of self or other, whose existence and meaning is continuously negotiated, revised and revitalized'.[4] Claims to ethnic membership arise and change according to situationally variable circumstances and interests.

Furthermore, Kasfir[5] convincingly shows that primordialism overlooks 'the fact that new ethnic groups were suddenly appearing under colonial rule—sometimes in rural areas, but more inexplicably, in the towns'. In many parts of the world, but perhaps best documented in Africa, new ethnic identities and groups are being created which claim, and receive from some researchers, primordial status. These new primordials (a shocking contradiction in terms) are 'made', not 'given'. In some cases they are 'reinterpretations of the old in terms of the apparently powerful and privileged arguments of the new';[6] in such cases we might have to admit that some old realities and resources were being activated which might arguably be part of a 'primordial heritage'. However, in other cases, appropriate cultural givens, or 'objective indicators', may be lacking, and 'they can often be constructed—as many local enthusiasts and political entrepreneurs set out to do during the colonial period'.[7] This same study goes on to discuss how a seemingly primordial ethnic identity or group 'may be carefully constructed by an upwardly mobile entrepreneur looking for a political base, or by introducing ethnic disputes into the civil service or university'.[8]

The upshot of these comments is that ethnic behaviour or ethnic groups cannot be taken as unproblematic evidence of primordial realities or sentiments. There are of course long-standing (although, we would still argue, not given or underived) social realities out there, but not every ethnic action represents a genuine age-old culture. Lal, for instance, refers to 'ethnicity by consent', by which she means

> the creation of ethnic cultures and identities by people who are not related to one another by descent but who nonetheless lay claim to primordial sentiments and ties and who are committed to a special style of life and a set of conventions which they transmit to their children.[9]

She also describes 'compulsory ethnicity' as 'the institutionalization of ethnic identification as a basis of collective claims concerning the distribution of scarce resources', such as could result from affirmative action programmes, quota systems, or even certain social service practices.

This discussion begins to involve the issue of ethnic mobilization, which is too great a topic to engage in the present article.[10] Let it be said, however, that ethnic mobilization must be mobilization along some particular lines and that these lines have tended to be taken, by 'native' and scholar, as primordial. Whatever the other dimensions of mobilization, it may, as we have seen, involve (1) the activation of cultural resources which are real enough but which were relatively 'dormant' and not previously the subject of strong 'primordial sentiment', or, (2) the literal creation, either of new groups which did not previously exist, coalesced around pre-existing cultural resources, or actually of new cultural resources which did not previously exist.

Ineffability

Primordialism has tended to treat the identification of 'primordial' attachments as the successful and inevitable end of analysis. About such attachments or identities, nothing more can be said. Indeed, nothing more apparently need be said, because, in Geertz's own words, the objects of primordial attachment—the 'congruities of blood, speech, custom, and so on'—seem to have 'an ineffable, and at times overpowering, coerciveness in and of themselves'.[11] Primordial bonds are distinguished from other kinds of bonds 'at least in great part' by their 'unaccountable absolute import'.[12]

It might be argued that Shils and Geertz, in their seminal formulations of the concept, intended to say that ethnic members themselves regard the attachments that they experience as ineffable and unquestionable—not necessarily that the attachments are impervious to social analysis. It is well known that social actors are often unable to explain their feelings and behaviours, at least not in a sociologically interesting and useful way; there is nothing surprising in that. However, sociologists ought not to be satisfied with this layman's view of the world. Unfortunately, regardless of the possible intentions of Shils and Geertz, subsequent analysts have frequently interpreted them to mean, and have thus carried on as if, primordial attachments are ineffable and hence unanalysable for sociologists.

This situation is particularly curious in view of the literature cited above, as well as that which will be cited below, which adds many analytical subtleties to this supposedly ineffable phenomenon. Even in this brief review we have not only seen social analysts speaking lucidly about ethnic bonds, but we have also seen ethnic actors—what Kasfir[13] would call 'ethnic entrepreneurs'—consciously manipulating ethnicity.

Primordialists, those who defend a Shilsian/Geertzian approach to ethnic phenomena, are frequently pitted against so-called 'circumstantialists', who argue that ethnic feelings arise out of specific social conditions. Spicer, for one, has offered a concept to link ethnicity to circumstance: the concept of 'opposition'.[14] Simply put, when a group (an 'ethnie') experiences opposition to incorporation into a wider society or comes under explicit threat or attack, ethnic feeling is generated. Here is a perfectly lucid analytical idea, and one that, unlike so many others, can be empirically tested. However, several attempts to 'resynthesize' primordialism and circumstantialism through concepts such as Spicer's have betrayed themselves by reintroducing apriority and ineffability in an unintelligible way. For instance, Scott,[15] employing Spicer, suggests that 'the greater the degree of opposition, the greater the primordial sentiments engendered'. If we take the word 'engender' literally (as 'to cause to exist or to develop'), then we are being asked to believe that such phenomena are at once primordial and caused—and in analytically-undecipherable manner. Lest there be any doubt, Scott goes on to say that primordial sentiments 'have to be elicited by some *experience*. . . . Hence, primordial sentiments have to be tied to circumstances'.[16] Logic dictates that if this be true, either these phenomena are not primordial in the strong sense, or the primordialists need to redefine the concept. We tend to believe, agreeing that circumstances and experiences are important, that the former is the case, and that any attempt to redefine the concept would probably redefine it out of existence.

Affectivity

Another way in which primordial phenomena have been distinguished from other social phenomena, and rendered unapproachable, is by reference to their affective quality. All the terminology of primordialism suggests affect: attachment, bond, tie, sentiment. In fact, as McKay says directly,[17] primordialism 'focuses our attention on the great emotional strength of ethnic bonds'.

We are hardly critical of this; recognizing the emotional quality of human social life, above its mere rational or instrumental aspect, is crucial and has been the concern of many scholars in recent years. However, whether acknowledging this is tantamount to accepting the previous two features of primordialism, or ultimately to accepting primordialism itself, remains to be seen.

The emotional strength of ethnic feelings is attributed by some analysts to the connection between ethnicity and kinship. Horowitz,[18] for example, argues that ethnicity should be regarded as a greatly extended form of kinship because the idea of common ancestry 'makes it possible for ethnic groups to think in terms of family resemblances ... and to bring into play for a much wider circle those concepts of mutual obligation and antipathy to outsiders that are applicable to family relations'. Indeed, the needs served by kinship, the nurturance and support provided by family, are also met through the mutuality of ethnic group membership; the idiom of the family is frequently encountered in the context of ethnicity. We would agree that the strength of emotion evinced through ethnic attachments may well derive from their similarities to family ties—or, rather, that the similarities between the two ties derive from general features of human bonding capabilities. Nevertheless, to the extent that primordial ties are likened to the feelings one has for family and kin, it is crucial for us to recognize the nature and source of such bonding.

However, conceiving of the primordial in this way has led to a controversy and a fallacy. The controversy centres on whether primordial ties are qualitatively different from other kinds of ties, or groups based on these respective ties. Hechter,[19] among others, argues that primordial ties are distinct, whereas Hoben and Hefner[20] argue that they are not. Horowitz[21] comes down somewhere in between, suggesting that there is a continuum in the ways in which people organize and categorize themselves, such that the affective and the instrumental would be viewed as poles rather than opposites. It is not really necessary at this juncture to enter this debate, although we are inclined to believe that affective ties are, or at least can be, qualitatively different from other types. Scott, for instance, maintains that without primordialism (in the ethnic member's experience and in the sociologist's analytical vocabulary) 'we would have people acting ... without passion, in a wholly sober, rational manner'.[22] Again, while we agree, as do most social theorists, that human beings are not wholly sober and rational agents, 'primordial' seems to have inflated in this analysis to be synonymous with 'emotional'. In fact, as we proceed, we shall encounter again the sense that 'primordial' is meant predominantly to communicate the notion of 'emotional'—and worse, that the notion or understanding of emotion being offered is incomplete and unacceptable.

This brings us to the fallacy, which is more central to our present purposes. It essentially suggests that these emotional, affective ties are not born in social interaction but are somehow just there, implicit in the relationship (kin or ethnic) itself. This leads to a mystification of emotion, a desocializing of the phenomenon, and in extreme cases can lead to the positing of a biological imperative of bond-formation. In other words, if bonds simply *are*, and if they are to have any source at all, then they must have a genetic source. Sociobiological explanations thus become, curiously, the last bastion of any kind of analytic enterprise, albeit a dead-end one.

The source of this fallacy, and the cause of most of the confusion regarding the primordial concept, is the failure of sociology and anthropology to deal intelligibly with emotion. Primordial ties are likened to kinship, but here again the assumption is that kin simply are bonded. Family affection appears 'underived'; how much more so must we consider higher-level and more abstract affections and identities. There is no awareness of the genesis, of the 'sociology', of bonding or identity-formation. We should look elsewhere for insights into the process of bonding, to bring these to bear on the problem of primordial sentiments—and perhaps of emotion in general. [...]

Conclusion

In this article we have argued, by example and by logic, that primordialism is a bankrupt concept for the analysis and description of ethnicity. If primordial is to mean 'from the beginning', *a priori*, ineffable, and coercive—which it must if it is to be genuinely primordial—then the evidence suggests conclusively that the term is only inappropriately assigned to most of the ethnic phenomena of our day. If primordial, on the other hand, is restricted in meaning but widened in application to refer to emotion, then it reveals itself as unnecessary and unfortunate baggage in ethnic analysis.

Ethnicity is surely an affect issue, making it distinct from strictly material or instrumental issues, but this by no means makes it primordial, since emotion is not necessarily or ordinarily primordial but has a clear and analysable sociogenesis. In fact, in the end primordialism belies the same faulty approach which has already come under fire in the realms of culture and affect—taking phenomena that are simply 'already existing' and 'persistent' and reifying and mystifying them into things that are 'natural', 'spiritual', and 'have always existed and always will'. The fact, and it is a problematic fact at best, that ethnics experience their identities as such, or that ethnic sentiments 'are able to pass from practice to practice without going through discourse or consciousness'[23] lends no support to primordial theory and does not call into question the social origins of ethnic attachments. Social science has already overcome, or is in the process of overcoming, this obstacle in the analysis of general cultural phenomena, and when this realization strikes scholars of ethnicity we are sure that the sociological usage of primordialism will be dramatically curtailed, if not discontinued altogether, because of its lack of empirical support and its inherent social passivity and anti-intellectualism, and it will be replaced with empirical research of the sort that we have outlined above.

['The poverty of primordialism: the demystification of ethnic attachments', *Ethnic and Racial Studies*, 16: 2 (1993), 187–92, 199–201.]

STEVEN GROSBY

8 The Inexpungeable Tie of Primordiality

There are a number of unsolved problems about the historically variable, yet persistent beliefs about the significance of birth or nativity, in particular about the connections through both birth to particular biologically related persons—parents and offspring—and birth in a specific territory. These are beliefs about the creation and transmission of life; they are cognitive references to the objects around which various kinds of kinship are formed; they have been described by the term 'primordial'.[1] Why are such beliefs so persistent and ubiquitous? Why do human beings attribute significance to the biological phenomena of descent and kinship, and the locale of nativity? That they have done so and continue to do so is beyond dispute. Indeed, the very existence of this journal, *Ethnic and Racial Studies*, bears witness to the evidently inexpungeableness of primordial ties, and the strength and pervasiveness of those ties in the world today.

One sociological problem about primordiality is whether or not the attachments which are constitutive of the family represent an existentially primary pattern of human relationship. This has long been the assumption of, but by no means only of, psychoanalytic theory. Of course, the family is a most important association for the development of the infant into a person—what sociologists call socialization. Even prior to that development there is the attachment of the parents and the grandparents to the child as their child, the child which is significant to them because it is biologically linked with them. Nevertheless, from everything we know historically and anthropologically about the human species, the infant has never merely belonged to its immediate family; the child has also belonged *from birth* to the larger cultural collectivity, whether a lineage, a clan, a tribe, a city-state, a nation, or a national state. As biologically necessary as the parents of the infant are in the generation and transmission of the substance of life—the substance has historically often been described through the imagery of flesh and blood, the infant develops into a person through its participation in the objectified, past and current, achievements of the lives of the many individuals of the larger cultural collectivity. It does this by participation in, for example, the language of the larger cultural collectivity; in learning the language of its society. The infant participates in the culture of the larger society; it becomes a member of that society; it shares in its collective consciousness through the assimilation and use of the language. The life and the development of the life of the infant have always been dependent upon *both* the immediate family and the larger collectivity. Yet, and herein lies the problem, we attribute the properties which we see as constitutive of the family to the larger collectivity, for example, in the historically ubiquitous use of terms like home in 'homeland', father in 'fatherland', or mother in 'motherland'. Primordial properties are seen as fundamental in the larger collectivity as well as in the family.

Another problem was suggested by Husserl[2] when he referred to the 'horizon of ownness' (*Eigenheitshorizont*) as primordial (*das Primordinale*). This is, according to Husserl, the area and the objects with which we are *familiar.* The problem lies in the fact that the area with which we are familiar, the primordial, is subject to structural variation and extension, both spatially and temporally, for example, one considers the entire territory of one's country and its past to be in some way 'one's own'. This structural extension of the 'horizon of ownness' is possible because of the openness of the human mind.[3] Yet, the directions of that openness are influenced by numerous historical and social factors, including and especially beliefs. The fact that the boundaries of the 'horizon of ownness' may vary through time and from one civilization to another does not in any way invalidate either the fact that human beings perceive primordial objects or the explanatory power of the category of the primordial.

A further complication arises when we ask what might be the connection between the former, sociological problem of relations of birth—kinship in all its various manifestations—which are often described by the image of the family and this latter, phenomenological formulation of familiarity and its structural extension. One is immediately struck by the common etymology in the English language of the terms 'familial' and 'familiar'. Does this common etymology suggest a limit on the extension of familiarity arising from the significance we attribute to nativity? (I note in passing that historical expressions of relatively consistent universalism, for example, Buddhism[4] and Catholicism,[5] have time and time again made 'compromises' with the primordial relations of birth, with the family, ethnicity, and nationality.) In many discussions about ethnicity and nationality, it appears fashionable, after Talcott Parsons,[6] and evidently more palatable to refer to the seemingly rigid limit on the extension of 'familiarity' as 'particularism'. It seems to me that behind this suggestive, yet evasive term of particularism are to be found the persistent primordial attachments of kinship, the ties to one's own: one's own children, one's own 'people', and one's own land.

These and other problems surrounding primordiality deserve our attention and require explanation. Unfortunately, these difficult and fundamental problems are not taken up by Eller and Coughlan[7] in their recent broadside against the category of the primordial, 'The poverty of primordialism'. Instead, they present a farrago of arguments which is noteworthy both in its misunderstanding of primordiality and, thus, in its evasiveness in dealing with the phenomena of ethnicity and nationality.

The only description of ethnicity given by Eller and Coughlan in their article is that ethnicity is 'an affect issue'; it is an 'emotional attachment' which is 'born out of social interaction'. Repeatedly throughout their article, the authors refer to the 'emotional underpinnings', 'emotional basis', 'emotional attachment', and 'strength of emotion' of ethnicity. Furthermore, they appear to think that 'primordialism is essentially a question of emotion or affect'. These observations are evidence of blindness to the fundamental features of primordiality, ethnicity, and nationality. Such observations reveal the total failure of the authors to see that emotions are aroused by the cognition of an object. The emotions accompany the cognitive perception of the object—in this case, it is the cognition of the property of kinship. Such observations are all too indicative of the current intellectual disarray of sociology and anthropology in the United States, where the terms 'social interaction' and 'social construction' have been excuses for ignorance pretending to be knowledge.

One of the few contributions which sociology has made to our understanding of social phenomena has been the development and further refinement of certain classifications of the fundamental patterns of human experience. Well known examples of such classificatory schema are Tönnies's[8] distinction between *Gemeinschaft* and *Gesellschaft*, Troeltsch's[9] distinction between church and sect, Weber's[10] typologies of social action and legitimate authority, Parsons's and Shils's[11] pattern variables, and Shils's[12] distinction between primordial, personal, sacred, and civil ties. All these classifications refer explicitly or implicity to cognitive perception and the affective responses to the perceived properties of objects. In opposition to the crude simplicities of materialism in its various manifestations—behaviorism, economic determinism, or, in the currently fashionable terminology of Eller and Coughan, 'rational calculus of self interest' and 'social construction', all the above classificatory schemas recognized that there is a plurality of orientation of human action, and, furthermore, that there is a particular constellation of beliefs specific to and constitutive of each orientation. These classificatory schemas recognized certain fundamental uniformities in human action and hence in human societies.

These insights—found, for example, in the work of Tönnies, Weber, Scheler, Schmalenbach, Parsons, and Shils—recognized the distinction between the cognitive—beliefs—and the affectual—emotions. I acknowledge that the obscure relation of emotion to cognition is of the utmost relevance to ethnicity and nationality, for example, the possibility that one element of patriotism may be the 'positive' emotion of the love of one's own, while one element of nationalism may be the 'negative' emotion of the hatred of the other. Given the matter at hand, we need not take up this important problem because the argument of Eller and Coughlan takes place at a much cruder level of analysis. Nowhere in their article is there any acknowledgment of the necessary existence of the *objects* of emotions and feelings, that is to say with regard to ethnicity and nationality, *beliefs* about ancestry and territory.

Eller and Coughlan apparently do not see that affects have objects; if they did, they might also become aware that the objects have to be perceived. They would then see that the solidarity of any collectivity is not at all simply a matter of emotion. They seem to think that differences between collectivities are a matter of degrees of emotion—objectless emotion unaccompanied by cognition. But that is obviously not so. Perhaps their elementary confusion is a consequence of the reductionism which is today so common throughout the social sciences, where qualitatively different beliefs are reduced to some putatively uniform 'real' cause, for example, 'interest', 'power', or, it would seem, 'emotion', thereby denying the relative independence of the achievements of the mind and the plurality of orientation of human action.

Primordiality according to Eller and Coughlan is 'essentially a question of emotion or affect'. Nothing could be less true. The term refers to a particular pattern of orientation of human society. One element of any orientation is its cognitive referent. This was understandably taken for granted by Shils in his article, 'Primordial, personal, sacred, and civil ties'.[13] It is assumed in his and Geertz's[14] use of the terms 'attachments' and 'ties'. The cognitive referent in 'attachments' or 'ties' is explicitly referred to a number of times in Shils's article as can easily be observed in his formulations: 'classification of the *properties* of objects', 'the *qualitative properties* of the individual', 'states of mind entailing *beliefs*', 'certain *features* or *characteristics* of the person', 'certain especially *significant* relational *qualities*' (my emphasis). The objects in the primordial attachments have to do with kinship; these objects include a common territory of origin and residence, and biological connection. Once again, 'attachments' or 'ties' to objects necessarily entail beliefs about those objects; these objects must be cognized in order to become objects of attachments. This obvious sociological point is not understood by Eller and Coughlan.

It is an act of interpretative cognition that we perceive something to be in the category of the primordial. Primordiality only asserts that human beings classify themselves and others in accordance with primordial criteria. It does not say that the referents of the criteria necessarily exist in the form in which those who refer to them believe. It does say a) that human beings do make classifications of the self and the other in accordance with such criteria, and b) that on the basis of these classifications, they form groups, membership in which influences the conduct of their members.

Apparently it can no longer be taken for granted in academic sociological discourse that one's interlocutors know that the primordial ties of kinship and locality entail beliefs. Apparently it can no longer be taken for granted that it is understood that beliefs are necessary components in the constitution of the collective consciousness, the consensus, of a collectivity. Eller and Coughlan's repeated use of the empty and evasive term 'social interaction' obscures precisely this constitutive necessity of belief as a component in human action and in the existence of ethnicity and nationality. It is remarkable that nowhere in their article is there a single attempt to explain what the authors mean by their repeated use of the term 'identity' in 'ethnic identity'. To do so would have brought our authors face to face with the existence of what they seek to deny but which is all around them, namely the significance which human beings attribute to relations of descent, the ties of primordiality.

Very little in human affairs is 'social interaction', at least as Eller and Coughlan appear to use the term, that is, to connote random, behavioural—emotional—encounters. Rather than merely interacting, human beings act in ways that are meaningful to one another; that is, they participate in historically evolving patterns of belief and action. The individual participates in these given, a priori bounded patterns. The patterns are the legacy of history; they are tradition. Many traditions, too, are constituted by cognitive beliefs focused on primordial objects. Ethnic groups and nationalities exist because there are traditions of belief and action towards primordial objects such as biological features and especially territorial location.

It is to belabour the obvious to point to the historical development and variation of such beliefs and the institutions which bear them. The interesting, significant point is that kinship, which is a pattern of real and presumed biological connectedness, is a recurrent and pervasive pattern of human orientation, albeit with historical variation. Eller and Coughlan's diatribe against primordialism is actually a rejection of both sociology's classification of the plurality of orientation of human action and the bearing of history through tradition on that orientation. Their disregard of tradition and its corollary of the disregard of the fundamental features of human existence are conveyed by their repeated use of the frivolous clichés of the day, such as 'socially constructed'. The existence of a historically pervasive and recurring pattern of primordial attachment suggests that the significance that human beings attribute to biological connection is neither capricious nor accidental. Why should this be?

One's parents give one life. The locality in which one is born and in which one lives nurtures one; it provides the food necessary for one's life. The larger collectivity in which one is born and in which one lives protects one's life from the potentially threatening chaos of the external world. One's parents have the power to give life to one; nature has the power to make plentiful or barren the area in which one lives; the national state has the power to protect one's life and all that which is *familiar* to one. To some extent, these powers over life can be purposely manipulated, although, even then, the consequences of such manipulation are often unforeseen. To some extent these powers remain beyond our manipulation; that is one of the reasons why human beings stand in awe of them: they remain *ineffable* and *coercive*. Herein lies a part of the reason for the significance that human beings attribute to primordial relations attendant on birth: the family, the locality, and one's own 'people' bear, transmit, and protect life. This is why human beings have always attributed and continue to attribute sacredness to primordial objects and the attachments they form to them. This is one of the reasons why human beings have sacrificed their lives and continue to sacrifice their lives for their own family and for their own nation.

The above observations on primordiality are by no means new. They are merely a modest extension of Tönnies's[15] recognition of the significance that human beings attribute to descent and land and Weber's[16] recognition of the charismatic importance of the blood relationship (*Sippen*—or *Erbscharisma*). Eller and Coughlan, in so far as they are aware of it, disapprove of this tradition of sociological analysis and its recognition of the ineffable, the coercive, and the sacred in human affairs, including in ethnicity and nationality. They object to 'the mystical and spiritual language' used to describe the attachments to family and kin.

Perhaps Eller and Coughlan ought to raise their sights a bit higher, beyond the concept of the primordial, and object to Weber's concept of charisma as being 'unsociological, unanalytical, and vacuous', for charisma—certainly ineffable and coercive—is the gift or grace of god. It is of course of secondary importance that something was said by Tönnies or Weber or Shils. It is, however, of the utmost importance that human beings hold beliefs about the gift, preservation, and continuation of life and order some of their actions in accordance with those beliefs.

Understanding better the social phenomena of ethnicity and nationality is our task. Let us not be diverted from that task by either Eller and Coughlan's pedantic objection to 'terms [which] are not typically found in the sociologists' lexicon' or their callow political litmus test of acceptability as expressed in their objection to 'a concept specifically drawn from sociological discourse that can be shown to shore up the structures of social and racial inequality'. By such a statement, have our authors unwittingly let the cat out of their bag? When all is said and done, is it politics that drives their argument?

['The verdict of history: the inexpungeable tie of primordiality—a response to Eller and Coughlan', *Ethnic and Racial Studies*, 17: 2 (1994), 164–71.]

PIERRE VAN DEN BERGHE

9 Does Race Matter?

Do social races have any biological underpinning?

At a trivial level, the answer to that question is an obvious 'yes'. A social race is *defined* as a group sharing physical (as distinguished from cultural) attributes.[1] But *must* there be such a linkage? Do physical differences between groups always lead to social differences? More generally, do physical phenotypes always matter socially? And, if so, why?

My theory, first stated a decade-and-a-half-ago, is very simple.[2] All social organisms are biologically programmed to be nepotistic, i.e. to behave favourable (or 'altruistically') to others in proportion to their real or perceived degree of common ancestry.[3] Social organisms evolved to be nepotistic because altruistic investment in unrelated organisms is biologically wasted and therefore *could* not evolve, as Darwin clearly saw well over a century ago. The evidence, both human and non-human, for rampant nepotism is overwhelming. The bibliography on humans alone now runs into several hundred titles. Favouring kin among humans is sometimes conscious, sometimes unconscious, and biologically, it does not matter which. But, consciously or unconsciously, we must be able to discriminate according to degree of biological relationship to ourselves, if our beneficence to others is to increase our inclusive fitness.

For the most fundamental mammalian social tie, the mother–infant one, a simple mechanism is typically present: identification and imprinting shortly after birth by sight, sound, olfaction or a combination of these. Experimental switching of neonates has demonstrated these simple recognition mechanisms in many mammalian species. But often, and certainly for humans, the situation is much more complex. More than most (perhaps all) other organisms, humans recognise and make fine gradations of kinship, and dispense their largesse or their nastiness accordingly.[4]

Being intelligent and opportunistic animals, humans use all possible clues of relatedness, with a preference for the ones that are reliable, quick and cheap. Since it pays, in fitness maximisation terms, to be a fine-tuned discriminator of kinship in a wide range of situations involving hundreds or even thousands of relationships, any readily identifiable, unfalsifiable marker of probable common ancestry will be used. Specification of a few simple properties of the marker itself, of the social circumstances of the individual, and of the ecological conditions of the social encounter can lead one to good behavioural predictions. For example, it can be predicted that, among social mammals with heavy biparental investment in offspring, parenthood will be 'tested' by males more than by females, because paternity is exposed to much more uncertainty than maternity. Mothers *know* their babies are theirs; fathers cannot be so sure, and therefore will look much more for physical resemblance, especially for signature-like rare characteristics such as a mole on the nose. Women concerned with paternal investment in their offspring, on the other hand, can be expected to stress the physical resemblance of their babies to their mates more than to themselves. 'Isn't he his father's spitting image?'

Let us now widen the focus from kinship in the narrow sense, to that form of extended kinship we call race or ethnicity. Both racial and ethnic groups are socially defined by real or putative common descent, and the distinction between the two types of groups is merely in the relative salience of biological or cultural *markers* of membership. My contention is that, in both cases, the social concern is with common biological descent, *even when the markers are primarily cultural.*

There are three main objections to my formulation of ethnocentrism and racism as extended forms of biologically rooted nepotism.

(1) The common descent of ethnic groups is often a myth, not a biological reality. Therefore, my argument is invalid. To which I reply: A myth, to be effective, has to be believed, and a myth of ethnicity will only be believed if members of an ethnic group are sufficiently alike in physical appearance and culture, and have lived together and intermarried for a sufficient period (at a minimum three or four generations) for the myth to have developed a substantial measure of biological truth. The Emperor of Japan can effectively claim to be the father of the Japanese nation in a way that Queen Victoria could never validate her claim as mother of India. Ethnicity or race cannot be invented or imagined out of nothing. It can be manipulated, used, exploited, stressed, fused or subdivided, but it must correlate with a pre-existing population bound by preferential endogamy and a common historical experience. Ethnicity is *both* primordial *and* instrumental.

(2) If ethnicity and race are both rooted in the biology of nepotism, why is it that most ethnic groups stress cultural markers of membership rather than heritable physical ones? The answer here is quite simple: because most ethnic groups seek to differentiate themselves from their immediate neighbours in situations where some short-distance migration and intermarriage take place. Therefore, most ethnic groups *look* so much like their neighbours that they *must* rely on cultural markers of distinction. The proof of the biological pudding is that, where physical, genetic markers do a reliable job of differentiating between groups, they *are* used. In fact, the conditions under which racial groups do emerge are quite predictable: they appear after long-distance migration of sizeable groups across visible genetic clines: slavery, colonialism, indenture, voluntary migration, military conquest are so many examples, especially across large geographical barriers such as oceans or deserts. And racial groups can only survive as long as interbreeding remains relatively

infrequent. Three or four generations of 25 per cent or more exogamy typically erode both racial and ethnic boundaries, and lead to the formation of new ethnic groups. Both race and ethnicity are *not* immutable, but their mutability is a function of exogamy over several generations.

(3) If biological nepotism is extended to large groups, which, under modern conditions, often comprise millions of individuals, has not the concept been diluted to the point of meaninglessness, and reduced to a mere analogy?

Of course, the more distant the biological relationship between two individuals, the more diluted the benefits of nepotism become. Indeed, the biological model predicts that the preference is proportional to the degree of relationship. Relatedness is relative. Ego is at the core of a set of concentric circles defining declining degrees of relationship: nuclear family, extended family, lineage, clan, dialect group, subethnicity, nation. These levels of relatedness are imbedded into one another. Circumstances and interests will determine the level of solidarity which is activated at any given place and time, in a classical fission-and-fusion scheme such as British anthropologists have described for African segmentary lineage societies. But the principle of nepotism, however diluted, suffuses all levels, and there is no *a priori* reason why nepotistic discrimination should stop at any particular point, unless it can be displaced by a superior strategy of fitness maximisation. Brothers *do* murder each other, but not gratuitously and not as easily as strangers. When they do, there is usually a big payoff, such as a throne, an inheritance or a harem. To affirm the operation of nepotism, even in large groups, is not to deny the operation of other principles of cooperative behaviour (such as class solidarity), or fitness maximisation (such as deceit and treachery). The size of the group dilutes the effectiveness of solidary behaviour whatever the base of solidarity, but not more so for ethnic groups than for other social groups such as classes, corporations, clubs or army units, and perhaps even *less*. Ethnic and racial groups can be politically mobilised, even on a huge scale, with greater ease and rapidity, than other social groups, especially under external threat from an enemy who is himself defined in ethnic or racial terms.[5]

Does the biology of social race explain the etiology of racism in contemporary societies?

Better put, does my theory of the biological genesis of social race predict and explain contemporary racism better than competing theories? The answer, I think, is yes, not because it supplants other theories, but because it complements them at a higher level of theoretical generality. It provides a predictive scheme of when, where and why racism can be expected to wax and wane, on a world-wide basis, without having to invoke any special cultural, psychological or historical causes.

Racism, defined as discriminatory behaviour based on inherited physical appearance, can be expected to arise whenever variance in inherited physical appearance is greater *between* groups than *within* groups. This is a relatively rare event, except when two or more hitherto isolated populations migrate across large geographical obstacles. It is even rarer for intergroup variance to *remain* greater than intragroup variance for long, because contact generally brings about interbreeding. So, racism will appear after long-distance migration, but will only persist as long as social barriers to exogamy prevent intermixture, and thus the recreation of a more typical situation where intragroup genetic diversity exceeds intergroup differences. Racism cannot be sustained long if racial membership cuts across the microkinship of the family. Precisely *because* social race is an extension of the principle of nepotism, it cannot long survive interbreeding. Even the rare exceptions, such as relations between white and brown Afrikaners in South Africa, confirm the rule: the 'races' only survived the interbreeding of slavery because of the reimposition of an endogamous caste system after slavery.

Having specified the objective conditions which lead to the rise and the decline of racism, does it follow that racism will inevitably accompany these conditions? Unfortunately, I think the answer is, again, affirmative. Why? Because we are not only selfish maximisers, but intelligently opportunistic ones. Sociality is synonymous with discrimination. Only a fool behaves indiscriminately towards all. We must constantly decide when to be nice or nasty, trusting or suspicious. In the last analysis, we have only two bases for doing so: reciprocity and nepotism. Reciprocity is tricky, unstable, open to cheating, and often dependent on costly information or past experience. It only works between *individuals* who *know* one another well and who expect to *continue* interacting in a mutually beneficial way without deceit or coercion. For nepotism to yield its genetic reward, the only requirement is correct assessment of relatedness. It works best if the cost of that assessment is minimised, that is, if the assessment is reliable, easy and fast.

These simple principles enable us to predict which markers of group membership will be used under what conditions. Where neighbouring groups look alike physically, cultural markers do a better job of assessing group membership than genetic traits. Not all cultural markers are equally good. The *beret* may be a symbol of Basque ethnicity, but it is not reliable. Indeed, it has been usurped by millions of Frenchmen, Spaniards and others. Military uniforms are used for ready recognition of friend and foe from a distance, but they too are open to cheating. That is why costume is frequently a *symbol* of ethnicity, but never a *test* of it. Facial scarification is much more reliable than dress because it cannot easily be undone. Cultural markers of ethnicity which permanently change physical appearance are common: circumcision, tooth filing, tattoos and so on. Language is also a common marker. Even though it is strictly cultural, it is learned early in life and difficult to 'fake' in adulthood, because few people retain the ability to mimic the phonetics of a language learned after puberty. Until recent migrations, someone who spoke your dialect without a foreign accent was most likely to be a native fellow ethnic. But the drawback of language as a marker is that, though reliable, it is fairly slow. You have to ask questions before you shoot, and sometimes you cannot afford the delay.

Let us turn to biological markers. They only work between groups that look quite different. Between Zulus and Boers in South Africa, they worked with complete efficacy: you could shoot at 500 metres and never make a mistake. Norwegians and Swedes, on the other hand, could never be racists towards one another, even if they wanted to. They have to listen to one another before they can tell who is who. The Nazis tried to be racists with Jews but their biological markers worked with perhaps 10 to 15 per cent reliability. In practice, they used mostly cultural markers: circumcision, synagogue attendance, the Star of David, denunciations, surnames, etc. Nazi racial theory ludicrously outstripped the reality of genetic differences. They actually had a very difficult time picking out Jews from their Gentile neighbours, especially in the assimilated Jewry of Western Europe.

Physical markers, in short, only 'work' under the limiting and rare condition of genetic heterozygosity being greater between groups than within. If such a condition is present, however, does it follow that racism is inevitable? Not by a long shot, because most genotypic differences are phenotypically hidden by recessivity or are so cryptic as to be useless for purposes of quick and easy group membership ascription. Blood types, for instance, must be tested by antigens from a blood sample, and the test is slow and costly enough that soldiers in combat are *culturally* tagged (or, in the case of the SS in Nazi Germany, even tattooed) for their genotype.

In practice, then, only a few inherited phenotypes are culturally utilised to form social races, and they are chosen, not for their behavioural significance, but simply for their *visibility.* Skin pigmentation is the most widespread because it is the most visible from the greatest distance and subject to only a limited range of environmental variation. (The genetics of skin colour are still poorly understood and are probably under the control of four to six different loci.) Facial features (notably eye, lip and nose shape), hair texture and physical stature are also used where they are diacritic. For example, in Rwanda and Burundi where the Hutu–Tutsi–Twa distinction is marked by large group differences in height, stature is widely used as a criterion. It works better in Rwanda where a rigid caste system hindered interbreeding, than in the more fluid social structure of Burundi, but, in both cases, the physical distinction was used as a quick and dirty basis for sweeping genocidal action (against the Tutsi in Rwanda, against the Hutu in Burundi). A particularly gruesome atrocity against the Tutsi in Rwanda was to amputate them at the knee to cut them down to size.

This double condition of greater inter- than intragroup heterozygosity *and* high phenotypic visibility predicts when, where and why physical phenotypes get transmuted into social races. The reason why racism became the great pandemic of the nineteenth and twentieth centuries was simply the sudden acceleration of large-scale, long-distance migration across wide genetic clines. The social consequences were enormous and noxious because racial distinctions are peculiarly invidious and immutable, well beyond cultural distinctions. All group distinctions between in-group and out-group are designed to exclude potential competitors from competition for scarce resources, but racial distinctions are especially nasty because they are almost totally beyond individual control. You can learn a language, convert to a religion, get circumcised or scarified, adopt a dress style, but you cannot become tall or white.

In practice, social race is always a social stigma for the subordinate group, and all attempts to pretend otherwise have been singularly unsuccessful. Pragmatically, in terms of policy, it means that institutionalisation of racial categories, however innocuous or even benevolent it may appear, is frequently noxious in its consequences. I am thinking of such measures as racial questions on censuses, race-based affirmative action and similar measures, which have generally had the effect of reinforcing stigmatised racial distinctions.[6]

Conclusion

Let us now close the circle on the relationship between genes and behaviour. I have repeatedly stressed that behaviour, human and non-human alike, can only be understood within an evolutionary framework that gives equal weight to genes and environment acting in concert. For humans, culture is, of course, a large part of the social environment of our species. A genetic effect on behaviour can be direct and result from natural selection, even when it leads to a reduction in fitness (e.g. overeating when food is available, leading to obesity in affluent societies, but providing valuable caloric storage in unstable hunting and gathering economies characterised by cycles of feast and famine; or the craving for drugs which mimic the pleasurable sensations of natural enzymes).

The case of racism, however, is different. The linkage between genes and behaviour is clear, but it did not evolve by natural selection. Racism is conceivably a case of culture 'highjacking' genes which were selected for different ends (e.g. skin pigmentation regulating exposure to sun radiation in different latitudes), and making them serve a totally different social agenda. Yet, that social agenda itself had an underlying biological programme: fitness maximisation through nepotism. Finally, but not less importantly, that social agenda itself had an enormous feedback effect on the life chances of different groups, on their reproductive success, and therefore, in the final analysis, on the course of human evolution itself.

We are only in the infancy of understanding the co-evolution of genes and culture, but understand it we must if we are to make sense of our behaviour, especially behaviour, such as racism, which does not *seem* to make sense.

['Does race matter?', *Nations and Nationalism*, 1: 3 (1995), 359–68.]

JOSHUA FISHMAN

10 Ethnicity as Being, Doing, and Knowing

Language and ethnicity

The contempt for ethnicity and its passionate rejection by the bulk of modern Western intellectuals make it imperative that we recognize Herder and the social, cultural, anthropological tradition derived from his seminal contributions. We need to recognize and appreciate that ethnicity is a powerful experience. Sex roles are not the same as sexism; religious beliefs are not the same as religious bigotry; and the phenomenon of ethnicity is not identical to ethnocentrism or racism.[1] Ethnicity must therefore be approached seriously, even sympathetically, as a social dimension that has received too little attention and too much abuse during the past two centuries. That approach will benefit the Eastern European specialist and all of social theory.

Ethnicity is 'being'

Ethnicity in the pre-mobilized state is the untutored and largely unconscious ethnicity of everyday life and ethnographers have catalogued how members of various ethnic collectivities discuss and recognize that phenomenon. The extent to which ethnicity is intuitively defined and experienced as part of an actor's 'being' (as distinct from his 'doing' and 'knowing') is often overlooked in a literal sense. Ethnicity has always been experienced as a kinship phenomenon, a continuity within the self and within those who share an intergenerational link to common ancestors. Ethnicity is partly experienced as being 'bone of their bone, flesh of their flesh, and blood of their blood.' The human body itself is viewed as an expression of ethnicity and ethnicity is commonly felt to be in the blood, bones, and flesh. It is crucial that we recognize ethnicity as a tangible, living reality that makes every human a link in an eternal bond from generation to generation—from past ancestors to those in the future. Ethnicity is experienced as a guarantor of eternity.

The sense of 'being' of ethnicity pre-dates the Hebraic and Hellenic *Weltanschauung* of familial kinship. The externalist is concerned whether that view of ethnicity is real and commonly accepted, but the members of ethnicity aggregates recognize that it is the view itself that matters, not its validity according to external criteria. The feeling of being related to others as closely as to brothers, sisters, parents, grandparents, sons and daughters is one of the most powerful motivations of humankind. That feeling simultaneously transcends death and promises eternal life, while tangibly demonstrating familial roots, and perpetuation of the lineage. Above all, ethnicity is a universal mystery to be shared with other great and powerful forces.

Just as ethnicity is a bodily and directly experienced reality, language is also a bodily experience. Language and speech are elements of identity experienced in the self and issued from the self. Speech is fashioned by the tongue and teeth and other bodily organs. Language is assumed to be inherited in the same ways as other physical gifts and capacities. Language and ethnicity are tangible features of identity related to the other perceived bodily attributes: sex, intelligence, skill, strength, wit and temperament. Individuals belonging to a given ethnic aggregate supposedly differ from members of other ethnic groups in physical appearance (although not only on that basis). That difference together with differences in language, temperament, and intellect (all features related to physical attributes), mark and keep them members of their group.

Exclusively biological interpretations of human behavior lead to racism, but ethnicity extends beyond the biological or 'being' dimension. Ethnicity in the modern era is a consciously manipulated, massive and dynamic social factor that has resulted in unspeakable racial abuses. However, modern man has perpetrated similar horrors for philosophical, political, economic and religious reasons unrelated to ethnicity. Modern man's capacity for committing horrible acts is a by-product of modernity basically unrelated to ethnicity or to the biological assumptions of ethnicity in particular. Thus, while there is a racist potential in modern ethnicity, that potential is not sufficient to damn the phenomenon. The racist potential in ethnicity suggests the need to recognize the emotional investment involved. The biological component of ethnicity is just as pliable, escapable, interpretable, and compromisable as the non-biological bases of human aggregation. Each folk theory, whether within or outside an ethnicity cluster, has escape hatches and allows for transformation—each has its own rites of passage and its own supernatural ways of interpreting paternity and changing the meaning of 'being.' Nevertheless, the biological component is one of the most powerful features of any ethnicity cluster and an awareness of this component usually results in a socio-cultural consolidation which makes further transformation difficult. The metaphors of blood, bones and flesh joined by the emotive experience of tears, pain, joy and laughter produce the least transient experiences within the realm of ethnicity. It is significant that ethnic languages are always thought to preserve, not merely to evoke, the bio-emotional experiences of revered ancestors.

Languages link past and present generations in a peculiarly sensitive web of intimacy and mutuality. The link between language and ethnicity in modern Eastern Europe perpetuates a poignant sense of identity widely recognized by ethnic collectivities elsewhere as well. Modern theory may deride the link between language and ethnicity as irrational and fanciful but that derision neither explains nor reduces its power.

Ethnicity is 'doing'

John Stuart-Mill recognized that the modern polity required a particular kind of civility behavior, 'doing,' if it was to achieve stability, and he recognized that ethnicity was a disruptive rival. Marx also recognized that the modern economy required proletarian unity, a particular kind of 'doing' to curb the evils of capitalism and to more widely share the bounty of modern technology. He also recognized ethnicity as a disruptive rival. Parsons recognized that existence in a modern urban society requires an achieved status, a particular kind of 'doing' unrelated to the principle of 'doing' within ethnicity. The 'doing' of ethnicity is related to the common paternal lineage shared by all that places transcendental responsibilities on each actor. The physical heritage of ethnicity creates expressive obligations and opportunities for behaving as the ancestors behaved and preserving their great heritage by transmitting it to generation after generation. The 'doings' of ethnicity are thus more meaningful than the goal-directed behavior theoretically involved through civility, rationality, or other such mundane approaches. The 'doings' of ethnicity preserve, confirm, and augment collective identities and the natural order. Ethnic 'doings' promise solutions to current problems and to problems yet unstated and unknown.

Ethnic 'doings' are often linguistically encumbered, dependent, and expressable only within traditional ethnic networks. Songs, chants, sayings, prayers, invocations, formulas, rites, jokes, and riddles are all required, recognized, expected, rewarded, and undetachable from ethnic communities. They are viewed and fully available only through the linguistic systems to which they are naturally related.

'Doing' is ultimately more negotiable than 'being' since behavior and linguistic media are subject to change, but even these changes are subject to authentication before the resulting behavior is justified. The changes are limited to the revitalization and recapture of authentic linguistic expressions. When linguistic shifts occur they will always tend to relate partially and symbolically to the ancestral patrimony befitting the 'corpus mysticum.'

Obviously, the language component, just as the entire ethnic behavior pattern, tends toward periodic revitalization. Current needs and problems are always a factor in ethnicity. The past always needs to be recaptured, used, interpreted, and exploited to resolve current problems. Thus, ethnicity is more than a means of preserving the past; it also has the potential for giving direction and providing group identity during change. The authentication of behavior has a potential for completing increasingly novel and modern social tasks. Even so, the authentication process increasingly depends upon language. Eastern Europe exemplifies how ethnic authenticity has been used for new 'collective' purposes and how language has been used to authenticate those purposes and maximize their attainment.

Ethnicity is 'knowing'

Classical Hebraic and Greek theories stress ethnicity as 'knowing,' i.e. they derived philosophy and even cosmology from an ethnic basis. However, ethnic 'knowing' has deep roots in all cultures. The physical authenticity of ethnicity requires that we 'do' what is authentic and promises that we will appreciate infinitely more as a result. Authentic ethnic responses permit people to be wise in special ways, more sensitive to inter-personal vibrations. They allow people to react to unique stimuli and to intuit what others cannot grasp. Ethnicity is a *Weltanschauung* that helps to explain origins, clarify eternal questions, rationalize human destiny, and purports to offer an entre to universal truths.

Ethnic 'doings' and 'knowings' are commonly considered to be impossible in any language other than the authentic. However, ethnicity is not necessarily Whorfian[2] since authentic language is not necessarily an active agent or a causative factor. Rather, it is more often a reflective or merely a traditionally linked factor. In either case the language of authenticity is a genuine and altogether frugal route to wisdom derived from authentic 'being' and 'doing.' Wisdom requires an authentic medium since any other mode of expression would be inadequate, shallow, and self-limiting in expressing the treasures that need to be enjoyed and sensed. This link between language and ethnic 'knowing' is still vibrant in Eastern Europe where language is a vehicle of communication, an identifier and authenticator of individuals within groups, and of groups in relation to their heritages of wisdom. Language permits an exquisitely refined and unique awareness of eternal verities so it contributes a unique meaning to life and deserves a unique devotion and dedication from the living. Since the wisdom derived from the language of authenticity is unspecified and unlimited it is likely to provide insights into current and future problems and salvation, even as it has so many times in the past. Language movements are built around this putative association so that authentic languages could be more fully established, protected, and cultivated. The masses in such movements have not been motivated by any objective 'need' to unify modern economies and polities with their linguistically embedded school systems.[3] On the contrary, they are motivated by the subjective need to unite with their brothers and sisters in applying their authenticated wisdom to the solutions of current problems. No external knowledge or objective scepticism can replace the validity of language and ethnicity. Objectivity and external observation cannot replace the human being's need to belong intimately, inter-generationally, authentically. At best, we can only attempt to understand that need if we do not experience it ourselves.

Ethnicity and irrationality

Traditionally Western European intellectuals have debunked ethnicity—and have tended to ascribe it to disruptive and disadvantaged peoples. They have never recognized it in themselves or in their own unmarked societies. They have denied the mutability, manipulability, and purposiveness of ethnicity and therefore the functionality of the link between language and ethnicity. Those denials need to be examined both with respect to their validity, as well as to assist in understanding the subjective nature of ethnicity. That examination will emphasize the limitations of modern Western European social theory as an approach to an understanding of ethnicity.

Mutability

Western European and American social theories often unwittingly arose from the changes resulting from the industrial revolution. Of course, the industrial revolution was itself a by-product of the prior characteristics and experiences of Western Europe. Accordingly, those theories are often unjustifiably harsh in their analysis of the mutability inherent in ethnicity. Ethnicity is exceptionally prone to change in terms of membership, content, and saliency[4] and since ethnicity claims and stresses authenticity, its mutability may be viewed as a flaw which invalidates and discredits it as a social phenomenon. That critique frequently involves the vulgarization of ethnicity, a treatment that would be sharply rejected by the advocates of other theories. The pristine, unaltered ethnic nation is a myth, but so is the notion of a super-ethnic proletariat or intelligentsia. Furthermore the observations made of a phenomenon in constant change may still be valid. Theories of social change should observe changes in ethnicity with interest rather than citing change to discredit the validity of its role. Because political science and sociology tend to reject ethnicity as a causal factor in social change it is damned if it does change and damned if it doesn't. That irrational and infantile rejection of ethnicity is probably related to its preverbal-nonverbal origins. The role of ethnicity in social change has been prematurely denied without having been fully and constructively examined.

However, those involved in the study of ethnicity as a legitimate social concern view the mutability of ethnicity in one of two ways. It may be viewed as a decline of interest justifying renewed dedication, effort, and devotion to pristine authenticity. In this sense, some of the advocates as well as some of the critics of ethnicity react similarly by rejecting mutability. However, their conclusions differ greatly; the advocates are drawn to greater commitment and the critics to greater repulsion. Another kind of 'within the fold' reaction to the evidence of mutability accepts change as the essence of ethnicity. The mainspring or essence of authenticity is believed to be the preordained 'wisdom' essential to the acceptance of necessary and desirable change, growth, alteration and self-correction. This change-accepting rationale belies the notion that ethnicity is a 'backward looking' or 'ancestor worshiping' ethos. Actually, ethnicity is neither, rather it is an experience of deeply rooted, intimate and eternal belonging. The operating principle of ethnicity is authenticity which operates to reject as well as validate mutability, depending on the particular social, historical, and personal environment. Ethnicity movements exploit mutability just as other modern movements do.

Language academies established to preserve 'the authentic spirit' of particular languages while entrusted with their modernization exemplify the penchant that ethnicity systems have for simultaneously pursuing authenticity and modernization (mutability). For example, the 'great Sun' theory, which viewed all European languages as repositories of Turkish genius, and the exploitation of Graeco-Latin roots in Talmudic and Medieval Hebrew, make it clear that authenticity is directional in inspiration and outcome. The desire to be modern 'in an authentic way' (in 'our own way' while remaining 'true to our own genius,' and so as to 'preserve our own heritage') tells us a great deal about the depth of commitment and adaptability of ethnicity. That kind of commitment and adaptability can be studied best in Eastern Europe where the simultaneous urge toward authenticity and modernization has been massive and intensive. Those who sneer at fabricated peasant costumes, folk songs, folk dances and folk derivations of communism and democracy defy understanding the phenomenon they seek to explain. However, ethnicity continues to become multi-faceted because of its ability to indigenize the modern world.

Manipulability

The need to belong deeply and intimately to an ethnic aggregate is a powerful motivation. Consequently, ethnicity has motivated movements in all possible directions on the political compass. Ethnicity has been unjustly criticized because of its purportedly greater manipulability. The anti-ethnic revulsion that followed the Nazi and Fascist excesses resulted because those excesses were confused with ethnicity. It should be noted that ethnicity movements in the early nineteenth century were largely moderate and libertarian. The Greek, Polish, Italian and Irish movements toward independence all adhered to the kind of self-respect that permits respectful acceptance of other nations. This view was also typical of early South Slavic and East Slavic ethnicity movements. However, following the success of the Junkers in unifying Germany, and that of the Tsarists in subverting the revolution of 1905 the manipulation of ethnicity was increasingly dominated by militant and messianic-cataclysmic symbols. At the same time socialist movements also became more militant, apocalyptic, and cataclysmic in method and theory. The earlier socialist tradition of gradualism was paralleled by the traditional gradualistic approach of those who advocated ethnicity. The 'excesses of ethnicity' have more than been matched by the excesses of non- or anti-ethnic modernization and secularization. Secular messiahs and totalitarian democracies have[5] visited indescribable horrors upon vast populations without reference to ethnicity. The clashes between these movements on the domestic and, increasingly on the international stages, foreshadow greater dangers ahead. Nevertheless, ethnicity alone is often the whipping boy.

In everyday traditional life ethnicity is not nearly as manipulable as it is on the modern politicist arena. The quiet, self-defining routines of habitual comfort and authenticity is the core of ethnicity. The manipulation of ethnicity to attain political, economic or cultural goals is a modern manifestation and is certainly one of the least unique features of ethnicity. Indeed, it is often the enemy of unmobilized ethnicity. The immemorial nature of unmobilized ethnicity and its power when mobilized are patent and potent in Eastern Europe. The use of language to achieve mobilization is clear but the authenticity of language pre-dates mobilization, manipulation, and that is further subjective proof of the continuity between authenticity and modernization.

['Social theory and ethnography', in Peter Sugar (ed.), *Ethnic Diversity and Conflict in Eastern Europe* (Santa Barbara, ABC-Clio, 1980), 84–97.]

WALKER CONNOR

11 Beyond Reason: The Nature of the Ethnonational Bond

For the sake of clarity, we begin by noting that nationalism and patriotism refer to two quite distinct loyalties: the former to one's national group; the latter to one's state (country) and its institutions. For people, such as the Japanese, who possess their own ethnically homogeneous *nation-state* and for *staatvolk*, such as the French, who are culturally and politically preeminent in a state, even though other groups are present in significant numbers, the fact that nationalism and patriotism are two different phenomena is usually of little consequence. For such people, the two loyalties tend to blur into a seamless whole. But in a world containing thousands of ethnonational groups and less than two hundred states, it is evident that for most people the sense of loyalty to one's nation and to one's state do not coincide. And they often compete for the allegiance of the individual.

For example, a Basque or Catalan nationalism has often been in conflict with a Spanish patriotism, a Tibetan nationalism with a Chinese patriotism, a Flemish nationalism with a Belgian patriotism, a Corsican nationalism with a French patriotism, a Kashmiri nationalism with an Indian patriotism, a Québèc nationalism with a Canadian patriotism. The list could be lengthened several times over. Nationalism and patriotism are vitally different phenomena and should not be confused through the careless use of language.

We know from the comparative study of nationalism that when the two loyalties are perceived as being in irreconcilable conflict—that is to say, when people feel they must choose between them—nationalism customarily proves the more potent. You have been privileged in your lifetime to witness one of history's most vivid illustrations of the relative strength of these two loyalties: the very recent case of the Soviet Union, wherein a beleaguered Soviet President Gorbachev only belatedly discovered that a sense of loyalty to the Union of Soviet Socialist Republics (what, for seventy years had been termed *Soviet patriotism*) was no match for the sense of nationalism demonstrated by nearly all of the peoples of the Soviet Union, including even the Russian nation. And obviously, events within what, until recently, was known as the Federal Republic of Yugoslavia certify that Albanian, Bosnian, Croatian, and Slovene nationalism has each proven itself far more potent than a Yugoslav patriotism.

To understand why nationalism customarily proves to be a far more powerful force than patriotism, it is necessary to take a closer look at national consciousness and national sentiment. What, for example, is the nature of the bond that both unites all Poles and differentiates them from the remainder of humanity? Until quite recently it was the vogue among prominent writers on nationalism to stress the tangible characteristics of a nation. The nation was defined as a community of people characterized by a common language, territory, religion, and the like. Probing the nation would be a far easier task if it could be explained in terms of such tangible criteria. How much simpler it would be if adopting the Polish language, living within Poland, and adhering to Catholicism were sufficient to define membership in the Polish nation—were sufficient to make one a Pole. But there are Germans, Lithuanians, and Ukrainians who meet these criteria but who do not consider themselves Polish and are not considered Polish by their Polish fellow citizens.

Objective criteria, in and by themselves, are therefore insufficient to determine whether or not a group constitutes a nation. The essence of the nation is a psychological bond that joins a people and differentiates it, in the subconscious conviction of its members, from all nonmembers in a most vital way.

With but very few exceptions, authorities have shied from describing the nation as a kinship group and have usually explicitly denied any kinship basis to it. These denials are customarily supported by data showing that most nations do in fact contain several genetic strains. But this line of reasoning ignores the dictum that it is not *what is* but *what people perceive as is* which influences attitudes and behavior. And a subconscious belief in the group's separate origin and evolution is an important ingredient of national psychology.

In ignoring or denying the sense of kinship that infuses the nation, scholars have been blind to that which has been thoroughly apparent to nationalist leaders. In sharpest contrast with most academic analysts of nationalism, those who have successfully mobilized nations have understood that at the core of ethnopsychology is the sense of shared blood, and they have not hesitated to appeal to it. Consequently, nationalistic speeches and proclamations tend to be more fruitful areas for research into the emotional/psychological nature of nationalism than are scholarly works. Too often such speeches and proclamations have been precipitously dismissed as propaganda in which the leadership did not truly believe. But nationalism is a mass phenomenon, and the degree to which its inciters are true believers does not affect its reality. The question is not the sincerity of the propagandist, but the nature of the mass instinct to which he or she appeals. [...]

Unlike most writers on nationalism, then, political leaders of the most diverse ideological strains have been mindful of the common blood component of ethnonational psychology and have not hesitated to appeal to it when seeking popular support. Both the frequency and the record of success of such appeals attest to the fact that nations are indeed characterized by a sense—a feeling—of consanguinity.

Our answer, then, to that often asked question, 'What is a nation?' is that it is a group of people who feel that they are ancestrally related. It is the largest group that can command a person's loyalty because of felt kinship ties; it is, from this perspective, the fully extended family.

The sense of unique descent, of course, need not, and *in nearly all* cases *will not*, accord with factual history. Nearly all nations are the variegated offsprings of numerous ethnic strains. It is not chronological or factual history that is the key to the nation, but sentient or felt history. All that is irreducibly required for the existence of a nation is that the members share an intuitive conviction of the group's separate origin and evolution. To aver that one is a member of the Japanese, German, or Thai nation is not merely to identify oneself with the Japanese, German, or Thai people of today, but with that people throughout time. Or rather—given the intuitive conviction that one's nation is unique in its origin—perhaps we should say not *throughout time* but *beyond time*. Logically, such a sense of one's nation's origin must rest upon a presumption that somewhere in a hazy, prerecorded era there existed a

Japanese, German, or Thai Adam and Eve. But logic operates in the realm of the conscious and the rational; convictions concerning the singular origin and evolution of one's nation belong to the realm of the subconscious and the nonrational (note: not *ir*rational but non-rational).

This distinction between reason and the emotional essence of the nation was expressed in a tract written a few years back by a person in solitary confinement within the Soviet Union. He had just been found guilty of antistate activities in the name of Ukrainian nationalism. He wrote:

> A nation can exist only where there are people who are prepared to die for it; . . .
> Only when its sons believe that their nation is chosen by God and regard their people as His highest creation.
> I know that all people are equal.
> My reason tells me that.
> But at the same time I know that my nation is unique . . .
> My heart tells me so.
> It is not wise to bring the voices of reason and of emotion to a common denominator.[1]

The dichotomy between the realm of national identity and that of reason has proven vexing to students of nationalism. With the exception of psychologists, people trained in the social sciences tend to be uncomfortable in confronting the nonrational. They are inclined to seek rational explanations for the nation in economic and other 'real' forces. But national consciousness resists explication in such terms. Indeed, in a strong testament to the difficulty of explicating national consciousness in any terms, Sigmund Freud, who spent so many years exploring and describing what he termed 'the unconscious,' acknowledged that the emotional wellsprings of national identity defied articulation. After noting that he was Jewish, Freud made clear that his own sense of Jewishness had nothing to do with either religion or national pride. He went on to note that he was 'irresistibly' bonded to Jews and Jewishness by 'many obscure and emotional forces, *which were the more powerful the less they could be expressed in words*, as well as by a clear consciousness of inner identity, a deep realization of sharing the same psychic structure.'[2]

Having noted that national identity defied articulation in rational terms, Freud made no attempt to further describe the national bond and the feelings to which it gives rise, but there is no mistaking that the sentiments he was trying to express are the same as those more concisely and enigmatically summed up in the German maxim, 'Blut will zu Blut!'—a loose translation of which might be 'People of the same blood attract!' A nineteenth-century author, Adolph Stocker, expanded on this sentiment: 'German blood flows in every German body, and the soul is in the blood. When one meets a German brother and not merely a brother from common humanity, there is a certain reaction that does not take place if the brother is not German.'[3] 'German' in this passage could, of course, be replaced by English, Russian, Lithuanian, etc. without affecting the passage's validity. Indeed, the thrust of the passage is remarkably similar to the sentiment expressed by a young Chinese nationalist revolutionary (Chen Tiannua) around 1900:

> As the saying goes, a man is not close to people of another family. When two families fight each other, one surely assists one's own family, one definitely does not help the 'exterior' family. Common families all descend from one original family: the Han race is one big family. The Yellow Emperor is a great ancestor, all those who are not of the Han race are not the descendants of the Yellow Emperor, they are exterior families. One should definitely not assist them; if one assists them, one lacks a sense of ancestry.[4]

No matter how described—Freud's interior identity and psychic structure, or blood-ties, or chemistry, or soul—it is worth repeating that the national bond is subconscious and emotional rather than conscious and rational in its inspiration. It can be analyzed but not explained rationally.

How can we analyze it? It can be at least obliquely analyzed by examining the type of catalysts to which it responds, that is to say, by examining the proven techniques for reaching and triggering national responses. And how has the nonrational core of the nation been reached and triggered? As we have seen in the case of numerous successful nationalist leaders, not *through* appeals to reason but *through* appeals to the emotions (appeals not to the mind but to the blood).

The nonrational core of the nation has been reached and triggered *through* national symbols, as historically varied as the rising sun, the swastika, and Britannia. Such symbols can speak messages without words to members of the nation, because, as one author has noted, 'there is something about such symbols, especially visual ones, which reach the parts rational explanation cannot reach.'

The nonrational core has been reached and triggered *through* nationalist poetry because the poet is far more adept than the writer of learned tracts at expressing deeply felt emotion, as witness the following words written in 1848 by a Romanian poet to describe the Romanian nation:

> It is in it that we were born, it is our mother;
> We are men because it reared us;
> We are free because we move in it;
> If we are angered, it soothes our pain with national songs.
> Through it we talk today to our parents who lived thousands of
> years back;
> Through it our descendents and posterity thousands of years later
> will know us.

The nonrational core has been reached and triggered *through* music popularly perceived as reflecting the nation's particular past or genius; the music may vary in sophistication, embracing the work of composers such as Richard Wagner, as well as folk music.

The core of the nation has been reached and triggered *through* the use of familial metaphors which can magically transform the mundanely tangible into emotion-laden phantasma: which can, for example, mystically convert what the outsider sees as merely the territory populated by a nation into a motherland or fatherland, the ancestral land, land of our fathers, this sacred soil, land where our fathers died, the native land, the cradle of the nation, and, most commonly, the *home*—the *home*land of our particular people—a 'Mother Russia,' an Armenia, a Deutschland, an England (Engla land: land of the Angles), or a Kurdistan (literally, land of the Kurds). Here is an Uzbek poet referring to Uzbekistan:

> So that my generation would comprehend the Homeland's worth,
> Men were always transformed to dust, it seems.
> The Homeland is the remains of our forefathers
> Who turned into dust for this precious soil.[5]

A spiritual bond between nation and territory is thus touched. As concisely stated in the nineteenth-century German couplet, 'Blut und Boden,' blood and soil become mixed in national perceptions.

It is, then, the character of appeals made through and to the senses, not through and to reason, which permit us some knowledge of the subconscious convictions that people tend to harbor concerning their nation. The near universality with which certain images and phrases appear—blood, family, brothers, sisters, mother, forefathers, ancestors, home—and the proven success of such invocations in eliciting massive, popular responses tell us much about the nature of national identity. But, again, this line of research does not provide a rational explanation for it.

Rational would-be explanations have abounded: relative economic deprivation; elite ambitions; rational choice theory; intense transaction flows; the desire of the intelligentsia to convert a 'low,' subordinate culture into a 'high,' dominant one; cost-benefit considerations; internal colonialism; a ploy of the bourgeoisie to undermine the class consciousness of the proletariat by obscuring the conflicting class interests within each nation, and by encouraging rivalry among the proletariat of various nations; a somewhat spontaneous mass response to competition for scarce resources. All such theories can be criticized on empirical grounds. But they can be faulted principally for their failure to reflect the emotional depth of national identity: the passions at either extreme end of the hate-love continuum which the nation often inspires, and the countless fanatical sacrifices which have been made in its name. As Chateaubriand expressed it nearly 200 years ago: 'Men don't allow themselves to be killed for their interests; they allow themselves to be killed for their passions.'[6] To phrase it differently: people do not voluntarily die for things that are rational.

[*Ethno-nationalism: The Quest for Understanding* (Princeton University Press, 1994), 196–8, 202–6.]

FREDRIK BARTH

12 Ethnic Groups and Boundaries

The main theoretical departure consists of several interconnected parts. First, we give primary emphasis to the fact that ethnic groups are categories of ascription and identification by the actors themselves, and thus have the characteristic of organizing interaction between people. We attempt to relate other characteristics of ethnic groups to this primary feature. Second, the essays all apply a generative viewpoint to the analysis: rather than working through a typology of forms of ethnic groups and relations, we attempt to explore the different processes that seem to be involved in generating and maintaining ethnic groups. Third, to observe these processes we shift the focus of investigation from internal constitution and history of separate groups to ethnic boundaries and boundary maintenance. Each of these points needs some elaboration.

Ethnic group defined

The term ethnic group is generally understood in anthropological literature[1] to designate a population which:

1. is largely biologically self-perpetuating
2. shares fundamental cultural values, realized in overt unity in cultural forms
3. makes up a field of communication and interaction
4. has a membership which identifies itself, and is identified by others, as constituting a category distinguishable from other categories of the same order.

This ideal type definition is not so far removed in content from the traditional proposition that a race = a culture = a language and that a society = a unit which rejects or discriminates against others. Yet, in its modified form it is close enough to many empirical ethnographic situations, at least as they appear and have been reported, so that this meaning continues to serve the purposes of most anthropologists. My quarrel is not so much with the substance of these characteristics, though as I shall show we can profit from a certain change of emphasis; my main objection is that such a formulation prevents us from understanding the phenomenon of ethnic groups and their place in human society and culture. This is because it begs all the critical questions: while purporting to give an ideal type model of a recurring empirical form, it implies a preconceived view of what are the significant factors in the genesis, structure, and function of such groups.

Most critically, it allows us to assume that boundary maintenance is unproblematical and follows from the isolation which the itemized characteristics imply: racial difference, cultural difference, social separation and language barriers, spontaneous and organized enmity. This also limits the range of factors that we use to explain cultural diversity: we are led to imagine each group developing its cultural and social form in relative isolation, mainly in response to local ecologic factors, through a history of adaptation by invention and selective borrowing. This history has produced a world of separate peoples, each with their culture and each organized in a society which can legitimately be isolated for description as an island to itself.

Ethnic groups as culture-bearing units

Rather than discussing the adequacy of this version of culture history for other than pelagic islands, let us look at some of the logical flaws in the viewpoint. Among the characteristics listed above, the sharing of a common culture is generally given central importance. In my view, much can be gained by regarding this very important feature as an implication or result, rather than a primary and definitional characteristic of ethnic group organization. If one chooses to regard the culture-bearing aspect of ethnic groups as their primary characteristic, this has far-reaching implications. One is led to identify and distinguish ethnic groups by the morphological characteristics of the cultures of which they are the bearers. This entails a prejudged viewpoint both on (1) the nature of continuity in time of such units, and (2) the locus of the factors which determine the form of the units.

1. Given the emphasis on the culture-bearing aspect, the classification of persons and local groups as members of an ethnic group must depend on their exhibiting the particular traits of the culture. This is something that can be judged objectively by the ethnographic observer, in the culture-area tradition, regardless of the categories and prejudices of the actors. Differences between groups become differences in trait inventories; the attention is drawn to the analysis of cultures, not of ethnic organization. The dynamic relationship between groups will then be depicted in acculturation studies of the kind that have been attracting decreasing interest in anthropology, though their theoretical inadequacies have never been seriously discussed. Since the historical provenance of any assemblage of culture traits is diverse, the viewpoint also gives scope for an 'ethnohistory' which chronicles cultural accretion and change, and seeks to explain why certain items were borrowed.

However, what is the unit whose continuity in time is depicted in such studies? Paradoxically, it must include cultures in the past which would clearly be excluded in the present because of differences in form—differences of precisely the kind that are diagnostic in synchronic differentiation of ethnic units. The interconnection between 'ethnic group' and 'culture' is certainly not clarified through this confusion.

2. The overt cultural forms which can be itemized as traits exhibit the effects of ecology. By this I do not mean to refer to the fact that they reflect a history of adaptation to environment; in a more immediate way they also reflect the external circumstances to which actors must accommodate themselves. The same group of people, with unchanged values and ideas, would surely pursue different patterns of life and institutionalize different forms of behaviour when faced with the different opportunities offered in different environments? Likewise, we must expect to find that one ethnic group, spread over a territory with varying ecologic circumstances, will exhibit regional diversities of overt institutionalized behaviour which do not reflect differences in cultural orientation. How should they then be classified if overt institutional forms are diagnostic? A case in point is the distributions and diversity of Pathan local social systems. By basic Pathan values, a Southern Pathan from the homogeneous, lineage-organized mountain areas, can only find the behaviour of Pathans in Swat so different from, and reprehensible in terms of, their own values that they declare their northern brothers 'no longer Pathan'. Indeed, by 'objective' criteria, their overt pattern of organization seems much closer to that of Panjabis. But I found it possible, by explaining the circumstances in the north, to make Southern Pathans agree that these were indeed Pathans too, and grudgingly to admit that under those circumstances they might indeed themselves act in the same way. It is thus inadequate to regard overt institutional forms as constituting the cultural features which at any time distinguish an ethnic group—these overt forms are determined by ecology as well as by transmitted culture. Nor can it be claimed that every such diversification within a group represents a first step in the direction of subdivision and multiplication of units. We have well-known documented cases of one ethnic group, also at a relatively simple level of economic organization, occupying several different ecologic niches and yet retaining basic cultural and ethnic unity over long periods (cf., e.g., inland and coastal Chuckchee[2] or reindeer, river, and coast Lapps[3]).

In one of the following essays, Blom (pp. 74 ff.) argues cogently on this point with reference to central Norwegian mountain farmers. He shows how their participation and self-evaluation in terms of general Norwegian values secures them continued membership in the larger ethnic group, despite the highly characteristic and deviant patterns of activity which the local ecology imposes on them. To analyse such cases, we need a viewpoint that does not confuse the effects of ecologic circumstances on behaviour with those of cultural tradition, but which makes it possible to separate these factors and investigate the non-ecological cultural and social components creating diversity.

Ethnic groups as an organizational type

By concentrating on what is *socially* effective, ethnic groups are seen as a form of social organization. The critical feature then becomes item (4) in the list above, the characteristic of self-ascription and ascription by others. A categorical ascription is an ethnic ascription when it classifies a person in terms of his basic, most general identity, presumptively determined by his origin and background. To the extent that actors use ethnic identities to categorize themselves and others for purposes of interaction, they form ethnic groups in this organizational sense.

It is important to recognize that although ethnic categories take cultural differences into account, we can assume no simple one-to-one relationship between ethnic units and cultural similarities and differences. The features that are taken into account are not the sum of 'objective' differences, but only those which the actors themselves regard as significant. Not only do ecologic variations mark and exaggerate differences; some cultural features are used by the actors as signals and emblems of differences, others are ignored, and in some relationships radical differences are played down and denied. The cultural contents of ethnic dichotomies would seem analytically to be of two orders: (i) overt signals or signs—the diacritical features that people look for and exhibit to show identity, often such features as dress, language, house-form, or general style of life, and (ii) basic value orientations: the standards of morality and excellence by which performance is judged. Since belonging to an ethnic category implies being a certain kind of person, having that basic identity, it also implies a claim to be judged, and to judge oneself, by those standards that are relevant to that identity. Neither of these kinds of cultural 'contents' follows from a descriptive list of cultural features or cultural differences; one cannot predict from first principles which features will be emphasized and made organizationally relevant by the actors. In other words, ethnic categories provide an organizational vessel that may be given varying amounts and forms of content in different socio-cultural systems. They may be of great relevance to behaviour, but they need not be; they may pervade all social life, or they may be relevant only in limited sectors of activity. There is thus an obvious scope for ethnographic and comparative descriptions of different forms of ethnic organization.

The emphasis on ascription as the critical feature of ethnic groups also solves the two conceptual difficulties that were discussed above.

1. When defined as an ascriptive and exclusive group, the nature of continuity of ethnic units is clear: it depends on the maintenance of a boundary.

The cultural features that signal the boundary may change, and the cultural characteristics of the members may likewise be transformed, indeed, even the organizational form of the group may change—yet the fact of continuing dichotomization between members and outsiders allows us to specify the nature of continuity, and investigate the changing cultural form and content.

2. Socially relevant factors alone become diagnostic for membership, not the overt, 'objective' differences which are generated by other factors. It makes no difference how dissimilar members may be in their overt behaviour—if they say they are A, in contrast to another cognate category B, they are willing to be treated and let their own behaviour be interpreted and judged as A's and not as B's; in other words, they declare their allegiance to the shared culture of A's. The effects of this, as compared to other factors influencing actual behaviour, can then be made the object of investigation.

The boundaries of ethnic groups

The critical focus of investigation from this point of view becomes the ethnic boundary that defines the group, not the cultural stuff that it encloses. The boundaries to which we must give our attention are of course social boundaries, though they may have territorial counterparts. If a group maintains its identity when members interact with others, this entails criteria for determining membership and ways of signalling membership and exclusion. Ethnic groups are merely or necessarily based on the occupation of exclusive territories; and the different ways in which they are maintained, not only by a once-and-for-all recruitment but by continual expression and validation, need to be analysed.

What is more, the ethnic boundary canalizes social life—it entails a frequently quite complex organization of behaviour and social relations. The identification of another person as a fellow member of an ethnic group implies a sharing of criteria for evaluation and judgement. It thus entails the assumption that the two are fundamentally 'playing the same game', and this means that there is between them a potential for diversification and expansion of their social relationship to cover eventually all different sectors and domains of activity. On the other hand, a dichotomization of others as strangers, as members of another ethnic group, implies a recognition of limitations on shared understandings, differences in criteria for judgement of value and performance, and a restriction of interaction to sectors of assumed common understanding and mutual interest.

This makes it possible to understand one final form of boundary maintenance whereby cultural units and boundaries persist. Entailed in ethnic boundary maintenance are also situations of social contact between persons of different cultures: ethnic groups only persist as significant units if they imply marked difference in behaviour, i.e. persisting cultural differences. Yet where persons of different culture interact, one would expect these differences to be reduced, since interaction both requires and generates a congruence of codes and values—in other words, a similarity or community of culture.[4] Thus the persistence of ethnic groups in contact implies not only criteria and signals for identification, but also a structuring of interaction which allows the persistence of cultural differences. The organizational feature which, I would argue, must be general for all inter-ethnic relations is a systematic set of rules governing inter-ethnic social encounters. In all organized social life, what can be made relevant to interaction in any particular social situation is prescribed.[5] If people agree about these prescriptions, their agreement on codes and values need not extend beyond that which is relevant to the social situations in which they interact. Stable inter-ethnic relations presuppose such a structuring of interaction: a set of prescriptions governing situations of contact, and allowing for articulation in some sectors or domains of activity, and a set of proscriptions on social situations preventing inter-ethnic interaction in other sectors, and thus insulating parts of the cultures from confrontation and modification.

Poly-ethnic social systems

This of course is what Furnivall[6] so clearly depicted in his analysis of plural society: a poly-ethnic society integrated in the market place, under the control of a state system dominated by one of the groups, but leaving large areas of cultural diversity in the religious and domestic sectors of activity.

What has not been adequately appreciated by later anthropologists is the possible variety of sectors of articulation and separation, and the variety of poly-ethnic systems which this entails. We know of some of the Melanesian trade systems in objects belonging to the high-prestige sphere of the economy, and even some of the etiquette and prescriptions governing the exchange situation and insulating it from other activities. We have information on various traditional polycentric systems from S.E. Asia integrated both in the prestige trade sphere and in quasi-feudal political structures. Some regions of S.W. Asia show forms based on a more fully monetized market economy, while political integration is polycentric in character. There is also the ritual and productive cooperation and political integration of the Indian caste system to be considered, where perhaps only kinship and domestic life remain as a proscribed sector and a wellspring for cultural diversity. Nothing can be gained by lumping these various systems under the increasingly vague label of 'plural' society, whereas an investigation of the varieties of structure can shed a great deal of light on social and cultural forms.

What can be referred to as articulation and separation on the macro-level corresponds to systematic sets of role constraints on the micro-level. Common to all these systems is the principle that ethnic identity implies a series of constraints on the kinds of roles an individual is allowed to play, and the partners he may choose for different kinds of transactions. In other words, regarded as a status, ethnic identity is superordinate to most other statuses, and defines the permissible constellations of statuses, or social personalities, which an individual with that identity may assume. In this respect ethnic identity is similar to sex and rank, in that it constrains the incumbent in all his activities, not only in some defined social situations. One might thus also say that it is *imperative*, in that it cannot be disregarded and temporarily set aside by other definitions of the situation. The constraints on a person's behaviour which spring from his ethnic identity thus tend to be absolute and, in complex poly-ethnic societies, quite comprehensive; and the component moral and social conventions are made further resistant to change by being joined in stereotyped clusters as characteristics of one single identity.

The associations of identities and value standards

The analysis of interactional and organizational features of interethnic relations has suffered from a lack of attention to problems of boundary maintenance. This is perhaps because anthropologists have reasoned from a misleading idea of the prototype inter-ethnic situation. One has tended to think in terms of different peoples, with different histories and cultures, coming together and accommodating themselves to each other, generally in a colonial setting. To visualize the basic requirements for the coexistence of ethnic diversity, I would suggest that we rather ask ourselves what is needed to make ethnic distinctions *emerge* in an area. The organizational requirements are clearly, first, a categorization of population sectors in exclusive and imperative status categories, and second, an acceptance of the principle that standards applied to one such category can be different from that applied to another. Though this alone does not explain why cultural differences emerge, it does allow us to see how they persist. Each category can then be associated with a separate range of value standards. The greater the differences between these value orientations are, the more constraints on inter-ethnic interaction do they entail: the statuses and situations in the total social system involving behaviour which is discrepant with a person's value orientations must be avoided, since such behaviour on his part will be negatively sanctioned. Moreover, because identities are signalled as well as embraced, new forms of behaviour will tend to be dichotomized: one would expect the role constraints to operate in such a way that persons would be reluctant to act in new ways from a fear that such behaviour might be inappropriate for a person of their identity, and swift to classify forms of activity as associated with one or another cluster of ethnic characteristics. Just as dichotomizations of male versus female work seem to proliferate in some societies, so also the existence of basic ethnic categories would seem to be a factor encouraging the proliferation of cultural differentiae.

In such systems, the sanctions producing adherence to group-specific values are not only exercised by those who share the identity. Again, other imperative statuses afford a parallel: just as both sexes ridicule the male who is feminine, and all classes punish the proletarian who puts on airs, so also can members of all ethnic groups in a poly-ethnic society act to maintain dichotomies and differences. Where social identities are organized and allocated by such principles, there will thus be a tendency towards canalization and standardization of interaction and the emergence of boundaries which maintain and generate ethnic diversity within larger, encompassing social systems.

Interdependence of ethnic groups

The positive bond that connects several ethnic groups in an encompassing social system depends on the complementarity of the groups with respect to some of their characteristic cultural features. Such complementarity can give rise to interdependence or symbiosis, and constitutes the areas of articulation referred to above; while in the fields where there is no complementarity there can be no basis for organization on ethnic lines—there will either be no interaction, or interaction without reference to ethnic identity.

Social systems differ greatly in the extent to which ethnic identity, as an imperative status, constrains the person in the variety of statuses and roles he may assume. Where the distinguishing values connected with ethnic identity are relevant only to a few kinds of activities, the social organization based on it will be similarly limited. Complex polyethnic systems, on the other hand, clearly entail the existence of extensively relevant value differences and multiple constraints on status combinations and social participation. In such systems, the boundary maintaining mechanisms must be highly effective, for the following reasons: (i) the complexity is based on the existence of important, complementary cultural differences; (ii) these differences must be generally standardized within the ethnic group—i.e. the status cluster, or social person, of every member of a group must be highly stereotyped—so that inter-ethnic interaction can be based on ethnic identities; and (iii) the cultural characteristics of each ethnic group must be stable, so that the complementary differences on which the systems rest can persist in the face of close inter-ethnic contact. Where these conditions obtain, ethnic groups can make stable and symbiotic adaptations to each other: other ethnic groups in the region become a part of the natural environment; the sectors of articulation provide areas that can be exploited, while the other sectors of activity of other groups are largely irrelevant from the point of view of members of any one group.

[*Ethnic Groups and Boundaries* (Boston: Little, Brown and Co., 1969), 10–19.]

ABNER COHEN

13 Ethnicity and Politics

The Informal Nature of Political Ethnicity

In the light of the foregoing discussion, a number of points can be made which can help in isolating the phenomena and processes of ethnicity.

Firstly, contemporary ethnicity is the result of intensive interaction between ethnic groupings and not the result of complete separatism. This is contrary to what one may call 'the glue theory of tribalism' which has been suggested by some writers. This theory states that during the colonial period, the colonial powers had acted as 'glue' in sticking together within the framework of new, artificially established, centralized states, some diverse 'tribal' groups, and that once the glue was removed when the colonial powers withdrew, each package state began to disintegrate and to fall into its original parts. It is of course true that many of the new states of Africa were originally created by the colonial powers. But during the colonial period a great deal of integration between the constituent tribal groups had taken place and this had given rise to increasing interaction between these groups. In British West Africa, this interaction was limited because of the policy of Indirect Rule and also because the strategic positions of centralized power were held by the foreign rulers. But the protective umbrella of Indirect Rule made it possible for some tribal groups to develop vital interests of their own while other tribal groups became relatively underprivileged. When the British withdrew an intense struggle for power ensued. The privileged became exposed to the danger of losing power and had to mobilize their forces in defence while the underprivileged aligned themselves to gain power.

Further and more bitter struggles broke out over new strategic positions of power: places of employment, taxation, funds for development, education, political positions, and so on. In many places the possibilities of capturing these new sources of power were different for different tribal groups, so that very often the resulting cleavages were on tribal lines. As a result of this intensified struggle, many tribal groups mobilized their forces and searched for ways in which they could organize themselves politically so as to conduct their struggle more effectively. In the process of this mobilization a new emphasis was placed on parts of their traditional culture, and this gave the impression that here there was a return to tribal tradition and to tribal separatism when in fact tribalism in the contemporary situation was one type of political grouping within the framework of the new state.

Secondly, tribalism involves a dynamic rearrangement of relations and of customs, and is not the outcome of cultural conservatism or continuity. The continuities of customs and of social formations are certainly there, but their functions have changed. As Gluckman pointed out a long time ago, 'where in a changing system the dominant cleavage is into two culture-groups, each of these groups will tend to set increasingly greater value on its own endo-culture, since this expresses the dominant cleavage'.[1]

Thirdly, ethnicity is essentially a political phenomenon, as traditional customs are used only as idioms, and as mechanisms for political alignment. People do not kill one another because their customs are different. Men may make jokes at the strange customs of men from other tribes but this by itself will not lead to serious disputes. If men do actually quarrel seriously on the grounds of cultural differences it is only because these cultural differences are associated with serious political cleavages. On the other hand men stick together under the contemporary situation only because of mutual interests. The Hausa of Sabo are united *vis-à-vis* the Yoruba because their unity is essential for their livelihood and for safeguarding their assets in the land and the buildings of the Quarter. Another tribal group may unite in order to mobilize votes in elections, to gain new benefits in development funds, or even to prevent the relatively scarce supply of women of the ethnic group from being taken by outsiders.

Finally, ethnic grouping is essentially informal. It does not form part of the official framework of economic and political power within the state. Otherwise, i.e. if an ethnic grouping is formally recognized, either as a state or as a region within a federal framework, then we are no longer dealing with ethnicity but with national or international politics. Thus according to this usage interaction between the regions of Nigeria should not be called ethnicity. Similarly the relations between various 'native authorities' during the colonial period cannot be called ethnicity since ethnic groupings under native authorities were officially recognized and a great part of their political organization was formally institutionalized. It is only when, within the formal framework of a national state or of any formal organization, an ethnic group informally organizes itself for political action, that we can say that we are dealing with ethnicity. Informally organized political groupings of this type have been called by different names. Bailey, borrowing a term from Easton, has called them 'parapolitical structures', and described them as those political structures 'which are partly regulated by, and partly independent of, larger encapsulating political structures; and which, so to speak, fight battles with these larger structures in a war which for them, seldom, if ever, ends in victory, rarely in dramatic defeat, but usually in a long drawn stalemate and defeat by attrition'.[2] Wolfe refers to the same kind of groupings when he states that 'the formal framework of economic and political power exists alongside or intermingled with various other kinds of informal structures which are interstitial, supplementary, parallel to it'.[3]

[*Custom and Politics in Urban Africa* (Berkeley: University of California Press, 1969), 198–201.]

14 Ethnic Groups and Ethnic Identity Formation

There are three ways of defining ethnic groups—in terms of objective attributes, with reference to subjective feelings, and in relation to behavior. An objective definition assumes that though no specific attribute is invariably associated with all ethnic categories, there must be some distinguishing cultural feature that clearly separates one group of people from another, whether that feature or features be language, territory, religion, color, diet, dress, or any of them. The problem with objective definitions is that it is usually extremely difficult to determine the boundaries of ethnic categories in this way.[1] The difficulty with subjective definitions is that they make it impossible to answer the basic question of how a group of people arrives at subjective self-consciousness in the first place. Behavioral definitions are really a form of objective definition since they assume that there are specific, concrete ways in which ethnic groups behave or do not behave, particularly in relation to and in interaction with other groups. Behavioral definitions merely suggest that there are cultural differences between ethnic groups, but that the critical distinctions reveal themselves only in interaction with other groups.[2] But, the existence of explicit codes of behavior and interaction is rather more characteristic, more all-pervasive, and more evident in simple than in complex societies in which people may establish their separateness with reference to specific attributes without adopting an entirely distinct code of behavior.

Subjective definitions will not, therefore, serve the analytical purpose of this book, which is to specify the conditions for the formation, persistence, and transformation of ethnic identities over time, whereas interactive definitions lack the universality required. The most appropriate definition for the aims of this book is one that begins with objective cultural markers but which also recognizes that they are susceptible to change and variation. Any group of people dissimilar from other peoples in terms of objective cultural criteria and containing within its membership, either in principle or in practice, the elements for a complete division of labor and for reproduction forms an ethnic category. The objective cultural markers may be a language or dialect, distinctive dress or diet or customs, religion or race. The inclusion in the definition of the phrase 'contains within its membership, either in principle or in practice, the elements for a complete division of labor and for reproduction' is designed to emphasize the cultural basis of ethnicity and to distinguish ethnic categories from other social categories based on class or gender or age grades.

Ethnicity is a sense of ethnic identity, which has been defined by De Vos as consisting of the 'subjective, symbolic or emblematic use' by 'a group of people . . . of any aspect of culture, in order to differentiate themselves from other groups.'[3] This definition can be used for the analytic purposes required here by altering the last phrase to read 'in order to create internal cohesion and differentiate themselves from other groups.' An ethnic group that uses cultural symbols in this way is a subjectively self-conscious *community* that establishes criteria for inclusion into and exclusion from the group. At this point, matters of descent, birth, and a sense of kinship may become important to ethnic group members, for the methods of inclusion and exclusion into the group often involve the explicit or tacit adoption of rules of endogamy and exogamy. Ethnicity or ethnic identity also involves, in addition to subjective self-consciousness, a claim to status and recognition, either as a superior group or as a group at least equal to other groups. Ethnicity is to ethnic category what class consciousness is to class.

Ethnicity is an alternative form of social organization and identification to class, but it is a contingent and changeable status that, like class, may or may not be articulated in particular contexts or at particular times.[4] Ethnic groups that use ethnicity to make demands in the political arena for alteration in their status, in their economic well-being, in their civil rights, or in their educational opportunities are engaged in a form of interest group politics which became prominent in the United States during the 1960s and 1970s and which sought to improve the well-being of group members as individuals.[5] However, some ethnic groups in other contexts go further and demand that corporate rights be conceded to the group as a whole, that they be given not just individual educational opportunities on the same basis as others, but that they be given control over the public system of education in their areas of concentration so that they can teach the history, language, and culture of their group to their own children. They demand a major say for the group in the political system as a whole or control over a piece of territory within the country, or they demand a country of their own with full sovereignty. In the latter case, the ethnic group aspires to national status and recognition. Insofar as it succeeds by its own efforts in achieving any one of these goals either within an existing state or in a state of its own, it has become a nationality or a nation.[6] A nation, therefore, may be seen as a particular type of ethnic community[7] or, rather, as an ethnic community politicized, with recognized group rights in the political system.[8] [. . .]

This process of development of communities from ethnic categories is particularly associated with the early stages of modernization in multiethnic societies where languages have not yet become standardized, where religious groups have not become highly structured and compartmentalized, and where social fragmentation is prevalent. However, the transition may occur even in postindustrial societies such as the United States, where Negroes have become Blacks, Mexican-Americans Chicanos, and many other ethnic groups have rediscovered their origins and identities.

The second stage in the transformation of ethnic groups involves the articulation and acquisition of social, economic, and political rights for the members of the group or for the group as a whole. Depending upon the perceived needs and demands of the group, its size and distribution, its relations with other groups, and the political context, demands may aim at relatively modest civil, educational, and political rights and opportunities for the individual members of the group or for recognition of the group's corporate existence as a political body or nationality. Insofar as an ethnic group succeeds by its own efforts in achieving and maintaining group rights through political action and political mobilization, it has gone beyond ethnicity to establish itself as a nationality.

The delineation of the process of nationality-formation in this manner suggests several problems that require explanation. First, what are the conditions under which ethnic groups become communities and under which ethnic demands, ethnic competition, and ethnic conflict take place? Second, what are the conditions under which an ethnic community is likely to make the major demand for status as a nationality and what are the requirements for success? Third, how does one explain the transformations that take place in the culture, behavior, and boundaries of a people as it undergoes the movement from ethnic group to nationality? Fourth, since it is also evident that ethnic and nationality movements frequently ebb and flow over time within the same group, how can one explain the resurgence of ethnicity and nationalism among diverse groups of people at different times and in different places? The focus of the remainder of this chapter will be on the first two questions, but the analysis will also touch, at several places, on the last two.

Ethnic differentiation: from ethnic groups to communities

The movement from ethnic group to community is a transition that some groups never make, that others make initially in modern times, and that still others undergo repeatedly at different points in time. In the first category are the various 'lost' peoples and speakers of diverse dialects who have merged into or are merging into other peoples—the Cornish in the United Kingdom, the Frisians in Holland, the Sorbs and Wends of Eastern and Central Europe, the Maithili-speaking people and numerous other dialect-speakers in north India. In the second category are the newly-formed ethnic groups and nationalities of the nineteenth and twentieth centuries—the Welsh and the Irish, the nationalities in Austria-Hungary, the Ibos in Nigeria, the Naga tribes in northeastern India and most of the language communities of contemporary India, the Malays in Malaysia. In the last category are the ancient peoples of the world, Jews, Han Chinese, Egyptians, and the major nationalities of Western Europe.

What are the conditions that determine whether or not one group will merge into another group, or will establish or reestablish and redefine its identity? The richness of a group's cultural heritage, the stage of development of its language, and the distinctiveness of its religious beliefs do not by themselves predetermine that one group of people will be more internally solidary than another and will be more likely to perpetuate itself through time. Absence of or loss of a distinctive language has not prevented Blacks in the United States or Celtic groups in the United Kingdom, or non-Hebrew, non-Yiddish speaking Jews in the United States from acquiring or maintaining a sense of ethnic identity. By the same token, over the centuries in Europe, old, fully standardized, written languages—Latin, Anglo-Saxon, Provencal, Low German, Church Slavonic—some of them spoken by peoples occupying compact geographical areas, have been 'submerged' while other languages have replaced or absorbed them.[9] Moreover, despite the fact that European culture, civilization, and science have for centuries been dominated increasingly by the three great languages, English, French, and German, this has not prevented 'the growth of linguistic diversity in Europe from 16 [standard] languages in 1800 to 30 in 1900 and to 53 in 1937'[10] and the attendant development of language communities among many of them.

Distinctive minority religious groups in modern times have often developed into ethnically selfconscious communities, but it has also often happened, particularly in Eastern Europe and in South Asia, that religious differences have been used or even created to establish or emphasize between peoples barriers that have non-religious origins. The attempt to establish a Uniate Church in Bulgaria, which culminated in the development of a separate hierarchy of Eastern Orthodoxy, has over time served to reinforce the ethnic separateness of Bulgarians from Greeks, but it was not religious distinctiveness that intially inspired the rise of Bulgarian ethnic consciousness. Islam in non-Muslim states has often provided a strong basis for Muslim separatism, but again it is not the distinctiveness of Islam as such in relation to other religions that is decisive, for the degree of Muslim communal self-consciousness varies in different contexts. For example, in Eastern Europe, Islam has served more effectively as a basis for ethnic separatism in Yugoslavia than in Albania.[11] Nor can Jewish religious distinctiveness explain Jewish ethnic separatism that culminated in Zionism, for often enough Jews chose to assimilate in Eastern Europe when conditions were favorable. In South Asia, Sikhism as a distinctive religion has its origins in the early sixteenth century, but it was not until the late nineteenth and early twentieth centuries that a militant body of believers began the process that continues up to the present day, i.e., of shaping and defining the boundaries of the Sikh community to conform to a particular view of Sikh orthodoxy and instilling in large segments of the Sikh population a sense of communal solidarity and separateness from Hindus.[12]

The process of creating communities from ethnic groups involves the selection of particular dialects or religious practices or styles of dress or historical symbols from a variety of available alternatives. It will be shown below that it is always the case that particular social groups, leaders, or élites stand to benefit and others to lose from the choices that are made.

Ethnicity and élite Competition

Ethnic communities are created and transformed by particular élites in modernizing and in postindustrial societies undergoing dramatic social change. This process invariably involves competition and conflict for political power, economic benefits, and social status between competing élite, class, and leadership groups both within and among different ethnic categories. Several scholars of ethnicity and nationality have pointed out that modernization and industrialization in large, multiethnic societies tend to proceed unevenly and often, if not always, benefit some ethnic groups or some regions of a country more than others.[13] However, inequality between different ethnic groups or culturally distinct regions does not by itself spur the development of communal or national consciousness. Speakers of an unstandardized local dialect in a backward rural region of a modernizing country may very well go on speaking their language and cultivating their fields without becoming concerned that their language is being neglected and without developing any sense of solidarity.[14] They may do so either because they are completely in the backwash of modernization, remote from urban lifestyles and only marginally affected by new educational opportunities and new means of mass communication and transportation, or because the locally powerful economic, religious, and political élites find it to their advantage to cooperate with external authorities and adopt the language and culture of the dominant ethnic group in order to maintain or enhance their own power. Relevant examples here are the Anglicized Welsh aristocracy in Wales in the nineteenth century, the Polonized Lithuanian nobility in Lithuania, and the Magyarized Romanian nobility in Transylvania. This kind of cooperation between internal élites and external authorities usually leads to a situation of persistent ethnic differences among the mass of the people, but without the articulation of ethnic demands.

Ethnic selfconsciousness, ethnically-based demands, and ethnic conflict can occur only if there is some conflict either between indigenous and external élites and authorities or between indigenous élites. Four sources of élite conflict that may spur the development of ethnic communalism or separatism in preindustrial or early modernizing societies are those (*a*) between a local aristocracy attempting to maintain its privileges against an alien conqueror; (*b*) between competing religious élites from different ethnic groups;

(*c*) between religious élites and the native aristocracy within an ethnic group; and (*d*) between native religious élites and an alien aristocracy.

[*Ethnicity and Nationalism* (New Delhi, Newbury Park, London: Sage Publications, 1991), 18–20, 22–6.]

MICHAEL HECHTER

15 Ethnicity and Rational Choice Theory

Rational choice considers individual behaviour to be a function of the interaction of structural constraints and the sovereign preferences of individuals. The structure first determines, to a greater or lesser extent, the constraints under which individuals act. Within these constraints, individuals face various feasible courses of action. The course of action ultimately chosen is selected rationally: in Parson's words,[1] 'individuals adapt means to their ends in such a way as to approach the most efficient manner of achieving them'. When individual preferences are assumed to be known, transitive and temporally stable, behaviour can be predicted in the face of any combination of structural constraints.

How can these assumptions be justified in macro-sociological research, especially when rational choice theorists also assume that each individual may have a set of preferences that is unique?

Whereas a certain (but unknown) proportion of every individual's preferences are idiosyncratic, the rest (such as preferences for wealth, honour and power) are commonly held by many others. These common preferences impel everyone in the group to act similarly. Some of the idiosyncratic preferences may result in singular action, but so long as the common preferences are known (a significant caveat, and one to which I will return below), then the idiosyncratic ones will cancel one another out and their average will be zero.

This may be true enough, but how can these common preferences ever be known? They can't be assumed *a priori*, for there is no practical limit upon them: as the adage has it, *chacun à son goût*. But it can be expected that everyone will prefer more wealth, power and honour to less, because attaining these goods often makes it easier for individuals to attain other (perhaps more idiosyncratic) goals. Although it would be foolish to predict the behaviour of any given individual, the law of large numbers allows predictions for the aggregate to be rather precise.[2]

According to such reasoning, individuals will only fulfil their corporate obligations when they receive a net benefit by doing so. As a result, both collective action and social order depend on the belief of most people that free riding and crime do not pay.[3] The rational actor will commit crime to attain his or her goals, unless deterred by the fear of incarceration (or some other punishment). Similarly, in large groups, where informal social controls lose their efficacy because individual networks rarely overlap, collective action is problematic because free riding is hard to detect.

Now unlike the other theories—both of which are curiously static—this one is eminently capable of explaining *changes* in behaviour. The mechanism it proposes in this respect is refreshingly simple. Changing relative prices leads to corresponding changes in behaviour: the more costly it is for people to choose a traditional course of action to achieve a given benefit, the more likely it is that they will consider an innovative alternative to reach the same end. Further, the causes of these price changes are endogenous to the explanation, since they are at least partly the result of a myriad of independent individual decisions which together comprise aggregate demand. Aggregate demand, in turn, pushes supply.

In contrast to both normative and structural theories, then, rational choice offers the prospect of arriving at predictive statements, rather than at the *post hoc* descriptions for which sociologists have had to settle too frequently in the past. This is a cherished goal for those who are committed to the development of a more scientific discipline. Three examples should suffice to illustrate something of the range of applications of rational choice theory in the field of ethnic and race relations.

Sowell[4] uses rational choice principles to explain patterns of racial discrimination in the job market. Consider a society having a low-status racial group whose members command a relatively low price in the labour market. Distancing typically occurs as a result of this kind of racial hierarchy: thus, members of the high-status group prefer to limit their social interaction with low-status individuals. If it is assumed that employers are profit-maximisers, and if they cannot effectively collude against the members of a particular group, then racial discrimination in hiring should be greater in non-profit-making organisations and regulated industries than in unregulated and profit-making enterprises.

Why should this be so? Even if all employers prefer to exclude low-status workers from their firms, whenever their pay is lower than their productivity there is an economic incentive to hire them. However, if employers are prevented from maximising profits by government regulatory agencies, or are legally non-profit-making, then they have no opportunity to earn more profit by hiring relatively inexpensive (and racially low-status) labour. Regulated industries are usually controlled by political bodies, so their hiring policies are less subject to economic constraints and more subject to political ones. This fact suggests an additional implication: should public objections to racial discrimination arise, the racial hiring policies of regulated industries will undergo a more rapid turn-around than those of unregulated industries.

Landa[5] seeks to explain why ethnically homogeneous middlemen are so much more common in Third World societies than in developed ones. Her argument begins with the problematic nature of exchange in rational choice theory. If two parties to a contract are both wealth-maximisers, what keeps either of them from abrogating the contract whenever this becomes profitable? In societies where contract law is both well-developed and easily enforced, the judicial system is often sufficient to deter traders from breach of contract. But this remedy is unavailable in countries with poorly developed or non-existent judicial systems. In such settings, ethnically homogeneous networks provide traders with the best alternative means of insuring against breach of contract.

Rational traders will choose to participate in the least costly type of trading network. They are likely to choose ethnically homogeneous trading networks because these economise on co-ordination and enforcement costs. On the one hand, traditional codes of conduct (think of the Confucian or Talmudic codes) can have many of the same effects as systems of contract law. On the other hand, confining trade to members of one's own ethnic group permits one to take advantage of an informationally efficient screening device. This allows the merchant to predict the contractual behaviour of a potential trading partner with a high degree of accuracy. For these reasons, then, the prevalence of ethnically specialised middlemen should be greatest (*ceteris paribus*) in societies having the least developed judicial systems.

Finally, Hechter, Friedman and Appelbaum[6] seek to predict the conditions under which ethnic collective action will arise. In their view, the likelihood of collective action does not rest on factors—like the degree of inter-ethnic inequality, or changing levels of relative deprivation—that affect members' desires for structural change in the society at large. Instead, the members of any ethnic group will engage in collective action only when they estimate that by doing so they will receive a net individual benefit.

In this regard, ethnic organisations are critical for two basic reasons. First, they are the major source of the private rewards and punishments that motivate the individual's decision to participate in collective action. Second, because the individual's benefit/cost calculation depends in part upon his estimate of the probability of success of any collective action, organisations can play a key role by controlling the information available to their members. When members have few alternative sources of information, organisations can easily convince them that the success of a contemplated collective action is a real possibility, perhaps even a foregone conclusion. On this basis, the likelihood of ethnic collective action varies positively with organisational resources, monitoring capacity, solidarity, control over information, history of equitable distribution of collective benefits, and adoption of non-violent tactics, while it varies negatively with organisational size, and the capacity of antagonists—including the state—to punish prospective participants.

Structural factors alone cannot account for such phenomena. In each instance adequate explanation requires the establishment of a link between the structural constraints on the one hand and the preferences that motivate individual behaviour on the other. Rational choice theory offers the best current hope of wedding micro- and macro-levels of analysis into a logically consistent whole that is also empirically falsifiable.[7]

However, it also raises two basic questions which, as yet, have no convincing answers. To be fully satisfactory, a theory that accounts for behaviour as the result of an interaction between individual preferences and structural constraints must be able to explain the determinants of both these parameters.

The question about preferences arises in the context of social order problems (including the problem of collective action). Whereas normative and structural theorists are overly optimistic about the realisation of social order, rational choice theorists instead tend to be overly pessimistic.

In their view, a rational person will only comply with group norms—and thereby contribute to the maintenance of social order—when there is a positive or negative sanction, or selective incentive, for so doing. This is as true for the economist's analysis of the provision of public goods as it is for the game theorist's analysis of co-operation in the Prisoner's Dilemma.[8] Since it is costly to provide such sanctions, the key prediction of rational choice theory is that the realisation of social order is highly problematic.

Sociologists traditionally part company with rational choice theorists in their assessment of the sufficiency of sanctions or selective incentives as causes of social order. Rational choice theorists argue that sanctions are necessary *and* sufficient for the attainment of social order in large groups. On the other hand, many sociologists feel that there is more social order than can be explained on the basis of sanctions alone.

This question, I submit, is one of the core issues separating sociological from rational choice analysis. Whereas rational choice theorists attend only to external constraints on individual action, in addition to these sociologists return again and again to admittedly fuzzy notions like 'charisma', 'legitimacy', and 'internalised norms' in their explanations of human behaviour. This is because they are often more aware of the monitoring costs that are necessary to control deviants or free riders than are rational choice theorists.

Careful rational choice analysis reveals that selective incentives represent only one of three types of monitoring cost that must be incurred if deviance or free riding is to be curtailed in large groups.[9] Selective incentives are necessary but insufficient causes of an individual's decision to comply with the obligations imposed in any social order. In addition, there are two other costly requirements that many rational choice theorists tend to ignore.

On the one hand, groups must be able to detect whether or not an individual actually does comply. Call the attendant costs the costs of monitoring.

On the other, groups must ensure that each member receives the particular sanction or selective incentive which is appropriate to his or her past behaviour: that is, rewards for compliance, and punishment for non-compliance. This activity entails the costs of properly allocating the sanctions.

Now when monitoring and allocation costs are added to the costs of providing the sanctions themselves, it is evident that free riding and deviance are likely to be even *more* pervasive in large groups than many rational choice theorists appreciate. Hence there is probably more ethnic collective action than can be explained solely by the provision of selective incentives. Likewise, there is probably far more obedience to the law than can be explained solely by police deterrence.

Can this problem be resolved within current rational choice theory? At this point the best that can be said is maybe. Several familiar means of economising on control costs in large groups seem to be consistent with rational choice principles. I shall mention only three of them here. First, groups can adopt specific institutional arrangements—such as profit-sharing, group rewards or communal distribution rules more generally—that give members incentives to monitor each other. Second, they can provide public sanctions that make a spectacle of apprehended deviants, thereby convincing many others to walk the straight and narrow path. Third, sanctions need not be imposed every time someone deviates; decades of research in experimental psychology have shown that intermittent sanctioning is even more effective than the constant variety.

However, there may be another kind of solution as well. Perhaps under certain conditions individuals can be induced to maximise some collective rather than individual utility schedule. Were this the case, then people would want to act in the interests of their ethnic or racial group and would not even be tempted to take a free ride. What might account for the development of such a preference?

Many people feel that rational choice has an Achilles' heel, and that this is the problem of preference-formation. 'Preference' is the generic term used in rational choice analysis to designate internal states. Together with environmental constraints that impose costs, preferences help determine individual action. Yet since they cannot be measured, their independent role is accorded too little importance. Claims for their insignificance can only really be justified by making very stringent assumptions—that preferences are temporally stable, transitively ordered, and not endogenously determined. Even some of the most ardent proponents of rational choice sheepishly admit that these assumptions are questionable.[10] In consequence, rational choice sometimes seems as if it is a hollow shell that has too little relevance for the study of non-economic phenomena.[11]

There can be no doubt that the problem of preference-formation is a most difficult one. *De gustibus non est disputandum* can be read as a warning to all those who believe this question is tractable. Because of its difficulty, the economists—with their customary generosity—have smirkingly bequeathed it to the sociologists. Not for nothing do they believe in rational choice! We should certainly look this gift horse carefully in the mouth. Even so, we are not totally ignorant of processes of preference-formation, and, as a matter of fact, there is much material in the literature on ethnic and race relations that bears on the issue.

Where do preferences come from? It appears that they can be formed through both selection and learning mechanisms.[12] Selection mechanisms favour individuals with adaptive preferences—to take a trivial example, inhabitants of the tropics who like cold drinks—as against maladaptive ones—inhabitants of the tropics who like hot drinks. People with maladaptive preferences are likely to be less wealthy, healthy, happy and ultimately long-lived than people with adaptive preferences. As such, they are less likely to transmit their preferences to others on account of their reduced life-expectancy as well as their disproportionate lack of 'success', however relativistically this is defined—unsuccessful people are not likely to be viewed as worthy of emulation. Thus, in whatever ways preferences are transmitted, adaptive ones will tend to be selected over maladaptive ones.

But many preferences, probably the majority of them, are intrinsically neither adaptive nor maladaptive: consider preferences for eating scones as against croissants, or for doing sociology as against anthropology. Many such preferences result from learning processes, and particularly from modelling. A major determinant of the distribution of these preferences is differential association, because this is the factor that limits the feasible set of models, or persons whose behaviour is available for observation. Further, there is wide agreement that childhood experiences have a privileged status during the rest of a person's life. For these reasons, families are often capable of transmitting preferences across the generations.

From this it follows that critical loci for the study of preference-formation include the family as well as other institutions that encourage differential association. Many kinds of minority groups fill this bill.

Consider groups that successfully resist assimilation into their host society. Whether they are in relatively newly established Utopian communities or in ancient ethnic ones, the members of such groups appear to be acting on the basis of preferences, or values, widely discrepant from those held in the surrounding community. Here, then, is a rich body of evidence about differential preference-formation.

Rural 'intentional communities' have been established in many parts of the world, but especially in the United States.[13] Typically, these communities attempt to be economically autarkic—that is, to approach the ideal of an *oikos* economy. Since in virtually every instance membership provides a lower standard of living and less freedom of dress, sexual behaviour and inter-personal relations generally than is available in the host society, how are such groups able initially to attract members, to mould the preferences of succeeding generations, and to retain the allegiance of their adult members?

Initial recruitment is not terribly problematic because it is guided by self-selection. The benefits which such communities can provide for their members need not be universally attractive. At a minimum, membership in an intentional community offers relief from loneliness (which is attractive to the lonely); a heavy dose of directedness (which is attractive to those with low self-esteem),[14] and, often, economic security (which is attractive to the economically insecure). Such benefits can have an extremely narrow appeal: the Shakers, for example, gave physically unattractive women with reduced marital prospects a chance to lead stable, respectable and celibate lives in nineteenth-century America.

Retaining members in succeeding generations is a different task because, unlike their parents, the children do not voluntarily choose to become members. A community's success in influencing their preferences—so that they come to value community membership more than the lures of the host society—has much to do with its chances of survival. But how can this bit of preference-formation be managed? Perhaps the most common mechanism of preference-formation in such communities is the systematic limitation and distortion of information about alternatives existing beyond the group's boundaries. Here the guiding maxim seems to be that it is hard to prefer something if you do not know it exists.

But limiting information in the intentional community is no simple task: it is far easier to do in small and geographically isolated communities (as in many 'tribal' societies) than in the midst of vast national societies like the contemporary United States, where information is aggressively trumpeted through the air waves and other mass media. Even among the Amish—a prototypically successful intentional community—the adults cannot be naïve about conditions in surrounding Pennsylvania towns. What keeps them from passing this knowledge on to their children, and thereby piquing their interest in defection?

Amish parents are likely to present information about the surrounding society to their children in an unfavourable light in order to warn them away from temptation, because they believe that their own salvation depends upon keeping their children in the faith. But parental incentives to colour and limit information about the outside world do not have to rest on such fundamentalist religious beliefs. The status[15] and style of life of parents in all such groups depend on the continued existence of their communities. Should these groups fail to survive, then the parents' livelihoods cannot be sustained, and their remaining prospects tend to be unremittingly bleak.

If parents are motivated selectively to inform their children about life in the wider society, this limitation of knowledge typically continues in secondary socialisation. Most critically, such groups prevent their children from attending state-supported schools.[16] Often ownership of radios and televisions is forbidden; in the case of one Seattle commune that I studied, programmes deemed suitable for watching were carefully screened by elders.

By controlling education, intentional communities not only maximise their chances of moulding children's preferences—giving them a taste for community-provided benefits and an aversion to those provided in the outside world—but also raise their exit costs by denying their children access to the kind of training that would enable them to compete successfully in the external labour market.[17]

Most urban ethnic and racial groups do not persist for these reasons. Few parents in such groups are as strongly motivated to keep their children by their side as are the parents in the intentional community. The persistence of urban ethnic and racial minorities is most often due to limitations of opportunity emanating from outside group boundaries, that is to a panoply of forces that channel group members into distinctive positions in a cultural division of labour.[18]

The case of the Gypsies, however, is an interesting exception.[19] Far from attempting the kind of economic autarchy that permits substantial limitation of information, the Gypsy economy is highly dependent on the *gaje* world. As is well-known, Gypsies tend to cluster in extremely narrow occupational niches—serving as coppersmiths, fortune-tellers, musicians, horse-traders, and so forth.

Although the barrier separating the Rom from the *gaje* is to a degree permeable, the Gypsies probably manage to retain a large majority of their young within the group. Due to their economic interdependence, it is much harder to do this by limiting their children's knowledge of outside opportunities, as each family's welfare depends almost entirely on the exploitation of such opportunities. How, then, are Gypsies so successful in retaining their young?

A common explanation is that Gypsy survival is due to strongly held Gypsy beliefs that the *gaje* world is polluted, and only the Rom are clean. Here again, parents have a strong personal incentive to inculcate such beliefs in their children. Since Gypsy children contribute to household income, their defection would diminish it. Further, the Gypsies have developed ample means of warding off assimilationist pressures. They have an ability to remain anonymous in urban society by avoiding registration at birth, for school, for the census, for the draft and with the local tax authorities. By denying their children the training necessary to enable them to compete successfully in the labour market, the Rom ensure their continued economic dependence on the Gypsy community.

Altogether this suggests that preferences tend to be formed and moulded in solidary communities. Community solidarity, in turn, is sustained by dependence and monitoring mechanisms[20] that operate in a fashion wholly consistent with rational choice principles. Hence, I suspect that a close reading of the evidence about religious, ethnic and racial assimilation would reveal that rational choice theory does a reasonably good job of accounting for gross differences in inter-group preferences.

This would be significant, for it would do away with a persistent criticism of rational choice analyses: namely that to be falsifiable such explanations have to specify individual preferences *ex ante*, but that in practice they are always specified *ex post*. There seems to be no intrinsic reason why group preferences cannot be inferred from detailed case-studies, and then employed for the purposes of prediction.

['A rational choice approach to race and ethnic relations', in D. Mason and J. Rex (eds.), *Theories of Race and Ethnic Relations* (Cambridge University Press, 1986), 268–77.]

MICHAEL BANTON

16 The Actor's Model of Ethnic Relations

The theoretical approach which I favour starts not from any prior conception of the ethnic group or the nation, but from the human individual, socialized and optimizing, and belonging to more than one social group. For this purpose I take an imaginary individual, Husin Ali, a clerk working in 1989 for a multinational engineering firm in Petalingjaya, a suburb of Kuala Lumpur.[1] A sample of residents in that locality was told that Husin Ali had been patronizing Mr Ah Kow's grocery shop, noted for its cheapness and nearest to his house. He had been told that someone called Ahmad was about to open a second grocery shop in the neighbourhood. Respondents were asked whether they thought that Husin Ali would transfer his custom to the new shop. The research assumed that the names of the three individuals would be taken as signs that Husin Ali and Ahmad were Malays and Ah Kow a Chinese Malaysian. Some respondents, so it was thought, would expect that Husin Ali would want to shop with Ahmad because he was a fellow Malay, while others would expect him to shop wherever the goods were cheapest.

There were two main reasons for expecting Husin Ali to change to Ahmad. Firstly, the possibility that the personal satisfaction he would derive from helping a co-ethnic would outweigh any greater price of the goods bought. Secondly, the possibility that he would be influenced by a concern for the judgements of his peers, who would approve his patronizing a co-ethnic and disapprove of his shopping with a Chinese Malaysian when he could quite easily have helped Ahmad.

There are some circumstances in which virtually all Malays will feel bound to align themselves with their co-ethnics in dealings with Chinese Malaysians, such as in situations of political competition, and some circumstances in which an individual will have an unconstrained choice whether or not to interpret the situation in ethnic terms. This requires us to recognize the existence in Malaysia of ethnic roles, that is, of relationships in which the parties' conduct is governed by shared beliefs about their mutual rights and obligations.[2] As hypothesized, respondents were found to be divided in their predictions about whether Husin Ali would see shopping for groceries as a relationship governed by ethnic roles. One finding of this research was that in many circumstances what we, perhaps unwisely, called ethnic loyalty, was a less important determinant of Malay alignment than my coworker expected. At a time when ethnic nationalism is often misrepresented as resembling a living force, it is important to note our finding that self-interest in saving money or gaining social status, and sentiments of obligation to a friend, neighbour or fellow worker, were often more influential than ethnic identification.

Having considered Husin Ali's personal sentiments, we can move to a further variable: whether his relations with his peers were competitive or cooperative. Since we did not cover this in the Petalingjaya research, I take an example from a very different location, concerning language use in Catalonia, as presented by David Laitin.[3]

Industrial growth in the Catalan-speaking region has encouraged the immigration of workers speaking Castilian Spanish. The Catalan government promoted the regional language although some Catalans preferred that their children should in primary school learn to speak Castilian, as it is a world language and the official language of the state. The immigrants might have been expected to resist programmes favouring Catalan. A possible explanation of why they did not resist is offered by Laitin's ingenious application of game theory. Taking first the position of the immigrant worker seeking a strategy that will enable his or her children to climb the social ladder, he concludes that a parent will envisage his or her child as having to compete with the children of other immigrant parents. Will they see that their children learn Catalan? If they do, then the first parent's child will be at a disadvantage unless he or she has also learned it. Laitin has noticed that the alternatives assume the form of the game known as the prisoner's dilemma. Likely payoffs depend upon the decisions of the actor's peer. Assigning scores to the various outcomes if the actor chooses an assimilation or a cultural maintenance strategy, and the competitor does likewise, he provides a highly plausible interpretation of why they were content for their children to attend Catalan-speaking schools.

This model requires considerable elaboration because in the prisoner's dilemma the two prisoners are unable to communicate with one another. If they could communicate and agree upon a common strategy they might do better. Laitin's application of the model assumes that the Castilian-speaking immigrants chose to compete as individuals rather than as a group, in the belief that the pay-offs would be the greater this way. An immigrant might well believe that he or she would be better off were all immigrants to get together and compete as a group. Someone would have to organize the group, since others would find it in their interest to be free-riders. The prospective organizer would then have to contend with the Hechter equation.[4] Would the benefits of collective action be sufficient to compensate him or her for the effort involved in organizing it?

As Laitin observes, immigrant families often want their children to be introduced to the cultural traditions of their familial homeland. They are accustomed to particular rituals and ceremonies as ways of marking the stages of the life cycle. Other peoples' rituals do not have the same meaning for them. They want to maintain their own rituals, ceremonies and fiestas as ways of marking the phases of the calendar. Who among them is to assume the burden of organizing such events? My point is that there is an interrelation between the capacity of a group to compete collectively in the public sphere, such as taking up a stand regarding language maintenance, and their collective organization in the private sphere. As Mancur Olson[5] has taught us, collective action is often a by-product of an organization established for some other purpose. A group which has its own private festivities will be more solidary in its dealings with other groups, so one way of promoting group competition is to begin in the private sphere.

The position in Catalonia suggests that there may be a contrast in this respect between an immigrant group and the settled population. The immigrants may have come alone or as nuclear families, disposed to compete on an individual basis. The settled population is more likely to see them as an entity and to respond cooperatively to their presence. Collective action among the settled population could therefore be subject to lower costs than among the immigrants, and less vulnerable to free-riding. Malays would dispute that such a conclusion can be applied in their country because they see Chinese Malaysians as cooperating more successfully with one another than they are able to do. (Their perception may not be accurate, and may reflect only a general tendency for individuals to perceive a competitor group as more cooperative than their own.[6]

These accounts of Petalingjaya and Catalonia point to a process by which ethnic boundaries are often dissolved. Some situations continue to evoke ethnic alignment, but the pattern of social relations changes with the introduction of new relationships, such as those deriving from motoring, the market for consumer goods, paying taxes, using new technology, and many kinds of employment, which are seen as independent of ethnic definitions. Twenty-eight years ago I argued that it can be helpful to conceive of roles as arrayed on a scale. At one end are basic roles, like those of gender, which are relevant in many or most situations. At the other end are those roles which are largely independent of other relationships, such as those created by leisure time pursuits. The scale records the relative frequency with which a particular role is socially relevant.[7] In circumstances of ethnic tension, such as those of the former Yugoslavia, ethnic roles that have been towards the middle of the scale have been pushed up to the basic end.[8] At other times ethnic roles may move towards the independent end because other definitions have become relatively more potent. Ethnic definitions can lose ground to other social definitions, such as those of religion, class, nation or friendship. They can also weaken if self-interest is allowed greater legitimacy at the expense of social obligation. Change in ethnic relations often comes about not because people change the value they place upon association with co-ethnics, but because they change their ideas about which relationships are to be governed by ethnic norms. The research in Petalingjaya suggests that the consumer market can be a solvent of ethnic particularism.

Actor and observer models

A name, or a person's appearance, can be a sign of a role that person is expected to play. How do we decide whether a name or some other feature of a person is a sign of an ethnic role? How is it to be distinguished from a sign of a national role? To answer these questions it is best to begin by comparing what we think of conventionally as ethnic and national roles with other ascribed roles, such as those of race and gender.

There is no way in which we can tell *a priori* the extent to which respondents in Petalingjaya took the names Ah Kow and Ahmad as signs of ethnic, national and religious roles. This is an empirical question. The significance given to a name or other attribute will vary from one subject to another and from one situation to another. The social scientist, however, seeks criteria for distinguishing ethnic from national and religious significance in empirical research. To sort out what is entailed, it is best to begin by differentiating two kinds of models of the social structure: those of the actor and the observer. The resident of Petalingjaya rarely employs any concept of ethnicity. He or she uses a practical language embodying proper names, such as Malay, Chinese, and Indian. Anyone who speaks this language knows that persons assigned to these categories vary in their cultural distinctiveness. In the languages they use, the costume they wear, the use they make of their leisure, etc., some are more culturally distinctive, and in this sense, more 'ethnic', than many of the adolescents who listen to the same pop music, eat similar foods, and mix readily. Some Malays may perceive some Chinese as being more orientated towards China, and in this sense more 'national'. Some Malays, too, are more concerned with the promotion of Islam, and may consider a difference in ethnic origins unimportant by comparison with profession of the faith. There have been similarities in the former Yugoslavia where some have seen others as Serbs and Croats without employing any concepts of ethnicity, nationality or religion. It is the observer who decides that a particular attitude is to be labelled ethnic, national or religious. It is also the observer who notes that group boundaries are more easily maintained when they incorporate elements from nationality and religion as well as ethnic descent.

An actor's model is one which he or she uses to navigate a course through daily life, helping to identify the shallow water, the best channels, and the likely reactions of other vessels. An observer's model uses abstract concepts like that of ethnicity in place of proper names; it seeks to distinguish ethnic, national and religious attributes in order to compare relations in Petalingjaya or Bosnia-Herzegovina with some other locality, and in this way learn about the causes of tolerance and intolerance. The observer looks for regularities of which the actors are unaware or about which actors have insufficient information. In so doing, the observer often comes to mistaken conclusions which take a long time to clear up.

One such confusion was that of race. It makes no sense to distinguish ethnic from racial relations in Petalingjaya or the former Yugoslavia. Racial theories were advanced in the mid-nineteenth century as observer models. They asserted that underlying the actors' models of their social relations there were zoological determinants which the actors ought to learn about and take as guides to policy. When many yielded to the apparent plausibility of these theories, in Europe, North America, and regions influenced by them, the theories became constituents of actors' models of their societies. We now recognize the theories to have been ill-founded and pernicious. There would be benefits could we stop using the idiom of race, but this is not a practical prescription. Firstly, race is too important in many actor models, and secondly we need the word 'race' as part of the rationale for all the legislation, international and national, which has been designed to combat discrimination based on ideas of race.

In English-language usage ethnic groups are commonly regarded as subdivisions of racial groups. A physical feature is taken to indicate that an individual is to be assigned to a racial category while a cultural feature is taken as a sign that the individual is a member of an ethnic group. So a nation, like perhaps the United States, may be seen as divided into racial groups which in turn are divided into ethnic groups. In Petalingjaya and the former Yugoslavia the nation has been divided into groups which the actors identify by proper names but which observers have called either racial or ethnic, though contemporary opinion prefers the latter. These groups are constituted by both inclusive and exclusive processes. Malays, Chinese and Indians in Petalingjaya wish to preserve some of the cultural characteristics of their groups, and share a fellow-feeling with group members. These are inclusive processes. The non-members are regarded, and treated, as different by others in certain circumstances; this is exclusion. It appears that in Bosnia some people have been forced by Serbian politics into ethnic categories, becoming Bosnian Serbs instead of Serb Bosnians, and forced to regard their ethnic identity as more important relative to other identities than they used to do. Whereas previously they could have placed obligations to a friend, neighbour or fellow worker before an obligation of shared ethnicity alone, they have been forced by processes which we do not yet fully understand, to change their priorities. If so, this is a more striking example of the importance that exclusive processes can acquire.[9] [. . .]

The signs of ethnicity

Though both language and costume can be signs of ethnic self-assignment, they differ in their social implications. We need always to remember that no-one can hear, see, smell, taste or touch ethnicity. As an influence upon behaviour it is something we can know only through the things that are taken as signs of it. Personal names are frequently interpreted as signs of ethnicity. They are particularly open to manipulation, in that a person may change a name to make it less distinctive, or, indeed to make it more distinctive, as many African Americans have adopted African names or, if members of the Nation of Islam, have taken X as a family name.

In reviewing the signs of ethnicity, it is useful to start with the definition of ethnic group adopted by the House of Lords in the case of *Mandla v Dowell Lee*.[10] Notice how, in Lord Fraser's speech, he distinguished between the factors constituting an ethnic group, and the signs by which it is to be identified. He said that for a group to constitute itself an ethnic group for the purposes of the 1976 Act, it must 'regard itself, and be regarded by others, as a distinct community by virtue of certain characteristics'. It must have 'a long shared history, of which the group is conscious as distinguishing it from other groups, and the memory of which it keeps alive'. So whether it has the requisite consciousness is signified by its members' behaviour. Such a group must also have 'a cultural tradition of its own, including family and social customs and manners'. Again, the definition specifies both the necessary condition and the signs for deciding whether or not a group meets it. Certain other characteristics, of geographical origin or descent, language, literature, religion and size, though not essential, may be relevant. They, too, may be signs of the presence of an ethnic group. While this definition is based upon the meaning that the word ethnic has acquired in English, it might be employable in other cultures too.

From studies of discrimination in applications for employment we have learned that accent, address and birthplace may be taken as signs that an applicant belongs to a minority. Studies in Belfast have also illuminated the process of 'telling', the ways in which people 'tell' whether someone else is

Catholic or Protestant.[11] In principle, the processes are no different from those by which people assess the class status of those they encounter. The features which can be taken as signs of social position are varied, and it will often be impossible to tell if the ethnic or the national sign has been influential. This is one of the reasons why empirical research should not depend upon any assumption that the actor and the observer share the same conception of what is ethnic or national.

['Modelling ethnic and national relations', *Ethnic and Racial Studies*, 17: 1 (1994), 2–7, 9–10.]

Section III

Ethnicity in History

INTRODUCTION

This section considers some accounts that attempt to uncover the long history of ethnic ties in various parts of the world.

William McNeill, the renowned world historian, places the ubiquity of ethnicity in the context of factors that have prevailed for much of history, namely, nomadic conquest and enslavement, long-distance trade, and endemic disease and the need to replenish urban labour forces. All of these conduce to the establishment of polyethnic hierarchies in civilized centres. Only at the margins of the civilized world, in Japan and north-west Europe, did more ethnically homogeneous states manage to survive.

In the ancient world ethnicity was widespread, although nationality in the political sense was rare. It can be found among the ancient Israelites (Grosby 1991) and to some extent in ancient Greece. Moses Finley uses Meinecke's distinction between *Kulturnation* and *Staatsnation* to illuminate the dichotomy in ancient Greece between the *polis* (city-state) and Hellas as a cultural world separate from the unintelligible barbarians. Because of their fierce *polis* loyalties and their dispersion, most Greeks were unwilling to convert their cultural allegiances into unified political forms. The same has been true, at various periods of its history, of Japan. After the dissolution of the Heian empire and the rise of the Kamakura Shogunate in 1192 Japan experienced long periods of political disunity matched by a strong sense of common Japanese ethnicity and culture, despite the importation of Buddhism. The roots of Japanese cultural unity, according to Jean-Pierre Lehmann, lie in the superimposition of language, territory, race, and, to some extent, religion.

A crucial part in the development of ethnicity over the long term has been played by what John Armstrong calls 'archetypal diasporas'. Jews and Armenians are particularly well-known examples of polyglot communities who have settled in trading enclaves after being forced to leave their homelands for economic or political reasons. Using an 'ethno-symbolic' approach, Armstrong attributes their persistence over nearly two millennia to, in particular, the role of their sacral myths, texts, and liturgies, sacred languages, and their decentralized religious organization. For Robert Bartlett, language and law complement religion as factors that reinforce ethnic differences and group competition. Examining the interaction of ethnic groups in Eastern Europe, as well as in Ireland and Spain, Bartlett shows how language acted as a badge of ethnic difference from early medieval times, giving rise to a growing linguistic nationalism in the later Middle Ages.

What these readings demonstrate is the widespread nature of ethnic ties and their strategic importance for economic and political life, prior to the onset of modernity.

WILLIAM H. MCNEILL

17 Pre-modern Polyethnicity and Ethnic Homogeneity

Ancient, medieval, and early modern disease patterns were such as to require cities to import labor; and in many instances, when spontaneous immigration from the nearby countryside proved insufficient, resort to enslavement supplied the shortfall, moving across wider cultural boundaries and greater distances to bring an unfree labor force into action. The result, needless to say, was ethnic mixture and pluralism on a grand scale in major centers of imperial government, and less complex mixing in provincial urban centers whose catchment area for immigrant labor was smaller and less variegated than the catchment areas needed to sustain imperial capitals.

Only in remote and barbarous lands did ethnic homogeneity prevail. Migratory tribesmen and other uncivilized communities could indeed maintain the simplicity and solidarity of society that allowed rulers and ruled to belong to the same cultural and biological community. Yet even in such communities, strangers sometimes intruded, perhaps only as temporary sojourners, tempting local taste with strange and exotic trade goods and showing what human skill and effort could achieve.

This points to a third factor in civilized life that assured ethnic mingling: the exchange of goods across cultural boundaries through some sort of organized trade. Valued goods originating in identifiable localities—items like obsidian flakes from the Aegean island of Melos or the native copper from Lake Superior's shores—traveled very long distances in prehistoric times, though exactly how they moved from hand to hand is unknown. When written records begin to cast new light, long-distance trade had already become a specialized occupation; a find of merchants' records from Asia Minor shows that laws and customs for the conduct of caravan trade were already well developed as early as the nineteenth century BC in the ancient Near East.

But in proportion as the import of goods became part of everyday activity, another kind of social and cultural mixing of peoples became normal and necessary. Merchants coming from afar were liable to linger, at least until they could accumulate a suitable return cargo; and some set up permanent residence to act as agents for their fellows and/or to perform other specialized services within the host community. Long-distance trade therefore gave birth to permanent communities of aliens in major urban centers. These trade and skill diasporas, like ancient slavery, attained legal definition from very early times, as the rights of merchants prescribed by the laws of Hammurabi show.

Centuries later, beginning about 500 BC, the rise of portable and universal religions—i.e. Buddhism, Judaism, Christianity, and Islam together with some less successful faiths like Manicheanism—provided an effective cultural carapace for trade diasporas, insulating them from their surroundings in matters of faith and family as never before. Portable and universal faiths, in fact, permitted followers of a religion that differed from that prevailing in the environing society to maintain a corporate identity indefinitely, generation after generation. The Jewish ghettoes of western Europe illustrate this possibility, in contrast to such a group as the Lombards, who gave their name to medieval London's financial center, but in the long run failed to maintain a separate existence in a society whose religion they shared.

In the most active and ancient centers of Eurasian civilization, i.e., in the Middle East and immediately adjacent regions, therefore, mingling of diverse peoples in urban centers through conquest, through enslavement, and through long-distance trade resulted in the creation of a series of social niches inhabited by one or another ethnic group. Such groups entered into conventional and relatively well-defined relations with one another, in accordance with a peck order of social prestige and deference. Upheavals in such arrangements occurred whenever a new conquest took place, and other shocks—for example, the rise of a new religious movement such as that associated with the name of Sabbatai Sevi among the Jews of the Ottoman empire in the seventeenth century—could alter ethnic alignments and balances rather abruptly. But in normal times, between such bouts of change, governments presided over an ordered ethnic diversity, and no one supposed that uniformity was desirable or that assimilation to a common style of life or pattern of culture was either normal or possible.

Further away from the Middle Eastern center the ethnic intermingling and complexity of human groupings lessened; and one can find some close analogues to the nation-state of modern times in sufficiently remote or marginal places. Japan, for example, was never successfully invaded by outsiders after the ancestors of the Japanese people established themselves on those islands in prehistoric times. Whatever ethnic diversity initially existed among those ancestors disappeared before historic records begin, save always for the gulf that separated the Japanese from the Ainu, whose share of the islands was gradually pushed back to the marginal northernmost parts of the archipelago. Chinese and Korean high culture came to Japan in due season, borne partly by Buddhist missionaries. But the Japanese quickly took the initiative in importing civilized skills and knowledge from the mainland, so that few foreigners ever found lodgment in the islands. To be sure, a handful of skilled Korean potters preserved a separate existence for centuries, and Japanese seamen may have brought some slaves into the country. But, in general, the Japanese preserved their ethnic homogeneity by defeating even the most formidable invaders, like Kublai Khan's Mongols, and by choosing for themselves what to admit to their homeland and what to reject or repel.

Japan's prickly autonomy and comparative isolation were well illustrated by the reception accorded European missionaries and traders in the sixteenth century. Initially, the newcomers were welcomed, conversion to Christianity became fashionable in some circles, and European guns were both admired and imitated with extraordinary success. But when European connections that went along with Roman Catholicism threatened to affect the political loyalties of a portion of the Japanese people, the central government ruthlessly repressed the new faith and drove out resident Europeans, cutting the Japanese off from the rest of the world almost completely.

More than any other civilized land, therefore, the Japanese islands maintained ethnic and cultural homogeneity throughout their history and at least in principle constituted a nation-state under the suzereignty of the emperor, even in ages of political fragmentation when military power and command rested in practice with clan leaders and their bands of sword-wielding samurai.

Unlike Japan, China was subject to recurrent conquest from the steppes, and Chinese settlers, as they penetrated southward from the initial core region of the Yellow River valley, engulfed a great number of other peoples who did not at once merge into the Chinese body social as undifferentiated subjects of the emperor. Moreover, in China's imperial eras, from the time of the Han dynasty onwards (202 BC to 220 AD), professional armies extended the emperor's political jurisdiction into central Asia and other borderlands, where an enormous diversity of peoples—Turks, Tibetans, Mongols, Manchus, Koreans, to name only those familiar to westerners—shared subjection with the Chinese to the dictates of a distant court.

China, therefore, did not retain anything like the isolation and ethnic homogeneity that characterized Japanese society. Willy-nilly, it belonged to the great Eurasian ecumene, subject to all the stresses and strains of living in uncomfortable proximity to peoples of different language, culture, and skills. Political and ethnic boundaries never coincided exactly. Instead, Chinese conquest of borderlands alternated with conquest of part or all of China by peoples coming from those same borderlands.

Yet there is a sense in which Chinese civilization did attain and maintain a far greater cohesion than was true of civilizations in Europe, western Asia, and India. This resulted from the way Confucianism became institutionalized. Admission to the Chinese managerial élite came to depend less on inherited status than on mastery of the Confucian classics and of the style of life and thought they inculcated. This allowed persons of diverse background to become fully and completely Chinese simply by becoming learned. From about the tenth century AD suitably educated mandarins staffed the government, managed the court, and dominated society. Even Genghis Khan's heirs found the services of Confucian administrators indispensable. As a result, in 1368, when Chinese rebels successfully overthrew what the educated classes firmly felt to be an alien, barbarian regime, and brought a new native-born dynasty, the Ming, to power, any lingering foreign taint imposed upon China during the Mongol era was systematically repudiated and suppressed in the name of a restored and purified Confucian orthodoxy.

But this should not disguise from us the fact that earlier in China's long history far greater openness to innovation coming from the west had prevailed. The reception of Buddhism is, of course, the great monument to China's earlier readiness to borrow from abroad; and with Buddhism came a variety of secular changes like the enlarged scope for commerce and some technical skills and ideas (e.g. monumental sculpture) that remained central to later Chinese civilization.

The truth of the matter, it seems to me, is this: until about 1000 AD, China was ready and willing to learn from foreigners whenever they had anything worthwhile to teach because, up to that time, China's level of skills and attainment was no greater than that of other civilized communities. But between about 1000 and, say, 1450, China did spurt ahead and surpass the rest of the world in wealth, skill, and population. Marco Polo's awed account of the wonders of Cathay shows how a traveled and sophisticated European reacted to Chinese accomplishments in the late thirteenth century. A few decades later, Ibn Battuta's more cursory report of what he saw in China records a similar reaction, though China's complete indifference to Islam depressed that learned and pious Moslem traveler.

These experienced foreigners' reaction to Chinese wealth and skills lets us understand better how the Chinese educated classes, accustomed after about 1000 to finding only inferiors outside Chinese borders, were deeply offended by the Mongol conquest, so that when the barbarian yoke was thrown off in 1368 the liberated Chinese elites were intent above all on keeping foreigners at arm's length. Looking backward was more comfortable than looking outward, even after a new barbarian dynasty, the Manchu, subjugated China in the mid-seventeenth century. The resulting defensive posture effectively insulated China from European probes in the early modern period after blunting imperial overseas explorations that might, under other circumstances, have led to a Chinese discovery of America on the one hand and of Europe on the other.

Such a history, I think, shows that the xenophobic unity of Chinese high culture in modern times was more a deliberate and exaggerated pose among the educated than a social reality. In fact, foreigners played an absolutely crucial role in China's history, even in those centuries when Chinese rulers and thinkers were most eager to repudiate them. Both Ming and Manchu dynasties actually presided over a multinational empire in which the numerical superiority of the massed Chinese peasantry supported a Confucian governing elite without itself entirely belonging to that privileged world.

Indeed, local dialects and ways of life varied substantially even within China proper, making the Chinese less like a single European nation than like the Latin (or Germanic) peoples of Europe—i.e., culturally and linguistically akin, but diverse enough in language and custom to constitute separate nationalities. If the papal monarchy had prevailed in medieval Europe and been able to keep the German and Latin nations under a single overarching administration, entrusting government to clerics, trained in church law and using Latin for administrative purposes, the Chinese pattern of imperial unity would have been nearly replicated at the other end of the ecumene; but of course that was not how things turned out in the Far West.

[*Polyethnicity and National Unity in World History* (Toronto University Press, 1986), 14–22.]

MOSES FINLEY

18 The Ancient Greeks and their Nation

The *failure* of the Greeks to unite politically has been an almost unchallenged concept among historians of antiquity ever since.[1] Implicit is the modern identification of nation with nation-state, with its corollary that any 'nation' which neither united nor even strove to unite politically suffered from inherent defects, failed, whether in the nineteenth century or in the fifth and fourth centuries BC 'The important and *perhaps somewhat disheartening* fact.... The failure of the Greeks *to realize their potentiality as a nation*...' (my italics).[2] As living ideology such a simple doctrine is understandable enough, often effective and not rarely catastrophic. As an analytical tool, it crumbles quickly. 'The tendency has always been strong to believe that whatever receives a name must be an entity or being, having an independent existence of its own.'[3] In what sense may one legitimately say that the Greeks failed to do something that, demonstrably, they never conceived of, as either a possible or a desirable end? In what sense, indeed, were the Greeks a nation at all if we insist on equating nation with nation-state?[4]

When Herodotus was writing, Greek communities, most of them tiny, severely restricted in population and in space, were scattered from Phasis at the eastern end of the Black Sea all the way to Marseilles.[5] The Greek peninsula itself was solidly Greek, as were the islands in the seas around it. The western coast of Asia Minor (modern Turkey), most of Sicily, the southern tip of Italy from Naples down were heavily Greek, but they also contained substantial non-Greek populations. Elsewhere in the extensive territory in which there were Greek communities they tended to be more or less non-contiguous little dots in an alien world of Scythians, Thracians, Libyans, Gauls and dozens of others. Unless prevented by another power, each community had its own government, its own coinage, calendar and laws, its own temples and cults. The variations were infinite, yet Herodotus could speak, without descending to nonsense, of their common language, religion and customs. These were the grounds on which every one of the innumerable scattered communities was accepted to be as Greek as every other, in its own opinion and in the judgment of the rest (discounting the inevitable local claims to a superior brand of Hellenism). They also had a common label for all other peoples—*barbaroi*. Its deployment was a clear signal of a qualitative differentiation, commonly but not always with a pejorative implication.

Paradoxically, it can be argued that both the dispersion of the Greeks among barbarian nations and the absence of a central Greek political or ecclesiastical authority served as centripetal forces holding their common culture together. The former compelled them to cling to their Hellenism, their identification with other Greeks, as a means of retaining self-identity. The latter prevented the emergence of regional loyalty, rebellion, heresy and similar centrifugal forces familiar from later epochs in European history. The several Greek dialects remained recognizably and intelligibly Greek for many hundreds of years, in contrast to the transformation of late Latin into Romance languages. So did art and architecture; religion, too, though in this sphere the variations, changes and accretions were bewildering in their number and range.

I am of course suggesting not that any Greek offered these arguments against unification, but that *we* must propound such propositions if we wish to explain, not evade, the history of the Greek 'nation'. Instead we are commonly served up with a mixture of tautology, rhetoric and mysticism resting on the notions of immanence and failure. In an influential work on the history of nationalism in Germany, written at the beginning of this century, Friedrich Meinecke gave currency to the categories of *Kulturnation* and *Staatsnation*. 'We may distinguish between an earlier period, in which nations on the whole had a more plantlike and impersonal existence and growth, and a later period, in which the conscious will of the nation wakens in that it feels itself to be a great personality (even if only through the instrumentality of its leaders) and claims the hallmark and right of the developed personality, namely, self-determination.'[6] Individual Greek city-states never emerged from the vegetable state.[7] Why not? Even if one accepts Meinecke's metaphorical formulation as meaningful, the key question has still to be answered. In 1800 one could have said of the Prussians that they were Germans culturally but Prussians politically, as the ancient Athenians were Greeks culturally but Athenians politically. Why did the situation undergo a radical change in the former instance, not in the latter?

'The failure of the Greeks to realize their potentiality as a nation'—so runs a widely accepted view—'was due to several causes of which the particularism of the *polis* was only one (though an important one)'.[8] This is a tautology disguised by the (misused) word 'cause'. City-state particularism was no fixed entity, neither was it a mere prejudice, pure emotionalism. The *polis*, wrote Aristotle, exists by nature and is prior to the individual (*Politics* 1253a19–20). 'A *polis* has its proper scale like all things, animals, plants, inanimate instruments. Each will lose its power [to function properly] if it is excessively small or excessively large; it will either be robbed of its own nature entirely or it will be defective.... A state composed of too many... will not be a true *polis* because it can hardly have a true constitution. Who can be the general of a mass so excessively large? And who can be herald, except Stentor?... The optimum size of a *polis* occurs when the numbers are the greatest possible for self-sufficiency, while living within sight of each other' (*Politics* 1326a35–b24).

These sentences are the culmination of a complex, coherent argument, in which the components are Aristotle's concept of nature, his doctrine of the mean, and his ethics, with its systematically developed notions of justice, community (*koinonia*), virtue and the good life.[9] City-state 'particularism', for Aristotle at least, was the outcome of all these elements, and if they constituted a powerful block to what we call 'nationhood', they point in directions wholly unrelated to any modern theory or ideology on the subject. To charge Aristotle with being blind to the potentiality of the Greek nation, to its right to self-determination as a developed personality, is therefore a sterile, meaningless way of looking at the distant past.

Aristotle died a year after Alexander the Great, whose exploits initiated important changes in the realities of the city-state, but, as we shall see, no equally fundamental shifts in attitudes to nationhood. All Greek thinkers, philosophers, poets, historians, were equally 'blind' to the idea of a *Staatsnation*. And when they began to probe into the components of Herodotus' 'definition' of Hellenism, into the Greek *Kulturnation*, they found themselves troubled and confused, unable to formulate an agreed, or even fully consistent, conception. Common language seemed obvious enough as a starting point. Common descent was a stereotype, and it is doubtful that many Greeks took it very seriously.[10] Common religion, symbolized by such Panhellenic institutions as the oracle at Delphi and the quadrennial games in honour of Zeus at Olympia, had its ambiguous side. 'Homer and Hesiod', wrote the sixth-century BC philosopher Xenophanes, 'have attributed to the gods everything that is disgraceful and blameworthy among men: theft, adultery and deceit.... If cattle and horses and lions had hands or could draw with their hands and produce works of art as men do, the horses would draw their gods horselike, the cattle cowlike, and give them bodies, as every species has its own.'[11] Xenophanes' target was not merely Homer and Hesiod but the traditional conception of the Olympic gods and, so to speak, the Olympic morality, which the two poets had fixed in as scriptural a way as is possible in a culture without a sacred book.

'Much learning does not teach reason, understanding. Otherwise Hesiod would have learned it.... But Hesiod is the teacher of most. They are convinced that he knows the most, he who does not even know day and night. There's one for you.'[12] That bitter comment by Heraclitus was an expression of the great rationalist movement in Greek philosophy, in open conflict with the majority. Aristophanes' *Clouds* is an effective, though caricatured, presentation of the popular response; the 'Republic of wise men' of the founder of Stoicism, Zeno, is the extreme counter-statement. But the battle was not always restricted to intellectual debate; the last third of the fifth century BC witnessed a series of impiety trials in Athens that began with the exile of Anaxagoras and closed with the death of Socrates.[13] The same Heraclitus, it is to be noted, found the faculty of rational thinking to be a peculiarly Hellenic trait: 'Eyes and ears are poor witnesses for man if he has the soul of a barbarian.'[14] Plato rejected that but was equally opposed to the traditional morality and theology: he banned from his Republic all poetry, Homer in particular, 'with the sole exception of hymns to the gods and encomia of the good' (*Republic* 607A).

Obviously a determination of what the Greeks or any segment of the Greeks meant by common religion and common customs, Hellas and Hellenism, cannot be made by the prevailing method of selecting apt quotations, overt programmatic statements. What is required is a systematic, quantitative where appropriate, multivariate analysis of everything in the available documentation that pertains to national consciousness; of the casual as of the programmatic references, of the unintended as of the intended meanings, of the silences, too, and always in correlation with the precise context in which something is said or is not said.[15]

What I mean by the silences is quickly illustrated from the *Works and Days* of Hesiod, an 800-line poem which is a brilliant compound of apparent autobiography, myth, moral indignation with a prophetic undercurrent of doom, farmer's almanac, and instruction in ritual.

It was Hesiod, apparently, who first gave literary expression to the belief that all Greeks had a common progenitor, Hellen, grandson of Prometheus and great-great-grandson of Heaven and of Ocean. Hence the collective name, Hellenes. Yet in the *Works and Days* there is no role for the Hellenes. Kinsmen, neighbours and the community make up the whole of his set of identifications. 'A man grows eager to work when he considers his neighbour, a rich man who hastens to plough and plant and put his house in good order; and neighbour vies with his neighbour as he hurries after wealth.... A bad neighbour is as great a plague as a good one is a great blessing; he who enjoys a good neighbour has a precious possession' (lines 21–24, 346–48).[16] For those 'who practise violence and cruel deeds far-seeing Zeus, the son of Cronos, ordains a punishment. Often even a whole community (*polis*) suffers for a bad man who sins and devises presumptuous deeds, and the son of Cronos lays great trouble upon the people, famine and plague together' (lines 238–43).

A note of doom hangs over the *Works and Days*, at its blackest in the account of the five ages of man. 'Would that I were not among the men of the fifth generation.... For now truly is a race of iron, and men never rest from labour and sorrow by day and from perishing by night; and the gods shall lay sore trouble upon them.... And then Aidos and Nemesis, with their sweet forms wrapped in white robes, will go from the wide-pathed earth and forsake mankind to join the company of the deathless gods: and bitter sorrow will be left for mortal men, and there will be no help against evil' (lines 174–201). All mankind is threatened, unlike 'O ye children of Benjamin, gather yourselves to flee out of the midst of Jerusalem, and blow the trumpet in Tekoa, and set up a signal of fire on Bethhaccerem; for evil appeareth out of the north, and a great destruction.... Be thou instructed, O Jerusalem, lest my soul depart from thee; lest I make thee desolate, a land not inhabited' (Jeremiah vi, 1, 8). The Hebrew prophet had one and only one point of reference, his people, his nation, while the Greek poet had several, of which his nation was not one. The moment he left the daily concerns of his farmers to consider more universal matters, he leaped from the community to the human race.

Hesiod and his farmers had little contact with non-Greek states. When war disturbed the closed circle of their existence, as happened often enough, the enemies who raided his fields and destroyed his crops, and against whom he retaliated in kind while serving in his community's militia, were as Greek as themselves. Finally, there came a time when old Greece (as we may call it) was invaded by a foreign power, Persia. In assemblies and councils everywhere decisions were urgently debated. Should the great Persian armies be resisted at the probable cost of rout and perhaps extinction, or should discretion prevail and the best possible bargain be made with the invaders? No doubt orators made frequent use of the increasingly pejorative word 'barbarians' in the debate, but nothing in the actual behaviour suggests that the basis for decision was any different from what it was when the threat came from another Greek state or coalition (except in so far as the Persian threat was unprecedented in its scale). In the *Persians*, a tragedy produced in Athens eight years after the decisive Greek naval victory at Salamis, Aeschylus gave the call to battle: 'Advance, O sons of the Hellenes, liberate your country' (lines 402–3). However, one should not draw implications too quickly. The appeal is identical, even to the key word, liberate (from slavery), with Thucydides' version (1.124) of the Corinthian plea to Sparta in 432 BC to take the initiative against Athens: 'Believing that the city that has been establishing itself as a tyrant in Hellas has been established against all alike . . . let us attack it and reduce it, so that we ourselves may live safely in the future and the Hellenes now enslaved be liberated.'[17]

After all, the trouble with the Persians started in Asia Minor, and there the Greeks had lived in their cities for more than half a century in quiet acceptance of Persian suzerainty. Why they finally revolted is unclear, but it was certainly not because they had come to the conclusion that their Greek nationhood was incompatible with barbarian rule. Mutual animosities among the Asia Minor Greeks had a long history behind them. Herodotus himself was not immune. If these animosities had not led to outright war for some decades, that was only because the Persians would not permit it. Everywhere else that Greek communities were established among other nationalities they warred with each other as freely as on the Greek peninsula itself.

None of this is to suggest that Hellas had no meaning whatever. But it is essential to catch the right contextual note. Every ancient Greek, living in a complex society, belonged to a multiplicity of groups.[18] By the time of Herodotus and Thucydides the list of possibilities, apart from purely informal groups which should not be underestimated, included the family and household; the neighbourhood or village; the occupational group or military unit; the community and its political subdivisions (whether in a highly structured city-state like Athens or in the looser, more primitive societies of Thessaly or Aetolia); the *ethnos*, a category (for which there is no English equivalent) of regional subdivisions of the Hellenes, normally larger than a *polis*, such as the Boeotians or Arcadians; a social stratum; the age-group and the table-fellowship. It is self-evident that the interests and demands of these varied groups were not always consonant, and often enough conflicting. It is also self-evident that the nature and intensity of an individual's ties, institutional and psychological, to each group with which he had an affiliation varied substantially—according to the context or activity; according to his status within the group (few were egalitarian) and within the social hierarchy itself; according to his own self-image, aspirations and ambitions, lack of ambition or feeling of deprivation.

[*The Use and Abuse of Ancient History* (London: Hogarth Press, 1986), 121–7, 233–5.]

JEAN-PIERRE LEHMANN

19 The Cultural Roots of Modern Japan

As a preliminary understanding, it is useful to apply to Japan the various criteria for the development of nationalism referred to earlier: the religious, the territorial, the linguistic and the ethnic. It will be seen how all combined to allow Japanese nationalism to develop untrammelled by barriers which have beset, in one way or another, most other societies attempting to form themselves into nations.

Territory

The Japanese territory is clearly defined, even if it has slightly expanded or contracted over time. Essentially the Japanese nation comprised the three islands of Kyushu, Shikoku and Honshu. In the latter part of the nineteenth century a programme of colonisation was carried out in the northern island of Hokkaido; although the Russians may have occasionally cast an expansionist glance in that direction in the past, Hokkaido nonetheless indisputably became recognised as part of Japan. To the majority of the Japanese these four islands are effectively what is meant and included in the nation of Japan. Both to the north and the south there are areas of some ambiguity.

To the north-west of Hokkaido lies the elongated island of Sakhalin, while to the north-east are the Kuril islands, stretching all the way up to Kamchatka. Sakhalin was visited by both Russian and Japanese navigators from the seventeenth century onwards. In the modern era sovereignty over Sakhalin has alternated between the Japanese and the Russians, while at times they divided it into half. At the end of the Second World War there were somewhere in the region of 400,000 Japanese living in Sakhalin, the great majority of whom were repatriated to Japan, and the island is now, along with the Kurils, a separate *oblast* of the USSR with Yuzhno-Sakhalinsk as its capital. The Japanese do not dispute Russia's jurisdiction over Sakhalin. The question of the Kurils is different. Here again, possession has alternated between Japan and the USSR; at the Yalta Conference the Russians were ceded the Kurils at the same time as their jurisdiction over the whole of Sakhalin was recognised. Today, however, the Japanese claim the two islands in greatest proximity to Japan, Kunashiri and Etorofu (Kunashir and Iturup as they are known in the USSR) and this is a matter of dispute between Japan and the Soviet Union; it is unlikely, however, to lead to war between the two countries. The ordinary Japanese will not think of Etorofu and Kunashiri in terms comparable to, say, the way the ordinary Frenchman felt about Alsace-Lorraine in the period 1871–1918. The Soviet presence on these islands is strategically uncomfortable, economically unfortunate (fishing) and psychologically upsetting. In the consciousness of the Japanese, however, these islands are not an integral part of the Japanese nation.

The same comment might be made of another chain of islands which extends for approximately 400 miles from southern Japan to the northern tip of Formosa, collectively known as the Ryukyu islands, the largest of which is Okinawa. Originally the Ryukyus formed an independent kingdom. By the fourteenth century Chinese supremacy was established; but in keeping with Chinese custom the king of Naha (capital of Okinawa) retained a degree of sovereignty as long as he paid tribute to the Chinese emperor. The Ryukyus served as a meeting place and trade entrepôt between China and Japan and by the fifteenth century the Shimazu realm (Satsuma) of Southern Kyushu had already established a special relationship with the islands. In 1609 the Satsuma fief actually conquered the Ryukyus, annexed the northern islands of the chain, and made the king at Naha a vassal of the *daimyo* (feudal lord) of Satsuma; a strange situation developed whereby the king of Naha paid tribute both to Peking and to Kagoshima (capital of Satsuma). After the revolution of 1868 the king was brought to Tokyo and in 1879 the Ryukyu islands were administratively metamorphosed into the Okinawa prefecture. The Chinese put up only token resistance and so both *de facto* and *de jure* the Ryukyus became administratively a part of Japan. This does not mean, however, that the Ryukyus figure in the Japanese perception of what constitutes their nation. In April 1945 two Allied offensives converged on the island of Okinawa which capitulated in June. It is true that 85 per cent of the defenders died in battle and it is also true that the fall of Okinawa was instrumental in the resignation of the Cabinet of General Koiso Kuniaki (1880–1950). At the same time, however, the government could still claim that the sacred soil of Japan had not been trampled upon by an enemy foot. The Ryukyus lie on the periphery of the true Japanese nation.

So far as the four main islands are concerned, however, the territory of the Japanese nation is both clearly defined within the Japanese consciousness and internationally recognised. The advantages of this situation cannot be overemphasised. Territorial wars have plagued many of the nations of the world; Japan has been immune from these. This clear recognition of what constitutes the national territory has also been a major factor in developing a concept and ideology of territorial nationalism. Nor, and this is a very important point, are there rival nationalisms claiming attachment to any piece of territory. Japanese territorial nationalism is also singularly reinforced by linguistic, religious and ethnic considerations.

Language

Sati àl-Husri's definition of the most important unifying precept of a nation, a common language, admirably fits the Japanese case. It is true that a fisherman from Tohoku (north-east Japan) would have had difficulty conversing with a farmer from the southern part of Kyushu; there were regional dialects, but no significant linguistic barriers. In this respect again Japan stands out in stark contrast to many of the countries of the world. In fact one can go further than this. Not only do the Japanese have a single unifying language, spoken by no other nation, but it is a very difficult language for a foreigner to master. Francis-Xavier (1506–52), the Basque Jesuit missionary, described the Japanese language as an invention of the devil in order to impede the progress of Christian proselytism. The Japanese language, therefore, is not only a unifying factor, but also a defence mechanism. Hence linguistic nationalism could also be a potent force.

Religion

The religious factor in Japan is a somewhat complicated one. At the risk of some oversimplification, one can say that it consists of an amalgam of the purely indigenous Shinto along with the importation from outside of Buddhism and Confucianism—the latter two, however, in spite of being originally extraneous have, over the centuries, taken on a marked indigenous hue. Leaving aside matters of metaphysics, as far as national consciousness is concerned the following points can be made. The Shinto religion is inextricably associated with both the territory and people of Japan. Just as the Japanese language is spoken in no other nation, similarly Shinto is practised only in Japan; it is not an evangelising religion. (The only exception here was the establishment of Shinto shrines in Taiwan, Korea and Manchuria in the pre-Second World War years as part of the programme of the 'japanisation' of these colonised people.) Japan was perceived both in esoteric literature and in popular mythology as the 'land of the gods' (*shinkoku*). The initial xenophobic resistance to the Western incursion of the mid-nineteenth century—*joi*, or the movement to 'expel the barbarians'—had a certain millenarian coloration to it.

Having said that, it is also the case that although religion, mainly in the form of Shinto, may have contributed to a sense of national consciousness, religious nationalism as such, in a manner akin to Christian or Islamic societies, is not a characteristic feature of Japan in the modern era. As noted above, the Japanese embraced both Shinto and Buddhism—Confucianism is more of a moral philosophy than a religion. On the whole the two religions have co-existed quite harmoniously and in fact have exerted reciprocal influences over each other. Although one or the other may have experienced periods of ascendancy, the Japanese people are not divided between Shintoists and Buddhists in the sense that, say, the Indians are between Muslims and Hindus and the Northern Irish between Catholics and Protestants. Religious fervour, though discernible in a few sects, is not a marked feature of Japanese history, philosophy or society, nor is there a tradition of religious exclusivism. There have been conflicts in Japanese history in which monks and temples were involved; it would not be accurate, however, to describe these as religious wars, since the fighting was primarily concerned with the temples' temporal powers, not their spiritual beliefs.

Japan, in contrast to so many societies, has been spared the problem of significant religious minorities and the violent confrontations that these seem invariably to invite or provoke. While religion in Japan, therefore, has not been a determining influence on the development or coloration of Japanese nationalism, it has been a contributory factor, even if only passively, to modernisation. Thus, Japan's progress was not to be significantly impeded by strong reactionary religious groups—such as the *ulema* in parts of the Islamic world, for example the *mollahs* in Iran today, or, for that matter, the Roman Catholic Church in Europe and Latin America—nor by deeply held popular religious shibboleths. This is not to say that the process of modernisation was enthusiastically embarked upon by one and all, far from it, but that the forces of opposition did not enjoy the degree of religious sanction which they had in other societies.

Race

There is no such thing as the Japanese race, in the sense of a distinct racial species. The Japanese, however, have perceived themselves as a distinct racial group and this perception has played an important function in the development of Japanese national cohesiveness and nationalism. This unifying concept of a common race is further underlined by the absence of significant ethnic minorities, something which in so many other societies has acted as a disruptive force. There are groups which are discriminated against: the aboriginal inhabitants of Japan—the descendants of whom, the Ainu, are contained exclusively in the northern island of Hokkaido; Koreans living in Japan; and an indigenous outcaste group known as the *eta*, whose origins and role will be discussed in a later chapter. Without in any way wishing to minimise the plight of these people, nevertheless from an historical perspective the point is that they were not of a sufficient magnitude to threaten the viability of the nation.

In the age of nationalism the Japanese arrived on the scene singularly well equipped. The potential for creating a unified nation was certainly there. Ultimately the strongest manifestation of Japanese nationalism is the territorial, though it is buttressed by the linguistic and racial. What this means in real terms is that the instinctive reaction is to defend the territory and to preserve Japanese sovereignty over it. Cultural considerations, though by no means totally insignificant, are nevertheless of secondary importance. Religion in Japan may not have been a strong force for nationalism, nor, however, was it a significant impediment to change. It is the combination of these factors which set out Japan's uniqueness.

[*The Roots of Modern Japan* (London: Macmillan, 1982), 6–10.]

JOHN ARMSTRONG

20 Archetypal Diasporas

Many investigations of modern nationalism, in seeking to explain its manifestations in nineteenth-century philological myths, find diaspora nations hard to interpret. There are, to be sure, modern versions of Jewish and Armenian nationalism based ostensibly on linguistic distinctiveness. Even these versions are more concerned with adapting ancient myths to the currently dominant assumption that a nation must be territorial. I do not intend to criticize resort to such fashionable secular myths; under certain conditions it constitutes an indispensable defensive reaction to others' xenophobia. All the same, it is crucial to be clear about the essential difference between a collectivity that has maintained a sharp identity for centuries or millennia and one that is the product of the diffusion of nationalist ideology. The intensity of identity produced by older sacral myths—based on but not always coextensive with distinctive religions—has never been exceeded by modern secular myths.

Elsewhere I have termed diaspora ethnic collectivities that have maintained such persistent sacral myths 'archetypal diasporas.' Archetypal diasporas that have survived (including the remnant of Parsees, mainly in India, but retaining sacral centers in Iran) have been sustained by the highly concrete component of their myth that points to their sacral locus of origin as well as by a distinctive alphabet.[1] The ambiguous circumstances of David's founding of Jerusalem as a sacral capital for a hitherto nomadic people were noted in chapters 2 and 6. Perhaps the tensions involved in Jewish adaptation to an urban center made nostalgic attachment to it stronger after its destruction by the Romans. Thenceforward dispersed Jews could perceive Jerusalem not as an urban life style but as a purely sacral symbol. One small indication of the intensity of identification with Jerusalem will suffice. The Chinese, like late medieval Western aristocrats, identify a family by the location of its ancestral graveyard. Over the centuries, Jews have been just as concerned with their burial places, hoping to rest in Jerusalem. When, as was usually the case, this turned out to be impracticable, they avoided referring in their epitaphs to any other place of origin, preferring to stress instead the solidarity of all Jews.[2]

Armenians created a similar center of intense attachment in Echmiadzin, a small city near Yerivan in what is now Soviet Armenia. They assert that the head of their distinctive church, the Catholicos, has been consecrated in Echmiadzin (originally called Vagharshapat) ever since the fourth century. Repeated attempts—by Byzantines, Ottomans, and most recently by anti-Soviet Armenians—to establish rival sacral centers have never succeeded.

As is the case for other theological aspects of ecclesiastical history, exploration of the doctrinal bases of the Gregorian church, as the Armenians' faith came to be known, would exceed the scope of this work. Given the paucity of general knowledge on the subject, however, some reference to the issues that divided Gregorians from larger Christian bodies is indispensable. The main divergence from the neighboring Christian church of Byzantium was a peculiar formula concerning the relationship between the divine and the human natures of Christ. Some observers have termed this formula 'Monophysite.' Historically, it is true, Armenians have preferred symbols near to the latter belief. For example, the sixth-century Gregorian church, like St Hripsimeh's near Echmiadzin, originally had a single apse window; during the seventh century, Byzantine occupying forces introduced three windows to symbolize the triumph of the orthodox doctrine of the Holy Trinity. Later, popes seeking church unification urged Gregorians to mix water with the wine of consecration to symbolize the two natures of Christ.[3] Armenian theological scholars reject the Monophysite label, in contrast to the Copts, pointing out that Gregorians admit Christ's real human nature, although not the true mortality of his body. Gregorian rejection of the Council of Chalcedon (451), Armenian scholars contend, came about because the council confused the two natures. In any case, a schism had arisen between the Gregorians and the orthodox Byzantine church decades before this doctrinal divergence when the former insisted on consecrating its own ecclesiastical head. The Gregorians argued—there is a parallel to French rejection of the 'Donation of Constantine'—that because Armenia had never belonged to the Roman empire, it need not recognize Constantinople's ecclesiastical jurisdiction.[4]

It is striking to observe how, in its origin, the Armenian ethnoreligious myth endeavored to assimilate components of the established Jewish identity. The surviving branch of the Arsacid dynasty in Armenia claimed ancient Jewish origin. St Gregory the Enlightener apparently came from this family. About AD 300, when Roman Christians were still subject to persecution, he collaborated with his lay relatives in a manner familiar from Central European experience to impose Christianity from above. Church leadership (which also was almost hereditary) at first was designated by the title *kahanaiapet*, derived from Hebrew for 'high priest.' Many Armenian nobles, such as the Bagratids, also asserted descent from Jews deported to Armenia in the first century BC by the Armenian pagan king Tigranes, who had carried out an ephemeral conquest of Syria. St Gregory also endeavored to relate earlier Armenian history to the Jews in order to share their role as God's Chosen People. Old Testament models of belief, hope, and conduct were frequent sermon themes. A high place was accorded a warrior saint such as Judas Maccabeus, and the prominence of liturgical prayers for Armenian victory is notable. Perhaps alone among Christian churches, the Gregorians have maintained the custom of ritual sacrifice of lambs in centers such as Geghard Monastery in a remote mountain district of Soviet Armenia.[5]

When one scrutinizes the history—as far as it can be known—of both Jews and Armenians, one detects curious parallels, even if the ancestral relationship is fictitious. Jews were seminomadic; Armenians apparently were sedentary in their earliest period. Both areas of settlement, however, lay athwart the great trade routes from the Mediterranean area to farther Asia. Their location constituted at once the curse and the opportunity of both peoples. Situated in hardly defensible positions between the Persian empires and the Hellenistic polities, both were exposed to repeated devastation. Ultimate subjugation for Jews came from the Roman Hellenistic side, for the Armenians from the Moslem Turkic successors of the Persians. Both Jews and Armenians developed large diaspora elements long before foreign force compelled complete dispersion. Some accounts place the number of Jews in Egypt at one million (14 percent of the total population), and there were other large colonies throughout the Mediterranean world before it was united by

Rome. Armenians moved in very large numbers to the Byzantine empire before their country was crushed between it and the Moslems. It is significant that at the start of their history both ethnic groups were renowned as warriors. Jewish mercenaries enjoyed some prominence in the early Middle East; Armenians constituted the best recruiting base for Byzantium in the seventh century AD. A recent Soviet study identifies some thirty-eight Armenian families among the three hundred top aristocratic families of tenth- to eleventh-century Byzantium. Almost all of the Armenian elite began as military commanders and regional governors, although many families then moved into Byzantine civil administration.[6]

After the final subjugation of their home territories, neither Jews nor Armenians had opportunities for prominent military careers—in fact, they became so well known as extremely unmilitary peoples that the Ottomans exempted both from the *devshirme*. Only after the holocausts suffered by both groups in the twentieth century did they revert, with remarkable distinction, to military traditions. During the long intervening period, Armenians and Jews alike turned to commercial occupations, that is, to roles usual for groups denied access to governing and military command positions. The extraordinary accumulation over the centuries of skills and aptitudes required in modernizing polities has led me to categorize such groups as 'mobilized diasporas.'[7] Both Jews and Armenians had obtained a long head start in acquiring commercial skills before their ultimate dispersions at times when other occupations were still open to them. No doubt most Jews—about one hundred thousand—in the great commercial metropolis of the Roman empire, Alexandria, were in commerce or liberal professions. Before the Persian Shah Abbas deported them to his capital in the sixteenth century, the Armenians of Julfa in the Transcaucasian homeland for several centuries had constituted the focal point for Armenian trading colonies stretching from Lvov to India.

Nevertheless, the dispersions accelerated the process by which both groups became 'middleman minorities.' For the Armenians, to be sure, final dispersion never took place in the sense that they ceased to occupy a small, fairly compact territory, although since 1915 this area has existed only within the Russian polity. In retrospect, one can locate the initial step that reduced the Armenian homeland to this vestige in the 1830–40 Ottoman implantation among sedentary Armenian peasants of Kurdish semi-nomadic mountaineers. The latter were entitled as Moslems to bear arms, in contrast to the Armenians, who were left almost defenseless.[8] The sources of the Armenian Holocaust, therefore, are closely related to the age-old incompatibility of nomadic and sedentary ways of life and the recurrent temptation of Islamic regimes to resort to nomadic auxiliaries.

In chapter 4 some account was presented of the extraordinary utility of Jews and Armenians to multiethnic polities lagging in modernization, like

Poland-Lithuania and the Ottoman empire. Much of this usefulness derived from the diasporas' technological knowledge in fields as diverse as medicine, luxury goods artisanry, and shipbuilding. Unquestionably, however, their greatest utility was for long-distance commerce. Both Jews and Armenians derived considerable advantages from their ability to cross the Islamic-Christian frontier. As long as they were widely tolerated, Jews performed a major service in exchange of knowledge as well as ideas between the two civilizations. Later, Armenians enjoyed a similar precarious toleration because their 'heretical' position kept them from being identified with either Orthodox or Catholics.[9] It appears that both Jews and Armenians were more highly appreciated as middlemen by Moslem than by Christian elites. For example, the Armenian community in the Crimea was instrumental in capturing the Black Sea commerce for the Ottomans from Italian merchants.[10]

Factors generated by their special backgrounds as diasporas were also important in enabling Armenians and Jews to conduct trade in diverse, often hostile environments. A network of protective family relationships provided contacts and shelter along the trade routes. Usually the solidarity engendered by such contacts was sufficient to make business dealings among diaspora members predictable.[11] If necessary, however, each community had its religious tribunals (usually recognized by the authorities of the broader polity for cases internal to the diaspora) to enforce probity. The Ottoman *millet* system extended such broad jurisdictional, welfare, and taxation authority to Armenian and Jewish communities that a narrow elite control emerged among them. In the first half of the nineteenth century, for example, Ottoman policy enabled the 7 percent of the Armenian *millet* residing in Constantinople to dominate all major institutions of the ethnic group.[12]

It is important to emphasize, however, that even when effective communications with the church hierarchy was impracticable the Gregorian Christian church appears to have been able to maintain uniformity almost entirely through community tribunals and informal pressures. Even less formally centralized subsystems enabled archetypal diasporas to maintain, through intensive communication networks, a high degree of uniformity in ethical expectations. Such uniformity was, in turn, a strong force for perpetuating identity.[13]

The degree to which both Jews and Armenians acquired a polyglot capacity was an extremely important factor in their usefulness to large polities. Part of their linguistic ability arose from their international contacts; it was also fostered by the requirement at any early age to adjust to a difficult sacral written language that was not commonly spoken. So important were linguistic skills that, for example, the 1569 treaty between France and the Ottoman sultan was composed by the interpreters for both sides in Hebrew. In circumstances like the sixteenth-century conflict between the Habsburgs and the Ottomans, a Jew such as Joseph of Nasi, who understandably hated the former, could become indispensable as diplomatic adviser to the sultan by use of a network of Jewish informants attached to the European Courts.[14]

Ethnoreligious identity was certainly prior to and more important than occupational roles. Nevertheless, such roles became so involved with identity that whole ranges of activity were excluded, whereas other activity was accepted by the diaspora communities as unavoidable. The special occupational roles held by Armenians and Jews were critically important for the exchange relationships that elites of both groups maintained with dominant polity elites. From the point of view of this section, however, the main issue is the effect of separate occupational niches upon the identities of the diasporas themselves. The circumstances of Islamic and Christian environments appear to have affected the diasporas differently. Islamic society, especially in cities, was not only highly segmented; this segmentation was accepted as the natural order of things. More specifically, as S. D. Goitein points out, the lack of strict territoriality in jurisdiction of the Islamic law schools made a non-territorial Jewish religious law system seem natural. Conversely, even in Carolingian West Europe after the disappearance of the Syrian commercial colonies, 'Jews' and 'merchants' became synonymous terms, just as 'Jews' and 'moneylenders' were synonymous in eighteenth-century England.[15] Consequently, Jews in the West and both Jews and Armenians in Poland were the objects of harsh stereotyping. In Moslem countries, both diasporas were prominent in specific roles, but other ethnic groups also had their allocated places in the occupational spectrum. Some diaspora roles in Islam incurred opprobrium from other minorities—for example, the requirement that Jews dispose of bodies of executed persons. The Ottoman requirement that Jews throw the ecumenical patriarch's body in the Golden Horn during the Phanariot massacre of 1821 led, for example, to violent Greek reprisals against Jews.[16] Generally, however, neither role opprobrium nor role competition appears to have been as intense in Moslem societies as in European Christian environments even where the latter (as in Poland–Lithuania) had many occupational niches for different groups.

Apparently, a major factor prior to industrialization—which increased tensions in many modernizing societies—was the agrarian ethos of both nobles and peasants in Christian countries. This ethos tended to stereotype townsmen, especially those who were alien in belief and appearance, as parasites. Such stereotypes of Germans were apparent in Poland and Hungary before Jews were prominent there and in Spain were directed against Genoese. Of course, Moslem nomads also had their stereotypes of cowardly, grasping, talkative townsmen. But the overwhelmingly urban model for Islamic religion and culture precluded such feelings from emerging as dominant trends except during periods of nomadic incursion when all city dwellers suffered alike.[17]

Religious belief remained the heart of diaspora identity. Complete adherence to boundary mechanisms in matters like endogamy was strongly enforced by the same system of community tribunals that adjudicated commercial quarrels. The development of a distinctive Armenian alphabet about a century after the adoption of Christianity meant that Armenians were isolated from the propaganda of Zoroastrians using Pahlevi texts and Nestorian heretics using the Syriac alphabet. Theological communication with Byzantium, although constant until Chalcedon, was rendered more difficult.[18]

In later periods, the peculiar languages of the diasporas were often reduced to symbols of religious identity, for members usually conversed in adaptations of foreign languages. Hebrew had been replaced by Aramaic before the first-century dispersion from Palestine. After the Arab conquest, Jews throughout the Islamic world shifted to Arabic, whereas those in the northern Mediterranean areas adopted variants of Romance. Most of the latter, moving northward, developed Yiddish from Old High German, whereas the Iberian Jews at some point during the *reconquista* shifted to variants of the Spanish dialects. Somewhat divergent from standard Castilian, a form of this language (Ladin) for centuries remained the speech of Jewish refugees in the Ottoman empire. Armenians adopted languages like Polish when they were distant from their rural ethnic area. Throughout these processes of linguistic shift, Scriptures and liturgy remained in the original sacral languages. Strong border guard mechanisms were retained against employing foreign linguistic elements, however convenient or prestigious they might be, that suggested deviation in the direction of a hostile faith. Very probably a less obvious resort to linguistic boundary mechanisms appeared in the perpetuation among Jewish physicians in Poland of Arabic (regarded as the vehicle of a relatively tolerant faith) and Greek instead of the Latin medical terms current among Christian physicians.[19] Latin might have opened doors to communication with the dominant elites, but, as Joseph II's effort to 'make the Jews regular citizens' (that is, to Germanize them by eliminating their Yiddish 'jargon') demonstrated, their identity would have been imperiled by such intercourse. Indeed, Jews in the Habsburg dominions encountered strong Jewish community opposition when they wished to enter general schools or universities.[20] Armenians reacted in much the same way; children were forbidden to learn Latin which was identified with the dreaded 'Latin' church. 'Better the Armenian faith in Hell than to get to Heaven with the Latin.'[21]

There is considerable merit to Joseph Laurent's generally sympathetic criticism of the Gregorian church:

> Because it had become exclusively Armenian in its recruitment, the dedication of its members, its faith, and its tendencies, it lacked the power to struggle against national

customs, being unable to invoke against their recalcitrance the authority of a general Christian organization above the very concept of nationality. At every level of the hierarchy, the Armenian church was the prisoner of those whom it had to direct or combat, because the church was merely for them and of them.[22]

Certainly the Armenian ecclesiastical organization has been identified for fifteen hundred years with a single ethnic group. Although unable to engage in extensive proselytizing, the church, like Judaism, Islam, and larger Christian denominations, has persisted in its concept of a worldwide mission in the divine plan. For the Gregorians, this mission was in practice largely confined to the Caucasus region, 'Iberia' (Georgia), and 'Albania' (present-day Dagestan).[23] Given the way the universal missions of larger religious bodies have occasionally been diverted—not necessarily perverted, for the balance of human values achieved through national identity has not yet been determined—it would be imprudent to reject the peculiar combinations of religion and ethnicity that diasporas have achieved.

[*Nations before Nationalism* (Chapel Hill: University of North Carolina Press, 1982), 206–13.]

ROBERT BARTLETT

21 Language and Ethnicity in Medieval Europe

Conquest and colonization created on the frontiers of Latin Christendom societies in which different ethnic groups lived side by side, and everywhere in the frontier zone of Latin Europe race relations were thus a central issue. It is worth stressing at the outset that, while the language of race—*gens*, *natio*, 'blood', 'stock', etc.—is biological, its medieval reality was almost entirely cultural. If we take a classic medieval formulation of the criteria of ethnicity, that of the canonist Regino of Prüm, writing around the year 900, we find that he offers four categories for classifying ethnic variation. 'The various nations,' he writes, 'differ in descent, customs, language and law' (*diversae nationes populorum inter se discrepant genere, moribus, lingua, legibus*). His first criterion, 'descent', is basic to modern forms of racism. The most notorious twentieth-century variants either, like colour racism in the USA, seize on clear biological markers or, like Nazi anti-Semitism, insist on invisible biological differences in the absence of such markers. In the Middle Ages racism of this kind was relatively insignificant. In these circumstances Regino's other criteria—customs, language and law—emerge as the primary badges of ethnicity. In contrast to descent, they share a common characteristic: all three are malleable. They can, indeed, with varying degrees of effect, be transformed not only from one generation to the next, but even within an individual lifetime. New languages can be mastered, new legal regimes adopted, new customs learned. To a point, therefore, medieval ethnicity was a social construct rather than a biological datum. If we define, say, 'German' and 'Slav' by customs, language and law rather than by descent, the grandchildren of Slavs could be Germans, the grandchildren of Germans Slavs. When we study race relations in medieval Europe we are analysing the contact between various linguistic and cultural groups, not between breeding stocks.

The term 'customs' (*mores*) referred to dress, domestic rituals, dietary habits, hair-styles and a host of other habitual practices that distinguished different populations. They were often critically important as differentiae of such groups. In Ireland, the English government legislated against the adoption of Irish hair-styles by loyal subjects: 'the degenerate English of modern times who wear Irish clothes, have their heads half shaved and grow their hair long at the back . . . making themselves like the Irish in clothing and appearance'. The Irish responded by a comparable assertion of identity through hair-style, and one sixteenth-century Irish poem attacks 'You who follow English ways, who cut short your curling hair'. It is indicative that one way to disguise oneself as a member of another race was to adopt their hair-styles. Pagan Slavs of the early twelfth century supposedly scalped German victims and 'after scalping them, they disguise themselves with their scalps and burst into Christian territories, passing themselves off as Christians'. Similarly, in 1190, Muslims trying to slip through the blockade of Acre shaved their beards (as well as putting on Frankish clothes and placing pigs on deck).

Language

Language had a particularly important role in defining nationality. Medieval ecclesiastics and scholars, with their biblically based belief in the common descent of mankind and their theory of an original community of language, found it natural to see the post-Babel differentiation of language as the first step in the formation of races or peoples. 'Races arose from different languages, not languages from different races,' as Isidore of Seville, the schoolmaster of the Middle Ages, put it. The same point is expressed even more pithily by another Latin author: 'language makes race' (*gentem lingua facit*). The power of the linguistic bond was recognized. As a fourteenth-century chronicler reported: 'those who speak the same language are entwined in tighter bonds of love'. These tighter bonds of love often manifested themselves, as we shall see, in a sharper hatred of those of a different language, for, as is apparent to the present day, 'wars and various tribulations have arisen from the diversity of tongues'.

As the vernaculars emerge into literary and documentary record in the High Middle Ages, they reveal large tracts of Europe possessing a relatively high degree of linguistic and cultural homogeneity and dominated by more or less standard languages: examples are English in England, Languedoil north of the Loire, Languedoc south of it, Low German in north Germany, High German in south Germany. There were, naturally, variations in dialect and some areas of linguistic overlap, but one can still see a clear contrast between these core areas and the conquered and colonized peripheries, which were characterized by a ubiquitous mixture and intermingling of language and culture. In the central zone the languages of different areas adjoined, of course, but the fringe zone saw a pluralism of language within the same territorial limits, differentiated by race and class. Although there were enormous linguistic variations within the area in which, say, High German or Languedoc were spoken, they normally took the form of dialectical variation over space. As one travelled from Trier to Vienna or from Béarn to Provence, one would notice the shift from one local variant to another. In complete contrast, the conquered and colonized peripheries of Europe were familiar with languages of completely different language families being spoken in the same settlement or street. The interplay of languages was thus a common and sharply recognizable feature of the frontiers of Latin Europe. Here it was not at all surprising to observe that 'many of our people now speak various languages in the streets', as the Bohemian chronicler Peter of Zittau remarked. When Pope John XXII excommunicated the Franciscan minister-general, Michael of Cesena, in 1329, the letters notifying this action to Cracow were first read out there in Latin and then 'expounded to the people in the vernacular, both in Polish and in German, so that they might be understood better and more clearly by everyone'. The streams, hills and settlements of the frontier zones began to show signs of a double identity: 'the place is called *woyces* in Slavic and *enge water* in German', explains one east Pomeranian document. Names of human settlements underwent similar linguistic transformation. The Irish Ellach in Meath, for example, came to be named Scurlockstown after its new holders, the immigrant Scurlag family—the English suffix 'town' being an indelible mark of the regions of colonization and partial anglicization in eastern and southern Ireland. In New Castile a village known in Arabic as Algariva was rebaptized with the assertive Romance named Villafranca. [. . .]

A growing strand of linguistic nationalism or politicized linguistic consciousness emerges in the later Middle Ages. A symptom of the identification of language and people in the use of the word for language in contexts where it almost certainly means 'people'. The West Slav word *jazyk* denoted both 'language' and 'people', and when the fourteenth-century Czech nationalist writer known as Dalimil employs the term *jazyk cesky*, it is impossible to say in every instance whether the linguistic or the ethnic connotation is greater. The German translation of Dalimil uses *zung*, i.e. 'tongue', and this has a similar semantic complexity, *Iaith*, the Welsh word for 'language', was likewise 'charged in contemporary parlance with a far greater range of attributes than the purely linguistic one'. It is characteristic that the Welsh word for 'those who do not speak Welsh' could be equated with that for 'aliens'. In Latin documents *lingua* enshrines the same ambiguity. Thus when the citizens of Cork refer to the *Hybernica lingua* as the king's enemies, it is only possible to translate this as 'the Irish race'. The Hospitallers in the Levant were grouped into 'tongues' according to their place of origin in western Europe. In all these instances a semantic ambiguity points to a conceptual one—ethnic and linguistic identity tended to blur into one another.

The sense of belonging to a language community could become the basis, not simply for a feeling of belonging or fellowship, but also for political claims. When Przemysl Ottokar II of Bohemia appealed for Polish support in his year of crisis, 1278, he (or, rather, his Italian notary) invoked the closeness of Czechs and Poles based upon physical proximity, ties of blood and the fact that 'the Polish nation . . . is united with us in harmony of language'. The same linguistic affinity again served political purposes in 1300, when Ottokar's successor, Wenceslas II, was offered the Polish throne. The Polish envoys reportedly said: 'there will be one king for us and the Bohemians and we will live together amicably under a common law. For it is fitting that those who do not differ much in speaking the Slavic language enjoy the rule of a single prince.' The Polish claim to Pomerelia, raised in opposition to the Teutonic Knights, was supported by the argument 'that there is one and the same language in Poland and Pomerelia and that all the people who customarily reside there speak Polish'. At about the same time, but almost a thousand miles to the west, the Bruce incursion into Ireland of 1315–18 also enlisted the rhetoric of linguistic kinship. In 1315, while planning the expedition, King Robert wrote a letter to the Irish which begins: 'Since we and you, our people and your people, free since ancient times, have sprung from one national stock, and a common language and common custom stir us to come together eagerly and joyfully in friendship . . .' Donal O'Neill's justification of his recognition of Edward Bruce as king, contained in the Remonstrance of 1317–18 addressed to John XXII, informed the pope that 'the kings of lesser Scotia [Scotland] all trace their blood to our greater Scotia [Ireland] and retain to some degree our language and customs'.

The counterpart to these aggressive claims that used linguistic community as an argument were defensive protestations, such as the accusations, raised especially in the later Middle Ages, that an enemy wished to destroy the native language. Such charges were not limited to the frontiers of Latin Europe. In 1295, when Edward I of England was trying to muster support in his struggle with Philip IV of France, he charged that the French king intended to invade England and 'wipe out the English language completely from the land'. It was clearly, however, the kind of rumour or accusation that would arise naturally in the ethnically divided societies of the frontiers. According to one Polish chronicler, the Teutonic Knights intended 'to exterminate the Polish language' (*ydyoma Polonicum*). Accusations of this type were not mere paranoid fantasies, for some examples of attempts at forcible language change can be found. In addition to the rules governing the language of the law court (to be discussed below), there were some other general attempts at linguistic prescription and proscription. In 1495, for example, Bishop John IV of Wrocław (Breslau) ordered the inhabitants of his village of Woitz (Wójcice) to learn German within five years or be expelled. More systematic and persistent were the rules that the colonial government and the English settlers in Ireland applied to the use of the native Irish language. On the one hand, they repeatedly legislated that settlers should not use the native tongue. 'We have ordained,' runs an ordinance of Edward III of 1359–60, 'that no one of English descent shall speak in the Irish tongue with other Englishmen . . . but every Englishman should study the English language.' Conversely, there was an effort to spread English among the native population. In the 1380s English envoys were trying to get the pope to command the prelates of Ireland that 'they should get their subjects to learn the English language'. Attempts were made to enforce these regulations. In Waterford a certain William Power was imprisoned in 1371 'because he could not speak English' and released only when he found pledges to undertake that he would learn the language; and in the fifteenth century the same city admitted apprentices to the freedom of the city only if they were of 'Inglish aray, habite and speche'. But such precepts were unusual and, one may surmise, rarely effective. Cultural legislation, even in the modern state, always faces an uphill struggle. In medieval circumstances it cannot have been enforceable. Language change there certainly was, but it was the result of migration and cultural adaptation, not of administrative prescription.

Language death is the most dramatic example of language change. Languages which were spoken by rural and lower-class rather than by urban and upper-class speakers and which were not written down for documentary and literary purposes might shrivel and die. There are several instances from the fringes of Latin Europe. Prussian, for example, a Baltic language akin to Lithuanian and Latvian, which was spoken by the native population of Prussia, had died out by the seventeenth century, swamped by the German of immigrants and rulers. A simple catechetical literature was produced in Prussian after the Reformation, but this was too little too late. A note on the cover of one of the surviving Prussian texts records that 'This Old Prussian language has completely disappeared. In 1677 a single old man, who lived on the Courland Spit and who still knew the language, died.' The language was entered on the list of written tongues only to be inscribed almost at once on that of dead ones. Wendish, the Slavic spoken west of the Oder, also disappeared in the later Middle Ages. Only in Lausitz do Slav speakers, the Sorbs, survive to this day (now with their own protected status and institutes for Sorb studies). Elsewhere the various branches of Wendish slowly died. One Polabian innkeeper and farmer, Johannes Parum Schultze, who lived in the so-called 'Hanoverian Wendland' around Lüchow and Dannenberg, wrote in 1725: 'I am a man of forty-seven years of age. When I and three other people in our village have gone, then no one will rightly know what a dog is called in Wendish.'

In Spain it was Arabic which gradually retreated before the triumphant Romance languages. A graphic presentation of the documentation surviving from Toledo in the 140 years after the Christian conquest of 1085 (see Figure 3) shows that in the first hundred years of Christian rule Arabic was used more frequently than Latin or Romance for purposes of record and that in the late twelfth century, possibly due to immigration of Mozarabs from a Muslim Spain polarized by the fanatical Almohads, Arabic was actually increasingly frequent as a language of documentary literacy. The early thirteenth century, however, saw a quite discernible shift, as, for the first time, Latin and Romance documents became more common than Arabic (131:111 for the period 1201–25). The trend developed dramatically. By the 1290s there are only one or two Arabic documents per year, at a time when total output of records is ever increasing. In the fourteenth century the trickle of Arabic dries up. A fundamental linguistic transformation had taken place.

[*The Making of Europe* (Harmondsworth: Penguin, 1994), 197–9, 201–4.]

Section IV

Ethnicity in the Modern World

INTRODUCTION

The serious sociological investigation of ethnicity in the modern world owes much to the American tradition of immigration and race studies of R. E. Park. This tradition tended to assume the assimilation of overseas immigrants by western liberal-democratic societies like the United States. It therefore came as something of a shock when Nathan Glazer and Daniel Moynihan (1963 and 1975) asserted the vigorous resistance of ethnic groups in New York, defined in familial, historical, interest, and religious terms, to the pressures of White Anglo-Saxon Protestant assimilation. For Glazer and Moynihan, the modern metropolis re-created ethnic groups and generated ethnic activity and communal politics, revitalizing ethnic ties and converting them into political interest groups. This theme was taken up by Daniel Bell on a larger canvas. The revival of ethnic ties is not simply the result of the plural nature of most societies world-wide, but stems from the fact that, unlike class, ethnicity combines affect with material interests. The decline of class allegiances in the new 'service society' allows ethnicity to play a much greater political role and achieve a new salience. For Herbert Gans, on the other hand, the secular trend of assimilation retains its power in America. Though the lower classes are bound into their ethnic communities through organizations, the middle and upper classes have been increasingly detached from their ethnic roots and in the third generation ethnicity has become a voluntary life-style. Ethnicity has become largely a matter of symbols and traditions which are individual and largely optional.

In Europe the situation is very different. For Winston James (1989), Britain represents an exclusionary society, which homogenizes the complex identities of Afro-Caribbeans into a single colour line. James explores Afro-Caribbean reactions and their relative failure to make common cause with the very different cultures of Asian immigrants. Stuart Hall takes the story further, arguing that the initial mobilization around Blackness in this situation has given way to a hybridized set of identities among minorities who seek to contest stereotypes and marginalization. One consequence is to reveal the problematic nature of Englishness. For Étienne Balibar, the ethnicity of majorities is also largely constructed as a means of creating the ideal of the nation through continuous time. For this purpose, language and race narratives furnish modes of closure that give a sense of naturalness to the ethnicized nation.

Others attribute to ethnicity a greater sociological reality. Rogers Brubaker, for example, shows how, in contrast to the more civic French conception of the nation which sought to assimilate minorities, Germany adhered to a markedly ethno-cultural understanding, with profound consequences for their contrasting approaches to immigration and naturalization policies. In the Middle East ethnicity is an essential part of the fabric of society. Bassam Tibi argues that we should understand *ethnies* as including the centrifugal forces of the stateless, segmentary 'tribe', which has traditionally been pitted against the state. There are also important economic ramifications of ethnic groups. Walter Zenner explores some of these in relation to 'middlemen minorities' and various economic theories of their functions in the modern labour market. For Zenner, it is less their economic than their social and cultural properties that distinguish and explain their activities and persistence over the centuries. This links ethnicity in the modern world with pre-modern ethnic ties and sentiments.

NATHAN GLAZER AND DANIEL P. MOYNIHAN

22 Beyond the Melting Pot

Perhaps the meaning of ethnic labels will yet be erased in America. But it has not yet worked out this way in New York. It is true that immigrants to this country were rapidly transformed, in comparison with immigrants to other countries, that they lost their language and altered their culture. It was reasonable to believe that a new American type would emerge, a new nationality in which it would be a matter of indifference whether a man was of Anglo-Saxon or German or Italian or Jewish origin, and in which indeed, because of the diffusion of populations through all parts of the country and all levels of the social order, and because of the consequent close contact and intermarriage, it would be impossible to make such distinctions. This may still be the most likely result in the long run. After all, in 1960 almost half of New York City's population was still foreign-born or the children of foreign-born. Yet it is also true that it is forty years since the end of mass immigration, and new processes, scarcely visible when our chief concern was with the great masses of immigrants and the problems of their 'Americanization,' now emerge to surprise us. The initial notion of an American melting pot did not, it seems, quite grasp what would happen in America. At least it did not grasp what would happen in the short run, and since this short run encompasses at least the length of a normal lifetime, it is not something we can ignore.

It is true that language and culture are very largely lost in the first and second generations, and this makes the dream of 'cultural pluralism'—of a new Italy or Germany or Ireland in America, a League of Nations established in the New World—as unlikely as the hope of a 'melting pot.' But as the groups were transformed by influences in American society, stripped of their original attributes, they were recreated as something new, but still as identifiable groups. Concretely, persons think of themselves as members of that group, with that name; they are thought of by others as members of that group, with that name; and most significantly, they are linked to other members of the group by new attributes that the original immigrants would never have recognized as identifying their group, but which nevertheless serve to mark them off, by more than simply name and association, in the third generation and even beyond.

The assimilating power of American society and culture operated on immigrant groups in different ways, to make them, it is true, something they had not been, but still something distinct and identifiable. The impact of assimilating trends on the groups is different in part because the groups are different—Catholic peasants from Southern Italy were affected differently, in the same city and the same time, from urbanized Jewish workers and merchants from Eastern Europe. We cannot even begin to indicate how various were the characteristics of family structure, religion, economic experience and attitudes, educational experience and attitudes, political outlook that differentiated groups from such different backgrounds. Obviously, some American influences worked on them in common and with the same effects. But their differences meant they were open to different parts of American experience, interpreted it in different ways, used it for different ends. In the third generation, the descendants of the immigrants confronted each other, and knew they were both Americans, in the same dress, with the same language, using the same artifacts, troubled by the same things, but they voted differently, had different ideas about education and sex, and were still, in many essential ways, as different from one another as their grandfathers had been.

The initial attributes of the groups provided only one reason why their transformations did not make them all into the same thing. There was another reason—and that was the nature of American society itself, which could not, or did not, assimilate the immigrant groups fully or in equal degree. Or perhaps the nature of human society in general. It is only the experience of the strange and foreign that teaches us how provincial we are. A hundred thousand Negroes have been enough to change the traditional British policy of free immigration from the colonies and dominions. Japan finds it impossible to incorporate into the body of its society anyone who does not look Japanese, or even the Koreans, indistinguishable very often in appearance and language from Japanese. And we shall test the racial attitudes of the Russians only when there are more than a few Negroes passing through as curiosities; certainly the inability of Russians to get over anti-Semitism does not suggest they are any different from the rest of mankind. In any case, the word 'American' was an unambiguous reference to nationality only when it was applied to a relatively homogeneous social body consisting of immigrants from the British Isles, with relatively small numbers from nearby European countries. When the numbers of those not of British origin began to rise, the word 'American' became a far more complicated thing. Legally, it meant a citizen. Socially, it lost its identifying power, and when you asked a man what he was (in the United States), 'American' was not the answer you were looking for. In the United States it became a slogan, a political gesture, sometimes an evasion, but not a matter-of-course, concrete social description of a person. Just as in certain languages a word cannot stand alone but needs some particle to indicate its function, so in the United States the word 'American' does not stand by itself. If it does, it bears the additional meaning of patriot, 'authentic' American, critic and opponent of 'foreign' ideologies.

The original Americans became 'old' Americans, or 'old stock,' or 'white Anglo-Saxon Protestants,' or some other identification which indicated they were not immigrants or descendants of recent immigrants. These original Americans already had a frame in their minds, which became a frame in reality, that placed and ordered those who came after them. Those who were like them could easily join them. It was important to be white, of British origin, and Protestant. If one was all three, then even if one was an immigrant, one was really not an immigrant, or not for long.

Thus, even before it knew what an Italian or Jew or an Irishman was like, the American mind had a place for the category, high or low, depending on color, on religion, on how close the group was felt to be the Anglo-Saxon center. There were peculiarities in this placing. Why, for example, were the Germans placed higher than the Irish? There was of course an interplay to some extent between what the group actually was and where it was placed, and, since the German immigrants were less impoverished than the Irish and somewhat more competent craftsmen and farmers, this undoubtedly affected the old American's image of them. Then ideology came in to emphasize the common links between Englishmen and Germans, who, even though they spoke different languages, were said to be really closer to each other than the old Americans were to the English-speaking, but Catholic and Celtic, Irish. If a group's first representatives were cultured and educated, those who came after might benefit, unless they were so numerous as to destroy the first image. Thus, German Jews who arrived in the 1840's and 1850's benefited from their own characteristics and their link with Germans, until they were overwhelmed by the large number of East European Jewish immigrants after 1880. A new wave of German Jewish immigrants, in the 1930's, could not, regardless of culture and education, escape the low position of being 'Jewish.'

The ethnic group in American society became not a survival from the age of mass immigration but a new social form. One could not predict from its first arrival what it might become or, indeed, whom it might contain. The group is not a purely biological phenomenon. The Irish of today do not consist of those who are descended from Irish immigrants. Were we to follow the history of the germ plasm alone—if we could—we should find that many in the group really came from other groups, and that many who should be in the group are in other groups. The Protestants among them, and those who do not bear distinctively Irish names, may now consider themselves, and be generally considered, as much 'old American' as anyone else. The Irish-named offspring of German or Jewish or Italian mothers often find that willy-nilly they have become Irish. It is even harder for the Jewish-named offspring of mixed marriages to escape from the Jewish group; neither Jews nor non-Jews will let them rest in ambiguity.

Parts of the group are cut off, other elements join the group as allies. Under certain circumstances, strange as it may appear, it is an advantage to be able to take on a group name, even of a low order, if it can be made to fit, and if it gives one certain advantages. It is better in Oakland, California, to be a Mexican than an Indian, and so some of the few Indians call themselves, at certain times, for certain occasions, 'Mexicans.' In the forming of ethnic groups subtle distinctions are overridden; there is an advantage to belonging to a big group, even if it is looked down upon. West Indian Negroes achieve important political positions, as representatives of Negroes; Spaniards and Latin Americans become the representatives of Puerto Ricans; German Jews rose to Congress from districts dominated by East European Jews.

Ethnic groups then, even after distinctive language, customs, and culture are lost, as they largely were in the second generation, and even more fully in the third generation, are continually recreated by new experiences in America. The mere existence of a name itself is perhaps sufficient to form group character in new situations, for the name associates an individual, who actually can be anything, with a certain past, country, race. But as a matter of fact, someone who is Irish or Jewish or Italian generally has other traits than the mere existence of the name that associates him with other people attached to the group. A man is connected to his group by ties of family and friendship. But he is also connected by ties of *interest*. The ethnic groups in New York are also *interest groups*.

This is perhaps the single most important fact about ethnic groups in New York City. When one speaks of the Negroes and Puerto Ricans, one also means unorganized and unskilled workers, who hold poorly paying jobs in the laundries, hotels, restaurants, small factories or who are on relief. When one says Jews, one also means small shopkeepers, professionals, better-paid skilled workers in the garment industries. When one says Italians, one also means homeowners in Staten Island, the North Bronx, Brooklyn, and Queens.

[*Beyond the Melting Pot* (Cambridge, Mass.: MIT Press, 1963), 12–17.]

DANIEL BELL

23 Ethnicity and Social Change

Most societies in the world today are 'plural societies.' By plural societies, I simply mean the existence of segmented sociological groups which can establish effective cultural and political cohesion within the society and make cultural, economic, or political claims on the society, on the basis of that group identity.[1] Sometimes these cohesions are direct and primordial; sometimes these cohesions are created out of adversary conflicts.

In most countries, and this has been true historically, the plural society was a product of conquest in which various minority groups were subjugated by force and incorporated into a society. In North America, however, the plural society was created largely out of the free mingling of peoples through immigration, and with impressed black slaves brought by traders.[2]

Until fairly recently, there was little overt competition between these plural groups. In colonial countries or empires, an open system of overt domination kept most of the indigenous peoples subjected. In multigroup societies such as the United States, the oldest settler segment exercised customary social and economic dominance. But with the destruction of imperialist rule in former colonial countries, and the erosion of the older authority structures in the industrial west, competition between the plural groups today has become the norm.

Except where minorities (or majorities even) are openly repressed (for example, South Africa, Angola), competition between plural groups takes place largely in the political arena. The reason is simple. Status competition is diffuse and lacks a specific site. Economic competition is dispersed between interests and occupations. But political competition is direct and tangible, the rewards are specified through legislation or by the direct allocation of jobs and privileges. The very nature of interest-group rivalry, where the plural groups are evidently distinct, makes it certain that the political arena becomes the most salient in the competition for the chief values of the society.

There is a second general reason why the political arena has become so salient. This is the 'shrinkage' of the economic order in advanced industrial societies. For two centuries, as Emile Durkheim pointed out seventy years ago, 'Economic life has taken on an expansion it never knew before. From being a secondary function, despised and left to inferior classes, it passed on to one of first rank. We see the military, governmental and religious functions falling back more and more in face of it.'[3] In effect, the economic order 'swelled up' as if to encompass, almost, the entire life of society and the 'horizontal' divisions of the economic order, that of capitalist and worker, became the central socio-political division of the society as well. But now, as I have pointed out earlier, the economic order in almost all advanced industrial societies has become increasingly subordinated to the political system: first, because of the need to manage the economic system; and second, because the rise of noneconomic values (environment, ecology, health, culture, freer personal styles—elements subsumed under that phrase 'the quality of life') has led to the demand for the control of economic production.

The third major reason for the centrality of the political order is that the major processes of modernization—the transformation of societies—in Africa, Asia, the Soviet Union, and to some extent, Latin America, are being carried out 'from the top,' by elites, and through the force and coercion available only through the political system. Marx may have felt that social change is initiated in society in the economic substructure, but the most striking fact of the industrialization of the Soviet Union and the transformation of peasant agriculture into communes in China is that these are 'directed' efforts, carried out by political means.

But politics is more than just the arena of interests or of social transformations. Politics is also the arena of passions, where emotions can be readily mobilized behind one's own flag, and against another group. The 'risks' of such inflamed political competition is that issues may not be negotiable (as they are when tied to interests alone), but become 'causes' that invite violent conflict and even civil war.

In the western world, up to the seventeenth and the eighteenth centuries, such passions were expressed largely in religious terms, even where, as in the religious rhetoric of the English civil war, they masked a political content. Today the clashes are in overt political terms, though behind some of the political rhetoric lurk the passions of secular religions, the national, class, or ethnic embodiments of ideological politics.

In the nineteenth century, particularly in Europe, the most potent ideology was nationalism. Nationalism joins culture and politics in a common purpose. It brings together the high-born and the low and gives those, even of the meanest circumstance, a pride in being able to feel at one with the highest classes in the country, and in a common culture and history. Nationalism has the appeal of unifying a country behind a common loyalty, and focusing emotional aggression against an outside neighbor. For this obvious reason, where there has been a strong, aggressive nationalism, class and ethnic rivalries have been subdued or muted. As World War I and other wars have shown, country rather than class had the overriding appeal, even among workers.

It is questionable whether in the western world today that kind of inclusive nationalism any longer has such a compelling power. It may be that nationalism has an emotional power within Yugoslavia, or in eastern Europe, or in Northern Ireland, but these are almost entirely instances of national groups subordinated to a larger political entity whose cultural and social dominance is resented. There is much less emotional nationalism in the state of Eire itself, than in Northern Ireland. The nationalism of Ukrainians and Uzbeks within the Soviet-dominated world is a weapon for independence; under conditions of independence, would the passions remain?

If one takes the western powers, those along the Atlantic littoral, is there much emotional patriotism in Great Britain, France, Western Germany, Italy, or the United States? For one crucial fact, nationalism was an ideology fashioned by intellectuals who created the consciousness of a common culture out of the myths, folklore, songs, and literature of a people. Nationalism, to that extent, was a product of romanticism, with its emphasis on history and nature, against the rationalism of modern life. But that kind of romanticism is no longer attached to the mystical notion of an 'organic' nation, and the intellectuals have decamped from patriotism.[4]

The second fact is that almost all these western societies are 'fatigued.' Nations and peoples, where circumstances are favorable, often display 'historical energies' which drive them forward to seek a place on the stage of history. These are the upsurges which reflect a military or economic vitality of a people. The historic drive of the western powers took place in the century between 1850 and 1950, largely in industrialization and imperialism, and took pride in technological achievement and empire. Yet those forces now seem spent, frayed by internal problems or exhausted in internecine wars; and few of those countries display that sense of 'national will,' which is what unites historical destiny with national purpose. Nationalism in these countries is at a low ebb.

And that creates a problem for them. The historical lesson is that societies undergoing rapid social change, or nation building, or territorial or political expansion, can escape or postpone internal political difficulties—the fear of established groups for the loss of privilege, the demand of disadvantaged groups for the reallocation of privilege—by mobilizing the society against some 'external' force, or for some common ideological purpose. Yet both ends are spent.

In the American hemisphere, the external force, initially, was 'nature,' and the energies of the society were channeled into the opening and developing of a large new continent. Later, the source of internal cohesion became some ideologically defined outside enemy. In the United States, in the 1950s, there was a large degree of social unity because the society was mobilized during the Korean war and after, against the threat of communism. When that ideological threat, which had been defined in monolithic terms, began to dissipate (though great power rivalry remained), the internal social divisions in the society that had been held in bound erupted. A large number of structural changes had been taking place in the society—the creation of a national society and a communal society—and the claims of disadvantaged social groups, such as the blacks and the poor.[5] Those now, inevitably, came to the fore, and they, too, were expressed in political terms.

The crucial question for all politics is what are the social bases of cohesion and cleavage—the objective basis for cohesion (interests), and the subjective basis for a common symbolism and shared consciousness (emotional tie); what determines the composition and character of corporate groups? Analytically speaking, there are two kinds of social movements: symbolic and expressive movements whose ties are primarily affective; and instrumental groups whose actions are bound by a set of common, usually material, interests.

Social units that are entirely symbolic-expressive are of two sorts: they may be simply fraternal, such as veterans' organizations reliving old glories, and thus become attenuated; or, if they are oriented to action, their life may be transient, since the need to heighten and mobilize feelings—in order to keep their zeal alive—drives them to extremes (for example, the Weathermen in student politics). Where social units are entirely instrumental, it becomes difficult to extend their range beyond the limited interest which impelled the organization, so, lacking any emotional basis for cohesion, either new interests have to be found, or the attachments and purposes of the organization become diminished. In short, the problem for symbolic-expressive groups is that while they can be mobilized quickly in periods of stress and peak experience, without a sustained, continuing interest which is real, and which has tangible payoffs for the members, the movements burn themselves out. The problem for instrumental organizations is the need to readapt themselves to new purposes when the old goals have become realized.

Those social units are most highly effective, clearly, which can combine symbolic and instrumental purposes. In the political history of our times, it is clear that 'class' and 'ethnicity' have been the two such dominant modes of coherent group feeling and action, and we can raise the general question, under what conditions has one or the other become most salient for action, or under what conditions might the two be fused?

Class, in industrial society in the last two hundred or so years, has justly been defined in terms of property relations, and class issues as the conflicts between those who have to sell their labor power and those who buy it. Working class politics, in that period of time, has been oriented either to the complete change of the system, or a sharing of power within it.

The fundamental fact is that few working class movements in the advanced industrial societies in recent years have had a revolutionary purpose. Even those which, rhetorically, still seek such a change, such as the Communist-dominated labor movements in France and Italy, no longer act that way in practice. Their chief effort is to have an effective voice over the control of working conditions. Since the end of World War II, industrial conflict in most countries has been institutionalized. This does not mean, necessarily, that all militancy vanished, nor that some of the economic conflicts may not spill over into politics, as in Italy, where parliamentary impasses threaten to polarize the society, or England, where the successive governments, Labor and Tory, have sought to restrict the activities of the unions. But it does mean two things: that some rough and ready rules of the game have tended to limit the conflict, and to force some negotiated solutions; and that these conflicts, as Ralf Dahrendorf has put it, had become 'institutionally isolated' so that there was little carry-over from the job to other areas of life; the occupational milieu lost its ability to mold the personality and behavior of the worker; and the industrial issues were no longer the overriding issues that polarize a society.[6]

The second fact is that structural changes in the society have tended to reduce the role of property and introduce a new criterion, that of technical skill, as the basis of class position. In more immediate terms, the changeover in most western societies from a goods producing to a service economy expands the proportion of white-collar jobs and emphasizes education as the mode of access to the expanding technical and professional vocations. The working class, as a proportion of the labor force, is shrinking, and the new service occupations and professional positions rarely carry the history or traditions of the older working class forms of activity. Thus, there is not a single but a double-based economic class system, of property and skill, in the society.[7]

One important consequence of the institutional change is that 'class' no longer seemed to carry any strong affective tie. To put it most baldly, what had once been an ideology had now become almost largely an interest. The labor movements in western industrial society have always been a cleft stick. On the one end, they have been part of a 'social movement' which seeks to transform society; on the other, a 'trade union' seeking a place within it. As a social movement, labor sought to mobilize affect as a means of maintaining a permanent hostility to an employer class, husbanding its zeal until the 'final conflict.' As a trade union, it has had to live on a day-to-day relation with particular employers and even, at times, adopt their point of view and interest, in order to save their jobs against competitive employers and other unions. The institutionalization of bargaining, necessarily, has meant a lowering of ideological sights. (One interesting indicator is the decline of 'labor songs' as a means of inspiring emotions; the only such songs in recent years have been those of the black civil rights movement.) The 'social movement' aspect of labor, with all the attendant aspects that the ideology sought to stimulate—fraternal organizations, cooperatives, theater and cultural groups—is no longer a 'way of life' for its members. The union has focused on the job, and little more.

The further fact, in the United States at least, is that this 'interest' often has been converted into a quasi-monopoly job position—either by the direct exclusion of blacks from certain occupations (a situation largely true in the building trades until recently), the operation of a 'merit' system as in teaching, which tends to restrict the opportunities of latecomer blacks for rapid advancement, or even the normal 'seniority' system in most union agreements, which acts to keep blacks and other minorities in the lower paying positions. For these reasons, one finds blacks often hostile to trade unions and, even though the overwhelming majority of them are workers, we find them in the unions emphasizing the 'ethnic' as against their 'class' identities. For the blacks, particularly, and more so for the radical blacks, the question whether they organize in 'race' or 'class' terms is a crucial one. Given the fact that their advancement has come largely through political pressure, and the ability to make gains by mobilizing votes, the emphasis, overwhelmingly, has been in race or nationalist terms.

In a plural society, class cuts across ethnic lines. Sometimes class becomes congruent with ethnicity, where there is a bipolar situation in which one ethnic group is economically predominant and another ethnic group economically exploited. More often than not, in the advanced countries at least, ethnicity cuts across class lines and members of the different ethnic groups are both in the economic majority and economic minority. Where class issues become attenuated, and communal questions come to the fore, understandably, the ethnic tie becomes more salient.

The conversion of the working class into an 'institutional interest,' with an elaborate bureaucratic structure of its own, is a process that has taken place primarily within the last twenty-five years. During that time the economic locus of conflict diminished. And where interests became institutionalized and instrumental, the adversary conflicts which tend to polarize emotions also diminished; for this reason the saliency of an identity as a worker tended to attenuate. At the same time, within this period, the political arena became more central. Where this has taken place on the local and community level, as has been evident in this period, interest-group unionism has become less important and other group memberships have come to the fore. For this double reason, ethnicity has become more salient in the last decade.[8]

Ethnicity has become more salient because it can combine an interest with an affective tie. Ethnicity provides a tangible set of common identifications—in language, food, music, names—when other social roles become more abstract and impersonal. In the competition for the values of the society to be realized politically, ethnicity can become a means of claiming place or advantage.

Ethnic groups—be they religious, linguistic, racial, or communal—are, it should be pointed out, *pre-industrial* units that, with the rise of industry, became cross-cut by economic and class interests. In trying to account for the upsurge of ethnicity today, one can see this ethnicity as the emergent expression of primordial feelings, long suppressed but now reawakened, or as a 'strategic site,' chosen by disadvantaged persons as a new mode of seeking political redress in the society.

Two historical factors are relevant here. One, which I have pointed to, is the loss of social dominance of the old social elites, a situation which derives from the breakup of the 'family capitalism,' which joined family directly to economic power in the western world.[9] Within the family system there has been an erosion of the social authority, of the major 'family' names in high society, particularly of the WASPs. One finds less of 'society' and more of 'celebrity,' less emphasis on large social estates and great houses, and more on movement and travel. If there is a 'social hierarchy' in the United States, it tends to hide itself, rather than flaunt its position as in the Gilded Age.

The second historical fact is the breakup of imperialism, which I discussed previously from the point of view of its significance for ideological developments. Imperialism has been looked at largely in economic and political terms, but clearly it had a cultural component which emphasized the superiority of the older nations and which had extraordinary psychological effects on the personalities of those who lived under imperialist rule. The resurgence of ethnicity, in that respect, is part of the broader historical upsurge against imperialism, reflected now, on the cultural side. Since no group can now claim explicit superiority, each group can emphasize its own language, religion, and culture as of intrinsic value and can assert a pride in the aggressive declaration of one's own ethnicity. Ethnicity becomes a badge that one can wear more openly and show as a mode of personal self-assertion.

These two facts, social and cultural, merge with the changed context of economic advancement and political organization. In industrial societies, access to economic and professional position becomes defined increasingly by technical criteria. In the modernizing world, as well, achievement becomes linked with technical competence, which involves higher education, specialized skills, and professional achievement. The one route largely open is the political one. One can move ahead by mobilizing a following, become elected to office or get a job by supporting a victorious candidate; or one can make demands for quotas or some other means of enforcing an allocation of position on some criterion other than the technical and professional.

In this context, claims are made on the basis of ascriptive or group identity rather than individual achievement, and this is reinforced by the nature of the political process which emphasizes some group coherence as a means of being effective in that arena. *What takes place, then, is the wedding of status issues to political demands through the ethnic groups.* In the recent historical situation, ethnic groups, being both expressive and instrumental, become sources of political strength.

In sum, there would be three reasons for the upsurge of the salience of ethnic identification:

1. In the greater mingling of peoples, with the expansion of more inclusive, yet attenuated, identities, in the simultaneous development of a culture that is more syncretistic and a social structure that is more bureaucratic, the desire for some particular or primordial anchorage becomes intensified. People want to belong to 'smaller' units, and find in ethnicity an easy attachment.

2. The breakup of the traditional authority structures and the previous affective social units—historically, nation and class—in turn make the ethnic attachment more salient.

3. The politicization of the decisions that affect the communal lives of persons makes the need for group organization more necessary, and ethnic grouping becomes a ready means of demanding group rights or providing defense against other groups.

What I think is clear is that ethnicity, in this context, is best understood *not* as a primordial phenomenon in which deeply held identities have to re-emerge, but as a strategic choice by individuals who, in other circumstances, would choose other group memberships as a means of gaining some power and privilege. In short, it is the *salience* not the *persona* which has to be the axial line for explanation. And because salience may be the decisive variable, the attachment to ethnicity may flush or fade very quickly depending on political and economic circumstances.

The paradox is that with more syncretism and intermingling, formal ethnic attachments may weaken, as evidenced by the high degree of intermarriage between groups, yet, if one wants to, one can now identify oneself more readily, and without lessened esteem, in ethnic terms, and make claims on that basis of that identity. The simple point, then, is that ethnicity has become fully legitimate—and sometimes necessary—as an identity, and this carries over, in a political situation, into a group attachment.

['Ethnicity and social change', in N. Glazer and D. P. Moynihan (eds.), *Ethnicity: Theory and Experience* (Cambridge, Mass.: Harvard University Press, 1975), 160–71.]

HERBERT J. GANS

24 Symbolic Ethnicity

Symbolic ethnicity can be expressed in a myriad of ways, but above all, I suspect, it is characterized by a nostalgic allegiance to the culture of the immigrant generation, or that of the old country; a love for and a pride in a tradition that can be felt without having to be incorporated in everyday behavior. The feelings can be directed at a generalized tradition, or at specific ones: a desire for the cohesive extended immigrant family, or for the obedience of children to parental authority, or the unambiguous orthodoxy of immigrant religion, or the old-fashioned despotic benevolence of the machine politician. People may even sincerely desire to 'return' to these imagined pasts, which are conveniently cleansed of the complexities that accompanied them in the real past, but while they may soon realize that they cannot go back, they may not surrender the wish. Or else they displace that wish on churches, schools, and the mass media, asking them to recreate a tradition, or rather, to create a symbolic tradition, even while their familial, occupational, religious and political lives are pragmatic responses to the imperatives of their roles and positions in local and national hierarchical social structures.

All of the cultural patterns which are transformed into symbols are themselves guided by a common pragmatic imperative: they must be visible and clear in meaning to large numbers of third generation ethnics, and they must be easily expressed and felt, without requiring undue interference in other aspects of life. For example, Jews have abstracted rites de passage and individual holidays out of the traditional religion and given them greater importance, such as the bar mitzvah and bas mitzvah (the parallel ceremony for 13-year-old girls that was actually invented in America). Similarly, Chanukah, a minor holiday in the religious calendar has become a major one in popular practice, partly since it lends itself to impressing Jewish identity on the children. Rites de passage and holidays are ceremonial; and thus symbolic to begin with; equally important, they do not take much time, do not upset the everyday routine, and also become an occasion for family reunions to reassemble family members who are rarely seen on a regular basis. Catholic ethnics pay special attention to saint's days celebrating saints affiliated with their ethnic group, or attend ethnic festivals which take place in the area of first settlement, or in ethnic churches.

Consumer goods, notably food, are another ready source for ethnic symbols, and in the last decades, the food industry has developed a large variety of easily cooked ethnic foods, as well as other edibles which need no cooking, for example, chocolate matzohs which are sold as gifts at Passover. The response to symbolic ethnicity may even be spreading into the mass media, for films and television programs with ethnic characters are on the increase. The characters are not very ethnic in their behavior, and may only have ethnic names—for example, Lt. Colombo, Fonzi, or Rhoda Goldstein—but in that respect, they are not very different from the ethnic audiences who watch them.

Symbolic ethnicity also takes political forms, through identification or involvement with national politicians and international issues which are sufficiently remote to become symbols. As politicians from non-Irish ethnic backgrounds achieve high state or national office, they become identity symbols for members of their group, supplying feelings of pride over their success. That such politicians do not represent ethnic constituencies, and thus do not become involved in ethnic political disputes only enhances their symbolic function; unlike local ethnic politicians, who are still elected for instrumental bread-and-butter reasons, and thus become embroiled in conflicts that detract from their being symbols of ethnic pride.

Symbolic ethnicity can be practiced as well through politically and geographically even more distant phenomena, such as nationalist movements in the old country. Jews are not interested in their old countries, except to struggle against the maltreatment of Jews in Eastern Europe, but they have sent large amounts of money to Israel, and political pressure to Washington, since the establishment of the State. While their major concern has undoubtedly been to stave off Israel's destruction, they might also have felt that their own identity would be affected by such a disaster. Even if the survival of Israel is guaranteed in the future, however, it is possible that as allegiances toward organized local Jewish communities in America weaken, Israel becomes a substitute community to satisfy identity needs. Similar mechanisms may be at work among other ethnic groups who have recently taken an interest in their ancestral countries, for example the Welsh and Armenians, and among those groups whose old countries are involved in internal conflict, for example the Irish, and Greeks and Turks during the Cyprus war of 1973.

Old countries are particularly useful as identity symbols because they are far away and cannot make arduous demands on American ethnics; even sending large amounts of money is ultimately an easy way to help unless the donors are making major economic sacrifices. Moreover, American ethnics can identify with their perception of the old country or homeland, transforming it into a symbol which leaves out its domestic or foreign problems that could become sources of conflict for Americans. For example, most American Jews who support Israel pay little attention to its purely domestic policies; they are concerned with its preservation as a state and a Jewish homeland, and see the country mainly as a Zionist symbol.

The symbolic functions of old countries are facilitated further when interest in them is historical; when ethnics develop an interest in their old countries as they were during or before the time of the ancestral departure. Marcus Hansen's notion of third-generation return was actually based on the emergence of interest in Swedish history, which suggests that the third generation return may itself only be another variety of symbolic ethnicity. Third generations can obviously attend to the past with less emotional risk than first and second generation people who are still trying to escape it, but even so, an interest in ethnic history is a return only chronologically.

Conversely, a new symbol may be appearing among Jews: the Holocaust, which has become a historic example of ethnic group destruction that can now serve as a warning sign for possible future threats. The interest of American Jews in the Holocaust has increased considerably since the end of World War II; when I studied the Jews of Park Forest in 1949–1950, it was almost never mentioned, and its memory played no part whatsoever in the creation of a Jewish community there. The lack of attention to the Holocaust at that time may, as Nathan Glazer suggests, reflect the fact that American Jews were busy with creating new Jewish communities in the suburbs.[1] It is also possible that people ignored the Holocaust then because the literature detailing its horrors had not yet been written, although since many second generation American Jews had relatives who died in the Nazi camps, it seems more likely that people repressed thinking about it until it had become a more historical and therefore a less immediately traumatic event. As a result, the Holocaust may now be serving as a new symbol for the threat of group destruction, which is required, on the one hand, by the fact that rising intermarriage rates and the continued decline of interest and participation in Jewish religion are producing real fears about the disappearance of American Jewry altogether; and on the other hand, by the concurrent fact that American anti-semitism is no longer the serious threat to group destruction that it was for first and second generation Jews. Somewhat the same process appears to be taking place among some young Armenians who are now reviving the history of the Turkish massacre of Armenians some sixty years later, at a time when acculturation and assimilation are beginning to make inroads into the Armenian community in America.

I suggested previously that ethnicity *per se* had become more visible, but many of the symbols used by the third generation are also visible to the rest of America, not only because the middle class people who use them are more visible than their poorer ancestors, but because the national media are more adept at communicating symbols than the ethnic cultures and organizations of earlier generations. The visibility of symbolic ethnicity provides further support for the existence of an ethnic revival, but what appears to be a revival is probably the emergence of a new form of acculturation and assimilation that is taking place under the gaze of the rest of society.

Incidentally, even though the mass media play a major role in enhancing the visibility of ethnicity, and in communicating ethnic symbols, they do not play this role because they are themselves ethnic institutions. True, the mass media, like other entertainment industries, continue to be dominated by Jews (although less so than in the past), but for reasons connected with anti-semitism, or the fear of it, they have generally leaned over backwards to keep Jewish characters and Jewish fare out of their offerings, at least until recently. Even now, a quantitative analysis of major ethnic characters in comedy, drama and other entertainment genres would surely show that Catholic ethnics outnumber Jewish ones. Perhaps the Jews who write or produce so much of the media fare are especially sensitive to ethnic themes and symbols; my own hypothesis, however, is that they are, in this case as in others, simply responding to new cultural tendencies, if only because they must continually innovate. In fact, the arrival of ethnic characters followed the emergence and heightened visibility of ethnic politics in the late 1960s, and the men and women who write the entertainment fare probably took inspiration from news stories they saw on television or read in the papers.

I noted earlier that identity cannot exist apart from a group and that symbols are themselves part of a culture, and in that sense, symbolic ethnicity can be viewed as an indicator of the persistence of ethnic groups and cultures. Symbolic ethnicity, however, does not require functioning groups or networks; feelings of identity can be developed by allegiances to symbolic groups that never meet, or to collectivities that meet only occasionally, and exist as groups only for the handful of officers that keep them going. By the same token, symbolic ethnicity does not need a practiced culture, even if the symbols are borrowed from it. To be sure, symbolic culture is as much culture as practiced culture, but the latter persists only to supply symbols to the former. Indeed, practiced culture may need to persist, for some, because people do not borrow their symbols from extinct cultures that survive only in museums. And insofar as the borrowed materials come from the practiced culture of the immigrant generation, they make it appear as if an ethnic revival were taking place.

Then, too, it should be noted that even symbolic ethnicity may be relevant for only some of the descendents of the immigrants. As intermarriage continues, the number of people with parents from the same secular ethnic group will continue to decline, and by the time the fourth generation of the old immigration reaches adulthood, such people may be a minority. Most Catholic ethnics will be hybrid, and will have difficulty developing an ethnic identity. For example, how would the son of an Italian mother and Irish father who has married a woman of Polish-German ancestry determine his ethnicity, and what would he and his wife tell their children? Even if they were willing, would they be able to do so; and in that case to decide their children's ethnicity, how would they rank or synthesize their diverse backgrounds? These questions are empirical, and urgently need to be studied, but I would suggest that there are only three possibilities. Either the parents choose the single ethnic identity they find most satisfying, or they become what I earlier called pan-ethnics, or they cope with diversity by ignoring it, and raise their children as non-ethnic.

The emergence of symbolic ethnicity

The preceding observations have suggested that symbolic ethnicity is a new phenomenon that comes into being in the third generation, but it is probably of earlier vintage and may have already begun to emerge among the immigrants themselves. After all, many of the participants in the new immigration were oppressed economically, politically and culturally in their old countries, and could not have had much affection even for the village and regions they were leaving. Consequently, it is entirely possible that they began to jettison the old culture and to stay away from ethnic organizations other than churches and unions the moment they came to America, saving only their primary groups, their ties to relatives still left in Europe, and their identity. In small town America, where immigrants were a numerically unimportant minority, the pressure for immediate acculturation and assimilation was much greater than in the cities, but even in the latter, the seeds for symbolic ethnicity may have been sown earlier than previously thought.

Conversely, despite all the pressures toward Americanization and the prejudice and discrimination experienced by the immigrants, they were never faced with conditions that required or encouraged them to give up their ethnicity entirely. Of course, some of the earliest Jewish arrivals to America had become Quakers and Episcopalians before the end of the nineteenth century, but the economic conditions that persuaded the Jamaican Chinese in Kingston to become Creole, and the social isolation that forced Italians in Sydney, Australia, to abolish the traditional familial male–female role segregation shortly after arriving, have never been part of the American experience.[2]

Some conditions for the emergence of symbolic ethnicity were present from the beginning, for American ethnics have always been characterized by freedom of ethnic expression, which stimulated both ethnic diversity, and the right to find one's own way of being ethnic that are crucial to symbolic ethnicity. Although sacred and secular ethnic organizations which insisted that only one mode of being ethnic was legitimate have always existed in America, they have not been able to enforce their norms, in part because they have always had to compete with other ethnic organizations. Even in ethnic neighborhoods where conformity was expected and social control was pervasive, people had some freedom of choice about ethnic cultural practices. For example, the second generation Boston Italians I studied had to conform to many family and peer group norms, but they were free to ignore ethnic secondary groups, and to drop or alter Italian cultural practices according to their own preference.

Ethnic diversity within the group was probably encouraged by the absence of a state religion, and national and local heads of ethnic communities. For example, American Jewry never had a chief rabbi, or even chief Orthodox, Conservative and Reform rabbis, and the European practice of local Jewish communities electing or appointing local laymen as presidents was not carried across the ocean.[3] Catholic ethnics had to obey the cardinal or bishop heading their diocese, of course, but in those communities where the diocese insisted on an Irish church, the other ethnic groups, notably the Italians, kept their distance from the church, and only in parochial schools was there any attempt to root out secular ethnic patterns. The absence of strong unifying institutions thus created the opportunity for diversity and freedom from the beginning, and undoubtedly facilitated the departure from ethnic cultures and organizations.

Among the Jews, symbolic ethnicity may have been fostered early by self-selection among Jewish emigrants. As Liebman points out, the massive Eastern European immigration to America did not include the rabbis and scholars who practiced what he called an elite religion in the old countries; as a result, the immigrants established what he calls a folk religion in America instead, with indigenous rabbis who were elected or appointed by individual congregations, and were more permissive in allowing, or too weak to prevent, deviations from religious orthodoxy, even of the milder folk variety.[4] Indeed, the development of a folk religion may have encouraged religious and secular diversity among Jews from the very beginning.

Still, perhaps the most important factor in the development of symbolic ethnicity was probably the awareness, which I think many second generation people had already reached, that neither the practice of ethnic culture nor participation in ethnic organizations were essential to being and feeling ethnic. For Jews, living in a Jewish neighbourhood or working with Jews every day was enough to maintain Jewish identity. When younger second generation Jews moved to suburbia in large numbers after World War II, many wound up in communities in which they were a small numerical minority, but they quickly established an informal Jewish community of neighborly relations, and then built synagogues and community centers to formalize and supplement the informal community. At the time, many observers interpreted the feverish building as a religious revival, but for most Jews, the synagogue was a symbol that could serve as a means of expressing identity without requiring more than occasional participation in its activities.[5] Thus, my observations among the second generation Jews of Park Forest and other suburbs led me to think as far back as the mid 1950s that among Jews, at least, the shift to symbolic ethnicity was already under way.[6]

The future of ethnicity

The emergence of symbolic ethnicity naturally raises the question of its persistence into the fifth and sixth generations. Although the Catholic and Jewish religions are certain to endure, it appears that as religion becomes less important to people, they, too will be eroded by acculturation and assimilation. Even now, synagogues see most of their worshippers no more than once or twice a year, and presumably, the same trend will appear, perhaps more slowly, among Catholics and Protestants as well.

Whether the secular aspects of ethnicity can survive beyond the fourth generation is somewhat less certain. One possibility is that symbolic ethnicity will itself decline as acculturation and assimilation continue, and then disappear as erstwhile ethnics forget their secular ethnic identity to blend into one or another subcultural melting pot. The other possibility is that symbolic ethnicity is a steady-state phenomenon that can persist into the fifth and sixth generations.

Obviously, this question can only be guessed at, but my hypothesis is that symbolic ethnicity may persist. The continued existence of Germans, Scandinavians, and Irish after five or more generations in America suggests that in the larger cities and suburbs, at least, they have remained ethnic because they have long practiced symbolic ethnicity.[7] Consequently, there is good reason to believe that the same process will also take place among ethnics of the new immigration.

Ethnic behavior, attitudes, and even identity are, however, determined not only by what goes on among the ethnics, but also by developments in the larger society, and especially by how that society will treat ethnics in the future; what costs it will levy and what benefits it will award to them as ethnics. At present, the costs of being and feeling ethnic are slight. The changes which the immigrants and their descendants wrought in America now make it unnecessary for ethnics to surrender their ethnicity to gain upward mobility, and today ethnics are admitted virtually everywhere, provided they meet economic and status requirements, except at the very highest levels of the economic, political, and cultural hierarchies. Moreover, since World War II, the ethnics have been able to shoulder blacks and other racial minorities with the deviant and scapegoat functions they performed in an earlier America, so that ethnic prejudice and 'institutional ethnism' are no longer significant, except again at the very top of the societal hierarchies.

To be sure, some ethnic scapegoating persists at other levels of these hierarchies; American Catholics are still blamed for the policies of the Vatican, Italo-Americans are criticized for the Mafia, and urban ethnics generally have been portrayed as racists by a sometime coalition of white and black Protestant, Jewish, and other upper-middle class cosmopolitans. But none of these phenomena, however repugnant, strike me as serious enough to persuade many to hide their ethnicity. More important but less often noticed, white working class men, and perhaps others, still use ethnic stereotypes to trade insults, but this practice serves functions other than the maintenance of prejudice or inequality.

At the same time, the larger society also seems to offer some benefits for being ethnic. Americans increasingly perceive themselves as undergoing cultural homogenization, and whether or not this perception is justified, they are constantly looking for new ways to establish their differences from each other. Meanwhile, the social, cultural and political turbulence of the last decade, and the concurrent delegitimation of many American institutions have also cast doubt on some of the other ways by which people identify themselves and differentiate themselves from each other. Ethnicity, now that it is respectable and no longer a major cause of conflict, seems therefore to be ideally suited to serve as a distinguishing characteristic. Moreover, in a mobile society, people who move around and therefore often find themselves living in communities of strangers, tend to look for commonalities that make strangers into neighbors, and shared ethnicity may provide mobile people with at least an initial excuse to get together. Finally, as long as the European immigration into America continues, people will still be perceived, classified, and ranked at least in part by ethnic origin. Consequently, external forces exist to complement internal identity needs, and unless there is a drastic change in the allocation of costs and benefits with respect to ethnicity, it seems likely that the larger society will also encourage the persistence of symbolic ethnicity.

Needless to say, it is always possible that future economic and political conditions in American society will create a demand for new scapegoats, and if ethnics are forced into this role, so that ethnicity once more levies social costs, present tendencies will be interrupted. Under such conditions, some ethnics will try to assimilate faster and pass out of all ethnic roles, while others will revitalize the ethnic group socially and culturally if only for self-protection. Still, the chance that Catholic ethnics will be scapegoated more than today seems very slight. A serious economic crisis could, however, result in a resurgence of anti-semitism, in part because of the affluence of many American Jews, in part because of their visibly influential role in some occupations, notably mass communications.

If present societal trends continue, however, symbolic ethnicity should become the dominant way of being ethnic by the time the fourth generation of the new immigration matures into adulthood, and this in turn will have consequences for the structure of American ethnic groups. For one thing, as secondary and primary assimilation continue, and ethnic networks weaken and unravel, it may be more accurate to speak of ethnic aggregates rather than groups. More important, since symbolic ethnicity does not depend on ethnic cultures and organizations, their future decline and disappearance must be expected, particularly those cultural patterns which interfere with other aspects of life, and those organizations which require active membership.

Few such patterns and organizations are left in any case, and leaders of the remaining organizations have long been complaining bitterly over what they perceive as the cultural and organizational apathy of ethnics. They also criticize the resort to symbolic ethnicity, identifying it as an effortless way of being ethnic which further threatens their own persistence. Even so, attacking people as apathetic or lazy, or calling on them to revive the practices and loyalties of the past have never been effective for engendering support, and reflect instead the desperation of organizations which cannot offer new incentives that would enable them to recruit members.

Some cultural patterns and organizations will survive. Patterns which lend themselves to transformation into symbols and easy practice, such as annual holidays, should persist. So will organizations which create and distribute symbols, or 'ethnic goods' such as foodstuffs or written materials, but need few or no members and can function with small staffs and low overheads. In all likelihood, most ethnic organizations will eventually realize that in order to survive, they must deal mainly in symbols, using them to generate enough support to fund other activities as well.

The demand for current ethnic symbols may require the maintenance of at least some old cultural practices, possibly in museums, and through the work of ethnic scholars who keep old practices alive by studying them. It is even possible that the organizations which attempt to maintain the old cultures will support themselves in part by supplying ethnic nostalgia, and some ethnics may aid such organizations if only to assuage their guilt at having given up ancestral practices.

Still, the history of religion and nationalism, as well as events of recent years, should remind us that the social process sometimes moves in dialectical ways, and that acculturative and assimilative actions by a majority occasionally generate revivalistic reactions by a minority. As a result, even ethnic aggregates in which the vast majority maintains its identity in symbolic ways will probably always bring forth small pockets of neo-traditionalism—of rebel converts to sacred and secular ways of the past. They may not influence the behavior of the majority, but they are almost always highly visible, and will thus continue to play a role in the ethnicity of the future.

['Symbolic ethnicity: the future of ethnic groups and cultures in America', *Ethnic and Racial Studies*, 2: 1 (1979), 9–17.]

WINSTON JAMES

25 The Making of Black Identities

It was from such a cultural milieu—albeit one persistently punctuated by African resistance[1] to the European value system foisted upon them during the colonial era—that the post-war Caribbean migrants to Britain emerged.[2] In the 'mother country' no regard was paid to the complex hierarchy of shades; the pattern of racism which the Caribbean migrants experienced here did not correspond to the complexion hierarchy which they had left behind in the Caribbean. They were regarded monolithically as 'coloureds', 'West Indians', 'blacks', 'immigrants', and even 'wogs', with no reference to differential shades. As an Indo-Trinidadian writing about his experience in Britain as a student in the early 1960s accurately observed:

> Leaving the West Indies and coming to Britain is like entering a land where the natives suffer from a curious kind of colour blindness in the contemplation of human groups. This special form of blindness manifests itself in an insensitivity to racial discriminations and variant shades within the category 'black'. It registers two crude categories, black and white.
>
> The West Indian consciousness is outraged by the crudity of the categorisation. In the rarefied atmosphere of the mother country, the delicate instrument ceases to function. All West Indians are black.[3]

A compatriot of the author of the above, a man of Portuguese-Madeiran extraction, was outraged by the shade blindness of the British. 'I was accepted as a white person in Trinidad. For all practical purposes,' he complained, 'I am coloured in England.'[4] Over the years this dichotomy of black/white in

British 'race relations' has helped to undermine, if not totally destroy, this hierarchy of shades of black which the Caribbean working class had itself, by and large, adhered to. The erosion of this hierarchy of shades, not the means by which it has been undermined in Britain, is without doubt, a positive political development. In a moving and courageous autobiographical essay by a 'light skinned' (her expression) Trinidadian woman studying in Britain during the early 1960s, the following conclusion was reached:

> The whole experience of living in England, though at first almost traumatic, is of extreme value for the West Indian student, particularly the light coloured student. I have no knowledge of what the experience does for the African or Indian, but I cannot help feeling that the consequences for the light coloured West Indian student are more wide ranging. He [sic] has removed an incipient white-type colour prejudice; he has his position as a member of one of the coloured races clearly outlined for the first time; he has a whole series of class prejudices overturned; he has the colonial myth of his almost British personality completely destroyed. In the end realization of this makes it impossible for him to be bitter about his stay in England. The English have at last rendered him a service.[5]

The second way in which the experience of migrating to Britain has entailed political demystification for Caribbean migrants is to be found in the undermining of island chauvinism. Divided by the expanse of the sea—the distance between Port of Spain (Trinidad) and Kingston (Jamaica) is equivalent to that from London to Moscow—and mutual suspicion in the Caribbean, the passage to Britain has brought Jamaicans, Barbadians, Grenadians, Kittians, Guyanese, Trinidadians, etc., in close proximity to each other for the first time. Although island loyalties still remain, the people of the Caribbean have been brought together by London Transport, the National Health Service and most of all, by the centripetal forces of British racism, to recognise their common class position and common Caribbean identity. No doubt the remnants of island chauvinism still linger on in the metropolis,[6] but it is equally true that this phenomenon has waned over time.

The somewhat innocent journey to Britain has also served as an unparalleled eye-opening experience to the 'West Indian pioneers'. In the Caribbean few have ever seen the European in the class location of the working class,[7] they had never associated Europeans with subordination and poverty. As a Guyanese female migrant related:

> I learnt very early to associate being white with being wealthy. A man who left my village long before I was born returned when I was about ten. He brought back a red-skinned woman with him. Probably she was no more than a whore he picked up in Georgetown, but she was very fair with long hair down her back. She must have been a half-caste, or something. But this man, I think his name was Adam, could not afford to give her a car and servants. You know, every day I expected the police to come and arrest Adam for making this white or near white woman walk around the village barefoot, carrying tin cans of water on her head? Yet all the time we were walking

barefoot. That was the point, black was something you associated with poverty. Now and again I would be taken to Georgetown and I would see the girls in offices working away at typewriters. I wanted to be able to be a typist too, but never dared to tell anyone, for working in an office meant a pale skin. I had an aunt who used to work for some white people in New Amsterdam. I went there once and saw the little fair-haired children skipping about the place. My aunty warned me that if they spoke to me, I should be very polite and should never forget to call them 'master' and 'miss'. My aunty would never work for a black man even if he was made of gold. She would never call a little black boy master, or a little black girl miss. It was all so very confusing.[8]

An Indo-Trinidadian male confessed: 'I had not the slightest idea of the existence of a working class in Britain.'[9] The shock of discovering the existence of a working class in Britain is by no means confined to those who lack a formal education. As George Lamming informs us the *petit bourgeoisie* also experience a sense of bewilderment at discovering that Britain has *white* workers. To him the shock of this discovery has not so much to do with lack of knowledge about England, *per se*, but more with the strength and persistence of what he calls 'the *idea* of England'.[10] Like whites in the Caribbean, the white Britons *as a whole* are conceived to be above manual labour.

On arriving in Britain the scales fell abruptly from the Caribbean migrants' eyes.

As Mrs. Stewart put it 'In Jamaica we used to take white people as gods. We always look up to them; they put on such a way you can't understand. People I know work for whites and would make their bath and bring them coffee, like slaves. The whites put themselves on such a pedestal, you really thought they were something.' Thinking back to her previous attitude, she gave a bitter laugh. For in England whiteness is no longer synonymous with high status occupations, large incomes, and authority; many whites are members of the working class performing menial tasks and living in relative poverty. 'What makes things strange,' one man told me, 'is that when I came over here, I was surprised to see the state of a lot of the English. I expected something else, not a lot of drunks some even begging. That's what I don't rightly understand. A lot of white folks see us as worse than them. Some of the time it's not even true.'[11]

There are two particularly noteworthy consequences of such experiences. Firstly, they help to destroy the erroneous association of white people *qua* whites with superordination; the mystique of whiteness dissolves in the air of a class-stratified English society. And secondly, coupled with their experiences of racism in Britain, they generate a corresponding valorisation of blackness on the part of Caribbean people.[12] Indeed, the whole experience of living in a white racist society has helped to forge a black identity where in many cases such an identity did not previously exist, or not consciously thought about. 'The colour of your skin matters here. In Jamaica it is class not colour,' stated, albeit far too categorically, one of Foner's respondents. Another told her 'I think most of my friends *feel* Jamaican. The English helped us to do it.'[13] Needless to say the English also helped Afro-Caribbean people in Britain to *feel* 'West Indian' and *feel* 'black',[14] in fact so much so that in one study as many as 70 per cent of the interviewees felt that all Jamaicans were in the same social class.[15] Overwhelmed by the pervasiveness of the class-blind racism in Britain, the Afro-Caribbeans have themselves, understandably, become somewhat blinded by the class differentiation and class formation taking place amongst people of their own colour and cultural background. The *Labour Force Survey* has shown that although Caribbean people in Britain are overwhelmingly concentrated within the ranks of the working class, they are nevertheless by no means all located within this category.[16]

It would be a mistake to believe that the first generation of Afro-Caribbeans regard their experience of living in Britain as an unmitigated disaster. They experience racism and they occupy in their vast proportion the lowest rung of the social hierarchy of Britain. Nevertheless, in material terms, the overwhelming majority enjoy a standard of living in Britain which many could only have dreamt of back in the Caribbean.[17] It is therefore not unexpected that their conception of Britain is an ambivalent one. As one migrant explains:

> These have been the hardest years of my life. I think about them, and I ask myself, Sonny, tell the truth, coming here, was it a good decision or not? Think before you answer, like your dead mother used to say. So I think. And I answer, 'Yes,' it was good that we came, and that we stayed. I found work, my wife is happy, happy enough. My children are happy and healthy. I thank the good Lord for all of that. I thank Him everyday, just as my dead mother told me I should. I pray to Him and I ask Him. I wish too. I wish this could be like this and that could be like that. I wish I were with my family, my father, my brother, my cousins. I wish I lived in a newer home, and made more money. I wish I would have come here and be treated like I was equal by all these people. But I came as someone they thought was a dope smuggler, and that's about the way they treat me.[18]

Another expressed the same sentiments but more concisely: 'It's all right here basically but we are kind of treated inferior.'[19]

In recent years, with the rise in unemployment, many more than hitherto are returning home.[20] But even more feel 'trapped' within Britain because they are incapable of mobilising the financial wherewithal to resettle in the Caribbean. [...]

Most second-generation Caribbeans in Britain have either lived in this country since early childhood or were actually born and brought up in Britain. In other words, they have either spent the greater proportion of their lives in the 'Mother Country' or have resided here for all their lives. This important characteristic of 'the second generation' has profound implications for their view of themselves and the world in which they live.

Unlike their parents, they compare their position and life-chance within British society, not with the conditions of pre-independent Caribbean society, but with their white British counterparts. Consequently their experience of racism in Britain is more immediate and their perception of the phenomenon is more uncluttered. It is therefore no surprise that their opposition to British racism is more instantaneous and more forthright. Not for them the consolation 'It's all right here, basically, *but* we are kind of treated inferior': for them it is 'It is not all right here, *because* we are treated as if we are inferior.' Their consciousness of themselves as a black enclave within British society is therefore even greater than that of their parents. It is true, as one commentator has written,[21] that their commitment to a sense of blackness is by no means even but, nevertheless as an aggregate, it is no doubt true that the vast majority consider themselves to be black and belonging to an oppressed minority within British society.

The power of island chauvinism has waned among the first generation, but for the second and indeed third generations of Afro-Caribbeans in Britain we can declare with almost complete certitude that this politically debilitating disease has hardly infected them. Even in the cases where these prejudices have been transmitted by parents to the young child, racism in the school ensures that it never takes root. As one member of this generation eloquently declared: 'As you grow older you just see them [small islanders] as black. When you're in school you all get harassed together, and see yourself as one—*all a we is one.*'[22]

Separated from any immediate and far-reaching experience of the society of their parents, surrounded by a sea of white hostility, many have been attracted to ideas of the Rastafarian 'movement' in an attempt to make sense of and survive their travail in Babylon. In essence, a plebeian form of *négritude*, the signal contribution of the Rastafarian 'movement' is the affirmation of pride of race and the celebration of the African provenance. Despite its well-recognised, but poorly understood, weaknesses and silences, the 'ideology' of Rastafarianism has made a tremendous contribution to the black counter-culture against the spell of white supremacy.

Unlike their parents, who have less attachment to Britain, the second generation of 'Caribbeans' are, willy-nilly, black Britons. They might speak a form of the Jamaican language and sport Rastafarian locks, but in Kingston many would not be understood and many more would not be able fully to understand the language of their Jamaican counterparts. The second generation are therefore, by default, creating new cultural forms based largely, but by no means exclusively, upon the legacy of their parents and foreparents. They are also forging new forms of resistance, like their North American counterparts, aimed at the specific problems which they face within British society. [...]

In short there has been a high degree of convergence in the experiences and political perspectives of black parents and their offspring in Britain which many commentators, blinded by their stereotype of the 'generational conflict' among Afro-Caribbean people, have hardly recognised.

Like all nationalities or ethnic groups, Afro-Caribbean people in Britain have erected boundaries in relation to those with whom they identify. In this case boundaries have been established which exclude the people whom many would regard as 'natural allies' of Afro-Caribbean people in Britain. Although the situation is quite dynamic, it is fair to say that at present Afro-Caribbeans do not on the whole identify with people of Asian descent in Britain.[23] Nor, it should be said, do Asian people identify with Afro-Caribbean people in Britain. [. . .]

Anyone who moves among Afro-Caribbean and Asian people in Britain with eyes to see and ears to hear would readily recognise that there does exist some antagonism, or, more typically perhaps, a tacit agreement of a peaceful, but cold co-existence, between the two groups. [. . .]

On balance it is fair to say that a relative state of indifference, if not antagonism, prevails over the more positive developments, mentioned above, between Afro-Caribbeans and Asians.

So, what are the bases of this problem?

Firstly, as the comments cited above indicate, there do exist major cultural differences between people of Asian descent and those of Afro-Caribbean origin. The mutual ignorance of, if not downright disrespect for, each other's culture and the internalisation by each of the British stereotype of the other help to explain this state of affairs.[24]

Secondly, aspects of Afro-Caribbean antipathy towards Asians are rooted in the Caribbean background. To augment labour supply and to increase their control over the labour forces, the plantocracy, throughout the Caribbean, as well as others elsewhere, turned to the Indian subcontinent after the enslavement of Africans had come to an end.[25] This system, known as 'Indian indentureship', lasted from the 1830s to 1917, at which time, thanks largely to Indian nationalist opposition in the subcontinent, this barbaric practice, very much akin to slavery, came to an abrupt end. The motives, organisation, practices and consequences of induced Indian immigration to the Americas are well documented.[26] The important point here is this: the process was specifically and expressly geared at breaking the increased power of the formerly enslaved Africans within the newly-created labour market. Elaborate strategies were conscientiously devised by the plantocratic bourgeoisie and its state to create the maximum division between Africans and the newly arrived and cruelly deceived Asians in the Caribbean. These, unfortunately, were extremely effective; the African and Indian exploited and oppressed were thoroughly divided;[27] mutual strike-breaking, for instance, was virtually a commonplace in late-nineteenth century Guyana. The animosities between the groups, though less intense than hitherto, exist to the present day.

Thirdly, the differences in the distribution, spatial as well as industrial, and location of Asians and Afro-Caribbeans in Britain—differences which do exist and which are often overlooked—also militate against the cohesion of these two groups in their fight against racism.[28]

Fourthly, racism in its concrete operation does not affect both groups in an identical manner. The specificities of the rhythm of Asian migration to Britain, for instance, have meant that people from the Indian sub-continent, not those from the Caribbean, have felt the brunt of racist immigration controls in Britain. Afro-Caribbeans for their part, undergo an exceptionally high degree of state harassment on a day-to-day level. The perceived differences in the problems which each group come up against, *vis-à-vis* the state, have hampered united action based upon common priorities.[29]

Finally, clearly identifiable differences in the *distribution* of Asians and Afro-Caribbeans within the class structure of Britain, and the lack of coincidence and unevenness of the respective dynamic of their class formation work against the development of unity of perspective on British racism and, even more, against combined political action.

There are thus a whole series of factors which inhibit the boundaries of the Afro-Caribbean fraternity *vis-à-vis* people of Asian descent in Britain, and vice versa. These need to be urgently and seriously addressed if the struggle against racism, being carried out—almost by default—on a daily basis by each group, is to be more effectively waged.

['The making of Black identities', in R. Samuel (ed.), *Patriotism: The Making and Unmaking of British National Identity* (London and New York: Routledge, 1989), ii. 234–41, 243–4.]

STUART HALL

26 The New Ethnicities

Another element inscribed in the new politics of representation has to do with the question of ethnicity. I am familiar with all the dangers of 'ethnicity' as a concept and have written myself about the fact that ethnicity, in the form of a culturally constructed sense of Englishness and a particularly closed, exclusive and regressive form of English national identity, is one of the core characteristics of British racism today.[1] I am also well aware that the politics of antiracism has often constructed itself in terms of a contestation of 'multi-ethnicity' or 'multi-culturalism'. On the other hand, as the politics of representation around the black subject shifts, I think we will begin to see a renewed contestation over the meaning of the term 'ethnicity' itself.

If the black subject and black experience are not stabilized by Nature or by some other essential guarantee, then it must be the case that they are constructed historically, culturally, politically—and the concept which refers to this is 'ethnicity'. The term ethnicity acknowledges the place of history, language and culture in the construction of subjectivity and identity, as well as the fact that all discourse is placed, positioned, situated, and all knowledge is contextual. Representation is possible only because enunciation is always produced within codes which have a history, a position within the discursive formations of a particular space and time. The displacement of the 'centred' discourses of the West entails putting in question its universalist character and its transcendental claims to speak for everyone, while being itself everywhere and nowhere. The fact that this grounding of ethnicity in difference was deployed, in the discourse of racism, as a means of disavowing the realities of racism and repression does not mean that we can permit the term to be permanently colonized. That appropriation will have to be contested, the term disarticulated from its position in the discourse of 'multiculturalism' and transcoded, just as we previously had to recuperate the term 'black', from its place in a system of negative equivalence. The new politics of representation therefore also sets in motion an ideological contestation around the term, 'ethnicity'. But in order to pursue that movement further, we will have to retheorize the concept of *difference*.

It seems to me that, in the various practices and discourses of black cultural production, we are beginning to see constructions of just such a new conception of ethnicity: a new cultural politics which engages rather than suppresses *difference* and which depends, in part, on the cultural construction of new ethnic identities. Difference, like representation, is also a slippery, and therefore, contested concept. There is the 'difference' which makes a radical and unbridgeable separation: and there is a 'difference' which is positional, conditional and conjunctural, closer to Derrida's notion of *différance*, though if we are concerned to maintain a politics it cannot be defined exclusively in terms of an infinite sliding of the signifier. We still have a great deal of work to do to *decouple* ethnicity, as it functions in the dominant discourse, from its equivalence with nationalism, imperialism, racism and the state, which are the points of attachment around which a distinctive British or, more accurately, English ethnicity have been constructed. Nevertheless, I think such a project is not only possible but necessary. Indeed, this decoupling of ethnicity from the violence of the state is implicit in some of the new forms of cultural practice that are going on in films like *Passion* and *Handsworth Songs*. We are beginning to think about how to represent a non-coercive and a more diverse conception of ethnicity, to set against the embattled, hegemonic conception of 'Englishness' which, under Thatcherism, stabilizes so much of the dominant political and cultural discourses, and which, because it is hegemonic, does not represent itself as an ethnicity at all.

This marks a real shift in the point of contestation, since it is no longer only between antiracism and multiculturalism but inside the notion of ethnicity itself. What is involved is the splitting of the notion of ethnicity between, on the one hand the dominant notion which connects it to nation and 'race' and on the other hand what I think is the beginning of a positive conception of the ethnicity of the margins, of the periphery. That is to say, a recognition that we all speak from a particular place, out of a particular history, out of a particular experience, a particular culture, without being contained by that position as 'ethnic artists' or film-makers. We are all, in that sense, *ethnically* located and our ethnic identities are crucial to our subjective sense of who we are. But this is also a recognition that this is not an ethnicity which is doomed to survive, as Englishness was, only by marginalizing, dispossessing, displacing and forgetting other ethnicities. This precisely is the politics of ethnicity predicated on difference and diversity.

The final point which I think is entailed in this new politics of representation has to do with an awareness of the black experience as a *diaspora* experience, and the consequences which this carries for the process of unsettling, recombination, hybridization and 'cut-and-mix'—in short, the process of cultural *diaspora-ization* (to coin an ugly term) which it implies. In the case of the young black British films and film-makers under discussion, the diaspora experience is certainly profoundly fed and nourished by, for example, the emergence of Third World cinema; by the African experience; the connection with Afro-Caribbean experience; and the deep inheritance of complex systems of representation and aesthetic traditions from Asian and African culture. But, in spite of these rich cultural 'roots', the new cultural politics is operating on new and quite distinct ground—specifically, contestation over what it means to be 'British'. The relation of this cultural politics to the past; to its different 'roots' is profound, but complex. It cannot be simple or unmediated. It is (as a film like *Dreaming Rivers* reminds us) complexly mediated and transformed by memory, fantasy and desire. Or, as even an explicitly political film like *Handsworth Songs* clearly suggests, the relation is intertextual—mediated, through a variety of other 'texts'. There can, therefore, be no simple 'return' or 'recovery' of the ancestral past which is not re-experienced through the categories of the present: no base for creative enunciation in a simple reproduction of traditional forms which are not transformed by the technologies and the identities of the present. This is something that was signalled as early as a film like *Blacks Britannica* and as recently as Paul Gilroy's important book, *There Ain't No Black in the Union Jack*.[2] Fifteen years ago we didn't care, or at least I didn't care, whether there was any black in the Union Jack. Now not only do we care, we must. [. . .]

['The new ethnicities', in J. Donald and A. Rattansi (eds.), *Race, Culture and Difference* (London: Sage, 1992), 256–8.]

ÉTIENNE BALIBAR

27 Fictive Ethnicity and Ideal Nation

I apply the term 'fictive ethnicity' to the community instituted by the nation-state. This is an intentionally complex expression in which the term fiction, in keeping with my remarks above, should not be taken in the sense of a pure and simple illusion without historical effects, but must, on the contrary, be understood by analogy with the *persona ficta* of the juridical tradition in the sense of an institutional effect, a 'fabrication'. No nation possesses an ethnic base naturally, but as social formations are nationalized, the populations included within them, divided up among them or dominated by them are ethnicized—that is, represented in the past or in the future *as if* they formed a natural community, possessing of itself an identity of origins, culture and interests which transcends individuals and social conditions.[1]

Fictive ethnicity is not purely and simply identical with the *ideal nation* which is the object of patriotism, but it is indispensable to it, for, without it, the nation would appear precisely only as an idea or an arbitrary abstraction; patriotism's appeal would be addressed to no one. It is fictive ethnicity which makes it possible for the expression of a pre-existing unity to be seen in the state, and continually to measure the state against its 'historic mission' in the service of the nation and, as a consequence, to idealize politics. By constituting the people as a fictively ethnic unity against the background of a universalistic representation which attributes to each individual one—and only one—ethnic identity and which thus divides up the whole of humanity between different ethnic groups corresponding potentially to so many nations, national ideology does much more than justify the strategies employed by the state to control populations. It inscribes their demands in advance in a sense of belonging in the double sense of the term—both what it is that makes one belong to oneself and also what makes one belong to other fellow human beings. Which means that one can be interpellated, as an individual, *in the name of* the collectivity whose name one bears. The naturalization of belonging and the sublimation of the ideal nation are two aspects of the same process.

How can ethnicity be produced? And how can it be produced in such a way that it does not appear as fiction, but as the most natural of origins? History shows us that there are two great competing routes to this: language and race. Most often the two operate together, for only their complementarity makes it possible for the 'people' to be represented as an absolutely autonomous unit. Both express the idea that the national character (which might also be called its soul or its spirit) is immanent in the people. But both offer a means of transcending actual individuals and political relations. They constitute two ways of rooting historical populations in a fact of 'nature' (the diversity of languages and the diversity of races appearing predestined), but also two ways of giving a meaning to their continued existence, of transcending its contingency. By force of circumstance, however, at times one or the other is dominant, for they are not based on the development of the same institutions and do not appeal to the same symbols or the same idealizations of the national identity. The fact of these different articulations of, on the one hand, a predominantly linguistic ethnicity and, on the other, an ethnicity that is predominantly racial has obvious political consequences. For this reason, and for the sake of clarity of analysis, we must begin by examining the two separately.

The language community seems the more abstract notion, but in reality it is the more concrete since it connects individuals up with an origin which may at any moment be actualized and which has as its content the *common act* of their own exchanges, of their discursive communication, using the instruments of spoken language and the whole, constantly self-renewing mass of written and recorded texts. This is not to say that that community is an immediate one, without internal limits, any more than communication is in reality 'transparent' between all individuals. But these limits are always relative: even if it were the case that individuals whose social conditions were very distant from one another were never in direct communication, they would be bound together by an uninterrupted chain of intermediate discourses. They are not isolated—either *de jure* or *de facto*.

We should, however, certainly not allow ourselves to believe that this situation is as old as the world itself. It is, on the contrary, remarkably recent. The old empires and the *Ancien Régime* societies were still based on the juxtaposition of linguistically separate populations, on the superimposition of mutually incompatible 'languages' for the dominant and the dominated and for the sacred and profane spheres. Between these there had to be a whole system of translations.[2] In modern national formations, the translators are writers, journalists and politicians, social actors who speak the language of the 'people' in a way that seems all the more natural for the very degree of distinction they thereby bring to it. The translation process has become primarily one of internal translation between different 'levels of language'. Social differences are expressed and relativized as different ways of speaking the national language, which supposes a common code and even a common norm.[3] This latter is, as we know, inculcated by universal schooling, whose primary function it is to perform precisely this task.

That is why there is a close historical correlation between the national formation and the development of schools as 'popular' institutions, not limited to specialized training or to elite culture, but serving to underpin the whole process of the socialization of individuals. That the school should also be the site of the inculcation of a nationalist ideology—and sometimes also the place where it is contested—is a secondary phenomenon, and is, strictly speaking, a less indispensable aspect. Let us simply say that schooling is the principal institution which produces ethnicity as linguistic community. It is not, however, the only one: the state, economic exchange and family life are also schools in a sense, organs of the ideal nation recognizable by a common language which belongs to them 'as their own'. For what is decisive here is not only that the national language should be recognized as the official language, but, much more fundamentally, that it should be able to appear as the very element of the life of a people, the *reality* which each person may appropriate in his or her own way, without thereby destroying its identity. There is no contradiction between the instituting of *one* national language and the daily discrepancy between—and clash of—'class languages' which precisely are not different languages. In fact, the two things are complementary. All linguistic practices feed into a single 'love of the language' which is addressed not to the textbook norm nor to particular usage, but to the 'mother tongue'—that is, to the ideal of a common origin projected back beyond learning processes and specialist forms of usage and which, by that very fact, becomes the metaphor for the love fellow nationals feel for one another.[4]

One might then ask oneself, quite apart from the precise historical questions which the history of national languages poses—from the difficulties of their unification or imposition, and from their elaboration into an idiom that is both 'popular' and 'cultivated' (a process which we know to be far from complete today in all nation-states, in spite of the labours of their intellectuals with the aid of various international bodies)—*why the language community is not sufficient* to produce ethnicity.

Perhaps this has to do with the paradoxical properties which, by virtue of its very structure, the linguistic signifier confers on individual identity. In a sense, it is always in the element of language that individuals are interpellated as subjects, for every interpellation is of the order of discourse. Every 'personality' is constructed with words, in which law, genealogy, history, political choices, professional qualifications and psychology are set forth. But the linguistic construction of identity is by definition *open*. No individual 'chooses' his or her mother tongue or can 'change' it at will. Nevertheless, it is always possible to appropriate several languages and to turn oneself into a different kind of bearer of discourse and of the transformations of language. The linguistic community induces a terribly constraining ethnic memory (Roland Barthes once went so far as to call it 'fascist'), but it is one which none the less possesses a strange plasticity: it immediately naturalizes new acquisitions. It does so *too quickly* in a sense. It is a collective memory which perpetuates itself at the cost of an individual forgetting of 'origins'. The 'second generation' immigrant—a notion which in this context acquires a structural significance—inhabits the national language (and through it the nation itself) in a manner as spontaneous, as 'hereditary' and as imperious, so far as affectivity and the imaginary are concerned, as the son of one of those native heaths which we think of as so very French (and most of which not so long ago did not even have the national language as their daily parlance). One's 'mother' tongue is not necessarily the language of one's 'real' mother. The language community is a community *in the present*, which produces the feeling that it has always existed, but which lays down no destiny for the successive generations. Ideally, it 'assimilates' anyone, but holds no one. Finally, it affects all individuals in their innermost being (in the way in which they constitute themselves as subjects), but its historical particularity is bound only to interchangeable institutions. When circumstances permit, it may serve different nations (as English, Spanish and even French do) or survive the 'physical' disappearance of the people who used it (like 'ancient' Greek and Latin or 'literary' Arabic). For it to be tied down to the frontiers of a particular people, it therefore needs an extra degree [*un supplément*] of particularity, or a principle of closure, of exclusion.

This principle is that of being part of a common race. But here we must be very careful not to give rise to misunderstandings. All kinds of somatic or psychological features, both visible and invisible, may lend themselves to creating the fiction of a racial identity and therefore to representing natural and hereditary differences between social groups either within the same nation or outside its frontiers. I have discussed elsewhere, as have others before me, the development of the marks of race and the relation they bear to different historical figures of social conflict. What we are solely concerned with here is the symbolic kernel which makes it possible to equate race and ethnicity ideally, and to represent unity of race to oneself as the origin or cause of the historical unity of a people. Now, unlike what applied in the case of the linguistic community, it cannot be a question here of a practice which is really common to *all* the individuals who form a political unit. We are not dealing with anything equivalent to communication. What we are speaking of is therefore a second-degree fiction. This fiction, however, also derives its effectiveness from everyday practices, relations which immediately structure the 'life' of individuals. And, most importantly, whereas the language community can only create equality between individuals by simultaneously 'naturalizing' the social inequality of linguistic practices, the race community dissolves social inequalities in an even more ambivalent 'similarity'; it ethnicizes the social difference which is an expression of irreconcilable antagonisms by lending it the form of a division between the 'genuinely' and the 'falsely' national.

I think we may cast some light on this paradox in the following way. The symbolic kernel of the idea of race (and of its demographic and cultural equivalents) is the schema of genealogy, that is, quite simply the idea that the filiation of individuals transmits from generation to generation a substance both biological and spiritual and thereby inscribes them in a temporal community known as 'kinship'. That is why, *as soon as* national ideology enunciates the proposition that the individuals belonging to the same people are interrelated (or, in the prescriptive mode, that they should constitute a circle of extended kinship), we are in the presence of this second mode of ethnicization.

The objection will no doubt be raised here that such a representation characterizes societies and communities which have nothing national about them. But, it is precisely on this point that the particular innovation hinges by which the nation form is articulated to the modern idea of race. This idea is correlative with the tendency for 'private' genealogies, as (still) codified by traditional systems of preferential marriage and lineage, to disappear. The idea of a racial community makes its appearance when the frontiers of kinship dissolve at the level of the clan, the neighbourhood community and, theoretically at least, the social class, to be imaginarily transferred to the threshold of nationality: that is to say, when nothing prevents marriage with any of one's 'fellow citizens' whatever, and when, on the contrary, such a marriage seems the only one that is 'normal' or 'natural'. The racial community has a tendency to represent itself as one big family or as the common envelope of family relations (the community of 'French', 'American' or 'Algerian' families).[5] From that point onward, each individual has his/her family, whatever his/her social condition, but the family—like property—becomes a contingent relation between individuals. In order to consider this question further, we ought therefore to turn to a discussion of the history of the family, an institution which here plays a role every bit as central as that played by the school in the discussion above, and one that is ubiquitous in the discourse of race.

['The nation form', in É. Balibar and I. Wallerstein, *Race, Nation, Class* (London: Verso, 1991), 96–100.]

ROGERS BRUBAKER

28 Civic and Ethnic Nations in France and Germany

For two centuries, locked together in a fateful position at the center of state- and nation-building in Europe, France and Germany have been constructing, elaborating, and furnishing to other states distinctive, even antagonistic models of nationhood and national self-understanding. In the French tradition, the nation has been conceived in relation to the institutional and territorial frame of the state. Revolutionary and Republican definitions of nationhood and citizenship—unitarist, universalist, and secular—reinforced what was already in the ancien régime an essentially political understanding of nationhood. Yet while French nationhood is constituted by political unity, it is centrally expressed in the striving for cultural unity. Political inclusion has entailed cultural assimilation, for regional cultural minorities and immigrants alike.

If the French understanding of nationhood has been state-centered and assimilationist, the German understanding has been *Volk*-centered and differentialist. Since national feeling developed before the nation-state, the German idea of the nation was not originally political, nor was it linked to the abstract idea of citizenship. This prepolitical German nation, this nation in search of a state, was conceived not as the bearer of universal political values, but as an organic cultural, linguistic, or racial community—as an irreducibly particular *Volksgemeinschaft*. On this understanding, nationhood is an ethnocultural, not a political fact. [...]

The politics of citizenship *vis-à-vis* immigrants is similar in form in France and Germany but sharply different in content. In both cases it pivots on national self-understanding, not on state or group interests. But the prevailing elite self-understandings are very different.[1] The French understand their nation as the creation of their state, the Germans their nation as the basis of their state. There is a strong assimilationist strand in the prevailing French self-understanding that is lacking in the prevailing German self-understanding. France is not a classical country of immigration, but it is a classical country, perhaps *the* classical country, of assimilation.[2] And schemes of self-understanding referring originally to the assimilation of the French periphery by the Parisian center have been easily and in a sense automatically and unconsciously transferred to the assimilation of immigrants.[3] In the last two decades both the desirability and the possibility of assimilating immigrants have been contested, as has the legitimacy of the Jacobin-Republican model of internal assimilation. Yet the prevailing elite understanding of nationhood, while contested, remains more assimilationist in France than in Germany. As a result, the idea of North African immigrants being or becoming French remains much more plausible and natural than the idea of Turkish immigrants being or becoming German.

Despite similar immigrant populations and immigration policies, French and German citizenship policies *vis-à-vis* immigrants remain sharply opposed. In part, this reflects the absence of compelling state or group interests in altering definitions of the citizenry. But it also reflects the fact that existing definitions of the citizenry—expansively combining *jus soli* and *jus sanguinis* in France, restrictively reflecting pure *jus sanguinis* in Germany—embody and express deeply rooted national self-understandings, more state-centered and assimilationist in France, more ethnocultural in Germany. This affinity between definitions of citizenship and conceptions of nationhood makes it difficult to change the former in fundamental ways. In France, the center-right government headed by Jacques Chirac was unable, in 1986–87, to adopt even a mildly restrictive reform of citizenship law, in part because its opponents were able to mobilize effectively by appealing to the prevailing elite national self-understanding. In Germany, naturalization policies were liberalized in 1990. But there is no chance that the French system of *jus soli* will be adopted; the automatic transformation of immigrants into citizens remains unthinkable in Germany. And liberalized naturalization rules alone will do little to further the civic incorporation of immigrants. Immigrants as well as Germans continue to associate the legal fact of naturalization with the social and cultural fact of assimilation, yet neither German political culture in general nor the specific social, political, and cultural context of the postwar immigration is favorable to assimilation. Add to this the fact that dual citizenship is permitted only in exceptional cases, and it seems likely that naturalization rates will remain quite low, and that the citizenship status and chances of immigrants in France and Germany will continue to diverge.

I should emphasize that I am not trying to account for the fine details of particular policy outcomes. Clearly these depend on a host of factors unrelated to patterns of national self-understanding. The policymaking process is highly contingent. Yet if elite understandings of nationhood have little bearing on the timing or detailed content of legislative change, they do help explain the otherwise puzzling persistence of broadly different ways of defining the citizenry. They limit the universe of debate and make a fundamental restructuring of citizenship improbable.

It might be objected that the appeal to elite understandings of nationhood is unnecessary. In the absence of pressing interests in citizenship law reform, on this argument, differences would persist out of mere inertia. This ignores the fact that there are pressures for convergence, although these do not arise in the first instance from state or group interests. In Germany, the anomaly of settlement without citizenship has generated widespread demands, endorsed even by the present center-right government, for easier access to citizenship. In France, the automatic attribution of citizenship to immigrants who, nativists argued, were neither assimilated nor assimilable, generated a strong campaign on the right for a more restrictive citizenship law. Mere inertia explains nothing.

But suppose the argument from inertia were reformulated. French and German definitions of the citizenry, it might be argued, are resistant to fundamental modification not because they are consonant with political and cultural traditions, but simply because they are *legal* traditions. The expansive French combination of *jus sanguinis* and *jus soli* was established a century ago; its roots extend back to the Revolution and even to the ancien régime. And German states—Prussia and other states before unification, Imperial Germany, the Weimar Republic, the Third Reich, and both German states after 1949—have relied exclusively on *jus sanguinis* ever since citizenship law was first codified in the early nineteenth century. The citizenship law of both countries has been modified in detail on numerous occasions over the years.

But the broad patterns—the mix of *jus soli* and *jus sanguinis* in France, the system of pure *jus sanguinis* in Germany—have long been fixed. They have taken on the inertial weight and normative dignity of tradition. This inertial force is only increased by the gravity and symbolic centrality of citizenship. States do not tinker with the basic principles of citizenship law as they might with the fine print of the tax code. The appeal to self-understanding, on this argument, is unnecessary. France and Germany continue to define their citizenries in fundamentally different ways because they have been doing so for more than a century.

This is more satisfactory than the crude argument from inertia. But tradition can not be equated with duration. The longevity of a practice alone does not establish its 'traditional' quality. Tradition is a constructed, not a purely objective property.[4] The appeal to tradition is an elementary form of political rhetoric. To present a policy or practice as traditional can contribute to its preservation by investing it with normative dignity and thereby raising the political cost of challenging it. Tradition is therefore a contested category. Policies and practices are the objects of representational struggles that seek to deem them 'traditional' or to deny them this dignity—instances of the general and perpetual struggle over the representation and characterization of the social world.[5] The appeal to tradition that was central to the French mobilization against the attempt to curb *jus soli* was not an appeal to endurance as such. It was an appeal to legitimate endurance, to the endurance of something deserving to endure, to an enduring consonance between a legal formula and a political-cultural self-understanding. Thus opponents of citizenship law reform characterized *jus soli* as a specifically *Republican* tradition, while proponents of the reform contested this characterization, arguing that *jus soli* reflected not Republican principles but the military and demographic needs of the state. In Germany too appeals to tradition invoked not simply the endurance of a legal form but rather the enduring congruence between a legal form (*jus sanguinis*) and a principle of political-cultural self-understanding (that Germany is not a country of immigration).

Endurance matters, but it is not alone decisive. Long-standing practices do have normative force, but only when the practices have some material or symbolic value or meaning that cannot be reduced to, although it may be strengthened by, their perdurance. The long-standing French and German definitions of the citizenry have indeed assumed the inertial weight and normative dignity of tradition. But this does not mean that self-understandings are irrelevant. If *jus soli* in France and *jus sanguinis* in Germany are construed and defended as traditions, this is not simply because of their endurance, but also because they embody and express deeply rooted habits of national self-understanding. They are understood and defended as legal traditions because of their consonance with political and cultural traditions. It is this consonance that gives their long endurance its normative force.

The crystallization of *jus soli* in France and of pure *jus sanguinis* in Germany occurred at the high noon of the European nation-state, in the decades before the First World War. Today, many observers have argued, Western Europe is moving decisively beyond the nation-state. Thus even if French and German definitions of citizenship remain sharply opposed, national citizenship may wane in significance, along with the nation-state itself. Just as the nation-state is being eroded from above and from below,[6] ceding some functions and capacities to supranational and others to subnational institutions, so too national citizenship may be eroded by the development of forms of supranational and subnational citizenship. In the postnational Europe of the future, the decisive instances of belonging, the decisive sites of citizenship, might be Europe as a whole on the one hand and individual regions and municipalities on the other.[7]

In the long run this postnational vision may come to fruition.[8] For the foreseeable future, however, the nation-state and national citizenship will remain very much—perhaps too much—with us. It is not only that, as Western Europe moves fitfully *beyond* the nation-state, multinational Yugoslavia and the Soviet Union have disintegrated *into* nation-states. It is not only that a powerful German nation-state has been recreated in the heart of Europe. It is also that throughout Western Europe nationhood has been revived as a political theme, and nativism as a political program, in response to the unprecedented immigration of the last thirty years.

Despite restrictive immigration policies in place in most Western European states for nearly two decades, the populations of immigrant origin have become larger and more diverse. This trend shows no sign of abating. For demographic reasons alone—to say nothing of economic, political, or ecological reasons—south–north migratory pressure is bound to increase. And at this writing, the countries of Western and Central Europe are bracing for a large influx of migrants from economically distressed and politically unstable regions of Eastern Europe and the former Soviet Union.

To some observers the ethnic heterogeneity that has been introduced, or reinforced, by immigration, together with the encroachments on sovereignty that are entailed by membership of the European Community, show that Western European countries can no longer be considered nation-states. But this is to mistake the nature of the nation-state. The nation-state is not only, or primarily, an ethnodemographic phenomenon, or a set of institutional arrangements. It is also, crucially, a way of thinking about and appraising political and social membership.[9] Because this way of thinking remains widely influential, debates about the citizenship status of immigrants remain in large part debates about nationhood—about what it means, and what it ought to mean, to belong to a nation-state.

We have followed these debates as they have unfolded in France and Germany, where distinctive and deeply rooted understandings of nationhood have found enduring expression in sharply opposed definitions of citizenship. But one could well follow them elsewhere. At this writing, for example, the incipient successor states to the Soviet Union are establishing their own citizenships. These are intended to serve as instruments of closure against unwanted immigrants, as means of strengthening the 'stateness' of these new nation-states, and as symbolic expressions of sovereignty. The politics of citizenship, in this setting, is a politics of identity, as in France and Germany; but it is also, to a greater extent than in Western Europe, a politics of interest. In the context of proportionally much larger minority populations, high ethnic tension, and potential violence, much more is at stake. For Latvians and Estonians, for example, who comprise only a small majority of the population of their respective states, it matters a great deal how citizenship is defined; as it does, reciprocally, for the large Russian immigrant minority in these states. Some radical nationalists have urged that citizenship be restricted to descendants of citizens of interwar Latvia and Estonia; others have argued that citizenship must be open to all residents.[10] Similar debates have been occurring in other breakaway polities.

Emigration from the Soviet Union and its successor states has engendered another set of problems concerning definitions of citizenship and understandings of nationhood. The emigration, at this writing, is primarily one of ethnic affinity, comprised of persons leaving the former Soviet Union for an external homeland to which they belong in ethno-cultural terms. This is the case, above all, of Jews and ethnic Germans, who have automatic citizenship rights in Israel and Germany, based on ethnoreligious and ethnocultural understandings of nationhood. But there are many other ex-Soviet nationalities with external ethnic 'homelands.' These include over a million Poles, 437,000 Koreans, 379,000 Bulgarians, 358,000 Greeks, and 172,000 Hungarians. How will the receiving states respond to these potential immigrants? Will they institute ethnocultural 'laws of return' like those of Israel and Germany, granting automatic citizenship to immigrants? Or will they decline to acknowledge these potential immigrants as members of their nation, or—even if they are acknowledged as members of the nation—decline to grant them privileged access to membership of their state?[11]

Citizenship and nationhood are intensely contested issues in European politics, east and west. They are likely to remain so for the foreseeable future. Those who herald the emerging postnational age are too hasty in condemning the nation-state to the dustbin of history. They underestimate the resilience, as well as the richness and complexity, of an institutional and normative tradition that, for better or worse, appears to have life in it yet.

[*Citizenship and Nationhood* (Cambridge, Mass.: Harvard University Press, 1992), 1, 184–9, 243–4.]

BASSAM TIBI

29 Old Tribes and Imposed Nation-States in the Middle East

One major contention of this essay is that most societies in the Middle East lack a homogeneous national population, the basic requirement of the externally imposed nation-state.[1] Despite the structural dissolution of the tribe as a premodern social organization, tribal identity and solidarity are still salient features of Middle Eastern societies. This section focuses on the tribal element and its relationship to current social-science debates on ethnicity.[2] The tribal fragmentation of many Middle Eastern societies has obstructed the establishment of a homogeneous population that undergirds the national community with national symbols and loyalties. Indeed, most of the Middle Eastern states, in varying degrees, accommodate diverse communities characterized by their own local symbols and loyalties. Pan-national ideologies (e.g., Arab nationalism) or local-national ideologies (e.g., Algerian or Syrian nationalism) have been mostly the concern of intellectuals and have failed to strike deep roots in the fragmented communities of many Arab states.[3] The question remains: how do we explain this fragmentation in individual states? Is it tribal, ethnic, or just sectarian?

Social scientists concerned with the Middle East have adopted the concept of ethnicity as an analytical tool for depicting the subsocietal divisions in nation-states without a national (i.e., homogeneous) community. Is the term *ethnie* simply another word for tribe, thus indicating a change in the nomenclature, or does ethnicity introduce a new analytical concept for dealing with our topic? Louis Snyder suggests 'the term [ethnicity] has assumed so many diverse meanings that it would be best to reject it.'[4] Before reaching such a definitive judgment we would do well to ask why scholars talk of ethnies instead of tribes. European historians usually refer to social groupings in premodern periods of their own history as ethnies but refer to similar entities in non-European history disparagingly as tribes. Thus, tribalism is seen as an Arab or African social phenomenon but not as something European. Social scientists in general, and students of the Middle East in particular, now avoid the term *tribe*, referring instead to prenational social groupings as ethnies, since they want to be free of the Eurocentric connotations of tribe.

Whereas contemporary Arab intellectuals make disparaging reference to *qabaliyya* (tribalism), in contrast to their praise of *qawmiyya* (nationalism), we cannot overlook the fact that those who claim descent from the prophet Muhammad (*ashraf*) are proud of their tribal (Qurayshite) origin. Meanwhile, anthropologists who work on the Middle East are familiar with avowed tribal descent of common local people who cannot claim *ashraf* descent. Furthermore, in the Arab context the adjective *tribal* does not bear the negative connotation that it does in the African context. More important, unlike in Africa, the terms *tribe* and *ethnie*, as employed by Smith, cannot be used synonymously when dealing with the Middle East. Thus, it makes sense to continue to use the term *tribe* as a subdivision of the ethnie, or ethnic community, in the Middle Eastern context. Let us turn to the example of the Alawites of Syria, who are ethnically Arabs and are organized into four different tribes. In terms of their interrelation with the rest of the Syrian community, the Alawites can be viewed as an ethnie. Even though they are Arabs, they distinguish themselves from other Arabs by embracing a myth of common descent and a common belief. A closer look at relationships within the Alawite community compels us, however, to employ the concept of the tribe. On this level we cannot equate tribe with ethnie since the Alawites are subdivided into four tribes: Matawira, Haddadin, Khayyatin, and Kalbiyya. The current ruling elite in Syria is recruited from the Matawira tribe and more specifically from the Numailatiyya clan.[5] It is obvious that we cannot refer to these tribes as separate ethnic communities, nor can we simply view them as an Alawite sect since they are not only split into four tribes but also religiously subdivided into Shamsis, Qamaris, and Murshidin.

At this juncture it is difficult to concur with Milton Esman and Itamar Rabinovich, who employ the concept of ethnicity as a general framework and impose it on the Syrian context without a single reference to tribes. Esman and Rabinovich subscribe to the concept of ethnicity in explaining the existing subdivisions within contemporary Middle Eastern nation-states. They define ethnicity as 'collective identity and solidarity based on such ascriptive factors as imputed common descent, language, customs, belief systems and practices (religion), and in some cases race or color.'[6] Basically, Esman and Rabinovich, and the contributors to their volume, are interested in what repercussions have followed from the adoption or imposition of the European model of the sovereign nation-state on the Middle East. They correctly hold to the view that the rise of 'ethnic' (or tribal) politics in the Middle East is related to '(1) control by the modern state of political and economic resources that are vital to the security and well-being of its inhabitants, and (2) tensions between the pluralism of society and claims of the state to regulate the lives of all who live in its territorial boundaries. . . . The [adopted] European model of sovereign state . . . was the threat to minorities, and in some cases to majorities, that exacerbated tensions among the various ethnic group communities in the Middle East and between those communities and the new states.'[7] Hence, these new states are only nominally nation-states based on the concept of nationalism, which suggests the preexistence of a national community that in fact never existed. Reaching beyond Esman and Rabinovich, it might be fruitful to differentiate between ethnies (as subnational divisions in the communities of the modern nation-states of the Middle East) and tribes. Thus, we can refer to the Berbers of Morocco, the Alawites of Syria, the Dinka of Sudan, and the Kurds of Iran, Iraq, Turkey, and Syria as ethnies without overlooking that they are subdivided and organized along tribal lines. This reasoning leads us to infer that the concept of ethnicity cannot be substituted for that of tribe. Ethnicity can be referred to as a supercategory that helps delineate differences in a prenational community. It reveals the ethnic origin of existing nations, on the one hand, and the subsocietal divisions of communities in the process of developing themselves into nations, on the other. Nevertheless, it fails to provide insights into the inner structures of ethnies and to provide tools needed for analyzing them. Thus, the concept of ethnicity continues to be useful, but not as an outmoded definition of tribe.

We can no longer equate tribes with nomads and rural populations. In Syria, for instance, the Alawites are prominently represented in the populations of major towns such as Damascus, Aleppo, and Hama as well as in Latakia. They also constitute major segments of the ruling military and civilian elites in the current Syrian regime whose members, according to Hanna Batatu, are 'chosen with extreme care and it seems unlikely that preference in selection would not have been given to men with close *tribal* links to Hafiz al-Asad. Many of them are even said to be from his birth place, the village of Qardaha.'[8] In the case of the Alawite tribe of al-Matawira we are dealing with a tribal community whose kinsmen have advanced to the ruling political elite. There are other cases in which tribespeople have ended up in towns, but on the lower end of the socioeconomic scale, without losing their tribal identity. This is true of the southern Sudanese Dinka people, who now live in the slums of Khartoum. In short, tribal affiliations are subethnic societal divisions in the nation-states of the Middle East. Tribal affiliations continue to exist despite the fact that Middle Eastern societies have undergone essential transformations.

A similar problem raised by the equation of tribes and ethnies is the equation of ethnic entities with sectarian groups, as in the case of the Shi'a of Iraq. As in Syria, where the Sunni-Alawite conflicts are not simply sectarian, in Iraq the tensions between the Sunni establishment represented by the kinsmen of Saddam Husayn (the clientele of Takrit) and the underground Shi'a are not solely sectarian either. Batatu has shown that this element among the Shi'a is of a rural origin. He brings to our attention the fact that

> for very long and well into the first decades of this century vast segments of the countryside were the home of semi-tribal groups. . . . At the same time it is necessary to remember that many of the rural Shi'is were of relatively bedouin origin and the bedouin have not been known for the vigor of their religion. . . . One other relevant factor, which needs to be stressed, is that not a few of the tribes, to which the rural Shi'is belong, were relatively recently converted to Shi'ism. For example, the important tribes of Rabi'ah, Zubayd, and Bani Tamim turned to Shi'ism only within the last 180 years or so.[9]

Moreover, it is the tribal element that explains this conversion to Shi'ism and not vice versa.

Earlier I emphasized autonomy, or at least a certain degree of it, as a major trait of a tribe. This helps explain why tribes stand in opposition to the state as a central monopolizer of power and why they resist being subdued by it. As Batatu argues, 'Shi'ism's antigovernmental motif, its preoccupation with oppression . . . and its miracle play representing Husayn's passion accorded with the instincts and suffering of tribesmen-turned-peasants and must have eased the tasks of the traveling Shi'a mu'mins,' who helped convert the Bedouins to Shi'ism.[10] Thus, to reduce Shi'i hostility directed against the Iraqi state to a sectarian explanation completely ignores the tribe–state dimension of the conflict.

In the final analysis, to understand the complexity of the existing societal subdivisions in Middle Eastern nation-states, we must recognize how intertwined ethnicity and sectarianism are with tribalism. In this sense the tribe, not as a social organization but rather as a referent of identity and group solidarity, is the most important element of what we may call ethnopolitics.[11] It is a central element in the current crisis of the Middle Eastern nation-state, and it has contributed in certain cases (such as Lebanon and Sudan) to the nation-state's disintegration. We must keep in mind that to date there exists no alternative to the nation-state since all units of the international system have to be structured along nation-state lines.

To view any ethnic community as a variety of a nation is as wrong as viewing tribes as ethnies. Ethnic communities have existed throughout history, whereas the emergence of nations is an entirely modern phenomenon that dates from the second half of the eighteenth century. Consequently, the collective cultural units and sentiments related to ethnicity are different from those of the nation. Ethnic bonds did not simply disappear when nations emerged. Anthony Smith does not subscribe to the analyses of the modernists who assert the utter novelty of the nation by insisting that there had been a radical break between premodern units and the modern, collective unit of the nation.[12] Nor does he accept the analyses of the primordialists who, in contrast, question the novelty of the nation and regard it as simply an updated version of older large collective units. Rather, Smith subscribes to the view that there has been a greater measure of continuity between the prenational ethnic ties and the new national ones. It is within this context that he looks to the concept of ethnie as an ethnic community and to its symbolism.[13] Smith's analysis seems helpful to the *problématique* of this essay insofar as it highlights the historical conditions under which ethnies were transformed into nations. It helps us understand why in the Middle East ethnic groupings of tribes like the Alawites, Druzes, Berbers, and Kurds were not transformed into nations encompassing other ethnic-tribal segments as well. In conceding the ethnic origins of nations, Smith points out that 'important changes within collective units and sentiments... have occurred within a preexisting framework of collective loyalties and identities, which has conditioned the changes as much as they have influenced the framework.' From this conclusion, he infers the need 'for a type of analysis that will bring out the differences and similarities between modern national units and sentiments and the collective cultural units and sentiments of previous eras, those that I shall term ethnie.' In Smith's view, the core of ethnicity 'resides in this quartet of myth, memories, values, and symbols and in characteristic forms or styles and genres of certain historical configurations of populations.'[14] This concept promises to be more useful than Esman and Rabinovich's for conceptualizing the status of tribes as subethnic entities in the course of state formation. Esman and Rabinovich, among others, indicate common language and ethnic descent as major characteristics of ethnicity without taking into consideration that the tribes of the Alawites, the Druzes, and even the Palestinians (whom they qualify as an ethnie) not only share Arabic as a common language but also claim a common Arab ethnic origin.[15] Even a narrower concept of ethnicity, one confined to drawing distinctions between Arabs and non-Arabs, does not provide a way out of the impasse. Neither approach helps us integrate the inquiry about the tribes and the state into the concept of ethnicity.

At this juncture we may conclude that ethnies are best characterized by the quartet of *myths, memories, values*, and *symbols* in their respective historical configurations. In this sense ethnicity also encompasses Arab tribes whom we have defined as a subethnic unit since an ethnic grouping (for example, the Druzes or Alawites) is composed of many tribes, however interrelated.

There remain the questions of why modern European industrial societies not only required but also attained cultural homogeneity by melding various ethnies into single nations and why Middle Eastern societies have so far failed to do the same. Industrialization and modernization in Europe were comparatively organic; moreover, they were indigenous processes of social change that accommodated the various ethnic origins of the nation. In the Middle East, as in other parts of the Third World, processes of modernization have been rapidly and externally induced and thus have proceeded unevenly. These processes, notes Smith, 'necessarily uproot villages and entire regions, eroding traditional structures and cultures and throwing many people out of their environments into the one dominated by anonymity and conflicts of modern urban centres.... The urban melting pot fails to assimilate the newcomers into the dominant literate culture through the education system.'[16] Those who under such conditions cannot be absorbed rely on their ethnic-tribal kin groups as reference groups; they can survive only through maintaining the network of prenational tribal loyalties and ties. Social conflicts over scarce resources assume an ethnic or, in an even narrower sense, tribal character. The cities of Khartoum and Casablanca provide ample evidence of this process. When subethnic tribes like the Alawite Matawira in Syria are capable of obtaining control of the state, not only do underdogs become topdogs but they also instrumentalize their prenational tribal ties to maintain their control.[17] Ironically, the national ideology of Arabism serves as a legitimizing formula in this tribal setup in Syria. This leads us to inquire into the quality of the modern state in the Middle East and also to ask why the institutional transplant of the nation-state has failed to take root in the Middle East and engender the needed national community. Why does tribal identity persist when the structural framework for the social reproduction of tribal life no longer exists? A closer discussion of the emergence of the nation-state in Europe and its extension to the Middle East, owing to the spread of the European international economy and the globalization of the European system of nation-states, may produce some preliminary answers.

['The simultaneity of the unsimultaneous: old tribes and imposed nation-states in the modern Middle East', in P. S. Khoury and J. Kostiner (eds.), *Tribes and State Formation in the Middle East* (Berkeley and Los Angeles: University of California Press, 1991), 137–43.]

WALTER ZENNER

30 Middlemen Minorities

The term *middleman minority* comes from Howard Paul Becker, an American sociologist who was influenced by the German classics. His writing on the subject can be seen as an indirect response to Sombart's association of commercial success with the Jewish race. In his various formulations, Becker endeavored to prove that those traits which may be associated with the Jews appear in other ethnic groups noted for their commercial acumen, such as the Scots, the Chinese, the Parsis, and the Armenians. In all of these groups, one finds enterprise connected to what he called a 'Chosen People complex,' but later was referred to as 'ethnic solidarity' or a 'separatist complex.'[1]

Becker's comparisons placed equal stress on several middleman groups, thus focusing attention on comparison. From 1940, when his first essay appeared, through the 1950s, most writing on the subject was still entwined with socioeconomic explanations of anti-Semitism.[2] There also were some valuable sociological writings dealing with anti-Semitism and European Jewry along these lines in the 1960s. By the late 1960s, however, increasing emphasis was placed on the trading minorities of Africa and Asia, who were perceived as comparable to the Jews in terms of pariah capitalism. This new interest accompanied concern with economic development and interethnic tensions in those regions. The formulations of Shibutani and Kwan, Blalock, Jiang, McClelland, Hagen, Wertheim, and others reflect this new thrust.[3]

In 1973, Edna Bonacich wrote a provocative article in which she argued that the middleman-minority theory was applicable not only to the study of early modern Jewry in Europe and the trading minorities of the Third World, but also to Asians and other small businessmen in the United States. Through their willingness to work hard for low profits and their ethnic solidarity, they filled niches of the economy which were too expensive for the large corporations to fill. At the same time, they could arouse the hostility of their native competitors, the native workforce against whom they might discriminate when employing their co-ethnics and their customers. She thus explains widely separated phenomena such as black riots which destroyed small businesses often owned by Jews and Asians in the United States during the 1960s and 1970s, the internment of Japanese in California during World War II, and anti-Indian riots in South Africa. While seeing communal solidarity as supporting the small businesses, she does not argue in her later articles and books that such groups are necessarily permanent minorities.[4] Her work is linked to that of other contemporary sociologists, especially Ivan Light and Howard Aldrich. It is marked by a highly critical stance toward the capitalist status quo.

Bonacich's approach is based on the assumption of several labor markets which divide the working class of capitalist societies into mutually antagonistic segments.[5] Her thinking was part of a general revival of Marxist thought in the United States and Western Europe during the 1970s. In dealing with middleman minorities, there has also been renewed interest in Abram Leon's pamphlet on the Jewish question, which suggested that the Jews in certain periods and places should be seen as a 'people-class,' a concept that combines ethnicity with the Marxist view of classes as groups with conflicting interests and differential access to the means of production and strategic resources.[6] Another Marxist current, that which views capitalism as having created a single-world system, is also useful in the interpretation of the roles of commercial ethnic groups.[7]

Another figure whose work integrated consideration of middleman minorities into a broader approach to the study of complex societies is Abner Cohen. For him, there is a continuous dialectical relationship between the symbols which mark different cultures and the way these symbols are used to further the political and economic interests of the bearers of those cultures. Such interest groups are based on primary relationships, whether ethnic or otherwise, and such groups are more important than the larger classes discerned by sociologists. The use of symbols to maintain group boundaries can thus be seen as a cultural strategy. In fact, many groups in traditional and modern societies find that their interests are guarded better through invisible organizations such as cousinhoods, membership in a common set of social clubs, religious ties, and informal networks, than through a highly visible, formally recognized institution. At times, ethnic groups may need to heighten their visibility as strangers to maintain their interests, while in other instances they may wish to lower their profile and appear to be an integral part of the society.[8]

An example of such invisible organization is the trading diaspora which maintained the long-distance caravan trade in West Africa in the recent past. The Hausa were one ethnic group which had such a diaspora, and they were similar to medieval Jewry in this regard.

Cohen considers the trading diaspora as a special organization in which a stable structure must allow for the mobility of its personnel. It must be a dispersed, but interdependent, set of communities. Often a diaspora is denied resort to the regular exercise of organized physical coercion, and it must find other means to maintain authority. To accomplish this, the diaspora may have stringent requirements for group membership, such as religious adherence or genealogical relations, special means of communication, and power exercised through regulation of credit.[9] [...]

A summary of middleman minority theories

In previous sections of this chapter, the development of the study of middleman minorities was reviewed historically. In this section, the features of the different theories will be summarized. Consistent among all these theories is the question of whether the most significant independent variables are those derived from the setting in which the minority finds itself or from the character of the minority itself, as well as how these factors affect each other. In extreme formulations a racist would see only factors stemming from the personalities of the minority members, while an extreme economic determinist might ignore any factors other than those arising from the total economic context. A third focus is on the immediate situation confronting the minority and majority group members when they interact, which may synthesize the two views.[10]

The aspects of the middleman situation which draws the attention are:

1. External conditions of the larger society and the economic niches of the minority
2. The situation of the stranger/sojourner/pariah
3. The attributes of the minority: (a) culture; (b) internal cohesion; and (c) objective visibility
4. Socioeconomic explanations of anti-Semitism

Cohen more than others has focused attention on the internal organization of the minority. This kind of discussion is helpful in understanding acculturation, separatism, and assimilation as it affects middleman groups. It focuses our attention on how groups may be labeled strangers or pariahs rather than merely assuming that any ethnic group specializing in trade or consisting of those who are self-employed is considered to be alien by its neighbors.

At the present time, the interest in the relationships between ethnicity and economics is active. There have been several symposia at scholarly meetings on middleman minorities and related topics. New works in the field are appearing, and research is spreading beyond a small core of social scientists.

Refutation

Opposition and refutation of middleman-minority theories exist. Those who deny the comparability of the different groups obviously fit into this category. To a certain extent, so do those such as Sombart and Milton Friedman who see middleman minorities as simply capitalists without special characteristics.

A recent refutation of economic competition as a root-cause of ethnic conflict was put forth by Donald Horowitz. In this argument, he presents arguments against Bonacich among others.

Horowitz marks out the field of his comparison as one in which ethnic groups are not ranked into rigid castes, although some ranking is always present. In most empirical cases, as in Africa and Asia, he claims that economic competition is limited by an ethnic division of labor. Recruitment to work in particular industries or sectors is through kin and former locals. Particular ethnic groups express preferences for jobs which usually avoid friction with other groups.

Sometimes, members of the majority group do compete directly with minority businessmen. In those cases, however, they frequently get little support from majority clients of the minority middlemen. In cases where governments give preferences to majority businesses in order to break the minority's monopoly, they, in fact, may create commercial rivalries.

Horowitz also cites many instances in which clients could have vented their anger on minority middlemen during periods of instability and chose not to. He tends to attribute hostility against commercial minorities to elites, such as university students. The latter are overrepresented in attitudinal studies. Horowitz, in general, diminishes the role of realistic economic interests as the foundation of ethnic political conflict.

In the conflict of unranked groups, he gives group entitlement a prime role. This term refers to the group's sense of its worth and legitimacy (for example, its honor). He believes that, when this psychology of group comparison is combined with the analysis of intragroup variability, the political party system, and other institutional constraints, one can explain the passionate and symbolic aspects of group conflict. Horowitz, as a political scientist, is uninterested in the reasons for ethnic occupational specializations which has engaged sociologists like Light and Bonacich. He also may overly diminish the importance of economic causes for ethnic antagonism. Still, there is considerable convergence between his views and those expressed in this book.[11]

External conditions and economic niches

In explaining the particular economic conditions which give rise to the specialization of certain ethnic groups as middlemen, several social scientists have pointed to the existence of a status gap. The status gap has been defined as 'the yawning social void which occurs when superordinates and subordinate portions of a society are not bridged by continuous, intermediate degrees of status.'[12] A status gap in the literal sense, however, need not be present to provide for open niches in an economic system which beg for filling. Several social settings have such openings which, whether or not they are full status gaps, will be discussed here.

An agrarian society based primarily on a subsistence economy may develop a status gap with the introduction of luxury goods through monetary trade. In such a setting, the feudal lords of the ruling elite disdain commercial activity and the peasantry does not possess the necessary skills. The classic case is that of Jews in the medieval-European economy prior to the Crusades.

Very similar is the situation of a newly conquered colonial area, ruled by an imperial elite and in which the indigenes lack the knowledge and skills to participate fully in the export and import economies. In both of these situations, there is a situation of complementarity as the traders occupy a new niche and have not displaced others.

In some settings, a particular region already has a trading group which is oriented to the old internal market. The incorporation into a wider world market, however, entails different knowledge and skills; the old trading group may be displaced by a different ethnic group oriented to a new export-import market. The Jews in sixteenth-century Poland are typical of this situation. In that period, they played an increasing role in the export of grain, while Christian merchants were not as involved in this trade. Jews were, however, excluded from trade with Muscovy.[13]

In advanced capitalist societies, large corporations such as supermarket chains may close retail outlets in remote rural areas or in impoverished urban slums. In state socialist economies, similar openings appear because of deficiencies in the state monopoly. There, black and gray markets appear. While ethnic specialization in the Soviet countereconomy has not been studied, the Soviet Georgians and the Jews have played prominent roles.[14] A debate continues as to whether the status gaps of preindustrial and colonial societies are comparable to the vacant niches in modern capitalist and socialist economies.[15]

Status gaps may be filled either through the immigration of traders, which is comparable to importing contract labor, or through the rise of an indigenous commercial class. Different societies have followed a variety of strategies in filling these gaps. It is presumed by some authors that indigenous entrepreneurs are more nationalistic, while those who immigrate are more oriented to an international market.[16]

From the perspectives of native and alien traders, the situation may be one of competition rather than complementarity, especially when one variety of skillholder has displaced another. After the Jews filled the initial status gap in medieval Europe, they were, in turn, displaced by a Christian bourgeoisie. In other situations, minority and alien traders may continue to have advantages over the natives. It is often unclear as to who is objectively a minority member or an alien, but it is in such situations of transition in which members of each group are concerned with their own group's merit.

Situation of the stranger/sojourner/pariah

Those who become traders and other middlemen are often distinguished from both the ruling elite and the masses by some ethnic markers, including religion, race, language, or some previous status. They are thus strangers to the majority. A problem in trying to make generalizations in terms of strangers and related concepts is that they depend heavily on the perceptions and folk categories of both minority and majority groups. In some areas, people from the next village are as foreign as are people from another country. When making generalizations, positivistic social scientists are often loath to deal with these native perceptions on their own terms. We prefer a single category such as *ethnic, race*, or even *stranger* to trying to equate the relationships between *infidel* and *believer* under medieval Christendom, Islam with castes in South Asia, and *brown-yellow* relations in Indonesia. In speaking about sojourning and settling, one must disentangle the complicated motives of migrants from the complex perceptions of permanent residents. It is important to realize that terms such as *stranger* are a type of shorthand.

Social thinkers have introduced the concept of the stranger in terms of a model of an isolated folk society beginning to be connected to a larger world through trade. The outsider has advantages in monetary dealings precisely because he does not face the same kinds of demands for reciprocity which confront members of the group. This reduces the stress of commerce which threatens the 'folk' moral order, and the trader, in turn, is threatened by the moral demands of this society. His opportunism and mobility aid him in remaining objective. Often, he belongs to a different ethnic group than do his clients. On this aspect, Brian Foster wrote, 'The ethnic difference has the effect of reducing the conflict inherent in face-to-face commercial transactions.'[17]

The fact that the trader is a stranger gives him a paradoxical advantage. He is attractive as a confidant because he is socially distant. He is more likely to keep a secret and aid the natives in doing certain things without the knowledge of the latters' sometimes antagonistic kin. A variety of roles from moneylender to court physician are thus open to the stranger. Especially important for the trader in this aspect are credit relationships. At the same time, he is stigmatized and barred from competing for authority and prestige.

If the trader treats his clients as objects, he and his fellows may be treated similarly. While medieval cities took varying degrees of wealth into account in assessing taxes of citizens, all Jews were obliged to pay the same tax, regardless of economic position.

Still, the tension and conflict arising from commerce are not eliminated by traders belonging to a different ethnic group than the people surrounding them. The tension is simply shifted from the interpersonal level to another in dealing with it. Shifting the conflict to the level of interethnic relations is made possible by the police power of the state.[18]

Societies with governments can back up the definitions which develop. They may encourage the separatism of the minority. The definition of a caste hierarchy in India is one example. Another is the way in which traditional Christian and Muslim states have tolerated infidels but suppressed heretics. Modern colonial and national governments allow the importation of labor and control stranger groups through designated leaders. They make laws and rules preventing them from owning land or entering civil service. They limit eligibility for citizenship and thus may actually facilitate the creation of a class of sojourners. Through inhibiting contact or facilitating assimilation they may create or disperse a class of strangers. The alien minority can serve the elite as taxpayers, tax collectors, concessionaires, or providers of credit and luxury goods. Because the strangers are relatively weak and lack authority (although not always power), they provide the rulers with deniability for wrongdoing and a ready scapegoat. They are given protection, except when their services as scapegoats are needed. Their relationship with the elite makes them ready servants of power, yet, as strangers, they are suspected of treason. The strangers' proximity to power may also offend the honor of the legitimate elite and mass majority members.[19]

The insecurity of the strangers' position—especially when their original intention was only to sojourn in a particular place—makes it unlikely that they will invest extensively in land or in heavy industry. In a period of economic nationalism, this subjects strangers to the charge of sending money out of the country and exploiting the natives. A problem in dealing with the liquid investments of minorities is the difficulty in defining liquidity because investments in diamonds, stocks, or even truck farms can all be considered as relatively liquid.

For those leaders who are interested in mobilizing their peoples to produce more, to invest in the local economy, and to achieve both economically and intellectually, there is a disadvantage in importing strangers who may be considered as pariahs or infidels. Persons with such stigmas are not considered to be models for majority elite behavior. For example, no Pole before World War II would model himself after a Jew. On the other hand, if the economic innovators—even members of religious and ethnic minorities—can sell themselves as being integrally native, then their behavior is likely to provide a model. The difference between stranger and native is not absolute and is a question of cognition as well as objective features.[20]

[*Minorities in the Middle* (Albany: State University of New York, 1991), 7–9, 11–17.]

Section V

Ethnicity, Religion, and Language

INTRODUCTION

Of the various markers and attributes of ethnicity, religion and language have been pre-eminent. While linguistic diversity or Babel has been almost universal, religion has provided the most intense energy for many pre-modern *ethnies*. This is especially marked in those *ethnies* that have evolved a myth of ethnic election. Using an 'ethno-symbolic' approach, Anthony Smith explores the concept and consequences of myths of chosen peoples, both in pre-modern epochs and into the modern era of nationalism, and distinguishes various patterns of national identity on the basis of different ethnic myths, symbols, and memories. Cynthia Enloe broadens this discussion of the multiple relationships between religion and nationalism. She focuses particularly on the uses of religion by ethnic groups, and the superimposition of certain evangelical religious traditions and particular ethnic communities. In contrast, Paschalis Kitromilides shows how Greek Orthodoxy contributed in some measure to the survival of a Greek-speaking *millet* but was compromised politically during the Greek War of Independence, and thereafter the Byzantine Orthodox *ecumene* was fragmented into its respective ethno-linguistic 'imagined' communities after 1821.

Language community has been the other great ethnic marker and mobilizer. Jaroslav Krejči and Vítězslav Velímský examined ethnicity in Europe in a multi-dimensional manner, and their research, set out in detailed tables, reveals the importance of language differentiation in Europe's array of peoples. In 1979, of the 73 ethnic groups, 60 are classified as defined by language, and 59 by a compact territory, and only in 36 cases was the political history important. Language is also important, according to Jacob Landau, both for diaspora *ethnies* like the Jews and Greeks, and for Turkish and Arab immigrants in Europe. Here the mass media, as well as multicultural education in the host society, reinforce their ethno-linguistic cultures. For John Edwards, language, in addition to its public communicative role, is an important private symbolic resource for ethnic groups. Private and symbolic markers persist because they promote the continuation of group boundaries without hindering social mobility. Symbols like a written language and history are vital constructs of missionaries and intellectuals, according to LeRoy Vail. Like other scholars, Vail rejects the idea of African tribalism and primordialism. In southern

Africa, missionaries have been especially prominent in reviving traditions and creating ethnic boundaries and pasts.

ANTHONY D. SMITH

31 Chosen Peoples

It is worth recalling first the very different factors and hypotheses from which a comparative analysis of the patterns of ethnic survival can depart. The ones usually highlighted are political in nature: the degree of a community's autonomy, its political will to survive and its leadership qualities. Sometimes analysis will focus on economic and ecological variables; the possession of specific homelands, their location, extent and population, and the presence of various material resources, facilities and skills for the support of a community. Yet another set of hypotheses treats *ethnies* as networks of communication, and seeks to ascertain how customs, language and other symbolic codes bind the members of communities together over generations.[1]

Each of these approaches, and the hypotheses that derive from them, can make valuable contributions to the study of ethnic survival, and they merit further intensive comparative investigations. It is worth remembering, however, that ethnic communities can, and have, survived over long periods without political autonomy, without a homeland of their own, even without a common language—as the linguistic divisions in Switzerland remind us—though this is rare. In such cases, other social and psychological factors appear to compensate for these absences.

This suggests that we need to pay more attention to the subjective elements in ethnic survival, such as ethnic memories, values, symbols, myths and traditions. The reason is that long-term ethnic survival depends, in the first place, on the active cultivation by specialists and others of a heightened sense of collective distinctiveness and mission. The members of an ethnic community must be made to feel, not only that they form a single 'superfamily', but that their historic community is unique, that they possess what Max Weber called 'irreplaceable culture values', that their heritage must be preserved against inner corruption and external control, and that the community has a sacred duty to extend its culture values to outsiders. Persians, Armenians, Poles, Russians, Chinese, Koreans, Japanese, Americans, Irish, English and French, to name but a few, have all cultivated this sense of uniqueness and mission by nurturing ethnic values and traditions, through myths of distant origins and symbols and memories of a golden age of former glory.[2]

We can go further. Myths of common ancestry and memories of a golden age may unite and inspire the members of an ethnic community over several generations. Yet what is even more important for ethnic survival is to cultivate a *myth of ethnic election*. Those communities that managed to formulate and cultivate such a belief have succeeded in prolonging the specific collective life of their members over many generations. The creation and dissemination by specialists of the belief that 'we are a "chosen people"' has been crucial for ensuring long-term ethnic survival.

A myth of ethnic election should not be equated with plain ethnocentrism. Ethnic communities have quite commonly regarded themselves as the moral centre of the universe and as far as possible affected to ignore or despise those around them. A myth of ethnic election is more demanding. To be chosen is to be placed under moral obligations. One is chosen on condition that one observes certain moral, ritual and legal codes, and only for as long as one continues to do so. The privilege of election is accorded only to those who are sanctified, whose life-style is an expression of sacred values. The benefits of election are reserved for those who fulfil the required observances. The classical expression of such beliefs among the ancient Israelites is to be found in the book of Exodus (ch. 19):

> Now therefore if ye will obey my voice indeed and keep my covenant, then shall ye be a peculiar treasure unto me from all peoples; for all the earth is mine; and ye shall be unto me a kingdom of priests and an holy nation (Exodus 19:5–6; cf. Deuteronomy 7:6–13 and 10:12–22).

The covenant here refers to a code of morality, law and ritual, set out in detail in the book of Deuteronomy, which the Israelites must observe if they are to remain chosen and redeemed by God. Only by keeping these laws and ceremonies can the community and its members be saved.[3]

Election myths in the Middle East and Europe

Even in antiquity, the Jews were by no means the only people to have believed that they were 'chosen'. Intimations of such ideas can be found over a millennium earlier in ancient Egypt and Mesopotamia. In the lands of Sumer and Akkad (now southern Iraq), the scattered city-states, while prizing their independence, acknowledged their ethnic kinship, particularly in times of crisis. The kings of one or other of the city-states united the Sumerians periodically, while worship of Enlil, chief god of the Sumerian pantheon, at his shrine in Nippur, acted as a religious focus for the Sumerian city-states. During the Sumerian revival under the Third Dynasty of Ur in the late third millennium BC, a greater sense of common ethnicity found expression in nostalgia for an earlier Sumerian golden age. Yet the sense of ethnic election was muted and indirect. It was vested in the king, as Enlil's representative on earth, and it was through kingship that any covenant between the gods and the community was mediated.[4]

Ethnocentrism was more marked in ancient Egypt. The land of Ptah was compact, united and more homogeneous than the lands of Sumer and Akkad. There was greater emphasis on divine election of the 'god-king', notably in the political propaganda of New Kingdom Pharaohs like Tuthmosis III,

Hatshepsut and Horemhab.[5] There was correspondingly less stress on the community's election, with or without moral conditions. At the same time, the characteristic Egyptian sense of cultural superiority to aliens, those who lived outside 'the land' (of Egypt), was accentuated after the Theban Pharaohs had driven out the Asiatic Hyksos dynasty in the sixteenth century BC. Once again, however, the sense of election rose and fell with the monarchy and the state, though it lingered on into hellenistic and Roman epochs.[6]

We cannot be sure, but a clear-cut theology of communal election in the ancient world seems to have originated in ancient Israel, though the forms of that relationship owed much to Near Eastern, especially Hittite, models. The central Israelite belief was that the sole God, the Lord of the universe, is working out His purpose for all His creatures, and has chosen a particular people to bring salvation to humanity. God's favour, however, is conditional on the fulfilment by the chosen of detailed moral and ritual codes. 'You only have I known of all the families of the earth; therefore I will punish you for all your iniquities'. Amos's prophetic judgement is unequivocal.[7] Later prophets, responding to the social and geopolitical position of Israel, hemmed in between Egypt and Assyria, elaborated on the moral dimensions of divine election. God's promise to Abraham that 'in thee shall all the families of the earth be blessed' is transformed by the Second Isaiah into the belief that Israel, the suffering servant, is chastised in order to bring salvation to all peoples. God uses Israel's enemies, the Assyrians and Babylonians, to redeem a purified Israel and thereby the world; while the Exodus from Egypt and the Covenant at Sinai are part of God's redemptive plan for humanity as a whole.[8]

Such a conception imposes a heavy burden on the chosen. They are continually required to live up to strict moral standards. Backslidings are liable to severe punishment. This affords great scope for prophets, judges, sages and other moral crusaders to warn their kinsmen and thereby periodically to reaffirm the distinctive qualities and unique destiny of the community. Later, this close relationship with God, with its inescapable moral demands on the community, became the social and psychological mainspring of Jewish survival in their long diaspora.[9]

Ideas of ethnic election, dynastic and communal, can be found among several other peoples of the ancient Near East. Here I can only mention a few. Among the Persians, the belief in ethnic chosenness has surfaced in various guises during their long history. The great Achaemenid kings, Cyrus and Darius, inherited the idea of the monarch's divine election from earlier empires and reserved for themselves the characteristic virtues of the Medes and Persians: truth, order and justice. Cyrus records how he 'constantly sought after order and equity for the black-headed people [of Babylon]' whom Marduk made him conquer; while Darius's rock inscriptions at Behistun emphasize the wisdom of living according to the precepts of the great

Persian god, Ahura-Mazda, and dwell on the special mission of a Persian king to his many subjects.[10]

Such themes were taken up much later by the Sassanid Persian rulers of Iran. The Zoroastrian temple religion was encouraged, and in the sixth century AD Chosroes I instigated a revival of old Persian symbols, myths and rituals. To this period, too, we can trace the origins of the *Book of Lords*, which recorded the exploits of the great Persian aristocratic families, chosen warriors defending Iran against the land of Tur'an. Though the Zoroastrian state religion ultimately failed to mould the Persians into a moral community, it did help to instil a sense of unique identity and destiny, which laid the basis for the New Persian cultural renaissance.[11]

Much later, under the Safavid dynasty in the sixteenth century, the adoption of Islamic Shi'ite beliefs gave a new moral dimension to Persian identity. The present century has seen a fervent renewal of Shi'ite national-religious community and missionary destiny—in contrast to the abortive attempts of the Pahlavis to recreate ancient Aryan imperial traditions.[12]

Further west, a powerful myth of election emerged in the mountain kingdom of Armenia after its conversion to Orthodox Christianity by St. Gregory in AD 301. The Romans and Byzantines contended for several centuries with the Persian Sassanid monarchs for control of Armenia, which finally lost its chance of independence after the disastrous battle of Avarayr in AD 451, despite a brief revival under the Bagratids in the ninth century. In this respect, Armenia resembled the Judean kingdoms, from which its rulers and nobles claimed descent. Both stood at the strategic crossroads of warring empires, and both peoples were spurred by political adversity to form a moral community and reinterpret their historical destinies in spiritual terms. The growing theological rift with Byzantine Orthodoxy, especially after the Council of Dvin (AD 554), and Armenian pride in being the 'first Christian nation', cemented their belief in ethnic election and divine mission, a belief that the Armenian clergy nurtured throughout the Armenian diaspora.[13]

Yet another Christian realm whose legitimacy rested on a dynastic myth of election was the Ethiopian kingdom of Aksum and its successors. The Aksumite kings may have adopted their Monophysite form of Christianity in the fourth century from Coptic sources, but it retained many Judaic features, brought perhaps from the southern Arab kingdoms. Successive Ethiopian kingdoms on the Abyssinian plateau derived their legitimacy from the symbolism of the Lion of Judah and the claim to royal descent from Solomon and the Queen of Sheba through Menelik. In the so-called 'Solomonic' dynasty from the thirteenth century, the ruling Christian Amhara nobles began to participate in this royal myth of election, which inspired a cultural revival and mobilized the community for resistance to Muslim invaders and the Falashas.[14]

We need not dwell at length on the powerful myths of election that have surfaced periodically among the Arabs and their kingdoms, notably during the Islamic conquests and in the period of the Crusades. The fact that Islam, like Christianity, is a world-religion, has not prevented the emergence of narrower ethnic myths within its domain. In some ways, Islamic allegiance has added a crusading fervour. Particularly among the Arabs, it has stimulated a pride in their language, culture and achievements and a sense of election and collective destiny that continue to exert a powerful influence on Middle Eastern politics to this day.[15]

Myths of election also helped to sustain ethnic communities in Europe. The ancient Greek encounter with the Persian empire had produced a heightened ethnocentrism, a sense of moral and cultural superiority to the surrounding 'barbarians', even a pan-Hellenic ideology—though, unlike the foundation myths of the Romans, it never succeeded in uniting the Greek city-states into a moral or political community. Only after the adoption of Orthodox Christianity in the Roman East, did Hellenism gradually acquire a moral dimension. The Byzantine Christian ideal was essentially dynastic and universal; yet it slowly became centred on the Greek-speaking inhabitants of an empire which by the ninth century had lost its western and eastern provinces, and which came to adopt Greek as its language of state in place of Latin and foster a classical Greek revival.[16] Much later, especially after the Crusader sack of Constantinople in AD 1204, a defensive Byzantine Hellenic population became even more convinced of its elective status and imperial mission—as if the destiny of the world hung on the correct liturgical observance of the only true Christian doctrine in the only genuine Christian empire.[17]

When that empire was at last extinguished in AD 1453, the same dream found a home further north and fed the burgeoning imperial ambitions of the Muscovite Russian state. The realm of the Russian Tsars became the sole bastion of Orthodoxy in an heretical world, the Third Rome, proclaimed by the Orthodox Russian clergy in the early sixteenth century. In the words of one of their leaders, Joseph of Volokolamsk monastery: 'In piety, the Russian land now surpasses all others'. From Ivan the Terrible on, the Tsar was elevated into a redeemer-figure, a 'father' to his chosen people in holy 'mother Russia'. By the nineteenth century, Slavophiles came to regard the Russian peasant community as the repository of truth, purity and wisdom—a religious conception that fed Tolstoyan and populist ideals and one that persists to this day in the writings of some neo-Russian nationalists.[18]

Similar myths can be found further west. They emerged, for example, in the Frankish kingdom in the eighth century, which the reigning Pope Paul likened to a 'new kingdom of David', occupying a place like that of the people of Israel. Similar language was used much later by Pope Boniface at the end of the thirteenth century, when he stated that '. . . the kingdom of France is a peculiar people chosen by the Lord to carry out the orders of heaven'—a status and mission that Joan of Arc, and many French leaders after her, have fought to retain and execute.[19]

Similar beliefs could be found in contemporary Scotland, in the language of the Declaration of Arbroath of 1320, in the growing sense of Swiss Confederation from 1291, among the defeated Welsh and Irish, in Hussite Bohemia, in Elizabethan England, in Calvinist Holland and, across the ocean, in the American colonies and Catholic Mexico.[20]

In all these instances, myths of ethnic election have helped to mobilize communities and ensure their survival over long periods. Because the ethnic myth is a dramatic tale that links the present with a communal past, and one that is widely believed, it helps to draw the members into a distinctive community, conferring on them a special aura, that of 'the elect'. Through its symbolism, it strives to unify different classes and regions, spreading ethnic culture outwards from the urban centres and the specialist strata, who guard the traditions, thereby creating a more participant society.[21]

Myths of ethnic election may also strengthen a community's attachment to its historic territory. By regarding the homeland as God-given, it ties the elect to a particular terrain. Only the sacred land and the sanctified soil are fit for the elect, and they can only be redeemed in the land where their fathers and mothers lived, their heroes fought and their saints prayed. To be worthy of forefathers who laid down their lives in these holy mountains and by the banks of these sacred rivers, must we not return to the ancient virtues and forsaken ways? The Swiss, who recall the heroism of Sempach and Morgarten, who extol the shining purity of the Jungfrau, who to this day re-enact the drama of William Tell, have they not converted an egalitarian myth of chosenness into the basis of their state and society, the condition of their continued freedom and prosperity?[22]

Finally, myths of ethnic election can incite a community to expansion and war. The conviction of possessing the only true faith, and a higher morality and civilization, has inspired and justified many a missionary movement and imperialist drive to those who 'live in darkness'—be it medieval Armenians seeking converts in the Caucasus, Arabs engaged in righteous *jihad*, or Western nations imposing white 'civilization' on Asians and Africans.[23]

Patterns of ethnic survival

In pre-modern eras, myths of ethnic chosenness spread to most areas of the world: to the Americas, Southern Asia, the Far East and Africa, as well as to Europe and the Middle East. Yet the belief in ethnic election has operated in different ways. Here I shall briefly distinguish four patterns of ethnic persistence and four ways in which myths of election help to sustain ethnic communities.

1. I call the first pattern *imperial-dynastic*. The myth of election is attached to the ruling house and dynasty, from which the community tends to take its main symbols and culture, and with which it is always associated. Thus, the Norman myths, within Normandy, were elaborated by clerics and chroniclers around the exploits of the ruling dukes from Rollo in AD 913 onwards. The chroniclers assumed that the Norman community shared in the special status and glory of its ruling house as a *regnum*, a kingdom of common customs and descent.[24]

This conjunction of dynasty, land and people was repeated on a grander scale in the later Western kingdoms of France, England and Spain. In all three, myths of election centred on the ruling house, with coronation and anointing ceremonies underlining the semi-divine status of the monarch. Over the centuries the kingdom and its people came to share in this elective status, as John of Gaunt's eulogy of England, 'This other Eden, demi-paradise', reminds us; until the point where the people themselves become the elect as citizens of a modern nation.[25] Poland illustrates clearly this process of transfer. In the medieval and Renaissance periods, the Polish myth of election was attached to the kingdom and its Catholic rulers. With the decline of the dynasty and the dissolution of the state in the late-eighteenth century, the people gradually became the focus of collective redemption. Sections of the nineteenth-century Polish intelligentsia, notably the great poet Adam Mickiewicz, interpreted Poland's role as that of a 'suffering Christ' among the nations, soon to rise again—while the Polish Catholic Church remained sufficiently close to the people to furnish an ethnic resource into this century. So, Poland avoided the fate of those aristocratic *ethnies*, where royal defeat and destruction of the state entailed the demise of the community itself, as occurred in Burgundy or ancient Assyria; instead, Poland was transformed after 1918 into a citizen-nation.[26]

2. A second pattern of ethnic survival, the *communal-demotic*, attaches the myth directly to the people in their sacred land. In these cases the community has usually been conquered and is struggling to preserve its former rights and way of life, claiming that its members are the original inhabitants and their culture is the vernacular. That was the claim of Celtic communities in Wales and Ireland. The Welsh myth of election pictured the community as the lost tribes of Israel, a latter-day chosen people, whose original form of Christianity had been transplanted to ancient Britain by Joseph of Aramathea. Together with the Welsh language, folk poetry and the medieval bardic contests, these beliefs helped to nurture a sense of unique Welsh identity, especially after the English conquest and the incorporation of Wales.[27]

Ireland exhibited a similar mixture of pagan and Christian motifs in its election myths. The Irish 'golden age' was variously located in the pagan Celtic era of the High Kings of Tara, and the heroes of the Ulster cycle of ancient sagas; or in the great epoch of Irish monastic learning, art and missionary activity after St Patrick's conversion of Ireland in the fifth century. The latter period, especially, furnished rich materials for later Irish myths of election, as literary scholars, archaeologists and poets in the eighteenth and nineteenth centuries envisaged the national restoration of an original Irish community in its *insula sacra*, its sacred island home.[28]

3. The third pattern is that of the *emigrant colonist*. Again the myth is attached to the people; but this time to a people on the move. They have left or fled their old homelands and are bent on building new communities in new homelands, often with little regard for the indigenous inhabitants. The elect are the immigrants and their descendants. Theirs is a settler community and mission. They carry with them their values, memories and traditions, regarding themselves as chosen by God for a providential destiny that will abolish the old order and inaugurate a new society.

The prototype here is the biblical exodus of the children of Israel from Egypt across the Red Sea. It has served as a model of their destiny for Anglo-Saxon tribes crossing the Channel into Britain, after the Roman legions had been withdrawn, the land of milk and honey being replaced by England's green and pleasant land.[29] Many centuries later another crossing, this time of an ocean by the Pilgrim Fathers fleeing religious oppression, became part of the foundation charter of the new American homeland, with its promise of freedom in a new Jerusalem.[30]

4. A final pattern, that of *diaspora-restoration*, also attached the myth of election to a community on the move; only this time it was to one moving in a reverse direction, back to the old homeland. The return of the community to its ancestral home from which it had been exiled became the precondition of collective redemption. Zionism is the classic instance, with its secular fulfilment of ancient Jewish religious aspirations. Yet we meet the same pattern among Armenians yearning to return to Mount Ararat, among eighteenth-century diaspora Greeks longing for a restoration of Hellas, among Liberians and other Black Americans intent on returning to Africa, and latterly among some communities deported by Stalin to distant parts of the Soviet Union. In each of these cases, as the great Greek educator, Adamantios Korais, so clearly realized, the restoration of a diaspora to its ancestral home involved not merely the physical return of a people, but also its spiritual regeneration through education and political mobilization.[31]

These four patterns of ethnic persistence and renewal do not pretend to be exhaustive. However, they reveal the importance of beliefs in chosenness for ethnic survival. They also show the different ways in which such beliefs operate. Sometimes they fuel expansion, sometimes popular revolt, at still other times mass migration and movements of restoration. They also expose the community to different risks: the ossification of the ethnic community through overdependence on the state, popular instability and extremism, dissipation of communal energy through schism or assimilation. These dangers are familiar to ethnic leaders. In each generation priests, scribes, prophets, bards, mandarins, even nobles, have warned the people of these dangers, and by prescribing remedies for communal ills have actively cultivated the sense of ethnic identity and destiny.

Each of these patterns also reveals certain key factors in ethnic survival. *Warfare* and a warrior ethos are generally prominent in the dynastic-imperial pattern. The elect consist of righteous warriors under their redeemer-princes and faithful caliphs, and ethnic chosenness is borne on the spears and shields of missionary knights such as the Hungarian or Catalan nobility. As with the battles of the ancient Israelites against the Philistines, memories of victory and defeat became incorporated into the sacred history of a chosen people and its warrior-deity.[32]

Popular revolt stands at the heart of the communal-demotic pattern. Theirs is no simple fate of passive endurance, but rather the ideal of a purified people, mobilized in defence of its heritage. Vernacular mobilization is the *leitmotiv* of survival among Irish and Basques, Czechs and Georgians, Kurds and Sikhs, and many more communities that have drawn on their native languages, traditions, symbols and memories for comfort and inspiration.[33]

Wandering has become the dominant theme of both emigrant and diaspora patterns. For the first, it is a migration to the promised land, with a providential destiny that excludes indigenous peoples and slaves. For the diaspora type, long exile evokes a fervent nostalgia, an ardent desire to recover an original home exclusive to the chosen community.[34]

['Chosen peoples: why ethnic groups survive', *Ethnic and Racial Studies*, 15: 3 (1992), 440–9.]

CYNTHIA ENLOE

32 Religion and Ethnicity

There is no consensus on what constitutes ethnicity but there is growing agreement that it is both objective and subjective. Ethnicity involves cultural attributes that can be observed, but those attributes must be of conscious value to a collection of people to amount to ethnicity. There is a growing agreement among scholars that ethnicity requires a sense of belonging and an awareness of boundaries between members and nonmembers, however vague and mutable those boundaries may be from situation to situation or from time to time.[1]

Ethnicity is difficult to define because it is composed of an intertwining *cluster* of attributes and not a singular cultural characteristic. Language, religion, territory and custom—by themselves—are insufficient to identify, or sustain, an ethnic group. Moreover, the cluster of attributes assigned a collective value by a group will vary. A common language is a typical component of the ethnic cluster, but it is neither necessary nor sufficient to distinguish ethnicity. The linguistic component in the ethnic cluster is verified by Austria's Slovene population and a government language census used as a basis for general Slovene mobilization. Yet clear ethnic boundaries among Africans and East Indians survived in Guyana long after the British successfully made English-speakers out of both groups.

This essay will explore the effect of religious differences on intergroup boundary visibility and maintenance between two ethnic groups to determine whether there is something peculiarly intense or profound about religion when it is a part of ethnic differentiations and the gap between communities is especially wide. Eastern European societies have experienced an historically high level of interethnic contact. Ethnic boundaries in that region are rarely maintained by the sheer physical remoteness often found in Asia or Africa. Thus an investigation of how ethnic boundaries and group integrity are maintained and the role played by religion in that process is especially rewarding in analyzing Romania, Yugoslavia and Czechoslovakia.

Religion appeals to a suprahuman or supraempirical authority to formulate explanations, judgments and goals. But in practice religions are markedly diverse. For instance, the extent to which supra-empirical authorities are explicitly and coherently defined differs widely. This is the basis of conventional distinctions between the 'Great' religions (Hinduism, Islam, etc.) and the presumably 'lesser' religions (animism, eclectic folk versions of the Great religions, etc.). The explicit organizational structures used to implement clerical authority and the extent of hierarchy and integration in those organizations also differ among religions. Thus Roman Catholic Christianity stands out because of its explicit, elaborate and hierarchical organization and animist religion is distinguished by its low degree of explicit organization and clerical professionalism. Religions can also be categorized according to the extent of their taboos determining dress, diet and other behaviors. Finally, religions differ in their approach to evangelical proselytizing. Islam and Christianity have ardently pursued converts and thus have absorbed a diverse range of cultural groups, Judaism has been remarkably nonevangelical.

The kind of religion—along these lines of distinction—as part of an ethnic group's communal package will determine how porous the ethnic boundaries are, how capable a group is of withstanding outside pressures to assimilate, and how prone the group will be to absorb outsiders through intermarriage or conversion. The type of religion confessed by group actors is also a significant factor in interethnic dynamics. The most tense interethnic relationship occurs when two ethnic groups confess different religions, each religion is theologically and organizationally elaborate and explicit, and when those religions have generated taboos operative in the routine aspects of life, for instance diet. The intensity is increased when each religion has a tradition of evangelism. This situation approximates the situation in contemporary

Lebanon but it is *not* applicable to the situation between Malays and Chinese in Malaysia, between Walloons and Flemings in Belgium, or between Great Russians and Ukrainians in the Soviet Union.

Therefore, when assessing what religion adds to ethnic identification and inter-ethnic relations, it is essential to note that there are critical differences among religions which bear directly on how ethnicity is expressed and maintained collectively. It is not simply a matter of 'religion' being a part of the boundary setting package, but *which* religion.[2] To add another complexity the boundaries may often be affected by a *sect* of a major religion. Some ethnic boundaries persist when persons are all Muslims, all Hindus or all Christians but the distinction between Sunni and Shiite Muslims is a salient factor in Iraqi ethnic politics; and there are divisions between Lebanese Christians—Maronite, Orthodox and Catholic.

Ethnic communalism does not appear to be lessened when groups are distinguished by sectarian differences rather than by major religious confessional orientations. Interethnic hostility, however, may be particularly acute when each ethnic group is convinced that its own interpretation of the basic theology is correct while the other's is corrupted. Moreover, when the religious beliefs of two ethnic groups are relatively close the other differences may become especially important since they are necessary for boundary maintenance. Richard Gambino observes that Italian-Americans traditionally felt more antagonism toward Irish-Americans than against Jews or Protestants because of what they perceived to be the deviations of Irish Catholicism.[3] This suggests that when ethnic boundaries are firmly established on extrareligious grounds, group members who appear to be religiously identical will have a stake in denying religious homogeneity.

The most common way of rendering the extent to which religion sustains ethnic boundaries operative in the study of ethnicity has been to focus on rates of *intermarriage* which is, in a sense, the 'bottom line' of ethnicity. The rate of intermarriage is not determined by religious rules exclusively since class and racial factors are also important in reducing or promoting intermarriage. Marriage is a sacred act in most cultures and religious divisions are significant even when they operate in company with class and racial factors. The rising rate of intermarriage between gentiles and Jews in the United States has alarmed many Jewish leaders who believe it indicates a lowering of the religious quotient in the American Jewish ethnic package and a weakening trend. In contrast secularization has been deliberately promoted in the Soviet Union and the State has encouraged cross-ethnic and cross-confessional marriages. Nonetheless Muslims (who themselves are ethnically diverse) are less likely to marry non-Muslims than they are to marry Muslims.[4]

It may be futile and unrealistic to separate religion and ethnic identity. Many individuals behave as if their ethnic affiliation and professed religion are one and the same: to be born Croatian is to be born Catholic. But there have been attempts in the United States to pry religion and ethnicity apart analytically. American political analysts have questioned (as have the elected politicians they advise) the existence of a 'Catholic vote' and wondered, on the other hand, if 'ethnic votes' determine polling outcomes. Historically analysts have been interested in the immigrant experience (or assimilation experience). That interest has raised questions about the interplay of religion and foreign nationality in shaping behavior in the American society. Most such questions are directed toward Catholic-confessing ethnic groups because of the American preoccupation with Church and State and because Catholic groups have presumably had the most electoral impact. Actually the effort to distinguish religion and ethnicity is just as valid for Protestants and other religious subgroups.

If ethnicity is merely religion in disguise, then holding religion constant should reveal few significant differences among ethnic groups. A recent study of American Catholics' political attitudes and values revealed wide-ranging differences among Catholics and those intra-Catholic differences fell into distinctly ethnic patterns. Furthermore, the survey was most directly related to spiritual values and not concerned with such differences as US foreign policy *vis-à-vis* Poland or Ulster, questions that would normally elicit group differences. For example, 76 percent of the Irish Catholics opposed miscegenation laws, whereas 58 percent of the Italian Catholic respondents and 66 percent of the Polish Catholic respondents agreed with those laws. Likewise, only 32 percent of the Irish Catholics favored legalized abortion when a mother 'is married and doesn't want any more children,' while 43 percent of the Italian Catholics favored legalized abortion. The same study also found that ethnic attitudinal differences persist among American Protestants along ethnic group lines although the differences were less wide-ranging overall. For instance, 37 percent of German Protestants favored legalized abortion whereas 57 percent of the Scottish Protestant respondents did so.[5] Kathleen Frankovic made an important related attempt to determine whether religion is simply the *class* phenomenon in disguise by studying religion's impact on American political behavior. She found that in voting behavior and issue orientations, 'No matter what type of class measures were used—income, education, occupation, or even residence in urban areas—religious distinctiveness remained relatively high.' Furthermore, Frankovic found little evidence that interreligious differences in political behavior were being diluted over time in the United States.[6] Thus if religion is a factor which helps to sustain ethnic boundaries it is not losing sufficient impact to lend credence to 'end of ethnicity' predictions. Moreover, a cross-national Gallup Poll survey conducted in 1976 revealed that 56 percent of American respondents considered their religious beliefs 'very important' to them, while only 5 percent labeled them 'not at all important.' The same survey found, however, that only 17 percent of West Germans and 12 percent of Japanese considered their religious beliefs 'very important.'[7]

Many nation-states have been formed on the assumption that religion and ethnicity were separable, but that when an overwhelming majority of citizens all confessed an identical religion—ethnicity would lose saliency and functional value. This was the hope underlying the formation of Israel and the postcolonial establishment of Pakistan. It is increasingly obvious, however, that even when religion is a constant, ethnic boundaries remain and sometimes ethnic group members even hold them in greater esteem. Being Jewish has not eliminated the sense of the Russian Jew's ethnic integrity inside Israel. This is not as surprising as it first appeared to observers because, according to a study by Jeffrey Ross, recent Russian Jewish immigrants in Israel do not think of their Jewish identification as a religious identity, but rather as a *national* identification. Only 8.1 percent of Ross' sample of new Russian Jewish immigrants considered themselves to be religious.[8] Similarly, Bengalis in precivil war Pakistan assigned more and more value to their supra-Islamic ethnic distinctiveness. There was a growing interaction between Muslim and Hindi Bengalis across the India-Pakistan border as the rift between East and West Pakistan Muslims widened. The civil war was not just territoriality masquerading as ethnicity; today Western Pakistan is all Muslim yet it is still threatened by interethnic conflict.

Within some multiethnic and multi-religious states there is a feeling that religion may cause less system-threatening cleavages than ethnicity. Thus political parties with religious orientations are formed to comprise two or more ethnic groups—at least at election time. Political integration in Belgium typically involved ethnically crosscutting religious and secular parties. When these parties—Socialist and Catholic—collapsed or split into communal wings the existence of the Belgian state appeared to be in serious jeopardy. The Belgian political system, in other words, tolerated political mobilization based on religion but could not withstand political mobilization based on ethnicity without a new constitutional and elitist formula for integration. The Netherlands and West Germany also experienced formalized religious cleavages in social and political affairs which have not caused the profound anxiety occasioned by, past and potential, ethnic changes.

Finally, in order to see how much religion contributes to the intensity and the sustenance of ethnicity it is possible to examine ethnic groups that are internally divided along religious lines. There are few multireligious ethnic groups and their relative scarcity suggests that religion is the root of ethnic differentiations or that religious distinctiveness is a key to ethnic saliency. The overseas Indian ethnic group is internally divided more often than not by religion. Indian ethnic communities in Malaysia, Guyana, Trinidad, Uganda, and Great Britain are divided between Muslims and Hindus and, in smaller numbers, by Christians. A cursory review of those Indian communities suggests that (1) the existence of religious heterogeneity has not made Indian qua Indian ethnicity less real for its members than ethnicity for religiously homogenous groups, (2) religious diversity frequently hinders efforts by Indians to mobilize communally to pursue Indian interests. Thus in Guyana common local political gossip suggests that the largely African ruling party has deliberately exploited the religious split among the Guyanese Indians intending to coopt Muslim Indians. The Indian political party in Guyana, however, is secular and does not depend on religious appeals. Despite being a majority in Guyana, the Indians have failed to translate their numbers into an effective political mobilization.[9] The divisions among the Indian population in Britain are linguistic, caste, country of previous residence and religious, and those divisions have hampered Indian political development in labor, immigration and housing policy.[10]

One of the most prominent religiously divided ethnic groups in Eastern Europe is the Czech community. That community is divided between Catholics and Protestants, but the Czechs have sustained a strong sense of ethnic boundaries. Similarly, Albanian ethnic nationalism has flourished in recent generations despite intraethnic divisions.

Religious homogeneity may not be the *sine qua non* of ethnic boundary maintenance but religious pluralism within a community still has genuine consequences in the operation of the community in society at large.

['Religion and ethnicity', in P. Sugar (ed.), *Ethnic Diversity and Conflict in Eastern Europe* (Santa Barbara: ABC-Clio, 1980*b*), 350–60.]

PASCHALIS KITROMILIDES

33 Orthodoxy and Nationalism

Despite its effectiveness, the process of nation-building through the imaginative construction of a sense of ethnic community brought to the fore the fundamental, and theoretically inescapable, antinomy between Orthodoxy and nationalism. The ensuing conflict in moral values dramatized the essential incompatibility between the imagined community of religion and the imagined community of the nation. The community of the faithful, which in evangelical Christianity had been formed against all earthly distinctions of race, class and sex, of freedom and slavery, of wisdom and ignorance, provided the doctrinal backdrop of the universal Church and Orthodox ecumenicity. The community of the Orthodox Church therefore remained indifferent to the new concepts of national identities and secular states; and when these concepts formed the bases of alternative communities for its faithful, it met the challenge with open hostility.

A whole tradition of Balkan national historiography is nevertheless premised on the assumption that Orthodox Christianity and the Orthodox Church played a major role in nation-building, by preserving collective identity under the Ottomans and by preparing the advent to independence. The Orthodox Church, in short, is assumed to have cemented national identity in the years of captivity. This assumption runs throughout conventional twentieth-century Balkan historiography, both secular and ecclesiastical, especially in Greece, where official rhetoric has perpetuated it as a fundamental ideological tenet. The role of the Church in modern Greek history has consequently become the focal point of controversy between conventional and revisionist schools of historical writing. However, both apologists and critics of the Church are asking ideologically motivated questions which inevitably obscure the real historical issues. The relation between Orthodoxy and nationality can only be understood as a historical problem. On certain levels of analysis and in specific historical contexts the assumption about 'Orthodoxy as guardian of nationality' can indeed be shown to be borne out by the evidence. But it is far from a straightforward, self-evident or conceptually unproblematical issue.

The Orthodox Church in the Balkans did contribute to the preservation of collective identity under Ottoman rule by institutionalizing and safeguarding the distinction of the Christian subjects from their Muslim rulers.[1] But the distinction was religious, not national, in content. One of the greatest anachronisms of Balkan, and for that matter European, historiography has been the injection of national content into that traditional religious distinction. Furthermore, the Orthodox church, and especially its monastic institutions, preserved the languages and the medieval imperial memories of the Balkan peoples, a heritage that in time was to be politicized by nationalism and made the basis of historiographical anachronisms. The Church, however, as an institution of the Ottoman state remained a supranational organization and, by virtue of its own doctrinal principles, a non-national one. It was only the confusions arising from the coincidence that power in the Orthodox Church was wielded by a Greek-speaking hierarchy that created 'ethnic' antagonisms within it before the age of nationalism. It was the eventual abandonment of the ecumenicity of Orthodoxy, and the 'nationalization' of the churches, that brought intense national conflicts into the life of the Orthodox Church and nurtured the assumption concerning the affinity between Orthodoxy and nationality.

The fundamental antinomy contained within the original relationship derived from a deeper contradiction between secular history and theological principles. The historical record is replete with instances of this antinomy, which are sources of embarrassment for the proponents of conventional views on both the lay and ecclesiastical sides. The embarrassment, like the intensification of the antinomy itself, is a direct product of the total success achieved by the imaginative process of constructing national communities, which of course has radically transformed not only self-images and conceptions but also moral codes. To reconstruct the story of the antinomy between Orthodoxy and nationalism would be tantamount to rewriting the ecclesiastical history of south-eastern Europe and the Middle East in the last two centuries, and naturally cannot be attempted here. Only a brief historical illustration of the process will be presented below, in order to hint at the radical interruption of the Orthodox religious tradition involved in the 'nationalization' of the churches which followed the advent of the national states.

The earliest instances of the cleavage can be traced in the confrontation of the Church with the advocates of cultural and ideological change associated with the Enlightenment. The conflict was articulated after 1789, when it became clear to traditional religious leaders where the intellectual changes and the liberal principles of the Enlightenment were leading. The active opposition of the Patriarchate of Constantinople, especially under Patriarch Gregory V (1797–8, 1806–8 and 1818–21), to the spread of the Enlightenment in Greek education and culture and to the Greek national movement which sprang from it, constitute the clearest sign of the antinomy between Orthodoxy and nationalism. Gregory V condemned, by appealing to the principles of Orthodox doctrine, both the radical republicanism of Rhigas Velestinlis in 1798 and the outbreak of the Greek Revolution in 1821. The classic statement of the Church's position came in the militant conservative tract *Paternal Instruction* (1798), attributed to patriarch Anthimos of Jerusalem (1788–1808) but probably written by Gregory V himself, which counselled the pious to submit to Ottoman rule and warned against the pernicious consequences of revolutionary plans for the souls of the faithful.[2] The Greek experience was not unique. Another instance of the opposition between the Orthodox church and nationalism arose with the vehement reactions of the Serbian hierarchy against the cultural and linguistic reforms advocated by Vuk Karadzic.[3]

The advent of independent states in the Balkans, seeking to solidify their independent status through the proclamation of the independence of their churches, dramatized the extent of the impact of nationalist ideas upon Balkan politics. These gestures, which broke centuries-old traditions and sought legitimization through a nationalist reinterpretation of the ecclesiastical past of the Balkans, brought to the fore an antinomy between Orthodoxy and nationalism that had been in the making since the pre-Independence, Enlightenment period. The unilateral declaration of the autocephaly of the Orthodox Church in Greece (1833), Romania (1865), Bulgaria (1870) and Albania (1922–37) created serious canonical problems with the Patriarchate of Constantinople. In the case of Bulgaria, the intense national conflicts which underlay ecclesiastical issues caused the problem to escalate into a full-scale schism lasting over seventy years (i.e. until 1945). Only the Orthodox Church in Serbia, with its stronger traditions and older religious institutions, acceded peacefully to autocephaly in 1879 by following the canonical step of receiving administrative independence conferred by the synod of Constantinople itself.

It is ironical that the Church of Greece was the first to break away from the Greek-controlled Patriarchate of Constantinople, thus setting an example for the non-Greek churches in the northern Balkans to follow. As already noted, the independence of the Church of liberated Greece from the Patriarchate of Constantinople was urged quite early in the War of Independence by the Greek Enlightenment's leading political thinker. Adamantios Korais insisted that it was unthinkable for the clergy of free Greece to submit and obey the instructions of a Patriarch still held captive by the nation's oppressors. Korais's argument crystallized the conflict between Orthodoxy and nationalism that was to rage in the Orthodox world, and especially in south-eastern Europe, for the rest of the nineteenth century. Almost half a century later it was echoed by the Romanians, in their efforts to create their own autocephalous national church.

While the regional churches of the Balkan states were thus nationalized by becoming components of the nation-states' modern administrative structure, the Ecumenical Patriarchate in the Ottoman Empire kept its distance from the new nationalism. This placed serious obstacles in the way of those attempting to use the Church's powerful structure and authority in order to promote the imaginative construction of national identity. Ubicini noted in the 1850s that 'the clergy in Turkey, as elsewhere, are of the ecclesiastical party and of that alone'.[4] It was this party which was opposed to the new nationalists, 'the party of Hellenism' whose proponents, still few according to Ubicini, 'simply desired to be annexed to Greece'.[5] The Patriarchate, through a series of acts and pronouncements of its holy synod, made official and clear its opposition to nationalism and condemned as uncanonical initiatives motivated by nationalist considerations.

Although the first occasion for such reactions on the part of the Patriarchate was the autocephaly of the Church of Greece, the solemn and public condemnation of national claims in the Church, and of attempts to turn it into an instrument of nationalism, was provoked by the Bulgarian schism in 1870. In August 1872 the Ecumenical Patriarch, along with the other Orthodox Patriarchs of Alexandria, Antioch and Jerusalem and the archbishop of Cyprus, convened a major synod which issued a condemnation of 'phyletism', by which was essentially meant nationalism.

> The question of what basis racism—that is, discriminating on the basis of different racial origins and language and the claiming or exercising of exclusive rights by persons or groups of persons exclusively of one country or group—can have in secular states lies beyond the scope of our inquiry. But in the Christian Church, which is a spiritual communion, predestined by its Leader and Founder to contain all nations in

one brotherhood in Christ, racism is alien and quite unthinkable. Indeed, if it is taken to mean the formation of special racial churches, each accepting all the members of its particular race, excluding all aliens and governed exclusively by pastors of its own race, as its adherents demand, racism is unheard of and unprecedented . . . All the Christian churches founded in the early years of the faith were local and contained the Christians of a specific town or a specific locality, without racial distinction. They were thus usually named after the town or the country, not after the ethnic origin of their people.[6]

The synod concluded by issuing the following condemnation of racism:

> We renounce, censure and condemn racism, that is, racial discrimination, ethnic feuds, hatreds and dissensions within the Church of Christ, as contrary to the teaching of the Gospel and the holy canons of our blessed fathers which support the holy Church and the entire Christian world, embellish it and lead it to divine godliness.[7]

The condemnation of 'phyletism' crystallizes the antinomy of Orthodoxy and nationalism. Appeals to Christian doctrine and Orthodox traditions nevertheless could not stem the tide of new forces in world history. The nationalization of the regional Orthodox churches proceeded apace. The Bulgarian church became the major instrument for the promotion of Bulgarian national claims in Macedonia in the second half of the nineteenth century.[8] To counter this, Greek bishops in the area took increasingly militant nationalist stands, to such a point that the national struggles in Macedonia were primarily fought over the control of churches and ecclesiastical jurisdictions. Albanian prelates were soon to be added to the complex picture, as they in turn assumed the leadership of the Albanian nationalist movement.[9] Nationalist struggles and ecclesiastical politics in the Balkans became intertwined in an intense, often violent contest over the loyalties of the faithful.

Meanwhile the newly independent churches were going through their domestic crisis over relations with the national states. The Church of Greece went through its crisis in the first twenty years of independence, ending with the total submission of the Church to the state. The Romanian Church underwent a parallel experience in the period from the 1880s to the 1920s, involving domestic conflicts with the state and external conflicts with the Ecumenical Patriarchate. The conflicts with the state involved issues of Church administration and civil jurisdiction in Church affairs. The independence of the Church of Romania was considered a necessary complement to national independence. In claiming autocephaly from Constantinople, the Romanians used an argument strikingly similar to that of Greek nationalists almost half a century earlier. The dependence of their Orthodox Church on the Ecumenical Patriarchate was considered a national humiliation since the Patriarch, situated in Constantinople, the capital of their former masters, had remained a prisoner of the Ottoman state.[10] Once the desire for ecclesiastical independence was canonically settled with the official recognition of Romanian autocephaly by Patriarch Joachim IV in 1885, a remarkable attempt was made to endow the Romanian Church with a distinct national past of its own. This interest in the history of Romanian Orthodoxy culminated with the publication in 1908–9 of Nicolae Iorga's two-volume *History of the Romanian Church and the Religious Life of Romanians.*

The full nationalization of the Church of Romania came with its unilateral elevation to patriarchate in the context of the creation of 'Greater Romania' after World War I. In a way, the creation of the Romanian patriarchate in 1925 was the last symbolic act in a process which over several decades produced the imagined community of the Romanian nation. Church and nation finally became one, in spite of earlier conflicts between the Orthodox hierarchy and nationalist intellectuals, especially in Transylvania.[11] Despite the original conflicts with nationalism, through the cunning of history the elevation of the regional Orthodox churches of the Balkans to patriarchates became a final act in the affirmation of national identity and autonomy.[12] Serbia accomplished this in 1920 and Bulgaria, after the termination of the schism and under communist rule, in 1953. In this case, too, although Serbia proceeded canonically and peacefully, Bulgaria proclaimed its patriarchate unilaterally and was not recognized by Constantinople until 1961.

Notwithstanding its condemnation of 'phyletism', the Ecumenical Patriarchate did not remain immune from the challenge of nationalism. The struggle against pan-Slavism in Macedonia and its more specifically ecclesiastical guise, the fight against the encroachments of the Bulgarian Exarchate on the administrative jurisdiction of the Patriarchate in Macedonia and Thrace, brought about a common front between the nationalist claims of the Greek state in Macedonia and the insistence of the Patriarchate on the defence of its canonical rights. As a consequence a gradual differentiation took place within the ranks of the hierarchy of the Patriarchate, involving the elevation to the episcopate of a younger generation of militant nationalists with a mandate to counter the expansion of the Exarchate. The exigencies of the struggle eventually led these bishops to see eye-to-eye with Greek policy-makers as to the priorities and strategy of the defence of Greek and Patriarchal interests in Macedonia. Thus, by the turn of the twentieth century, a whole new mentality shaped by the values of nationalism crept gradually into the politics of the Ecumenical Patriarchate, the condemnation of 'phyletism' of a few years earlier notwithstanding. The new bishops were among the best-trained and ablest men in the hierarchy and included such dedicated nationalists as Germanos of Kastoria and Chrysostom of Drama, who openly advocated the subordination of the policies of the Orthodox Church in the Ottoman Empire to the directives of the national centre at Athens.

This stand represented a radical break in the tradition of the Patriarchate, which had followed a policy of accommodation with the Ottoman state, knowing full well from the long experience of centuries that loyalty to the Sublime Porte was the key to the survival of both the Church and its flock in the Empire and the guarantee of the Patriarchate's traditional privileges. This was the view of the Ecumenical Patriarch Joachim III (1878–84 and 1901–12), who took a firm stand against the militancy of the new bishops and insisted on the independence of the Patriarchate from Athens. The violent struggle that ensued between the Patriarch and the nationalist bishops was symptomatic of the attempt to 'nationalize' even the centre of supranational Orthodoxy under the onslaught of Balkan nationalism.[13] At about the same time, similar conflicts between nationalist and traditional parties in the hierarchy occurred in the Orthodox churches of the Middle East. The Patriarchate of Antioch experienced such a crisis when in 1897 its Arab bishops, urged on by years of Russian propaganda and after a protracted struggle, forced the resignation of their Cypriot-born patriarch Spyridon, the last in a long line of Greek Orthodox patriarchs of Antioch.[14] Even the smallest of the Orthodox churches, the insular Church of Cyprus, was subject to the pressures of nationalism. A protracted conflict over the succession to the archepiscopal throne, lasting from the death of Archbishop Sophronios in 1900 to 1909, ended with the election of the nationalist Cyril II (1909–16). From this point on, the Church of Cyprus assumed the leadership of the Cypriot nationalist movement which opposed British rule in the name of union with Greece.

As a consequence of these ecclesiastical struggles and the gradual nationalization of the regional Orthodox churches, the unity of the 'Orthodox commonwealth', which for almost ten centuries had extended over the whole of eastern Europe and the Middle East, was irrevocably broken. The imagined community of Orthodox Christianity, which since the conquest had determined the common identity of the Orthodox Christian subjects of the sultan, was destroyed. It was gradually replaced by the new sense of community cultivated by the national states, which, after administratively and linguistically homogenizing their societies, found in religion a powerful additional support for their national unity and external aspirations. Clearly, however, religion came last in the struggle to forge new national identities and did not become a functional element in national definition until the nation-states had nationalized their churches. Whereas language had provided the initial criterion in delineating the imagined communities of the hoped-for nations, Orthodoxy was enlisted last, its powerful psychological and symbolic force helping to cement the unity of the new nations which the states had created.

['"Imagined communities" and the origins of the national question in the Balkans', *European History Quarterly*, 19: 2 (1989), 177–85.]

There are firstly five objective factors which can contribute to the identification of a group as a nation: territory, state (or similar political status), language, culture and history. When positive answers to all of these criteria coincide there can be little doubt that the respective community or population is a nation; then usually the sixth, subjective criterion, national consciousness, is also present. But there are situations where some, or even most of the objective criteria are missing and yet the community feels itself to be a nation. Whether the rest of the world, especially the interested neighbours, are or are not willing to acknowledge the group in question as a separate nation is, in the long run, irrelevant. The subjective factor of consciousness is the ultimate factor which eventually decides the issue of national identity.

As national consciousness is a factor, the presence of which is not always easy to ascertain, we shall simply suppose its presence in all cases of well-established nations (taken for granted not only by themselves but also by their neighbours) and also in the case of those ethnic groups which in addition to some objective characteristics do possess a cultured elite capable of defending in an articulate way their claim for a separate ethnic identity.

In order to realise which of the objectively assessable criteria, such as language, culture, history, territory and political status, are present and consequently are supposed to contribute to the national identity and its awareness, an attempt will be made to list all European ethnic groups according to these criteria. This will also help us to understand the relative importance of individual criteria.

For a deeper insight into the many-faceted reality it is sometimes not enough to ascertain whether a particular criterion is present or not; we may need also to ask in what form it is present. This would be especially useful with regard to questions such as whether an ethnic group lives in a territory of its own; whether it is settled in a more or less compact way; whether it has its own more or less sovereign state or only a federated or autonomous unit; whether it speaks its own language which distinguishes it from all other ethnic groups or not etc.

Considering all such circumstances, relevant for our classification, we arrive at a taxonomy or scheme in which the six defining characteristics (territory, political status, history, culture, language and consciousness) are amplified in twenty types in the following way:

(1) *Territory*: there are three basic types of relationship of an ethnic group to a geographical area:
  (a) the main body of the ethnic group lives in *compact* settlements in the territory;

(b) the group lives *mixed* with another in the territory;
(c) the group has no country of its own and is scattered over a wider area (*diaspora*).

(2) With respect to *political status*, the following alternatives are envisaged:
(a) sovereign *state*;
(b) equal position of the nationality with others within a state or federation; both these cases may be, in our scheme, labelled as *federated* status, i.e. federated with respect to ethnic issues;
(c) *autonomous* status within a state or federation;
(d) no status of self-government at all

(3) *History* in our scheme is conceived mainly in political terms; its type is assessed as to whether it can be related to the respective ethnic group, i.e. whether or not the ethnic group had over a longer period of its history a state or similar political formation of its own. If it had its own territorial political framework during at least some substantial part of its history, we shall classify this case of political history as *related*. If an ethnic group shared its political history with another, as for instance the Catalans with the Spaniards in the Aragonian kingdom, or Slovaks with Magyars in the Hungarian kingdom, then the position can be classified as *unrelated*. If neither alternative was the case, then there would be no political history noted in this scheme.

Related political history, whether continuous or interrupted, is assumed also in cases when there was a plurality of states in the territory of the respective nationality, most of which contributed to the promotion or upholding of national tradition and/or consciousness, as in medieval Germany or Italy or the twin Romanian principalities of Wallachia and Moldavia.

(4) With regard to *culture* the question is whether the primary basis of the particular culture is (a) *language*, (b) *religion*, (c) *political conditions*, irrespective of whether past or present, or possibly (d) a special *way of life*.

(5) As the existence of one's own *language* is not a necessary condition for national identity, the basic question is whether the group possesses its own language or whether it shares it with another group. If it has its own language, then the strength of national consciousness may vary according to whether that language has developed into a literary form or whether it has remained more or less at the stage of a spoken vernacular (dialect).

These alternatives allow for a set of combinations. One ethnic group can use two languages of which both or only one may be a literary language; in the latter case the other would be a mere spoken vernacular (a specific dialect).

The alternatives in our classification then are (a) own (literary language); (b) shared (literary and spoken language in common with another ethnic group); (c) own and shared; in this last case the native language may be either a literary one or a mere dialect which however can also be partly used for writing.

In individual cases it may sometimes be difficult to decide whether a particular language can be truly considered as a literary one. This would especially be the case with languages which could not fully develop their literary form due to political circumstances (when the ethnic group has been incorporated into the nation state of a kindred ethnic group or an alien ethnic group with a strong unifying linguistic policy). Nevertheless, in those cases where one of the languages used by a bi-lingual ethnic group can hardly be considered as anything more than a mere dialect (this usually happens to be the indigenous language), a note 'dialect' is used instead of 'own' in our classification.

(6) As a *national consciousness* reflects the salient characteristics of the nationality, its typology can be drawn with respect to these characteristics. In our scheme the following alternatives are envisaged: (a) *ethnic*, if the basis is language and associated culture, (b) *political*, if the basis is a separate political unit (state) the significance of which is supported either by historical tradition or by a particular socio-economic system and (c) *both*, if ethnic and political elements are so closely intertwined that it would be arbitrary to consider one of them more important.

Religion is not considered to be a sufficient cause of or reason for national consciousness. Wherever it has assumed the role of being the main mark of differentiation between what otherwise appear to be kindred people, it seems in fact to be a substitute for another determinant. It is a rallying point for those who either have abandoned another, more pertinent, expression of ethnic identification such as language (Jews, and Ulstermen of both denominations), or who, having lost their special political status of belonging to the dominant group within an empire which had been horizontally stratified in religious communities, cannot accommodate themselves within a differently patterned framework (Serbo-Croat-speaking Muslims in Yugoslavia). [. . .]

Even if Europe is conceived in its narrowest geographical confines (with the eastern frontier on the Ural mountain range and the Manych lowlands), 73 ethnic groups can be identified. These groups are of course of very different magnitudes, from several tens of thousands to a hundred million; this diversity may also be a particular factor of sociological relevance. Therefore, in our tables, an indication of the numerical strength of each nationality is added to the six characteristics. The data are based on censuses in 1970 or 1971 or estimates related to that period.

For the convenience of the reader, Europe has been divided into five geographical areas, each of which reveals a different stress on, or pattern

Table 1: *Western Europe*

	1 Territory	2 Political status	3 History	4 Culture	5 Language	6 Consciousness	7 Population in mills.
Alsatians	compact	none	unrelated	language	shared & dialect	ethnic	1.4
Basques	compact	autonomous[1]	unrelated	language	own	ethnic	0.9
Bretons	compact	none	related	language	own	ethnic	1.0
Catalans	compact	autonomous	unrelated	language	own	ethnic	6.5
Channel Islanders	compact	autonomous	related	politics	shared & dialect	ethnic & political	0.12
Corsicans	compact	none	unrelated	language	shared & dialect	ethnic	0.25
English	compact	state	related	language	own	ethnic & political	45.0
French[2]	compact	state	related	language	own	ethnic & political	50.0
Galicians	compact	none	unrelated	language	shared & own	ethnic	1.7
Irish	compact	state	related	religion	shared & own	ethnic & political	3.5[3]
Manx	compact	autonomous	related	politics	shared	political	0.06
Portuguese	compact	state	related	language	own	ethnic & political	9.0
Scots	compact	autonomous[4]	related	politics	shared[5]	ethnic & political	5.5
Spaniards	compact	state	related	language	own	ethnic & political	25.0
Welsh	compact	none	related	language	shared & own	ethnic	2.7

Notes:

1. Concerns Basques only in Spain (*c.* 0.8 million).

2. Including Occitans.

3. Including Catholics in Northern Ireland; from the ethnic point of view the *c.* one million Protestants can be considered as a particular branch of Scottish or English or combined British nationality. Their characteristics would be: territory—mixed; self-government—at present none; political history—related; culture—based primarily on religion; language—shared; consciousness—mainly based on political history coupled with religious affiliation.

4. In contrast to the Welsh, Scots are classified as an autonomous ethnic group because Scotland's union with England is based on a kind of constitutional contract which enabled Scotland to preserve a wide range of legal and cultural peculiarities and which within the common political institutions can more easily be altered than the autonomous or federated status of some ethnic groups elsewhere.

5. Gaelic being spoken by under 2 per cent of the Scottish population and not being a common Scottish issue, is not considered relevant for the identification of Scottish nationality.

Table 2: *Northern Europe*

	1 Territory	2 Political status	3 History	4 Culture	5 Language	6 Consciousness	7 Population in mills.
Danes	compact	state	related	language	own	ethnic & political	5.0
Faroese	compact	autonomous	unrelated	language	own	ethnic	0.03
Finns	compact	state	related	language	own	ethnic & political	4.3
Icelanders	compact	state	related	language	own	ethnic & political	0.2
Lapps	mixed	none	none	language	own	ethnic	0.05
Norwegians	compact	state	related	language[1]	own	ethnic & political	4.0
Swedes	compact	state	related	language	own	ethnic & political	8.0

Note:

1. Virtually two languages: the *rigsmål*, used mainly in cities, is a newly adapted Danish; the *landsmål*, used mainly in the countryside, is the old dialect adapted for literary purposes.

Table 3: *West Central and Southern Europe*

	1 Territory	2 Political status	3 History	4 Culture	5 Language	6 Consciousness	7 Population in mills.
Austrians	compact	state	continuous	political	shared	political	7.5
Belgians:							
Flemings	compact	federated	unrelated	language	shared	ethnic & political	6.0
Walloons	compact	federated	unrelated	language	shared	ethnic & political	3.0
Bruxellois[1]	compact	none	unrelated	language	shared	political	1.0
Dutch	compact	state	continuous	language	own	ethnic & political	13.0
Frisians[2]	compact	autonomous	unrelated	language	own	ethnic & political	0.6
Furlanians	compact	none[3]	unrelated	language	shared & own	ethnic	*c.* 0.5[4]
Germans[5]	compact	state	related	language	own	ethnic & political	60.0[6]
Greeks	compact	state	related	language	own[7]	ethnic & political	8.6
Italians	compact	state	related	language	own	ethnic & political	53.0
Luxembourgers	compact	state	related	political	shared & dialect	political	0.35
Maltese	compact	state	unrelated	language	own & shared	ethnic & political	0.32
Sardes (Sardinians)	compact	autonomous[8]	unrelated	language	shared & own	ethnic	1.2
Swiss:							
German (Alemannic)	compact	federated	related	language	shared & dialect	ethnic & political	4.2
French (Romand)	compact	federated	related	language	shared	ethnic & political	1.2
Italian	compact	federated	unrelated	language	shared	ethnic & political	0.8[9]
Romansh	mixed	none[10]	unrelated	language	own	ethnic & political	0.06
Turks	compact	state	related	language	own	ethnic & political	4.5[11]

Notes:

1. French-speakers in the 19 parishes of the *Agglomération* and the six parishes 'with facilities'.
2. In the Netherlands only; East and North Frisians in the Federal Republic of Germany are waning mini-ethnies of several thousand speakers only.
3. Although there is an autonomous region Friuli-Venezia Giulia, Furlanians here are outnumbered by Italian-speaking people; they are, however, allowed to use their own language when dealing with the authorities. There is also a small Slovene minority in the region.
4. Including Ladins (*c.* 20,000) living as a tiny minority in the autonomous province of Trentino-Alto Adige. The Friulian and Ladin languages are considered by some linguists as Italian dialects, by others, together with the Romansh (in Switzerland), as a separate group of Raeto-Romance languages.
5. The differentiation between subgroups identified by distinct dialects and/or autonomous regions is not considered. It is assumed that such a regional consciousness, even in the most explicit case of the Bavarians, does not break out of the general framework of the German nation with its common literary language and ethno-political consciousness.
6. Including West Berlin but excluding guest workers.
7. Virtually two languages: the modern one resulting from the spoken vernacular (*demotic*) and a rather bookish language from the official *kathareiusa* which is more in line with ancient tradition.
8. Sardinia enjoys an autonomous status as a region. The ethno-linguistic situation of Sardinia is, to say the least, ambiguous. An attempt to explain it at some length will be made in Chapter 13.
9. Including Italian guest workers.
10. In the once predominantly Romansh-speaking canton Grishun (Graubünden in German) Raetians (or Ladins as some of them call themselves) are now outnumbered by Alemannic Swiss. These, as well as the Italian-speaking minority, are provided with better educational and also cultural opportunities than the Raetians.
11. European part of Turkey (minus its non-Turkish population) plus Turkish minorities in Bulgaria, Greece and Yugoslavia.

Additional note:

Sicilians cannot, in the light of our indicators, be considered as a separate ethnic group in spite of their status of autonomy. Aostans (Valdôtiens) and German-speaking people of the South Tirol (Südtiroler) are considered as parts of French and Austrian ethnic communities respectively.

Table 4: *East Central Europe*

	1 Territory	2 Political status	3 History	4 Culture	5 Language	6 Consciousness	7 Population in mills.
Albanians	compact	state[1]	unrelated	language	own	ethnic & political	3.6[2]
Bulgarians	compact	state	related	language	own	ethnic & political	7.7
Croats	compact	federated	related	religion	shared	ethnic & political	4.5
Czechs	compact	federated	related	language	own	ethnic & political	9.6
Germans	compact	state	related	political	shared	political	16.9[3]
Gypsies	diaspora	none	none	lifestyle	own & shared	ethnic	*c.* 2.0
Hungarians	compact	state	related	language	own	ethnic & political	12.3[4]
Macedonians	compact	federated	unrelated	language	own	ethnic & political	1.2
Montenegrins	compact	federated	related	political	shared	political	0.5
Poles	compact	state	related	language	own	ethnic & political	33.0[5]
Romanians	compact	state	related	language	own	ethnic & political	18.5
Serbs	compact	federated	related	religion	shared	ethnic & political	8.4[6]
Slovaks	compact	federated	unrelated	language	own	ethnic & political	4.5
Slovenes	compact	federated	unrelated	language	own	ethnic & political	1.7
Sorbs (Lusatians)	mixed	none	unrelated	language	own	ethnic	0.07
Yugoslav Muslims[7]	mixed	autonomous[8]	unrelated	religion	shared	political[9]	1.7

Notes:

1. An autonomous region in the Serbian Republic of federal Yugoslavia.
2. Of which 1.3 million in Yugoslavia.
3. Not including about 2.7 million Germans living in the USSR and other East-Central European countries.
4. Including 2.7 million in Romania, Czechoslovakia and Yugoslavia.
5. Not including one million Poles living in the USSR.
6. Including 0.3 million who declared themselves Yugoslavs.
7. Officially recognised as a separate nationality.
8. In view of being the largest ethnic group in Bosnia-Hercegovina which is one of the six republics constituting the Yugoslav federation.
9. In the sense of being a community whose identity was created by political circumstances. Type of communal consciousness similar to that of Protestants in Northern Ireland.

General note:

Before the Second World War, however, there were more than 4 million ethnic Jews in that area. In some countries they could even declare Jewish nationality at the censuses.

Table 5: *Eastern Europe (European part of the USSR excluding the northern slope of the Caucasus)*

	1 Territory[1]	2 Political status[2]	3 History	4 Culture	5 Language	6 Consciousness	7 Population in mills.[3]
Bashkirs	mixed	autonomous	unrelated	language	own	ethnic	1.2
Belorussians	compact	federated[4]	unrelated	language	own[5]	ethnic & political	9.1
Chuvash	compact[6]	autonomous	none	language	own	ethnic	1.7
Estonians	compact	federated	unrelated	language	own	ethnic & political	1.0
Jews	diaspora	none[7]	none	religion	shared & own[8]	ethnic	2.1
Kalmyks	mixed	autonomous	none	language	own	ethnic	0.13
Karelians[9]	mixed	autonomous	none	language	own	ethnic	0.15
Komi	mixed	autonomous	none	language	own	ethnic	0.5
Latvians	compact[10]	federated	unrelated	language	own	ethnic & political	1.4
Lithuanians	compact	federated	related	language	own	ethnic & political	2.7
Mari	mixed[6]	autonomous	none	language	own	ethnic	0.6
Moldavians/Romanians	compact	federated	related	language	own	political[11]	2.8
Mordovians	mixed[6]	autonomous	none	language	own	ethnic	1.3
Russians	compact	federated	related	language	own	ethnic & political	129.0
Tatars	mixed[6]	autonomous	interrupted	language	own	ethnic	5.9
Udmurts	mixed	autonomous	none	language	own	ethnic	0.7
Ukrainians	compact[10]	federated[4]	unrelated	language	own	ethnic & political	40.7

Notes:

1. Territory is classified as mixed wherever the share of the respective ethnic group does not exceed 50 per cent of the population in the corresponding Union Republic or Autonomous Republic.

2. Entries in this column present a dilemma: the *de jure* status may not coincide with the *de facto* status. The entries in Table 4.5 refer obviously to the *de jure* status. A *de facto* entry concerning the Russians should read 'state', and some appropriate new categories would have to be coined for the Union Republics and the Autonomous Republics. (Suggestions: 'non-self-governing cultural distinctiveness' for the former, and 'marginally above none' for the latter.)

3. Figures refer to the population who in the territory of the USSR as a whole declared themselves as belonging to the particular nationality at the 1970 census. Their number may considerably differ from the population in the corresponding republics or regions.

4. Embellished by separate membership of the United Nations.

5. The Belorussian language established its identity in the sixteenth and seventeenth centuries, but became widely used for literary purposes only after 1917.

6. A significant proportion (50 per cent or more) of the ethnic group lives outside the official territory.

7. The Jewish Autonomous Region is on the Chinese border; it has barely 0.2 million population (mostly Russian); over 99.5 per cent of Soviet Jews live in the diaspora.

8. Yiddish was widely used in Central Europe from the sixteenth century, but is now found mainly in the USA and the USSR.

9. Karelian is a Finnish dialect which, for political reasons, is considered a separate language.

10. Concerns only rural areas. A separate entry 'mixed' would be appropriate for the town population.

11. The unity or duality of the ethnic consciousness of the Romanian/Moldavian pair is as debatable as that of the Germans in the FRG and the GDR. For details see Chapter 9.

Table 6: *Classification of European Nationalities (Ethnies)*[1]

SYNOPTIC TABLE

Defining characteristics	Type	West	North	West Central & South	East Central	East	Europe as a whole
Territory	compact	15	6	17	13	8	59
	mixed	—	1	1	2	8	12
	diaspora	—	—	—	1	1	2
Political status	state	5	5	8	6	—	24
	federated	—	—	5	7	7	19
	autonomous	5	1	2	1	9	18
	none	5	1	3	2	1	12
History (political)	related	10	4	9	9	4	36
	unrelated	5	2	9	6	5	27
	none	—	1	—	1	8	10
Culture	language	11	7	16	10	16	60
	religion	1	—	—	3	1	5
	political conditions	3	—	2	2	—	7
	special way of life	—	—	—	1	—	1
Language	own	7	7	7	10	16	47
	own & shared	6	—	5	1	1	13
	shared	2	—	6	5	—	13
Consciousness	political	—	—	3	3	1	7
	ethnic	8	2	2	2	10	24
	both combined	7	5	13	11	6	42
Totals		15	7	18	16	17	73
of which with less than one million population		4	3	6	2	5	20

Note:

1. Four more (Bruxellois, Galicians, Sardinians and Kalmyks) than in J. Krejci, 'Ethnic problems in Europe', in S. Giner and M. S. Archer (eds.), *Contemporary Europe, Social Structures and Cultural Patterns* (London: Routledge & Kegan Paul, 1978); Bruxellois (*Francophones*) and Walloons, though belonging to the same French linguistic community, regard themselves as ethnically distinct from each other. Galicians and Sardinians were added for ethno-linguistic reasons and their national consciousness, so far established in a rather vague way, was given the benefit of the doubt. Kalmyks were added because the geographical area of Europe under consideration was slightly enlarged. Chapter 9 deals additionally with eleven ethnic groups confined to the northern slope of the Caucasus.

of, individual defining marks and their types. These areas are (1) West; (2) North; (3) West Central and South; (4) East Central; and (5) East. The Centre is divided between the East on one side, and West and South on the other, according to the political criterion. Nationalities living in countries whose governments profess Marxism-Leninism as their state doctrine are summed up in Table 4, while Table 3 contains all the other countries of Central and Southern Europe. The East includes only nationalities whose main bodies are living in the European part of the USSR. The numbers of their population, however, refer to the USSR as a whole. Also, at this stage, we do not consider the five dwarf states (Andorra, Liechtenstein, Monaco, San Marino and Vatican City) whose combined population barely exceeds one hundred thousand.

There is, however, one important factor which the tables do not indicate: the type and magnitude of fragmented ethnic groups. These are parts (fragments) of nations detached from their main bodies in the nation states and living in states dominated by other nationalities. This special case of ethnic minorities will be considered at a later point (in Part Two, especially Chapter 6).

Table 6 gives summarised information on the regional distribution of the 73 European ethnic groups or nationalities (Germans being counted twice and Occitans lumped together with French). It shows that the most frequent types of individual characteristics are (a) the territory of compact settlement and (b) language as the basis of the culture; 59 and 60 groups have been classified in these respective categories. Religion provides the basic identification of an ethnic group *vis-à-vis* its neighbours in five cases and a special (more or less nomadic) type of life in one or two particular cases (if Lapps, who in the table are characterised by language, are included with Gypsies). In the remaining seven cases the basis for a certain cultural differentiation from the main ethnic body, with whom the language is shared, relates to political conditions, namely the existence of a separate state.

Forty-seven ethnic groups can be identified by their exclusive use of their own literary language. Thirteen ethnic groups are in a sense bi-lingual: they speak both their own special language and a language which they share with another ethnic group. Of these, in eight cases the native language is more or less a literary one, whereas in the remaining five cases it has remained at the level of a dialect. In another 13 cases both the spoken and literary language of the respective group is the same as that of kindred people in another, usually neighbouring state.

Looking at it from the political angle, in 1979 only 24 ethnic groups had a state of their own. If nationalities who share a state with other nationalities on at least formally equal terms (our category of federated status) are included, the number increases to 43; of these, however, five are branches of broader linguistic communities (Flemings, Walloons, Alemannic, Romand and Italian-speaking Swiss) with whom they share their literary language and from whom they differ almost solely because of their separate statehood.

In terms of political history the position is also variegated. Only in 36 cases can the political history before the nineteenth century be related to the respective ethnic group. In 27 cases the political history was related to a body which was virtually multinational, the unifying factor of which was usually a dynasty.

In ten cases no political history in the proper sense can be traced before the twentieth century.

National consciousness can be classified in 42 cases as based both on ethnic and political identification. In 24 cases a prevalence of ethnicity in the national consciousness can be ascertained; only in seven cases was the national consciousness primarily due to political circumstances and development. In the case of the Swiss and Belgians the ethnic aspects of consciousness are stressed in internal rather than external relationships.

Finally, we can identify in Europe two ethnic groups (Jews and Gypsies) who have, at least within the European context, no political and territorial basis (i.e. no type of self-government and no political history) and whose collective consciousness is wholly based on a particular type of culture. In the case of the Jews it is based primarily on religious tradition, in the case of Gypsies on a special, more or less nomadic, way of life.

The difference in the nature of European nationalities becomes more significant if they are scrutinised in the regional breakdown. Most political nations (identified in our tables by the political base of their culture) are in Western and Central Europe. Of the twelve ethnic groups without any status of self-government (by the mid-1980s), five are in the West, one in the North, three in West Central Europe, two in East Central Europe, and one in the East. In contrast to this, the three Western parts of Europe have a high number of ethnic groups with their own political history.

[*Ethnic and Political Nations* (London: Croom Helm, 1981), 44–6, 49–60.]

JACOB LANDAU

35 Diaspora and Language

The relevance of the language factor in determining the relations of a diaspora with its host country and its home country, respectively, is well illustrated in the case of a relatively new diaspora, the Turks in Western Europe. In contradistinction to such diasporas of migrant workers as the Spaniards, Portuguese or Italians, the Turks have been migrating to seek work in Western and Northern Europe—at least in sizable numbers which allow us to consider them a diaspora—only since the early 1960s. In Federal

Germany (on which we have to focus, due to limitations of space), the number of Turkish workers rose from 7,000 in October 1961 to 18,500 in July 1962 and reached a peak of 615,827 in mid-1974,[1] stabilizing somewhat after that. Taking into account workers' families and the fact that some have come illegally (and are not registered statistically), the magnitude of the quantitative problems is evident: close to two million Turks in Federal Germany alone. They constitute the largest contingent among foreigners there, 33 percent as compared to 14 percent Yugoslavs, 13 percent Italians, 6 percent Greeks, 5 percent Asians, 4 percent Spaniards and 25 percent other nationalities (according to the *Frankfurter Allgemeine Zeitung*, 14 May 1982). Other issues are no less relevant, as unemployment is growing in all of Western Europe which, as an urbanized, highly industrialized society, appears more prone to friction with disparate diasporas residing in its larger centers of population than a rural pre-industrialized community.

Much of the current research on the Turkish diaspora in Western Europe has focused on socio-economic issues,[2] emphasizing their labor relations, residential patterns and acculturation difficulties. The strains imposed upon relations between the government of Turkey and those of Western Europe, primarily that of Federal Germany, have been overlooked. Nevertheless, there is no doubt that the facts of life resulting from the presence of a large diaspora of Turkish workers have already affected responses to Turkey's moves to join the European Common Market; some Western European representatives have intimated that they were apprehensive of being 'flooded' by Turkish workers.[3] Tensions between the Turkish government and several others, which have left an impact on almost all official-level negotiations, are only one side of this coin. The other is individual reactions; one hears a great deal about German personal animosity towards Turkish *Gastarbeiter* and their families (expressed, sometimes, in unfunny jokes), but much less about resentment by Turkish intellectuals, mirrored in the Turkish press and probably fed by the feeling that their government is becoming increasingly dependent upon Western Europe.

Moreover, little to no mention is made of the language factor in this context. Obviously, Turkish is different from German, but so are Portuguese and Serbo-Croatian. However, the difference lies not merely in vocabulary or pronunciation, as with Portuguese and Serbo-Croatian; Turkish is also worlds apart in its syntax, which may well be the expression of a particular mentality. Turkish is an agglutinative language of the Altaic group, in which word order is disparate and word formation is achieved by the addition of numerous enclytic suffixes. This is why it is so laborious for foreigners to learn Turkish, and for Turks to acquire other languages. One could compare this with a left-handed person having to master physical skills with his right hand; it can be done and it has been done, but with tremendous efforts and with results of which one may only seldom boast. Of course, many, possibly most, educated

Turks have achieved fluency in one or more foreign languages. However, these have little representation among the *Gastarbeiter* in Western Europe, many of whom belong to the less educated middle or lower class of the unemployed in their home country. Even if prospective employers select the best of the job-seeking population, most still belong to the peasant or poorer urban groups, with serious cultural and linguistic difficulties of acculturation to their new milieu in Western Europe. The same applies to their families, except for children born abroad or those who migrated at a very early age. It has been well-documented by now that the unavoidable daily contact of Turkish children with their peers in the host country is a constant source of friction.

Hence Turkish diasporas in Western Europe maintain close ties with their home country. This is most understandable concerning Turks intending to spend only a few years in Western Europe and then return home; perhaps these do not belong essentially to a diaspora. However, even the others regularly listen to Turkey's radio broadcasts; Turkish newspapers are flown in daily in matrixes and printed locally in Federal Germany and the Netherlands; Turkish politicians campaign among them and the Turkish *Gastarbeiter* are much more concerned about Turkish than Western European politics; and their own *imams* lead them in prayer. Of particular interest is that—insofar as it can be ascertained—these patterns continue with their children, that is, in the second generation, all of whom speak Turkish at home and in the 'quarter', and many of whom study it as well. In this respect, the Turks in Europe seem to differ from other diasporas in which the second generation adapts and the third assimilates. One example of the latter kind which comes to mind is that the Syrian-Lebanese diaspora in the United States, which arrived there chiefly in the late nineteenth and early twentieth centuries. These Arabs formed a diaspora (*mahjar*, in Arabic) with its own Arabic newspapers and literature,[4] but with no meaningful political connections with their home country. Even nowadays, when the political connection of Arab diasporas with their home countries has become noticeable (chiefly since the 1975 civil war in Lebanon), they are nonetheless very low-key and moderate in scope, as is characteristic of assimilated migrants' descendants. However, one must remember that the *mahjar*'s first generation was led intellectually by such figures as Jubran Khalil Jubran and his peers. Furthermore, they were Christians and were usually acquainted with at least one foreign language, generally French or English. Also, the United States at the turn of the century was a more pluralistic society than some parts of Europe today. The special case of the Turkish diaspora in Western Europe, in the present generation, is their overall separateness from their host countries in language, culture and religion, as well as in the nature of their sojourn abroad, which some of them consider to be only temporary.

There is another difference between these two cases, even if the Turkish diaspora in Western Europe is too recent to allow us to draw a comprehensive comparison. The Turkish children of this diaspora not only speak Turkish at home, of course, but many also study it in special government-organized classes, at least in Federal Germany, where wide-scale experiments have been initiated to teach these foreign children their own language and culture. We may safely predict that both now and in the foreseeable future, the second generation will hardly adapt and will certainly not assimilate in their host countries. The children of the Arab *mahjar*, on the other hand, speedily became part of society in their adoptive host countries, particularly in the United States, since the late nineteenth century. This was largely brought about by the fact that most of the second generation—and the whole of the third—had no opportunity to study Arabic at school (barring a few exceptional cases), even if they spoke it at home. Hence the rapid adaptation and even assimilation into their host countries. Grants for the study of Arabic, offered by several of the wealthier home countries, are primarily awarded to university students and therefore have not yet changed the overall situation. The relations of Arab immigrants' descendants with their home countries were maintained, when at all, on two principal levels: sentimental (family ties) and economic (business connections). Political relations with the home countries have been generally rare and sporadic. A comprehensive examination of the Lyndon Baines Johnson archives in Austin, Texas, revealed the amazing fact that relatively little White House political lobbying on Middle East affairs was carried out by Americans of Arab extraction (the few such attempts were practically always accomplished by the same individuals). No less revealing, Arab *mahjar* fundraising for the home countries has usually been sporadic, becoming organized and institutionalized only during the last decade, when the need arose to assist financially a Lebanon ravaged by civil war.

The situation varies markedly among Greek Americans, both in their lobbying in the Cyprus case[5] and in their fundraising. The facts that Arab Americans are fewer in number than Greek Americans and that Greece is poorer than some Arab states provide only a partial explanation of these differences. While one cannot be certain of the role of the language factor in the above instances, it is nonetheless interesting to note that Greek American children seem to devote much more time than Arab American ones to the study of their home country language. According to the 1960 US Census, modern Greek was the mother tongue for 173,031 of the foreign-born. The overall figure is undoubtedly larger if one considers knowledge of Greek among those born in the United States as well. From a survey of Greek speakers in the United States, carried out at approximately the same time,[6] it emerges that the Greek Orthodox Archdiocese of North and South America operated 16 day schools in the US, in which not only were Greek language studies emphasized, but instruction in subjects like history and religion was usually conducted in Greek. Community churches also maintained about 450 afternoon schools at which Greek history and religious studies were offered in Greek. This situation is actually only one facet, albeit an important one, in a basic controversy internally dividing the Greek American community for the last sixty years. Two major trends, essentially contradictory in nature, were represented since the 1920s by the Greek-American Progressive Association (GAPA), striving for the preservation of Hellenic culture among Greek immigrants to the US and their children, and the American Hellenic Educational Progressive Association (AHEPA), campaigning for smoother and speedier Americanization. In the 1960s, GAPA comprised some 10,000 members and AHEPA about 25,000.[7] These obviously represented basically different orientations on the linguistic and cultural levels towards home country and host country, respectively. Again, perhaps it was not coincidental that GAPA, although smaller than AHEPA, was generally more active in lobbying for the interests of Greece and of Greek diasporas in Turkey and Cyprus.[8]

A parallel, although not identical, situation prevails among parts of the Greek diaspora in present-day Federal Germany; the issue of schooling Greek children has complicated relations between the two governments. Briefly stated, in the Rhine/Main area, where many Greek *Gastarbeiter* reside, two groups of parents repeat the disputes of Greeks in the US, but more bitterly so. An integration-oriented Association of Greek Parents in Frankfurt and its vicinity has been opting for the education of their children in German schools. Their main argument: many of the children will remain in the Federal Republic, hence they should be proficient in German. A more home-country oriented group of parents, Athena, wish their children to study the Greek language and culture in Greek schools. Their main argument: many Greek children will want to return home some day and a good knowledge of Greek would be extremely important for their careers there; meanwhile the authorities wish to integrate them in German schools in order to produce uneducated people for cheap labor. Thus Athena has promoted the establishment of tuition-free Greek elementary and secondary schools. In 1982, some 34,500 youngsters were enrolled in the former and another 2,500 in the latter. It is a sign of the popularity of those Greek schools that pupils have been commuting up to 50 kms daily to attend them, sometimes in overcrowded classes of up to sixty pupils, who huddle together often using outdated textbooks. The Greek *Gymnasium*, or secondary school, in Stuttgart, inaugurated in 1977, is one such example out of ten. Its 450 pupils, all Greeks, aged seventeen to eighteen, study each afternoon on three levels in 17 classrooms. The aim of all the students is to obtain the *Abitur*, the coveted graduation-diploma required for registration at a German university. Since the German universities tend to refuse to recognize the validity of the certificates of some of these schools, the Greek Consulate in Frankfurt has been drawn into the controversy. It was recalled that the Greek Government was contributing 15 million marks annually towards the upkeep of these schools. Negotiations between the two governments led nowhere; as a result, the government of Andreas Papandreou recently accorded official recognition to Greek schools abroad (including about 40 in Federal Germany), as well as the right of admission to universities in Greece. Under a previous agreement between the two states, this grants automatic admission rights to the universities of Munich and Frankfurt as well.[9]

In this context, Jewish diaspora schoolchildren should also be mentioned. This group has apparently been investigated to a greater extent than several other immigrant groups with regard to educational pursuits. Although I have been unable to find detailed overall data regarding their recent instruction in Hebrew, data are readily available about Jewish studies, which very frequently comprise some Hebrew. Recent research carried out on a world-wide basis[10] has established that 37 percent of the total of 1,325,500 Jewish children (outside Israel), aged 6–17, were enrolled in Jewish schools during the late 1970s. A breakdown of this 37 percent indicates that 13 percent were enrolled in day schools and 24 percent in part-time Jewish education; in other words, of those receiving some Jewish instruction, about one-third were enrolled in day schools and two-thirds were receiving part-time Jewish schooling. The data are heavily dominated, of course, by the figures in North America. They indicate an overall decline of almost one-third since the 1960s, which fits the general trend in many Jewish diasporas. The tantalizing questions, to which no definite answer can be offered by the present state of our knowledge are: Is there any correlation between this study of Jewish subjects and Hebrew in the various diasporas, on the one hand, and political and economic involvement in Israel's affairs, on the other? Does this study of Hebrew have any impact on the attitudes of Jewish diasporas towards their host countries? In other words, one wonders how the generation gap in this particular case affects political lobbying for, and voluntary financing of, the home country. A definite answer is particularly hazardous in this instance in that practically no Jewish diasporas (with the exception of Israeli emigrants who in 1983 numbered about 390,000 world-wide), came originally from the State of Israel—while most Italian diasporas came from Italy, and so forth—although many Jews abroad tend to consider Israel as their home country nonetheless.

['Diaspora and language', in G. Sheffer (ed.), *Modern Diasporas in International Politics* (London: Croom Helm, 1986), 87–93.]

JOHN EDWARDS

36 Symbolic Ethnicity and Language

In the first chapter I referred to the distinction between communicative and symbolic aspects of language and throughout the book I have mentioned differences between public and private manifestations of ethnicity generally. With regard to language the point is that while, ordinarily, communicative and symbolic facets co-exist, they are separable. Among mainstream populations the language of daily use is usually also the variety which carries and reflects group culture and tradition. Among minority groups, or within groups in which language shift has occurred in the reasonably recent past, the value of language as a symbol can remain in the absence of the communicative function.[1] The Irish example demonstrates a continuing attachment for a language no longer widely spoken, whose communicative revival is neither feasible nor generally desired. Eastman[2] has argued, similarly, for the notion of an 'associated' language which is connected with group identity but which is not used regularly or, indeed, known at all.[3]

Ignorance of the communicative-symbolic distinction can lead to lack of clarity and misdirected effort. If revivalists emphasise language mainly in communicative terms when mounting their campaigns, and if their appeals are directed towards groups where shift has occurred, then they: (a) will be unsuccessful in the promotion of language use; (b) may reintroduce, under the mantle of pluralism, a sort of *anomie*;[4] and (c) may promote a cynical view of any and all efforts on behalf of group identity. In 1976, for example, I described a bilingual education programme for French children in Vermont. As part of the study of the effects of this programme, parents (who spoke French) were asked to rate themselves along linguistic lines. About 55 per cent saw themselves as mainly English; another 13 per cent felt they were in some transitional period between French and English. There were other families in the programme who did not meet the criterion of speaking French at all. Yet the project had been established, by well-meaning outsiders, precisely to bolster communicative French usage. The most cursory survey of the area showed that most families were well settled—originally from Quebec, they were not new immigrants—thought of themselves as Americans and retained French for private purposes. The programme, in its ignorance, attempted to sustain a changing identity through public language use, via the children. When it ended, because of local unwillingness to pick up the financial reins from the federal funding agency, it left in its wake a cynicism which extended to all forms of active intervention in defence of identity. It seemed too, that this failure to influence a public marker of groupness actually weakened the desire for private elements—especially among the children, whose increasing lack of interest in the language transferred itself to other features of their French background.

A distinction between communicative and symbolic language mirrors a more general one between public and private ethnic markers. It is the force of the argument so far that, for practical reasons, we should expect public and non-symbolic characteristics to be relatively early casualties in assimilative or modified pluralistic contexts. Private and symbolic markers, on the other hand, continue to exist because they promote the continuation of group boundaries without hindering social mobility and access. It should be noted that *some* public markers persist for a long time; this is because they are both public *and* symbolic. Dress, ornamentation, dance, song—these may disappear as ordinary markers of group life while persisting (or re-emerging) as symbolic markers, albeit public ones. In this case, their appearance is often limited to special festivals, 'days' and the like, may be linked to commercial interests, and can become available to anyone interested, group member or not.

A very useful discussion of symbolic ethnicity, to which I have already briefly alluded, has been provided by Gans.[5] He states that the new ethnicity has not affected basic processes of acculturation and assimilation, but there *is* a new interest in 'roots'. This is not intense enough to lead to any revival, but it does give rise to renewed ethnic symbolism. This, in Gans' words, is 'an ethnicity of last resort, which could, nevertheless, persist for generations' (p. 1). Ultimately, however, even this will disappear, according to Gans. Consequently, there has been no essential disruption of so-called 'straight-line theory', i.e. that which predicts the gradual absorption of minorities. However, because of upward mobility, ethnic groups have become more visible and have adopted ethnic symbols; this has led to attention from 'journalists and essayists' who have been largely responsible for propounding the idea of an 'ethnic revival'.[6] All of this implies that Hansen's[7] famous notion of the third-generation 'return' to ethnicity is, if true, essentially limited to symbolic manifestations, e.g. the returning grandsons do not often want to learn the ancestral language.[8]

If symbolic ethnicity and private markers are the aspects which remain, it follows that active intervention on behalf of minority identity may be non-productive or, indeed, counter-productive. There is no evidence to suggest that meaningful aspects of ethnicity can be held in place for any reasonable length of time by such action, much less the ones that are usually dealt with (like language), which are visible and public markers highly susceptible to change. It is instructive here to consider that Greeley—clearly in favour of ethnic persistence—acknowledges that the 'core of ethnic residue' endures precisely because 'little if any self-consciousness about ethnic heritage is required and because behavior patterns are intimate and interpersonal',[9] that residual characteristics remain because they do not evoke social penalty, and that groups 'will rather quickly relinquish ethnic characteristics that are an obstacle to American achievement'.[10]

It can of course be argued that a trade-off between public and private, symbolic and non-symbolic ethnicity is bad if all that remains to a group is some symbolic 'residue'. Thus Smolicz[11] observes that 'residual ethnicity obscures the fact of ethnic cultural degeneration... ethnic culture gets steadily shallower'. But is change degeneration? Does Smolicz bewail the inevitable? The force of history suggests simply that the transition to residual ethnicity occurs widely and that it is not a phenomenon fought against by most ordinary group members. Retention of public, visible markers is unlikely, with or without official support and encouragement, given the social realities bearing upon majority–minority relations—except, of course, where group segregation is preferred (rare) or enforced (indefensible).

[*Language, Society and Identity* (Oxford: Basil Blackwell, 1985), 110–13.]

LEROY VAIL

37 The Creation of Ethnicity in South Africa

The creation of ethnicity as an ideological statement of popular appeal in the context of profound social, economic and political change in southern Africa was the result of the differential conjunction of various historical forces and phenomena. It is the very unevenness of their co-appearance and dynamic interaction that accounts for the unevenness of ethnic consciousness in the region. One may discern three such variables in the creation and implanting of the ethnic message. First, as was the case in the creation of such ideologies elsewhere, for example in nineteenth century European nationalism, it was essential to have a group of intellectuals involved in formulating it—a group of culture brokers. Second, there was the widespread use of African intermediaries to administer the subordinate peoples, a system usually summed up in the phrase 'indirect rule', and this served to define the boundaries and texture of the new ideologies. Third, ordinary people had a real need for so-called 'traditional values' at a time of rapid social change, thus opening the way for the wide acceptance of the new ideologies.

What emerges perhaps most clearly from these studies is the fact that intellectuals carefully crafted their ethnic ideologies in order to define the cultural characteristics of members of various ethnic groups. These intellectuals could be European missionaries, as the studies by Harries, Ranger, Vail and White, and Roberts make clear. Or, as Harries, Vail and White, Jewsiewicki and Papstein show, they could be European anthropologists and historians. And, in all cases in this volume, local intellectuals—whether Afrikaner, 'coloured' or African—were intimately involved in the process and, where it was possible, they were ready to work hand in hand with their European counterparts.

The role of missionaries was especially crucial in at least one—and sometimes all—of three ways, and it is evident that their influence upon the development of African history in the twentieth century has been far greater than they have been given credit for over the past two decades. First, missionaries themselves were often instrumental in providing the cultural symbols that could be organized into a cultural identity, especially a written language and a researched written history. Samuel Johnson long ago recognized that 'languages are the pedigree of nations', and missionaries accepted this dictum wholeheartedly. They had the skills to reduce hitherto unwritten languages to written forms, thereby delivering the pedigrees that the new 'tribes' required for acceptance. Again and again, in the chapters by Giliomee, Butler, Harries, Ranger, Vail and White, and Penvenne, to mention only some, language stands as the central item in the assemblage of a cultural package. Where these languages have been African languages, it was the missionaries who chose what the 'proper' form of the language would be, thus serving both to further unity and to produce divisions by establishing firm boundaries.[1]

In addition to creating written languages, missionaries were instrumental in creating cultural identities through their specification of 'custom' and 'tradition' and by writing 'tribal' histories, a process discussed in the chapters by Ranger, Vail and White, and Jewsiewicki. Once these elements of culture were in place and available to be used as the cultural base of a distinct new, ascriptive ethnic identity, it could replace older organizing principles that depended upon voluntary clientage and loyalty and which, as such, showed great plasticity. Thus firm, non-porous and relatively inelastic ethnic boundaries, many of which were highly arbitrary, came to be constructed and were then strengthened by the growth of stereotypes of 'the other', as the essays by Siegel and Papstein show.

Second, and of considerable practical importance, European missionaries, assuming that Africans properly belonged to 'tribes', incorporated into the curricula of their mission schools the lesson that the pupils had clear ethnic identities, backing up this lesson with studies of language and 'tribal custom' in the vernacular. The importance of such education is made clear in the chapters by Ranger, Vail and White, and Jewsiewicki. Thus, mission education socialized the young into accepting a tribal membership, and to be a member of a 'tribe' became 'modern' and fashionable through its close association with education.

Third, and finally, missionaries educated local Africans who then themselves served as the most important force in shaping the new ethnic ideologies. These people—usually men—were keenly aware of the forces that were pulling apart their societies and, with the examples of nationalism in Europe derived from their own mission education before them, they sought to craft similar local movements as a means of countering these problems. Despite their own western-style education, they realized that such a construct would best be understood and accepted if it were put in a cultural idiom easily accessible to the people. Thus, in formulating their new ideologies, they looked to the local area's past for possible raw material for their new intellectual bricolage.[2] Like their European predecessors during the initial stages of nineteenth century nationalism, they 'rediscovered' the 'true values' of their people and so defined the 'ethnic soul'. Their cultural strongbox was the 'customs' and 'traditions' of the people, identification with which they saw as giving an automatic, ascriptive cultural unity to 'their' people as they confronted the challenge of colonialism and the impact of industrialization. Virtually every study in this volume demonstrates the role of educated people as key actors in the creation of such ideology.

In those societies where missionaries did not work, or where they did work but did not introduce education along western lines, or where African intellectuals emerged only at a late period or not at all, the development of ethnic ideologies was either stalled or never occurred. The unevenness of education in southern Africa largely determined the unevenness of the development of ethnic consciousness, as is brought out in the essays by Vail and White, Macmillan, Siegel, and Papstein. In many locales it is only today, after the post-independence expansion of education and the emergence of local intellectuals, that the process of creating such ethnic ideologies and 'forging traditions' has emulated what happened earlier in other societies.

It was not sufficient, however, that there should be local intellectuals—white or black—interested in the recovery of the ethnic past. A second, more instrumental factor was also required, and this is explored most fully in the chapters by Harries, Vail and White, Marks, Jewsiewicki, and Papstein. All of southern Africa was under direct European administration of various types, and by the period after World War I, virtually all administrations were engaged in implementing systems of indirect rule, using African 'traditional' authorities as intermediaries between the white administration and the ruled. Thus, if language in the form of written discourse was central in specifying the forms of culture, indirect rule provided the institutional framework for articulating these forms. Communication between the European administrators and subordinate Africans was distinctly tribal in its tone and content. Africans were talked to in terms deemed suitable, and these terms were ethnic. In the cases of the 'Cape Coloureds' and the Luso-Africans of Mozambique, and, to some extent, the Afrikaners, for whom the conventions of indirect rule were not suitable, they were simply denied representation, as the studies by Goldin, Penvenne, Giliomee and Butler indicate.

There were several reasons for the European policy of indirect rule. First, there was the realization that the use of so-called 'traditional' African leaders could be markedly less expensive than the employment of expensive European officials. Second, administrators assumed that Africans were naturally 'tribal' people. If the natural ethnic units could be strengthened, it would help ensure their continuation as discrete 'tribal' groups and prevent the emergence of 'detribalized' Africans of whom whites were deeply suspicious. This, in turn, would slow the emergence of any potentially dangerous territory-wide political consciousness that might develop. The remarks of a British War Office official in 1917 reflect these divide-and-rule tactics:

> [The] spirit of nationality, or perhaps it would be more correct to say, of tribe, should be cultivated and nowhere can this be done with better chance of success than in British East Africa and Uganda, where there are numerous tribes ethnographically quite distinct from one another. It is suggested that in each ethnographically distinct district the schools should, as far as possible, form integral parts of the tribe and centres of folk-lore and tradition. . . .
>
> . . . a method may also be found whereby the efforts of missionaries may also assist in the cultivation of national spirit. This it seems might be done by allowing only one denomination to work in each demographic area and by not allowing the same denomination to work in two adjacent areas.[3]

Third, by the end of World War I it was becoming increasingly evident that the chronic absence of men from rural societies was producing great social stresses. The administrators became convinced that the rural disintegration occurring before their eyes could be slowed, if not stopped, by the encouragement of 'traditional authorities' to use 'traditional sanctions' in exercising control over the rural areas to counter the forces of social decay.

This acceptance of indirect rule by European administrations obviously gave opportunities to African political authorities to augment their personal power. More importantly, I suggest, it gave opportunities to the intellectuals of the areas concerned—both European missionaries and African members of the educated petty bourgeoisie—to implement their ideological programmes through alliances with the newly recognized chiefs. This process is a theme of several essays in this volume, including those by Vail and White, Marks, Jewsiewicki and Papstein. In this way the cultural ideals contained in their new ideologies could be at least partially actualized in the day-to-day workings of African administrations under indirect rule. Ethnic identity, thus, came to be specified not only by the written histories, grammars, and accounts of 'traditional customs' produced by local culture brokers, but also—and in many respects, far more importantly—by the actual operation of the administrative mechanisms of indirect rule. This aspect of the development of ethnic identity was the consequence of the dynamic interaction of African initiative with the expectations of European administrators and forward-looking missionaries. It should be remembered, however, that the subordinate peoples did not have a free hand in their work as they had to operate within the severe constraints imposed by racist administrators who were ever alert to check initiatives deemed either unseemly or dangerous, something brought out clearly in the chapters by Marks, Macmillan, Jewsiewicki and Siegel, among others.

The presence of intellectuals, the socialization of ethnic ideas through mission schools and through the actual operation of administrative systems under indirect rule to strengthen 'tribal' rule were, however, by themselves inadequate to produce a broad acceptance of an ethnic ideology. The ideology itself needed a *raison d'être* and an appeal, and it was this appeal that constitutes the third factor in our model of the growth of ethnicity in southern Africa.

The ideologies of nationalism have often been described as 'Janus-like'. They are in one aspect profoundly reactionary, looking backwards to a Golden Past: they concentrate upon its heroes, its historical successes, and its unsullied cultural purity, and are decked out with the mythic 'rediscovered' social values of that past. In Africa, the explicit association of such ethnic ideologies with chiefs and headmen whose position was often firmly rooted in the past was an additional factor in accentuating the backward-looking face of ethnicity. Yet these ideologies were also clearly products of the present, concerned with current conditions, and they typically exhibited a forward-looking concern for the future. Nationalism—and tribalism—have thus appeared uncertain and ambiguous to many observers.

Yet when one looks closely at the situation in southern Africa, one comes to realize that the ethnic message's backward-looking aspects and its forward-looking concerns have been in no way contradictory. The emphases on past values, 'rediscovered' traditions, and chiefly authority were truly conservative—that is, they were calculated to conserve a way of life that was in the process of being rapidly undermined by the forces of capitalism and colonialism. Forward-looking members of the petty bourgeoisie and migrant workers alike attempted to shore up their societies and their own positions in them by embracing ethnicity and accepting tribal identities.

As the chapters by Vail and White, Marks, and Jewsiewicki show, ethnicity appealed to the petty bourgeoisie because its forward-looking aspects ensured them a leadership role in the newly defined 'tribe' as the well-informed interpreters of 'tribal tradition'. Their position as allies of chiefs further legitimized their role, blunting consciousness of the class divisions that were then appearing in local societies. In this situation, it was generally accepted that they also had a duty to improve their own social and economic positions 'for the good of the tribe'.

Far more importantly, ethnicity appealed strongly to ordinary African men, not primarily because it gave them a sense of psychological comfort, as the primordialist interpretation argues, but because it aided them in bringing a measure of control to the difficult situations in which they found themselves in their day-to-day life. The word 'control' is crucial. It was the element of control embedded in tribal ideologies that especially appealed to migrant workers, removed from their land and families and working in far distant places. The new ideologies stressed the historical integrity of the tribe and its land and, especially, the sanctity of the family and its right to land.[4] Land stood at the very centre of ethnic ideologies.

The place of women was also a central issue dealt with in ethnic ideologies. In the early decades of the century bridewealth steadily inflated in value, and women thus represented a greater 'investment' by men in cattle or money. With most men absent as migrant labourers, women were also becoming more important to the day-to-day survival of the family through their work on the land. Yet such valuable women naturally often sought to act independently, even to the extent of seeking divorces or leaving the rural areas illegally to move to industrial and urban areas. This produced acute conflict between the genders. Therefore an emphasis on the need to control women and a stress on the protection of the integrity of the family came to be intrinsic to both ethnic ideologies and the actual institutional practices of indirect rule. The studies by Vail and White, Marks, and Jewsiewicki show this with special clarity. Ethnicity's appeal was strongest for men, then, and the Tswana proverb to the effect that 'women have no tribe' had a real—if unintended—element of truth in it.

Ethnic ideologies helped to provide the control necessary to minimize migrants' natural anxieties about what occurred at home. In the system of indirect rule, the chiefs were of central importance. It was they, with their new official histories, their new censuses and lists, their new courts and records, all of which employed for the first time that most fundamentally powerful invention, writing, who were now able to exercise a greatly increased degree of surveillance over both women and land in the absence of the men. It was they who brought into daily practice those 'rediscovered traditions' which emphasized control in the name of 'custom'. The old dictum that 'all politics is local' was especially valid throughout southern Africa. African men and their lineages accepted that it was in their essential interest to support the new structures of chiefs, their courts, and their educated petty bourgeois spokesmen and agents. It was also for this reason that men, when returning at the end of their contracts from the mines or farms or plantations, gave chiefs the gifts that constituted one of their most important sources of income. The good chief was a proxy who protected the interests of the migrant workers and, for that, they were ready—if not eager—to reward him materially. In effect, the bureaucratized chief of the newly constituted 'tribe' had replaced the lineage head or independent patron of earlier times, and the old language of kinship came to be employed as metaphor to sustain and legitimize this new, obviously non-kinship relationship.[5]

It was for very real reasons of exercising at least a measure of control over land and women, thereby bringing at least a measure of peace to their minds, that African men welcomed the new ethnic ideologies which involved augmenting powers of chiefs in a situation of rapid social decay. Ethnicity, insofar as it was a mechanism of such control, may be interpreted, then, as a form of popular male resistance to the forces that were reshaping African lives throughout southern Africa. It was for this reason also that the appeal of ethnic ideologies was strongest amongst those who were migrant labourers. The ethnic identity that was rooted in the realities of the countryside was, rather incidentally, strengthened in the workplace, where migrants found themselves in the company of, and often in competition with, workers from other cultural groups, a situation which generated sets of largely negative ethnic stereotypes and is explored in the chapters by Jewsiewicki, Siegel and Papstein.

Men came to think of themselves as belonging to particular ethnic groups, then, not because they especially disliked their fellow workers, nor because being a member of the group made them feel good, but rather because the ethnic apparatus of the rural area—the chiefs, 'traditional' courts, petty bourgeois intellectuals, and the systematized 'traditional' values of the 'tribe' as embodied in the ethnic ideology—all worked to preserve the very substantial interests which these men had in their home areas. Without ethnicity—or tribalism—the migrants would have been less able to exercise the control that was necessary for them to assure the continuation of their positions in rural societies and their ultimate retirement in their home areas.

In those situations in which labour migrancy was not a pressing reality (the Afrikaners, the 'Cape Coloureds', the Luso-Africans of Mozambique and, to a lesser extent, contemporary Swaziland and Ciskei—see Giliomee, Butler, Goldin, Penvenne, Macmillan and Anonymous, respectively) or in areas from which men did not emigrate in large numbers, such as southern Zambia and central Malawi, the ethnic message has clearly had less popular appeal, reaching no further than the petty bourgeoisie in most cases. In the case of the Afrikaners effective class alliances between the bourgeois elements of society and the 'poor whites' were brought into being only in the 1940s and afterwards. In the case of the 'Cape Coloureds' and the Mozambican Luso-Africans—and possibly Swaziland and the Ciskei—the gaps between well-off and poor were too great to be 'easily overcome by appeals to ethnicity, as is suggested in the chapters by Goldin, Penvenne, Macmillan and Anonymous. In these situations, class identity—or at least class tension—has tended to overshadow ethnicity.

[*The Creation of Tribalism in Southern Africa* (London: James Curry Ltd. and Berkeley: University of California Press, 1993), 11–16.]

Section VI

Race and Ethnicity

INTRODUCTION

The study of the interrelations of race and ethnicity has inspired a vast literature, which lies outside the scope of this Reader. However, given the importance of this topic-area, we have included a few readings which reveal the overlapping nature of the two concepts and their empirical referents.

The concept of a 'plural society' has provided a major point of departure in the study of ethnic and race relations. Initially developed for the study of colonial societies in South-East Asia by J. S. Furnivall, it was reformulated by M. G. Smith, who distinguishes between culturally homogeneous societies with normative integration and societies deeply divided along ethnic and cultural lines and held together mainly by coercion. In plural societies the ethnic and cultural segments are institutionally separated and incorporated differentially and unequally into the national state. Since the Second World War overseas immigrants have experienced varying degrees of unequal incorporation in western societies. John Rex describes the reception of immigrants from the Caribbean, Algeria, Turkey, and South Asia, and discusses attempts to integrate them through policies of multiculturalism which combine a commitment to racial equality and justice with a respect for cultural diversity.

The concept of 'race' is not, as has been thought, exclusively European or wholly modern. Frank Dikötter shows that in imperial, as well as modern, China national identity has been strongly infused with racial ideas that have long accorded superiority to Han Chinese. Later, western racist ideas reinforced this sense of Han superiority and underpinned the world-view of communist China. In Africa, as Immanuel Geiss's analysis of Pan-Africanism reveals, intellectuals oscillated between cultural, continental, and racial-biological definitions of the African within an anti-colonialist framework. Geiss links the Pan-African movement with other 'Pan-' movements like Pan-Slavism, which distinguish groups of peoples on ethnic and cultural grounds, with important political consequences.

In nineteenth-century Europe the confusion of language, ethnicity, and race spawned the dubious concept of an 'Aryan race', which sought to undermine both Christian and Enlightenment ideas of a universal humanity. But, as Leon Poliakov shows, the roots of this denial are to be found in the polygenetic conceptions of some Enlightenment thinkers themselves, and this in turn allowed anti-Semitic and racist ideas to achieve pseudo-scientific status. In the twentieth century these ideas found fertile soil in the structural conditions of plural societies all over the world. Leo Kuper describes in vivid detail the genocidal effects of this confluence of ideas and plural structures, especially in decolonizing societies like Algeria, Rwanda, and India. The climax of this process was reached in twentieth-century Armenia and Nazi Europe, where large-scale instability resulted in the stigmatization and premeditated murder of whole peoples. Scholars continue to debate the causes of genocide, but a crucial factor, Fein argues, is the rise of new élites within declining states for whom minorities are outside the universe of moral obligations.

38 The Plural Society

Pluralism is a condition in which members of a common society are internally distinguished by fundamental differences in their institutional practice. Where present, such differences are not distributed at random; they normally cluster, and by their clusters they simultaneously identify institutionally distinct aggregates or groups, and establish deep social divisions between them. The prevalence of such systematic disassociation between the members of institutionally distinct collectivities within a single society constitutes pluralism. Thus pluralism simultaneously connotes a social structure characterized by fundamental discontinuities and cleavages, and a cultural complex based on systematic institutional diversity. In this paper I try to isolate the minimal conditions essential and sufficient to constitute pluralism. I try also to show how such conditions generate and sustain social cleavages that distinguish pluralities, while other combinations of institutional and social differences differ in their structural expression. Having summarily indicated some of the principal forms that social pluralism may take, I review briefly the modes and conditions by which it may be stabilized or transformed.

Pluralism may be defined with equal cogency and precision in institutional or in political terms. Politically these features have very distinctive forms and conditions, and in their most extreme state, the plural society, they constitute a polity of peculiar though variable type. Specific political features of social pluralism center in the corporate constitution of the total society. Under these conditions the basic corporate divisions within the society usually coincide with the lines of institutional cleavage, reinforcing and generally converting them into deep and rigid inequalities in social and political life. The enforcement and maintenance of these corporate divisions and inequalities are then normally identified with the preservation of social order and stability. Any modification in the political and social relations between these corporate divisions involves corresponding changes in the conditions of social structure. To seek out the conditions essential for this coincidence of corporate boundaries and institutional discontinuity, we have therefore to discover the minimal degrees and forms of institutional divergence which are required to facilitate, promote, or enjoin the sectional closures that plural polity incorporates; and conversely, we need to inquire how various alternative forms of corporate organization may establish, preserve, or foster institutional differentiation, or reduce or deny its public significance, while permitting its persistence or dissolution equally. In effect, we need first to determine the circumstances and ways in which these modes of corporate organization and institutional differentiation interact to support, reinforce, dislocate, or modify one another, and then to identify the conditions requisite for their stabilization or transformation.

To analyze the institutional and political conditions of pluralism, it is first necessary to distinguish pluralism from its principal alternatives, and to indicate how its variable range governs its structural significance.

Since institutions are collective modes of action, organization, and orientation, both normative and cognitive, institutional differentiation correspondingly distinguishes collectivities that differ in organization, standardized procedures, norms, beliefs, ideals, and expectations. Quite commonly, all the members of a distinct society share an identical system of institutions. The boundaries of such societies are defined by the maximum span of the institutional system on which their social organization and cohesion are based. Such conditions of institutional homogeneity, which are characteristic of simple societies, represent the polar opposite of the systematic institutional diversity that constitutes pluralism.

Many societies, including the most highly developed industrial societies, seem to stand midway between these extremes. In these societies the entire population, or at least the overwhelming majority, share a common system of basic institutions, while being systematically differentiated at the secondary level of institutional organization in which alternative occupational, political, and religious or ethnic structures predominate. Societies with this combination of common and exclusive institutional affiliations are properly distinguished by their pervasive heterogeneity from the conditions of homogeneity and pluralism already described. These types of societies differ significantly in structure, complexity, modes of integration, and in their capacities for self-generated development. Though institutional homogeneity and high levels of organizational complexity are mutually exclusive, and no industrial society is ever institutionally homogeneous, social heterogeneity or pluralism is equally consistent with industrial or preindustrial levels of economic and technological organization. Thus the institutional classification is independent of economic or technological criteria.

The most extreme and politically significant expression of pluralism is to be found in the 'plural society,' as J. S. Furnivall appropriately labeled internally autonomous and inclusive political units ruled by institutionally distinct numerical minorities.[1] The subjugated majority of the population in a plural society may or may not share a single common system of institutions; often the people are internally subdivided by their differing institutional allegiances; but in all cases they simultaneously differ in their political status and in their institutional practice and organization from the discrete minority who rule them. In their colonial phase, all recently independent African states were plural societies;[2] and despite independence, most of these ex-colonies retain their plural character with marginal alteration. Thus pluralism and colonialism are not homologous. Colonialism is merely one mode of pluralism, characteristically instituted in the form of a plural society. However, pluralism is by no means confined to plural societies, although it is in those units that it has its purest expression and most profound effects.

One of the major problems that faces emergent nations with a recent colonial past consists in effecting the transition from pluralism to the heterogeneity requisite for their transformation into cohesive national units. Such transformations have not yet occurred in several Latin-American societies, despite relatively long histories of independence. Of European states that faced a similar predicament at an earlier date, we need merely mention Spain, Portugal, Russia, Germany, and France to indicate the various difficulties, processes, and outcomes involved. One of our concerns in this paper is to detect as best we can the most general conditions requisite for those processes of societal transformation and enhanced political integration on which 'modernization' directly depends.

A society is a self-sufficient, self-perpetuating, and internally autonomous system of social relations. Such a system distinguishes a population occupying a specific territory; but as a system of social relations, the society is clearly distinct from territory or population. The society is the structure of relations through which the population of members is internally organized as joint occupants of a given area. Changes in population mass or composition, or more obviously in territory, do not themselves directly constitute changes in the social system, although they undoubtedly affect it in many ways. It is with differences in the systems of social relations which constitute societies that the distinctions between pluralism, homogeneity, and heterogeneity are directly concerned.

Social relations are either institutionalized or optional in their base, individual or collective in their form. The range and conditions that govern optional relations at both the individual and collective levels are themselves institutionally prescribed and regulated. Thus the inclusive autonomous system of social relations which constitutes a society is directly or indirectly institutionalized. If the members of the society share a common system of institutions, then they will also share a common framework and pattern of social relations; and their internal differentiation by corporate and personal status will be governed by uniform criteria and principles. If the aggregate is institutionally heterogeneous in its base, then the system of institutionalized relations in which its society consists will be correspondingly heterogeneous in character and form. In consequence, members will differ in the significance they attach to those criteria and principles that regulate their corporate and personal identity and status placement. If the society consists of collectivities divided by fundamental institutional differences, then, within the corresponding corporate divisions whose interrelations constitute the societal level of organization and integration, there will be corresponding diversity of institutionalized relations. In such conditions, members of differing social sections occupy significantly differing positions in relations with one another. In consequence, societies with homogeneous, heterogeneous, and plural institutional systems differ correspondingly in character and structure.

['Institutional and political conditions of pluralism', in Leo Kuper and M. G. Smith (eds.), *Pluralism in Africa* (Los Angeles: University of California Press, 1969), 27–30.]

JOHN REX

39 Multiculturalism in Europe

After 1945 the economically successful countries of Western Europe faced shortages of unskilled labour as well as offering niches for entrepreneurs in areas of business which indigenous entrepreneurs were unwilling to occupy. They also needed professional skills which had to be provided from outside. Professional migrants were, however, not thought of as problematic in their countries of settlement, representing more of a problem to their sending societies, which saw themselves as suffering a brain drain. The main problem groups in the countries of settlement, therefore, were seen to be the largely unskilled immigrant groups and 'pariah' traders.

The different West European countries drew their immigrants from different countries and received different kinds of immigrants according to their historic circumstances. The United Kingdom drew upon Ireland, and then, primarily on former colonial territories in the Caribbean, the Indian subcontinent, East Africa and the Mediterranean. France turned to southern European countries, particularly to Portugal, and to its former colonial territories in the Maghreb and in more distant overseas departments and former colonies, including the Caribbean, Africa and the Far East. Germany, having no former empire to turn to, recruited guest workers from Southern Europe and from Turkey. The Netherlands faced a variety of immigrant problems, including those of returning settlers and their allies from Indonesia, those of migrants with Dutch citizenship from Surinam and the Antilles, and those of Turkish and Moroccan guest workers. Belgium recruited Italians and then Moroccans. Sweden, already having large numbers of Finns, also began to recruit in the same labour markets as the other North Western European countries. Additionally, all of these countries attracted a variety of asylum seekers and others fleeing from conditions of political disorder.

Obviously there is great variety in these patterns of migration and this summary statement also clearly excludes a number of smaller immigrant minority groups in each of the countries concerned. There are clearly dangers, therefore, in any attempt to make a generalisation about all immigrant problems. What is clear, however, is that there were certain patterns in the way in which these countries defined the 'immigrant problem'. The United Kingdom was preoccupied with questions of colour: the term immigrant was used as a social construction referring primarily to darkskinned people from the Caribbean, Asia and Africa, although, so far as South Asians were concerned, there were also problems of cultural and religious difference within this category. France became increasingly concerned with its Algerian immigrants and with what was often seen as the 'threat' of Islamic identities. In Germany anxieties were focused on Turkish guest workers, who were not necessarily thought of primarily as Muslims, but simply as temporary residents. In the Netherlands there was less colour consciousness than in the United Kingdom, making it possible to assimilate the Surinamese more easily than was the case with British West Indians, but, increasingly, as can be seen from the Report of the Netherlands Scientific Council for Government Policy, entitled *Immigrant Policy* (1990), the focus of attention was on the third of the immigrant population from Morocco and Turkey.

Of course, it can and should be argued that any intelligent policy towards immigrant settlement would have needed to take account, one by one, of the problems of, and those presented by, each separate immigrant group. Nonetheless it was clear that two related but separate problems had to be dealt with in every case. One was the question of political, social and economic inequality. The other was the accommodation of cultural difference.

The relatively straightforward problem of inequality was dealt with in different ways in the different countries and in different policy traditions. Where there was a guest worker policy there could, by definition, be no political equality, though it was still possible for governments and political organisations to argue about the ways in which non-citizens could have equal social rights. Where immigrants had citizenship rights, on the other hand, the primary focus of the debate about equality had to be on combating racial and ethnic discrimination.

This latter situation was most clearly evident in the United Kingdom, which, recognizing the similarities between the problems of its Caribbean immigrants and those of blacks in the United States, set up relatively elaborate institutions concerned with bringing about 'racial' equality. While such institutions were often appropriate for dealing with black Caribbean migrants whose situation paralleled that of black Americans, they were extended in Britain to deal with the problems of South Asians, whose migration often had a different trajectory and whose problems were primarily those of cultural rather than racial difference. Not surprisingly there was some objection on the part of Asians to having their problems dealt with in this way[1] and, when it was suggested that similar institutions should be set up in continental Europe, European social scientists pointed out that the British concentration on 'racial' equality was not really relevant to their problems.[2] Generally, they did no more than try to combat discrimination through the normal courts.

A further feature of the situation in continental Europe was an unwillingness to use the term 'race', which was widely thought to be disreputable after the experience of Nazism. Problems of inequality were often referred to as the inequality of ethnic rather than racial groups, though, paradoxically, their inequality was often explained in terms of the 'racism' of majority groups. In the United Kingdom, too, the Marxist sociologist R. Miles[3] argued forcefully that the focus of attention should be on racism rather than race relations and his view was widely shared by many non-Marxists.[4]

Concern about equal treatment of the members of minority groups was shared by those influenced primarily by French republican ideas,[5] and by socialists and social democrats committed to the ideals of the welfare state.[6] These traditions were, however, silent on the question of how far cultural difference should be tolerated or encouraged. Indeed, the likelihood was that any tradition which based itself upon the notion of equality would be cautious about the recognition of cultural differences, which might become markers for inequality. The problem facing those who campaign for multiculturalism was therefore to show that the recognition of cultural diversity was compatible with and did not undermine, those institutions which were concerned with guaranteeing equality between individuals and classes.

I have, myself, argued for an ideal concept of egalitarian multiculturalism which deals with both of these questions.[7] In doing this, I have found it useful to base the concept on a 1968 statement by the British home secretary in which he defined 'integration' as involving 'not a flattening process of uniformity', but 'cultural diversity, coupled with equal opportunity, in an atmosphere of mutual tolerance'.[8] I have suggested that this statement involves the simultaneous recognition of two cultural domains, one a shared political culture of the public domain, centring around the idea of equality, the other that of a number of separate cultures in the private or communal domain, involving shared language, religion, customs and family practices.

What this concept of egalitarian multiculturalism seeks to avoid above all is the sort of situation imagined by left-wing critics of multicultural policies. What they argue is that multiculturalism has usually been simply a rhetoric which disguises inequality and ghettoisation, or a means of marking groups as minorities so that they can be controlled, manipulated or subjected to unequal treatment.[9] I agree with these critics that what has usually passed as multiculturalism does have these characteristics,[10] but this by no means brings into question the *ideal* which I have proposed. It is possible to combine the recognition of cultural diversity with a fight for individual equality, and I would argue that it is only if it does this that any concept of multiculturalism is acceptable in a democratic society.

It may still be asked why cultural diversity should be encouraged if individuals are in any case offered all the gains and benefits of equality in a modern democratic society. In answering this question I have given three reasons:[11] the first is what I call the Durkheimian one, namely that some kind of intermediate group between the individual family and the state is necessary to provide the individual with moral and emotional support and to prevent a situation of anomie;[12] the second is that individuals need the networks and cultural ideals which their group offers if they are to have the solidarity which is necessary in their fight for equal rights, and that it is this solidarity deriving from ethnic mobilisation, rather than the benign behaviour of governments, which can act as a guarantee of equality; the third is based on the utilitarian argument that we do not know whether new cultures may not have some objective validity, and that the possible gains of recognising them outweigh any possible dangers.

There is, of course, a danger in reifying minority cultures and I do not want to suggest that they should be recognised in unchanging traditional forms, but I know of no ethnic minority culture which has this form. What strikes me about them is that they themselves are a response to circumstances and that, while they are always in some measure concerned with maintaining cultural forms for the reasons given in the previous paragraph, they are also shaped by their experience as individual members of a minority group engaged in the struggle to achieve equality. What we may say happens is that as a result of their struggles for equality the civic culture becomes part of the minority culture.

A further point to be made here is that ethnic minority communities do not simply act on their own. They enter societies in which other disadvantaged groups are engaged in the struggle for equality and they must necessarily interact and form alliances with these groups. Indeed, within an established class and party system, they cannot act without the aid of these groups. What they have to counter, however, is the process of what Parkin[13] calls 'double closure'. This is what happens when an indigenous group fighting for equality and having made gains for itself, seeks to exclude others from benefiting from those gains. In joining in class struggles immigrant minorities have to form parties within parties and unions within unions to ensure that their interests are defended.

One other realistic point has to be made in reviewing European experience in dealing with the question of multiculturalism. This is that the indigenous majority culture cannot be seen simply as one amongst a number of cultures. Nor should it even be argued that this culture will inevitably be modified through absorbing into itself bits and pieces of new minority cultures. There are, of course, superficial elements of minority cultures, like those concerned with cuisine, which do affect the majority culture, but they are unlikely to transform it fundamentally, and there are many cultural and institutional features of the societies in which immigrants settle which they will, therefore, have to accept as providing the framework in which they now have to live their lives. *Inter alia*, these include the official language of the society, its economic institutions and its criminal and civil laws. Accepting these and living within their constraints is the price which immigrants have to pay, and are usually willing to pay, for the advantages of immigration. On the other hand, I believe that it is to be expected that immigrant minorities will make their contribution to a developing national culture through their campaigns against injustice and through their own 'high', literary, or aesthetic cultures.

Finally, I should like to make clear what the egalitarian ideal of multi-culturalism means when it uses the term 'integration'. It does not simply mean proportionate representation in educational and economic institutions, as the recent Dutch report referred to above appears to imply. Nor does it simply mean legal citizenship. For my own part, I would draw on another idea from Durkheim's *Division of Labour*. This is Durkheim's argument that a modern society based upon organic solidarity must have a moral basis. In criticising Spencer's view of economic exchange, he writes 'the image of the one who completes us becomes inseparable from ours... It thus becomes an integral and permanent part of our conscience....'.[14] Similarly, I would argue that, quite apart from the warm moral and emotional support which groups provide for their members, the nature of the relationships between minority groups and national societies on the political level must itself be moral. The individuals who negotiate with one another do not simply have an external relation with each other; they become united in their consciences and their pursuit of justice. Only when this sort of relationship exists on the public level, will what I mean by integration have been achieved. Integration should therefore be seen as a moral and social psychological question.

['Multiculturalism in Europe and America', *Nations and Nationalism*, 1: 2 (1995), 246–50.]

FRANK DÍKÖTTER

40 The Idea of 'Race' in Modern China

The emergence of a racial consciousness (1793–1895)

Thought in ancient China was oriented towards the world, or *tianxia*, 'all under heaven'. The world was perceived as one homogeneous unity named 'great community' (*datong*). The Middle Kingdom, dominated by the assumption of its cultural superiority, measured outgroups according to a yardstick by which those who did not follow the 'Chinese ways' were considered 'barbarians'. A theory of 'using the Chinese ways to transform the barbarian' (*yong xia bian yi*) was strongly advocated. It was believed that the barbarian could be culturally assimilated (*laihua*, 'come and be transformed', or *hanhua*, 'become Chinese'). In the Age of Great Peace, the barbarians would flow in and be transformed: the world would be one.

Western incursions from the end of the eighteenth century onwards blatantly contradicted this traditional conceptual framework: Westerners were unwilling to pay homage to the Chinese court (the Macartney mission of 1793); they rejected the tribute system which had traditionally regulated contacts with barbarians; they refused to be culturally assimilated; and, mysteriously, they failed to turn into Chinese.

The most dramatic consequence of this new historical development was that the sheer physical presence of Westerners in the beginning of the nineteenth century demonstrated the relativity of China's own world-view. Chinese literati increasingly discovered that the well-established symbolic universe in which they operated was neither total nor absolute.

The Westerner was often negated by being perceived as a devil, a ghost, an evil and unreal goblin hovering on the border of humanity. Many texts of the first half of the nineteenth century referred to the English as 'foreign devils' (*yangguizi*), 'devil slaves' (*guinu*), 'barbarian devils' (*fangui*), 'island barbarians' (*daoyi*), 'blue-eyed barbarian slaves' (*biyan yinu*), or 'red-haired barbarians' (*hongmaofan*).

Racial stereotypes, grafted upon the barbarian imagery that the Chinese had developed since the incipient stage of their civilization, contributed to the cultural defence of the menaced symbolic universe. The traditional social perception of skin colour was central to this process of stereotyping: 'The Chinese call the barbarians "devils", and differentiate them according to their skin colour', wrote Xu Shidong (1814–1873).[1] The white ones are cold and dull as the ashes of frogs, the black ones are ugly and dirty as coal', explained Jin He (1819–1885).[2] The hairy appearance of the foreigner was frequently underlined. For one observer, 'the white ones are really ghosts; the sounds of their speech are similar to birds, their shins and chest are covered with hair, their green eyes suffer when they look in the distance'.[3]

The repulsive physical features of the foreigner were interpreted as the outward manifestation of an innate inadequacy. In the absence of anatomical knowledge, speculations about the inner physical organization of the barbarian's body could confirm his non-humanity. Yu Zhengxie (1775–1840), a major scholar remembered for his strong interest in research and his liberal ideas, believed that foreigners had only four chambers in the heart, whereas the Chinese had seven. He also thought that Westerners had four testicles.[4]

Absence of familiarity with physically dissimilar people contributed to the gradual appearance of a racial consciousness in China after the middle of the last century. Racial consciousness often first appears among those who have extended contact with a phenotypically different outgroup. The Canton area in particular and the coastal regions generally first developed a sense of racial identity that was to spread gradually to most of the country. Familiarity with outgroups led both to an increased relativization of the ingroup's cosmological position and to an increased specification of the ingroup's identity.

Intellectuals directly exposed to foreigners were vital in the activation of a racial consciousness. After the 1840s, scholar-officials involved in foreign affairs became increasingly aware of the need for a less Sino-centric perspective. Officials like Lin Zexu (1785–1850), Xu Jiyu (1795–1873) or Wei Yuan (1794–1856) compiled world geographies concerned with more practical valuations of the outside world. By a process of positive differentiation between themselves and other non-Western people, they enhanced their own identity. Xu Jiyu's influential account presented Africa as a desperately chaotic continent, inhabited by retrograde black barbarians. 'It is scorching, miasmatic, and pestilential. Its climate and its people are the worst of the four continents.'[5] Others compared Africa to the *hundun*, or Chaos, the primeval state of the Universe according to Chinese folklore. It was precisely those who attempted to make China adopt a more practical vision who were the most eager to denigrate coloured people. The relativization of the ingroup commanded the conceptual debasement of specific outgroups. Africans functioned as a negative identity for those who attempted to depart from the culturalistic assumptions of the traditional Chinese universe. Stereotypes and misperceptions largely facilitated the emergence of a racial identity, which was vital in the process of relativization and adaptation.

The reformers and the idea of race (1895–1902)

The decisive phase in the process of gradual erosion of China's Sinocentric view of the world was its defeat in the Sino-Japanese war of 1894. The Japanese victory led to an outpouring of patriotic agitation in the country. In a general atmosphere of intellectual ferment, study societies created by the scholar class to discuss political issues sprang up in most parts of the country. Journals and newspapers published by concerned scholar-literati spread ideas of reform. The main concern was the survival of China as a racial unit and as a sovereign state in the face of foreign aggression.

Yan Fu (1853–1921) was perhaps the most outspoken and influential proponent of a new world-view based on racial differences:

> There are four main races on the earth: the yellow, the white, the brown and the black. The yellow race's territory is contiguous with the north of Siberia, extending to the South China Sea, bordered by the Pacific and up to the Kunlun mountains in the west. They have prominent cheek-bones, a shallow nose, long eyes and straight hair. The white race dwells west of the salted lakes of the Ural, on the territory conquered by ancient Rome. They have blue eyes and curly hair, a prominent forehead and deep-set sockets. On the many islands south of Vietnam, west of Luzon and east of India is the brown race. The black race is the lowest.[6] They live in Africa and in the territories around the tropics. They are the so-called black slaves.[7]

Yan Fu's vision was articulated on the notion of race: it drew a dividing line between the western barbarians and the traditional barbarians. He undertook a transfer of China's sense of identity from a cultural unity, traditionally opposed to various barbarians that can eventually be annihilated through a process of absorption, to a racial unity, faced with aggressive alien races in an international context of struggle for survival. In the context of racial struggle, Yan warned against the Western sway over the yellow breed or, worse, the weeding out of the entire yellow race: 'They will enslave us and hinder the development of our spirit and body... The brown and black races constantly waver between life and death, why not the four hundred million of yellows'.[8]

Yan Fu's racial bias was clear in his brief presentation of Darwin, which focused exclusively on the theory of struggle for survival. Instead of conveying the individualistic approach of Darwin, Yan pictured evolution as a process of constant struggle between races. Group cohesion, Yan Fu believed, was the principle by which 'the race is strong and the group can stand'.[9]

The inauspicious spectre of interracial war, along with the threat of racial extinction, overshadowing China's future, conveyed a heightened sense of urgency to the intellectuals' discussions of the country's shortcomings in its confrontation with the West. The problem of the survival of the Chinese as a racial unit was the paramount concern shared by the majority of writers of that decade. Liang Qichao (1873–1929), whose writings exerted a lasting influence on two generations of intellectuals, borrowed Yan Fu's ideas of racial identity and racial struggle, but added the American Indians to his classification of races. He divided mankind into five main races: the white, the yellow, the red, the brown and the black races.

This association, which prevailed until 1949, was the pure product of the Chinese inclination for well-ordered symmetrical patterns. Chinese literati preferred to view the world in well-defined colours corresponding to clear-cut continents, similar to the ancient custom of associating the barbarians of the four quarters with different colours: the red or black Di, the white or black Man, the pitch-dark Lang, all surrounding the Imperial Centre, symbolized by the colour yellow.

Ethnocentric reactions of the reformers were mainly directed against the Westerners. Though the coloured people were evidently absent from the social unit with which China was physically confronted, they too were continuously approached in the intellectuals' writings. Ranking appears to be the key phenomenon underlying the Chinese interest in darker people. By downgrading the coloured races, collective self-esteem was enhanced. The Chinese negative perception of Africans was largely a phenomenon of compensation.

In the universe of the reformers, the dominating white and yellow races were opposed to the darker races, doomed to racial extinction by hereditary inadequacy. Liang Qichao perpetuated traditional Confucian ideas about hierarchy by continuously dividing his five races into dichotomous couples like 'noble' (*guizhong*) and 'low' (*jianzhong*), 'superior' (*youzhong*) and 'inferior' (*liezhong*), 'historical' and 'ahistorical'. Tang Caichang (1867–1900) opposed 'fine' (*liangzhong*) to 'mean' (*jianzhong*) races,[10] projecting the social hierarchy that characterized traditional China upon the outside world: in the hierarchy of the Qing dynasty, citizens were divided into 'common people' (*liangmin*) and 'mean people' (*jianmin*). Tang constructed antithetical couplets with the four races that Yan Fu's essays had introduced: 'Yellow and white are wise, red and black are stupid; yellow and white are rulers, red and black are slaves; yellow and white are united, red and black are scattered'.[11] He particularly loathed Australian aborigines, who 'are pitch black, have emaciated limbs, resemble macaques and are more repulsive than the oran-utang one can see in Malaysia'.[12]

Liang Qichao persistently denied any sense of equality to the coloured peoples. India did not flourish 'because of the limitations of her race. All the black, red, and brown races, by the microbes in their blood vessels and their cerebral angle, are inferior to the whites. Only the yellows are not very dissimilar to the whites'.[13] For Liang,[14] blacks and browns were simply lazy and stupid. The reformer Kang Youwei (1858–1927), perhaps the most acclaimed Chinese philosopher of the last hundred years, expounded a utopian vision of the world in a work called *Datongshu*, or 'One World'. Kang[15] wanted to eliminate the darker races in order to achieve universal harmony. Darker races were inferior and should be eradicated. He proposed to whiten the darker races by dietary change, intermarriage, and migration; those who resisted should be eliminated by sterilization.

Racial identity remained the prerogative of reform-minded scholars until the beginning of this century. From the conservatives' point of view, discussions on racial matters were taboo, as they implied a degree of relativization that undermined the bases of their Sino-centric universe. This point is best illustrated by a document entitled the 'Scholars' Covenant', drawn up in 1898 by a group of scholars critical of the reformers. The sixth point of the covenant lambasted the vitiated language of the reformers, and denounced the use of terms like 'yellow race' (*huangzhong*) or 'white race' (*baizhong*).[16] The concept of race introduced a comparative perspective that constituted a menace to the Confucian distinction between civilized Chinese and foreign barbarians.

The general image that emerges from the reformers' writings is that of a yellow race engaged in a merciless war for world supremacy with the white race. This outlook was mainly dictated by China's traditional dichotomous view of a world divided between Chinese and barbarians. The lack of any pluralistic world-view predisposed China to perceive mankind in antithetical terms of dominating and dominated races.

Race, however, was only one form of group definition that the reformers embraced. Group definition is a notion that can only exist in a relational context with other groups. The complexity of this network of relations can persuade a group to adopt more than one self-definition, and some of these may have a certain degree of overlap. These definitions possess a high degree of flexibility, and may vary considerably as a result of the changes in the perceptions and the valuations that the ingroup has about outgroups. In the case of the reformers of the last decade of the nineteenth century, Confucianism still exerted a lasting influence as a religio-moral faith. Kang Youwei's movement for the 'preservation of the faith', for instance, tried to promote Confucianism as a national religion by giving it an institutional legitimation. Despite the many attacks of the reformers on the traditional culturalist world-view, Confucianism remained a powerful form of ethico-spiritual identity.

The revolutionaries and the nation-race (1902–1915)

Race was only consecrated as the ultimate form of group definition by the generation of revolutionaries at the beginning of this century. Whereas the reformers perceived race as a biological extension of the lineage (*zu*), encompassing all people dwelling on the soil of the Yellow Emperor, the revolutionaries excluded the minorities from their definition of race, which was narrowed down to the Han, the country's main ethnic group. Nationalism was perceived as a key to racial survival (*baozhong*) for the radical Chinese students studying in Japan during the first decade of this century. The concept of nationalism was couched in terms borrowed from the Japanese. *Minzuzhuyi*, from the Japanese *minzokushugi*, exerted the most lasting influence upon the political terminology of the Chinese students. The term literally meant 'racism', and expressed a nationalist vision based on a common race. The overlap of meaning of the term *minzu*, signifying both race and nation, contributed to the emergence of a concept of nationalism characterized by a vivid racial consciousness. The constant juxtaposition of *guo*, 'country', to *zhong*, 'race', in set phrases like 'love the race love the country' (*aizhongaiguo*), or 'national boundaries and racial boundaries' (*guojiezhongjie*) also contributed to the infusion of racialist ideas into the Chinese nationalist vision.

The myth of blood was realized by elevating the figure of the Yellow Emperor to a national symbol. Hailed as the first ancestor (*shizu*) of the Han race, his portrait served as the frontispiece in many nationalist publications. From the middle of 1903 onwards, the radical journals established by students studying in Japan started using dates based on the supposed birthday of the Yellow Emperor, initiator of the Chinese race. Liu Shipei (1884–1919) advocated a calendar in which the foundation year corresponded to the birth of the Yellow Emperor: 'The reformers see the preservation of the religion as a handle, so they use the birth of Confucius as the starting date of the calendar; the purpose of our generation is the preservation of the race, so we use the birth of the Yellow Emperor as a founding date'.[17]

The Yellow Emperor remained a powerful figure for many decades. Despite the historian Gu Jiegang's criticism of the mythical foundations of the figure of the Yellow Emperor in the 1920s, he was still officially revered in 1941 as the founder of the nation and the initiator of the race.[18]

The main feature of Chinese intellectual thought since the 1890s was the preoccupation with the idea of group. The revolutionary nationalists completed the transition from group to race. Zhang Binglin (1869–1936), like many other nationalists, expanded the racial basis of Yan Fu's writings and explicitly associated the principle of *qun* ('group', 'flock') with racial strength. In his article 'On bacteria' (1899),[19] he explained how racial power was proportional to the ability to group (*hequn*): the inferior black, brown, and red races prostrated before the yellow race because they had failed to group. On the other hand, the yellow race was dominated by the white race. The whites had vanquished the yellows because of their greater ability to group.

Traditional values reinforced the concept of racial grouping. Confucian values of filial piety and ancestor worship paved the way for the cult of the Yellow Emperor. Racial loyalty came to be perceived as an extension of family loyalty. The family, often corresponding to the clan in China, was seen as the unit by which the race was composed. The revolutionary Chen Tianhua (1875–1905) actively integrated traditional values into a pattern of racial solidarity in his influential writings:

> As the saying goes, a man is not close to people of another family [*xing*, surname]. When two families fight each other, one surely assists one's own family, one definitely does not help the foreign [*wai*, 'exterior'] family. Common families all descend from one original family: the Han race is one big family. The Yellow Emperor is a great ancestor, all those who are not of the Han race are not the descendants of the Yellow Emperor, they are exterior families. One should definitely not assist them; if one assists them, one lacks a sense of ancestry'.[20]

Kin terms were infused into a racial rhetoric that called forth emotional dispositions usually reserved for close relatives: 'The racial feeling comes from the birth onwards. For the members of one's own race, there is surely mutual intimacy and love; for the members of a foreign race, there is surely mutual savagery and killing'.[21] Kin terms fostered the much needed bonds of association and group loyalty.

Contrary to the reformers, who had expressed their ideas of sociopolitical renewal in a frame still dominated by a reference to the past, the nationalists successfully broke away from the culturalist tradition. They elaborated a new sense of identity that narrowly focused on the Han race, pictured as a perennial biological unit descended from a mythological ancestor. Until 1915, however, the nationalist vision of blood and soil remained chiefly confined to the political arena. The idea of race would only reach a much wider audience with the New Culture Movement.

Race after the New Culture Movement (1915–1949)

The New Culture Movement started in 1915 and lasted for several years. It was characterized by a totalistic and iconoclastic attack on the traditional cultural heritage.[22] Many new scholars, often educated in either Japan or the West, were determined to integrate foreign science and culture into the intellectual revolution of their country. They invited the youth to part with the stagnant elements of traditional culture and to accept foreign democracy, science and culture as the founding elements of a new order.

Spurred by this intellectual revolution, the idea of race made rapid progress, infiltrating most domains of intellectual activity. The successive attacks unleashed against the traditional heritage since the middle of the nineteenth century had dramatically undermined the bases of a well-established collective identity and had led to the artificial separation of race and culture. Racial exclusiveness was the warrant for successful cultural iconoclasm. With the New Culture Movement, Western social sciences became an instrument to debunk the traditional culture and to boost racial identity. Science and age-old stereotypes constantly intermingled to accommodate ethnocentric feelings of biological exclusiveness.

The concept of the evolution of species led to the idea of original purity. Visions of a pure and vibrant race were projected into an idealized past to compensate for the nation's degraded position in the new world order created by the West. Science and myth wove a fabric on which the frustrated mind could visualize its fantasies. Wei Juxian,[23] to take but one example, published an article inquiring into the origins of the Han race that was entirely based on mythology. Wei saw the Xia as the genuine descendants of the Yellow Emperor. The Yin, the author believed, descended from the Emperor Yan and had intermarried with the Xia to generate the actual Han race. Wei situated the Xia's place of origin on the Caucasus: they were a pure and white race. The Yin, however, were merely red-skinned barbarians from a part of China now known as Sichuan province. White and red had given birth to the yellow Hans. Wei Juxian maintained the myth of purity by locating the source of pollution in an alien group.

Archaeology was in search for evidence of human beginnings in China. Lin Yan, for instance, carefully examined all the theories that traced the origins of the 'Chinese race' down to alien migrations, but rejected them for lack of scientific proof. Like many of his contemporaries, he cited the Peking Man discovered at Zhoukoudian to prove that the 'Chinese race' had existed on the soil of the Middle Kingdom since the very beginning. He concluded that the country had been inhabited by 'the most ancient original mankind' on earth.[24] Modern archaeology had to corroborate China's traditional ethnocentric theories. Science was infused in age-old myths to revitalize Sinocentric beliefs that could provide a sense of biological continuity so essential in an age of anxiety.

The transition from cultural universalism to racial nationalism took place in an age dominated by Western racial theories. The tension accumulated by the superiority–inferiority complex of the Chinese *vis-à-vis* Western racial arrogance was often released in depreciative descriptions of the coloured people. In physical anthropology, Africans were simply referred to as the 'black slave race' until the end of the 1920s. Gu Shoubai,[25] perhaps the most popular writer on physical anthropology in the 1920s, divided blacks into a 'little black slave race' (*xiao heinu zhongzu*) and a 'standard black slave race' (*zhun heinu zhongzu*). Gong Tingzhang,[26] another influential pseudo-scientist, reproduced a picture of a black in suit and tie; the caption read: 'Black slave from Africa'. Gong believed that blacks and Australians had small brains and had only attained the level of civilization of Chinese 'stupid peasants' (*yunong*),[27] a remark that reveals how easily native prejudice was projected on newly discovered peoples.[28] Professor Chen Yinghuang[29] believed that the purpose of anthropology was to study all the races, from the Chinese and the English 'down to the black slaves and the dwarf slaves', an age-old derogatory term for the Japanese.

Doubts about the biological foundations of the race led to the flourishing of eugenics, the pseudo-science of race improvement.[30] The pressure of the superiority–inferiority complex felt by many educated Chinese was relieved by dichotomization: intellectuals were designated as the superior elements of the race, whereas the lower classes were branded inferior. By transferring the myth of superiority from race to class, the intellectuals set themselves up as a privileged social group, holder of racial purity. The task of the eugenists was to eliminate the inferior classes or to raise them up to the level of the superior class: in both cases, the nation's purity would be recovered and its superiority regained. The popularity of eugenics among the educated classes thus reflected both their concern with national revival and their sense of racial identity.

Conclusion

It was only after 1949 that the concepts of race and class would merge, giving the country a new sense of identity. Racial discrimination was expressly forbidden by the Chinese Communist Party after 1949.[31] Widespread propaganda under the supervision of reformed anthropologists attempted to rectify racial thinking,[32] it also fostered the idea that only Westerners could indulge in 'racism', as the Chinese were now the leaders of the victimized coloured people in the historical struggle against white 'imperialism'.

The idea of racial exclusiveness became taboo, but the underlying ideas that had led to its expression failed to disappear. The messianic idea of a universal mission of unification (the *datong*, or 'One World' ideal) was now expressed in a phraseology based on the concept of class struggle, whereas the artificial dichotomization between Chinese and Westerners in biological terms of 'race' was merely reformulated in social terms of 'class'. Moreover, racial prejudice in China has tended to reappear during periods of internal and external tension. During the Sino-Soviet rift, race made an official reappearance when the Communist party increasingly harped on the theme of biological differences between Soviets and Chinese. With the gradual rapprochement of the two superpowers nowadays, the idea of racial identity could prove to be dangerously tempting in an isolated China.

['Group definition and the idea of race in modern China', *Ethnic and Racial Studies*, 13: 3 (1990), 421–31.]

IMMANUEL GEISS

41 Pan-Africanism and European Imperialism

It is still difficult, perhaps even impossible, to provide a clear and precise definition of Pan-Africanism. It is a complex problem which can best be approached historically. By looking at its various manifestations we can arrive at simple and comprehensive formulae, compare them with objective reality and modify them continually in the light of modern knowledge.

By Pan-Africanism we understand:

1 Intellectual and political movements among Africans and Afro-Americans[1] who regard or have regarded Africans and people of African descent as homogeneous. This outlook leads to a feeling of racial solidarity and a new self-awareness and causes Afro-Americans to look upon Africa as their real 'homeland', without necessarily thinking of a physical return to Africa.
2 All ideas which have stressed or sought the cultural unity and political independence of Africa, including the desire to modernize Africa on a basis of equality of rights. The key concepts here have been respectively the 'redemption of Africa' and 'Africa for the Africans'.
3 Ideas or political movements which have advocated, or advocate, the political unity of Africa or at least close political collaboration in one form or another.

Even this provisional definition is unsatisfactory and will not please everyone. But it will serve as a working tool for historical analysis, if used with due caution.

In addition to the difficulties encountered in defining the concept, two other factors make the history of the Pan-African movement complex and difficult to comprehend. Firstly, developments occurred simultaneously on three continents—in North America (USA and the West Indies), in Africa (especially West Africa) and Europe (especially England)—sometimes influencing one another but sometimes in isolation. Secondly, these developments must be seen within the framework of the general history of Africa, America and Europe, so that one always has to bear in mind a fair amount of world history, even though one cannot draw the line as precisely as one might wish.

Furthermore, Pan-Africanism developed on different planes of varying significance. If we take the political aspect in each period as the criterion, we may distinguish six such planes.

1 Pan-Africanism frequently took the form of a movement of all coloured and colonial peoples, which has been called since Bandung the 'Afro-Asian solidarity movement', or the 'Pan-Colonial' or, earlier, 'Pan-Coloured' movement.
2 In most cases Pan-Africanism was understood as 'Pan-Negroism', i.e. was defined primarily in racial terms. This view ignored Arabic North Africa and concentrated on the solidarity between Black Africans and Afro-Americans.
3 Only after the unity of the whole African continent had become the goal, and Afro-Americans of the New World had been excluded, did Pan-Africanism attain the form from which it derives its name and the meaning generally associated with it today.

   Two sub-categories may be further distinguished: the drive for the unity of Black Africa south of the Sahara and that for the unity of the entire continent including the Arabic north.
4 A regional union has frequently been regarded as a preliminary stage on the road to continental unity, especially in British West Africa during the earlier years. Only in very recent times have such ideas been taken up in other regions as well, notably in East Africa.
5 The fifth plane to be considered is the national one. Until a short time ago it was at this level that concrete action as a rule took place, whereas theoretical discussions, propaganda and agitation were oriented mainly to the supra-national plane.
6 Nationalism frequently first developed on a tribal level (e.g. in the case of the Fanti).

Pan-Africanism has hardly ever been a clearly defined, precise or rational concept. On the contrary, it has been (and still is) a matter of hazy, vague emotions—a vision or a dream, as Du Bois put it.[2] Nevertheless it is possible to isolate a rational kernel from the chaos of declarations and proclamations, even though this rational element is all too often subordinated to a feeling of resentment and despair at the injustice prevalent in the world and at White domination. Here one has to be particularly careful about the way in which one launches upon a critical analysis, and the definitions outlined above will be found helpful. For what may at first sight appear to the unsympathetic European (if he takes any notice of these ideas at all) as products of the fevered imagination of frustrated and half-educated negroes—a hotchpotch of confused and ill-digested notions—emerge when viewed historically as an unconscious, inarticulate demand by Pan-Africans[3] for equal rights for Africans and people of African descent. Its opposition to the idea and practice of racial discrimination and hierarchical relationships among men, makes Pan-Africanism *par excellence* the ideology of decolonization in Africa.[4] It stands for the economic, technological, social and political modernization of a whole continent.

Pan-Africanism is thus predominantly a modern movement. It is the reaction of the most advanced, most intensively Europeanized Africans and Afro-Americans to contact with the modern world. Its representatives have been Africans or Afro-Americans who in many cases had an academic education in Europe, America or West Africa, or who were exposed for a long time to modern influences in their own country. They embraced the European and North American principles of equality and democracy and on this basis elaborated their own ideology of emancipation from White supremacy. Africans who completed their studies in Europe or in the USA, or who stayed there voluntarily for a considerable length of time and then returned to their African homelands, acted as a ferment of modernization upon traditional society; like the Afro-Americans, they protested against racial discrimination and European colonialism, turning against their White masters the very political and intellectual principles they had learned from them.

A process of this kind is not uncommon in history. One finds it wherever an advanced culture comes into contact with a stagnant and backward society, wherever the conflict between the old and the new produces a fresh awareness in a society that has been stirred into movement. It usually leads to a division between those who unreservedly want rapid and consistent modernization and those who want to preserve what is traditional, or at least to progress slowly. Between the element favouring radical modernization and that favouring conservation one finds an intermediate group which in one way or another would like to combine the old and the new. For them, as for the conservatives, a largely idealized past serves as a useful means of formulating their new self-awareness.

Parallels to this aspect of Pan-Africanism can be discovered in the recent history of almost all modern societies. In Germany the Romantics invoked the medieval empire as a response to the challenge of the French Revolution.[5] The Slavs looked back to their history in medieval times, in shaking off foreign economic, social and political domination, and on this basis developed a modern national consciousness. This led to the revival of so-called 'unhistorical' nations, to demands for national self-determination, and ultimately to the emergence of individual nation states. In Russia there was a sharp cleavage between 'Westerners' and 'Slavophils', between exponents of rational, modern Western ideas and those Romantics who sought to revive the country's own traditions.[6]

These parallels may help us to understand the African cultural renaissance and the political movement of Pan-Africanism. These are ambivalent reactions to modernizing influences and to the White supremacy associated with them. In this case, too, we may observe the dialectic of cultural contact, the tension between the (few) advocates of consistent modernization and those who favour some kind of combination of the new and the old. It is worth bearing in mind that Pan-Africanism is but one instance of a universal phenomenon, which takes different forms according to time, place and historical setting.[7] Just as Pan-Slavism and Slav nationalism were closely linked, so Pan-Africanism and African nationalism are interconnected. Pan-Africanism may be seen as African nationalism extended to embrace either the entire African continent or Black Africa alone.

The reaction of the most modernized Africans and Afro-Americans to contact with the modern world reflects three simultaneous processes: the transition from a gradual modernization of society to new levels of 'social aggregation'; the clash between modern and traditional elements; and an attempt to integrate them. For a century African society has been evolving from traditional agrarian forms to more modern ones. This results at first in an inevitable confusion and a bewildering eclecticism; this is probably best represented by Nkrumah and his philosophy of 'Consciencism',[8] a deliberate attempt to combine ideas of a traditional African character with ideas from the Arabic–Islamic world and from Western Europe (with Marxism–Leninism being treated as a Western influence).

It is inevitable that the relatively sudden and massive confrontation of a traditional and largely isolated society with the modern world should lead to a long period of transition and confusion. For the modern world is itself no compact, uniform, rational structure; it has developed in a complex process of chaotic and violent conflict. For this reason Pan-Africanism reflects the tensions and contradictions of the modern world, especially as they have been transplanted to African soil, as well as the confusion that springs from the blending of modern and traditional African elements. This explains the frequent vacillations between traditionalism and modernism which one can observe time and time again among exponents of Pan-Africanism.

These considerations enable us to define Pan-Africanism in both a narrower and a broader sense. The narrower definition is limited to the political movement for the unification of the African continent, perhaps to the Pan-Negro movement (planes 3 and 2). The broader definition includes cultural and intellectual movements, even those that aim at a wider solidarity, i.e. anti-colonialism or Afro-Asianism. A distinction of this kind roughly corresponds with that drawn by George Shepperson between 'Pan-Africanism' (in the narrower sense) and 'pan-Africanism' (in the broader sense).

With some justification the beginning of Pan-Africanism in the narrower sense may be dated as recently as 1958, when two Pan-African conferences were held on African soil (both in Accra), and the 'diaspora' first began to return to the 'promised land' of Africa. If this is so, the period before 1958 is only the prehistory of Pan-Africanism, and one can distinguish between a 'narrower' and a 'broader' prehistory corresponding to the narrower and broader definitions of the term. Its prehistory in the narrower sense begins with the first Pan-African conference in London in 1900; that in the broader sense goes back to the late eighteenth century.

Prior to 1900 there was no Pan-Africanism in the narrower sense, either in name or form. If Pan-Africanism proper was a reaction to classical European imperialism and colonialism, approximately from the 'scramble for Africa' (in the late nineteenth century) onwards, the first quasi-Pan-African impulses may be considered as a reaction to what might be called European 'proto-imperialism' in the eighteenth and nineteenth centuries, characterized by the slave trade across the Atlantic and by slavery and racial discrimination in the New World. By analogy one may speak of a 'proto-Pan-Africanism' before 1900.

An attempt to study Pan-African prehistory in the broader sense requires an investigation into the historical conditions for its appearance in about 1900. One would have to describe and analyse the soil from which Pan-Africanism could spring, including the social changes in Africa (especially British West Africa), the West Indies and among Afro-Americans in the USA from the late eighteenth century. Moreover, from the late eighteenth century onwards individual Africans and Afro-Americans formulated ideas which may be categorized as 'Pan-African' in the broader sense or as 'proto-Pan-African'. One thus faces the problem of exploring the tradition of Pan-Africanism before it appeared in articulate guise in 1900, i.e. its historical continuity.

[*The PanAfrican Movement* (London: Methuen, 1974), 3–8.]

42 The Aryan Myth and Biblical Universalism

Now that we have reached the end of our enquiry, what lesson can be drawn from it? We said at the beginning that the search for origins, the attempt to find one's identity through one's ancestors, has always been the concern of human groups in every age and culture. This may be inferred *a priori* by analogy with the individual, and it is confirmed in the writings of the anthropologists quoted in the introduction to this book. We have not attempted to investigate this subject in every human culture but have confined ourselves to examining the myths of origin of the principal European nations. One might describe these myths as compromises between pagan memories, dynastic ambitions and the teachings of the Church. These compromises were influenced by the strength of ancestral memories and by historical vicissitudes and they took the most varied forms; but usually they showed distinct preference for Germanic stock or blood. We have also seen how the tendency embodied in the ruling dynasty to claim a distinct and superior descent always clashed with the myth of Adam as a universal father—a myth which according to a rabbinical apologist, was intended to teach all men that they are in reality equal.[1]

The Judaeo-Christian tradition was both anti-racist and anti-nationalist, and the social structure and barriers of the Middle Ages, with its feudal, horizontal hierarchies, no doubt helped the Church to translate this ideal into reality. If all men were equal before God, vertical and geographical distinctions should make no difference to the value of human beings. Nevertheless, one exceptional case (which we should perhaps have examined more closely)[2] showed how restricted were the limits of this universal equality. During the Renaissance, the Spanish statutes relating to 'purity of blood' brought about a type of segregation similar to that of the racial laws promulgated in the twentieth century by the Nazis and Fascists. This case is highly instructive since it shows how, given appropriate circumstances, religious bigotry, under cover of a perverted theology, was able to bring about discrimination against Christians said to belong to a biologically inferior stock. Even so, though the 'inferior race' of the *conversos* (i.e. Christians of Jewish or Moorish descent) was persecuted by the Inquisition and, in the case of the Moors, expelled from Spain, it was not exterminated. No doubt the anthropology of the Church acted as a brake in the last resort, thus saving Christian honour.

The doctrine of the unity of the human race, about which people always had secret misgivings, was directly attacked by a number of leading philosophers of the Enlightenment. We have discussed the new anthropological ideas put forward in the eighteenth century at some length because such writers as Buffon, Voltaire, Hume or Kant, each in his own way prepared the ground for the racial hierarchies of the following century. We believe that we may thereby have put straight certain widespread misconceptions about historical development. When, among the ruins of the *ancien régime*, Adam died as a universal ancestor, first scientists and then philosophers affiliated Christian peoples to other patriarchs, and these were no longer Biblical but Indian. It should be emphasized that, at least to begin with, this genealogy did not imply any political exclusions. In fact the real founder of the Aryan myth, Friedrich Schlegel, was a supporter of total emancipation for the Jews. Once launched by the orientalists and the German myth-makers, the new theory gained ground rapidly to become internationally accepted and acquire, during the second half of the century, much the same status as the theory of spatial ether. Thereafter the theory of Aryan origins was propagated among the masses, mainly in support of anti-semitic campaigns, though other political passions such as Franco-German rivalry also helped it to spread. From about 1890 the theory began to be questioned, in part because of the widespread discussion which it aroused. It then passed from the scientists to the demagogues to become at last the official doctrine of the Third Reich when men designated as non-Aryans were sacrificed to the gods of racialism.

Before its final degradation, in the course of less than a century, to such depths of infamy, the Aryan theory was in the main current of scientific progress and appeared to be corroborated by linguistic discoveries. Hegel is an outstanding example of how it carried conviction with the most acute minds of the past. We have argued that the attraction which it exercised was due in part to the desire to abandon the anthropodicy of the Bible with its 'Jewish fables', and we noted the lordly disdain with which Goethe attributed descent from Adam to the Jewish people alone. The Indian fables, which had acquired popularity before the discovery of linguistic ties between India and Europe, could be used to diminish the influence of the Bible, as the writings of Voltaire or Herder show. So the Aryan theory does indeed belong to the tradition of anti-clericalism and anti-obscurantism; it is a product of the first gropings of the sciences of man as they tried to model themselves on the exact sciences and so strayed into a mechanistic and determinist blind-alley where they remained for a century.

In dealing with these questions we have drawn attention to the remarkable fact that the Bible took some account of the principles and distinctions which have been adopted by biological sciences only in the nineteenth century and by the sciences of man only in our own times. But scientists whose subject was biology often thought in terms of anthropology. When, for instance, Linnaeus heard that Réaumur had fertilized a chicken with a rabbit he at once exclaimed that this cast a disquieting light on the origin of the Negroes—though he added that, as a good Christian, he refused to attribute an animal origin to mankind.[3] Less fervent Christians did not share such scruples. Many gave their support, especially on grounds of polygenism, to those legendary beliefs on which the classical authors had already embroidered innumerable variations and which the Church, as the heir to Jewish tradition, had never been able to eradicate completely.

In what way did the Biblical account anticipate the theories of modern science? It did so by establishing, alongside the gulf between God and His creation, a similar gulf between man and the animals or between man and nature, as well as the gaps between the species. The only Biblical passage which assumes a different order of things seems like an echo of a pagan myth. It is in Chapter VI of Genesis where, in the story of the Flood, we are told that the 'sons of God' (b^{e}nê 'elōhîm) 'came in unto the daughters of men' and bore children to them and that these 'became mighty men which were of old, men of renown'. This reminds one of the descendants of Wotan or Zeus; but this race of demi-gods, once mentioned, is immediately suppressed, one might say censored, together with all other life on earth. That Creation survived is due to Noah's Ark alone. After this the censorship is absolute throughout the whole Bible text and in the commentaries. The species, according to the Talmud, promised as they left the Ark, not to fornicate with each other, and they never mingled again. The real meaning of the religious exclusiveness of the Mosaic law is its constant reminder to man, in all the circumstances of his life, of his unique position in the world.

It would probably be useless to ask why the Biblical account rejects the fantastic unions with which all mythologies are filled and why, by thus isolating man from other creatures, it appears to designate him as a creature apart—a 'cultural' as opposed to a 'natural' being—who has cast off certain biological bonds to set out on a journey from which there could be no return. At most one might compare Biblical anthropology to the insights of some Greek authors, as has been suggested by the Hellenist Pierre Vidal-Naquet. But it is more to the point to stress the persistence of the mythological error and to relate it to the animistic confusions of paganism and to the Aristotelian 'great chain of being'.

The problem then becomes one of explaining the constant and universal tendency to identify man with his environment or with 'nature'. What is the basis of this tendency (which every society has expressed in its own language whether poetical or pseudo-scientific)? What universal aspiration does it express? Today psychoanalysis provides us with a means of finding out. It relates that dream to the urge to recover the euphoria which characterizes the most archaic stage before individuation—the stage of 'primitive narcissism' when, as we are told by those who investigate these obscure beginnings, human beings feel that they are at one with the surrounding universe and each individual feels himself to be organically the Whole as though he were god in a pantheistic sense.[4] Thus the childish paradise of total happiness is in the final analysis that of the preconscious life in the womb, before the 'fall' into the world. One can extrapolate this view of the development of the human psyche to the psychic development of the human species; one can compare the emergence of consciousness in the individual with the process by which the human species itself emerged. And if we do so, do we not find, in mankind as a species, the same archaic longing for a great return to the beginnings, for a fusion with Mother Nature? Do not all mythologies bear witness to this longing?

The Mosaic tradition alone, by separating man from nature and overthrowing the idols of wood or stone, proclaimed the everlasting dream to be something illusory and sacrilegious, and in doing so it aroused permanent hostility—a hatred and resistance which was extended to the Jews who, whatever they might do or say, were in the eyes of the world the bearers of the Old Testament message. We have explained elsewhere how abuse directed against this stupid and barbarous people, whose superstitions swamped the West, was once a stock technique of anti-religious propaganda.[5] After its beginnings in the infant science of the Enlightenment, the struggle against the old demythologizing books, by way of historical and social changes of every kind, and involving every aspect of life, finally led to a war of extermination against men. The same link exists between the elaboration of the Aryan myth at the beginning of the nineteenth century when it arraigned the truth of the Biblical genealogies and its murderous consequences in our own times.

[*The Aryan Myth* (New York: Basic Books, 1974), 326–30.]

LEO KUPER

43 Genocide and the Plural Society

1. The subjection of peoples to alien subjugation, domination and exploitation constitutes a denial of fundamental human rights, is contrary to the Charter of the United Nations and is an impediment to the promotion of world peace and co-operation.
2. All peoples have the right to self-determination; by virtue of that right they freely determine their political status and freely pursue their economic, social and cultural development.
6. Any attempt aimed at the partial or total disruption of the national unity and the territorial integrity of a country is incompatible with the purposes and principles of the Charter of the United Nations.

[Declaration on the Granting of Independence to Colonial Countries and Peoples: General Assembly Resolution 1514 (XV) of 14 December 1960]

The plural society provides the structural base for genocide, the presence of a diversity of racial, ethnic and/or religious groups being the structural characteristic of the plural society, and genocide a crime committed against these groups. This is not to say that genocide is inevitable in the history of plural societies, but only that plural societies offer the necessary conditions for domestic genocide. The many genocidal conflicts in plural societies (as for example in India on partition, or in Bangladesh, or in Rwanda and Burundi) suggest an intimate relationship between the plural society and genocide.

I do not use the term plural society to mean simply the presence of a diversity of racial, ethnic and/or religious groups. The effect of this would be to classify the overwhelming majority of societies as plural societies. I use the term rather, in a tradition deriving from J. S. Furnivall, to describe societies with persistent and pervasive cleavages between these sections. It is a distinctive type of society, recognized as such in the literature under a variety of names—divided societies, communally fragmented societies, multi-ethnic or multiple societies, composite societies, segmented societies and internally colonized societies.

In the plural society, racial or ethnic or religious differentiation is elaborated in many different spheres. There is generally inequality in the mode of political incorporation, as in the constitutional provisions which exclude Africans from the vote for members of the South African parliament. Even where there is formal recognition of political equality, there may be practical inequality, as in Northern Ireland, where Protestants succeeded in maintaining an entrenched political domination over Catholics, notwithstanding a democratic constitution. The political inequality is usually associated with economic discrimination—in opportunities for employment, in wages, in access to the means of production. There is almost certain to be discrimination also in provision for education, sometimes with quite startling differences in expenditure for dominant groups as compared with subordinate. Segregation may be imposed in many spheres, including prohibition against intermarriage, or an increasing segregation may develop in the course of conflicts protracted over many years. Differences in culture and social organization may add further to division between the different sections.

The plural society, in its *extreme* form, is characterized by a superimposition of inequalities. The same sections are dominant or subordinate, favoured or discriminated against, in the political structure, in the economy, in opportunities for education, in human rights, in access to amenity. And issues of conflict tend also to be superimposed along the same lines of cleavage and inequality. These structural conditions are likely to be conducive to genocidal conflict. They aggregate the population into distinctive sections, thereby facilitating crimes against collectivities. The divisions being so pervasive, and relatively consistent in so many spheres, issues of conflict may move rapidly from one sector to another, until almost the entire society is polarized. A quite local racial disturbance, for example, of seemingly minor significance, may set off a chain of reactions—rioting at distant geographical points, demonstrations, strike action, police reprisals, reciprocal terrorism and violent political confrontation at a national level. So too, by reason of the superimposition of issues of conflict, particular issues, however specific in their origin, become generalized to a wide range of grievance. And if there is a long history of struggle, with its models, for the dominant group, of effective violent repression, and its memories, for the subordinate group, of past injustice and atrocity, it will give an emotional charge to the conflict, which may escalate to high levels of destructive violence. But this is by no means an inevitable development. A society which one might characterize as an extreme plural society on the basis of objective measures may remain quiescent for long periods, perhaps indefinitely, lacking the subjective reactions and opportunity to sustain a destructive conflict.

In the examples which follow, I have drawn on case studies of highly destructive violence to establish the argument of a genocidal potential in the conflicts between racial, ethnic or religious sections of a plural society. I would not personally describe each of the case studies as genocide. But they are all conflicts in which the charge of genocide has been made—though this charge is often made in a loose and exaggerated way. And they are all conflicts in which there has been massive slaughter, with episodes of genocidal massacre, whole communities of the target group being annihilated.

Colonization has been a major creator of plural societies, and many colonial and settler societies conformed to the extreme type of plural society. But colonies varied greatly in the manner of the initial colonization, in the structure of the relationships established, in the mode of decolonization, and in the violence attending these historical phases.

Many variables are relevant to these differences in colonial societies, and in the incidence of violent confrontation. There is the familiar distinction between limited settlement, as in the early Iberian pre-capitalist colonization of Central and South America, substantial settlement, as in Algeria and South Africa, and massive settlement, engulfing the indigenous peoples, as for example Indians in the USA and Canada, Maoris in New Zealand, Aborigines in Australia. Then there is the extent of intermarriage, with milder forms of racism prevailing where intermarriage was a predominant mode, as in Mexico, and maximal racism, with exclusion of intermarriage. The period of colonization, related to the forms of economic exploitation, is specially significant, as in the search for raw materials at the lowest possible cost in an earlier period, and for market outlets for finished goods at a later period. The time factor is also relevant to the ideological justifications and the policies of the different colonial powers. So too, of particular significance for the introduction of new groups, with increasing pluralism of the society, is the failure of attempts by the colonizers to enslave, or to harness to production, indigenous groups, and the consequent resort to slaves or contract labourers from the outside; and the need in certain situations to encourage the immigration of middlemen accustomed to a technological culture and a money economy.[1] This has been a source of small hostage groups in former colonies, and also of substantial populations, strong enough to challenge the indigenous peoples in the struggles for power on decolonization.

I have already discussed, in theories of genocide, the vulnerability of hunting and gathering groups in the process of colonization, and, more generally, the incidence of genocidal massacres in the establishment and maintenance of colonial domination. The colonization of Algeria in the nineteenth century, and its decolonization by revolution in 1954–61, are among the most bloody conflicts in the history of modern colonialism. The brutality of the initial conquest and 'pacification', with whole communities annihilated and areas of fair settlement and cultivation deliberately laid waste, was recalled in revolutionary writings, and became part of the political consciousness in the struggle for liberation, achieved by the Algerians at enormous cost in human life and in the uprooting of millions of Algerians from their traditional homes.

Fanon wrote in 1959, during the revolution, of 'the genocide that is rife in Algeria'. Sartre, as we have seen, was more cautious in the charge he made at the Russell Tribunal, introducing the qualification that the settlers could not carry massacre to the point of physical genocide, because of their need to exploit the native peoples; by exterminating the sub-proletariat in Algeria, they would have exterminated themselves as settlers.[2] I do not see how the Algerian struggle can really be described as genocide within the terms of the United Nations definition, but it was certainly marked by genocidal massacres. In 1945, at Sétif, and under police provocation, Muslims participating in the celebration of victory in the Second World War, spread through the city, savagely attacking and murdering the Europeans they encountered. This was followed by attacks in the countryside with armed bands of Muslims killing, raping, multilating, pillaging, burning. The French and settler reprisals were vastly more savage. There were summary executions and reprisal massacres of Arabs; Senegalese troops and legionnaires pillaged, burnt, raped and slaughtered in full freedom; a cruiser bombarded coastal areas; planes destroyed forty-four villages. In the final count, the French dead numbered 103, and there were some hundred wounded and mutilated. The French authorities estimated the Muslim dead as 1,500; the liberation movement placed the Muslim death toll at 50,000.[3]

In the Constantine area, during the course of the revolution, massacre and counter-massacre re-enacted the tragedy of Sétif. In Philippeville, in August 1955, Arabs mounted a devastating attack. At Constantine, bombs exploded throughout the city; and at El Halia, a mining centre in which fifty European families lived among 2,000 Arabs, under conditions of complete equality in employment, and seemingly in perfect harmony, the Europeans were relentlessly slaughtered. When the military finally arrived, wading through pools of blood, they found the bodies of men and women sexually mutilated, women and children with their throats cut and disembowelled by billhook. The reprisals in Constantine took the form of the indiscriminate slaughter of Arabs; in Philippeville, young Muslims were rounded up and shot down in the stadium, while the villages from which some of the assailants originated were destroyed by mortar. The toll of reprisals, according to the count of the revolutionary forces, was 12,000 Muslims dead or missing.[4]

To these pogrom-type massacres must be added the indiscriminate killing of Muslims or of settlers in the escalation of the struggle, with its increasing polarization and reciprocal cycles of terrorism, as in the discharging of a bomb in the densely populated Muslim Casbah, or the bombing of a European milk bar and other public places, or the Muslim terrorist attack followed by the settler *ratonnade* (pogrom), or Muslim massacre and massive French settler vigilante massacre, or the random gunning down of non-combatants.[5] In all this, one can see the genocidal potential of violent conflict in plural societies.

Where there were two tiers of domination in the colonial structure, decolonization was particularly charged with genocidal potential. Plural societies preceded colonial imperialism,[6] and in some cases, capitalist colonization of a plural society resulted in the superimposition of an additional layer of domination on an earlier domination. In a number of these societies, decolonization detonated explosive genocidal conflicts, as the earlier rulers and their one-time subjects engaged in violent struggle under the impetus of electoral contests in a democratic idiom, introduced by the colonial powers in the movement to independence.

A major genocide of this type was carried out by a minority of Tutsi against a Hutu majority in Burundi in 1972. In both Rwanda and Burundi, domination had been established centuries earlier by invading Tutsi pastoralists over Hutu agriculturalists and small numbers of Twa hunters and gatherers. Under Belgian mandate, the traditional lines of domination remained clearly defined in Rwanda in a relationship often described by commentators as caste. The sharpness of division was, however, somewhat softened by a great network of patron–client relationships, by a seeming acquiescence in inequality, and by loyalty to the Mwami, the king. The restraints on divisive ethnic confrontation broke down, however, under the impact of reforms introduced by the Belgian government, including a progressive system of electoral representation. Political parties consolidated on mainly ethnic lines, and terrorism, initiated by the Tutsi, and the violent reactions of Hutu, rapidly polarized the society, and escalated electoral contest to violent confrontation.

In March 1962, in one of the regions of Rwanda, the murder by Tutsi bands of two policemen in one raid, and of four Hutu (including one policeman and two civil servants) in another raid, led to massive indiscriminate reprisal in which between 1,000 and 2,000 Tutsi men, women and children were massacred and buried on the spot, their huts pillaged and burned and their property divided among the Hutu population. In December 1963, with Rwanda independent under Hutu domination, a minor, but threatening, invasion by Tutsi set off genocidal massacres. In the prefecture of Gikongoro, at the instigation of the local prefects, Hutu armed with clubs, pangas and spears methodically began to murder all Tutsi in sight—men, women and children. An estimated 5,000 were massacred in Gikongoro, and perhaps another 5,000–9,000 in other areas. The constitutional procedures established by the Belgian government with continuous United Nations intervention had served as catalyst for this escalating conflict in the plural society of Rwanda, terror and ultimately genocidal massacre becoming the instruments of political change.[7]

In Burundi, the colonial situation seemed promising for ethnic accommodation. Relations were more fluid. As in Rwanda, the Tutsi were a minority (some 14 per cent in a population of perhaps three-and-a-half million in the period of decolonization). There were divisions within the dominant stratum of dynastic families, and the Tutsi and Hutu were themselves internally divided. Regional differences, and differences in wealth, power and status among Tutsi and among Hutu, added to the structural complexity of the society, which offered many social bases, and the stimulus of varied interests, for the transcending of ethnic exclusiveness. And initially, in the movement to decolonization, political division did not flow along ethnic lines. But very rapidly the society became ethnically polarized, as Tutsi élite sought to eliminate their Hutu opponents by terrorism and assassination, and Hutu responded by counter-terrorism.

Within three years of independence, ethnic conflict had escalated to genocidal massacre. In 1965, on the failure of a Hutu attempted coup, and in reaction also to massacres of Tutsi in the countryside, the army, assisted by civilian defence groups, and the government acting through a Council of War, killed some 2,500 to 5,000 Hutu, virtually liquidating Hutu leadership. This was a precursor, as it were, to the genocide of 1972, which re-enacted, on a vastly destructive scale, the events of 1965. In the southern provinces of Burundi, Hutu rebels, with some assistance by rebels from Zaire, slaughtered and mutilated every Tutsi they could find and of whatever age or sex, as well as the few Hutu who refused to join them. In the reprisals in which some 100,000 Hutu were slaughtered, the employed and the educated and the semi-educated were the special targets for revenge, which was also directed indiscriminately against Hutu.[8] Nor did 1972 see the end of these massacres, which continued into 1973, with intermittent killings thereafter.

In India, the conflicts in the process of decolonization were aggravated by religious cleavages. At the time of partition, the relationship between the

British, Hindus and Muslims was hardly comparable to the two-tier structure of Rwanda under Belgian mandate. Hindus were in a great majority, some 300 million Hindus as against 100 million Muslims. They were separated from Muslims not only by their religion, but also by caste prohibitions on intermingling. They had been more ready than Muslims to seize the opportunities for British education, and they were largely the administrators of India for the British. It was mainly from their ranks too that India's businessmen, financiers and professionals were recruited.[9] To be sure, the great majority of Hindus and Muslims must have been living in equal poverty. Still, in an independent India, politically unified but communally divided, Hindus would have dominated the society.

Partition transformed this situation, giving dominance to the majority, Muslim or non-Muslim, in the partitioned sections. But the distribution of populations, with substantial religious minorities in areas dominated numerically by members of other religions, or with much intermingling of people of different religion, or with segregated enclaves, did not permit of an easy severance into a Hindu India and a Muslim Pakistan. The structure thus gave opportunity for the persecution of minorities, and for retaliation in massacre, as reprisal provoked counter-reprisal in areas of mixed living, and as atrocity against Hindus or Sikhs in Muslim areas, or against Muslims in areas of Hindu or Sikh dominance, set off counter-massacres in a continuous spiral of escalating violence.

Already massacres had started in some areas prior to partition, when communal sentiment became inflamed in the troubled course of constitutional negotiation. In Calcutta, following the proclamation by the Muslim League of 16 August 1946 as Direct Action Day, Muslim

> mobs howling in a quasi-religious fervor came bursting from their slums, waving clubs, iron bars, shovels, any instrument capable of smashing in a human skull... They savagely beat to a pulp any Hindu in their path and left the bodies in the city's open gutters... Later, the Hindu mobs came storming out of their neighbourhoods, looking for defenseless Muslims to slaughter. Never, in all its violent history, had Calcutta known twenty-four hours as savage, as packed with human viciousness. Like water-soaked logs, scores of bloated cadavers bobbed down the Hooghly river toward the sea. Other corpses, savagely mutilated, littered the city's streets. Everywhere, the weak and helpless suffered most... By the time the slaughter was over, Calcutta belonged to the vultures. In filthy grey packs they scudded across the sky, tumbling down to gorge themselves on the bodies of the city's six thousand dead.[10]

And the Calcutta massacres triggered off other massacres not only in neighbouring areas, but across the continent in Bombay.

Relationships were particularly explosive in the Punjab. This was a Muslim majority province, but Muslims constituted only about 57 per cent of the population of over 34,000,000 enumerated in the 1941 census. In the west they were markedly predominant: in the east both their numbers and dominance fell away. Here lay the homelands of the Sikhs who had ruled over most of the province only some hundred years earlier, and of the Hindu Jats, a peasantry also with martial traditions.[11] In the city of Lahore, almost equally balanced populations pressed their rival claims. The city of Amritsar, built around the Golden Temple, was the main religious and political centre of the Sikhs, who numbered some six million, concentrated mostly in the Punjab. And beyond these cities was the province's 'mosaic of communal pockets set haphazardly amongst one another'.[12]

Inevitably, partition into a Muslim west and a Hindu east was highly disruptive. Lahore went to Pakistan, Amritsar to India. The Sikhs, split in two by partition, became the principal actors in the tragedy of the Punjab. Five million Sikhs and Hindus were left in Pakistan's half of the Punjab, over five million Muslims in India's half.[13] It was an invitation to massacre.

Massacre in the Punjab had preceded partition. In the village of Kahuta, where 2,000 Hindus and Sikhs and 1,500 Muslims lived in peace, a Muslim horde had set fire to the houses in its Sikh and Hindu quarters with buckets of gasoline. Entire families were consumed by the flames. Those who escaped were caught, tied together, soaked with gasoline and burnt alive like torches. 'A few Hindu women, yanked from their beds to be raped and converted to Islam, had survived; others had broken away from their captors and hurled themselves back into the fire to perish with their families.'[14] In Lahore, a tolerant city of some 500,000 Hindus, 100,000 Sikhs and 600,000 Muslims, a Sikh leader had precipitated violence by hacking down a Muslim League banner with a cry of death to Pakistan. In the riots which followed, more than 3,000 were killed, most of them Sikh. On the eve of independence, 15 August 1947, the city was a scene of desolation. 'Almost a hundred thousand Hindus and Sikhs were trapped inside Old Lahore's walled city, their water cut, fires raging around them, mobs of Muslims stalking the alleys outside their *mahallas*, waiting to pounce on anyone venturing out.' In Amritsar, 'murder was as routine an occurrence in its bazaars and alleyways as public defecation. The city's Hindus devised the cruel tactic of walking up to an unsuspecting Muslim and splashing his face with a vial of nitric or sulphuric acid. Arsonists were in action everywhere.' While the city authorities were performing the independence day rituals, 'an enraged horde of Sikhs was ravaging a Muslim neighbourhood less than a mile away. They slaughtered its male inhabitants without mercy or exception. The women were stripped, repeatedly raped, then paraded shaking and terrified through the city to the Golden Temple, where most had their throats cut.' In the countryside, Sikh bands attacked Muslim villages and neighbourhoods. 'A particular savagery characterized their killings. The circumcised penises of their Muslim male victims were hacked off and stuffed into their mouths or into the mouths of murdered Muslim women.'[15]

Campbell-Johnson, Press Attaché to the last British Viceroy of India, wrote[16] that perhaps the most horrifying feature of the communal insanity was the lust of the strong to seek out the weak for massacre: hospitals and refugee trains were the special targets of these crazed assassins. There were periods of four and five days at a stretch during which not a single train reached Lahore or Amritsar without its complement of dead and wounded.[17] In some of the trains, almost all the passengers had been most horribly slaughtered. So too, the refugee columns on the roads became an easy target for loot and massacre.

Many of these genocidal massacres were carried out by mobs in murderous frenzy. They were not a centrally organized government-directed type of genocide. Hindu and Muslim leaders gave assurances of protection to minority communities, and on 22 July 1947, shortly before partition, spokesmen for the prospective governments of India and Pakistan in a joint statement solemnly guaranteed protection to all citizens. This guarantee, it was stated, 'implies that in no circumstances will violence be tolerated in any form in either territory. The two Governments wish to emphasize that they are united in this determination.'[18] There was seemingly a remarkable faith in the effectiveness of the projected boundary force. But the leaders had greatly underestimated the extent and destructiveness of the communal passions unleashed by partition, and they were powerless to control the conflagration in the Punjab.

[*Genocide* (Harmondsworth: Penguin, 1981), 57–66.]

HELEN FEIN

44 The Armenian Genocide and the Holocaust

I proposed an explanation of both the Armenian genocide and the Holocaust as emerging from the latent implications of the political formula adopted by a new elite in a state in decline, a formula legitimating the raison d'etat of the state as the vehicle for the destiny of the dominant group from which the victim is excluded by definition.[1] The theory inferred predisposing and facilitating conditions which were specified in both cases but abandoned the notion of a specific trigger or precipitant. These conditions are:

1. The victims have previously been defined outside of the universe of obligation of the dominant group. (This is a necessary but not sufficient condition for the third step.)
2. The rank of the state has been reduced by defeat in war and/or internal strife. (This is a predisposing condition toward a political or cultural crisis

of national identity in which the third step becomes more likely to occur....)

3. An elite that adapts a new political formula to justify the nation's domination and/or expansion, idealizing the singular rights of the dominant group, rises to power....
4. The calculus of costs of exterminating the victim ... changes as the perpetrators instigate or join a (temporarily) successful coalition at war.... The calculus changes for two reasons: the crime planned by the perpetrators becomes less visible and they no longer have to fear sanctions.[2]

This was exemplified in both genocides. In the Armenian case, one can show these correspondingly numbered states, processes, and events: 1) the exclusion of non-Muslims from the Islamic universe of obligation and their legal and social inferiority in the Ottoman Empire; 2) the decline of the Empire, shrinking gradually since the 17th century, in territory and population which were rapidly and steeply reduced by military defeats in the 20th century; 3) the rise of the Young Turks (coming to power in 1908) and their adaption of Pan-Turanian ideology as a new basis for legitimation of their right to domination; and 4) the alliance of Turkey with Germany and the Central Powers in World War I which rendered Turkey immune to protests and sanctions of the western Allies, diminishing the visibility of the Armenians and giving the Turks the opportunity to repudiate treaties with Russia and other allies (especially the 1913 treaty) which protected the Armenians.

In the case of Germany, the corresponding conditions are: 1) the preexistent exclusion of the Jews from the Christian universe of obligation over two millennia by the dominant church which defined them as deicides and stigmatized them; 2) the German defeat in World War I, the conditions of peace, and the decline in the rank and prestige of the German state; 3) the rise of the Nazi Party, which, from the beginning, defined the Jews as alien, and Hitler's conception of them as non-human; and 4) the decline in the visibility of the Jews, German motives to protect them for instrumental reasons and their accountability for them as World War II increased the number of Jews under German rule and led to the redefinition of the Final Solution from that of expulsion to that of the annihilation of the Jews (both of which presume the end is their elimination).

Nowhere do I assume that Hitler needed or used the Final Solution to legitimate his rule in 1939/41 as Baum[3] asserts repeatedly, misconstruing and never citing, but repeatedly referring to 'Fein's legitimation thesis'.[4] Hitler needed an ideology to legitimate the right of the state as agent of the *Volk*—the community based on the Aryan ideal-type—to exist and to expand in order to attain power in 1933. Baum develops the thesis that the extermination of the Jews was meaningless action, denying the self-proclaimed motives of its perpetrators. The tolerance for such action is explained by the lack of value consensus (attributed to status inconsistency) of German elites, employing a highly extended train of reductionism and regression.

Mazian[5]—whose general theory was discussed in Chapter 3—cites some similar preconditions as Fein.[6] Both Armenians and German Jews were defined as outsiders; both the Ottoman Empire and Germany had lost territory and experienced internal political strife; and in both cases the apparatus of the state was taken over by a 'powerful leadership with territorial ambitions forming a monolithic and exclusionary party.' Mazian views the victims' lack of a state of their own as an absence of an agency of social control which might check the genocidal state. Religious institutions are also agents of social control which might check the genocide in German occupied countries. The Islamic institutions utterly failed to check the Turkish genocide.

Some critics of such comparison deny the similarities between the annihilation of the Jews by Nazi Germany and of the Armenians by the Turks principally by emphasizing the difference between the prior interaction of the Armenians and Turks with that of Jews and Germans. For example, Dawidowicz (in a symposium on the uniqueness of the Holocaust) asserts:

> The Turks murdered the Armenians because the Armenians committed political acts and engaged in military stratagems which threatened Turkish hegemony.... the Turks had a rational reason for murdering the Armenians. That murder was a means to an end. The Germans, however, had no rational reason for murdering the Jews.... For the Third Reich the murder of the European Jews was not the means to an end, but the end itself.[7]

This raises many questions both about notions of rationality and of conflict. Dawidowicz's first assumption is simply wrong (see following discussion of Melson). Were it correct it would simply imply that the Turkish genocide was a retributive genocide, not that there was no genocide. Second, Dawidowicz ignores the existence of substantive rationality which is guided by an 'ethic of ultimate ends'[8] when the ends are evil as were those of the Nazis. Her limited concept of rationality prevents her from seeing how ultimate ends—the good of the Turks or Aryans—condition both perceptions of threat and the legitimacy of the means used against it. She ignores the extent to which the perception of threat is often a construction of the perpetrator through psychological mechanisms—selective generalizations, denial, displacement, and projection of blame—and ideological elaboration. If one accepts that the Nazis conceived of the Jews as a threat (so well documented by Dawidowicz[9] from Hitler's speeches and writing) one must also consider the evidence showing how the Young Turks' perception of the Armenians as a threat was the construction of their definition of Turkic identity.

Robert Melson examines the question of Armenian provocation in an arresting essay in which he concludes with a comparison of the massacre of the Armenians to the Holocaust.[10] Melson observes that there was no parallelism between the intentions, organization, and control of forces of Armenians and Turks:

> The truth of the matter is that the Armenians were not united under a single agency, even under a single political party, and they certainly did not have an army or a police force either to conquer the Turks or to defend themselves. Beyond an assumption of equality of power, the 'two-nations-same-land' argument assumes that Armenian national sentiment was somehow symmetric or equivalent to Turkish national sentiment.[11]

Melson concludes that it was the *ideological* transformation of the Young Turks, their rejection of the concept of a multi-national empire and embrace of an integral nationalism known as pan-Turkism or pan-Turanianism, which accounted for their decision to eliminate the Armenians.

After discarding the provocation thesis, Melson discriminates four factors which preceded both the Armenian and Jewish genocides as preconditions: 1) they were both communal minorities defined as unequal and persecuted; 2) both minorities modernized earlier and their relative success (compared to the dominant group) created 'tensions' with elements of the dominant majority; 3) 'the victimized group comes to be identified, either geographically or ideologically, with the enemies of the larger society and state'; 4) 'the larger society and the state experience a series of significant military and political disasters which undermine their security and worldview'.[12]

Melson's second condition is distinctive. It seems to me to be a likeness rather than a precondition and is superfluous and over-generalized (see discussion of middleman minorities in Chapter 3). Other theories which address the question of when MM's are endangered focus on the extent of competition between majority and minority, the social mobilization of lower strata of the majority group, and the pre-existence of an ideology (such as antisemitism) demonizing the minority.[13]

Dekmajian, comparing the Armenian case and the Holocaust, suggests that the pathology of the elites is another critical variable in both cases.[14] Dekmajian proposes that the crucial catalyst leading toward genocide—acknowledging other factors previously cited—is a pathological elite which strives to resolve its own identity crises stemming from the social marginality of its leaders. Such leaders embrace a new identity offered by radical ideologies which project blame for personal and national failures on scapegoats. He observes how many Young Turk ideologists and leaders involved in the massacres were of non-Turkish ethnic origin and how many Nazi leaders were *Volksdeutsche* born in peripheral areas in and outside Germany. Other criteria of marginality he uses are not well defined nor is their prevalence among leaders compared with their prevalence among the population at that time: personal failure, deprivation, 'declasse elements.' The extensive studies of Nazi Party members and leaders[15] are not drawn on to probe whether Nazi Party members did systematically differ as hypothesized from other Germans.

Dekmajian's proposition regarding the role of pathological elites deserves further examination; one could compare pre-genocidal situations where all the other necessary conditions specified exist but leaders do not elect a genocidal solution with those in which they do. To date, researchers analyzing psychological protocols of Nazi leaders imprisoned after 1945 (previously discussed in Chapter 3) did not agree that these were pathological individuals when such studies were based on blind appraisals: i.e. psychologists not knowing the subjects, not prejudiced by their deeds. There are no comparable studies of Turkish leaders who planned the massacres.

This brief review of some comparisons of the origin of the Final Solution and the Armenian massacres shows both the extent of agreement on underlying causes and the variety of other factors which may be adduced as contributing, predisposing or necessary causes. Given the diversity of focus and the tangled web of the phenomena, this variety is not as surprising as the degree of concurrence.

[*Genocide: A Sociological Perspective* (London: Sage, 1993), 71–5.]

Section VII

Ethnic Conflict and Nationalism

INTRODUCTION

Ethnic cleavages have provided the grounds for many conflicts throughout history. In the world of modern plural states, seeking to 'build nations' and create 'national identities', ethnic alignments may subvert such developments, especially where they coincide with economic inequalities. Michael Hechter's earlier model of 'internal colonialism' (see his article in *Nationalism* (1994)) sought to explain the persistence of ethnic sentiments and the revival of nationalism in the peripheral areas of industrial societies, notably Britain. John Stone's introduction to a special issue of *Ethnic and Racial Studies* summarizes both the model and the criticisms to which it has been exposed.

As important as economic factors has been the role of the modern state, notably under colonialism. Cynthia Enloe shows how colonial administrations sought to classify, divide, and absorb colonized populations in ethnic terms, and accorded special roles to peripheral groups such as the so-called 'martial races'. Colonial societies also saw increased competition between incorporated ethnic communities. In the post-colonial period this expresses itself in a politics of ethnic entitlement. For Donald Horowitz, these new states are characterized by a concern with political domination by ethnic groups; power is sought for its value in conferring status and this finds expression in the pursuit of symbolic goals such as language.

In many post-colonial national states ethnicity has also played a crucial role. In Latin America indigenous ethnic movements against the state have been recurrent. Florentia Mallon argues that the different political responses of their Indian communities are the result of quite dissimilar modern experiences in plural states like Peru, Bolivia, and Mexico. In Asia, by contrast, ethnic arithmetic in the new states, according to Selig Harrison, favours larger, central groups, at the expense of smaller, more peripheral communities like the Baluchs. In Pakistan this produces a political stalemate. The Baluchs cannot achieve their territorial goals, while the Pakistani state was unable to use Islam to dilute ethnic allegiances and create a unified nation. Brass, in his broad overview of ethnicity and caste in modern India, also emphasizes the role of the modern, unifying state in recognizing ethnic cleavages. At the same time, central élites often intervene in regional conflicts between opposed ethnic groups, who are differentially mobilized in the division of labour and whose allegiances may be cross-cut by other ties.

In South-East Asia ethnic relations display considerable variety, violent in Burma, fragile in Malaysia, and harmonious in Singapore. David Brown explores these different patterns of national integration and seeks to explain them in terms of different types of state and regime. Deniz Kandiyoti reveals a similar variety in the patterns of national reproduction, especially in Asia and Africa. Ethnic nationalism has had ambiguous effects on the status of women, both confining them as mothers in the home and liberating them as participants in the struggle for national emancipation.

As in the case of homeland *ethnies*, diaspora communities play an important economic and political role in the modern world. For Milton Esman, diaspora people, host society, and homeland form a triangular relationship which is conducive to support for nationalism in the homeland. The ability of diasporas to influence the course of events is conditioned by their access to resources, the opportunities offered by the host society, and their degree of solidarity. Diasporas are one example of 'peoples' who desire national self-determination. Hakan Wiberg explores the different conceptions of the term 'people' from a legal and international standpoint, in which the right of national self-determination has become restricted to ex-colonies. Ethnic claims for national independence which do not fit this conception have led to state repression and raised serious international problems across the world, from Bosnia and Chechnya to Sri Lanka and Burma.

These virulent conflicts have encouraged scholars and statesmen to consider different strategies of ethnic conflict regulation. According to Sammy Smooha and Theodor Hanf, these range from partition to various forms of national democracy (ethnic, consociational, and liberal); models which the authors apply to various geopolitical conflicts. John McGarry and Brendan O'Leary widen this discussion to include modes of conflict elimination and conflict management. Under the first heading they include partition, mass population transfer, and secession. Under the second they focus on hegemonic control, but also consider federalization, arbitration, and consociationalism as modes of accommodating ethnic demands with the integrity of states.

The proliferation of options for conflict regulation suggests the protean nature, unpredictability, and intractability of ethnic conflicts throughout the world. Clearly, ethnicity, which on one level is so important in the creation of nations, has also on another level proved to be a serious obstacle to nation-building in Africa, Asia, and to a lesser extent, Latin America.

One of the major challenges for the 'new world order' lies in managing the multiple conflicts arising from the dissolution of the Soviet Empire into successor states possessing substantial aggrieved ethnic minorities. Ray Taras explores four conditions under which such ethnic conflicts within states might spill over into the international arena and the Pan-European institutions that might contain them. He asks whether this revolt of ethnic 'sub-groups' against the national states is a threat to the formation of stable liberal democracies in Eurasia. Or can this revolt be viewed more positively, as the harbinger of a new interdependent post-nation-state order, in which the aggressive assertion of state sovereignty will give way to a global society which recognizes the rights of small ethnic nations?

JOHN STONE

45 Internal Colonialism

In recent years *Internal Colonialism* has become an increasingly popular concept in the analysis of race and ethnic relations. It has been applied to a wide range of situations including the black ghettos of America,[1] the Celtic fringe of Britain,[2] and the Palestinians in Israel.[3] Some scholars find it a useful analytical tool that helps to place patterns of ethnic and racial dominance in a broad comparative perspective; other scholars dismiss it as a misleading analogy that obscures more than it illuminates.[4] Whatever position one takes, there can be no doubt that internal colonialism is a highly controversial concept that needs to be tested against data drawn from many different societies, and this makes it an appropriate subject for the first special issue of *Ethnic and Racial Studies*.

The papers included in this issue, with the exception of Hechter and Levi's that was written specifically for the Journal, were originally presented to a panel of the International Studies Association in Washington DC during February 1978. They are written by specialists from a number of different disciplines—sociology, political science, social anthropology and history—and are based on evidence derived from a diverse range of societies which includes Canada, France, Finland, Italy, Alaska, Hungary and Romania. Given the variety of perspectives and the diversity of the empirical evidence, it is not surprising that the concept of internal colonialism meets with different responses from the different writers. Reece, Ritter and Alapuro find that it provides considerable insight into the social, economic and political relationships they are exploring; McRoberts and Verdery suggest substantial modifications and refinements to the basic model; and Palloni finds it largely inappropriate to the society and region that he is analysing.

It is possible to trace the origins of the concept of internal colonialism to at least as far back as the 1930s when it was used to characterize the relations between North and South in the United States.[5] The analogy between the situation of colonial domination and the position of racial and ethnic communities within industrial societies has only slowly become explicit in the writings of scholars. However, the argument is not new and it is interesting to remember that a major post-war debate between European apologists for colonialism and an American administration intent on dismembering European empires in the name of national self-determination centred around the so-called 'salt water fallacy'.[6] The Europeans maintained that 'colonialism' was not confined to relationships overseas and that the situation of the American Indians, if not the blacks, was colonial in essence. The same basic thesis was resurrected and recast in sociological jargon by the radical critics of the mid-1960s and soon became widely acceptable. Ironically, the Europeans who started the argument overlooked analogous colonial relationships within their own metropolitan boundaries and it took a North American scholar, Michael Hechter, to popularize the application of internal colonialism to the Celtic fringe of the United Kingdom and thus, by extension, to other long-established European states.

This is not to deny that there was some awareness of European ethnonationalism, to use Walker Connor's term,[7] before the late 1960s. It is perhaps no coincidence that the scholars with the greatest perception of the phenomenon had often been keen students of colonial societies, where the boundaries of nations and states[8] could not, by any stretch of the imagination, be seen as identical. Studying the problems of ethnic conflict, 'tribalism' and national integration in these situations might naturally suggest the need to reexamine the assumptions about the cohesiveness of the (inaccurately-named) 'nation-states' of Europe. For many of these assumptions were based on poor historical scholarship as well as certain biases within the social sciences themselves.[9] Thus Coupland's pioneering study, *Welsh and Scottish Nationalism* (1954), arose out of his earlier interest in colonial nationalism and, more recently, French Africanists like Yves Person and Christian Coulon have developed a strong concern with Breton and Occitan nationalism after many years studying nationalism in Africa.

Apart from providing the inspiration for the analogy, classical colonialism may also have influenced the development of ethnonationalist sentiment in a more direct way. A number of scholars have claimed that the end of empire, by reducing the material and occupational advantages resulting from membership of the tradition European state, has been an additional factor strengthening the appeal of micro-nationalism in Western Europe.[10] As in the arguments over the role of oil discoveries in the promotion of nationalist and separatist movements in, for example, Scotland, Biafra, or Cabinda, this remains a plausible, if unproven, hypothesis.

The first contribution to this issue focuses specifically on this recent resurgence of ethnonationalism—ethnoregionalism in Hechter and Levi's terminology—in the Western World. Three basic aspects of the problem are emphasized by the authors that are closely linked to the internal colonialism thesis. For, by defining inter-regional relationships as 'colonial', nationalist leaders have tried to inspire popular support for movements designed to promote greater autonomy, if not outright secession. Hechter and Levi analyse the social bases, intensity and timing of ethnic mobilization which can be seen as an answer to some of the criticisms raised against Hechter's original formulation of the thesis. Some of these critics have argued that the crude link suggested between ethnic separatism and capitalist industrialization does not hold in many cases so that, for example, the classic nineteenth century separatisms of Eastern Europe emerged prior to any significant capitalist penetration of largely rural areas. These regions lacked commodity markets, large scale production and a significant proletariat. Further criticisms point out that capitalist exploitation and development has not always followed cultural lines; that even where the model appears to fit it does not explain why separatist tendencies are stronger in one area rather than another; and that it certainly does not account for situations of regional 'over-development'.[11]

Hechter and Levi's addition of a segmental dimension to the cultural division of labour can be seen as one possible solution to the problem of explaining some of the diversity in ethnic mobilization. It might usefully be compared to the theory of ethnic conflict recently proposed by Mughan which emphasizes the relationship between modernization, relative deprivation and the distribution of power resources.[12]

Two further points raised by Hechter and Levi are of particular interest. The first is the extent to which ethnic sentiment is in part a product of the tolerance of the central state, for it has been noted in other contexts that the lack of success of many separatist movements can be closely linked to the strategies of central governments.[13] A second point is the emphasis on the international dimension of ethnonationalism. Perhaps one should include here the *deliberate* attempts to foster ethnic sentiment, or to suppress it, as a tactic in the international balance of power. This process was clearly illustrated in the 1975 agreement between the Shah of Iran and the Baathist leadership in Iraq which rapidly submerged the aspirations of Mustafa Barzani and his Kurdish followers in the waters of the Shatt-el-Arab. The role of India in the Bangladesh secession, and the activities of the Somalis, Russians and Cubans in the Ogaden are further reminders of the importance of international politics in the development of regionalism and the analysis of separatism.

The remaining papers in the issue select various aspects of the internal colonialism thesis and examine them in relation to case studies of specific societies. McRoberts draws a sharp distinction between the internal colonialism thesis and the idea of a cultural division of labour. He finds the second concept to be a much more flexible and valuable tool in analysing the historical and contemporary development of Quebec. For, as he points out, 'Quebec was at the same time, both core and periphery; a core to an Ontario periphery, but a periphery to a British core', and these relationships have changed over time. Furthermore, it is often more satisfactory to use the individual, rather than the region, as a basic unit of analysis, and particular attention should be paid to internal divisions within a cultural group instead of assuming a situation of cultural solidarity.

According to Reece, the internal colonialism analogy fits the Breton data rather well, and he documents the material exploitation and linguistic suppression of the region in considerable detail. However, the mere fact that Brittany is poorer than much of the rest of France does not tell us much about the process of ethnogenesis in Alsace, and the use of suicide rates as evidence for regional oppression (as all good Durkheimians would note!) raises a lot of interpretative problems. The paradox of increasing nationalist resentment at a time of significant material gains would seem to confirm Tocqueville's insight into the role of relative deprivation as a motivating force behind social action and political mobilization.[14]

Ritter, like McRoberts, notes specific deficiencies in most theories of modernization—which appear as the 'diffusion hypothesis' in Hechter's book on the Celtic Fringe—when applied to regional ethnicity. Both longitudinal and cross-sectional comparisons between settlers and indigenous groups within Alaska tend to confirm aspects of Hechter's model but show that it can be used as much within regions as between them. Alapuro also demonstrates this in describing the historical relationship between Finland and Sweden, and in his analysis of the party systems of the eastern region of Finland within the Finnish state.

Two further interesting points emerge from Verdery's historical study of inter-ethnic tensions in the Habsburg empire. First, she notes the manner in which the dynamics of internal colonialism can vary according to a society's position within the world economy, so that Transylvania could be regarded, to use Wallerstein's inelegant language, as a 'semi-periphery of the world system'. Second, she stresses the important part played by the Hungarian gentry in the ethnic agitation of the eighteenth and nineteenth centuries, which parallels the activities of similar groups in other nationalist movements. Thus, during the present century, the frustrated and 'overqualified' secondary school teachers produced by the French educational system have been disproportionately involved in ethnic activist movements.[15]

Finally, Palloni examines the internal colonialism model in relation to the Italian regional situation. He rejects it in favour of a system of personalised relationships, which he terms a clientelistic model, and argues that an alliance between the elites in the core and the peripheral elites gives a better explanation of the kind of social mechanisms at work. As is often the case when attempts are made to quantify complex social relationships, a relatively sophisticated methodology tends to be based on rather crude assumptions—the Christian Democrat vote is a somewhat unreliable index of support for the core. The fact that Rome does not feature as part of the core also suggests that care must be taken before regional units of analysis are used in preference to class or status divisions, or any other non-territorial bases of stratification.

This special issue does not reach any definitive conclusions about the broad merits of the internal colonialism thesis. It does suggest that internal colonialism raises almost as many questions as it answers, and, in this respect alone, it certainly has fulfilled a valuable function.

['Internal colonialism', *Ethnic and Racial Studies*, 2: 2 (1979), 255–8.]

46 Ethnic Soldiers

Almost every multi-ethnic society has one or two groups that have been stereotyped as being prone to, and adept at, soldiering. They include some of the most popular subjects in romanticized military history: Gurkhas, Bedouin, Scots, Sikhs, Ibans, Berbers, Cossacks, Maori, Mongols, Kurds, Zulus, Irish, Montenegrins. Such a list brings to mind deeds of daring, attitudes of fidelity and a communal exclusiveness that only the most persistent and imaginative outsiders can penetrate. But there are other more interesting attributes which these 'martial races' share.

All of the groups so commonly labelled as inherently 'martial' have been geographically distinct, usually occupying territories on the regional peripheries of the state—that is, the state as it was organized and delineated at the time when these groups were considered for special military treatment. This geographic concentration made them more visible as groups and made focused recruiting campaigns easier, for military recruiting is almost universally carried on in terms of spatial categories. Furthermore, the regions in which Gurkhas and their martial counterparts lived were typically remote, often mountainous. Whether their remoteness was in the mountains or on the plains or deserts, as was the case with Sikhs and Bedouin, these groups occupied territories near historic invasion routes. Initially this attribute might make recruiting difficult, but once incorporated into the military, it would allow the central state élites to employ such groups against dissident lowlands populations with less fear that they might intermingle and sympathize with the state élite's adversaries.

Such remote homelands also meant that, in many instances, the future 'martial races' had fought quite successfully against absorption into the expanded state (nation-state, empire or colony), skilfully using their knowledge of their rugged terrains to resist otherwise superior military opponents. In conducting such resistance, groups such as the Berbers or Montenegrins won begrudging respect from their encroaching enemies. While state élites first encountered them in circumstances which should have placed them in the 'least reliable' category, and thus on the outer rim of any state ethnic security map, élites were so impressed with their potential value to the state that they sought to enhance their reliability instead. This, of course, entailed risks, and in some instances—most notably Afrikaners' refusal to follow the British practice in recruiting Zulus into the South African army—commanders and their politicians determined that the now-defeated skilled fighters could not be made sufficiently loyal to serve the state military.

The perfect 'martial race' was an ethnic group that produced men who were both martial *and* loyal. This is at the heart of the 'Gurkha syndrome'.

The combination is not a natural one when, typically, the group only recently has waged protracted battles against the recruiting institution. The key ingredient necessary to make martial traits and allegiance compatible is *dependency.* By making an ethnic group dependent, the state élite can move it from the outer rim of the security map to a circle closer to the core. Those groups which have been defeated have little access to central authority and are frequently outnumbered within the newly consolidated state system. It is such vulnerability that permits recruiters to absorb them into the military with little fear of subversion or mutiny. For soldiering now becomes one of the very few means of livelihood which Gurkhas, Kurds and other such groups possess in the reordered politico-economic system. Furthermore, they are often objects of suspicion or contempt in the eyes both of other ethnic groups and the state élites. They are urged to see military service as a vehicle for gaining respect, legitimacy and protection in the larger social order of which they are now, albeit reluctantly, a part.

Groups labelled and employed as martial races also share certain intra-communal characteristics that have made them especially attractive to outside recruiters. They were conventionally categorized as 'tribes'. That is, they were perceived by state security planners—and those ethnographic observers who have advised the planners—as societies with rather confined societal boundaries in which bonds of personal allegiance and reciprocity play basic roles in locating authority and distributing power. In reality, of course, such groups as the Berbers in Algeria and Morocco, the Gurkhas in Nepal and the Montenegrins in Yugoslavia are not ethnographically uniform. But they were seen to share intra-ethnic attributes which became valuable to outsiders. That is, as will be underscored throughout this study, building militaries has been, in part, an ethnographic enterprise. Nowhere is this plainer than when state security planners were deciding how to go about absorbing such groups as the Gurkhas. Such ethnic groups were so openly acknowledged to be culturally distinct, even 'exotic', that security optimization demanded they be examined with an anthropologist's eye. Up to the present day, state security and academic ethnography have had a persistent, if uneasy, reciprocal relationship.

What was recognized within such communities was a mode of social organization that would enhance enlistments. Outsiders with state missions to perform would exploit existent, traditional authority structures in their recruiting. This was an eminently efficient recruitment strategy. Individual enlistment may be worth the effort if the state is recruiting *officers*, for they have to have special individual characteristics, and not too many persons have to be enticed at any one time. But, to fill the ranks, you need to bring in scores or even hundreds of men at a time. To fill the ranks, it is more efficient to operate through authority figures within a structured community who can draw upon existing bonds of obligation and credibility for the sake of bringing their communal subordinates into the army. Voters are mobilized in many societies in precisely the same fashion. All that is needed is (a) for those authority structures to stay intact so that communal élites maintain their superior status over subordinate members of the community, and (b) for outside military recruiters to make it rewarding for the communal élites to play this middleman role as suppliers of men to the ranks. Being gradually coopted in this manner, of course, makes indigenous élites less useful as buffers and bargainers for their ethnic followers.

Thus, while different from one another, the ethnic groups that came to fill the 'martial race' role in many armies shared certain conditions which made them both available for state military service and attractive to military recruiters. Above all, they were groups that had proved their soldiering skills in resistance to outside invasion, but, once defeated, were in positions of vulnerability and dependency. As we will see, this basic political weakness became a source of ethnic cohesion and also determined the security functions they performed in the larger state military establishment.

A group presumed by military commanders to possess a special soldiering aptitude was thought to be just that: composed of would-be soldiers (and would-be soldiers' wives, since a serviceable 'martial race' had to have a familial structure compatible with army life). It was rarely thought to be composed of would-be *officers*. There were exceptions to this widespread assumption, however. For instance, Berbers in Morocco came to be perceived of as potential officers, as were Sikhs in the Indian army. Significantly, neither group was a model of political weakness. The Sikhs in particular came close to occupying positions in the core of the state apparatus. For the most part, however, those ethnic group members who might on rare occasions achieve officer rank usually rose out of the ranks after displaying a marked capacity for cultural assimilation into the ethnic group that commanded the army and controlled state institutions.

To be a member of a martial race therefore entailed being exceptionally fit to perform the functions of an infantryman. Rarely would Gurkhas or Bedouin be recruited chiefly to serve as rank-and-file soldiers in logistical support units. They were seen to be most valuable in the front lines during combat. To carry out the role of competent, reliable infantryman, they had to be dependent on those ethnic outsiders who officered their units. For, it was assumed, such soldiers were traditionally accustomed to obeying authority if authority-wielders demonstrated competence. The symbiotic relationship between the ethnic 'martial race' in the ranks and the ethnic group dominating the officer corps was a microcosm of the larger ethnic security system which would maintain the state order.

Once in the army, the groups were typically organized in units of their own. Even if the rest of the army was intended to serve as a model of a genuinely integrated national institution—and this was itself uncommon—it was considered legitimate to keep the martial races in regiments that were explicitly communal. The state underscored the ethnic character of the 'martial races' symbolically as well as organizationally. There was deliberate cultivation of insignia and uniforms highlighting the distinction of the unit. Where ethnicity was so explicitly reinforced, it was intended to bolster morale among the recruits, who would presumably fight not just to defend the state but to uphold communal pride.

[*Ethnic Soldiers* (Harmondsworth: Penguin, 1980*a*), 26–30.]

DONALD HOROWITZ

47 Symbolic Politics and Ethnic Status

Santayana once spoke of the 'deadly significance of symbols.' How apt the depiction is for symbolic conflict in severely divided societies. Issues such as the status of languages, the names of towns and states, the identity of incumbents in honorific positions, national anthems, cow slaughter (in India), and the right (or sometimes duty) to wear particular garments have been significant and deadly at various times. In Kenya, public attention was riveted on the issue of whether a Kikuyu or a Luo became principal of the University of Nairobi, for its outcome seemed to foreshadow the general future of non-Kikuyu.[1] Loss of a similar job by an Ibo in Nigeria some years earlier had also become a *cause célèbre*. When it was proposed to change the name of Mysore state in India to Karnataka, there was bitter opposition. Karnataka was a name associated with the Lingayats, whose domination of the state was feared by others. When there were complaints that Malaysian Chinese were refusing to rise as the national anthem was played in theaters, parliament imposed criminal penalties.[2] In every case, what might have been seen as a minor issue involved deeper disputes over group status.

Demands for the symbolic recognition of status are not confined to multiethnic polities or to Asia and Africa. Insecure, declining, or rising groups frequently lay claim to a favorable distribution of prestige through the official invocation of symbols. Claims of this kind need have no direct effect on the distribution of tangible resources among the contending groups, but they usually connote something about future treatment: who will be discriminated against and who will be preferred. Although all political systems must cope with some such claims, in a multiethnic society the size and intensity of the symbolic sector, as a fraction of all demands, constitute an excellent indicator of malintegration.

In a study of the temperance movement in the United States, Joseph R. Gusfield has articulated the objectives of symbolic conflict in terms of status politics.[3] The origins of such a movement Gusfield finds in the propensity of groups to derive 'prestige and self-respect' from the harmony 'between their norms and those which achieve dominance in the society.'[4] When status uncertainties exist, efforts are made to obtain authoritative allocations of prestige. Since the distribution of prestige is partly determined by the symbolic action of public officials who ' "act out" the drama in which one status group is degraded and another is given deference,' groups make 'demands upon governing agents to act in ways which serve to symbolize deference or to degrade' opposing groups.[5] Politics thus constitutes one of the important 'rituals by which status is determined.'[6]

Politics has a commanding position for determining group status in post-colonial societies, for two reasons. First, non-political institutions have been relatively weak in such societies and cannot compete effectively with the state in the allocation of prestige. Second, under colonial rule, attributes and emoluments of ethnic status became matters of state policy. Standing above the groups, the colonial state became the arbiter of ethnic relations. In so doing, it displaced frequently less visible, *ad hoc*, more dispersed methods of handling such matters. The state became the focal point for ethnic claims, a role inherited by the post-colonial state. The imprimatur of government is therefore indispensable to satisfactory ethnic status.

The objective of symbolic demands is a public affirmation of legitimacy where legitimacy is contested. The precise issues chosen for symbolic emphasis depend on the issues that demarcate the contestants. The temperance issue illustrates this point, for the conflict-symbol—drink—was chosen for its utility in distinguishing nativist, Protestant, small-town groups from immigrant, Catholic, urban groups. Symbolic conflicts, however, also accentuate points of difference between the groups and generate countersymbols around which opposition to a symbolic claim can coalesce. In India, for example, as Hindu demands for cow protection increased, Muslim demands for the right to slaughter cows also intensified, and the Muslim Kurbani festival, at which cows were slaughtered, grew in importance.[7] Status conflicts can help shape group culture.

The ethnic uses of symbolic discourse

Symbolism is effective in ethnic conflict, because it clothes ethnic claims in ideas and associations that have acknowledged moral force beyond the particular conflict, thereby masking something that would otherwise be controversial. As 'Malaysian Malaysia' calls forth all the power of egalitarian principles diffused on a worldwide basis, so 'sons of the soil' evokes the sanctity of the home against intrusion. The larger principles in which a demand is cast provide justification and render it more difficult to deny the validity of the demand. The pursuit of conflict through symbols thus obscures their segmental character by linking them with universals and simultaneously avoids running afoul of prevailing local ideology. When, for example, 'communal,' including religious, demands were said to be illegitimate in India, the Sikhs, differentiated on the basis of religion, avoided the prohibition by casting their demands in terms of the Punjabi language instead. In politics, as in literature, the crux of any symbol lies in its ambiguity,[8] and that is also its value in conflict. Symbolism permits the purposeful confusion of meaning, so as to conflate segmental claims with a wider political morality.[9]

Viewing ethnic politics through the prism of status claims, several things become clearer. Foremost among these is the relationship of status to psychological elements in ethnic conflict. Status discontents, notes Gusfield, appear when the prestige accorded to a group is less than group members believe is merited.[10] Since social recognition affects self-esteem, much political behavior aims at bringing objective (or official) recognition into harmony with subjective or aspirational recognition.[11] Mass 'restiveness occurs when the state is not symbolically aligned with those who feel threatened.'[12] Status discontents flow, therefore, from a challenge to self-esteem or to place in a territory. Consequently, it can be expected that groups whose personal worth has been cast in doubt will be most vigorous in seeking authoritative reassurance. Group status and group psychology are not severable. They meet in struggles over the symbols of prestige and dominance. Similarly, those whose full membership in the polity is placed in doubt by exclusionary policies and symbols that connote exclusion are likely to advance their own symbolic claims to equality.

The politics of language and the language of politics

Jayakan Bahasa Kebangsaan—'Glorify the National Language'—read a neon sign in Kuala Lumpur. The national language referred to was Malay. It may seem odd to persuade people to glorify a language. It seems more appropriate, perhaps, to encourage them to learn and use it. But 'glorify' is an antonym for 'denigrate,' and the Malay language had occasionally been denigrated. In any case, more than just language was at stake. Under the colonial regime, the language of administration was the language of the ruler, and the status of the language denotes the status of the group that speaks it. In Assam, when Bengalis and hill people opposed making Assamese the official language of the state, a placard in their procession read 'Assamese is a donkey's language.' An Assamese counterprocession declared Bengali to be 'a goat's language.' A slur on the language is a slur on the people, and a 'glorified' language is a glorified—or at least securely positioned—people.

Language, then, is a symbol of domination. Groups claiming priority—Assamese, Malays, Sindhis, Sinhalese, Mauritanian Moors, Maharashtrians—demand that their language be given what they invariably call 'its rightful place,'[13] by which they mean exclusive official status. For groups uncertain about their worth, the glorification of the language is also intended to reflect a revised or aspirational evaluation. The status of the language is a symbol of newfound group dignity. Claims for official status for a language are typically demands for an authoritative indication 'that some people have a legitimate claim to greater respect, importance, or worth in the society than have some others.'[14] And conversely for resistance to official status: for many years, Somalia had no official script because Osmania, the leading script for Somali, was identified with the Darood who previously used it.

In more directly competitive terms, official status may aid group performance. For example, it has been commented that the Assamese language movement grew out of 'a deep feeling of mortification among Assamese-speaking people at the relative excellence of Bengali-speaking people, who surpassed them in the economic field and outdid them in competitive examinations, including university examinations.... It was thought that, once Assamese emerged as the official language, the Bengalis, for want of their efficiency in it, would automatically be put at bay.'[15] And so language issues are symbolically capable of weaving together claims to exclude others with claims to shore up uncertain group worth. Language is the quintessential entitlement issue.

Groups on the receiving end of such demands respond accordingly. The Bengalis demanded that Bengali be recognized as an alternative official language. Until a prohibition on such debate took hold in Malaysia, Chinese were wont to speak of multilingualism. Berbers in Algeria and Tamils in Sri Lanka have claimed linguistic 'parity.' All such demands go much beyond language. As the demand for a single official language reflects the desire for a tangible demonstration of preeminence, so linguistic parity is transparent code for equality more generally.

The matter of group worth finds its way into linguistic counterdemands as well. An advanced group, commanded to study, be examined, and work in the language of a backward group, quickly calls attention to the inadequacy of the language sought to be made official—to its simplicity, its shallow literary tradition, its underdeveloped grammar and vocabulary, the paucity of textbooks in the language, the unsuitability of the language for use in technical fields, and its general inferiority to the colonial language it is supposed to displace. The suitability of a language for official purposes and the degree to which it is in need of upgrading are measured by comparison to the European language that formerly held sway, just as the respective groups are measured in the same way. Whether the counterclaim is for multilingualism or parity, or for retention of the colonial language (as in Mauritania and India), the galling thing for advanced groups is to trade what is in their eyes a richer linguistic heritage for a poorer one. The Bengali statement on this is typical of that of Mauritanian Kewri, Malaysian Chinese, and Tamils in Sri Lanka and

India: 'Those concerned with academic standards may, of course, still wonder if the Assamese language can adequately cope with advanced teaching. . . .'[16] For a Bengali to have to work in Assamese is, from his perspective, to be demeaned.

The more the Bengalis object, the more the Northern Sudanese deprecate the contribution of the Southern tongues to human culture, the more the Tamils flaunt their Dravidian heritage, and the more the Kewri make sarcastic comparisons of Arabic to French, the more firmly do the denigrated groups insist on official status for their language. The objections raise the issue of worth more sharply.

Moreover, the backward groups have a rejoinder to these arguments. They may agree that their language is inadequate and in need of help, just as they agree that they themselves are inadequate and in need of help. Without official status, Sinhala will lose out to Tamil, it is said; and without a bootstrapping effort to improve and 'catch up,' neither the people nor the language can adapt to the competitive milieu. The inadequacy of the language becomes a point in favor of official status and especially in favor of the creation of language institutes to coin new terms, propagate correct usage, and in general enrich the language and cultivate the intellectuals who work in it (as well as employ them). If cultural superiority is in doubt, that, too, is something the state has the power to rectify. Politics can be used not only to confirm group status but to enhance it.

Consequently, in an array of states, the so-called vernacular intelligentsia has been in the front ranks of language policy proponents and language policy beneficiaries: Malay teachers and Chinese teachers, Moorish teachers and Kewri teachers, students and writers and filmmakers. And, as the hotbed of Malay language demands was the Malay language and literature institute, so the hotbed of Arabic language demands in Mauritania was the institute of Islamic studies.[17]

The role of such institutes and their personnel provides a further insight into the conflict-generating power of linguistic issues. Symbolic issues may transcend subethnic differences if symbols are selected for their breadth. Language often has this ethnic cohesion-building capacity. It is directly related to middle-class job and promotion prospects in the civil service and secondarily in the private sector. But it reaches far beyond the middle class and those dependent on it, to ordinary people 'far removed from rivalry over urban white-collar jobs,' as Robert N. Kearney points out of the Sinhala Only movement. 'The individual Sinhalese tended to identify his fortunes with those of his language and to see the status of his language reflected in his own sense of dignity and self-respect.'[18]

Language is therefore a potent symbolic issue because it accomplishes a double linkage. It links political claims to ownership with psychological demands for the affirmation of group worth, and it ties this aggregate matter of group status to outright careerism, thereby binding elite material interests to mass concerns. Needless to say, language is not the only issue that can do this. Official religion served the same function in Burma. At first, the 'special position of Buddhism' was 'recognized,' but in 1961 this equivocal phrasing was repealed by a State Religion Act that made Buddhism the official religion. The Act required the Public Service Commission, in recruiting candidates for government employment, to accord the same weight to a knowledge of Pali, the liturgical language, as to other subjects, a provision which reflected the careerist motivations of some proponents.[19] But the main support for the state religion movement came from the countryside, a fact which cannot be explained without reference to the significance of the state religion as a symbol of Burman hegemony. This is precisely the way it was interpreted by minorities, especially the Kachins and Chins. Religion, then, can sometimes link elite and mass concerns. But clearly it is more plausible to think that fluency in the working language of a bureaucracy will become an issue more often than will facility in scripture.

Language is so often an issue, in other words, not because there is something special about linguistic difference or something mystical and therefore conflict-producing about the process of communication. The reason is more mundane: in a multilingual state, there has to be a language policy to decide trivial and important issues of linguistic choice. What language will be spoken in parliament? Will letters sent to government offices in one language rather than another be returned? If not, what will be the language of reply? What about road signs? Such issues find their way to the symbolic agenda wherever linguistic differences coincide with ethnic differences and so can be used as a measure of group status. Where there is no such coincidence, other issues can and will be found. Land is a common issue that tests claims to primacy and equality. As the Guyanese are fond of saying, 'he who owns the land owns the country.'[20]

There is another side to language conflict, not captured by my analysis of the ethnic symbolism of language. Policy choices have consequences, not just for careers of members of one or another ethnic group, but for social-class mobility, for bureaucratic effectiveness, and for international contact. To opt for multilingualism usually means perpetuating the colonial language as the interethnic 'link,' thereby preserving the advantages of the advanced group, with its greater mastery of that language, and also preserving ties to universities in the former metropole. To choose an indigenous language is to make job recruitment more egalitarian classwise, but to discriminate ethnically, and also to diversify international educational contacts (since French or English is no longer the 'natural' second language, students may choose university training in a variety of countries). All of these consequences raise serious issues, not likely to be resolved by a careful process of weighing tradeoffs once symbolic claims are made.[21]

Far more likely is the imposition of a language over violent opposition or the imposition of an unsatisfying compromise: common formulae are to make one language 'national' and another 'official' or to except minority regions from the sway of the official language. Where civilian governments rule, the configuration of party competition or its absence will have much to do with the choice. Where military regimes rule, the ethnic composition of the regime will usually be determinative.

This much, however, is very clear. Symbolic claims are not readily amenable to compromise. In this, they differ from claims deriving wholly from material interest. Whereas material advancement can be measured both relatively and absolutely, the status advancement of one ethnic group is entirely relative to the status of others. That is an important reason for being precise about what is at stake in ethnic conflict. Ethnic claims are expressed in moral language and are not quantifiable. How does a policymaker divide up the 'glorification' of the national language? Some leaders have been notably more skillful than others at splitting symbols in ethnic conflict. But the task is inherently frustrating. That is why compromise outcomes are more likely in political systems that provide countervailing incentives for politicians and their followings to behave moderately in the assertion of group claims.

[*Ethnic Groups and Conflict* (Berkeley and Los Angeles: University of California Press, 1985), 216–24.]

FLORENCIA E. MALLON

48 Indigenous Peoples and the State in Latin America

In Tlatelolco, in the symbolically laden Plaza of the Three Cultures, there is a famous plaque commemorating the fall of Tenochtitlán, after a heroic defence organised by Cuauhtémoc. According to the official words there inscribed, that fall 'was neither a victory nor a defeat', but the 'painful birth' of present-day Mexico, the mestizo Mexico glorified and institutionalised by the Revolution of 1910. Starting with the experiences of 1968—which added yet another layer to the archaeological sedimentation already present in Tlatelolco—and continuing with greater force in the face of the current wave of indigenous movements throughout Latin America, as well as the crisis of *indigenismo* and of the postrevolutionary development model, many have begun to doubt the version of Mexican history represented therein.[1] Yet it is important to emphasise that the Tlatelolco plaque, fogged and tarnished as it may be today, would never have been an option in the plazas of Lima or La Paz. The purpose of this essay is to define and explain this difference by reference to the modern histories of Peru, Bolivia and Mexico. In so doing, I hope to elucidate some of the past and potential future contributions of indigenous political cultures to the ongoing formation of nation-states in Latin America.

As suggested by the plaque in Tlatelolco, the process and symbolism of *mestizaje* has been central to the Mexican state's project of political and territorial reorganisation. By 1970, only 7.8% of Mexico's population was defined as Indian, and divided into 59 different linguistic groups. Geographically and politically speaking, the Indian population tended to inhabit the periphery of the country: Oaxaca, Chiapas and Yucatán in the south; the Huasteca and the Tarascan and Huichol regions in the east and west, respectively; the Yaqui in the north. When new indigenous organisations were formed in the 1970s and 1980s, the country's central Nahua zone was not considered Indian; 'Great Councils' were set up for Otomis, Matlatzincas, Totonacs, and so on, but not for the Nahua. The Náhuatl group, the strongest and most numerous in Mexican territory, was considered instead the native counterpart to the conquerors in the mix that generated the 'cosmic race', the mestizo who occupies such a privileged place in the national mythology. In this context, the Indians of central Mexico are identified as improverished peasants, pure and simple, and they are supposedly looked down upon as rural poor rather than as Indians. It is in this sense that we can best appreciate the political content of the constructions of 'mestizo' and 'Indian' in Mexico, and better understand how Judith Friedlander, writing in 1975 and basing herself on a community in Morelos, could conclude that the category 'Indian' had no cultural content whatsoever, and served only as an instrument of class oppression.[2]

Generally speaking, the anthropological and historical literature for Mexico reflects this politically constructed division between a mestizo core and an indigenous periphery. Scholars writing on central Mexico have tended to use a class analysis: their subject is a peasantry undergoing proletarianisation. It is here where the literature on the Mexican Revolution is richest, and where the great debate between 'campesinistas' and 'proletaristas' was centred in the 1970s and 1980s. Indigenous cultures are the subject of study in peripheral regions: here are located the great anthropological traditions of Yucatán, Chiapas, Oaxaca, the Puebla highlands, the Yaqui Valley. Often these indigenous cultures have been studied outside of time, as scholars have searched for precolumbian continuities in the *cofradías*, fiesta complexes, and other customs. Only recently have the cultural and social processes of these peripheral regions become more historicised.[3]

The Peruvian case shows important differences. In 1961 the Indian population was calculated at approximately 47%, and concentrated in the area of the southern highlands known as the 'mancha india'. In contrast to Mexico, the Peruvian state has been unable to centralise its power through a unifying process of *mestizaje*, and has not relegated the Indian to the country's periphery. Instead, the political construction of 'Indianness' has been a bipolar one: Indian highlands, white and mestizo coast; white and mestizo cities, Indian countryside. In this context, *mestizaje* separates rather than unites the population: the *misti*, or highland mestizo, is a figure signifying domination. *Mistis* mediate between the city and the Indian communities by accepting privileges from the whites in order to dominate the Indians. Historically, during the twentieth century, becoming a mestizo in urban areas often meant cutting ties with the countryside and the community of origin.[4]

Peruvian social science has reflected and reconstructed these dualisms. In the 1960s and 1970s, sociologists and anthropologists tended to adopt a modernisation perspective through which to view 'traditional' (read 'Indian') political, social, and economic systems in the countryside. Commercialisation in the rural areas and migration to the city were seen as parallel processes that together would incorporate the Indian into the modern world, through cultural transformation. In the cases where this transformation was considered complete, it was called *mestizaje*; where it remained incomplete, it was termed 'cholification'. After the guerrilla movements of 1965 and the 1968 military revolution a new variant of dualism began to emerge, in which the Indian would disappear thanks to the development of capitalism, proletarianisation, and unionisation. In the place of indigenous peoples would emerge a socialist worker peasant alliance. But in the 1980s, with the beginnings of the present civil war, the failure of the military's development project and of the electoral left, once again the social science literature has fragmented and scholars have rediscovered the pure and idealised Indian, while the concept of the Andean utopia has gained ascendancy.[5]

Though Bolivia shares with Peru, in a general sense, the bipolar construction of Indian and white ethnicities, historically and culturally speaking this construction has a different internal dynamic. Rather than a highland-coast or urban-rural opposition, we find a variety of regional and ethnic fragments being constructed and recombined across time: Quechua and Aymara plateau versus Quechua and mestizo valleys: white elites versus Indian popular classes; a colonial silver economy centred in Sucre–Potosí versus a 'modern' tin economy in Oruro–La Paz. *Mestizaje* as a process seems to affect the Quechua more than the Aymara, and to occur more in the Cochabamba valley than on the La Paz plateau. And in the city of La Paz, the presence of Aymara intellectuals, students and entrepreneurs is impressive when compared to Peruvian cities.[6]

The distinction between plateau and valley, Aymara and Quechua, can also be discerned in scholarly production about Bolivia. On one side we find the anthropological works about Yura, K'ulta or the Norte de Potosí, which generally emphasise the continuities in Indianness—whether Quechua or Aymara—since before the Conquest, and contrast the Indian community with mestizo or white society. On the other side we have the literature on the 1952 Revolution, the Cochabamba Valley, or the mineworkers, which emphasises *mestizaje*, radical politics, and social movements oriented around class. Despite the analytical richness of many studies, the literatures tend not to dialogue between themselves, claiming instead that their object of study is the 'true' Bolivian reality. This occurred with the work of Tristan Platt about the nineteenth-century 'reciprocity pact' between Andean communities and the state, work which though based on the reality of the Norte de Potosí, was for quite a while accepted as a general model for Bolivia.[7]

In all three countries, these different political and intellectual constructions of ethnicity have had an impact on the role played by indigenous cultures and utopias in the elaboration of oppositional movements and ideologies. In Mexico during the twentieth century, with few exceptions (such as the Yaqui during the 1910 Revolution, and the COCEI in Juchitán during the 1980s), indigenous cultures and ideologies have been marginal to the big popular movements. In Peru, by contrast, already in the 1920s José Carlos Mariátegui noted that the Indian problem was inseparable from the land problem, suggesting that the construction of a truly Peruvian socialism needed to begin from the Indian. In recent years as well, there has been much talk of the Andean utopia—that only if one starts from Andean and indigenous traditions, from the visions of the future and of change constructed in the highlands of Peru, will it be possible to elaborate a truly successful and inclusive national project. In Bolivia as well, Katarismo was born in the 1970s, taking the name of Tupaj Katari, Aymara leader of the Andean civil war of 1781–2. Though seeking to form a multi-ethnic and multi-class alliance of peasants, students, workers, and intellectuals from around the country, Katarismo has taken as its unifying banner the indigenous and Andean traditions of the Aymara plateau, and it is there where the movement has had its greatest force.[8]

['Indian communities, political cultures and the state in Latin America, 1780–1990', *Journal of Latin American Studies*, 24 (1992), 35–40.]

SELIG S. HARRISON

49 Ethnicity and Politics in Pakistan: The Baluch Case

Significantly, while the Baluch, Sindhis, and Pashtuns comprise less than 30 percent of the population, they identify themselves historically with ethnic homelands that make up 72 percent of Pakistan's territory. To the ideologists of Pakistani nationalism, it is infuriating that the minorities should assert proprietary claims over such large areas of the country despite their numerical inferiority, and Islamabad consciously seeks to obliterate regional and ethnic identities in order to pursue modernization programs addressed to what is viewed as the greatest good for the greatest number of Pakistanis. But to most members of the minorities, the disparity between their population and their territorial claims is irrelevant, since 'Pakistan,' i.e., the Punjabis and Muhajirs, is perceived as having occupied and annexed their territories forcibly as an imperial power.

It is no accident that the smallest of the minorities, the Baluch, who see no hope for achieving significant power in Pakistani politics even under a democratic dispensation as a result of their numerical weakness, is the most alienated from Islamabad and the most responsive to secessionist appeals. Only the Baluch have waged significant armed insurgencies against successive Pakistani central governments, and only the Baluch have thrown up a broadly accepted leadership that is openly committed to achieving independence from Pakistan. By contrast, the Sindhis, while seriously disaffected from most regimes in Islamabad, have not yet produced an effective separatist movement, and the more calculating Pashtuns are content, for the moment, to use separatism as a thinly veiled bargaining weapon to win provincial autonomy and to exact economic and political concessions from the Punjabi-Muhajir elites. [...]

In seeking to mobilize a nationalist movement today, Baluch leaders can manipulate the powerful historical symbolism of a tortuous struggle for survival stretching back for more than two thousand years.[1] According to the most widely accepted Baluch legends, the Baluch and the Kurds were kindred branches of a tribe that migrated northward from Aleppo in what is now Syria shortly before the time of Christ in search of fresh pasture lands and water sources. One school of Baluch historians attempts to link this tribe ethnically with the original Chaldean rulers of Babylon; another with the early Arabs.[2] In any case, there is agreement that the Kurds headed toward Iraq, Turkey, and Northwest Persia, while the Baluch moved into the coastal areas along the southern shores of the Caspian Sea, later migrating into what are now Iranian Baluchistan and Pakistani Baluchistan between the sixth and fourteenth centuries.

Western historians regard the Aleppo legends as unsubstantiated, but scholars in Baluchistan and the West generally agree that the Baluch were living along the southern shores of the Caspian at the time of Christ. This consensus is based largely on linguistic evidence showing that the Baluchi language originated in a lost language linked with the Parthian or Medean civilizations which flourished in the Caspian and adjacent areas in the pre-Christian era.[3] As one of the older living languages, Baluchi is a subject of endless fascination and controversy for linguists. While it is classified as a member of the Iranian group of the Indo-European language family, consisting of Persian, Pashtu, Baluchi, and Kurdish, Baluchi is a separate language and is closely related only to one of the members of the Iranian group, Kurdish. In its modern form, it has incorporated borrowings from Persian,

Sindhi, Arabic, and other languages, but it has retained striking peculiarities of its own.

J. H. Elfenbein, the most authoritative student of the Baluchi language, divides Baluchi into six regional dialects: the Eastern Hill, Rakshani, Sarawani, Kachhi, Lotuni, and Coastal. While there is 'no doubt that all dialects are more or less mutually intelligible,' Elfenbein stresses, 'what differences do exist are deeply rooted' and complicate the development of a standard literary language.[4] The problems of standardization are aggravated by the lack of a universally accepted alphabet for Baluchi. There is a rich and ancient Baluchi folklore that has been handed down orally from generation to generation, but the first attempts to develop a Baluchi script were not made until about 150 years ago. By 1969, when a Baluchi textbook was prepared at McGill University, a distinctive Baluchi alphabet consisting of thirty-seven letters plus diacritics and special symbols, had evolved as an outgrowth of the nationalist movement. The authors of the textbook described it as a modified form of the Persianized Nastaliq style of the Arabic alphabet, which has been adapted to the sounds of Baluchi and contains a number of new letters.[5] But the Nastaliq script is not universally accepted by Baluch writers, and many Baluch nationalist works have been written in Urdu or English.

The Baluch have been remarkably successful in preserving their separate cultural identity in the face of continual pressures from strong cultures in neighboring areas. Despite the isolation of the scattered pastoral communities in Baluchistan, the Baluchi language, for all of its dialect difference, together with a widely shaped folklore tradition and value system, have provided a unifying common denominator for some five million people in seventeen major Baluch tribal groupings native to the 207,000 square-mile areas reaching from the Indus River in the east to the Persian province of Kerman in the west. This tradition has been strong enough to subsume and absorb the Brahui linguistic subgroup within Baluch society.[6] Politically, however, the Baluch record is a mixed one, marked heretofore by relatively brief interludes of unity and strong leadership among centuries of fragmentation and tribal strife.

The most impressive demonstration of Baluch political unity came in the eighteenth century when several successive rulers of the Baluch principality of Kalat succeeded in expanding their domain to bring most of the Baluch areas under one political umbrella. Mir Nasir Khan, who ruled Kalat for forty-four years beginning in 1749, set up a loose bureaucratic structure embracing most of Baluchistan for the first time and got the principal Baluch tribes to adopt an agreed system of military organization and recruitment.

During the early years of Nasir Khan's reign, Kalat was a tributary of the newly established state of Afghanistan, a salient historical fact which is cited by Afghan nationalists today as a justification for including Baluchistan in a 'greater Afghanistan.' Once he had established his army on a solid basis, however, Nasir Khan took on the Afghans militarily, fighting Ahmad Shah Durrani's forces to a standstill in 1758. Thereafter, Kalat enjoyed sovereign status until the arrival of the British, though it remained a military ally of Afghanistan.

Prior to the Nasir Khan period, the early Kalat rulers had paid tribute to Iran, and Nasir Khan himself was installed on his throne with the backing of the Persian Emperor Nadir Shah. But Nasir Khan rejected his tributary status following the assassination of Nadir Shah and the decline of centralized authority of Iran. He even made nominal claims of sovereignty for Kalat over the freewheeling Iranian Baluch areas. For their part, the Iranian Baluch never produced a unified kingdom of their own comparable to Kalat, though they consistently resisted Persian and Afghan incursions. Certain strong chieftains were able to establish localized confederacies covering much of Iranian Baluchistan, notably Dost Muhammad, who was beginning to forge a coherent kingdom in southeastern Iran when Reza Shah Pahlavi subdued his forces in 1928.

For Baluch nationalists today, Nasir Khan's achievements remain an important symbol, providing some semblance of historical precedent for the concept of a unified Baluch political identity. Indeed, Ghaus Bux Bizenjo, former Governor of Pakistani Baluchistan and a leading nationalist, argued in an interview with the author that Nasir Khan's successors would have succeeded in creating an enduring polity if it had not been for the deliberate manipulation of the internal divisions in Baluch society by the British Raj. Playing off rival chiefs against each other in the half century after Nasir Khan's death, Britain systematically divided the Baluch area into seven parts. In the far west, the Goldsmid Line gave roughly one-fourth to Persia in 1871; in the north, the Durand Line assigned a small strip to Afghanistan in 1893; and in British India, the Baluch areas were divided into a centrally administered entity, British Baluchistan, a truncated remnant of Kalat, and three other smaller puppet principalities.

In Bizenjo's view, the Baluch suffered this unhappy fate simply because they happened to live in an area of vital military importance to the British, in contrast to the more fortunately situated Afghans. It was historical accident, he explained, that gave the Afghans the opportunity for independent statehood denied to the Baluch. Thus, it served the interests of the British to foster a unified Afghanistan under their tutelage as a buffer state that would shield their Indian Empire from Russia. Conversely, it was necessary to divide the Baluch in order to assure unimpeded control of the resulting imperial frontier with this Afghan buffer. Nasir Khan's Baluchistan might have emerged in a buffer state role instead, Bizenjo contended, if the Russians had moved southward sooner than they did and if they had swallowed up Afghanistan before Britain embarked on its nineteenth-century 'forward policy.'[7]

It should be remembered that the nineteenth and twentieth centuries marked a major watershed for the Baluch, who had never lost their freedom before their conquest by the modern armies of Britain, Iran, and Pakistan. The Baluch bitterly resisted their forcible incorporation into Iran by Reza Shah in 1928 and later into the new state of Pakistan left behind by the British Raj in 1947. In the case of Iran, the Shah's iron repression kept the Baluch largely under control with the exception of a brief, Iraqi-supported insurgency until the Khomeini revolution led to a weakening of the central authority in 1979 and an outpouring of long-suppressed nationalist feeling. In Pakistan, by contrast, Baluch insurgents have waged an on-again, off-again guerrilla struggle ever since the departure of the British, culminating in a brutal confrontation with 80,000 or more Pakistani troops from 1973 to 1977 in which some 55,000 Baluch were involved, 11,500 of them as organized combatants. Casualty estimates during this little-known war ran as high as 3,300 Pakistani soldiers and 5,300 Baluch guerrillas killed, not to mention hundreds of women and children caught in the crossfire. At the height of the fighting in late 1974, United States-supplied Iranian combat helicopters, some manned by Iranian pilots, joined the Pakistani Air Force in raids on Baluch camps. The Baluch, for their part, did not receive substantial foreign help and were armed only with bolt-action rifles, homemade grenades, and captured weaponry.

Significantly, when they started their poorly prepared insurgency in 1973, the Pakistani Baluch were not fighting for independence but rather for regional autonomy within a radically restructured, confederal Pakistani constitutional framework. They were seeking the creation of a Baluch-majority province[8] as part of a larger redemarcation of provinces to be followed by a division of powers within which Islamabad would retain control over defense, foreign affairs, communications, and currency, while the provinces would have unfettered local authority over everything else, including the exploitation of natural resources and the allocation of development funds.

By the time the shooting subsided in 1977, however, separatist feeling had greatly intensified. The wanton use of superior firepower by the Pakistani and Iranian forces, especially the indiscriminate air attacks on Baluch villages, had left a legacy of bitter and enduring hatred. Since nearly all Baluch felt the impact of Pakistani repression, the Baluch populace has been politicized to an unprecedented degree.

There is now a widespread Baluch nationalist consciousness that cuts across tribal divisions. Islamabad, however, ignoring this emergence of nationalism, tends to think of Baluch society solely in terms of its traditional tribal character and organizational patterns. Baluch discontent is artificially stimulated by the tribal sardars (landholding tribal chiefs) to protect their feudal privileges, it is argued, and economic modernization will alleviate Baluch unrest by gradually eroding the sardari system. This argument is undercut by the fact that the central government has been more than willing to protect and extend the privileges of cooperative sardars. Most sardars have attempted to safeguard their privileges by avoiding direct identification with the nationalist movement, while keeping the door open for supporting the nationalist cause in time of confrontation between the Baluch and the central government, as in the case of the 1973–7 insurgency. The only exceptions are the chieftains of the two largest tribes, Ataullah Mengal and Khair Bux Marri, who are the principal leaders of the underground organizations working for independence.[9] Mengal and Marri, now in exile in London and Kabul respectively, have followers and allies in all of the major tribes.

To be sure, it is important to recognize the strength of tribal loyalties and the monolithic power of the sardar in the hierarchical Baluch social structure to mobilize and discipline his tribes. It was the unified support of nearly every tribe, acting on a tribal basis, that made the Baluch insurgency during the 1973–7 period so effective. At the same time, it would be a mistake to underestimate the significance of the ongoing process of urbanization and education that is taking place as a result of the slow but steady impact of economic change. By conservative estimates, out of a total Baluch population of some five million in Pakistan, Iran, and the Persian Gulf, there are 300,000 to 450,000 literates[10] who are providing volatile raw material and politically conscious leadership for the Baluch independence movement.

The inability of the Punjabi-Muhajir establishment to neutralize ethnic self-assertion with Islamic appeals has been particularly evident in the case of the Baluch. The Jama'at-i Islami and other Islamic fundamentalist groups in Pakistan are generally viewed by the minorities as agents of the Punjabi-Muhajir establishment. Jama'at leaders preach a pan-Islamic doctrine in which ethnicity—and nationalism—are explicitly repudiated as incompatible with Islam. For this reason Jama'at leaders enjoy less influence among the minorities than local Islamic dignitaries who consciously seek to minimize the potential for conflict between the claims of Islam and the claims of ethnic identity. In tribally based societies such as those of the Baluch and the Pashtuns, the Muslim divine stands apart from the tribal power structure and depends on varying degrees of partnership with the tribal chief. In certain parts of Iranian Baluchistan, as Philip Salzman has explained,[11] the *mawlawi* (religious scholar) has been able to challenge the power of the sardar, but the mullah (religious leader) in Pakistani Baluchistan is generally kept in a junior partnership role.

The great majority of the Baluch are Sunnis of the Hanafi rite. However, there is a cleavage between the Sunni majority and an estimated 500,000 to 700,000 Zikri Baluch, who live in the coastal Makran area and in Karachi. The Zikris believe in the Messiah Nur Pak, whose teachings supercede those of the Prophet Muhammad himself. This heresy has led to intermittent Sunni repression of the Zikris ever since the sect originated during the fifteenth century. The Zikris have generally been allied with the Baluch nationalist cause in contemporary Pakistani politics, except for a significant segment in Karachi, where the late Zulfiqar Ali Bhutto's Pakistan People's Party (PPP) has enjoyed substantial Zikri support.

One of the most significant indicators of the vitality of Baluch nationalism is likely to be the extent to which the Baluch are able to develop a standardized language rendered in a commonly accepted script. Although a lively literature has developed as an adjunct of the nationalist movement, Baluchi books, magazines, and newspapers reflect a widespread linguistic confusion rooted in the existence of six regional dialects.

The 1973–7 insurgency aroused unprecedented political awareness in Baluchistan, and the degree of psychological alienation from Islamabad now evident in Baluchistan is strikingly reminiscent of the angry climate that was developing in East Pakistan during the late 1960s.[12] In particular, the Baluch nationalist movement, like the Bangladesh movement, is fueled to a great extent by economic grievances.[13] Ever since the secession of Bengali East Pakistan in 1971, many observers have blithely compared Baluchistan to Bangladesh, predicting the inevitable emergence of an independent Baluchistan sooner or later. This comparison is valid up to a point, but on closer examination, it is apparent that there are important differences between the two cases. Baluch nationalism has not yet acquired the cohesion and momentum that Bengali nationalism had achieved in 1971. Baluch leaders are seeking to build a nationalist movement on the uncertain social and cultural foundations of a fragmented tribal society with a minuscule middle class; low literacy levels; a relatively undeveloped literature with three competing systems of transliteration; a narrow, albeit growing, base of nationalist activists; and a relatively recent tradition of mass participation in political life. By contrast, the Awami League, which led the Bengalis to independence, operated in a relatively homogeneous society with a significant middle class; a well-established cultural and literary life; a vital, standardized language; a broad base of nationalist activists; and a heritage of mass politicization dating back to the struggle against the British Raj. Moreover, the dispersion of the Baluch population poses peculiarly complex and intractable problems for Baluch nationalists. Bengali leaders faced some demographic adjustments in dealing with their Hindu and Bihari Muslim minorities, but these problems were of a lesser magnitude than those presented by the Baluch diaspora.

In military terms, the Bangladesh independence forces were not only protected by the physical separation of East Pakistan from West Pakistan by more than 1,000 miles of Indian territory, but they also received substantial assistance from the Indian Army in the critical stages of their struggle. Baluchistan is directly exposed to the adjacent provinces of Pakistan and Iran, and the Baluch had not yet found a foreign mentor in late 1984. To be sure, it is possible that the Baluch will receive Soviet or other foreign support at some point in the future, which might well enable them to overcome their handicaps. But in 1984 the prospects for achieving an independent Baluchistan remained uncertain, and slender possibilities thus still existed for political settlements between the Baluch and the Pakistani and Iranian central governments.

['Ethnicity and political stalemate', in Ali Banuazizi and Myron Weiner (eds.), *The State, Religion and Ethnic Politics: Afghanistan, Iran and Pakistan* (Syracuse, New York: Syracuse University Press, 1986), 270–7.]

PAUL BRASS

50 The Politics of Ethnicity in India

India's linguistic, religious, ethnic, and cultural diversities are proverbial. So are the political mobilizations and the violent conflicts and antagonisms which have arisen from time to time among and between persons from its distinctive cultural groups. However, it is important to note that neither political mobilization nor ethnic and cultural antagonisms flow naturally out of India's diversities. The 1971 *Census of India* enumerated 33 languages with speakers of more than one million, but only 15 of them have achieved any form of significant political recognition.

The 1981 census enumerates a tribal population of more than 50 million persons divided into hundreds of distinct groups. Many political mobilizations have occurred among several of the tribal groups from the nineteenth century up to the present, of which a few have developed into bitter, violent, and secessionist movements directed against non-tribals, against particular state governments, or against the Government of India itself. On the other hand, many tribal groups have not mobilized and have not rebelled. Moreover, the forms which tribal mobilizations have taken have been diverse. Some have focused on economic grievances, have appeared to be class-based, and have drawn support from Marxist political organizations. Others have focused on political demands and have been organized and led by tribal leaders and exclusively tribal political organizations.

The whole modern history of India has been deeply affected and badly scarred by conflict between separatist Muslim political leaders and organizations and the Indian National Congress and by continuing Hindu–Muslim riots and pogroms against Muslim minorities in some cities and towns. Even with respect to these conflicts and the associated violence, however, they must be contrasted against periods of Hindu–Muslim cooperation. Moreover, it must be noted and needs to be explained why such conflicts have occurred more intensely in some parts of the country and have been less intense or non-existent in others where Hindus and Muslims also live side-by-side.

In the 1980s, India has faced an extremely violent movement among militant Sikhs, some of whom have become secessionist. The Punjab, where most Sikhs live, has become virtually an embattled ground in which a violent guerrilla war is being waged between Sikh militants and the Indian police. Yet, Sikhs and Hindus have cooperated politically in the past and were never before considered to be hostile communal groups.

India has also been generally characterized as a society divided by caste and caste antagonisms. Various Indian censuses before the 1930s enumerated thousands of local castes and dozens of large caste clusters within each linguistic region. Caste mobilization and inter-caste conflict have occurred in India since the late nineteenth century among many such groups. Moreover, in the 1970s and 1980s, inter-caste conflict between so-called backward and upper caste groups became intense in several states. Once again, however, it needs to be stressed that such mobilizations and conflicts have occurred among specific groups in specific regions at particular times and not others.

Migration of persons from one lingustic region to another, particularly to the relatively less densely populated tribal regions of the country and to the northeastern state of Assam and to the major metropolitan centers such as Bombay and Delhi have also produced situations which have sometimes, but not always, led to migrant–nativist political conflicts.

Part II of this book deals with the major linguistic, tribal religious, caste, and migrant–non-migrant mobilizations and conflicts which have occurred in India since Independence. In the discussions which follow in the specific chapters dealing with these issues, the following themes and arguments concerning the source of ethnic and cultural political mobilizations and conflicts are stressed.

First, state recognition in both the pre- and post-Independence periods itself has been a critical factor in explaining the rise of some ethnic and cultural movements rather than others. The British gave official preference to the Bengali language in the east rather than to Assamese and Oriya and to Urdu in the north rather than Hindi. They provided separate electorates and other political concessions to Muslims and Sikhs. They allowed migration of plains people into tribal areas in central India but forbade it in some parts of the northeast. They patronized the non-Brahman movement in south India when Brahmans were leading the Indian National Congress there.

In the post-Independence period, the government of India and the state governments sought to change the balance of recognition among some groups. Hindi was adopted as the official language of the country and of the north Indian states, definitively displacing Urdu from its remaining bastions in Punjab and U. P. Assamese was adopted as the sole official language of Assam against the wishes of the large Bengali-speaking minority and many tribal groups. Separate electorates for Muslims and Sikhs were done away with, but reservations of legislative seats and administrative and educational places for Scheduled Castes and Tribes were retained or introduced.

State recognition sometimes worked in contrary ways. On the one hand, it strengthened some of the groups so recognized and weakened others. On the other hand, in some cases, it contributed to the development of counter-movements by non-recognized groups. The best examples of this type are the numerous movements among unrecognized 'backward castes' who have sought systems of reservations equivalent to those granted to Scheduled Castes and Tribes.

A second factor emphasized here, also a political one, concerns the specific policies and political strategies pursued by the central led state governments in relation to regional and sub-regional cultural entities. One general argument stressed below is that Indian state policy towards minorities has differed in the Nehru and post-Nehru periods. Under Nehru, the central government pursued pluralist policies in relation to major language and cultural movements, recognizing especially most of the large language groups among whom major mobilizations developed for the creation of separate linguistic states. At the same time, however, the Center sought to avoid direct involvement in regional conflicts among different ethnic and linguistic groups. The Center also turned a blind eye or took no action in relation to the discriminatory policies followed by dominant regional groups within the several states of the Union.

In the post-Nehru period, however, the central government has played a more directly interventionist role in regional conflicts between opposed ethnic, communal, and caste groups. It tolerated the disruptive and allegedly murderous and terrorist activities of Sant Jarnail Singh Bhindranwale in the Punjab in order to embarrass its main political rival, the Akali Dal, in that state. During the succession struggles after 1965 between Mrs. Gandhi and her rivals, the central Congress leadership in several states moved to displace upper caste leaders from state Congress organizations and replace them with backward caste persons and to mobilize the votes of the latter castes to defeat its rivals in the state Congress and in the opposition. The consequences of these interventions, some of which may justly be perceived as socially progressive, have nevertheless often had the consequence of intensifying inter-ethnic regional conflicts and of focusing some of them upon the central government itself.

A third factor influencing the mobilization of some groups and not others has been unevenness in rates of social change among different social groups leading in turn to imbalances in their relative access to jobs, educational advantages, and political power. Each region of India has a dominant language group and particular castes, usually of elite status, who have long held disproportionate shares of public employment, educational, and political opportunities. Challenges to the preponderant shares of dominant groups in various life opportunities do not usually come from those most oppressed but from persons from groups who have some resources but not others or from groups among whom processes of social change have begun such as to make elites among them acutely conscious of the disparities between the life chances of persons from their own group and persons from the dominant groups.

A related factor is the extent to which persons from different ethnic and cultural groups actually find themselves in competition for the same niches in the division of labor in society. Migrant laborers who go to areas of the country where the demand for farm or plantation labor is high may not come into conflict with local competitors, whose numbers may be much smaller than those of the migrants themselves. However, it is often the case that educated persons from different religious, language, caste, and other categories compete for the most prestigious and secure jobs in public service and for the educational opportunities to gain access to them. It is not surprising, therefore, that conflict between competing educated classes in search of scarce jobs has been among the most prevalent sources of ethnic conflict not only in India but throughout the developing world.

Another factor influencing the types of conflict which occur in India concerns levels of political action and levels of ethnic loyalties. India is a society which contains both multiple levels of political arenas and hierarchies of loyalties to cultural categories. At the level of the village and its surroundings, *jati*, the local aspect of caste may provide a basis for economic action, political organization, and social conflict. In a unit as large as a district, however, correspondingly larger units of political action or political coalitions across *jati* boundaries become necessary for effective political action. The unit of loyalty and political action may then become the caste category or caste cluster or a coalition of related castes. At the state level, only the largest caste categories with wide representation throughout large parts of a state may be able to act in solidary and politically effective ways. In many cases, such actions at the state level become impossible and other kinds of loyalties to faction and party become predominant. At the national level, caste becomes virtually ineffective as a basis for sustained political mobilization for the available caste categories at this level lack appropriate social or economic content.

Alternatives to caste as an organizing principle for political conflict also exist at every level in Indian politics, particularly from the district upwards. At those levels, categories such as Hindu and Muslim become more prominent, language loyalties become critical, one's status as a migrant or a 'son of the soil' may be decisive, or factional, party, and ideological bases for political division may prevail.

The three following chapters in part II deal with the major types of conflicts which have occurred in post-Independence politics in which different ethnic and cultural categorizations have been used as bases for political mobilization. Chapter 5 focuses on language conflicts, chapter 6 on conflicts involving non Hindu minorities and between tribals and non-tribals, and chapter 7 on caste mobilization, caste conflict, and migrant–non-migrant conflicts. The central argument which links the treatment which follows of these different sets of conflicts is that India's cultural diversities do not themselves provide inherent obstacles to national unity or inevitable sources of conflict. Conflicts between language, religious, and ethnic groups tend to center around issues of jobs, educational opportunities, and local political power. The roots of these conflicts have often been quite similar in the pre- and post-Nehru periods. However, a combination of increasingly assertive centralizing drives by the Indian state and its national leadership with an intensified struggle for power in center, state, and locality have contributed to the intensification of conflicts based on such categories in the post-Nehru era.

[*The Politics of India since Independence*, New Cambridge History of India, Vol. IV: 1 (Cambridge University Press, 1990), Introduction, 129–34.]

DAVID BROWN

51 Ethnicity, Nationalism and Democracy in South-East Asia

In the foregoing examinations of the differing characterizations of the state, ethnicity has been depicted as related, variously, to the collapse of traditional authority structures, to the state's managerial institutions, to the factional rivalries amongst political élites, to regional economic disparities, and to the class structure of society. Clearly, if each or any of these features of the political, social and economic environment were intrinsic to the nature of ethnicity, then the discussion would contain a central inconsistency. It has been argued here, however, that these aspects of the environment are only contingently related to ethnicity; while what is intrinsic to ethnicity is its ideological character—as a psychological and political kinship myth. Both the type of cultural attributes to which this myth attaches, and the kind of economic, political or social mechanisms by which it is engendered are, it has been argued, crucially influenced by the character of the state.

Thus the discussions have had two purposes: to offer explanations of the various patterns of ethnic politics in Southeast Asia, and to explore different models of the state so as to make explicit some of their ethnic implications. The intention has been to narrow the perceived gap, frequently evident in Southeast Asian studies, between the recognition and description of the unique politics of each country, and attempts at comparative and conceptual analysis. The resultant argument has been in two stages: that ethnic consciousness constitutes an emotionally powerful ideological response to the pattern of insecurities generated by the power structure of the state, and therefore that the character of the state constitutes the dominant influence upon the character of ethnic politics. The exploration of the different perspectives on the state thus offers a series of differing scenarios as to the development of ethnic consciousness and its relationship to state nationalism. The resultant explanations are distinct in that they employ the markedly different languages relating to class, corporatist, ethnocratic, clientelist or internal colonial models, but are comparable in terms of their common reference to the causal impact of the character of the state. It has not been suggested that the perspectives used for the examination of ethnicity in each country are of general validity; merely that they provide, in each case, an illuminating angle from which to examine some facets of that country's ethnic politics.

Such an approach begins to offer a basis for tackling the crucial question as to why countries which have many similarities in the cultural pluralism of their societies should nevertheless vary greatly in the character and consequences of their ethnic politics. Why is there endemic ethnic violence in Burma, fragile but generally non-violent ethnic relations in Malaysia, and generally harmonious ethnic relations in Singapore?

One crucial factor influencing the relative success of the different states in implementing their ethnic strategy relates to the capacity of the state. Whereas the Singaporean state has sufficient administrative and ideological capability to implement its ethnic management strategies in a reasonably competent way, the Burmese state has no such capacity, and merely has a disruptive impact upon the targeted communities. But to say that the state's ability to manage ethnicity depends on its capacity to manage ethnicity is clearly not very profound. The intention here, therefore, is to draw together some themes as to the relationship between the character of the state and the nature of ethnic politics which have been implicit in the discussions of the different types of state. The discussion will be limited to two factors which seem to have influenced the politics of each of the Southeast Asian states so as to inhibit the effective management of state–ethnic relations. These factors relate to the ambiguities evident in the states' portrayals of the nation, and to the role played in ethnic–state relations by the ideology of democracy.

There is no inevitable clash between the claims of ethnicity and the claims of state nationalism, and each of the models of the state which have been discussed offers a potentially feasible formula for achieving their reconciliation through state management of the ethnic–state relationship. But there is no denying that such efforts at ethnic management rarely seem to have been fully successful, though there are, as we have noted, major variations in the extent and form of the ethnic tensions which such failures have engendered.

The way in which ethnicity and state nationalism relate to each other depends in part upon the type of state nationalism adopted in a particular country. We have previously noted the distinction, deriving from Meinecke and Kohn, between the idea of the political nation, and the idea of the cultural nation.[1] In the first formulation—the political nation—the state claims that its people constitute a nation because they have willingly come together to form a community of equal citizens irrespective of their racial, religious or linguistic backgrounds. They are a nation because they wish and believe themselves to be a nation; and nationhood is defined in terms of the equal duties, rights and status of all citizens. Such a formulation of a political nation might seem to be particularly appropriate for societies, like those in Southeast Asia, which contain several ethnically conscious cultural communities. It would seem to imply, most clearly, a depiction of the nation as an overarching ethnically neutral community in which ethnicity is regarded as politically irrelevant to the national politics of meritocratic, democratic or universalistic procedures which are employed to define citizenship rights. Alternatively, the idea of the political nation may accommodate the idea of a community comprising ethnic components, with each component enjoying equal status, power, and access to resources, according to some formula of 'unity in diversity', consociationalism, or federalism.

The alternative formulation of the nation is as the cultural nation: the community which constitutes a distinct people with its own language, way of life, history and homeland. When a state claims to constitute such a cultural nation it is seeking to arrogate to itself the power of the kinship myth by portraying the whole society as an ethnic community. The claim to cultural nationhood allows the state to demand the allegiance of its people in ways that echo the imperative of ethnic loyalty. The nation is depicted as offering identity, security and authority to its members such as the family offers the child, and in return the nation demands the loyalty and allegiance the child owes to the family. The more that the state can point to, or itself generate, the common cultural attributes which define the cultural nation, the more claim it has to the allegiance of its members. Similarly, the more clearly an individual possesses the cultural attributes which define the national community, the more fully does that individual deserve the citizenship rights accruing to membership of the nation.

The distinction between the political nation and the cultural nation was originally intended and employed to refer to different types of nation-state. But what is apparent in the foregoing discussions of Southeast Asian politics is that instead of these states fitting neatly into one or other category, they each seek, in different ways, to employ both formulations. They claim somehow to offer equal citizenship rights to all citizens irrespective of cultural attributes, but they also define the nation in cultural terms so as to give priority of some kind to those possessing the attributes of cultural nationhood. It is this ambiguity or incoherence in the designation of the nation-state which hinders the effective management of ethnic–state relations.

The origin of this ambiguity in the definition of the nation is quite clear. The state élites consider cultural nationalism to offer a stronger basis for political cohesion and societal loyalty than does political nationalism; and indeed political nationalism is perceived to be both western in origin and colonialist in its connotations. Despite their cultural pluralism, each of the Southeast Asian societies can derive, from their pre-colonial history, an image of a set of dominant cultural attributes and values which form the core for the definition of contemporary nationhood. They therefore seek to portray the culturally plural society as one which is potentially culturally homogeneous, and which already has a cultural core around which nationhood can develop. For Burma this cultural core is Burman, for Singapore it is the idea of consensual Asian values, for Indonesia it is embodied in *Panca Sila*, for Malaysia it is the *Bumiputra* attribute, for Thailand it is the Central Thai monarchy and culture.

The employment of two different languages of nationhood leads to two incompatible definitions of citizenship. Those groups in society which do not possess, or do not fully possess, the attributes of cultural nationalism are nevertheless told by various clauses in their constitutions and laws, and by political leaders, that they inhabit a political nation which gives equal citizenship status and rights to all. But they are also told, in other clauses, laws, speeches and policies, that they are in some sense of lower status than those who possess the prescribed cultural attributes; that they are, in effect, second-class citizens. This produces a sense of confusion and grievance amongst those who perceive themselves as unfairly culturally marginalized by the state. The political implication of this is that such minority cultural groups become in varying degrees alienated from the state.

Clearly this clash is greatest in the Burmese case where the state has discriminated against those who have not assimilated into Burman culture, but it has produced varying degrees of resentment against the state amongst Indonesia's *santri* Muslims, Malaysia's non-Malays, and Thailand's non-Thai citizens. In Singapore it emerges as a confusion amongst those whom the state suggests are 'too westernized' or who possess Asian attributes other than those fostered by the state, but who have expected equal consideration in an avowedly ethnically neutral meritocracy. In such circumstances, the capacity of the state to manage state–ethnic relations is undermined by the extent of these resentments.

The ambiguities generated by the mixing of the two languages of political nationalism and cultural nationalism provide one element in explaining the problematical nature of ethnic politics in Southeast Asia, and the variations in the intensity of such problems. But there is another factor emerging out of the previous discussions which concerns the relationship between ethnic and state nationalism on the one hand, and the ideology of democracy on the other.

The claims of ethnic nationalism and of state nationalism are potentially negotiable and manageable so long as each party recognizes the legitimacy of the other's claims. In some respects, it might be expected that the impact of the dominant legitimatory argument of the twentieth century—the democratic argument—would be such as to promote the prospects for reconciliation between ethnic and state claims, since democracy appears to promise the politics of negotiation and compromise rather than the politics of confrontation and violence. But the way in which the democratic ideology has been repeatedly employed in the politics of ethnicity in Southeast Asia has been such as to reduce the possibilities for compromise and accommodation.

The most obvious way in which this occurs is in the argument frequently employed by state élites, that they wish to promote democracy in their societies but are inhibited from doing so, in varying degrees, by the ethnic pluralism which they portray as inherently anti-democratic in its implications. This argument is formulated in various ways. The 'siege' formulation of the argument portrays ethnicity in terms of the spectre of chaos; as an anti-democratic, irrational and absolutist tie which makes some variant of authoritarian rule an unfortunate necessity. Once this spectre of ethnic chaos is raised, it follows that all rational citizens will resist it and will voluntarily, and democratically, choose the option of unity, development and stability which is offered by the state. Democracy thus becomes redefined by the state as rational support for the state's restriction on the politicization of anti-democratic ethnicity. At its most extreme, this argument is used to justify the continuation of oppressive military rule in Burma, but it has also been used to legitimate the 'soft authoritarian' democracies of Malaysia, Thailand, Indonesia and Singapore.

A second formulation of ethnicity as anti-democratic portrays the state as the embodiment of a consensual Rousseauean general will, and then depicts attachments to the sub-national ethnic community as partial, self-interested attachments which threaten to undermine the national consensus and thence divide the nation. A third way of counterposing the democratic state with the undemocratic ethnic attachment is the frequent employment of the majoritarian principle. This was intended in democratic theory to refer to situations where individuals move between majorities and minorities on different issues as the balance of non-ascriptive opinions and interests repeatedly shifts. But it has been applied in culturally plural societies to legitimate the dominance of ascriptive cultural majorities. By this means the democratic argument is employed in the service of the majority cultural group claiming to represent the whole nation-state, which is therefore 'democratically' free to ignore the interests of the cultural minorities.

By such means, the state which claims to be democratic can promote its own claim precisely by depicting ethnicity as an anti-democratic and therefore illegitimate claim. Since there is immense pressure in the twentieth century for all states to claim such democratic legitimacy, there is a corresponding pressure to employ such a claim to reduce the bargaining power of ethnicity.

This tendency for the democratic argument to polarize state–ethnic relations is exacerbated by the parallel tendency for ethnic élites to similarly use the democratic argument to strengthen their claims against the state. The democratic argument that the individual has a right to the achievement of self-realization through taking a full and active part in public decision making, does not of itself imply that any particular grouping of individuals—in this case the ethnic community—has any corresponding right to self-determination. The ethnic nationalist claim to political autonomy cannot, in other words, be derived from the democratic argument about the political 'rights of man'. Nevertheless, the ethnic nationalist argument has frequently sought to make such a connection by means of analogy. In other words, minority cultural groups have frequently argued that, just as democracy grants the citizen the right of rebellion against an authoritarian state, so do a people—an ethnic nation—have a democratic right to assert their autonomy against the central state, which is depicted as alien and undemocratic. Thus, the ethnic minority portrays itself as the guardian of legitimate democracy, and the state as the alien and illegitimate opponent of democracy.

This use of the democratic argument both by the state and by the ethnic élites so as to portray each other as the illegitimate opponents of democracy, is one which does not necessarily produce confrontation between the state and ethnicity. None of the states examined have condemned all manifestations of ethnicity as threats to democracy; and not all ethnic élites have asserted their claims by denigrating the democratic credentials of the state. Nevertheless, it has generated suspicion and resentment in each case. The articulation of ethnic interests becomes inherently hazardous in such circumstances since it risks being labelled by the state as anti-democratic communalism. The danger has been, in each of the Southeast Asian states, that ethnic interests have been deemed democratically legitimate by the state only when they have been supportive of the incumbent régime. Ethnicity thus inhabits a shadow world—liable to be designated as subversive communalism at one moment, but applauded as the legitimate articulation of cultural values and interests at another.

The problem then, is not that ethnicity constitutes a primordial loyalty which inevitably attaches to fixed ascriptive cultural attributes and is necessarily absolutist and overwhelming, but rather that it is frequently perceived in such a way by state élites who portray it as a primitive and threatening force to be suppressed, subverted or tamed. It has been argued here that it is not the cultural attributes themselves which define and generate the ethnic attachment, but rather the variable patterns of status, power and economic insecurities in the social environment. Ethnic consciousness is indeed 'irrational' in the sense that it is a response to emotional needs for identity, security and authority. But it fulfils these needs in part by providing an ideological myth of continuity and permanence which facilitates the adaptation of individuals to changing situations of insecurity. If the contemporary state intervenes in society sufficiently to influence the cultural attributes, political options, and security threats with which members of the multicultural societies are faced, then it becomes clear that the form, political manifestations and political consequences of ethnicity are not fixed, but depend to a significant extent upon variations in the character of the state.

[*The State and Ethnic Politics in Southeast Asia* (London: Routledge, 1994), 258–65.]

DENIZ KANDIYOTI

52 Women, Ethnicity, and Nationalism

Debates about the nature of society within turn of the century modernist movements in the Middle East gave the position of women a prominent place. Just like Western colonisers who used the 'plight' of Oriental women as a hallmark of the savagery and depravity of the colonised and as a justification of the mission incumbent upon their own civilisational superiority, modernist reformers bemoaned the condition of women as a clear symptom of backwardness.[1] As Zubaida points out, the main enemy of early reformers was 'backwardness' rather than 'foreignness'. Although they were politically opposed to European domination, they were not culturally antagonistic to its civilisation.[2] At this stage, the emancipation of women could be presented as part and parcel of a national regeneration project articulated in the language of moral redemption. A pervasive feature of such 'feminism' was that rather than presenting itself as a radical break with the past, which it did in fact represent, it often harkened back to more distant and presumably more authentic origins. Islamic reformists could claim that early Islam had been corrupted by foreign accretions and bad government, and that early Islam was, in fact, totally compatible with progressist ideals. Those who emphasised ethnic rather than Islamic sources of national identity invoked a pre-Islamic past (in Central Asia for the Turks, in the Pharaonic era for Egypt and in the pre-Islamic dynasties for Iran) as the repository of national values implying a higher status for women than was the rule in their current societies. Similar tendencies were apparent in India with the invocation of a golden age of Hinduism that was not oppressive to women. The 'modern' was thus often justified as the more 'authentic' and discontinuity presented as continuity.

Before concluding, as does Gellner, that this is an instance of the 'pervasive false consciousness' of nationalist ideology, we must pause to consider the particular perils of a 'modernist' position on women and gender relations in many post-colonial societies.[3] Nationalism and secularism principally appealed to a narrow stratum of the bourgeoisie and bureaucracy who, despite their political credentials as anti-imperialists, could nonetheless be accused of succumbing to Western cultural hegemony. Moreover, representatives of more traditional ideologies such as the *ulama* (Muslim clergy) did not deny the need for technological progress, modern armies or more efficient administration. However, for the achievement of progress to proceed without undue dilution of national identity (a key dilemma of cultural nationalism), the central symbols of this identity must be preserved and safeguarded from contaminating foreign influences. Tensions between modernist and organicist, anti-modernist strands in nationalism found a natural focus around the personal status of 'modern' citizenry and, more particularly, around the place and conduct of women. Since they were operating essentially within the same symbolic universe, secular nationalists were at pains to establish the indigenous and patriotic credentials of their modernising projects. Women participating in nationalist movements were likewise prone to justify stepping out of their narrowly prescribed roles in the name of patriotism and self-sacrifice for the nation.[4] Their activities, be they civic, charitable or political, could most easily be legitimised as natural extensions of their womanly nature and as a duty rather than a right. Modernity was invested with different meanings for men, who were relatively free to adopt new styles of conduct, and women who in Najmabadi's terms, had to be 'modern-yet-modest'.[5]

Meanwhile, in what constituted an explicit reversal of Orientalist depictions of passive, veiled women, nationalist propaganda began portraying women unveiled, participating in athletic competitions, making public speeches and handling sophisticated technology. As Graham-Brown points out, these icons of modernity were less a comment on changing gender relations than a symbolic evocation of the dynamism of a 'new' nation.[6] Schick suggests that in such a context:

> a photograph of an unveiled woman was not much different from one of a tractor, an industrial complex, or a new railroad; it still merely symbolised yet another one of men's achievements. Once again reduced to mere objects, women were, in these images, at the service of a political discourse conducted by men and for men.[7]

Yet, women's stake in nationalism is far more complex than the foregoing suggests. On the one hand, nationalist movements invite women to participate more fully in collective life by interpellating them as 'national' actors:

mothers, educators, workers and even fighters. On the other hand, they reaffirm the boundaries of culturally acceptable feminine conduct and exert pressure on women to articulate their gender interests within the terms of reference set by nationalist discourse. Feminism is not autonomous, but bound to the signifying network of the national context which produces it.

In countries where the most prominent form of cultural nationalism is Islamic, for instance, feminist discourse can legitimately proceed only in one of two directions: either denying that Islamic practices are necessarily oppressive or asserting that oppressive practices are not necessarily Islamic. The first strategy usually involves counterposing the dignity of the protected Muslim woman against the commodified and sexually exploited Western woman. It is thus dependent on a demonified 'other'. The second depends on a 'golden age' myth of an uncorrupted, original Islam against which current discriminatory gender practices may be denounced as actually not Islamic. Although the implications of the first strategy are conservative and those of the second clearly more radical, they share the same discursive space; a space delineated by a nationalist discourse reproduced by men and women alike. Changing the terms of this discourse exacts a heavy price: alienation from the shared meanings which constitute a language of identity, affiliation and loyalty.

It may well be argued that there is no particular reason to single women out as prisoners of a discourse they share with men. However, their gender interests may, at times, dictate their own demands and produce divided loyalties with men of their class, creed or nation. Women may choose to either openly express or to suppress such divergences of interest, which they generally do at their own cost in both cases.

There is a wealth of evidence to suggest that, for women, the 'modern' is always perilously close to the 'alien', particularly when contemplated codes of behaviour can be identified as an outright betrayal of the expectations of their own communities. In this connection. Hatem relates how during Napoleon's Egyptian expedition some middle-class Egyptian women saw it as in their interests to be allied with the French.[8] Impressed by the apparent courteousness of French husbands, a group of women in Rosetta petitioned Napoleon to enforce similar relations within Egyptian families. The patriarchal backlash against Egyptian women who consorted with the colonists was apparently fierce, with alleged massacres of collaborators serving, in Hatem's view, to discipline women.

The notion that women's gender interests could be used to turn women into political 'fifth columnists' was an explicit article of official policy in at least one well documented social experiment carried out by the Bolsheviks in Soviet Central Asia between 1919 and 1929. Massell's study of the Soviet-sponsored mobilisation of Muslim women is a classic case of a modernising state 'liberating' women as a means of undermining traditional solidarities and identities based on kinship, custom and religion.[9] Molyneux also documents several instances where the emancipation of women was used as a tool for socialist transformation.[10]

Ironically, the very structures defined as backward, feudal or patriarchal by the modernising state are the ones that get redefined as ethnic markers or as symbols of 'national' identity, especially if they are forcibly obliterated by an authoritarian statist project. Indeed, the *khudzhum* (assault) in Central Asia had a radicalising effect that produced a rally around the symbols of Muslim identity. There was a substantial rise in attendance at prayers and meetings in mosques, widespread withdrawal of Moslem children (especially girls) from Soviet schools and, more tragically, a terrible wave of violence and killing of women who transgressed communal norms. More significantly, even those men who had exhibited pro-Soviet leanings at an earlier stage recemented their alliance with traditional elites, and women themselves retreated into traditional practices since they felt vulnerable and exposed.

Lest we imagine that these tensions are peculiar to the encounter between 'foreign' ruling elites and native populations, Vieille extends his analysis to all 'modernising' states of the periphery. The state, in his view, seeks to repudiate the separate existence of civil society. It intervenes increasingly in society and 'turns on the routine of day-to-day existence, polices it tightly and symbolically devalues it'.[11] This suppression of the private may elicit active resistance. Vieille goes as far as to interpret the Iranian revolution as 'a surging back of the "private" into the public and the colonisation by the private of the State'.[12] Men's honour is invested in the 'private', which has women at its centre, and the state's interventions in this realm only aim 'to deprive the citizen of his honour and divest him of his right to political participation'.[13] Here, the 'private', defined as 'backward' or 'patriarchal' by modernist reformers, is redefined as a site of radical resistance against a despotic state. With typical oversight, the notion that women themselves may have an independent right to political participation is not even entertained by Vieille, nor does the fact that the symbol of resistance happens to be a veiled woman elicit any unease.

It is not my intention to vilify the 'private' as the nexus of patriarchal oppression or to glorify it as a site of cultural resistance against the coercive intrusions of the state.[14] I think, instead, that the identification of the private with the 'inner sanctum' of group identity has serious implications for how women of different class, religious or ethnic background fare through the ups and downs of secular nationalism, since it determines whether they emerge as enfranchised citizens or as wards of their immediate communities.

The very language of nationalism singles women out as the symbolic repository of group identity. As Anderson points out, nationalism describes its object using either the vocabulary of kinship (motherland, *patria*) or home (*heimat*), in order to denote something to which one is 'naturally' tied. Nationness is thus equated with gender, parentage, skin-colour—all those things that are not chosen and which, by virtue of their inevitability, elicit selfless attachment and sacrifice.[15] The association of women with the private domain reinforces the merging of the nation/community with the selfless mother/devout wife; the obvious response of coming to her defense and even dying for her is automatically triggered.

I argued earlier that the emancipation of women was equated with modernity by nationalist movements whose reforms were meant to serve as a tool for social 'progress'. Nonetheless, definitions of the 'modern' take place in a political field where certain identities are privileged and become dominant, while others are submerged or subordinated. In this process, certain ethnic, religious, linguistic or even spatial (urban versus rural or tribal) categories may be devalued or marginalised. Likewise, secular notions of modern nationhood subordinate and sometimes seek to destroy alternative bases for solidarity and identity. The fact that these submerged identities can become foci of cultural resistance and even lead to contested definitions of nationhood does not necessarily imply that they are uniformly emancipatory, nor does it guarantee that they will have a progressive gender agenda. Wherever women continue to serve as boundary markers between different national, ethnic and religious collectivities, their emergence as full-fledged citizens will be jeopardised, and whatever rights they may have achieved during one stage of nation-building may be sacrificed on the altar of identity politics during another.

Women may be controlled in different ways in the interests of demarcating and preserving the identities of national/ethnic collectivities. As Anthias and Yuval-Davis point out, regulations concerning whom a woman can marry and the legal status of her offspring aim at reproducing the boundaries of the symbolic identity of their group.[16] Until recently, white South African women were not allowed to have sex with men of other groups, nor were women of higher castes in India. Similarly, Muslim societies do not normally condone their women marrying out of the faith, although no such strictures exist for men since Islam is transmitted through the male line.

Women are also considered to be the custodians of cultural particularisms by virtue of being less assimilated, both culturally and linguistically, into the wider society. Immigrant women reproduce their culture through the continued use of their native language, the persistence of culinary and other habits and the socialisation of the young. Even in their native land, women of minority communities retain their cultural separateness to a greater extent than men. For instance, a Kurdish woman in Turkey is less likely to learn Turkish than a Kurdish man who comes into more frequent contact with the dominant culture through compulsory military service, greater access to schooling, dealings with the state bureaucracy or work experiences. Finally, cultural difference is frequently signalled through the dress and deportment of women. Mandel, who analyses the 'headscarf debate' in Germany, suggests that Islamic dress has taken on an additional symbolic dimension among migrant Turks who feel threatened by the Christian, German milieu and its potentially corrupting influence: 'They see the headscarf as a symbolic border, delimiting two separate corporate groups, and affirming themselves as part of a moral community.'[17] Conversely, many Germans interpret the headscarf as a sign of the Turks' essential inability to assimilate into German society and a justification for denying them citizenship rights.

Drawing women out into variously defined 'national' mainstreams through mass education, labour force participation and formal emancipation has been a standard feature of secular projects. It should not surprise us to discover that the failure of such projects and the politicisation of religious and ethnic identities have direct consequences for women's rights.

MILTON J. ESMAN

53 Diasporas and International Relations

The term 'diaspora' has long been associated by historians and social scientists with the dispersal of the Jews from Palestine, their homeland, following their defeat by the Romans in AD 70. More recently, the concept has been generalized to refer to any population which has migrated from its country of origin and settled in a foreign land, but maintains its continuity as a community. Thus, our working definition of diaspora is 'a minority ethnic group of migrant origin which maintains sentimental or material links with its land of origin.' This definition excludes migrants who take over or form a state and become its dominant element, for example the British in Australia and New Zealand. It excludes groups such as the Afrikaners in South Africa who have severed their sentimental and economic ties with their country of origin. It explicitly excludes ethnic groups whose minority status results not from migration but from conquest, annexation or arbitrary boundary arrangements; such minorities as the Albanians in Yugoslavia or the Somali in Ethiopia may become involved in irredentist conflicts. These differ from diaspora politics and require separate treatment.[1]

Migration has been a continuous phenomenon throughout history, induced by political or religious oppression and, more frequently, by the search for improved economic opportunities. Migrations may be voluntary or compelled. The most conspicuous case of the latter was the transportation of Africans to slavery in the Americas, but the movement of contract labor to Malaysia, Fiji and the Caribbean plantations in the nineteenth century also had many features of compulsion. Rapid population growth, uneven economic development and greatly improved transportation, beginning in the mid-nineteenth century, have accelerated migratory movements. New, large-scale diasporas have appeared almost overnight: Turks in Germany; Jamaicans in Britain; Ghanaians in Nigeria; Indians, Pakistanis, and Bangladeshis in the Persian Gulf states; Cubans and Vietnamese in the United States; Colombians in Venezuela. In every continent migrations are producing fresh diasporas and there is no reason to believe that this phenomenon will diminish in importance.

Nor do diasporas quickly assimilate into the receiving society. The 'illusion of impermanence' has been shattered by the experience of the overwhelming majority of migrations during this century.[2] Through a combination of preference and social exclusion, they maintain their identity and solidarity over extended periods. After three generations the Armenian community in France, though French-speaking and well-established economically, retains its group solidarity and applauds, when it does not directly support, terrorist activities against Turkish targets. In many countries there are older diasporas and newer diasporas. Even within the same ethnic group mutual support and solidarity may be strained by tensions and conflicts between earlier and later arrivals.

Along with internal cohesion, migrant groups tend to maintain links with their country of origin. Communication with kinfolk and financial remittances to relatives are the most common form of exchange. Migrants may return to their home country for visits or for permanent repatriation; fresh flows of recruits may nourish the migrant community and help to maintain language, culture and personal contacts; nostalgic third generation migrants may visit their homeland to rediscover their roots. Migrant communities may look to the home country and perhaps to its government for cultural reinforcement in the form of teachers and religious leaders. They may take a vital interest in political developments in the home country and even try to influence them. Thus migrant communities not only retain their group identity and their institutions over extended periods, they also maintain continuing links, both material and sentimental, with their country of origin. These links become a dimension of international politics.

To most migrant groups, the concept of homeland is quite specific and clear. To Croats in Germany, Pakistanis in Kuwait, Koreans in Japan or Haitians in the United States, their homeland is unambiguous. Depending on historical experience, however, the 'homeland' may be a less specific point of reference. Deprived by slavery of tribal solidarity, and of specific historical memories, American Blacks tend to identify with all of Black Africa, rather than with a particular territory or cultural community. For centuries, Jews in the diaspora identified with historical memories of Jerusalem and the land of Israel, to which the Messiah would lead them on the day of redemption, but they had few, if any, live contacts with that land and no affinities with its governors. Most diaspora Jews now identify sympathetically with the State of Israel, though Palestine has not been the actual homeland of their fathers for nearly two millennia. To diaspora communities the homeland may be an ideological construct or myth, but no less significant to them than specific homelands to which other migrant communities relate.

The continuing links between diasporas and homelands can be politicized, and this is their major significance in the study of international relations. Diaspora solidarities can be mobilized and focused to influence political outcomes in the home country, to provide economic, diplomatic and even military assistance to the home country or to seek protection and help from its government. Likewise, the government of the home country may call on the diaspora community for economic or political support, and the host country's government may attempt to use the diaspora community to promote its interests vis-à-vis the home country. With their variable capacities, opportunities and propensities to exert influence on behalf of their domestic or external interests, diaspora communities can be regarded as interest groups and as political actors. When diasporas are involved in issues that extend beyond the borders of their country of residence, the significant actors, aside from the diaspora communities, are the host government and, to a lesser degree, transnational and international institutions.

In some situations, however, the option of politicization is foreclosed for diaspora communities. The Persian Gulf countries exemplify this situation. The very existence of large foreign communities is regarded by these wealthy, but weak, authoritarian regimes as an unfortunate economic necessity and a potential political danger. They thus insist on the complete political neutralization of their immigrant communities. Nevertheless, international transactions between the home governments, which provide the labor force, and the host governments are necessary to regulate the flow and status of the migrants for whom their home governments act in the internationally recognized role of protectors. Though these diasporas are required to be entirely passive, their presence and activities are subjects for interstate relations. This article will deal with such situations only in passing. It will concentrate on the more common and more interesting cases where diaspora communities can themselves be actors in international exchanges.

The scope and intensity of diaspora activities, including those that affect international relations, are determined by three factors: the material, cultural and organizational resources available to them; the opportunity structures in the host country; and their inclination or motivation to maintain their solidarity and exert group influence.

In his treatment of migrant communities in the Ottoman, Romanoff and Hapsburg empires, one scholar distinguishes between mobilized and proletarian diasporas.[3] Proletarian or labor diasporas have no economic resources other than their labor, few communication skills and limited organizational experience. They are incapable of articulating their group interests in their new environment and they have no access to decision-making circles. They are relegated to the bottom of the income, occupational and status hierarchies. Gradually, as they become proficient in the local language, begin to acquire occupational skills and economic resources, from their own organizations for mutual assistance, and develop cadres of locally-educated leaders who know how to exert influence on the political structures of their adopted country, labor diasporas can begin to impress their needs on the public agenda. The great majority of migrant communities begin as proletarian diasporas. Before they develop the skills, capabilities and access needed to promote their domestic or international group interests, at least one or perhaps several generations may be required.

In contrast, Armstrong speaks of mobilized diasporas—those which bring occupational or communication skills that are in short supply in their adopted country. Because these skills are valuable to the dominant native elites, the leading elements of the diaspora communities can enjoy material rewards and sometimes the social status that these scarce resources command; they gain access to the native elites, securing their patronage and protection. Because of their cosmopolitan contacts and their language skills, they are often prominent in diplomatic roles, though as foreigners with another homeland they may not be fully trusted by the patrons they are serving. In time, as social mobilization occurs in their host country and indigenous groups acquire these skills, the diaspora becomes less valuable to the native elites. Yielding to competitive domestic pressure, the native elites eventually withdraw their patronage and protection; the diaspora is then exposed to the fate of privileged but unpopular foreigners.

'Middleman minorities,' that is immigrant communities that fill economic niches in pre-modern societies between the peasantry and the ruling elites, represent a more contemporary version of Armstrong's mobilized diaspora. Among the larger and better known middleman minorities are the Chinese in Southeast Asia, Asians in East Africa and Lebanese in West Africa. Their economic skills were valued, both by colonial governments and by successor indigenous regimes. But, as highly visible, economically successful, non-assimilating foreigners, they become vulnerable targets for emergent nationalist, populist and Marxist intellectuals and for potential economic competitors. By partnership arrangements, in effect by sharing their wealth with local elites—e.g., the Chinese in Southeast Asia—they may buy protection and continue to prosper. With modernization, however, Armstrong predicts that local elites will eventually be forced to abandon them as undesirable or even subversive foreigners. Do the recent disasters visited on the Asians in Uganda and the Chinese in Vietnam presage similar consequences for the Asians in Kenya and the Chinese in Indonesia, as well as for all middleman diasporas in modernizing societies?

Like most dichotomies, the division between mobilized and proletarian diasporas is too crude. It would be more accurate to visualize a continuum between the two poles. Migrant communities have greater or lesser ability to influence their new environment according to the economic resources, occupational skills and communication capabilities they bring with them. Their integration varies with their original endowments and with the rate at which the migrants and their descendants acquire these capabilities. Contrast the experience of migrant communities that arrived in the United States during the same period: the Irish, a proletarian diaspora and the Germans, a relatively mobilized community. The Irish struggled over many decades to accumulate the necessary resources to exercise influence beyond their localities; the Germans moved much more rapidly. A similar contrast can be drawn between Iraqi and Moroccan communities in Israel, both of which immigrated in large numbers shortly after the independence of the State in 1948. The Iraqis were soon absorbed into the Israeli establishment; the Moroccans after 35 years remain the most depressed and discontented group among Israeli Jews.

The second factor affecting the ability of diasporas to function as an interest group is the opportunity structure in the host country. This denotes the degree of freedom available to them to organize and to promote their group interests. Some political systems tolerate the organization of interest groups, including ethnic minorities, and the exercise of influence on their behalf. Others discourage it or forbid it entirely. In the relatively open political system of the United States, ethnic interest groups are free to organize and operate in the political market place; in the Soviet Union, they are not. Jews in the US have taken advantage of the opportunity to organize and promote their domestic and international interests; in the Soviet Union, similar activities by Jews or any other ethnic group would be considered seditious. Migrant communities in France are relatively free to organize and promote their collective interests; in the Persian Gulf states, political or organizational activity, even by fellow Arabs, is categorically proscribed and punished by deportation.

Opportunities in some countries are not equally available to all migrant groups. Some minorities may encounter severe constraints, while others are free to pursue their interests, even on international issues. Blacks in South Africa are completely circumscribed, while Jews are highly organized. The main point is clear: activities by diaspora communities, including those that relate to international affairs, vary as much with the opportunities available to them in their host country as with their skills and resources.

['Diasporas and international relations', in Gabi Sheffer (ed.), *Modern Diasporas in International Politics* (London and Sydney: Croom Helm, 1986), 333–9.]

Let us start by presenting the three main candidates for definitions of 'people' or 'nation'. One of them, perhaps the most traditional one, makes the very concept superfluous: 'the totality of persons born or naturalized in a country and living under a single government'.[1] With this definition, the set of 'peoples' or 'nations' in the world will coincide with the set of states (at least when colonialism is completely abolished). If, instead, we make the relationship with states an open empirical question, there remain two main types of definitions, one subjective and one objective. The latter may be exemplified by saying that by a people is meant a population that constitutes a nation by some combination of such objective but personal criteria as common language, common culture, common race, common religion, etc. One main problem with this type of definition is that it does not appear possible to lay down any single criterion or any single combination of criteria which appears relevant everywhere, if 'relevant' is defined in terms of, *inter alia*, subjective collective identifications. In some cases, state loyalties override differences in several dimensions, in other cases they do not. In some parts of the world, differences in religion make two different peoples of a group with the same language, in others differences in language make people of the same religion identify themselves as different nations.

Nor are the criteria as 'objective' as they may appear. In areas where 'race' is defined as important, the line may be drawn between the 'lilywhite' and the rest, as in the traditional south of USA, or between the 'coal black' and the rest, as in parts of the Caribbean. When we deal with languages of the same family, it may often appear arbitrary what pairs of tongues are counted as different dialects of the same language, and what are counted as two different languages; and 'arbitrary' here means that the lines are often drawn on political rather than linguistic grounds, hence not 'objectively' in the intended sense.

Furthermore, unless we make habitat one of the objective criteria, we may well find situations where a 'people', as defined by some combination of objective criteria does not form the majority of the population in any connected geographical area, or even in any area at all.

If objective definitions entail some problems, this is also the case for a more subjective definition, say, eg, that a people is a group of persons that identify themselves as a people distinct from other peoples, on whatever basis they do it. As in the case of various objective definitions, this leaves us with categories whose size of dispersion appears to exclude independent statehood, or even other forms of forming a political unit.

If we set ourselves the task of interpreting the norm of self-determination, that imposes limits on what definitions are relevant and what are not. It appears, however, that no legal document lays down any generally accepted definition of 'people'. One of the most recent major treatises on national self-determination,[2] states that:

'(i) The term "people" denotes a social entity possessing a clear identity and its own characteristics
(ii) It implies a relationship with a territory, even if the people in question has been wrongfully expelled from it and artificially replaced by another population
(iii) A people should not be confused with ethnic, religious or linguistic minorities, whose existence and rights are recognized in article 27 of the International Covenant on Civil and Political Rights.'

These statements, taken together, hardly constitute a definition in any sense of that word which would satisfy a logician. It may rather be said that it lays down some criteria of adequacy that any legal definition must satisfy, and it then becomes interesting what it does and what it does not exclude. Thus, it appears that defining the citizens of any state as a people is perfectly consistent with all three conditions, apart from the ambiguity of 'identity'. In fact, the question is whether any other definition is entirely consistent with the three criteria taken together. For even if a group is clearly identified and in addition equally clearly territorial, condition (iii) might be used to relegate it from being a 'people' to being a 'minority', having no valid claims to self-determination. This depends on where we draw the line between 'people' and 'minority', on which the cited paragraph 27 does not enlighten us; nor does any other legally binding definition appear to exist. In practice, however, the 'state' connotation of 'people' seems rather strong in legal thinking, at least when manifested in verdicts and resolutions. One indication of this is the clause that tends to follow formulations of the right to national self-determination in many contexts, stating that nothing in that principle

> 'shall be construed as authorizing or encouraging any action which would dismember or impair, totally or in part, the territorial integrity or political unity of sovereign and independent States conducting themselves in compliance with the principle of equal rights and self-determination of peoples as described above and thus possessed of a government representing the whole people belonging to the territory without distinction as to race, creed and colour. Every State shall refrain from any action aimed at the partial or total disruption of the national unity and territorial integrity of any other State or country.'[3]

It would, however, be too strong an interpretation to say that 'state' and 'people' are treated as synonymous. The quotation indicates that in some circumstances, inhabitants in a sovereign state may be regarded as forming more than one people, and this had also been explicitly affirmed in cases with, eg, openly racist restrictions in enfranchisement.

Another way of formulating the question is by means of the term 'non-self-governing territory', which subsumes, *inter alia*, colonies, mandates and trust territories. Some clarification is provided in the Annex of Resolution (1541) (XV) of the General Assembly, which indicates that *prima facie* evidence of that status of a territory exists if it 'is geographically separate and is distinct ethnically and/or culturally from the country administering it' (principle IV), and adds that once this is established other elements may be brought into consideration, which may be 'inter alia, of an administrative, political, juridical, economic or historical nature', where the crucial issue is whether 'they affect the relationship between the metropolitan State and the territory concerned in a manner which arbitrarily places the latter in a position or status of subordination' (Principle V).

There has been considerable controversy after World War II as to how to make the definitions called for. At one end of the spectrum, we find the early position of the colonial powers, sometimes referred to as the 'Belgian thesis', to the effect that there are many cases of 'internal colonization' of peoples inside a state boundary, and at the other pole the position, also called the 'salt water theory of colonialism', according to which only overseas possessions count.[4] In the United Nations, where the 'Belgian thesis'—with considerable justification—was seen as an attempt to obstruct the struggle against colonialism, the latter interpretation has prevailed, both in the important general resolutions (eg 1514 (XV)), and in specific applications. One may see the case of Bangladesh as an indication of this. It appears difficult to find interpretations of the crucial phrases, in which it would not be seen as geographically separate and ethnically distinct from West Pakistan, in addition to which several authors have argued the existence of internal colonialism[5]—and yet no UN support was forthcoming for its self-determination; in fact, it had to wait for years for membership after *de facto* independence. From a political point of view, this is what to expect. A considerable majority of the members of the UN have a vested interest in not allowing interpretations according to which the relations between nationalities inside a state boundary would be open to international criticism in legal or other 'official' forms.

On the other hand, if the principle of self-determination has undergone changes in the past, we should also expect that changes will continue to emerge. For one thing, with a few more changes in political geography in the world, including achievement of self-determination in Southern Africa, Palestine, and a few remnants of European colonialism, at least one major argument against the 'Belgian thesis' would become obsolete, and it might be more possible for the United Nations to deal with other forms of national subjugation. Also, the fact that the vast majority of wars since 1945 have been fought inside the territory of one single country[6] might bring the United

Nations to seek increasing competence in dealing with at least some types of—in this sense—internal conflicts, given that—in another sense—they are *not* internal: most of them involve some form of armed foreign intervention, with or without legal pretext.

If we go by an interpretation of international law in terms of how it has been applied, it appears that the only body that can have the right to self-determination is a Non-self-governing Territory; and that in this category it is only possible to be included either by being under some form of formal colonial rule, or by being subjected to explicit and legal racism or similar forms of political discrimination, or by being under military occupation. Several resolutions concerning remaining European and United States colonies and dependencies illustrate the first point, those concerning different parts of Southern Africa the second point, and some resolutions concerning Palestine appear relevant to both the second and third points. In no single case do we find resolutions from the United Nations about concrete cases of any other type than these three.

Normally, the entire population of the territory classified as Non-self-governing is taken to be the subject of self-determination, so that smaller parts of the population are not seen as having such a right. The will of the entire population is to be found out, by investigations, by elections or by referendum. Administrative changes that have been made by colonial powers are usually not accepted, if they can be construed as aiming at 'balkanization'.[7] There have been some exceptions here: Ruanda-Urundi, British Cameroons, and to some extent British Togoland—but in all these cases existing administrative boundaries were taken into account. It should be added that the population entitled to self-determination does not necessarily consist precisely of the population living in the territory. It may also include people attached to the territory who have been evicted from it and presently live as refugees, the most notable example being the Palestinians.[8]

When does right apply? The legal answer appears to be 'once and for all'. Once the right has been exercised by a Non-self-governing territory, whatever the decision arrived at, it cannot be resuscitated as such, but is transformed into 'equal rights of nations' (which in this context clearly means 'states'). It should be noted that this does not mean that implemented mechanisms for such decisions are always recognized. Thus the United Nations, having taken upon itself the competence to decide what is and what is not a Non-self-governing Territory, on several occasions refused to recognize referenda (Gibraltar and Djibouti) or elections (Namibia and Zimbabwe) as proofs that the right to self-determination had been exercised. Nor have the Bantustans in South Africa been recognized as independent states.[9]

There are three ways, or have so far been three ways, of exercising the right to self-determination. The most common by far is the transformation of the Non-self-governing Territory into an independent and sovereign state. The second possibility, integration with an already existing state, is exemplified by a few cases of enclaves in Africa and India,[10] by Sabah and Sarawak joining Malaysia, by British Togoland and Cameroons, and a few other cases. The third way, finally, association with an existing state, is mainly exemplified in some cases of previous colonies, mainly in the early postwar period. Whereas, theoretically, the right to self-determination would include the possibility to revise such associations, there has so far been no case of the issue being reopened, even if attempts have been made, eg in the case of Puerto Rico.[11]

Summing this section up, we are bound to arrive at a 'pessimistic'[12] conclusion in so far as we judge the position of international law by the record of the United Nations.[13] It has little support to offer populations living inside the territories of recognized sovereign states, when they strive for independence or autonomy. We have already referred to the fate of Bangladesh, which is also the only postwar case of post facto recognition of a successful rebellion against anything else than a colonial power (in the traditional sense). Temporarily successful rebellions have never been recognized in any form, with the possible exception of some resolutions on Tibet,[14] and they have on occasions been actively counteracted by the United Nations, most notably in Katanga.

But then, it is questionable whether the UN action in Congo can be taken as any indication of what is the position of international law, especially since both France and the Soviet Union refused to contribute to the Congo operation, arguing that it was not legal. Generally speaking, rebellion, whether civilian or armed, falls outside the scope of international law, thus being in itself neither forbidden nor permitted, unless specific circumstances obtain. Thus, whereas rebellion is neither legal nor illegal, certain types of aid to rebels by foreign powers is illegal. Furthermore, the United Nations have long recognized the right of peoples under colonial rule to use force in their struggle for liberation, and thereby also the right of third party states to assist such liberation movements, without this being considered interference in the domestic affairs of the colonial power.[15] Hence, the second principle overrides the first one in colonial cases. It is less clear what the situation is in other cases of domination. Thus, Resolution 2649 (XXV) of the General Assembly in Article 1 'affirms the legitimacy of the struggle of peoples under colonial and alien domination recognized as being entitled to the right of self-determination to restore to themselves that right by any means at their disposal'.[16] There is, however, no general definition of the concept of alien domination; but it has been applied to Rhodesia, Namibia, South Africa and Palestine, that is, cases which come fairly close to colonial situations in the traditional sense.

As we have already indicated, it seems unlikely that the United Nations will go beyond this class of cases, until these cases have ceased to exist as such.

Whether such a hypothetical situation would lead to a change in legal positions must be left as an open question, even if most extrapolations from the present situation appear to point to a No.

['Self-determination as an international issue', in Ioann Lewis (ed.), *Nationalism and Self-determination in the Horn of Africa* (London: Ithaca Press, 1983), 46–51.]

SAMMY SMOOHA AND THEODOR HANF

55 Conflict-Regulation in Deeply Divided Societies

The broad range of alternatives[1]

The literature on comparative ethnic relations documents the wide range of alternatives employed to accommodate deep communal conflicts.[2] They include genocide, forced removal, territorial partition, imposed assimilation, involuntary segregation, power sharing, open society and many variations and combinations of them.

For illustrative purposes basic information was gathered on more than 30 societies with deep ethnic divisions. While they do not constitute a representative sample, they cover the main regions (Africa, Asia, the Middle East and Europe) and periods (both historical and contemporary societies). They are classified into eight forms of communal conflict-regulation which are variants or combinations of violence, partition, domination and accommodation.

The fact that these cases are widely scattered into eight different alternatives of conflict-management clearly indicates that there is no 'typical' way in which deeply divided societies handle their internal divisions. There is a striking contrast between the eleven countries in which violent conflict is still going on and the eight cases in which accommodation is reached. In the middle we have six cases of partition and eight cases of continued domination.

Let us briefly consider each of the eight categories.

1. *Ongoing violence*: Ethiopia, Sudan, Uganda, South Africa, Burma, Philippines, Sri Lanka, Northern Ireland, Iraq, Lebanon and Palestine (Greater Israel). The scale of violence in these countries is enormous. In Sri Lanka, for instance, a guerilla war, accompanied by indiscriminate violence and claiming thousands of lives, has been raging for a decade. The Arab government of Iraq used chemical weapons to quell its restive Kurdish population. A civil war since 1975 has devastated and paralyzed Lebanon. In bi-polar Northern Ireland, civil strife erupted in 1968, self-rule was later suspended and British troops were deployed in a failing attempt to keep law and order. The most recent round of unrest in South Africa began in 1984 and in the West Bank and Gaza Strip in late 1987. To our list of areas where deep-seated

communal violence has recently surfaced one should add Georgia, Azerbaijan and other Asian republics of the former Soviet Union.

2. *Partition after violence:* India and Cyprus. In both cases partition took place only after a civil war resulting in tremendous casualties, massacres and expulsions. British India was successively partitioned into India, Pakistan and Bangladesh. Since partition India and Pakistan went to war several times and the Kashmir question has not been resolved yet. Violence forced the reterritorialization of the two communities in Cyprus, but the Greek majority rejects the de facto partition of the island while the Turkish minority has so far failed to gain any international recognition of the mini-quasi-state it formed in the North.

3. *Preemptive partition*: Mali federation, Malaysia, United Kingdom of the Netherlands and Sweden. All these four states were peacefully partitioned: the Federation of Mali dissolved itself in 1960 into Senegal and Mali, in 1965 Singapore separated itself from Malaysia, and further back in history, in 1905 the Union of Sweden and Norway was terminated, and in 1830–31 Belgium withdrew from the United Kingdom of the Netherlands. In all four cases the pre-existing, nearly complete territorial separation between the ethnic groups facilitated partition and hence did not result in major minority problems.

4. *Unstable domination*: Cameroon, Chad, Jordan, Syria and the historical Second German Empire. All these cases show that large-scale violence does not necessarily yield stable domination. In Cameroon the Christian-animist South has shattered the ascendancy of the Islamic North, while in Chad years of civil war have culminated in the entrenchment of the Moslem North. In both cases the ethnic power balance has remained shaky. Syria is a borderline case. Since the early sixties the non-Sunny Alawite minority (10% of the population) has held power despite several insurrections and failed coups d'etat. Syrian minority rule has so far tried to weather the challenges through ruthless repression and propagation of pan-Arabism. In Jordan the Hashemite monarchy retains power with the support of the Bedouin population, but the Palestinian majority has frequently questioned its legitimacy. In 1970 the regime survived only by a military clampdown on the PLO-led Palestinian revolt.

The historical Second German Empire presents an interesting case of unstable domination of Protestants over Catholics. The expulsion of Austria in the aftermath of the 1866 civil war reduced the Catholics to a minority and the rulers of the new German state expressly perceived it as a Protestant empire. Bismarck's attempt to politically isolate the Catholic minority through the Kulturkampf failed, however. Only when the Weimar Republic extended the general franchise to Prussia, could the Catholics obtain an adequate share of power.

5. *Stable domination*: Egypt, Turkey and Burundi. Egypt represents a single case of centuries-old unchallenged domination of the Moslem majority over

the Coptic minority. The Copts enjoy higher standards of living but are grossly discriminated against in various areas. More complicated and historically more challenged by the minorities is the rule of the overwhelming majority of the Moslem Turks in Turkey. They consolidated their numerical and political dominance through partial expulsion and mass-killing of the Armenian minority during the First World War. Turkey has other non-assimilating minorities: the Kurds, the Shiite Halevis and the Syrian Christians, none of whom is recognized as a minority and therefore all are subjected to enormous pressures to assimilate. A third case of a relatively stable domination is that of Burundi, where the 14% Tutsi minority has ruled the Hutu majority for centuries. After a revolt in 1973 the Tutsi tutelage was retained only by a massacre of genocidal proportions, in which the death toll reached about 5% of the population. These three cases indicate that a precondition for a stable domination appears to be either a huge majority or the extensive use of violence.

6. *Accommodation after violence*: Austria, Yugoslavia, Switzerland and the historical Holy Roman Empire. In all these cases compromise and mutual agreement were reached only after bloody wars: in Austria after the civil war of 1934 and defeat in the Second World War, while in Yugoslavia also after the Second World War and mostly as a result of the interethnic joint struggle during the war. In Switzerland the foundations of the present consociational democracy were laid after the civil war of 1848.

The historical case of the Holy Roman Empire is an illuminating example of the imaginative forms of accommodation in the pre-nationalistic era. The Thirty Years' War in which between one third to one half of the population died, was ended by the Treaty of Westphalia in 1648. It established a system of power-sharing with numerous checks and balances between the various intolerant religious communities, and between the emperor, princes and elected heads of city-states. This system guaranteed remarkable civil rights, a purely defensive foreign policy and a period of relative stability and peace which lasted for more than one and a half centuries.

7. *One-way accommodation*: Rwanda and Indonesia. In these two cases a unilateral, far-sighted policy by the majority has accorded the minority considerable rights leading to relatively amicable coexistence. In contrast to Burundi, in Rwanda a successful Hutu revolt against the Tutsi minority in 1959–60 reversed the centuries-old dominance. For over a decade the Tutsi minority tried to regain power several times, to which the ruling Hutu majority responded with new repressive measures. In 1973 the Second Republic was established, which grants the Tutsi minority considerable social and political rights of co-determination under a strict system of proportional ethnic representation. The Tutsis are entitled to 10% of all places in schools and universities, in the civil service, in the ruling party and in government. In consequence, ethnic relations have improved enormously.

In Indonesia the Moslems, above all the Javanese Moslems, constitute the great majority of the population. The policies of the governing elite toward the ethnic, religious and regional minorities is of unconditional rejection and ruthless suppression of any separatist tendency on the one hand, and of acceptance of the acquiescent minorities on the other. Within the legal and political framework of a highly centralized state, the accommodating minorities enjoy de facto federalism and certain consociational arrangements. Governors and state officials in the provinces are usually drawn from the local population, so that minorities are actually administered by members of their own group. Minorities as a whole are even overrepresented in the central government. This successful policy of accommodation is facilitated by a political ideology of 'unity in diversity.'

8. *Preemptive accommodation*: Belgium and the Netherlands. In both cases consociational compromises were negotiated and implemented as preventive regulation of potential conflict. Consociational democracy was established in the Netherlands through the Dutch political reform of 1917. But as the conflict between the religious communities declined over the years, the preventive 'medicine' became superfluous and hence was later phased out. In contrast, Belgium has been undergoing a long process of constitutional reform since the sixties. The consolidation of consociationalism has so far proved necessary for averting serious conflicts between the Flemish and the Walloons.

Taken together, these cases bear out the great variance in handling intense communal conflicts. There is certainly a strong tendency in deeply divided societies to resort to violence as evidenced in the large proportion of cases of protracted violence, and even most of the cases of successful partition or accommodation followed bloody struggles. However, the instances of coexistence through compromise and preventive approaches, although less frequent, are also significant. The historical and comparative record also confirms that unilateral regulation through domination by one group inflicts prohibitive social costs and is therefore seldom stable. The necessity to negotiate conflict settlements also emerges from this finding.

The four strategies

While the range of historical and contemporary modes of conflict-regulation is large indeed, the question is what are the acceptable and workable options for our time. The legitimacy and effectiveness of strategies are closely interrelated. Regulatory measures which blatantly deviate from present international standards on human and collective rights would encounter greater opposition by the affected groups and occasionally even trigger international intervention. Unilateral or violent methods such as mass killing, large-scale expulsion, domination and forced assimilation were more effective in the past because authoritarian rule was generally more tolerated and the subjected populations could less readily mobilize and resist. The rapid spread of democratic ideas and institutions across the world has also diminished the effectiveness of non-democratic forms for handling communal conflicts.

There are essentially four contemporary options: partition, ethnic democracy, consociational democracy and liberal democracy.

Partition

Of all the four options, partition is the most problematic, both in acceptance and feasibility. The population movements in the world during the last four centuries have been enormous, producing ethnically heterogeneous states. The considerable ethnic mix within the new states which emerged after the Second World War resulted from artificial borders set up previously by the colonial powers. In consequence, it is impractical to redraw state boundaries in order to achieve reasonable ethnic boundaries. Such attempts would also be opposed by the states themselves on grounds of the right to sovereignty. Partition also does not make sense economically. Since the present world economic system favors large states and markets and the duplication of state apparatus is very costly, a further multiplication of the already too divisive and inefficient world state system is counterproductive.

These considerations are sound and broad enough to limit the use of partition as a corrective option only. In some cases the creation of new states is the lesser evil and must not be ruled out. This is particularly true for countries with a history of incompatible nationalisms and intense conflicts. To succeed, partition must be negotiated, agreed upon and internationally endorsed rather than imposed unilaterally. It should also allow for voluntary population exchange in order to avoid the formation of new minorities. Since the post-partition states continue to share regional interests, they can also agree on terms of cooperation, including a common market, a military alliance, or even a loose confederation.

Let us mention several likely cases. Following the Soviet Union and Yugoslavia, a strong European candidate for dissolution is Czechoslovakia. The separation of Kashmir from India is also a probable and reasonable development. By the same token, the independence of Eritrea, Southern Sudan and Tibet would make the nationality question more manageable in these areas.

Ethnic democracy

Ethnic democracy is a democracy in which the dominance of one ethnic group is institutionalized. Combining a real political democracy with explicit ethnic dominance, this peculiar brand of democracy has its own tensions and contradictions.

The system qualifies as a democracy according to the standard criteria of the extension of rights to the entire population. Two kinds of rights are granted: political rights (including a multi-party system, change of governments through fair elections and lack of military or foreign intervention in the political process) and civil liberties (including right of assembly and association, freedom of the press and independent judiciary). In this respect ethnic democracy is not a Herrenvolk democracy which is by definition a democracy limited to the dominant ethnic group only.

Yet ethnic democracy differs from other types of democracy in according a structured superior status to a particular segment of the population and in regarding the non-dominant groups as having a relatively lesser claim to the state and also as being not fully loyal. The manifestations of superior status are various but the most important ones relate to entry to the highest offices in the land and to the character of the state (its symbols, official language, religion, immigration policy). They may expressly be written into the constitution and other laws, or incorporated into the unwritten but clear rules of the game. Since the state is considered to be the expression of the national aspirations of the dominant group, the nation takes precedence over the state of civil society. Since the loyalty of those not belonging to the nation is somewhat suspect, caution is exercised in recruiting them to very sensitive positions of trust in the society (the security services and top political posts).

The contradiction between the two principles of organization which are built into ethnic democracy is evident in various spheres. Its most outstanding manifestations are restrictions on certain individual and collective rights and on the full expression of the national identity of the non-dominant groups. Although it may make concessions to minorities, ethnic democracy should not be confused with consociational democracy in which the state is by definition neutral and minorities are accorded equal status, proportional representation and veto power in areas of vital interest to them.[3]

Ethnic democracy is as yet not common because it is absent among the established democracies of the West, and deeply divided non-Western societies tend to be non-democratic. However, we shall illustrate this newly identified type of democracy below when we discuss in detail the case of Israel.

Ethnic democracy may serve as a viable option for non-democratic, deeply divided societies. Some of them may opt to democratize politically while keeping ethnic dominance. For instance, Egypt is classified above into the category of stable domination. If it becomes a democracy but without renouncing the official dominance of the Moslem majority, then it would be an ethnic democracy. Since nationalism in Eastern Europe tends to be integral and exclusionary as opposed to Western nationalism which tends to be open, inclusive and coterminous with citizenship, there is a strong possibility for some of the democratizing states there to become ethnic democracies.

Consociational Democracy

A. Lijphart[4] presents a model of consociational democracy and claims that it best fits plural societies. The underlying principle is that the deep divisions and disputes cannot be eliminated and hence should be taken as givens. The political system is run on the basis of compromise and power-sharing between the constituent ethnic groups, so avoiding majority rule which may antagonize the smaller or weaker groups. The government is a cartel of the elites of the major groups. These leaders are engaged in constant negotiation and reach decisions by consensus. Minority groups hold effective veto power over any resolution deemed detrimental to their vital interests.

Other rules of fair play facilitate the running of the system. They include proportional representation of all the main population groups in key political and administrative positions. The groups also enjoy institutional and sometimes even territorial autonomy. They keep separate schools, community organizations and a distinct identity while sharing certain overaching values, institutions and identity with the rest of society.

Switzerland, Belgium and Canada are considered Western consociational democracies. They have coped with their internal divisions and conflicts through the politics of accommodation and reconciliation between the different ethnic groups rather than by disregarding ethnicity or attempting to undermine it through assimilation. In principle, there is no institutionalized dominance of any group but rather equal to equal relations and proportional distribution of public resources.

Liberal democracy[5]

In a liberal democracy the individual is taken as the cornerstone of the deeply divided society while ethnic affiliations are ignored by the state. All individuals are accorded equal civil and political rights and judged by merit. They compete and are free to mix, integrate, assimilate, or alternatively form separate communities as long as they do not discriminate against others.

The privatization of ethnicity in liberal democracy maximizes individual rights but minimizes collective rights. Ethnic groups may establish their own educational system and communal organizations but must bear the expenses involved and keep certain standards. The state is also not obliged to recognize these communal organizations, to negotiate with their leaders, or to grant them any special status different from that given to any other voluntary association.

Liberal democracy fosters civility, namely, a common domain of values, institutions and identity, at the expense of communalism. It equates nationalism with citizenship and the state with civil society. All citizens, irrespective of their national or ethnic origin, are considered equal nationals. Although subcultures are allowed within a common core-culture, liberal democracy has a clear bias toward ethnic integration and assimilation. It has better chances to succeed in an immigrant society where discontinuity with the past and willingness to trade culture and identity for social mobility are much greater than in a society composed of indigenous groups.

Liberal democracy may face two kinds of challenge. One is a failure of the promise of equality or non-discrimination. A group, like the blacks in the United States, which finds itself permanently disadvantaged, may lose faith in the system and turn to ethnic struggle. The state may react by stricter implementation of a policy of non-discrimination or launching a temporary corrective program of affirmative action. A much more serious challenge, however, may come from groups, like the Bretons, Basques, and Occitans in France, which seek state recognition of their rights to a separate language and culture although they are not socioeonomically deprived. Similarly the Sikhs in predominantly liberal India today push for a separate state despite their privileged class position. To cite a historical case, the Sudeten German minority in the Czechoslovakian liberal democracy of the inter-war period, although not subject to individual discrimination, insisted on territorial autonomy in addition to linguistic rights. It finally turned against the state when this and an earlier demand to be annexed to Austria were rejected.

['The diverse modes of conflict-regulation in deeply divided societies', in A. D. Smith (ed.), *Ethnicity and Nationalism* (Leiden and New York: E. J. Brill, 1992), 27–34.]

JOHN MCGARRY AND BRENDAN O'LEARY

56 Eliminating and Managing Ethnic Differences

Partition and/or secession (self-determination)

Genocide and forced mass-population transfers are obnoxious from the perspective of modern liberalism or modern socialism. By contrast, partitioning territories to permit self-determination or secession can, in principle, respect the rights of ethnic communities. Partition, self-determination and secession are compatible with liberal democratic institutions (universal, periodic and competitive elections, alternations in power, and civic freedoms of expression, assembly and organisation), in that such states can, in principle, permit secessions and preserve democratic institutions. Partition resolves ethnic conflict, if it works, by breaking up multi-ethnic states, or by allowing divorce between those ethnic communities which do not wish to live together in the same state.

Between the years 1948 and 1991 only one new state, Bangladesh, was carved out of an existing state—if we exclude the very numerous cases of decolonisation of European and US-controlled territories in Asia, Africa and Latin America. However, since the collapse of the communist empires of Ethiopia, Yugoslavia and the Soviet Union secession has become a growth-industry, the in-vogue method of ethnic conflict-resolution. Iraq will be next if Iraqi Kurds are allowed to have their way. The secession of Quebec from Canada remains a possibility after Canadians overwhelmingly rejected a proposed constitutional settlement in a referendum in October 1992. There are secessionist or semi-secessionist[1] movements in Europe (e.g. amongst the Basque, Corsican, Northern Irish nationalist, Scottish, Slovak and Welsh peoples); in Africa (e.g. the Polisario movement in the Moroccan-controlled western Sahara, the Dinkas of the southern Sudan and a bewildering variety of communities in the Horn of Africa); in the new republics of the Commonwealth of Independent States (e.g. Nagorno-Karabakh wishes to secede from Azerbaijan, South Ossetia from Georgia, Crimea from the Ukraine, and the 'Dniester Republic' from Moravia); and in central and southern Asia (e.g. the Khalistan movement for a Sikh homeland, the Kashmiri independence movement, Tibetans in Communist China, and the multiple ethnic secessionists of Burma).

The normative idea behind principled partitions and secessions is the principle of self-determination.[2] The key problem with the principle of self-determination as a means of eliminating ethnic conflict is that it begs four questions:

- Who are the people?
- What is the relevant territorial unit in which they should exercise self-determination?
- What constitutes a majority?
- Does secession produce a domino effect in which ethnic minorities within seceding territories seek self-determination for themselves?

In what were Yugoslavia and the Soviet Union these questions are hardly academic. As Lieven and McGarry and Schöpflin show here they have given rise to multiple civil wars. There are many other hard cases in seeking to apply the doctrine of self-determination. In Transylvania there are two major populations (Hungarians and Romanians) mixed together in the same region along with other smaller communities. In Northern Ireland each ethnic community claims that it is part of another nation, and wishes the putative boundaries of that nation to be the relevant jurisdiction for decision-making (Chapter 6).[3] In Quebec, native Canadians, who occupy a huge proportion of the province's land-mass, are unwilling to secede from Canada with the

Francophone majority (Chapter 2). In the Punjab (Chapter 4) and Kashmir, Hindus vehemently oppose the very idea of secession. In Slovakia, the Hungarian minority fears that the secession of the Slovaks from Czechoslovakia will be detrimental to their interests.

The constitution of a majority for self-determination begs the question of a majority in what region? In moderately complex cases the principle of self-determination seems indeterminate. As Ivor Jennings remarked:

> On the surface [the principle of self-determination] seem[s] reasonable: let the people decide. It [i]s in fact ridiculous because the people cannot decide until somebody decides who are the people.[4]

Exercising the principle of self-determination is only straightforward where there is no large or disgruntled ethnic minority within the relevant region affected by the proposed secession *and* when the seceding area includes the great majority of those who wish to leave. Unfortunately it is difficult to think of instances where these optimum conditions have applied. Norway's secession from Sweden was an exemplary case. So was the case of Swiss Jura. Here, in an 'internal secession', plebiscites were held commune by commune to produce a result that split the new canton into two, along religious lines (Protestants voted to stay with Berne canton). By contrast the partitions of Ireland and India left significant minorities behind in Northern Ireland and Kashmir. Even when secessions seem straightforward, and the seceding areas appear reasonably homogeneous, new conflicts can emerge fairly rapidly. The Ukraine is a possible future example. Most commentators have focused on the dangers posed by the sizeable Russian minority, but less attention has been paid to the deep historical, cultural and geographical divisions between Catholic westerners (who were annexed by Stalin) and the Orthodox (who have been linked to Russia for some three centuries). After the glow of national liberation fades, so might Ukrainian national unity.

There have been some ingenious proposals about how to construct a normative liberal theory of secession,[5] which can answer Jennings's question: 'Who decides who are the people?' Beran advances the argument that every (self-defined) area within a liberal democratic state should be given the right to secede, provided the same right is extended to every sub-area within the proposed secessionist territory. This argument answers the serious accusation that self-determination creates a dangerous domino effect by saying two different things:

- there is nothing wrong with allowing a state to fragment on the principle of self-determination; and
- the fact that the seceding units themselves should grant the right of self-determination within their boundaries should put a prudential check on the aspiration to seek self-determination in territorially problematic zones.

Adam and Moodley accept the thesis that people should be entitled to secede from democratic states. They think that it is important to reduce the fears of the Zulu-based Inkatha and white extremists that a democratic South Africa will become a vehicle of ANC/non-Zulu black power (Chapter 10). They think that the inclusion of a secession clause in the new South African constitution will create incentives to accommodate ethnic minorities.[6]

However, the right of secession seems unlikely to be entrenched in many modern liberal democratic constitutions,[7] and secession is likely to continue to have a bad press amongst liberals and socialists. But with the collapse of the global cold war, there is now much greater room for successful secession and the alteration of borders artificially frozen by the strategic interests of the superpowers—as the reunification of Germany suggests. The cold war had elevated the stability of boundaries into a necessity: rather than face nuclear confrontation each superpower respected the boundaries of the other's client-states, at least in Europe. 'Globalisation' and the increasing power of supra-state organisations may also make some international boundaries less inviolate.

Secession remains an option very likely to produce violence, and problems (initially) as bad as the ones it is intended to solve. Partitions can lead to population movements, often involuntary ones, and populations on the move are highly vulnerable to massacre, as happened during and after the partition of the Indian subcontinent.[8] Whether implementing secession is straightforward, on Beran's lines or not, the proposal of any community to secede from any state is likely to encourage key elites in the affected states to behave in chauvinistic and warlike ways. Normally secessionist movements provoke elites satisfied with the existing state into mobilising 'Unionist' movements against traitors. It was ironic to watch American commentators warning the Soviet Union during 1990–1 to allow its republics the right to self-determination. As Gorbachev observed, Lincoln's heirs have short memories.

What can be said of a general nature about the circumstances under which secession/partitions are likely to be carried out? Three external phenomena matter most and need to be studied closely: the nature of the inter-state system (is it permissive or restrictive?); the aftermath of wars (which often lead to territorial transfers/partitions, often without any considerations of consent) and the disintegration of empires (although this observation is almost tautological).

People seek full self-determination, in the form of independent statehood, for a variety of reasons. The urge for self-government may be motivated by a reaction against ethnic discrimination and humiliation, by the pragmatic expectation that the new nation-state will have greater economic and political freedom, by the wish to have a state in which different public policies will be pursued, by the desire for power and prestige amongst nationalist elites, or to protect a given ethnic culture from extinction. Not much of a very general nature can be successfully sustained about the economic circumstances or motivations of full-scale ethnic secessionist movements.[9] One observer notes that secessions are demanded both by economically advanced groups (e.g. Basques, Catalans, Ibos, Lombards, Sikhs, Tamils) and by economically backward communities (East Bengalis, Karens, Kurds, Slovaks); and that the secessionist communities can be located in either backward or advanced regional economies.[10]

Most importantly enthusiasm for the principle of self- determination flows from the democratisation of the world. Democratisation means that the people are to rule. The statist declares that the people are all those who are resident in a given state or political unit's boundaries (the civic nationalist); the nationalist that they are the nation (the ethnic nationalist). In a few happy cases—Iceland—these two answers approximately coincide. However, in most cases the two definitions of the people do not coincide. In the general case the definition and championing of the people are up for grabs, and the possibility of partition/secession enters into the fabric of any state where the ethnic and civic nationalisms may point to different definitions of the nation.

Once democratisation poses the issue of the definition of the people a clustered set of issues automatically follows: the most important of which are the definition of citizenship, the possession of the franchise, the state's boundaries and the organisational structure of the state. These issues create incentives for political entrepreneurs to make party-building efforts out of ethnic cleavages, whether at the foundation of the state or afterwards. Politicians in multi-ethnic states have multiple incentives to play the ethnic card: whether it be Randolph Churchill playing the Orange card in the UK in the 1880s or Jean-Marie Le Pen playing the Algerian card in France in the 1980s. It is not possible to immunise the democratic process to exclude potentially explosive civic and ethnic issues. They are always there for mobilisation by the oppressed or the opportunist or both. Those who lose out politically under existing state arrangements and policies, whoever they may be, may always choose to redefine the rules of the game by playing the ethnic card in the arena of party politics.

A final reason why ethnic questions are potentially explosive, and raise the possibility that some people(s) will be tempted to exercise self-determination through secession is simple. Ethnic questions raise relatively non-tradable issues. Nationality, language, territorial homelands and culture are not easily bargained over. They create zero-sum conflicts, and therefore provide ideal materials for political entrepreneurs interested in creating or dividing political constituencies.

Having suggested reasons why democratisation increases the likelihood that political actors will seek self-determination for their community and thereby destabilise existing multi-ethnic states we must make two qualifications. First, destabilisation is likely to be contained if the relevant state or region exists in a milieu of other liberal democratic states. Thus far, in the twentieth century, liberal democracies have never gone to war against one another. Second, there are some circumstances under which the destabilising effects of democratisation upon multi-ethnic states can be muted, and inhibit the impetus to consider secession. These factors include:

- internal territorial segregation which permits self-government ('good fences make good neighbours');
- demographic dominance (where the large group is sufficiently secure not to fear the minority (or minorities) and behaves in a generous way);
- demographic stability (where one or more groups are not outgrowing or 'outfalling' one another); and
- a history of pre-democratic co-operation amongst ethnic political elites which gives the post-authoritarian state a reasonable chance of promoting accommodation. [...]

Hegemonic control

The most common system of managing as opposed to eliminating ethnic conflict practised in multi- or bi-ethnic states is that of 'hegemonic control', a concept first developed by Ian Lustick[11] 'although we use the term slightly differently.[12] Hegemonic control has been the most common mode through which multi-ethnic societies have been stabilised in world history. Imperial or authoritarian regimes controlled multiple cultures within their territories through coercive domination and elite co-option.[13] They suppressed latent divisions between ethnic communities which might otherwise have been manifested, especially in conditions of economic modernisation. The control was 'hegemonic' if it made an overtly violent ethnic contest for state power either 'unthinkable' or 'unworkable' on the part of the subordinated communities: ethnically-based slave-systems were exemplary cases of authoritarian hegemonic control. Hegemonic control in imperial or authoritarian regimes need not have rested, although it often did, on the support of the largest or most powerful ethnic community. What was necessary was control of the relevant coercive apparatuses: thus ethnic minorities in Burundi, Fiji (after 1987), Liberia (before 1980) and South Africa (until 1990–1) were able to sustain hegemonic control because of their control over security and policing systems. In Burundi the Tutsi govern through a form of control which Lemarchand calls 'authoritarian containment' (Chapter 7).

Hegemonic control is therefore coercive and/or co-optive rule which successfully manages to make unworkable an ethnic challenge to the state order. However, there is a key difference in coercive regimes which practise hegemonic control. In authoritarian empires there was usually no grand objective pursued to eliminate ethnic difference—although one might argue that the world religions propagated transcendent identities. By contrast, in communist hegemonic systems, a new transcendent identity was consistently proclaimed: one which would eventually eliminate ethnic differences as irrelevant to people's civic identities as citizens. However, after initial post-revolutionary fervour it was rare for this vision to be articulated as one which would utterly eradicate ethnic difference, and the policies of communist parties primarily focused on suppressing the politicisation of ethnic differences (Chapters 3 and 8).

In liberal democracies hegemonic control appears less feasible than in authoritarian regimes. Liberal democracies with statist conceptions of citizenship permit, indeed facilitate, ethnic organisation and mobilisation; and ethnic contests for state power become eminently 'thinkable' and 'workable' within liberal democratic or open institutions. Think of how Irish nationalism was facilitated by the democratisation of the United Kingdom, or of how ethnic nationalism was encouraged by glasnost in the Soviet Union. Similarly the breakdown of the Franco regime after 1975 facilitated ethnic challenges to the Spanish state (Chapter 9), although of a less severe variety. The liberal optimist might therefore conclude that democratisation spells doom to systems of hegemonic control.

However, systems of hegemonic control, or ethnic domination, can be constructed in formally liberal democratic states. The most obvious method is when formally liberal democratic institutions are monopolised by a minority of the state's population. Thus white South Africans and Rhodesians established forms of settler-control over other ethnic communities, while preserving liberal democratic rules for their own community. Citizenship and representative government were confined to the *Herrenvolk*. Minority control within a given region is very common: consider Serbian domination of Albanians in Kosovo, or the treatment of the majority Bengalis in what was East Pakistan. In Fiji, the native minority, frightened by electoral returns which threatened their participation in government, supported a coup in 1987 which shifted towards a system of minority hegemonic control (Chapter 11).

But hegemonic control can occur in states in which the majority or entirety of the relevant state's adult population have formal access to citizenship. Democracy in its most primitive meaning is understood as 'majority rule'. Where political 'majorities' constantly fluctuate, as people change their minds on the key policy or political issues of the day, then majority rule is a sensible decision rule, infinitely preferable to the kind of minority rule practised by emperors, military dictators or one-party regimes. However, where there are two or more deeply established ethnic communities, and where the members of these communities do not agree on the basic institutions and policies the regime should pursue, or where the relevant ethnic communities are not internally fragmented on key policy preferences in ways which cross-cut each other, then 'majority rule' can become an instrument of hegemonic control.

Northern Ireland (1920–72), and the deep South of the USA (*c.* 1870–*c.* 1964), are examples of regions within liberal democratic states where formal majoritarianism co-existed with hegemonic control over the relevant minority. The relevant majority monopolised the police and judicial systems, manipulated the franchise to consolidate their domination, practised economic discrimination in employment and the allocation of public housing, and institutional discrimination against the minority's cultural and educational system(s), and ruthlessly repressed minority discontent. As Noel shows, the Canadian state practised control over aboriginal groups (Chapter 2). Natives were policed through the white judicial system, denied certain privileges if they left reservations and denied the (federal) franchise if they remained on them (until 1961).[14] In India, the demands of Sikhs for an autonomous Punjab partly arose from their fear that Nehruvian tolerance had increasingly given way to Hindu chauvinism, presaging a move towards control as the preferred Hindu method of governing India (Chapter 4). Since 1969 Malaysia has been moving away from consociationalism towards control: prompting Mauzy to describe the present arrangements with the label 'coercive consociationalism' (Chapter 5).

The normative lesson is obvious: a majoritarian system of liberal democratic government, designed to create strong powers for the governing party, is no guarantee of liberty for ethnic minorities. A 'winner takes all' system in the presence of ethnic parties ensures that ethnic competition will be regarded as a zero-sum conflict. Where two or more ethnic communities wish to belong to different external nation-states the potential instability of majoritarian liberal democracy is even more obvious, and the temptations to establish a system of control by the majority are correspondingly greater.

Some maintain that systems of hegemonic control can be normatively defensible. Lustick maintains that control is often the only alternative to continuous war—he had in mind the Lebanon after 1976.[15] However, this quasi-Hobbesian reasoning (any state is better than none) is suspect. Consider first the consequences of universalising Lustick's argument. It would lead one to maintain, as some do, that the dictatorial CPSU and the Yugoslav League of Communists were morally justified precisely because they suppressed ethnic conflict in the Soviet Union and Yugoslavia, that one-party states in Africa and Asia are similarly defensible, and that the reimposition of Ba'athist control over the Kurds is preferable to continuous civil war in Iraq.

There are at least five further difficulties with universalising Lustick's limited defence of hegemonic control. First, the options in any given ethnic conflict are rarely simply between those of control and continuous ethnic war—although there will be plenty of political entrepreneurs seeking to advance precisely this argument. Second, some of the options (federalism/

cantonisation, arbitration and consociationalism) have some record of success in stabilising deeply divided societies in ways compatible with liberal democratic norms, whereas any system of control is easily convertible into a system for the execution of genocide, ethnocide, forced mass-population transfers and other violations of human rights. Third, partitionist or secessionist options are almost invariably more desirable than the imposition of control. If the relevant partition or secession is even moderately well executed it should ensure that more people can enjoy legitimate self-government than would be the case under a system of control. Fourth, under systems of control the subordinated minority will always seek to 'internationalise' their plight under the relevant hegemonic group or party/dictator, and thereby threaten the stability of the relevant regime as well as the international order. Therefore one can use stability arguments which are the converse of Lustick's. Fifth, if a system of control eventually breaks down, its practices will have added to the accumulated stock of ethnic grievances. Repression sidelines moderates, bolsters extremists and obstructs prospects for future accommodation, as Singh and O'Duffy demonstrate has been true in both the Punjab and Northern Ireland (Chapters 4 and 6, respectively). The same story is true of the West Bank and Gaza Strip. One might also argue in a realist fashion, although the evidence would need careful appraisal, that wars may sort matters out more successfully than exercising hegemonic control, and even create incentives for post-war co-operative behaviour.

[*The Politics of Ethnic Antagonism* (London: Routledge, 1993), 11–16, 23–6.]

RAY TARAS

57 Post-Soviet Ethnic Conflict and International Politics

What were, a short time earlier, internal affairs of the USSR suddenly became transformed into foreign policy questions for Soviet successor states. It is important to consider briefly international relations theory that focuses on ethnic conflicts. As this volume has documented, the last years of the USSR witnessed a process of nationalist awakening that engendered ethnic-based conflicts. What does international relations tell us about the metamorphosis of ethnic-grounded conflicts into international problems?

Ethnic conflict is the dominant form of contemporary political violence and occurs in most parts of the world.[1] Stephen Ryan described how such conflict was commonplace in the first world, manifested as ethnic revival; in the second world, triggered by erosion of central authority; and in the third world, saddled with the legacy of decolonialization (artificial borders, dominant cultural groups as neo-colonizers).[2] He then outlined how regional powers became involved in ethnic disturbances. In our study we considered the probability that Turkey, Iran, and even Afghanistan would be lured into the politics of Soviet Central Asia. Azerbaijan, too, was making pivotal choices in seeking Iranian or Turkish influence in its development. In all these areas, the existing ethnic balance of power was fragile and even subject to attack.

Ryan's argument is that states may intervene in an ethnic conflict for affective and instrumental reasons. Affective links range from ethnic solidarity with another state's minority to irredentist claims on that other state. Instrumental concerns focus on a state's pursuit of its own national interests; this includes the interrelated subjects of national security, balance of power, and geopolitics. For Ryan, 'Rarely... will affective concerns prompt action without fears relating to security and loss of geopolitical advantage.'[3] Further, third party management by a regional actor often has the effect of escalating rather than deescalating conflict, rendering it more complex and intractable.

Spillover of ethnic conflict into the international arena can occur under any of four sets of conditions. First, ethnic conflict and resulting instability may tempt outside powers to intervene in order to maximize their self-interest. Understandably, any Russian efforts at mediating conflicts in Central Asia or the Caucasus might be perceived by regional actors as manifestation of Russian neo-imperial self-interest. Secondly, when an ethnic group is spread over more than one state but is a majority in none, it can cause ethnic strife arising in one state to spill over to another. National assertion by Tatars, Ossetians, and Meshketiens in any number of former republics could produce a chain reaction. Thirdly and probably most commonplace, conflict can arise in situations where a dominant group in one state is separated from conationals making up a minority in another state. Political assertion by Russians resident in the other republics of the old USSR but also Ukrainians in Belarus and Moldova could be magnified in scale if endorsed by the governments of independent Russia or Ukraine. Fourthly, disaffected ethnic groups can resort to terrorism in their efforts to attain their objectives.

In the post-Soviet context, additional factors affecting violence-proneness need to be investigated. The most likely victims of ethnic conflicts are the many minority groups found on the territory of the former USSR. Some colluded with the center in the distant or recent past, thereby inviting ostracization in the new political order. In addition, a sense of relative deprivation may be greater when certain formerly subject peoples regain independence but others do not. Best known is the threat posed by the massive inventory of the former Red Army which, when combined with the desperate need for hard currency, can facilitate arms transfers to disaffected ethnic groups.

There can be a positive side to ethnic conflict. It can result in a process through which minority rights are asserted and their grievances addressed. As this study has shown, cross-national coalition building in striving for independence was a common feature, and matrioshka nationalism allowed some minority groups to ally or bandwagon with titular nationalities against the Kremlin, creating a positive sum game for both. However as Jacob Bercovitch reported, the crucial factor that determines 'whether a conflict relationship is expressed through acts of violence and hostility, or whether it produces a more fruitful form of interaction [is] the way it is managed.' Conflict management efforts need to devise 'a range of mechanisms to limit the destructive effects of a conflict and increase its potential benefits.'[4] This role is increasingly falling upon the Conference on Security and Cooperation in Europe (CSCE).

Ultimately the assessment of the new ethnic order carved out of the Soviet shell depends on one's vantage point. 'Inside-out' accounts of nationalism, compiled by the ideologues of a national community, are usually kind to the phenomenon; 'outside-in' analyses, carried out by external observers, are generally harsher. Some political theorists are skeptical of all forms of nationalism and a political philosopher like Michael Walzer is quick to point to the inadequacy of both socialist as well as nationalist ideologies. Suggesting that national liberation and socialist revolutions can each establish regimes as bad as those they replace, he observed:

> The movements they create, heroic in their origins, turn out later on to be lethargic, bureaucratic, corruptible. The victories they win are incomplete and compromised; and often they don't win. If the masses can be mobilized, they can also be demobilized and dominated. And, what is most striking, they can be demobilized and dominated by militant elites acting in their own name—though also in the name of detachment, science, and a false universalism.[5]

A pessimistic interpretation of the post-Soviet order would highlight how nationalism—in contrast to socialism—will not be blamed for a country's economic failures, cultural shortcomings, and social pathologies, thereby avoiding the accountability that Buber considered a central criterion. Yet nationalist programs in the new states are not immune from the virus that killed Marxism. It will not be surprising, then, if the incidences of injustice, poverty, and conflict in the region remain largely unchanged.

A more positive conclusion might be reached if we follow James Rosenau's reasoning about the road to postinternational politics. Characterizing turbulence in international politics in terms of a clash between centralizing and decentralizing tendencies, he recognized a global shift to subgroupism—a concept broader than but related to nationalism. Fragmentation of whole systems into subsystems was occurring more commonly, and 'whether such changes stem from systemic planning or subsystem stirrings, they amount to movement in the direction of what has here been called "subgroupism," a direction contrary to that of "nation-statism."'[6] Rosenau gave examples of this distinction: 'some subgroups, such as the Armenians, Kurds, and Tamils, are "nationalities" that coexist with other groups within nation-states. It is in order not to confound the demands of nationality groups for autonomy and recognition with the orientations focused on states as whole systems that the term "nationalism" has been eschewed here in favour of "subgroupism."' Thus 'the Armenian pressure for autonomy in the Soviet Union is viewed as a form of subgroupism, even though Armenian "nationalism" is the impetus behind the pressure.'[7]

Rosenau wrote before the Soviet breakup and presciently detected the forces that produced proliferation of subgroups. The global tendency towards decentralization accelerated as 'illusion of states as omnicompetent collectivities has been revealed by technological developments that render people ever more interdependent.'[8] James Mayall captured the paradoxical and contradictory nature of this same process: 'Ostensibly, the world has been made safe for nationalism,' yet 'the ideal of "true" popular national sovereignty has never been wholly domesticated.' If it had been, Mayall pursued, then a world consisting of about 8,000 identifiably separate cultures would not have been compressed into under 200 independent states.[9]

Mayall was sanguine about the possibilities of the international system being able to develop beyond the nation-state. By contrast Rosenau perceived the beginnings of postinternational politics in increased cooperation between and among sovereignty-bound and sovereignty-free actors. Global norms would crystallize as societies used performance criteria to evaluate governments. Virulent patriotism was on the decline and 'Unabashed assertions of sovereign rights will diminish in frequency and intensity as adequate proof and appropriate performance become increasingly salient as criteria of national conduct.'[10]

Whether the future world order was to consist of a restored state-system, a pluralist world order, or the emergence of a global society was not clear to Rosenau. It thus remains for future research to discover whether, in the Soviet case, triumphant subgroupism may lead more effectively than Marxism did to an order grounded in consensual norms. Francis Fukuyama's position was decidedly on the side of stressing the compatibility of nationalism with liberalism. Nationalist struggles were 'the birth pangs of a new and generally (though not universally) more democratic order' in the states that used to make up the Soviet external and internal empires. He contended that 'Nationalism in these cases is a necessary concomitant to spreading democratization as national and ethnic groups long denied a voice expressed themselves in favor of sovereignty and independent existence.' At the same time, he was convinced that nationalism would have a transitional character and fade in political importance over time.[11]

Fukuyama may have equated nationalism's transitional nature with the ebb and flow of national assertion. It is conceivable, then, that nationalism (or subgroupism) was just a wave that broke in the early 1990s, to be succeeded by more placid political development. But it seems risky to suggest nationalism will never revisit the region.

In a vast empire brutalized by Tsarist autocracy and Stalinism, observers have been unclear about how much subgroupism exists and how deep nationalism is rooted among the various peoples that were subject to Moscow's rule. Our collective endeavor has been to explore the richness of this ethnic mosaic and to track the directions that many peoples set out for at a remarkable moment of history.

['Conclusion: making sense of matrioshka nationalism', in Ian Bremner and Ray Taras (eds.), *Nation and Politics in the Soviet Successor States* (Cambridge: Cambridge University Press, 1993), 532–6.]

Section VIII

Transcending Ethnicity?

INTRODUCTION

What are the prospects for ethnicity at the end of the second millennium? Are we likely to see an end to recurrent waves of explosive ethnic conflicts? Can we preserve cultural diversity without endangering national identity? Will ethnic ties and sentiments fade away as more and more people are absorbed into the global economy and a cosmopolitan mass culture of consumerism?

For many, ethnic modes of national identification must give way to the broader civic identities of liberal-democratic societies. For Raymond Breton this is occurring, albeit at differential rates, in the English- and French-speaking communities of Canada. Even the strong ethno-linguistic identity of the Quebecois will probably be eroded by industrialization, secularization, and intermarriage, as has the much more diffuse English identity. Eric Hobsbawm is much more confident of the imminent demise of ethnicity and nationalism. The ethnic revival is a temporary, reactive phenomenon linked to fundamentalism, but lacking its universalist moral and practical basis. Ethnicity provides no guidance in a world of rapid global change. For an immigrant society like Australia, according to Stephen Castles *et al.*, the traditional resources of ethnic nationalism and racism have nothing to offer Australians in an era of globalization. Instead, they propose the vision of a 'real communality' preserving the best in multi-culturalism but with a genuine commitment to equality.

Other scholars are less sanguine about the prospects for ethnic dissolution. Alberto Melucci, for example, sees in ethnic movements the need to return to tradition in order to underpin mass networks in the face of an impersonal bureaucratic society. Ethnic movements have multiple functions for people in an industrial society, as an instrument for political pressure and rectification of historic wrongs and a means of providing personal and collective identity. Even globalization may act to reinforce ethnic identities and differences. This is apparent in Japan, according to Kosaku Yoshino, where business élites who are the main consumers of the Japanese literature on ethno-cultural uniqueness unintentionally reinforce national stereotypes even as they engage in international business ventures. Attempts to counter these national stereotypes in immigrant societies like Australia, the United States, and Canada have also run into difficulties, as John Hutchinson argues in his examination of centenary and bicentenary celebrations in these societies. The promotion of a civic, multi-cultural myth of immigrant nations has instead served to provoke an ethnic backlash among sections of the core ethnic population.

The debate about ethnic transcendence is very much open and interpretations and prognoses diverge widely. What is clear, however, is that ethnicity and ethnic conflict, at this moment, show no signs of abating, despite the attempts to construct larger regional (e.g. European) and global cultures.

In one type of nationalism, the society and institutions that are constructed are seen as founded on cultural unity. The basis of inclusion and exclusion is ethnic (e.g. ancestry, language, religion, 'cultural distinctiveness'). The attachment of individuals to the collective entity is primarily symbolic and socio-emotional rather than pragmatic or utilitarian. Hence, they are mobilizable for the pursuit of collective goals on the basis of loyalty to the collectivity rather than of personal benefits they can derive from membership in it. They are less likely to leave the group when membership in another collectivity is perceived as providing a higher standard of living. A central preoccupation is with the cultural character of the community and its preservation. Accordingly, although the impact of other groups on one's material well-being is important, the main threats that the group and its elite focus upon are those that pertain to its cultural and linguistic integrity and maintenance.

In this type of nationalism, multilingual and multicultural states do not make much sense: they are perceived as awkward and unstable; as likely to entail discrimination and therefore internal conflict; and, as a result they are seen as conducive to a lower quality of life. The ideal societies are those in which political and linguistic boundaries coincide. This type of nationalism has been labelled cultural, ethnic, or primary.

The other type emphasizes the instrumental dimension of societal institutions. Societies are constructed in order to acquire control over resources; to solve problems; and to defend members against enemies. Societies are seen as rational-legal entities. The preoccupation is with the domain or territory over which societal institutions have jurisdiction.

The basis of inclusion or exclusion is civic: it is by birth or on the basis of legally established criteria and procedures. Theoretically, anyone who meets the criteria can become a member. In addition, the criteria tend to pertain to the economic well-being or development of the society—not its cultural character. In this nationalism, the cultural is dissociated from the political.

The attachment of individuals to the social order is primarily utilitarian. The community is based on interest, not on symbolic identification. Comparison with other societies is in terms of the 'national product' and other indicators of economic development and of the standard of living. Culture is relatively easily sacrificed if a particular course of action is perceived as economically beneficial and if national sovereignty is preserved (so as to be able to make other advantageous moves in the future). This type of nationalism has been called political, civic, territorial, or secondary.

Since they are ideal types, few nationalisms correspond to these descriptions. There are few, if any, pure types in reality. The distinction is nevertheless useful. First, nationalistic ideologies and the accompanying definitions of collective identities do differ in the extent to which they emphasize one or the other orientation. Second, the existence of the distinction allows a comparison of situations where the distinction is irrelevant with those where it is. Third, nationalism can change in one or the other direction: from ethnic to civic or vice versa. Finally, there can be circumstances such that one of the orientations and the course of action that it inspires is in contradiction with the other. For instance, the economic conditions in which a collectivity finds itself and/or its materialistic values can have policy implications in contradiction with its desire to maintain its cultural heritage and distinctiveness. [...]

French-Canadian, like the initial British-Canadian nationalism, is based on an ethnic conception of society. Ethnocultural criteria serve to determine membership in the collectivity. Of course, the nationalism of French Canada did not include a sense of empire; of being a participant in a grandiose civilizational enterprise. It did, however, contain an element of 'messianism'; a sense of being a chosen people with a mission in the world. The conquest—military at first; political and economic subsequently—made it a minority and largely cut its ties with France. Its ethnic nationalism was primarily defensive (*la 'Survivance'*) and oriented to the past in contrast to the British-Canadian sense of participation in the present and continuing success of an empire.[1] Its concern was the preservation against external threats of a culturally defined type of society—a preservation sought through isolation from other collectivities. In spite of important differences, the nationalisms of British- and French-Canadians resembled each other in that both aspired to the construction of an ethno-culturally defined society. They differed primarily in the means at their disposal for the pursuit of their nationalistic ambitions.

Also like in English-Canada, a number of phenomena have progressively transformed French-Canadian society. It changed as a result of phenomena such as industrialization, urbanization, the diffusion of American culture, the Black awakening in the United States, and the movement toward self-determination in the 'Third World'. It is now a population with higher levels of education and of economic and political expectations; it is considerably secularized; its attitude toward the state is that of an instrument for collective advancement.

Many of these changes began relatively early in the century, but culminated in what came to be known as the 'Quiet Revolution' in the 1960s. As the term 'revolution' implies, the changes experienced by this traditional society were profound and involved almost all sectors of social life. A few of these transformations are particularly relevant for the present analysis.

Perhaps the most significant was the fact that the community underwent a shift from a minority to a majority conception of itself. This change is reflected, for instance, in the substitution of Quebecois for 'French-Canadian' as the acceptable self-denotation. Related to this is a shift from a pan-Canadian to a Quebec definition of the boundaries of the collectivity—a second reversal, so to speak; that is a reversal to the view that prevailed at the time of Confederation. It should be pointed out, however, that these shifts are not general throughout the entire collectivity. Indeed, there is considerable debate over the definition of the collective identity and over who the community includes or should include, as the confrontations between independentists and federalists clearly show.

Second, Quebec nationalism[2] has lost much of its defensive, past-oriented, and '*Survivance*' character to become assertive and oriented to development. Its aim is to acquire control of the structures and processes that can have an impact on its political, economic and cultural well-being. It also seeks to gain increasing control over its external relations with other collectivities.[3]

Third, partly because of the new aspiration to control events rather than to protect itself through isolation and partly because of the secularization trend, State (rather than Church) institutions have come to be seen as the critical instrument for the realization of collective ambitions. With a majority group self-conception and the aspiration to establish one's group as such, 'province-building' under the leadership of State authorities has a tenor in Quebec that is somewhat different from the one it has in other provinces.

Finally, the fertility rate has declined considerably (as it has done in other Western societies). The traditional mean used to maintain the numerical strength of the collectivity and the vitality of institutions that depends, in part, on numbers has been abandoned. On the one hand, the Church is now unable to implement its natality policy as it did in the past. State authorities, on the other hand, although equally preoccupied with the matter as were ecclesiastical authorities, have so far found it almost impossible to develop an alternative policy that would be moderately successful. It is in this context that the integration of immigrants within the French-speaking collectivity has become an important political issue.

As a result of these changes (and certainly of others), attitudes toward other groups changed, whether they were of British or of other origins. First, just like British-Canadian nationalists were confronted with a French population that would not assimilate, Quebecois nationalists with their majority group identity have to deal with an Anglophone population that will not go away either, at least not entirely. In this connection, I would venture to hypothesize that ultra-nationalists in Quebec are far from displeased, and may even rejoice, with the statistics showing an exodus of Anglophones from Quebec. Similarly, there is informal evidence[4] that ultra-nationalists in English Canada are quite pleased with the low level of fertility among French-origin Canadians.

Second, the presence of non-British, non-French groups—a presence that increased with the post-war immigration—also generated cultural anxiety among the Quebecois as it did (and still does) among British-origin Canadians. As noted earlier, the concern is with the possible undermining of the cultural character of the society and with the possible erosion of the public predominance of the language. However, the 'problem' that the non-British, non-French immigrants and ethnic groups poses for the French Quebecois is not the same as the one noted earlier in the case of British-origin Canadians. In Quebec, members of ethnic minorities have traditionally opted to join the English-speaking, not the French-speaking collectivity. They therefore did not threaten the French collectivity directly, but indirectly by increasing anglophone numbers and by reinforcing their institutions.

A study was carried out in the early 1970s in which francophones and immigrants in Quebec participated in group discussions about issues involved in the 1968–9 St Leonard school crisis. It was observed that relatively few of the statements of either francophone or immigrant participants made reference to the direct relationship between their respective ethnic groups. Over 75 per cent of the statements made by francophones:

> referred either to the dominance of the Anglophone upper class or to an alliance of Anglophones and immigrants against Francophones . . . Severe inter-ethnic conflict between Francophones and immigrants therefore had no independent existence, but depended upon the relationship of each group to the Anglophone dominant class.[5]

The prevailing view was that something should be done to constrain immigrants to speak French:

> Cultural nationalists tended invariably to take a hard line on the school question, demanding that immigrants forego their material interests by sending their children to French schools. For them, the cultural growth of the French Canadian nation depends not upon socio-economic transformation but rather upon constraining New Canadians to speak French.[6]

Thus, the French began to react to ethnic minorities the way British-origin Canadians had reacted in an earlier period. The expectation is that minorities should adopt the language and way of life of the majority and if they do not move spontaneously in that direction, they should be compelled to do so. Thus, the traditional opposition to immigrants is slowly being transformed into an expectation of 'Franco-conformity'.

The St Leonard school crisis that the above study dealt with was the beginning of the long process whereby French was legally imposed as the official language of Quebec and as the language to be operative in its public institutions. The Quebecois did what British Canadians had done earlier in response to a similar cultural threat. The specific nature of the threat was defined somewhat differently by the French in Quebec than it was decades ago by British-Canadian cultural nationalists. In addition, because of differences in the political, economic and demographic context (e.g. the predominance of English in North America), the means available to each group to deal effectively with the threat are quite different. Nevertheless, the character of the perceived threat in relation to their ethnic nationalism is fundamentally the same.[7]

At the moment the non-British, non-French population is not growing rapidly in Quebec. Significant economic development, however, would in all likelihood accelerate immigration. If immigrants were to continue to integrate primarily into the English-speaking community, the situation that existed prior to the Quiet Revolution would continue, namely that of a national minority facing the possibility of further minoritization by the growth of the linguistic group that is a majority everywhere else in the country (and the continent). Such a situation could reenforce the defensive, ethnic nationalism that has existed up to now and that remains latent. It could also give an impetus to separatist tendencies. Indeed, political independence would, in all likelihood, be perceived by some groups as the only effective way of dealing with such a demographic threat.

On the other hand, immigrants could become part of the French-speaking majority. The extent to which this is likely to take place depends on several factors and circumstances. Among those is the degree of success of the linguistic policies and programs of the Quebec government. Even though the legislation is fairly recent, there is evidence that it is affecting to some degree the direction of the integration of members of ethnic minorities. For instance, in 1985–6, 59.6 per cent of students whose mother tongue is neither French nor English were pursuing their primary and secondary education in French; only 23 per cent did so in 1976–7. Also the percentage of those of non-English and non-French mother tongues who did not speak French decreased from 52.8 to 37.7 between 1971 and 1981. The corresponding percentages among those of English mother tongues are 63.3 and 44.9.[8]

The integration of ethnic minorities in French Quebec will also depend on the extent to which any economic expansion is under the control of a French-speaking economic elite. This is important since those who define the rules of access to jobs control much of the system of incentives that determine the direction of linguistic assimilation. Needless to say, the extent to which the English-speaking economic gatekeepers will apply the regulations of 'La Charte de la Langue française' is also of critical importance in this regard. Indeed, they still control a large part of the Quebec economy and are likely to continue to do so in the future.

Finally,[9] it will also depend on the absence of ethnic discrimination, that is on the possibility for members of ethnic minorities to be upwardly mobile in the French-controlled part of the economy. As long as a minority self-conception existed, a common attitude among francophones was that opportunities for themselves were limited, sometimes severely so, and that they could therefore not be expected to 'give any of them away' to members of other groups. But the situation is different for people who think of themselves as constituting a majority group. To the extent that members of their group actually control significant resources, they are confronted with a new set of normative expectations with regard to their accessibility to minorities.

To the extent that immigrants adopt French in their private as well as their public lives, the collectivity will experience variants of the same social processes as did British-origin Canadians. They will be variants because the demographic, political and socio-economic circumstances are somewhat different from those prevailing four or five decades ago. One of the processes will be the progressive dissociation of language from ethnicity, as more and more people of different ethnic origins adopt the French language. The imposition of 'franco-conformity' will progressively yield the same results with regard to French as those brought about by the imposition of 'Anglo-conformity' with regard to English. In fact, to a considerable extent, a 'francophone' is already socially defined as someone who speaks French; not as someone who belongs to an ethno-cultural group. In other words, French will become less and less the distinctive *cultural* attribute of an ethnic community and more and more the *means* of communication of an economic and political collectivity.[10]

Religion will also become progressively dissociated from the ethnic culture. Traditionally, Catholic culture in French Quebec had a strong ethnic element; although part of the larger Church, it was very much an ethnic religion playing a critical role in '*La Survivance*' of the collectivity. But if the new trend continues, there will be an increasing number of French-speakers who will be Catholic but of different ethnic origins. Also, there will be Protestant, Jewish and Moslem French-speakers. As in the case of British Canada, the religious content of cultural attachments will decrease in importance as it will have little meaning for the members of 'other' ethnic origins. It will be difficult for French ethnicity to be defined by a religion embedded in the symbolism and values of its own culture.

Also, now that a 'Quebecois' identity is established, that a '*projet de société*' is ambitioned, and that the State is seen as the means to pursue it, membership cannot be defined in terms of ethnic attributes, but in terms of citizenship. As in English Canada, the collective identity has to be redefined in such a way as to incorporate the people of non-French origins who are legally members of the polity. As long as the French collectivity saw itself as a minority; as long as it was in a defensive position; it made socio-political sense that the ideological basis of its nationalism be ethnocultural. It was perhaps the most effective means of social and political mobilization. But to the extent that it effectively becomes a majority—in self-conception and in control of institutions—it will run into serious problems of legitimacy and loyalty unless it permits and supports full participation of minorities in its economy and polity and does not make them feel alien, as not having the 'right stuff', as being second class citizens. In other words, the political values and norms that prevail in Western societies, in Canada and in Quebec (as witnessed by the existing Charters of Rights) will exert pressure toward the full inclusion of minorities in public institutions.

Finally, to the extent that people of other ethnic origins are absorbed into the collectivity, the latter will find it increasingly difficult to conceive of its destiny in terms of its traditional historical experience (as British-Canadian nationalists had to abandon the idea that the destiny of the society they were building would be 'played out in and through the Empire'). Its past will have little significance, if any, for the new members. It will have to 're-write' its history in ways that make sense to them. The social construction of a new historical community in Quebec may be facilitated by the fact that the 'sense of history' has already begun to decline among the younger generation of French-Quebecois. *'Notre maitre le passé'* is a symbolic statement that is losing much of its meaning. The modernization trend and the spread of a present and future oriented business culture seem to have decreased the importance of the past in the collective consciousness. This change is also apparent in the relative political decline of cultural elites (e.g. clergy, intellectuals of education and of the media) and the ascendancy of economic elites within the French collectivity. The utilitarian dimension of its nationalism is gaining importance and may well come in conflict with its cultural aspirations. This is likely to generate a certain amount of cultural anxiety and of resistance (as it did among British-origin Canadians). Indeed, this is already taking place in connection with the perceived 'demographic crisis' and with what should be done to avoid what some anticipate will be a 'demographic catastrophe'.[11]

The low fertility rate is the object of a debate 'that looks increasingly like the next "national question", the real "to be or not to be" of the Quebecois'.[12] This debate seems to include three central preoccupations. First, that, in spite of the linguistic successes indicated earlier, people of non-French origins will in large proportions turn out be anglophones in the sense that even though they will *know* French, they will habitually *use* English. In addition, their commitment to the maintenance of the French language is likely to be weak. Thus although their inclusion is seen as essential, they cannot replace French-speakers of French origin.

Second, that the French 'ethnic' will disappear in Quebec. Demographer Henripin has been quoted as saying that 'if the birthrate stays the same, and if massive immigration makes up the difference . . . by 2080 only 12 to 15 per cent of Quebecers will be able to trace their ancestry to today's population'.[13] The following is an expression of the anxiety generated:

Mais quand un éditorialiste, un pasteur, un député ou un ministre proclame que la 'rédemption' du Québec dépend de l'immigration, je m'inscris, en faux—et vous devriez faire de même. Cette idée est une tromperie. Elle implique que l'ethnie canadienne-française ait renoncé à exister. De fait, un peuple qui se fie sur l'étranger pour garantir un niveau de ressources humaines sur son territoire a déja abdiqué devant la vie.[14]

Le Québec s'achemine inexorablement vers une configuration multi-ethnique et multi-culturelle. La population est-elle prête à prendre ce visage? Que devons-nous faire pour integrer les immigrants sans les assimiler mais sans nous perdre? (Pagé de l'Alliance des professeurs de Montréal.)[15]

Third, that Quebec will not only become multi-ethnic but multi-racial as well; and that it will also include non-Christian groups. That is to say, it will contain groups perceived as very difficult to assimilate. The cultural anxiety that this anticipation generates is largely as intense in Quebec as it is the rest of Canada.[16] An important difference, however, is that English-Canada had several decades of experience with 'white ethnics' before having to deal with the integration of non-white minorities. French Quebec has to cope with both simultaneously. In other words, it will have to undergo a more substantial change in a smaller period of time.

It seems fairly clear that the French community of Quebec is now going through the socio-cultural transition that British-Canadians began earlier in the century. Its nationalism, its cultural identity; its ideology concerning other groups and their position in Quebec society is in the process of transformation. The prevailing social definition of who 'really' belongs is in the process of changing; what constitutes the 'national interest' has become very ambiguous in this regard; the importance of *'les Anglais'* as a comparison group and as a threat to the survival of the collectivity is diminishing while that of other groups such as the immigrants, ethnic minorities, and non-white and non-Christian groups is increasing.

If the history of the evolution of English Canada can be any guide as to what we can expect in Quebec in this connection, a long and stressful process is to be anticipated. In fact, in English Canada, the transformation from an ethnic to a civic nationalism is not complete even though it has been under way for more than fifty years.

['From ethnic to civic nationalism', *Ethnic and Racial Studies*, 11: 1 (1988), 86–7, 93–102.]

ERIC HOBSBAWM

59 Ethnic Nationalism in the Late Twentieth Century

The characteristic nationalist movements of the late twentieth century are essentially negative, or rather divisive. Hence the insistence on 'ethnicity' and linguistic differences, each or both sometimes combined with religion. In one sense they may be regarded as the successors to, sometimes the heirs of, the small-nationality movements directed against the Habsburg, Tsarist and Ottoman empires, that is to say against what were considered historically obsolete modes of political organization, in the name of a (perhaps misconceived) model of political modernity, the nation-state. In another sense most of them are quite the opposite, namely rejections of modern modes of political organization, both national and supranational. Time and again they seem to be reactions of weakness and fear, attempts to erect barricades to keep at bay the forces of the modern world, similar in this respect to the resentment of Prague Germans pressed into a corner by Czech immigration rather than to that of the advancing Czechs. This is not only the case of small linguistic communities vulnerable to quite modest demographic changes, such as the thinly populated hills and coasts of Welsh-speaking Wales, or Estonia, whose one million or so Estonian speakers would in any case place it at the very lower limit of populations capable of maintaining a modern linguistic culture at all levels. It is not surprising that the most explosive issue in both areas is the uncontrolled immigration of monoglot speakers of the English or Russian language respectively. However, similar reactions are to be found among much larger populations whose linguistic/cultural existence is not, or does not seem, in any way threatened. The most absurd example of this is the movement, which acquired political clout in some states of the USA in the late 1980s, to declare English as the only *official* language of the US. For while hispanophone immigration is indeed sufficiently massive in some parts of the USA to make it desirable, and sometimes necessary, to address this public in its own language, the idea that the supremacy of English in the USA is, or is likely to be, in jeopardy, is political paranoia.

What fuels such defensive reactions, whether against real or imaginary threats, is a combination of international population movements with the ultra-rapid, fundamental and unprecedented socio-economic transformations so characteristic of the third quarter of our century [. . .]

Massive population mobility naturally intensifies this disorientation, as do economic shifts, some of them not unconnected with the rise of local nationalism.[1] Wherever we live in an urbanized society, we encounter strangers: uprooted men and women who remind us of the fragility, or the drying up of our own families' roots.

What, if anything, have such ethnic/nationalist reactions in common with the recent rise of 'fundamentalism' in many parts of the globe, which has been described as appealing to 'people who cannot tolerate random and haphazard existence and unexplained conditions (and thus) often converge on those who offer most complete, inclusive and extravagant world views'.[2] It is seen as 'always reactive, reactionary'. 'Some force, tendency, or enemy must be perceived as potentially or actually eroding, corroding, or endangering one's movement and what it holds dear.' The 'fundamentals' that fundamentalism stresses 'always come from some earlier, presumably primal and pure . . . stage in one's own sacred history'. They 'are used for setting boundaries, for attracting one's kind and alienating other kinds, for demarcating'. And they conform to George Simmel's old observation that

> Groups, and especially minorities, which live in conflict . . . often reject approaches or tolerance from the other side. The closed nature of their opposition, without which they cannot fight on, would be blurred . . . Within certain groups, it may even be a piece of political wisdom to see to it that there be some enemies in order for the unity of the members to be effective and for the group to remain conscious of this unity as its vital interest.[3]

The similarities with a number of recent ethnic/nationalist phenomena are evident, especially where these are themselves linked with, or seek to re-establish links with, a group-specific religious faith—as among (Christian) Armenians opposing (Muslim) Azeri Turks, or in the recent and markedly Old Testament phase of Likud Zionism in Israel, so different from the aggressively secularist, and even anti-religious ideology of the movement's founders.[4] It seems probable that the visiting extraterrestrial would see ethnic exclusiveness and conflict, xenophobia and fundamentalism as aspects of the same general phenomenon. Nevertheless there is one important distinction. Fundamentalism, whatever its religious version, provides a detailed and concrete programme for both individuals and society, even if it is one selected from texts or traditions whose suitability for the late twentieth century is not obvious. What the alternative to the present, degenerate and evil, society is, presents no immediate problem: women are once again hidden from sight, or married ones have their hair shorn; thieves are once again punished by having hands or legs cut off; alcohol, or whatever else is ritually prohibited, is banned; and Koran, or Bible, or whatever constitutes the authoritative compendium of eternal wisdom, provides complete practical and moral guidance on all subjects, as interpreted by those whose business it is to do so. The call of ethnicity or language provides no guidance to the future at all. It is merely a protest against the status quo or, more precisely, against 'the others' who threaten the ethnically defined group. For, unlike fundamentalism which, however narrow and sectarian in its actual appeal, draws its strength from the claim to *universal* truth, theoretically applicable to all, nationalism by definition excludes from its purview all who do not belong to its own 'nation', i.e. the vast majority of the human race. Moreover, while fundamentalism can, at least to some extent, appeal to what remains of genuine custom and tradition or past practice as embodied in religious practice, as we have seen nationalism in itself is either hostile to the real ways of the past, or arises on its ruins.

On the other hand nationalism has one advantage over fundamentalism. Its very vagueness and lack of programmatic content gives it a potentially universal support within its own community. Except in genuinely traditional societies reacting against the initial impact of modernity, fundamentalism appears to be, universally, a minority phenomenon. This may be concealed either by the power of regimes which impose it on their peoples, whether they like it or not (as in Iran), or by the capacity of fundamentalist minorities to mobilize strategically placed votes effectively in democratic systems, as in Israel and the USA. But it may be taken for granted that nowadays the 'moral majority' is not a real (electoral) majority, just as a 'moral victory' (the traditional euphemism for defeat) is not a real victory. Yet ethnicity *can* mobilize the vast majority of its community—provided its appeal remains sufficiently vague or irrelevant. There is little doubt that most non-Israeli Jews in the world are 'for Israel'; that most Armenians support the transfer of Nagorno-Karabakh from Azerbaijan to Armenia; and that most Flemings do their best not to speak French. Of course this unity crumbles as soon as the national cause is identified not with generalities, but with much more divisive specifics: not with 'Israel' in general, but with the policies of Begin, Shamir or Sharon; not with Wales in general but with the supremacy of the Welsh language; not with Flemishness as against Frenchness, but with a specific Flemish nationalist party.[5] To this extent movements or parties specifically committed to a 'nationalist' programme, mostly separatist, are likely to be the expression of sectional or minority interests, or to be politically fluctuating and unstable. The rapid changes in the membership and electoral fortunes of Scots, Welsh, Québécois and no doubt other nationalist parties of the past twenty years illustrate this instability. Such parties, as always, like to equate themselves with the sense of collective separateness, hostility to 'them' and the 'imagined community' which may be almost universally felt in their 'nation', but they are very unlikely to be the only expressions of such a national consensus.

[*Nations and Nationalism since 1780* (Cambridge University Press, 1990), 164–5, 167–70.]

STEVEN CASTLES, BILL COPE, MARY KALANTZIS, AND MICHAEL MORRISSEY

60 Australia: Multi-Ethnic Community Without Nationalism?

In this book we have looked at the development of a multi-ethnic society in Australia, and have outlined the problems this brings for the definition of the nation. We have examined the various ideologies developed in response—in particular at racism, assimilation and multiculturalism—and have shown their consequences for the policies and institutional structures of the state. We have drawn attention to parallels in the use of migrant labour and the development of ethnic minorities between Australia and other advanced western industrial countries. The most obvious specific features of the Australian case are the relatively large volume of immigration and settlement, and the policy of extending citizenship and full civil rights to all migrants who want them. In this final chapter, we will draw some conclusions from our analysis, and examine the various options open to Australians in the decades ahead.

Homogeneity, difference and the state

The world history of the last few decades has been marked by a contradiction: on the one hand technological change, improving communications and the growing integration of the world market are making the world smaller and more homogeneous; on the other hand, there has been a revived emphasis on difference, whether in terms of individual life-styles, group cultural identities, or assertion of national uniqueness. The 'ethnic explosion' observed around the world embodies this contradiction: ethnicity, which purports to derive from the common history and traditions of a specific group, arises in the context of states which are increasingly all-embracing, both in size and in function. The Australian model of multiculturalism, with its complex and ambiguous balance between separatism of the varied groups, and cohesion of society as a whole, is one—relatively successful and peaceful—way of managing this contradiction. Yet it is inherently unstable, because the institution on which it is premised—the nation-state as the fundamental human collective—has itself become questionable. This is apparent on three interrelated levels: the economic, the cultural and the political.

The economic level is the most obvious: the central form of organization of the contemporary economy is becoming less and less the nation-state and more and more the international institutions of industry and finance. In early free enterprise industrial development (such as nineteenth-century Britain) the state was meant to abstain from economic intervention, merely using its power to regulate social conflict and to maintain appropriate military forces and foreign policies. In the imperialist phase of industrial development (such as in Germany up to 1918) the state took an active role in a partnership with industrial and financial capital to set up large-scale production units, to capture markets, and to contain the labour movement. In the welfare (or Keynesian) phase of world development (in most advanced economies in the period 1945 to about 1970) the state was active in regulating the economy, providing the infrastructure needed for production and containing social conflict through policies of full employment and social security. Woe betide any state today that tries to take such an interventionist role. It will meet with an investment strike by transnational industry and finance, a capital flight by national industry and, should it try to take protectionist measures, disciplinary action by world economic institutions like the International Monetary Fund. The leeway for national economic policies has become very narrow indeed, as the Labor Government has found since 1983.

There are two possible courses for a reformist government: to toe the line laid down by international forces, reducing social justice policies to marginal redistributions between the employed and the poor; or to seek a completely new economic strategy, based on popular control and participation. The Hawke Government has chosen the former path. This reduces national economic policy to a mere interpretation of the parameters laid down by a seemingly objective and all-powerful world market. The government has become an administrative organ entrusted with the task of providing the legal, fiscal, transport, administrative and social infrastructure needed for the smooth functioning of the Australian part of the world economy.

The homogenization of world culture has taken a similar course: the shift of cultural production from the household or the local community to the world factory profoundly affects our ways of life. Most people wear jeans, drink Coca-Cola, use electronic media and eat factory-made food. Even the most committed 'Greenie' critic of modern culture flies by jet to protest conventions, and returns home to listen to 1960s 'hippie' rock on a compact disc player. The British eat spaghetti, the Africans white bread, the Asians wiener schnitzel; but it all derives from the plants of world agri-business. The point is that homogenization actually makes differentiation both possible and meaningless: we can all get everything everywhere, but it has ceased to have any real cultural significance. Whatever we do is a celebration of the cultural dominance of the great international industrial structure, but we can kid ourselves on the basis of appearances that our culture or sub-culture is different. As difference loses its meaning, our need for it as a focus of identity becomes ever greater, as do our acts of self-deception. The attempt to preserve static, pre-industrial forms of ethnic culture is an obvious example of this.

The increasing integration of the world results in a simultaneous homogenization and fragmenting of culture. We are all in the same boat, but this does not mean that there is a single and universal political answer. Socialist and communist movements of the past could point to a goal relevant to all workers and, in the final analysis, to all human beings (because all were destined to become workers): the abolition of capitalism. In a world where socialist movements have failed in the most advanced countries, and where the 'real socialism' of many less advanced countries does not appear as an attractive option, the politics of radical opposition has tended to become fragmented. The universalist party has been replaced by the single-issue movements, based on gender, ethnicity, sexual preference, environmental concern, the wish for peace and so on. These movements are interlinked, and people move between them, but they are not capable of putting forward a viable global economic and political alternative.

If the nation-state is increasingly irrelevant on both the economic and cultural levels, what is the point of having it at all, and what is its political task? The leading apologists of the modern world economy tell us that its rationality lies in its very anarchy. The neo-classical economists have returned to the idea of an 'invisible hand', which secures optimum efficiency in production and distribution (not optimum equality, of course). Any state intervention in this market mechanism is seen as disastrous. A world state would be a threat to the freedom of the market. So the economically weak nation-state remains a functional political unit. It is able to a limited extent to develop and maintain national ideologies and loyalties. It can manage class and racial conflicts. It can provide systems of social security, education and training needed to develop mass loyalty and to socialize the working population. Briefly: the nation-state is still the most effective agency of social control.

Problems of the Australian nation-state

But as the nation-state loses many of its former functions and powers, becoming more and more an empty shell, it suffers a crisis of legitimacy. It needs powerful ideologies to shore up its crumbling walls. Where are they to be found? Return to traditional ideas of national greatness is one possibility: reassertion of heroic episodes of history (the founding of the nation) and the restating of central values (the family, free enterprise, democracy). A war is a traditional way out. Who thought it would still work until Mrs Thatcher sent the Fleet to the Malvinas, and Reagan invaded Grenada, bombed Libya and mined the harbours of Nicaragua? Military might still appears a central component of the idea of national greatness in the USA. Reagan's main strength was his capacity to wield such images. Racism has proved a viable, though limited, ideology for post-Keynesian society in Britain, France, West Germany and other European nations. Economic strength and efficiency remain powerful stereotypes in West Germany and Japan.

In thinking about Australian nationalism as a particular phenomenon, it is as well to think first about nationalism as a general phenomenon.

According to the literature reviewed in Chapter Six, nationalism is heavily reliant on symbolic manifestations which create a sense of community (overarching or even negating class or gender divisions) and immortality (in which the loss of self in death is palliated by the continuing existence of the nation). Its essential references are to primordiality, nature and exclusion. The nation is constructed not only around the presumed existence of a 'race', culture or language but also around the *origin* of that entity in semi-mythological (non-historical) time, and around some unique and generally superior national destiny. Almost invariably the nation is constructed in a process of conflict with other nations over the question of territory. We speak of geographical areas as 'achieving nationhood' or 'joining the family of nations'.

In terms of these characteristics it can be seen that some nations may develop a sense of community and cohesion which is extremely strong in the sense that the national myth is explicit, passionately internalized by the bulk of the population and largely immune from question, dissent or satire at the level of public discourse. Conversely, some states which are recognized as nations develop no such integrative bonds or, at least, very weak ones.

In each individual case only a study of the history of this nation reveals why the sinews binding together the 'imagined community' are of steel or of cotton wool: but some generalizations can be made.

First, nationalism tends to be most intense and least problematic in those states which 'achieved nationhood' as a result of some relatively short and easily identifiable historical trauma. The war of liberation, the war of independence, the great patriotic war are the most potent symbols of nationalism. Anderson is quite correct to stress the iconographic power of the tomb of the unknown soldier, but how much more powerful an icon is the statue of the unknown soldier who 'fell' in the creation (or heroic defence) of the motherland or fatherland than he whose demise occurred in the process of slaughtering Zulus, Ashantis or Kikuyu?

Indeed, in some nations formed out of the breakdown of European imperialism, a revolutionary war of independence has been proposed as the essential crucible of the nation. This was the view, for example, of Amilcar Cabral, the leader and theoretician of Guinean independence, and it is also a dominant strain in the writings of Tito and Mao.

Second, nationalism is strengthened by the ability to legitimize itself by reference to a period of continuity extending back to some prehistoric (or quasi-historical) time. The posturings of the Mussolinis and Shah Pahlevis about the immemorial ancestries of their regimes made no historical sense, of course, but at an emotional level they were both functional and potent. If the nation is immortal it is as well that it should be primordial: if it has no visible end it is strengthened by having no proximate beginning. Also it should be stressed that historically located beginnings are not incompatible with an ideology of primordiality. Ireland did not become a nation after the events of 1916–21: it became 'a nation once again'. Indeed, the sense of periodic destruction of the state apparatus which exemplifies the nation is in itself a powerful image of the primordial strength of the nation. It lives on even though ground down and subjugated and national destiny is fulfilled as it emerges to 'freedom'.

Third, the sense of national identity can be strengthened by investing in a particular state a consciousness of unique responsibility for some chiliastic mission. The sense of being the 'leader of the free world' and the unique repository of democratic values is one obvious case in point, and the carnage that has taken place on the Persian Gulf is another. Perhaps this spirit is best summed up by Salman Rushdie who observed that Pakistani soldiers were advantaged in conflicts with Indians since the former faced the prospect of martyrdom followed by instant entry to paradise while the latter could look forward only to reincarnation (possibly in a form even less desirable than that of an Indian infantryman).

Are these sorts of nationalist option open to Australia? The answer is, in general, no. Moreover, we are fortunate that that is the case. Australia has got through two hundred years without too much of the violent, the dramatic and the heroic. It is a patriot's never never land: no colonial liberation struggle, no revolution, no civil war, no wars with foreign powers fought on its own soil. The struggles to subjugate the Aborigines have been collectively suppressed from the national memory. Of course, Australia has had some history as part of the British Empire, and it was in that guise that Australians died heroically at Gallipoli. But the most important battle to preserve Australian nationhood was fought vicariously, through the agency of the US Navy in the Coral Sea. The Eureka Stockade and the struggle of nineteenth-century democrats for Federation are not the stuff of which national legends are made. They cannot be mentioned in the same breath as the American War of Independence or the storming of the Bastille. And the idea that an Australian Prime Minister might start a war to pull the nation together is too laughable to mention. Sending a gunboat to Suva was not on, even just before a federal election.

Shared heritage and culture is also not for Australia, a viable ideology of the nation. The reasons, as we have described throughout this book, are the increasingly vocal claims of the Aborigines to cultural integrity and the post-war immigration programme, which has created a situation in which around a quarter of the population are of non-British origin. People of British descent are still a majority, but an ideology which excludes such a sizeable proportion of the population is fundamentally flawed. Moreover, the British tradition is all too ambivalent in Australia: first, because of the convict stigma attached to initial settlement; second, because of the long drawn-out struggle to gain a separate Australian identity—summed up in 'anti-pommie' feeling.

Economic strength and prosperity is no longer a candidate for the role of unifying ideology. It did play that role for many years: in the post-war boom, 'the Australian Way' was defined in terms of consumerism. Good tucker, an owner-occupied house on a quarter-acre block, a car and perhaps a boat were symbols of Australian-ness which were open to all irrespective of ethnic origin. With real wages declining, housing costs rising, and—for the first time—the percentage of owner-occupiers falling, material prosperity can no longer be a key to national unity.

Racism

What about racism as an instrument for securing social solidarity? By drawing the boundaries of the nation in an exclusionary way, racism creates an 'imagined community', drawing people together through affective links which transcend conflicting socio-economic interests. Racism has had this function for most of Australian history. The White Australia Policy was a central element of Australian nationhood from the late nineteenth century right through to the 1960s. If we look overseas, we see that racism has been a traditional and frequent instrument for constructing national solidarity in crisis situations. It currently plays this role in several advanced industrial countries, particularly in Western Europe, as described in Chapter Five.

Racism no longer works that way in contemporary Australia. It does exist in several forms: first, racism towards Aborigines has been continuous and intense throughout Australian history. At present, anti-Aboriginal racism takes the form of prejudiced attitudes, and of economic and social marginalization. Second, some migrant groups are victims of structural racism, through mechanisms of labour market segmentation (as outlined in Chapter Two). Third, the Blainey Debate of 1984, as an attempt to develop an embracing racist ideology, did point to the existence of racist attitudes which could be articulated and mobilized.

Yet the fact that the Blainey Debate did not lead to a substantial and lasting racist mobilization points to the non-viability of racism as an ideology of the Australian nation today. Anti-Aboriginal racism persists because of the structural marginality of black Australians. An ideology based on anti-migrant racism is a non-starter just because migrants are structurally incorporated: as workers, small business owners, professionals and as citizens with civil and political rights. There is no significant social grouping which has a material interest in their dis-integration. And even if there were, there is no conceivable mechanism to achieve this. Blainey and Ruxton were aware enough of this not to direct their campaign against immigrants in general, but against Asians (and, later, Africans). The difference of skin-colour seemed to offer a chance for exclusionary policies (as the example of Britain indicated). It did indeed prove possible to mobilize anti-Asian feeling, but only on the streets and in the pubs. There was no significant political force or interest group willing to take it up for their own ends; it corresponded with nobody's interests.

The material reason for the non-viability of anti-migrant racism in Australia is the sheer size of their contribution to society and the economy, together with their incorporation into the people as voting citizens. The ideological reason is the existence of the doctrine of multiculturalism, as a reasonably successful way of managing the potential conflicts of a multi-ethnic society. Multiculturalism does bear racist elements: the recourse to primordiality as a basis for ethnic identity; the acceptance of ethnic chauvinisms (and sexism) as acceptable elements of cultures. The neo-conservative project of multiculturalism (of the Fraser-Zubrzycki-Galbally type) trades on such regressive elements as aspects of a divide-and-rule strategy for social control in a multi-ethnic society. The social democratic variant of multiculturalism is open to this critique too, despite its generalist social policy aims, for it cannot manage without recourse to culturalism in the final analysis. Multiculturalism is based on a construction of community through a celebration and fossilization of differences, which are then subsumed into an imagined community of national cohesion. It is a necessary project for the contemporary Australian state, and one which makes an overt return to a racist definition of the nation impossible.

But that does not necessarily mean that the multicultural project can succeed. We argue that it is too contradictory and limited an ideology to gain wide and enduring support. To start with, multiculturalism is not an accurate statement of power relations in Australia, where there is still a clear link between ethnicity (or more accurately, migrant worker status) and socio-economic life chances. Second, multiculturalism postulates at best an equal chance to be unequal, in a society where inequality is growing and welfare declining. It fails to address the fundamental dimensions of inequality: the ways in which ethnicity overlays class and gender. Third, cultural pluralism can actually preserve and deepen inequality, by creating separate and inferior educational and social systems for different groups. Fourthly, multiculturalism, despite the declarations on its relevance to all Australians, is not an ideology that has much attraction for the Anglo majority. The constant changes and re-evaluations of multicultural policies indicates how contradictory and ephemeral the ideology is.

The answer to this dilemma is not to abandon multiculturalism, but to concentrate our efforts on combating the structural factors which maintain inequality. In the context of a struggle against economic and social marginalization, it will be possible to resolve the issue of ethnic separatism: all individuals and communities should have the right to cultural autonomy in a society based on equal social, economic and political rights for everyone irrespective of gender, race, ethnicity or class background. This implies combating racist and sexist attitudes and institutions, both in Australian society, and in all of its subcultures. Our society will continue to be made up of communities of varying character, but such variation must cease to be a focus for discrimination or disadvantage.

Options for Australia

What possibilities are available to Australia as we enter the third century of white settlement? We see four options:

1) Inequality plus imagined community

This means the continued integration of the economy as part of the world market, but with the development of a firm ideological basis for national identity, leading to a strong commitment to the Australian nation-state. This option, as spelt out by the New Right, seems highly unlikely to succeed, given the problems of Australian national identity described in this book. Attempts to create a general 'we-feeling' through sport, life-style symbols or indeed through the Bicentenary, have had no enduring success.

2) Inequality plus state repression

This is the 'Latin American' model, in which social and political divisions become too sharp to be accommodated in consensus-type parliamentary politics. If the Australian economy really moves into the 'Banana Republic' mode envisaged by Keating in 1986, and no equitable way of sharing the burden can be found, so that the billionaires get richer and the number of people in poverty grows, then a peaceful solution may not be possible. Under similar pressures, formally democratic states in Latin America (Chile, Uruguay) succumbed to military dictatorships in the 1970s. This option seems possible, but not likely, for consensus politics have certainly not broken down here yet.

3) Inequality plus fragmentation and quiescence

In this option the breakdown of social solidarity takes the form not of polarization, but of fragmentation. Politics becomes increasingly meaningless, as the lack of real power of parliaments can no longer be concealed. Since the decisions are made in the stock exchanges of Tokyo, London and New York, and in the international corporate bureaucracies, why bother anyway? The result is hopelessness, hedonism and retreat into the private sphere. Protest takes the form of life-styles and sub-cultural pressure groups, and can easily be co-opted by the leisure industries. Increasing drug and alcohol addiction, fundamentalist religion, mental illness and violence are products of the real powerlessness of the social being. Politics shift from interests to values, providing a focus for New Right ideologies of family, individuality and competition. This seems the most likely scenario of all, for it is simply an extrapolation of existing trends.

4) Equality plus real communality

An alternative to these less than inspiring possibilities is a society based on the best elements of national Australian tradition, the most important postulates of multiculturalism, and the needs and interests of the broad majority of the population. Such a political and cultural reorientation would transcend any idea of nationalism, nation-state or simply imagined community.

The Australian traditions which should be reasserted are not those of colonization or war, but those of the 'fair go', that is, of social justice for all. The image of Australia which should be brought back is that of the 'workingman's paradise', though the racist and sexist aspects of this ideal would need to be worked through and modified.

The aspects of multiculturalism worth maintaining are the principles of cultural self-determination and of cosmopolitan identity. They must be linked to measures to meet the specific needs of discriminated and disadvantaged groups, and include policies to overcome structural marginalization and labour market segmentation, and to combat racism and prejudice.

Above all, the history of white racism and genocide against the Aborigines must become a central theme of education and public debate, and an accommodation with the Aborigines must be achieved through payment of reparations and Land Rights legislation. Steps must be taken to improve dramatically the economic and social situation of the Aboriginal population, not through welfare measures, but through making adequate resources available to Aboriginal communities and these being placed under their own control.

Any such strategy must be based on an attempt to redefine the basis of social organization, and to move away from a political emphasis on the nation-state. Australian life today is determined as much by events on the local level, as by those on the level of world politics and economics. In Britain, it has been local politics which have provided hope in the wasteland of Thatcherism. There is no contradiction between attempts to build community and bring about change at the local level, political work in the national arena, and participation in world politics.

[*Mistaken Identity* (Sydney: Pluto Press, 1992), 139–48.]

ALBERTO MELUCCI

61 The Post-Modern Revival of Ethnicity

During the phase of industrial capitalism there was a close correspondence between the position occupied within productive relations and the cultures of the various social groups. These cultures were clearly characterized as 'class cultures' and, paradoxically, in this context the subordinate classes enjoyed a certain autonomy. That is, they were able to develop practices and forms of communication qualitatively different from those of the dominant culture.

The modernization of complex societies has a direct influence on these areas, throwing them into the great machine of mass culture. The multiplication of contacts and the constant flow of messages destroys the homogeneity of the individual cultures: the media transmits standardized models, while migration and mass tourism encourage the extinction of cultural practices bound up with specific territorial or social circumstances. The growing differentiation of roles breaks up the unity of individual groups and forces their members into networks of functional and atomized relations. Consequently, basic social functions are entrusted to bureaucratic organizations that intervene in the definition and regulation of social behaviour.

But the highly differentiated relations typical of complex societies are unable to provide forms of membership and identification to meet individuals' needs for self-realization, communicative interaction and recognition. The bureaucratic and impersonal nature of complex organizations makes them ill-suited to achieving these goals. On the other hand the safeguarding or revival of declining traditional ties may offer new channels of solidarity and identification.

Ethnic identity is one of these channels. A revival of ethnicity is not necessarily related to open discrimination but is a response to a need for collective identity which transcends the general status of the group and tends to be stronger precisely where an ethnic group's position is relatively strong. Parsons has suggested the term 'de-differentiation' to explain this need for a collective identity among particular groups.[1] He argues that there is a growing plurality of social roles in which the individual is called upon to act. Yet none of these roles is able adequately to offer the individual a stable identity. Selective mechanisms of de-differentiation thus come into being to provide identity via a return to primary memberships. Thus, ethnicity is revived as a source of identity because it responds to a collective need which assumes a particular importance in complex societies.

Theories of 'ethnic dislocation'[2] which view the revival of ethnicity as a reappearance of a type of solidarity 'dislocated' from that of class by industrialization, tend to ignore this fundamental change. Ethno-national conflict is rooted in the past and testifies to the continuity of historic questions and ancient solidarities, but within this legacy it also introduces discontinuous elements, associated with the transformation of complex societies. Without such roots the ethno-national struggle would lose its social foundation and disappear into merely symbolic demands. But without the new themes introduced by emergent collective needs it would be reduced to a form of resistance which is archaic, utopian and regressive.[3]

The ethno-national question must be seen, therefore, as containing a plurality of meanings that cannot be reduced to a single core. It contains ethnic identity, which is a weapon of revenge against centuries of discrimination and new forms of exploitation; it serves as an instrument for applying pressure in the political market; and it is a response to needs for personal and collective identity in highly complex societies.

Meanwhile, analyses of the various historical circumstances of different nation-states contain two long-standing political issues: inter-group relations in segregated societies; and pluralism and international relations among multi-racial states. Here the protagonists are the state and the international system. We thus pass from a structural and synchronic analysis of ethno-national collective action to a diachronic and conjunctural reconstruction of its motives, development and outcomes. The ethno-national movements are also historical actors and their main fields of action, from this point of view, are states and relations among states. Thus, while these movements expose problems related to the structure of complex societies, they are also rooted in history and the actual workings of nation-states and international relations.

If we are to grasp the meaning of the movements' action, we must avoid conflating the analysis of these historical and structural aspects. Unless we link their appearance with the transformation of complex societies they become simple historical by-products of the process of nation-building or incidental events in the narrative of international relations. If on the other hand we ignore their origins in 'national questions' and in their conflict with the states, we risk reducing them to mere cultural appeals in the name of diversity.

Many ethno-national movements develop their action on cultural groups, to ensure the protection and renewed vitality of group culture. This activity can be regressive and strongly conservative, or it can develop historical traditions in the context of a changing society. The reference to cultural traditions is valuable in creating new symbolic systems. Past codes and languages are used by these movements to express demands and conflicts unique to complex societies: in particular, the need for the autonomous self-determination of identity finds fertile soil in ethnic cultures.

The ethno-national struggle also affects the distribution of resources and social opportunities, revealing old and new inequalities: those crystallized by centuries of historical conflict and those resulting from processes of modernization and related developments.

At the political level the ethno-national movements bring to light two problems central to complex societies: first, they raise questions about the need for new rights for all members of the community, particularly the right to be different; and, second, they claim the right to autonomy, to control a specific living space (which in this case is also a geographic territory). In terms of political action this means fighting for new channels of representation, access for excluded interests to the political system, and the reform of the decision-making processes and the rules of the political game. It is not only a struggle against the historical legacy of the nation state, but also against the fundamentally changed state apparatuses. We must not forget that the need to reduce the complexity of highly differentiated systems and to make change predictable feeds new policies of rationalization that usually result in the normalization of everyday life. In some cases the ethno-national movements have managed to throw into question the overall logic of this development and to regain a form of control that takes into account the needs of the individuals and groups involved.

Rapidly accelerating processes of development have accentuated differentiation and multiplied communications. Even peripheral areas find themselves exposed to the demands of the models of the 'centre'. Meanwhile statutory constraints are weakened and traditional social structures are no longer able to ensure the cohesion of groups. They consequently suffer disintegration. As supra-national systems of exchange broaden the economic and political markets, dependence and the threat of desegregation become evident—along with the potential for the autonomy of the marginal regions.

The ethno-national movements offer a response to these processes. They both continue and break with historical nationalism. They are the final outcome of nation-building and represent one of the most striking cases of persistent exclusion from citizenship. On this particular battlefield ethno-national movements exert a massive presence. But they are not only the product of a system of international relations that have not yet come to terms with the gulf between political and cultural processes. As other criteria of group membership (such as class) weaken or recede, ethnic solidarity also responds to a need for identity of an eminently symbolic nature. It gives roots, based on a language, a culture and an ancient history, to demands that transcend the specific condition of the ethnic group. The 'innovative' component of ethno-national movements, albeit a minority issue bound up with their struggle against discrimination and for political rights, also has a predominantly cultural character. The ethnic appeal launches its challenge to complex society on such fundamental questions as the goals of change and the production of identity and meaning. The conflicts affecting the 'centre' of complex systems transpose themselves to the 'periphery', where they express themselves through the social relations and symbols supplied by the 'ethnic nation'. Difference is thereby given a voice which speaks of problems which transverse the whole of society.

[*Nomads of the Present* (London: Hutchinson Radius, 1989), 89–92.]

KOSAKU YOSHINO

62 Globalization and Ethno-Cultural Differences

[O]ne motivation behind thinking elites' concern with Japanese uniqueness in the 1970s (and 1980s) was to promote better communication between the Japanese and non-Japanese through exploration and articulation of the peculiarities of Japanese behaviour, which were assumed to be a possible obstacle to intercultural communication. Conscious recognition of the peculiarities of Japanese behaviour was therefore considered to be a step towards better intercultural understanding. [. . .] The many thinkers who participated in the exploration and discussion of Japanese distinctiveness included those who—reflecting on ultra-nationalism in the Second World War and determined not to repeat the errors of narrow-minded nationalism—wanted to see the emergence of internationally minded Japanese who could communicate effectively with foreigners and could make real contributions to understanding between people of different cultures. However, the resulting large increase in the discussions of Japanese uniqueness had the effect of emphasising the Japanese difference to the extent that commonality between the Japanese and non-Japanese was forgotten and that foreign residents were assumed from the beginning not to understand Japanese people because of the latter's supposedly unique mode of thinking and behaving. What started as a well-intentioned activity to facilitate international understanding thus often had the unintended and ironic consequence of obstructing communication by sensitising the Japanese excessively to their distinctiveness. [...]

The type of literature that deserves our special attention is that written and edited directly by the staff of big-business companies and designed [for fairly well-educated groups with an interest in intercultural communication such as businessmen and students]... Such literature, edited in the form of textbooks, handbooks and glossaries, deals in one way or another with the peculiarities of Japanese culture and society manifested, for example, in 'untranslatable' Japanese expressions, business and management practices, and company men's everyday lifestyle. Such [cross-cultural manuals] popularise the *nihonjinron* in such a way that it may be applied to practical use.

A dual-language handbook, *Nippon: The Land and its People* by Nippon Steel Corporation, Personnel Development Division, is an epitome of [cross-cultural manuals].[1] It contains a wide range of subjects on Japan and the Japanese including their national character, various aspects of linguistic/communicative and social culture (i.e. the non-assertive mode of communication, 'interpersonalism', various aspects of group behaviour, communal mentality), and business, management, decision-making processes, employment practices, and industrial relations. [...] Taiyō Kōbe Bank Ltd. also produced a dual-language cultural handbook entitled *The Scrutable Japanese*, which carries articles on various aspects of the lifestyle of Japanese company men.[2] [...] Similarly, Mitsubishi Corporation produced a dual-language *Japanese Business Glossary*.[3] According to the General Manager of the Corporate Communications Office of the company, the book is intended to introduce 'unique Japanese business practices and expressions in a light but informative form'.[4] What is characteristic about such [cross-cultural manuals] is that the ideas of Japanese uniqueness are popularised in such a manner as to be used in a practical context of cross-cultural interactions in which the Japanese are expected to explain things Japanese to the non-Japanese.

More illustrative of this point is the type of spoken English textbooks [...] in which the *nihonjinron* are summarised and edited in the form of dialogues so that the reader can use model sentences in explaining Japanese culture in English. The following dialogue is very illustrative (note that

Mr J stands for Mr Jones, an American, Mr S for Mr Suzuki, a Japanese businessman):

Mr S: Most Japanese tend to avoid doing anything that sets them off from others. They worry about what others think and change their behavior accordingly.
Mr J: That's probably one of the reasons why people talk about Japanese groupism.
Mr S: It's a factor. It's also why Japanese are poor at asserting themselves. We tend to speak and act only after considering the other person's feelings and point of view.
Mr J: You can't say that about most Westerners. In America, we try to teach our children to be independent, take individual responsibility, develop their imaginations and creativity... We also try to train them to think logically, and learn how to express their thoughts and opinions.
Mr S: Yes, I know... Foreigners often criticize us Japanese for not giving clear-cut yes or no answers. This is probably connected to our being basically a homogeneous society and our traditional tendency to try to avoid conflicts...[5]

In the 'age of internationalisation'—as so called by the Japanese—in which knowledge of cultural differences is considered essential in addition to a spoken command of English, this type of learning material which combines both language study and discussions on cultural differences is increasing. What is particularly important about this type of [cross-cultural manual] is that it can condition the way one expresses one's ideas of Japanese characteristics by providing the language (vocabulary, catch-phrases, etc.) one uses. (Foreign language students often memorise model sentences and use them in actual conversations.) We might even suppose that the particular cultural values can be subconsciously implanted into the person in this way. [...]

What is interesting about Japanese business elites' concern with the uniqueness of the Japanese patterns of communication is that it results from their stated concern to reduce cross-cultural misunderstandings that occur, or are expected to occur, between Japanese and non-Japanese. Their 'good intentions' are illustrated in the editorial comments in the literature published by various companies. For example, Mitsubishi Corporation intends their book to 'help smooth the way for better international communication'.[6] Also, the Nippon Steel Corporation published their book 'in the hope of making some further contribution to mutual understanding between the people of Japan and the people of other countries throughout the world'.[7] Similarly, the president of Taiyō Kōbe Bank explains the aim of their book, which is to 'make a contribution, if modest, to the promotion of an understanding of Japan and the Japanese people at a time when comprehension is badly needed to ease mounting trade tensions [and also to] help Japanese students who are destined to live in an era of internationalization, by providing hints about how things Japanese may be expressed in good English'.[8] Implicit in this statement are two characteristic ways of looking at the world: cultural reductionism and cultural relativism. By cultural reductionism I mean explanations of social, political and economic phenomena in terms of culture perceived to be characteristic of a nation. Here, conflicts resulting from trade imbalances between Japan and other countries are reduced to a cultural problem, that is, the failure of Westerners to understand, and the failure of Japanese to explain, the peculiarities of the Japanese patterns of behaviour. Furthermore, cross-cultural understanding is proclaimed through an extreme form of cultural relativism.[9] [...]

The concern of the Japanese business elite and, for that matter, the Japanese elite in general with cross-cultural understanding can be discussed within the framework of [some] themes of cultural relativism. First, the attempt of Japanese businessmen to improve cross-cultural understanding is made through the recognition and emphasis of cultural differences that exist and/or are believed to exist between Japan and other countries. Behind this attempt are the three propositions concerning cultural relativism: first, Japanese culture is unique and relative to Japanese history (historical relativism); second, because judgements of right and wrong are relative to the cultural background of the person making the judgement, Japanese patterns of behaviour and thought should be evaluated in their own light (ethical relativism); and third, because the ways in which we interpret events are conditioned by culture-bound concepts and theories, it is important for non-Japanese to recognise the uniqueness of the Japanese way of thinking and for the Japanese to point it out (relativity of knowledge).

The important issue to be considered from the point of view of cultural relativism concerns the perception of Japanese culture in relation to Western civilisation. Considering that the Japanese have almost always adapted themselves to the more 'central' or universal Western ways, cultural relativistic thinking as applied to the Japanese context is likely to result in the assertion of Japanese uniqueness because it involves the conscious attempt of the Japanese to challenge the assumption that the Western ways are the 'universal' ways and to emphasise that the Japanese ways should equally be respected in the community of world cultures. The following remark by the General Manager, Personnel Development Division, Nippon Steel Corporation is typical of this line of thinking:

> The Japanese are not good at explaining themselves or expounding their opinions. Geographical and historical factors have long kept Japan an isolated nation and the people have felt no need to explain themselves to the 'outside world'.
>
> Even after the country was opened up, we still had very little to say about ourselves. Compared with the torrent of knowledge and information that poured into Japan, the amount that flowed out was negligible.
>
> Mutual understanding among the community of nations is based on the principles of self-expression and mutual tolerance.

> Japan has now earned a position among the advanced countries of the world and must begin reflecting its new status in its international activities.... The likelihood of misunderstanding and friction arising between Japan and other countries will increase proportionally. From now on, it will be imperative for the Japanese to take every possible opportunity to assist people everywhere to obtain a broader and deeper understanding of Japan.[10]

If the attempt at 'international understanding' is made through the actively conscious assertion of Japanese uniqueness or through the extreme version of cultural relativism, the unintended consequence of such an 'internationalising' attempt can ironically be the enhancement of cultural nationalism because it fails to stress the commonality shared by different peoples. It is in this sense that businessmen's concern to improve intercultural communication and their cultural nationalism are often two sides of the same coin.

The other theme concerning cultural relativism is that, although cultural relativism developed as a reaction against racism, it had an ironic effect of promoting other types of race thinking.[11] The type of race thinking that concerns this study is what I called 'racially exclusive possession of particular cultural characteristics'. [S]trong emphasis on cultural differences between the 'particularistic' Japanese and the 'universal' others is likely to result in association of 'Japanese culture' with the 'Japanese race'. The linguistic and communicative modes of the Japanese in particular tend to be considered the exclusive property of the 'Japanese race'. In this sense, cultural relativism, which legitimates cultural differences, is inextricably associated with this form of 'race thinking' (or quasi-race thinking). It is in the association of 'race' (imagined) and culture that one of the main characteristics of Japanese cultural nationalism is to be found.

[*Cultural Nationalism in Contemporary Japan: A Sociological Enquiry* (London: Routledge, 1992), 37–8, 172–4, 177–81.]

JOHN HUTCHINSON

62 Ethnicity and Multiculturalism in Immigrant Societies

The two preceding chapters have explored how the intrinsic tension between ethnic identifications, which are necessarily exclusive and hierarchical, and the commitment to citizenship equality has created problems of stability both for communist and liberal-democratic states in modern Europe which are not ethnically homogeneous. It is chastening, therefore, to note a second lesson: namely, that even in New World societies with a relatively weak historical sense and without mythic claims to 'primordial' homelands, foundation myths are associated with a specific ethnic core population and with patterns of power and exclusion, and cannot easily be manipulated.

This was demonstrated when planners (of the Australian Bicentenary) cut against the symbolic grain of an ethnic settlement myth, identified with British Australia, by trying to convert the occasion into a festival of multiculturalism. Of course, this may show the need for a more neutral civic or political foundation myth, but the experience of Canada and the USA suggests that such myths are essentially contested in multi-ethnic societies. Indeed, such was the distaste of many Quebecois for the Canadian myth of Confederation that they converted the occasion into a celebration of the survival of a distinctive French culture. The Canadian Centenary was thus an important moment in the crystallization of a distinctive and exclusive Quebec national identity. It highlighted emphatically the deep-seated differences within Canada, that, in spite of all initiatives since 1967, may prove to be intractable.

A further fundamental challenge to the notion of a horizontal status order came in Australia and (to a lesser extent) the USA from the indigenous peoples, who not only drew attention to their history of exploitation, but also demanded recognition of themselves as founding peoples. How this can be reconciled in the long run with the essentially immigrant basis of the nation-state is unclear, despite recent land treaties in Canada and the 1992 Mabo High Court decision in Australia which recognized native land title. But in Australia at least, the international dimension of the festivals enabled Aborigines to force their concerns on to the national agenda and strengthened the formation of an indigenous intelligentsia which made links with international organizations and their equivalents in other countries.

Similar points might be made about the Colombus Quincentennial of 1992. Originally envisaged in celebratory terms with Italian and Hispanic Americans vying for the leading role, the commemorative occasion was captured by radicals in order to highlight the grievances of indigenous peoples in both North and Latin America, and their history of oppression under the European yoke.

This discussion may lead us to argue that the image of these societies, sometimes presented as pioneers of a post-national experiment in ethnic diversity, is mythical. There is a gap between the official self-image of such multi-ethnic societies as egalitarian, and the existence of ethnically based status hierarchies. This is not to deny that these societies are much more successful than the European nation-states in coping with ethnic diversity. There is a reality to the myth just as there is to that of the ethnic nation-state in Europe. But one might regard the claims (in their different varieties) to offer futuristic models of successful living together to an increasingly interdependent world, as a part of a drive for a national identity by relatively recently settled immigrant territories, which have to define themselves in an international order dominated by states with claims to a long historical ancestry.

This brings us to our third conclusion: that such festivals reveal both in their idioms and ambitions the status anxieties of these countries, formulated in a language of maturation. The fact that such nations still conceptualize themselves so has its absurd side, since the USA has claims to be the oldest modern state in possessing a continuous democratic constitution since 1788. Moreover, there is a deep ambivalence among national intellectuals imbued with a 'Peter Pan' complex, for to 'come of age' is to lose one's 'youth'.[1] This ambivalence is not simply rooted in historical peculiarity but is the local expression of twin and competing impulses felt by all national elites: for their countries to be acknowledged, on the one hand, as *distinctive* (based in this case on their *new* world origins and subsequent multi-ethnic migrant character); and, on the other, to be recognized as *normal* members of the established international political and economic community, as they become world actors and as industrial development detaches them from their pioneer roots.

There is no final resolution to these competing drives, and the concept of 'maturity' that emerges out of their interplay has no objective referent: 'maturity' entails not a surrender of distinctiveness by becoming like the old European nation-states but simply the will to face the future by overcoming the problems and illusions of the past. The continued use of this idiom, however, reveals the insecurity of societies without the dignity of a *usable* 'immemorial' lineage (*pace* the indigenous cultures) which, in defining themselves in futuristic terms, feel the need of a periodic stocktaking of their achievements and weaknesses as a platform for action.

For this very reason, the US, Canadian and Australian state festivals became the focus of existential and social anxieties, and of expectations that these anxieties would be resolved in a decisive way. But because 'maturity' is subjectively defined, the festivals generated conflict as groups, in the absence of a significant other, indulged their different expectations of the occasion. They, therefore, failed to function formatively *in the sense intended* as galvanizers of a once-and-forever transition. They became landmarks, however, in another sense: because of the very conflicts they engendered. For these conflicts elaborated options in a common idiom and, by highlighting the intensity of divisions, inspired fresh initiatives of national reconciliation.

Finally, such events confirm once again nationalism as a recurring force in modern societies, one which purports to provide new direction at times when established identities and institutions are shaken by geopolitical, economic or cultural challenges. As we've observed, the commemorations gained support in all three countries from those who saw a need to redefine their political communities as international actors in the post-war period. This was most salient for the USA which, now thrust into assuming the leadership of the West against world communism, faced the problems (painfully posed in the

Vietnam debacle) of reconciling an 'imperial' *Realpolitik* with its original revolutionary idealism. But influential figures in Australia and Canada, too, felt a need to construct new and autonomous identities for their societies from the 1960s onwards as the British 'Mother' country downgraded its Commonwealth links in favour of a European future. A second reason for the staging of these festivals was to restore national cohesion to societies wracked by internal conflict. In the USA there was the issue of race, in Canada the antagonisms between Quebec and English Canada, and in Australia increasing tensions over the questions of land rights, Asian immigration and multiculturalism.

Resolutions were proposed, but even had they been applied successfully, the respite would have been temporary, because of the new and often unpredictable challenges to which all societies are exposed. In recent years new demographic and immigration trends in the USA have provoked fears that by 2017 European Americans will be in a minority, and there have been prophecies of social and political instability. Whether this will come to pass remains to be seen, but such considerations do suggest the provisional nature of contemporary cultural and political identities and a long future for nationalism.

[*Modern Nationalism* (London: Fontana Press, 1994), 193–7.]

Notes

Extract 1

RICHARD SCHERMERHORN: *Ethnicity and Minority Groups*

1. Robert Bierstedt, *The Social Order* (McGraw-Hill, 1963).
2. Talcott Parsons, *Societies, Evolutionary and Comparative Perspectives* (Prentice-Hall, 1966).
3. Modified from M. G. Smith, 'Social and cultural pluralism', *Annals of the New York Academy of Science*, 83, art. 5 (20 Jan. 1957), 763–77.

Extract 2

ELISABETH TONKIN, MARYON MCDONALD, and MALCOLM CHAPMAN: *History and Ethnicity*

1. R. Just, 'Some problems for Mediterranean anthropology', *Journal of the Anthropological Society of Oxford*, 6: 3 (1978).
2. Ibid. 73.
3. G. Autenrieth, *A Homeric Dictionary*, trans. R. Keep (rev. edn., University of Oklahoma Press, 1958); H. G. Liddell and R. Scott, *A Greek–English Lexicon* (rev. edn., Clarendon Press, 1958); R. Cunliffe, *A Lexicon of the Homeric Dialect* (Blackie and Sons, 1924); J. P. Balsdon, *Romans and Aliens* (Duckworth, 1979); H. D. Rankin, *Celts and the Classical World* (Croom Helm, 1987).
4. W. D. Elcock, *The Romance Languages* (Faber and Faber, 1960), 37.
5. Just, 'Some problems', 72.
6. Ibid. 83.
7. Ibid. 76.
8. Cf. S. Wallman, 'Ethnicity and the boundary process in context', in J. Rex and D. Mason (eds.), *Theories of Race and Ethnic Relations* (CUP, 1986), 228–9.
9. Just, 'Some problems', 77.
10. N. Glazer and D. P. Moynihan, *Ethnicity—Theory and Experience* (Harvard UP, 1975), 1.
11. R. Schermerhorn, 'Ethnicity in the perspective of the sociology of knowledge', *Ethnicity*, 1 (1974), 1, citing E. C. and H. M. Hughes, *Where Peoples Meet: Racial and Ethnic Frontiers* (Free Press, 1952).
12. Ibid., citing id., *Comparative Ethnic Relations—A Framework for Theory and Research* (Random House, 1970), 12.
13. Ibid. 2.
14. Just, 'Some problems', 76.
15. See e.g. E. Leach, *Political Systems of Highland Burma* (Athlone Press, 1954); F. Barth (ed.), *Ethnic Groups and Boundaries: The Social Organization of Culture Difference* (Allen and Unwin, 1969); A Southall, 'The illusion of tribe', in P. Gutkind (ed.), *The Passing of Tribal Man in Africa* (Brill, 1970) (reprint of *Journal of Asian and African Studies*, 5: 1–2, special issue); E. Ardener, 'Language, ethnicity and population', *Journal of the Anthropological Society of Oxford*, 3: 3 (1972), repr. in

R. Moss and R. Rathbone (eds.), *The Population Factor in Tropical Africa* (University of London Press, 1975); id., 'Social anthropology and population', in H. Parry (ed.), *Population and its Problems* (Clarendon Press, 1974); C. Lévi-Strauss *et al.*, *L'Identité* (Presses Universitaires de France, 1977); A. Epstein, *Ethos and Identity: Three Studies in Ethnicity* (Tavistock, 1978).

Extract 4

THOMAS H. ERIKSEN: *Ethnicity, Race, Class and Nation*

1. N. Glazer and D. A. Moynihan (eds.), *Ethnicity: Theory and Experience* (Harvard UP, 1975), 1.
2. R. Williams, *Keywords* (Flamingo, 1976), 119.
3. R. Cohen, 'Ethnicity: problem and focus in anthropology', *Annual Review of Anthropology*, 7 (1978), 379–404.
4. M. Chapman, Maryon McDonald, and Elisabeth Tonkin, 'Introduction—history and social anthropology', in id. (eds.), *History and Ethnicity* (Routledge, 1989), 17.
5. P. van den Berghe, 'Class, race, and ethnicity in Africa', *Ethnic and Racial Studies*, 6: 2 (1983), 221–36.
6. M. Banton, *Race Relations* (Tavistock, 1967).
7. Id., *Racial and Ethnic Competition* (CUP, 1983), 106; cf. R. Jenkins, 'Social anthropological models of inter-ethnic relations', in J. Rex and D. Mason (eds.), *Theories of Race and Race Relations* (CUP, 1986), 177.
8. T. H. Eriksen, *Us and Them in Modern Societies* (Scandinavian UP, 1992).
9. Williams, *Keywords*, 213–14.

Extract 6

CLIFFORD GEERTZ: *Primordial Ties*

1. I. Berlin, *Two Concepts of Liberty*, New York, Oxford University Press, 1958, p. 42.
2. E. Shils, 'Political Development in the New States,' *Comparative Studies in Society and History*, 2: 265–292; 379–411, 1960.
3. E. Shils, 'Primordial, Personal, Sacred and Civil Ties,' *British Journal of Sociology*, June, 1957.
4. B. R. Ambedkar, *Thoughts on Linguistic States* (Delhi, 1955), 11. Noting that the modern bilingual states of Canada, Switzerland, and (white) South Africa might be quoted against him, Ambedkar adds: 'It must not be forgotten that the genius of India is quite different than the genius of Canada, Switzerland, and South Africa. The genius of India is to divide—the genius of Switzerland, South Africa and Canada to unite.'

Extract 7

JACK ELLER and REED COUGHLIN: *The Poverty of Primordialism*

1. A. Hoben and R. Hefner, 'The integrative revolution revisited', *World Development*, 19: 1 (1990), 18.
2. M. C. Waters, *Ethnic Opinions* (University of California Press, 1990).
3. J. Nagel, 'Constructing ethnicity: creating and recreating ethnic identity and culture', in N. Yetman (ed.), *Majority and Minority: The Dynamics of Race and Ethnicity in American Life* (6th edn., Allyn and Bacon, 1993).

4. Ibid. 2.
5. N. Kasfir, 'Explaining ethnic political participation', *World Politics*, 31 (1979), 368.
6. J. Spencer, 'Writing within: anthropology, nationalism, and culture in Sri Lanka', *Current Anthropology*, 31: 3 (1990), 287.
7. Kasfir, *op. cit.*, 370.
8. Ibid. 376.
9. B. B. Lal, 'Perspectives on ethnicity: old wine in new bottles', *Ethnic and Racial Studies*, 6: 2 (1983), 166–7.
10. But see J. Rothschild, *Ethnopolitics: A Conceptual Framework* (Columbia UP, 1981); S. Olzak, 'Contemporary ethnic mobilization', *Annual Review of Sociology*, 9 (1983), 355–74; J. Nagel and S. Olzak (eds.), *Competitive Ethnic Relations* (Academic Press, 1986).
11. C. Geertz, *The Interpretation of Cultures* (Basic Books, 1973), 259.
12. Ibid.
13. Kasfir, *op. cit.*
14. E. Spicer, 'Persistent identity systems', *Science*, 174: 4011 (1971).
15. G. M. Scott, 'A resynthesis of the primordial and circumstantial approaches to ethnic group solidarity: towards an explanatory model', *Ethnic and Racial Studies*, 13: 2 (1990), 163.
16. Ibid. 167.
17. J. McKay, 'An exploratory synthesis of primordial and mobilizationist approaches to ethnic phenomena', *Ethnic and Racial Studies*, 5: 4 (1982), 397.
18. D. L. Horowitz, *Ethnic Groups in Conflict* (University of California Press, 1985), 57.
19. M. Hechter, 'Theories of ethnic relations', in J. Stack, Jr. (ed.), *The Primordial Challenge: Ethnicity in the Contemporary World* (Greenwood Press, 1986).
20. Hoben and Hefner, *op. cit.*
21. Horowitz, *op. cit.*
22. Scott, *op. cit.*, 166–7.
23. P. Bourdieu, *Outline of a Theory of Practice* (CUP, 1977), 87.

Extract 8

STEVEN GROSBY: *The Inexpungeable Tie of Primordiality*

1. E. Shils, 'Primordial, personal, sacred and civil ties', *British Journal of Sociology*, 8 (1957), 130–45; C. Geertz, 'Primordial sentiments and civil politics in the New States', in id. (ed.), *Old Societies and New States* (Free Press, 1963).
2. E. Husserl, *Cartesianische Meditationen, Husserliana, Band 1* (Nijhoff, 1950).
3. M. Scheler, *Die Stellung des Menschen im Kosmos* (Francke, 1928).
4. B. L. Smith (ed.), *Religion and Legitimation of Power in Sri Lanka* (Anima, 1978); R. Gombrich and G. Obeyesekere, *Buddhism Transformed* (Princeton UP, 1988).
5. S. Mews (ed.), *Religion and National Identity*, Studies in Church History, vol. 18 (Blackwell, 1982).
6. T. Parsons, 'The kinship system of the contemporary United States', *American Anthropologist*, 45 (1943), 22–38; id. and E. Shils (eds.), *Towards a General Theory of Action* (Harvard UP, 1951), 77–91.
7. Jack Eller and Reed Coughlin, 'The poverty of primordialism: the demystification of ethnic attachments', *Ethnic and Racial Studies*, 6: 2 (1993), 183–202.
8. F. Tönnies, *Gemeinschaft und Gesellschaft* (American Book, 1940; first pub. 1887).

9. E. Troeltsch, *The Social Teaching of the Christian Churches* (University of Chicago Press, 1981; first pub. 1911).
10. M. Weber, *Economy and Society* (University of California Press, 1978; first pub. 1922).
11. Parsons and Shils, *op. cit.*
12. Shils, *op. cit.*
13. Ibid.
14. Geertz, *op. cit.*
15. Tönnies, *op. cit.*
16. Weber, *op. cit.*

Extract 9

PIERRE VAN DEN BERGHE: *Does Race Matter?*

1. Nearly thirty years ago, I distinguished race as 'a group that is socially defined but on the basis of physical criteria', from ethnicity which is 'socially defined but on the basis of cultural criteria' (van den Berghe, *Race and Racism* (New York: Wiley, 1967), 9–10. That definition is widely shared in the social science literature, e.g. E. Ellis Cashmore, *Dictionary of Race and Ethnic Relations* (London: Routledge, 1988), John E. Farley, *Majority–Minority Relations* (Englewood Cliffs, NJ: Prentice Hall, 1995), John Rex, *Race Relations in Sociological Theory* (New York: Schocken, 1970), Thomas Sowell, *Race and Culture: A World View* (New York: Basic Books, 1994), William J. Wilson, *Power, Racism and Privilege* (New York: Macmillan, 1973).
2. My main statement is contained in *The Ethnic Phenomenon* (1981), but the book was preceded by my 1978 article in *Ethnic and Racial Studies*. See also my 1986 piece in the Rex and Mason collection, *Theories of Race and Ethnic Relations*.
3. The biological basis of nepotism has now been firmly established in hundreds of social species of both vertebrates and invertebrates. Indeed, nepotism is one of the main mechanisms of sociality in all known social organisms. See Martin Daly and Margo Wilson, *Sex, Evolution and Behavior* (Belmont, Cal.: Wadsworth, 1983); Richard Dawkins, *The Selfish Gene* (Oxford: Oxford University Press, 1976); R. L. Trivers, *Social Evolution* (Menlo Park, Cal.: Benjamin Cummings, 1985); and E. O. Wilson, *Sociobiology: The New Synthesis* (Cambridge, Mass.: Harvard University Press, 1975), for a few book-length overviews of both the theoretical basis of, and the empirical evidence for, nepotism.
4. My 1979 book, *Human Family Systems*, was an attempt to reinterpret the conventional anthropology of marriage and kinship in terms of the evolutionary biology of mating and reproduction. More extensive biological accounts of human mating and reproductive systems can be found in Daly and Wilson *op. cit.*, and Donald Symons, *The Evolution of Human Sexuality* (Oxford: Oxford University Press, 1979).
5. I engage my critics at greater length in 'Ethnicity and the sociobiology debate', in John Rex and David Mason (eds.), *Theories of Race and Ethnic Relations* (Cambridge: Cambridge University Press, 1986).
6. Among the many critics of race-based measures to redress past racial inequities, see Dinesh D'Souza, *Illiberal Education* (New York: Vintage Books, 1992); Nathan Glazer, *Affirmative Discrimination* (New York: Basic Books, 1975); Richard J. Herrnstein and Charles Murray, *The Bell Curve* (New York: Free Press, 1994); and

Thomas Sowell, *The Economics and Politics of Race* (New York: William Morrow, 1983). Most of these critics have come from the political right, but I have argued for more radical 'affirmative action' based on socio-economic criteria, not race or ethnicity.

Extract 10

JOSHUA FISHMAN: *Ethnicity as Being, Doing, and Knowing*

1. Joshua A. Fishman, 'Language, Ethnicity and Racism', *Georgetown Roundtable on Languages and Linguistics* (Washington, DC: School of Languages and Linguistics, Georgetown University, 1977).
2. Joshua A. Fishman and Bernard Spolsky, 'The Whorfian Hypothesis in 1975: A Socio-Linguistic Re-Evaluation', in Haywood Fisher and Rogelio Diaz-Gucreso (eds.), *Language and Logic in Personality and Society* (New York: Academic Press, 1977).
3. Ernest Gellner, *Thought and Change* (Chicago: Chicago University Press, 1964).
4. Joshua A. Fishman, 'The Role of Ethnicity in Language Maintenance and Language Shift', *Harvard Encyclopedia of American Ethnic Groups.*
5. Jacob L. Talmon, *The Rise of Totalitarian Democracy* (Boston: Beacon, 1952).

Extract 11

WALKER CONNOR: *Beyond Reason: The Nature of the Ethnonational Bond*

1. Valentine Moroz, *Report from the Beria Reserve* (Chicago, 1974), 54.
2. The quotation inter-utilizes translated extracts in Leon Poloakov, *The Aryan Myth* (London, 1974), 287, and the more clumsy translation in *The Standard Edition of the Complete Psychological Works of Sigmund Freud, Vol. 20 (1925–6)* (London, 1959), 273–4.
3. Carlton Hayes, *A Generation of Materialism, 1871–1900* (New York, 1941), 258.
4. Frank Dikötter, 'Group Definition and the Idea of "Race" in Modern China (1793–1949)', *Ethnic and Racial Studies*, 13 (July 1990), 427.
5. Walker Connor, 'The Impact of Homelands upon Diasporas', in *Modern Diasporas in International Politics*, ed. Gabriel Sheffer (London, 1985).
6. Cited in Walter Sulzbach, *National Consciousness* (Washington, DC, 1943), 62.

Extract 12

FREDRIK BARTH: *Ethnic Groups and Boundaries*

1. e.g. R. Narroll, 'Ethnic unit classification', *Current Anthropology*, 5: 4 (1964).
2. W. Bogoras, *The Chuckchee* (American Museum of Natural History, New York, 1904–9), vol. i.
3. G. Gjessing, *Changing Lapps: A Study in Culture Relations in Northernmost Norway*, LSE Monographs on Social Anthropology, no. 13 (London, 1954).
4. Cf. F. Barth, *Models of Social Organization*, Royal Anthropological Institute of Great Britain and Ireland, Occasional Papers, no. 23 (1966), for my argumentation on this point.
5. E. Goffman, *The Presentation of Self in Everyday Life* (New York, 1959).
6. J. S. Furnivall, *Netherlands India: A Study in Plural Economy* (Cambridge, 1944).

Extract 13

ABNER COHEN: *Ethnicity and Politics*

1. M. Gluckman, *Analysis of a Social Situation in Modern Zululand* (Rhodes Livingstone Institute, Manchester, 1955; first pub. 1940–2).
2. F. G. Bailey, 'Parapolitical systems', in M. Swartz (ed.), *Local Level Politics* (Chicago, 1968).
3. E. R. Wolf, 'Kinship, friendship, and patron–client relationships', in M. Banton (ed.), *The Social Anthropology of Complex Societies* (London, 1966).

Extract 14

PAUL R. BRASS: *Ethnic Groups and Ethnic Identity Formation*

1. Even where it is possible to do so, argues Barth, the use of cultural attributes to identify ethnic boundaries may be superficial, confusing form with content: Frederik Barth, 'Introduction' and 'Pathan Identity and its Maintenance', in Fredrik Barth (ed.), *Ethnic Groups and Boundaries: The Social Organization of Cultural Difference* (Boston: Little, Brown, 1969), 15, 131–2.
2. Barth, 'Introduction,' *op. cit.*, and Harald Eidheim, 'When Ethnic Identity is a Social Stigma,' in Barth, *Ethnic Groups and Boundaries*, *op. cit.*, 15 and 39–57.
3. George de Vos, 'Ethnic Pluralism' in George de Vos and Lola Romanucci-Ross (eds.), *Ethnic Identity: Cultural Continuities and Change* (Palo Alto, Calif.: Mayfield Publishing Co., 1975), 16.
4. Cf. Joan Vincent, 'The Structuring of Ethnicity,' *Human Organization*, 33: 4 (Winter, 1974), 376–7. The same remarks apply to the concept of nationality or nation as used here; cf. Benjamin Akzin, *State and Nation* (London: Hutchinson University Library, 1964), 36 and Karl M. Deutsch, *Nationalism and Social Communication: An Inquiry into the Foundations of Nationality*, 2nd edn. (Cambridge, Mass: MIT Press, 1966), 23.
5. This point has been made by Nathan Glazer and Daniel P. Moynihan, 'Introduction', in Nathan Glazer and Daniel P. Moynihan (eds.), *Ethnicity: Theory and Experience* (Cambridge, Mass.: Harvard University Press, 1975), 7–10, but they over-generalize their argument to other societies where ethnicity is more than merely interest, and may be a stage on the way to a claim to national status.
6. Cf. Akzin, *State and Nation*, *op. cit.*, 10, 12, 29, 31–4, 46, 81, 133, 143.
7. Since the nation is defined here as a type of ethnic group and ethnic groups have been defined without reference to any specific attributes or set of attributes, it follows that the nation (or nationality) also is not to be defined by any particular attributes such as language, religion, territory, or any others. Cf. Anthony D. Smith, *Theories of Nationalism* (New York: Harper & Row, 1971), 18, 147–50, 181–5; Dankwart A. Rustow, *A World of Nations: Problems of Political Modernization* (Washington, DC: The Brookings Institution, 1967), 47–8; Rupert Emerson, *From Empire to Nation: The Rise to Self-Assertion of Asian and African Peoples* (Boston: Beacon Press, 1960), 102–87. For contrary views that see a close connection between language and nation or nationality, see Munro Chadwick, *The Nationalities of Europe and the Growth of National Ideologies* (New York: Cooper Square Publishers, 1973; reprint of 1945 edition); Carl J. Friedrich, 'Corporate Federalism and Linguistic Politics,' unpublished paper presented at the International Political

Science Association Congress, Montreal (1973), 3–5; and Ernest Gellner, *Thought and Change* (Chicago: University of Chicago Press, 1964), 163–5. The predominant European tradition has been to distinguish the terms 'nationality' and 'nation', using the former term for language groups and the latter to define the attachment of people of one or more language groups to a single state. Cf. Peter F. Sugar, 'External and Domestic Roots of Eastern European Nationalism', in Peter F. Sugar and Ivo J. Lederer (eds.), *Nationalism in Eastern Europe* (Seattle: University of Washington Press, 1969), 3–6. Emerson, who considers most other objective criteria unhelpful in defining the nation, insists, however, upon an inseparable relation between a nation and a 'national territory,' however loosely defined; *From Empire to Nation, op. cit.*, 105–9.

8. This definition follows Akzin, *State and Nation*, in not including independence, statehood, or sovereignty in the definition of the nation. Many definitions do insist on this latter criterion; for example, see Friedrich, 'Corporate Federalism', 4; another statement of Friedrich's definition in Karl W. Deutsch and William J. Foltz (eds.), *Nation-Building* (New York: Atherton Press, 1966), 11–12; and Oscar Jaszi, *The Dissolution of the Habsburg Monarchy* (Chicago: University of Chicago Press, 1961), 26. However, such definitions prepare the way for the confusion of the concept of the nation with that of the state from which much of the existing literature on nationalism suffers. Some leading scholars of nationalism have, however, avoided this confusion; for example, Emerson, *From Empire to Nation*, 95–102 and Deutsch, *Nationalism and Social Communication*, 104–5, who reserve the term nation-state for nations that have acquired sovereignty.

   The most troublesome issues arise when the nation is defined in terms of group solidarity without reference to the state, but nationalism is defined as the striving for statehood. Then, any demands made by nations short of that for statehood cannot be analysed in a study of nationalism! See Rustow, *A World of Nations*, 21.

9. Karl W. Deutsch, 'The Trend of European Nationalism—The Language Aspect,' in Joshua A. Fishman (ed.), *Readings in the Sociology of Language* (The Hague: Mouton, 1968), 599.

10. Ibid. 606.

11. For example, compare T. Zavalani, 'Albanian Nationalism,' in Sugar and Lederer, *Nationalism in Eastern Europe, op. cit.*, 68; and Paul Shoup, *Communism and the Yugoslav National Question* (New York: Columbia University Press, 1968), 107–9. Of course, the distinctiveness of Islam itself varies in different contexts, but this does not seem to be a significant factor as between Albanian and Yugoslav Muslims.

12. Paul R. Brass, *Language, Religion and Politics in North India* (New York: Cambridge University Press, 1974), 277–86.

13. See, for example, Robert H. Bates, 'Ethnic Competition and Modernization in Contemporary Africa', *Comparative Political Studies*, 4 (Jan. 4: 1974), 457–84; Gellner, *Thought and Change, op. cit.*, esp. 166 and 171–2; Chong-do Hah and Jeffrey Martin, 'Towards a Theory of Synthesis of Conflict and Integration Theories of Nationalism', *World Politics*, 27: 3 (Apr. 1975), 373–9; Michael Hechter, 'Towards a Theory of Ethnic Change', *Politics and Society*, 2: 1 (Fall, 1971), esp. 42–3 and 'The Persistence of Regionalism in the British Isles, 1885–1966', *The American*

Journal of Sociology, 79: 2 (Sept. 1973), 319–42; Robert Melson and Howard Wolpe, 'Modernization and the Politics of Communalism: A Theoretical Perspective', *American Political Science Review*, 64: 4 (Dec. 1970), 1112–18; and Smith, *Theories of Nationalism, op. cit.*, esp. 116–18, 132.

14. Consider, for example, the case of rural Slovaks even as late as the turn of the twentieth century who, upon emigrating to the United States 'were unaware of their specific national identity', knowing 'only that they were from a certain village in what was called Hungary, they were sternly ruled by people who spoke a different tongue, and they were very poor'. David W. Paul, *The Cultural Limits of Revolutionary Politics: Change and Continuity in Socialist Czechoslovakia* (Boulder, Col.: East European Quarterly, 1979), 195.

Extract 15

MICHAEL HECHTER: *Ethnicity and Rational Choice Theory*

1. T. Parsons, *The Structure of Social Action* (McGraw-Hill, 1937).
2. M. Hechter and D. Friedman, 'Does rational choice suffice? Response to Adam', *International Migration Review* (1984).
3. It is seldom recognised that the problems of collective action and social order are analytically similar. This similarity rests on the fact that each involves a collective-good situation (Olson 1965; Taylor 1982). Social order is a collective good that no rational egoist has an interest in upholding. Similarly, the rational member of a minority group may well profit from affirmative action legislation on the group's behalf, but will free ride on other people's efforts to attain this collective good. The danger in each case is that the collective good will not be provided at all because of free riding, or deviance, as it is known in the sociological lexicon.
4. T. Sowell, *Race and Economics* (David McKay, 1975), 165–7.
5. J. T. Landa, 'A theory of the ethnically homogeneous middleman group: an institutional alternative to contract law', *Journal of Legal Studies*, 10 (1981), 349–62.
6. M. Hechter, D. Friedman, and M. Appelbaum, 'A theory of ethnic collective action', *International Migration Review*, 16 (1982), 412–34.
7. M. Hechter (ed.), *The Micro Foundations of Macro Sociology* (Temple UP, 1983), and *Principles of Group Solidarity* (University of California Press, 1987).
8. See R. Hardin, *Collective Action* (Johns Hopkins UP, for Resources for the Future, 1982), for a recent review.
9. M. Hechter, 'When actors comply: monitoring costs and the production of social order', *Acta Sociologica*, 27: 3 (1984), 161–83.
10. R. Michael and G. S. Becker, 'On the new theory of consumer behaviour', *Swedish Journal of Economics*, 75: 4 (1973), 378–96; J. Hirschleifer, 'Economics from a biological viewpoint', *Journal of Law and Economics*, 20: 1 (1977); A. K. Sen and B. Williams (eds.), *Utilitarianism and Beyond* (CUP, 1982).
11. A. K. Sen, 'Rational fools: a critique of the behavioural foundations of economic theory', *Philosophy and Public Affairs*, 6: 4 (1977), 317–44; A. O. Hirschman, *Shifting Involvements: Private Interest and Public Action* (Princeton UP, 1982).
12. Hechter, 'When actors comply'.
13. C. Nordhoff, *The Communistic Societies of the United States* (Schocken Books, 1965; first publ. 1875); J. A. Hostetler, *Amish Society* (Johns Hopkins UP, 1963); R. Kanter,

Commitment and Community (Harvard UP, 1972); B. Zablocki, *The Joyful Community* (Penguin Books, 1971).

14. Zablocki, *op. cit.*
15. Since most such groups are highly stratified with respect to authority and consumption, if not ownership of property, and elders often occupy the position of an aristocracy, status considerations are by no means irrelevant in the intentional community.
16. The fact that the United States has so many intentional communities is partially explained by constitutional guarantees of religious freedom, as well as by generous tax incentives that are available to groups that manage to become identified as religions.
17. Abandoning the community also imposes significant social costs—most such groups deny members any contact with apostates—including contact of parents with children. Needless to say, successful intentional communities also rely on efficient control systems whose task is aided by norms against individual privacy. Here too there are significant parallels with primitive communities.
18. Hechter, 'Group formation'.
19. M. Banton, *Racial and Ethnic Competition* (CUP, 1983), 158–64.
20. Hechter, *Principles of Group Solidarity.*

Extract 16

MICHAEL BANTON: *The Actor's Model of Ethnic Relations*

1. M. Banton and Mohd-Noor Mansor, 'The study of ethnic alignment: a new technique and an application in Malaysia', *Ethnic and Racial Studies*, 15: 4 (1992), 599–613.
2. Some would call these identities rather than roles. Where a pattern of expected behaviour defines a relationship between two or more persons, I prefer to say that the expectation defines a role. Where the expected behaviour is more general and not associated with particular relationships, then it is convenient to say that it defines an identity, though that word is, of course, used in other senses too.
3. D. D. Laitin, 'Language normalization in Estonia and Catalonia', *Journal of Baltic Studies*, 23: 2 (1992), 149–66.
4. M. Hechter, D. Friedman, and M. Appelbaum, 'A theory of ethnic collective action', *International Migration Review*, 16 (1982), 112–34; M. Banton, *Racial Theories* (CUP, 1987), 136.
5. M. Olson, *The Logic of Collective Action: Public Goods and the Theory of Groups* (Harvard UP, 1965), 132–8.
6. As described in H. Tingsten, 'National self-examination', *Ethnic and Racial Studies*, 2: 1 (1979), 52.
7. M. Banton, *Roles: An Introduction to the Study of Social Relations* (Tavistock, 1965), 34.
8. Those who migrate and settle in another country can be expected to be less influenced by the ethnic definitions of the country they have left, so it is noteworthy that according to a recent Australian study 'The most widespread and violent form of inter-ethnic conflict is reported to be that between Croatian and Serbian or Yugoslav people, although this appears to have declined both in frequency and intensity in recent years', *Racist Violence*, p. 148.

9. Initially, I formulated my theory of racial and ethnic relations in three propositions (1983, p. 104). The second read 'Ethnic groups result from inclusive and racial categories from exclusive processes'. Shirley Dex (1985, p. 525) observed that this could stand as a definition statement. So when I restated the theory (1987, p. 125) and divided it into five sub-divisions, starting with the theory of boundaries, I included it as part of the first proposition regarding racial and ethnic boundaries. I now believe it would have been better placed in the second sub-division, the theory of signs, which is concerned with the ways in which intergroup relations are affected by the nature of the attribute taken as a sign of group or category membership.
10. 1983 1 All ER 106. The definition of ethnic group in Mandla's case was formulated in order to decide whether Mandla had a remedy arising from the prohibition of indirect discrimination, not to decide whether the alleged discriminator had acted on the grounds of the victim's ethnic origins.
11. F. Burton, *The Politics of Legitimacy: Struggles in a Belfast Community* (Routledge, 1978), 37–67; R. Jenkins, *Hightown Rules: Growing Up in a Belfast Housing Estate* (National Youth Bureau, Leicester, 1982), 30–1. Comparative studies of how people tell one another's ethnicity or nationality (or, in India, their caste) in everyday encounters could be illuminating.

Extract 18

MOSES FINLEY: *The Ancient Greeks and their Nation*

1. One notable protest is that of H. Strasburger, 'Der Einzelne und die Gemeinschaft im Denken der Griechen', *Historische Zeitschrift*, 177 (1954), 227–48, reprinted in *Zur griechischen Staatskunde*, ed. F. Gschnitzer (Darmstadt 1969), 97–122 (I shall cite the original pagination). Another, tendentious one will be noted later: H. E. Stier, *Grundlagen und Sinn der griechischen Geschichte* (Stuttgart 1945).
2. Walbank, 'Nationality in Roman History', 146–8. The Liddell-Scott-Jones Lexicon is similarly infected: for *patris*, originally a poetic feminine form of *patrios* which then entered ordinary speech, the basic definition given is 'one's fatherland, country', then, as a secondary sense, 'native town or village'. The fact is that *patris* normally means 'fatherland, country' only in the particular sense of 'native town or village'; see Stier, *op. cit.*, 117–19. Indeed, in Homer *patris* had the still narrower connotation of 'family estate': Strasburger, *op. cit.*, 230–32.
3. John Stuart Mill, quoted from C. K. Ogden and I. A. Richards, *The Meaning of Meaning* (10th edn., London 1949), facing p. 1.
4. In a posthumously published essay, 'La nation', *L'Année sociologique* (1953/4), 7–68, Marcel Mauss showed that the close conceptual link between nation and state underlines the notorious history of the difficulty in defining 'nation' satisfactorily. 'Nation', incidentally, cannot be translated into ancient Greek, and 'Hellas' was employed in a variety of senses, including 'old Greece' in the narrow sense of the Greek world before the great north-eastern and western expansion (e.g. Thucydides 1.2.1).
5. In the centuries after Alexander the Great, there was a considerable growth of Greek cities further east, into Asia Minor, in Syria and Babylonia, but that did not significantly alter the situation under examination.

6. *Weltbürgertum und Nationalstaat. Studien zur Genesis des deutschen Nationalstaates* (Munich and Berlin 1908), 7. I have quoted only a portion of the prolonged (and mixed) biological metaphor, partly because such phrases as 'Selbstbestimmungsdrang der Nationen' are beyond my powers as a translator.
7. Stier, *op. cit.*, 108–10, 167–70, criticizing Meinecke, denies this. The *polis*, he says, was a proper *Staatsnation*, but he disputes Meinecke entirely on the latter's terms, as is fitting for a historian closely associated intellectually with Spengler.
8. Walbank, 'Nationality in Roman History', 148. The further argument that the great dispersion of the Greeks precluded the political unification of the whole of Hellas is a red herring. Let us put aside Phasis or Sinope in Asia Minor, Marseilles in Gaul. There was no move to unite the Greek peninsula or Greek Sicily, where the conditions of contiguity and manageable size were fulfilled: each became a single Roman province before the end of the second century BC.
9. Aristotle's 'the *polis* is prior to the individual' is therefore a far more embracing notion than the superficially similar one to be found in the literature of the 'interactionist' school of social psychology, e.g., 'the temporal and logical pre-existence of the social process to the self-conscious individual that arises in it': G. H. Mead, *Mind, Self & Society*, ed. C. W. Morris (Chicago 1934), 186.
10. Behind the ideology of common descent lay larger views of human and ethnic origins, which the Greeks manipulated in various ways to set themselves above and beyond the barbarians; see E. J. Bickerman, '*Origines Gentium*', *Classical Philology*, 47 (1952), 65–81.
11. Xenophanes, frag. 11 and 15, Diels-Kranz ed.
12. Heraclitus, frag. 40 and 57, Diels-Kranz ed.
13. I have examined some of the implications in my *Democracy Ancient and Modern* (New Brunswick and London 1973).
14. Heraclitus, frag. 107. Epicurus held a similar view according to Clement of Alexandria, *Stromata* 1.15.67.1.
15. For a modest example of the discoveries made possible by such a quantitative analysis, see Helen H. Bacon, *Barbarians in Greek Tragedy* (New Haven 1961). I have refrained from using the technical term 'content analysis' employed in modern communication research because it appears to infuriate some, at any rate, among classical historians. Most of the current work seems to concentrate on the mass media, on propaganda and politics, or on psychotherapy, all in the contemporary world. For the historian, the most useful introduction is still B. Berelson, *Content Analysis in Communication Research* (1952, reissue New York 1971); cf. the introduction to part I, by K. Krippendorff, and the extensive bibliography in *The Analysis of Communication Content*, ed. G. Gerbner *et al.* (New York 1969). For an application of the techniques to a historical question, see e.g. G. Shapiro *et al.*, 'Quantitative Studies of the French Revolution', *History and Theory*, 12 (1973), 163–91.
16. Translations of Hesiod are by H. G. Evelyn-White in the Loeb Classical Library.
17. Cf. Aristotle, *Rhetoric* 1396a18: the Athenians 'enslaved the Hellenes, they reduced to slavery those who were bravest in fighting with them against the barbarians, the Aeginetans, the Potidaeans and all such others'.
18. I shall ignore the distinction suggested by R. K. Merton between 'groups' and 'categories', for, helpful though it is in certain analyses, it would introduce

an unnecessary complication into the present discussion; see Merton and A. K. Rossi, 'Contribution to the Theory of Reference Group Behavior', in *Readings in Reference Group Theory and Research*, ed. H. H. Hyman and E. Singer (New York and London 1968), 26–68, reprinted in part from Merton, *Social Theory and Social Structure* (rev. edn., Glencoe, Ill., 1957); 225–75. Hellas is of course a category in this terminology. There were other categories, which I have not bothered to include in my list, such as Lacedaemonians and Ionians.

Extract 20

JOHN ARMSTRONG: *Archetypal Diasporas*

1. Another diaspora important during the Middle Ages was the Nestorian Christian community, which one 15th-century traveler considered as important in 'the Indies' as the Jews were in the West. F. Nau, 'L'expansion nestorienne en Asie', *Annales du Musée Guimet, Bibliothèque de vulgarisation*, 40 (Paris, 1913). See also J. Richard, *La Papauté et les missions d'orient au moyen age, XIII–XV siècle* (Rome, 1977), 9 ff.; J. Joseph, *The Nestorians and their Muslim Neighbours: A Study of Western Influence on their Relations* (Princeton, 1961), 10 ff.; J. Dauvillier, 'Byzantins d'Asie Centrale et d'Extreme Orient au moyen age', *Revue des Études Byzantines*, 11 (1953), 70; C. Commeaux, *La Vie quotidienne chez les Mongols de la conquête* (Paris, 1972), 294, 307.
2. J. Juster, *Les Juifs dans l'empire romain*, 2 vols. (Paris, 1914), i. 418.
3. A. B. Yeremian, 'Sur certaines modifications subies par les monuments arméniens au VIIe siècle', *Revue des Études Arméniennes*, 8 (1971), 264; Richard, 201.
4. S. Der Nersessian, *Armenia and the Byzantine Empire* (Cambridge, Mass., 1945), 25–37; E. Ter-Minassiantz, *Die armenische Kirche in ihren Beziehungen zu den syrischen Kirchen bis zum Ende des 13 Jahrhunderts* (Leipzig, 1904), 91 ff.; A. Ter-Mikelian, *Die armenische Kirche in ihren Beziehungen zur byzantischem: vom IV bis zum XII Jahrhundert* (Leipzig, 1892), 14, 40, 75; S. Weber, *Die katholische Kirche in Armenien: Ihre Begründung und Entwicklung ver der Trennung* (Freiburg im Breisgau, 1903), 354ff.; J. Laurent, *L'Arménie entre Byzance et l'Islam depuis la conquête arabe jusqu'en 886* (Paris, 1919), 133 ff.
5. I rely on Laurent, 133 ff., and on recent personal observations, for the ritual sacrifice. On other points, see E. Sarkisyanz, *Geschichte der orientalischen Völker Russlands bis 1917* (Munich, 1961), 46 ff.; Weber, 229 ff.; A. Christensen, *L'Iran sous les Sassanides* (Copenhagen, 1936), 13, 230; H. Gelzer, 'Die Anfänge der armenischen Kirche', Königlich-Sächische Gesellschaft der Wissenschaft zu Leipzig, Philologisch-Historische Klasse, *Bericht über die Verhandlungen*, 65 (1895), 130–2.
6. A. P. Kazhdan, *Armyane v Sostave Gospodstvuyushchego Klassa Bizantiiskoi Imperii v XI–XII vv* (Yerevan, 1975), 146–50.
7. See J. A. Armstrong, 'Mobilized and proletarian diasporas', *American Political Science Review*, 70 (1976), 393–408, for additional bibliographical references and analysis of the exchange relationship between diasporas and dominant elites.
8. X. de Planhol, 'Géographie politique et nomadisme en Anatolie', *Revue Internationale des Sciences Sociales*, 11 (1959), 552. Cf. L. Nalbandian, *The Armenian Revolutionary Moment* (Berkeley, 1963), 26. The Kurds had been infiltrating the Armenian

area since the 13th century. C. Cahen, 'Le Probleme ethnique en Anatolie', *Cahiers d'Histoire Mondiale*, 2: 2 (1954), 352 ff.

9. S. Vyronis, Jr., *The Decline of Medieval Hellenism in Asia Minor and the Process of Islamicization from the Eleventh through the Fifteenth Century* (Berkeley, 1971), 199.
10. H. Inalcik, *The Ottoman Empire: The Classical Age, 1300–1600* (London, 1973), 129; B. Nolde, *La Formation de l'empire russe: études, notes et documents*, 2 vols. (Paris, 1952, 1953), ii. 141.
11. W. J. Fischel, *Jews in the Economic and Political Life of Medieval Islam* (London, 1937), 30; S. W. Baron, *A Social and Religious History of the Jews*, 2nd edn., vol. 16 (New York, 1976), 41; G. Deverdun, *Marrakech: Des origines à 1912*, vol. 1 (Rabat, 1959), 277; A. Sharf, *Byzantine Jewry from Justinian to the Fourth Crusade* (London, 1971), 98–9; A. J. Brawer, *Galizien wie es an Oesterreich kam* (Leipzig, 1910), 82–91.
12. S. Atamian, *The Armenian Community* (New York, 1955), 44; M. Grigorian, *Armenians in the Service of the Ottoman Empire* (London, 1977), 2 ff.; Nalbandian, 43 ff., 71 ff.
13. On differences in diaspora adaptability to peculiar ethical contexts, see E. Turczynski, *Konfession und Nation* (Düsseldorf, 1976), 71; W. O. McCagg, Jr., *Jewish Nobles and Geniuses in Modern Hungary* (Boulder, Col., 1972), 53; F. Braudel, *Civilisation matériel, economie et capitale, XV–XVIIIe siècle* (Paris, 1979), ii. 100. 127; iii. 415.
14. C. Roth, *The House of Nasi* (Philadelphia, 1948), 19, 67; S. Gerlach, *Tage-Buch* (Frankfurt, 1974), 155.
15. G. Kisch, *The Jews in Medieval Germany* (Chicago, 1949), 318; S. D. Goitein, *A Mediterranean Society: The Jewish Communities of the Arab World as Portrayed in the Documents of the Cairo Geniza*, 2 vols. (Berkeley, 1967, 1971), i. 66.
16. P. P. Argenti, *The Religious Minorities of Chios* (Cambridge, 1970), 172; M. Franco, *Essai sur l'histoire des Israélites de l'empire ottoman* (1897, repr. Hildesheim, 1973), 132, 160 ff.
17. D. N. Wilber, *The Architecture of Islamic Iran: The Il Khānid Period* (New York, 1955), 13; Fischel, 110; R. Brunschvig, *La Berbérie oriental sous les Hafsides*, 2 vols. (Paris, 1940, 1947), i. 397; S. Mendelssohn, *The Jews of Asia* (London, 1920), 10, 81; G. Schlumberger, *L'Epopée byzantine à la fin du dixieme siècle*, 3 vols. (Paris, 1896–1905), ii. 444. As discussed in ch. 3, the Castilians, despite their normal Mediterranean inclination to town life, adopted an antiurban ideology. The strong urban preference of the Italians, on the other hand, may have influenced their tolerance of Jews.
18. Laurent, 133; Weber, 405.
19. F. Valjavec, *Der Josephinismus* (2nd edn., Munich, 1945), 32; Brawer, 104 ff.
20. I. Beidtel, *Geschichte der österreichischen Staatsverwaltung, 1740–1848*, 2 vols. (Innsbruck, 1896, 1898), ii. 170; P. Mitrofanov, *Joseph II*, 2 vols. (Vienna, 1910), i. 267; G. Kisch, *Die Prager Universität und die Juden, 1348–1848* (Mährisch-Ostrau, 1935), 53.
21. R. Wallach, *Das abendländische Gemeinschaftsbewusstsein im Mittelalter* (Leipzig, 1928), 49.
22. Laurent, 145.
23. Weber, 515; but see Richard, 92, on Gregorian efforts to proselytize Turkic groups.

Extract 23

DANIEL BELL: *Ethnicity and Social Change*

1. The range and extent of such plurality are striking. The largest countries in the world, India, the Soviet Union, the United States, and China, are plural societies, as are most countries in Asia, Africa, and Latin America. In fact, the relatively homogeneous society is the rare exception in the world—Japan (though it has a despised caste, the Eta), the Scandinavian countries, France (though with a strong Breton separatist movement), Italy (if we include Sicily as culturally 'Italian' and if we minimize regional particularism)—and even where there have been strong and established national political institutions, as in Great Britain, we find distinctive nationalist movements such as the Scottish and the Welsh, and the predictions that within a decade there may be a new federal structure to British political life, rather than the present-day control from Westminster. For a review of the problems of plural societies, see the issue of *International Social Science Journal*, 'Dimensions of the Racial Situation,' 23: 4 (1971), especially the review article by Leo Kuper, 'Political Change in Plural Societies,' 594–607.
2. As Pierre L. van den Berghe has written: 'The plural societies of Asia, Africa and Spanish America more recently studied by sociologists and anthropologists have, in fact, been far more typical of conquest states than the frontier immigrant and/or slave plantation societies which underpinned much of the previous ethnic relations literature. In the more classical case of the conquest state, the indigenous population is subordinated and exploited but neither exterminated nor enslaved; the dominant group remains a minority and is not supplemented by massive and continuous immigration after the conquest; cultural and social pluralism of the various ethnic groups is fairly stable and long-lasting; and much of the immigration which takes place subsequent to the conquest is likely to take the form of an interstitial pariah merchant class, ethnically distinct from both the indigenes and the politically dominant minority. This is the pattern characteristic of most empires, including most of the colonial territories of the European powers in Asia and Africa. The United States, Canada, Australia, Argentina, Uruguay, Chile, Brazil and the West Indies are the exceptions, made possible by the low pre-conquest population density, low level of indigenous military and productive technology, and sensitivity of the natives to imported epidemic diseases.' 'Ethnicity: The African Experience,' *International Social Science Journal*, 23: 4 (1971), 508. To these patterns, one would have to add the Russian empire which represented a combination of conquest and amalgamation and which, in the Soviet form, despite the formal equality of the multiple peoples, still sees a Great Russian domination both politically (in that Russians occupy the key political positions in most of the constituent Republics) and culturally.
3. Émile Durkheim, *Professional Ethics and Civic Morals* (Glencoe, The Free Press, 1958), 10–11.
4. That romanticism, of course, is now channeled into the idea of 'liberation' and the renewed mystique of 'revolution.'
5. For a detailed discussion of the underlying structural changes in American society and the emergence of new social groups and constituencies, see my essay, 'Unstable America,' *Encounter* 34 (June 1970), 11–26.

6. What modern society does, writes Dahrendorf, is to separate industrial conflict from political conflict. Or, as Anthony Giddens writes, in emendation of this idea, '"conflict consciousness" is in a certain sense inherent in the outlook of the worker in capitalist society; "revolutionary consciousness" is not.' See Ralf Dahrendorf, *Class and Class Conflict in Industrial Society* (Stanford, Stanford University Press, 1959), 271–7; and Anthony Giddens, *The Class Structure of the Advanced Societies* (London, Hutchinson University Library, 1973), 201–2.

   What is striking in Giddens's effort to reformulate a theory of class in advanced industrial societies is the total absence of any discussion of ethnicity or ethnic divisions within the class structures. Truly, a one-eyed vision of modern society.
7. Whether the structural changes—the emergence of knowledge or skill as the basis of class—will bring a coherent class identity on the part of the new technical classes is an open question. The knowledge elites have long had a specific ethos, defined usually as 'professionalism.' And this conception of their role in the past has militated against a traditional class identification. Yet even though these groups are defined by a common ethos, in the post-industrial society, as I have argued, it is likely that the *situs*, or locale of work, such as a business corporation, the university, the government, or the military, may be more important than the *stratum* as the source for political organization and political claims for the elite constituencies so that politics, more likely than not, would be on corporative rather than class lines. Among the 'semi-skilled intellectuals,' like teachers, one finds an increasing readiness to accept trade unionism and forego the traditional guild and professional identification and this may represent a new kind of class organization. But it is doubtful whether this 'educated labor,' in the United States, at least, would become an active ideological force.
8. Involvement beyond the borders of the country—the Jews with Israel, the blacks with Africa, the 'new left' with national liberation movements—has been a conspicuous feature of the last decade, an 'internationalism,' again which contrasts with the small degree of internationalism of the trade-union movements in working-class issues.
9. For a discussion of this question see my essay, 'The Break-up of Family Capitalism', in my *The End of Ideology* (Glencoe, The Free Press, 1960).

Extract 24

HERBERT J. GANS: *Symbolic Ethnicity*

1. See Nathan Glazer, *American Judaism* (Chicago: University of Chicago Press, 2nd edn. 1972), 114–15.
2. On the Jamaica Chinese, see Orlando Patterson, *Ethnic Chauvinism* (New York: Stein and Day, 1977), ch. 5; on the Sydney Italians, see Rina Huber, *From Pasta to Pavlova* (St Lucia: University of Queensland Press, 1977), pt. 3.
3. For a study of one unsuccessful attempt to establish a community presidency, see Arthur A. Goren, *New York Jews and the Quest for Community* (New York: Columbia University Press, 1970).
4. Charles S. Liebman, *The Ambivalent American Jew* (Philadelphia: Jewish Publication Society of America, 1973), ch. 3. Liebman notes that the few élite rabbis who did

come to America quickly sensed they were in alien territory and returned to Eastern Europe. The survivors of the Holocaust who came to America after World War II were too few and too late to do more than influence the remaining Jewish orthodox organizations.

5. Gans, 'The Origin and Growth of a Jewish Community in the Suburbs', in M. Sklare (ed.), *The Jews: Social Pattern of an American Group* (New York: Free Press, 1958), 205–48.
6. See Herbert J. Gans, 'American Jewry: Present and Future', *Commentary* (May 1956), 422–30, which includes a discussion of 'symbolic Judaism'.
7. Unfortunately, too little attention has been devoted by sociologists to ethnicity among descendants of the old immigration.

Extract 25

WINSTON JAMES: *The Making of Black Identities*

1. It can hardly be over-emphasised the extent to which resistance was mounted by Africans in the Americas to their enslavement. The literature on the subject is a vast and growing one. Eugene Genovese has a detailed bibliographical essay in *From Rebellion to Revolution: Afro-American Slave Revolts in the Making of the New World* (Baton Rouge, 1979).
2. The distribution of migrants from the various territories during the early years of migration have been estimated to have been as follows. Jamaica, 1953–61: 148, 369. Barbados, 1955–61: 18,741. Trinidad and Tobago, 1955–61: 9,610. British Guiana, 1955–61: 7,141. Antigua, 1955–61: 4,687. Montserrat, 1955–61: 3,835. St Kitts-Nevis-Anguilla, 1955–61: 7,503. Dominica, 1955–61: 7,915. Grenada, 1955–61: 7,663. St Lucia, 1955–61: 7,291. St Vincent, 1955–61: 4,285. See C. Peach, *West Indian Migration to Britain* (London, 1968), 106–7.
3. K. Ramchand, 'The colour problem at the university: A West Indian's changing attitudes', in H. Tajfel and J. Dawson (eds.), *Disappointed Guests: Essays by African, Asian and West Indian Students* (London, 1965), 28.
4. A. M. Gomes, 'I am an Immigrant', in A. Salkey (ed.), *Caribbean Essays* (London, 1973), 53. Cf. P. Madoo, 'The transition from "light skinned" to "coloured"', in Tajfel and Dawson (eds.), *op. cit.*
5. P. Madoo, *op. cit.*, 61–2.
6. D. Pearson, 'West Indian communal associations in Britain: some observations', *New Community*, 5: 4 (Spring-Summer, 1977), and *Race, Class and Political Activism: A Study of West Indians in Britain* (Farnborough, 1981).
7. For the qualified exceptions of Barbados and Grenada, see F. Henriques and J. Manyoni, 'Ethnic group relations in Barbados and Grenada', in UNESCO, *Race and Class in Post-Colonial Society: A Study of Ethnic Group Relations in the English-Speaking Caribbean, Bolivia, Chile and Mexico* (UNESCO, Paris, 1977).
8. Cited in D. Hinds, *Journey to an Illusion: The West Indian in Britain* (London, 1966), 11–12.
9. Hinds, *op. cit.*, 15. Cf. S. Patterson, *Dark Strangers: A Study of West Indians in London* (Penguin, Harmondsworth, 1965), 15.
10. G. Lamming, *The Pleasures of Exile* (London, 1984), 25–7.
11. N. Foner, *Jamaica Farewell: Jamaican Migrants in London* (London, 1979), 51. Cf. R. Sherwood, *The Psycho-dynamics of Race: Vicious and Benign Spirals* (Brighton,

1980), 318–19 and P. Schweitzer (ed.), *A Place to Stay: Memories of Pensioners from Many Lands* (London, 1984), 30.

12. As Fanon recognised: 'It is the white man who creates the Negro. But it is the Negro who creates négritude.' And as the originator of the concept, Aimé Césaire has explained the adoption of the concept *négritude* was a conscious act of defiance, not a term haphazardly or fortuitously chosen. As for its root-word, *négre*, Césaire tells us: 'Since there was shame about the word *négre*, we chose the word *négre*.' See Fanon's *A Dying Colonialism* (New York, 1965), 47, and Césaire's interview with René Depestre in the former's *Discourse on Colonialism* (New York, 1972), 73–4. Césaire's prime work of African celebration of awareness is of course, *Return to My Native Land* (London 1969). Cf. Jean-Paul Sartre, *Black Orpheus* (Paris, 1976): an exceptional analysis of negritude and an authentic expression of Sartre's anti-imperialism and solidarity with the oppressed. This essay was to have a profound influence upon the young Franz Fanon.
13. N. Foner, *Jamaica Farewell: Jamaican Migrants in London* (London, 1979), 117 and 143 (emphasis in original). A St Lucien man concluded: 'I think people lose respect for us when we let them think we want to be black Englishmen. We are going to be reckoned with the black heads of this world, when they are being counted. We must see ourselves in this context' (D. Hinds, *Journey to an Illusion: the West Indian in Britain* (London, 1966), 16–17). Cf. P. Schweitzer (ed.), *A Place to Stay: Memories of Pensioners from Many Lands* (London, 1984), 32.
14. Indeed, Foner points out: 'Respondents generally used the term "black", "colored", "West Indian", and "Jamaican" interchangeably (many times in the same sentence) when speaking, both informally and in answer to direct questions, about their position in English society. This was so even though the interview questions always used the category Jamaican': N. Foner, *Jamaica Farewell: Jamaican Migrants in London* (London, 1979), 144.
15. Foner, *op. cit.*, 134–5.
16. See Office of Population Censuses and Surveys (OPCS), *Labour Force Survey, 1981* (HMSO, London, 1982), Table 4.25, p. 22. Cf. C. Brown, *Black and White Britain: The Third PSI Survey* (London, 1984), Tables 79 (p. 185), 91 and 92 (pp. 197–8), 95 (p. 201), 120 and 121 (pp. 223–4).
17. It must be said that this state of affairs is less a positive credit to Britain than a major indictment of the nation states of the Commonwealth Caribbean—many of which are unviable as economic entities—which Britain has plundered and disfigured over the centuries, and their mimetic indigenous ruling classes who, though nominally presiding over independent states, have kept intact the fundamental pillars of the social structure erected under colonialism.
18. Cited in T. Cottle, *Black Testimony: The Voices of Britain's West Indians* (London, 1978), 16.
19. N. Foner, 'The meaning of education to Jamaicans at home and in London', *New Community*, 4: 2 (Summer, 1975).
20. For a good index of this new mood among the older generation of Afro-Caribbeans in Britain, see the views expressed *in their own words* in the otherwise astonishing, insensitive and downright mocking articles by David Selbourne, 'The new black exodus: blacks who have their eyes set on home' and 'I'm getting

out before it fall on me', in *New Society* (19 May 1983 and 23 May 1983). It should be noted that the return migration of Caribbeans to the islands is by no means a new phenomenon. On the experience of the early returnees see Betty Davidson, 'No place back home,' *Race*, 9: 4 (1968) and H. Orlando Patterson, 'West Indian migrants returning home', *Race*, 10: 1 (1968).

21. B. Troyna, 'Differential commitment to ethnic identity by black youths in Britain', *New Community*, 7: 3 (Winter, 1979).
22. Caribbean Teachers' Association (ed.), *Black Youth Speak Out* (report of the CTA Youth Conference, 1984) (London, 1984), 42, emphasis in original.
23. Some years ago at least, similar, but less intense contradictions existed between Africans and Afro-Caribbeans in Britain (for some examples see S. Benson, *Ambiguous Ethnicity: Inter-racial Families in Britain* (Cambridge University Press, 1981), 40, 97–9). However, the largely identical nature of racism which they faced in their everyday life, the disproportionately large role which continental Africans played in the Black Power movement in Britain in the late 1960s (cf. Obi Egbuna, *Destroy This Temple: The Voice of Black Power in Britain* (London, 1971)) and the spectacular rise of pan-Africanist ideas via Ras Tafari in the mid-1970s in Britain, all helped to defuse tension.
24. In the Caribbean new migrants, Indians and others, quite quickly adopted the stereotype established by the dominant European culture of the African. The Africans in their turn saw the Indians largely through the spectacle of the hegemonic European stereotype. Cf. D. Lowenthal, *West Indian Societies* (London, 1972), 156 ff, and L. Braithwaite, *Social Stratification in Trinidad* (Kingston, 1975), 44 ff.
25. In the case of the British colonies in the Caribbean this epoch finally ended between 1834 and 1838.
26. H. Tinker, *A New System of Slavery: The Export of Indian Labour Overseas 1830–1920* (London, 1974); K. Laurence, *Immigration into the West Indies in the Nineteenth Century* (Aylesbury, 1971); J. La Guerre (ed.), *Calcutta to Caroni: The East Indians of Trinidad* (Port of Spain, 1974); and W. Rodney, *A History of the Guyanese Working People, 1881–1905* (London, 1981). The numbers of Indian indentured labourers brought into the Caribbean were as follows: British Guiana, 238,909; Trinidad, 143,939; Jamaica, 36,412; Martinique, 25,519; Guadeloupe, 45,000; Surinam, 34,304; Windward Islands, 10,026. Source: K. Laurence, *op. cit.*, 57.
27. By far the most thorough case study of these strategies of divide and rule in the Caribbean in relation to Africans and Asians is to be found in W. Rodney's posthumously published *A History of the Guyanese Working People, 1881–1905* (London, 1981), 174 ff.
28. This point is dealt with at length in W. James, 'The myth of the "black community"', in W. James and C. Gutzmore (eds.), *Inside Babylon: Caribbean People and Their Descendants in Britain* (Pluto Press, London, forthcoming).
29. For some recent indications of the differences in priorities of these two groups, see the survey results cited in M. Fitzgerald, *Political Parties and Black People* (London, 1984), 57. C. Brown, *Black and White Britain: The Third PSI Survey* (London, 1984), brings out a number of these differences on a whole range of issues: see especially Tables 116–19 and 135–8.

Extract 26

STUART HALL: *The New Ethnicities*

1. Stuart Hall, 'Racism and reaction', in *Five Views on Multi-Racial Britain* (London, Commission for Racial Equality, 1978).
2. Paul Gilroy, *There Ain't No Black in the Union Jack: The Cultural Politics of Race and Nation* (London, Hutchinson, 1987).

Extract 27

ÉTIENNE BALIBAR: *Fictive Ethnicity and Ideal Nation*

1. I say 'included within them', but I should also add 'or excluded by them', since the ethnicization of the 'others' occurs simultaneously with that of the 'nationals': there are no longer any historical differences other than ethnic ones (thus the Jews also have to be a 'people'). On the ethnicization of colonized populations, see J.-L. Amselle and E. M'Bokolo, *Au cœur de l'ethnie: ethnies, tribalisme et Etat en Afrique* (La Découverte, Paris, 1985).
2. Ernest Gellner, *Nations and Nationalism* (Blackwell, Oxford, 1983) and Benedict Anderson, *Imagined Communities* (Verso, London, 1983), whose analyses are as opposed as 'materialism' and 'idealism', both rightly stress this point.
3. See Renée Balibar, *L'Institution du français. Essai sur le colingualisme des Carolingiens à la République* (PUF, Paris, 1985).
4. Jean-Claude Milner offers some very stimulating suggestions on this point, though more in *Les Noms indistincts* (Seuil, Paris, 1983), 43 *et seq.* than in *L'Amour de la langue* (Seuil, Paris, 1978). On the 'class struggle'/'language struggle' alternative in the USSR at the point when the policy of 'socialism in one country' became dominant, see F. Gadet, J.-M. Gaymann, Y. Mignot, and E. Roudinesco, *Les Maîtres de la langue* (Maspero, Paris, 1979).
5. Let us add that we have here a sure *criterion* for the commutation between racism and nationalism: every discourse on the fatherland or nation which associates these notions with the 'defence of the family'—not to speak of the birth rate—is already ensconced in the universe of racism.

Extract 28

ROGERS BRUBAKER: *Civic and Ethnic Nations in France and Germany*

1. Popular understandings of nationhood may be much more similar. But the politics of citizenship depends on elite self-understandings, for formal citizenship, unlike, say, immigration, is not a salient popular issue.
2. The French political and intellectual elite is itself a remarkable product of assimilation. The habitual schemes of thought and expression deployed by professionals in the representation of the social and political world—politicians, journalists, high civil servants, intellectuals, and so on—are products of the labor of 'continuous normalization' imposed by centralized institutions such as the Ecole Normale Supérieure, the Ecole National d'Administration, or the Institut d'Etudes Politiques (P. Bourdieu, 'La représentation politique. Éléments pour une théorie du champ politique', *Actes de la recherche en sciences sociales*, 36–7 (Feb.–Mar. 1981), 3–24).

3. On the transfer of schemes of interpretation and understanding from one domain to another, see Bourdieu's discussion of the concept of habitus in *Outline of a Theory of Practice*, trans. Richard Nice (CUP, 1977), 82–3; and *Distinction: A Social Critique of the Judgement of Taste*, trans. Richard Nice (Harvard University Press, 1984), 170–5.
4. E. Hobsbawm, 'Introduction: Inventing Traditions', in id. and T. Ranger (eds.), *The Invention of Tradition* (CUP, 1983).
5. On representation struggles, see Bourdieu, 'L'identité et la représentation. Éléments pour une réflexion critique sur l'idée de région', *Actes de la recherche en sciences sociales*, 35 (Nov. 1980), 63–72; 'La représentation politique'; and *Distinction*, 479–84.
6. Kolinsky, 'The Nation-State in Western Europe: Erosion from "Above" and "Below"?'; Beetham, 'The Future of the Nation-State', in L. Tivey (ed.), *The Nation State* (Oxford: M. Robertson, 1981).
7. On the incipient development of European citizenship, see R. Aron, 'Is Multinational Citizenship Possible?', *Social Research*, 41 (1974), 638–56; A. C. Evans, 'European Citizenship: A Novel Concept in EEC Law', *American Journal of Comparative Law*, 32 (1984), 679–715; Andrew Durand, 'European Citizenship', *European Law Review*, 4 (1979), 3–14; Eberhard Grabitz, *Europäisches Bürgerrecht zwischen Marktbürgerschaft und Staatsbürgerschaft* (Cologne: Europa Union Verlag, 1970).
8. For an account of the recasting of membership asserting—in my view, prematurely—that the fundamental organizing and legitimating principles of membership are already postnational, based on universal personhood rather than national citizenship, see Yasemin Soysal, 'Limits of Citizenship: Guestworkers in the Contemporary Nation-State System', Ph.D. dissertation, Stanford University, 1991, ch. 8.
9. R. Brubaker, 'Immigration, Citizenship, and the Nation-State in France and Germany: A Comparative Historical Analysis', *International Sociology*, 5 (1990), 380–383.
10. id. 'Citizenship Struggles in Soviet Successor States', forthcoming in *International Migration Review*.
11. id. 'Political Dimensions of Migration from and among Soviet Successor States', Paper presented at conference on International Migration and the Security and Stability of States, Center for International Studies, Massachusetts Institute of Technology, 5–6 Dec. 1991.

Extract 29
BASSAM TIBI: *Old Tribes and Imposed Nation-States in the Middle East*

1. On this topic, and also with reference to the Middle East, see Hugh Seton-Watson, *Nations and States: An Enquiry into the Origins of Nations and the Politics of Nationalism* (London, 1977), esp. 239–71; and John Breuilly, *Nationalism and the State* (Manchester, 1982).
2. In addition to A. D. Smith, *Ethnic Origins of Nations* (Oxford, 1986) see Joane Nagel, 'The Ethnic Revolution: The Emergence of Ethnic Nationalism in Modern States', *Sociology and Social Research*, 68: 4 (1983–4), 417–34.

3. See Bassam Tibi, *Arab Nationalism: A Critical Inquiry* (New York 1981).
4. Louis Snyder, 'Nationalism and the flawed concept of ethnicity', *Canadian Review of Studies in Nationalism*, 10: 2 (1983), 263.
5. Hanna Batatu, 'Some observations on the social roots of Syria's ruling, military group and the causes of its dominance', *Middle East Journal*, 35: 3 (1981), 331–2. See also Patrick Seale, *Asad: The Struggle of the Middle East* (Berkeley, 1989), 8–11.
6. See Esman and Rabinovich (eds), *Ethnicity, Pluralism and the State in the Middle East* (Ithaca, 1988), 3. Rabinovich (155–72) refers to the Alawites of Syria and points out that the 'community's modernization and politicization during the past two decades' has been the structural background of the Alawite's 'spectacular rise from the fringes of Syrian public life to a position of power and dominance.' For Rabinovich, the explanation of this phenomenon 'remains a mystery' (162). The concept of ethnicity does not lead us out of this impasse.
7. Ibid. 3–4.
8. Batatu, 'Some Observations', 332; see also Seale, *Asad*.
9. Hanna Batatu, 'Iraq's underground Shi'a movements: characteristics, causes and prospects,' *Middle East Journal*, 35: 4 (1981), 583–4.
10. Ibid. 585.
11. Gabriel Ben-Dor, 'Ethnopolitics and the Middle Eastern State', 71–92, in Esman and Rabinovich (1988).
12. Smith, *Ethnic Origins of Nations*, 7–13.
13. Ibid. 13–16.
14. Ibid. 13, 15.
15. See Esman and Rabinovich, *Ethnicity*, 3–24.
16. Smith, *Ethnic Origins of Nations*, 10.
17. To this phenomenon Ghassan Salamé's formula *tamaddun al-sukkan wa tarayuf al-sulta* (the urbanization of the population and the ruralization of political power) applies. See Ghassan Salamé, Elbaki Hermassi, and Khaldun al-Naqib, *Al-Mujtama' wa al-Dawla fi al-Watan al-'Arabi*, ed. S. E. Ibrahim (Beirut, 1988), 215–18. Sociologically, the links between holders of state power, as a center of resource allocation, and their prenational tribal community can be characterized as a patron-client relationship. For an effort at grappling with this complicated issue, see John Waterbury, 'An effort to put patrons and clients in their place,' in Ernest Gellner and John Waterbury (eds), *Patrons and Clients* (London, 1977), 329–42.

Extract 30

WALTER ZENNER: *Middlemen Minorities*

1. Howard P. Becker, 'Constructive typology in the social sciences', in *Contemporary Social Theory*, H. Barnes, H. Becker, and F. Becker (eds.) (New York: Appleton, Century, 1940), 17–46.
2. W. Cahnman, 'Social-economic causes of anti-Semitism', *Social Problems*, 5 (1957), 21–9, Irwin Rinder, 'Strangers in the land', *Social Problems*, 6 (1958), 253–60; Sheldon Stryker, 'Social structure and prejudice,' *Social Problems*, 6 (1958), 340–54.
3. T. Shibutani and K. Kwan, *Ethnic Stratification* (New York: Macmillan, 1965), 168–98; Hubert Blalock, *Toward a Theory of Minority Group Relations* (New York: John Wiley, 1967), 82–3; and R. A. Schermerhorn, *Comparative Ethnic Relations* (New

York: Random House, 1970), 55, 72, 74, 77, 99, 106, 111–12, 147, and 151, reflect the 'race relations' view in middleman minority theory. David C. McClelland, *The Achievement Motive* (New York: Appleton-Century-Crofts, 1953) deals with the motives for entrepreneurship, although this approach was not often applied to middleman minorities. For critiques of this approach, see Abner Cohen, *Custom and Politics in Urban Africa* (Berkeley: University of California Press, 1972), and John Waterbury, *North for the Trade* (Berkeley: University of California Press, 1969), 103–15.

4. Edna Bonacich, 'A theory of middleman minorities', *American Sociological Review*, 38 (1973), 583–94; 'Class approaches to ethnicity and race', *Insurgent Sociologist*, 10 (1980), 9–23; 'Middleman minorities and advanced capitalism', *Ethnic Groups*, 2 (1980), 311–20; Jonathan H. Turner and Edna Bonacich, 'Toward a composite theory of middleman minorities', *Ethnicity*, 7 (1980), 144–58; and Edna Bonacich, Ivan Light, and Charles Choy Wong, 'Korean immigrant small business in Los Angeles', in *Sourcebook on the New Immigration*, R. B. Bryce-Laporte, D. Mortimer, and S. Couch (eds.) (New Brunswick, NJ: Transaction Books, 1980), 167–84.
5. On the split-labor hypothesis, see Edna Bonacich, 'A theory of ethnic antagonism: the split-labor market', *American Sociological Review*, 37 (1972), 547–59, 'The past, present and future of split-labor market theory', in *Research in Race and Ethnic Relations: A Research Annual* (Greenwich, Conn.: JAI Press, 1979), 17–64; and 'Class approaches to ethnicity and race', 9–23.
6. Abram Leon, *The Jewish Question—A Marxist Interpretation* (New York: Pathfinder Press, 1970).
7. I. Wallerstein, *The Modern World System*, vol. 1 (New York: Academic Press, 1974), 147–51, and vol. 2 (New York: Academic Press, 1980), 145.
8. Abner Cohen, *Two Dimensional Man* (Berkeley: University of California Press, 1974). The symbolic side of the dialectical relationship between symbols and power is best presented in his study of the Creoles of Sierra Leone. See Abner Cohen, *Politics of Elite Culture* (Berkeley: University of California Press, 1981). Incidentally, while the Creoles today are specialized as civil servants, they were a middleman group during the late nineteenth century.
9. Abner Cohen, 'Cultural strategies in the organization of trading diasporas', in *The Development of Indigenous Trade and Markets in West Africa*, C. Meillassoux (ed.) (London: Oxford University Press, 1971), 266–84. His analysis of trading diasporas is based on his study of Hausa cattle traders. See Cohen, *Custom and Politics in Urban Africa*.
10. For a classification of theories, see Bonacich and Modell, *The Economic Basis of Ethnic Solidarity: The Case of the Japanese-Americans* (Berkeley, University of California Press, 1981), 24–30.
11. Donald Horowitz, *Ethnic Groups in Conflict* (Berkeley and Los Angeles: University of California Press, 1985), 16–51; 105–25, and 141–228.
12. Rinder, 'Strangers in the Land', 253–60.
13. Wallerstein, *Modern World System*, i. 151.
14. On the 'black/gray market' in the Soviet Union, see Hedrick Smith, *The Russians* (New York: Quadrangle, 1976), 125–31; and Konstantin Simis, 'Russia's underground millionaires', *Fortune* (June 1981), 36–50.

15. See Bonacich, 'A theory of middleman minorities'; 'Class approaches to ethnicity and race'; 'Middleman minorities and advanced capitalism'.
16. At this point, Bonacich's discussion of middleman minorities overlaps with her split-labor market theory. See Bonacich, 'A theory of ethnic antagonism,' and 'Past, present, and future of split-labor market theory'. For the distinction between adopting skills by training indigenous skillholders or importing skillholders, see Abraham Hirsch, 'Importing and Adopting Skills', *Human Organization*, 24 (1965), 124–7.
17. Brian Foster, 'Ethnicity and Commerce', *American Ethnologist*, 1 (1974), 437–48.
18. Foster, 'Ethnicity and commerce'.
19. Blalock, *Toward a Theory of Minority Group Relations*; Foster, 'Ethnicity and commerce'; and Horowitz, *Ethnic Groups in Conflict*, 187–9.
20. Examples of 'middleman groups' who were quasi-natives include Scots and Dissenters in England, Old Believers in Russia, and Antioqueños in Colombia.

Extract 31

ANTHONY D. SMITH: *Chosen Peoples*

1. K. Deutsch, *Nationalism and Social Communication* (Boston, 1966); J. Krejci and V. Velimsky, *Ethnic and Political Nations in Europe* (London, 1981).
2. For Weber's phrase see M. Weber, *Economy and Society*, vol. 1, ed. G. Roth and C. Wittich (New York, 1968), iii, ch. 3, p. 926. For the Swiss case, see J. Steinberg, *Why Switzerland?* (Cambridge, 1976). For a discussion of myths of the 'golden age', see A. D. Smith, 'National identity and myths of ethnic descent', *Research in Social Movements, Conflict and Change*, 7 (1984).
3. This is the burden of the priestly book of Deuteronomy, esp. ch. 30; see R. M. Seltzer, *Jewish People, Jewish Thought* (New York, 1980), i. ch. 2.
4. S. N. Kramer, *The Sumerians* (Chicago, 1963), ch. 7; G. Roux, *Ancient Iraq* (Harmondsworth, 1964), ch. 10.
5. On this royal propaganda, see J. van Seters, *In Search of History* (New Haven and London, 1983), ch. 5, esp. 172–81, who quotes Hatshepsut's cliff-temple inscriptions in Middle Egypt: 'I have raised up that which had gone to pieces formerly, since the Asiatics were in the midst of Avaris in the Northland. They ruled without Re . . .' (174).
6. For the expulsion of the Hyksos from Egypt *c.*1580 BC, see B. G. Trigger *et al.*, *Ancient Egypt: A Social History* (Cambridge, 1983), 149–60, 173–4. For a comparison with Mesopotamian conceptions of divine kingship, see H. Frankfort, *Kingship and the Gods* (Chicago, 1948), 5–12, 299–312.
7. Amos 3: 2; but cf. the more universalist outlook at Amos 9: 7, which likens Israel to the Ethiopians, Philistines, and Syrians in God's eyes; cf. also Hosea 11: 1, for the idea of Israel as God's child.
8. See e.g. Isaiah 41: 8–10; 43: 1–21; 49: 14–18; also Jeremiah 2: 1–3; 4: 1–4; and 31 *passim*; Hosea 11: 13–14. See on this I. Zeitlin, *Ancient Judaism* (Cambridge, 1984).
9. See the classic study of Jewish messianism by J. Klausner, *The Messianic Idea in Israel* (London, 1956); cf. R. J. Werblowski, 'Messianism in Jewish history', in H. Ben-Sasson and S. Ettinger (eds.), *Jewish Society Through the Ages* (London, 1971),

30–45, and J. H. Yerushalmi, *Jewish History and Jewish Memory* (Seattle and London, 1983).

10. R. C. Dentan (ed.), *The Idea of History in the Ancient Near East* (New Haven, Conn., 1983), 86, 89–94.
11. R. Frye, *The Heritage of Persia* (New York, 1966), 239–61; *The Cambridge History of Iran*, Vol. 3 (Cambridge, 1983), pt. 1, ch. 3B.
12. P. Avery, *Modern Iran* (London, 1965); N. Keddie, *Roots of Revolution* (New Haven and London, 1981), chs. 1–3.
13. For the early history of Christian Armenia, see D. M. Lang, *Armenia, Cradle of Civilisation* (London, 1980), chs. 7–8. For the Jewish links, see J. Armstrong, *Nations Before Nationalism* (Chapel Hill, NC, 1982). For the evolution of Armenian Christianity, see A. S. Atiya, *A History of Eastern Christianity* (London, 1968), 315–28.
14. On the Solomonic tradition in the *Kebra Nagast* ('Glory of the Kings'), the Ethiopian national epic, see E. Ullendorff, 'The Queen of Sheba in Ethiopian tradition', in J. B. Pritchard (ed.), *Solomon and Sheba* (London, 1974), 104–14; and cf. Ullendorff, *Ethiopia and the Bible* (London, 1968) for more details, and D. Keesler, *The Falashas, the Forgotten Jews of Ethiopia* (New York, 1985), for the Falashas and Jewish elements in Ethiopian Christianity.
15. On these Arab dimensions of Islam, see J. Carmichael, *The Shaping of the Arabs* (New York, 1967), and B. Lewis, *The Emergence of Modern Turkey* (London, 1970). For the modern period, see H. Sharabi, *The Arab Intellectuals and the West* (Baltimore and London, 1970); for medieval Islamic identities, see Armstrong, *op. cit.*, ch. 3.
16. N. H. Baynes and H. St L. B. Moss (eds.), *Byzantium* (London and New York, 1969), ch. 1.
17. P. Sherrard, *The Greek East and the Latin West* (London, 1959); Armstrong, *op. cit.*, 178–81.
18. For the medieval Russian beliefs, see M. Cherniavsky, 'Russia', in O. Ranum (ed.), *National Consciousness, History, and Political Culture in Early-Modern Europe* (Baltimore and London, 1975), 18–43, and R. Pipes, *Russia under the Old Regime* (London, 1977), ch. 9. For 19th-century Slavophile ideals, see E. Thaden, *Conservative Nationalism in Nineteenth Century Russia* (Seattle, 1964); for recent neo-Russian expressions among the Orthodox and the nationalists, including *Pamyat* and *Veche*, see D. Pospielovsky, 'The "Russian Orientation" and the Orthodox Church', in P. Ramet (ed.), *Religion and Nationalism in Soviet and East European Politics* (Durham and London, 1989), 81–108.
19. See Armstrong, *op. cit.*, 152–9, and M. Bloch, *Feudal Society*, 2 vols. (London, 1961), ii. 431–7. For St Joan, see M. Warner, *Joan of Arc* (Harmondsworth, 1983). For a recent critical analysis of French myths of election, in Third Republic (and later) history texts, see S. Citron, *Le Mythe National* (Paris, 1988).
20. For the text and background of the Declaration of Arbroath, see A. A. M. Duncan, *The Nation of Scots and the Declaration of Arbroath* (London, 1970); for the Swiss beliefs, see H. Kohn, *Nationalism and Liberty* (New York, 1957). For a more general discussion, see Smith, *op. cit.*
21. G. S. Kirk, *Myth, its Meanings and Functions in Ancient and Other Cultures* (Cambridge, 1973); cf. H. Tudor, *Political Myth* (London, 1972) and L. Thompson, *The Political Mythology of Apartheid* (New Haven and London, 1985).

22. Kohn, *op. cit.*; G. Thürer, *Free and Swiss* (London, 1970).
23. For a clear example of Western cultural imperialism, that of the French in West Africa, see W. H. Lewis (ed.), *French-Speaking Africa* (New York, 1965). For a similar, if more aloof, imperialism in China, see F. Dikötter, 'Group definition and the idea of "race" in modern China', *Ethnic and Racial Studies*, 13: 3 (1990), 420–32.
24. R. H. Davis, *The Normans and their Myth* (London, 1976); cf. S. Reynolds, *Kingdoms and Communities in Western Europe, 900–1300* (Oxford, 1984), ch. 8.
25. For French myths of dynastic election, see E. H. Kantorowicz, 'Pro patria mori in medieval political thought', *American Historical Review*, 56 (1951), 472–92, and Armstrong, *op. cit.*, 152–9. For English/British myths, see H. Kohn, 'The origins of English nationalism', *Journal of the History of Ideas*, 1 (1940), 69–94; H. A. MacDougall, *Racial Myth in English History* (Montreal and Hanover, NH, 1982); and R. A. Mason, 'Scotching the Brut', *History Today*, 35 (Jan. 1985), 26–31.
26. O. Halecki, *A History of Poland* (London, 1955); N. Davies, *God's Playground*, 2 vols. (Oxford, 1982).
27. For Welsh myths, see G. Williams, *When Was Wales?* (Harmondsworth, 1985), and P. Morgan, 'From a death to a view', in E. Hobsbawm and T. Ranger (eds.), *The Invention of Tradition* (Cambridge, 1983).
28. J. Sheehy, *The Rediscovery of Ireland's Past* (London, 1980); J. Hutchinson, *The Dynamics of Cultural Nationalism* (London, 1987).
29. N. Howe, *Migration and Mythmaking in Anglo-Saxon England* (New Haven and London, 1989).
30. See E. L. Tuveson, *Redeemer Nation* (Chicago and London, 1968) and C. C. O'Brien, *God-land* (Cambridge, Mass., 1988) for American puritan providentialism. We meet the same sentiments in early settlement Australia, which 'is truly a land flowing with milk and honey', according to Barron Field's *Geographic Memoirs* of 1825 (cited in B. Smith, *European Vision and the South Pacific* (London, 1960), 185.
31. See the analysis of Korais in E. Kedourie, *Nationalism in Asia and Africa* (London, 1971), Introduction. For the birth of Zionism, see D. Vital, *The Origins of Zionism* (Oxford, 1975); for Armenian diaspora nationalism, see L. Nalbandian, *The Armenian Revolutionary Movement* (Berkeley, 1963) and C. Walker, *Armenia, the Survival of a Nation* (London, 1980); for back-to-Africa movements, including Garveyism, see T. Draper, *The Rediscovery of Black Nationalism* (London, 1970).
32. For Christian and Muslim warrior myths, see Armstrong, *op. cit.*, ch. 3; for Israelite beliefs, see M. Weinfeld, 'Divine intervention in war in ancient Israel and in the ancient Near East', in H. Tadmor and M. Weinfeld (eds.), *History, Historiography and Interpretation* (Jerusalem, 1986), 121–47; more generally see A. D. Smith, 'War and ethnicity', *Ethnic and Racial Studies*, 4: 4 (1981), 375–97.
33. B. Anderson, *Imagined Communities* (London, 1983), ch. 5; cf. S. Pech, 'The nationalist movements of the Austrian Slavs in 1848', *Social History*, 9 (1976), 336–56; A. D. Smith, 'The origins of nations', *Ethnic and Racial Studies*, 12: 3 (1989), 340–67.
34. For such immigrant nationalisms, see H. Seton-Watson, *Nations and States* (London, 1977), ch. 5; and compare the contemporary protests of Aborigines, American Indians and Mohawks.

Extract 32
CYNTHIA ENLOE: *Religion and Ethnicity*

1. Fredrick Barth, *Ethnic Groups and Boundaries* (Boston: Little, Brown & Co., 1969). The situational character of ethnic identity is persuasively described in Judith Nagata, 'What is Malay?', *American Ethnologist*, 1: 2 (1974), 331–50.
2. Donald E. Smith, *Religion and Political Development* (Boston: Little, Brown & Co., 1970), 33–56.
3. Richard Gambino, *Blood of My Blood: The Dilemma of The Italian Americans* (New York: Anchor Books, 1975), 235–7.
4. Ethel Dunn and Stephen P. Dunn 'Ethnic intermarriage as an indicator of cultural convergence in Soviet Central Asia', in Edward Allworth (ed.), *The Nationality Question in Soviet Central Asia* (New York: Praeger Publishers, 1973), 46.
5. Elmer Spreitzer and Eldon E. Snyder, 'Patterns of variation within and between ethno-religious groupings', *Ethnicity*, 2: 2 (June 1975), 124–33.
6. Kathleen A. Frankovic, 'The effect of religion on religious attitudes' (unpublished Ph.D. dissertation, Rutgers University, 1974), 1, 214–23.
7. Gallup Opinion Index, 'Religion in America, 1976', Report No. 130 (1976), 8.
8. Jeffrey A. Ross, 'Political mobilization of Jews in U.S.S.R.', Comparative Interdisciplinary Studies Section of The International Studies Association, *Working Paper #13* (1974), 13.
9. Ralph Premdas notes, however, that The Official Guyanese Indian association in the past was officially close to the Indian political party: Ralph Premdas, *Voluntary Associations and Political Parties in a Racially Fragmented State: The Case of Guyana. Occasional Papers No. 2* (Georgetown, Guyana: Department of Political Science, University of Guyana, 1972), 34–5. In Trinidad, Muslims in the East Indian Community are thought to be closer to the politically dominant Afro-Trinidadians than are either Hindu or Christian East Indians: Yogendra K. Malik, *East Indians in Trinidad* (London: Oxford University Press, 1971), 36–7.
10. Of the Indians in Britain (not including Pakistanis) 85% are Hindus, according to Ernest Krausz, *Ethnic Minorities in Britain* (London: Paladin, 1972), 19. An insightful profile of an Indian Muslim Kutchi refugee family in Britain in Jane Kramer, 'The Ugandan Asians', *New Yorker* (8 Apr. 1974), 47–93.

Extract 33
PASCHALIS KITROMILIDES: *Orthodoxy and Nationalism*

1. For a general appraisal referring to the whole of Eastern Europe, cf. Emanuel Turczynski, 'Nationalism and Religion in Eastern Europe', *East European Quarterly*, 5 (1972), 468–86. It is characteristic, however, that Dimitri Obolensky, 'Nationalism in Eastern Europe in the Middle Ages', in id., *The Byzantine Inheritance of Eastern Europe* (London, 1982), connects the appearance of phenomena of 'nationalism' in the Middle Ages only with those cases marked by 'the rise and consolidation of states'.
2. See Richard Clogg, 'The *Dhidhaskalia Patriki* (1798): An Orthodox Reaction to French Revolutionary Propaganda', *Middle Eastern Studies*, 5: 2 (May 1969), 87–115.

3. See Gale Stokes, 'Church and Class in Early Balkan Nationalism', *East European Quarterly*, 13: 3 (Autumn 1979), 259–70. See also Duncan Wilson, *The Life and Times of Vuk Stefanovic Karadzic 1787–1864* (Oxford, 1970), 46–9, 323–30.
4. M. A. Ubicini, *Letters on Turkey*, translated by Lady Easthope (London, 1856), ii. 236.
5. Ibid. 237.
6. In the semi-official translation quoted below the term 'phyletism' is rendered as 'racism', which may obscure the real target of the nineteenth-century condemnation. See Maximos, Metropolitan of Sardis, *The Oecumenical Patriarchate in the Orthodox Church* (Thessaloniki, 1976), 303.
7. Ibid. 308–9.
8. S. Zankow, *Die Verfassung der bulgarischen orthodoxen kirche* (Zurich, 1918), surveys the subject from the vantage-point of Bulgarian nationalism; while M. I. Gedeon (ed.), *Eggrapha patriarchika kai synodika peri tou boulgarikou zitimatos (1852–1873)* (Constantinople, 1908), codifies the official pronouncements of the Patriarchate of Constantinople on the problem. See also L. S. Stavrianos, 'L'institution de l'exarcat bulgare: Son influence sur les relations interbalkaniques', *Les Balkans*, 9 (1939), 56–69.
9. Stavro Skendi, *The Albanian National Awakening 1878–1912* (Princeton, 1967), 161–4, 174–5, 179–80, 296–302.
10. See George R. Ursul, 'From Political Freedom to Religious Independence: The Romanian Orthodox Church, 1877 to 1925', in Stephen Fischer-Galati, Radu R. Florescu, and George R. Ursul (eds.), *Romania between East and West. Historical Essays in Memory of Constantin C. Giurescu* (Boulder, 1982), 224.
11. Cf. the very interesting study by Keith Hitchins, *Orthodoxy and Nationality: Andreiu Saguna and the Rumanians of Transylvania, 1846–1873* (Cambridge, Mass., 1977).
12. It is interesting to note that the autonomous Church of Georgia, one of the oldest Orthodox churches in the Caucasus, raised the issue of its elevation to autocephaly and patriarchate during the visit of the Patriarch of Constantinople Demetrios I in August 1987. This suggests that the question of ecclesiastical status still remains a major concern and probably provides an outlet of national assertion and self-recognition in the absence of independent statehood.
13. On the historical and theoretical significance of these conflicts see Paschalis M. Kitromilides, 'To telos tis ethnarchikis paradosis', *Amitos sti mnimi Photi Apostolopoulou* (Athens, 1984), 486–507.
14. On the background, see Derek Hopwood, *The Russian Presence in Syria and Palestine 1843–1914: Church and Politics in the Near East* (Oxford 1969), 159–79. The dislocation of the Greek Patriarch of Antioch was considered 'the first real victory for Arab nationalism'.

Extract 35

JACOB LANDAU: *Diaspora and Language*

1. N. Abadan-Unat (ed.), *Turkish Workers in Europe, 1960–1975* (Leiden, 1976), 5.
2. R. E. Krane (ed.), *Manpower Mobility Across Cultural Boundaries: Social, Economic, and Legal Aspects* (Leiden, 1975); Abadan-Unat, *op. cit.*

3. J. M. Landau, *Johnson's 1964 Letter to Inönü and Greek Lobbying of the White House*, Jerusalem Papers on Peace Problems, no. 28 (Jerusalem: The Leonard Davis Institute for international relations, 1979).
4. I. al-Na'uri, *Adab al-Majhar* (Cairo, 1967).
5. Landau, *op. cit.*
6. T. Anderson and M. Boyer, *Bilingual Schooling in the United States*, 2 vols. (Washington, DC, 1970), ii. 232–4.
7. E. C. Vlachos, *The Assimilating of Greeks in the United States* (Athens: National Centre of Social Researches, 1968), 90–8.
8. Landau, *op. cit.*
9. U. Füssel, 'Accusations fly over row in Greek school', *The German Tribune* (Hamburg), 26 Dec. 1982, pp. 12–13, trans. from the *Frankfurter Rundschau*, 9 Dec. 1982; M. Zeiss, 'Abitur auf Griechisch', *Die Zeit*, 11 June 1982, p. 33.
10. G. S. Himmelfarb and S. Dellapergola, *Enrolment in Jewish Schools in the Diaspora* (Jerusalem: Institute of Contemporary Jewry, 1982).

Extract 36
JOHN EDWARDS: *Symbolic Ethnicity and Language*

1. J. Edwards, 'Ethnic identity and bilingual education', in H. Giles (ed.), *Language, Ethnicity, and Intergroup Relations* (London, 1977).
2. C. Eastman, 'Language, ethnic identity, and change', in J. Edwards (ed.), *Linguistic Minorities, Policies and Pluralism* (London, 1984).
3. C. Eastman and T. Reese, 'Associated language: how language and ethnic identity are related', *General Linguistics*, 21 (1981), 109–16.
4. D. Riesman, *Individualism Reconsidered* (New York, 1965).
5. H. Gans, 'Symbolic ethnicity: the future of ethnic groups and cultures in America', *Ethnic and Racial Studies*, 2 (1979), 1–20.
6. See also P. Hinton, 'Where have the new ethnicists gone wrong?', *Australian and New Zealand Journal of Sociology*, 17 (1981), 14–19.
7. M. Hansen, 'The third generation in America', *Commentary*, 14 (1982), 492–500.
8. Edwards, *op. cit.*; J. Fishman, *Language Loyalty in the United States* (The Hague, 1966); J. Smolicz, *Culture and Education in a Plural Society* (Canberra, 1979).
9. A. Greely, 'The persistence of diversity', *Antioch Review*, 39 (1981), 146.
10. Ibid. 147.
11. Smolicz, *op. cit.*, 87.

Extract 37
LEROY VAIL: *The Creation of Ethnicity in South Africa*

1. For an interesting, although not wholly convincing, assessment of the central role of language in the building of nationalism, see B. Anderson, *Imagined Communities: Reflections on the Origin and Spread of Nationalism* (London, 1983).
2. It should be noted that intellectuals discussed in the chapters of this volume are all literate intellectuals. The nature of the evidence makes it difficult to ascertain the nature of the thought and work of non-literate intellectuals, yet it should be kept in mind that such non-literate intellectuals have indeed worked to further

ethnic ideologies through oral genres. This whole topic is the subject of a forthcoming study by L. Vail and L. White.

3. Malawi National Archives, GOA 2/4/12, 'Mohammadanism and Ethiopianism', Circular letter, Lt. Col. French to Gov. Smith, 7 Aug. 1917.
4. M. Chanock, *Law, Custom and Social Order: The Colonial Experience in Malawi and Zambia* (Cambridge, 1985), is an important study that goes far in exploring the role of the perceived need to control women in the development of concepts of law during the colonial period.
5. The relevance of the language of kinship ties to the development of ethnic identity is explored, within a basically primordialist interpretation, in Horowitz, *Ethnic Groups in Conflict* (Berkeley and Los Angeles, 1985), 55–92.

Extract 38

M. G. SMITH: *The Plural Society*

1. J. S. Furnivall, 'Some Problems of Tropical Economy', in Rita Hinden (ed.), *Fabian Colonial Essays* (London: George Allen and Unwin, 1945), 161–84; and J. S. Furnivall, *Colonial Policy and Practice* (London: Cambridge University Press, 1948), 304–12.
2. Georges Balandier, 'The Colonial Situation', in Pierre L. van den Berghe (ed.), *Africa: Social Problems of Change and Conflict* (San Francisco: Chandler Publishing Co., 1965), 36–57; Adriano Moreira, 'Rapport général: Aspect juridique et politique', in *Ethnic and Cultural Pluralism in Intertropical Countries* (Brussels: INCIDI, 1957).

Extract 39

JOHN REX: *Multiculturalism in Europe*

1. T. Modood, 'The end of hegemony: the concept of Blacks and British Asians', in J. Rex and B. Dury (eds.), *Ethnic Mobilisation in a Multi-Cultural Europe* (Aldershot, 1994).
2. C. Neveau, 'Is "Black" an exportable category to mainland Europe?', in Rex and Dury, *op. cit.*
3. R. Miles, *Racism after 'Race Relations'* (London, 1993).
4. J. Rex, *Race Relations in Sociological Theory* (London, 1983), *Race and Ethnicity* (Milton Keynes, 1986), and 'The role of class analysis in the study of race relations—a Weberian perspective', in id. and D. Mason (eds.), *Theories of Race and Ethnic Relations* (Cambridge, 1986); M. Wieviorka, 'Ethnicity as action', in Rex and Drury, *op. cit.*
5. Wieviorka, *op. cit.*
6. F.-O. Radtke, 'The formation of ethnic minorities and the transformation of social into ethnic conflicts in a so-called multi-cultural society: the case of Germany', in Rex and Drury, *op. cit.*
7. J. Rex, *The Concept of a Multi-Cultural Society: Occasional Papers* (Warwick, 1986).
8. J. Rex and S. Tomlinson, *Coloured Immigrants in a British City* (London, 1979).
9. J. Rath, 'Minosering: De Social Constructe van Ethnische Minderheden', Ph.D thesis, University of Utrecht, 1991.
10. J. Rex, 'The political sociology of multi-cultural societies', *European Journal for Multi-Cultural Studies*, 2: 1 (1991).

11. J. Rex, 'Ethnic identity and the nation-state: the political sociology of multicultural societies', *Social Identities*, 1: 1 (1994) and 'The second project of ethnicity: transnational migrant communities and ethnic minorities in modern multicultural societies', *Innovation*, 7: 3 (1994).
12. E. Durkheim, *The Division of Labour in Society* (Glencoe, Ill., 1933).
13. F. Parkin, *Marxism and Class Theory* (London, 1979).
14. Durkheim, *op. cit.*, 61–2.

Extract 40

FRANK DIKÖTTER: *The Idea of 'Race' in Modern China*

1. A. Ying (ed.), *Yapian zhanzheng wenxue ji* (Collection of literary writings on the Opium War) (Peking, 1957), 836.
2. Ibid. 44.
3. Ibid. 143.
4. Li Ao, *Dubai, xia de chuantong* (Tradition descended as a monologue) (Taipei, 1988), 4.
5. Xu Jiyu, *Yinghuan zhilüe* (A brief survey of the maritime circuit) (Osaka, 1861), *juan* 8, p. 1a.
6. The expression 'lowest' reflects the Chinese belief in geographical determinism, thus having a latitudinal as well as an evolutionary connotation.
7. Yan Fu, *Yan Fu shiwen xuan* (Selected poems and writings of Yan Fu) (Peking, 1959), 20.
8. Ibid. 22.
9. Ibid. 9.
10. Tang Caichang, *Juedianmingzhai neiyan* (Essays on political and historical matters) (Taipei, 1968), 501.
11. Ibid. 468.
12. Ibid. 563.
13. Liang Qichao, *Yinbingshi quanji* (Complete works of Liang Qichao) (Shanghai, 1941), ii. 13.
14. Ibid. 52.
15. Kang Youwei, *Datongshu* (The one world) (Peking 1956).
16. Ye Dehui, *Yijiao congbian* (Documents of the campaign against the 1898 reform movement) (Taipei, 1970), *juan* 5, p. 17b.
17. Liu Shipei, 'Huangdi jinian shuo' (About a calendar based on the Yellow Emperor), in *Huangdi hun* (The soul of the Yellow Emperor) (repr. Taipei, 1968), 1.
18. Zhang Qiyun, 'Huangdi zisun' (Sons of the Yellow Emperor: speech made during the national festival of grave-sweeping, 5 Apr. 1941), in *Minzu sixian* (Nationalist thought) (Taipei, 1951), 1.
19. Tang Zhijun (ed.), *Zhang Taiyan zhenglun xuanji* (Selected political writings of Zhang Binglin) (Peking, 1977), 139.
20. Chen Tianhua, *Chen Tianhua ji* (Collected works of Chen Tainhua) (Changsha, 1982), 82.
21. Ibid. 81.
22. Lin Yu-Sheng, *The Crisis of the Chinese Consciousness: Radical Antitraditionalism in the May Fourth Era* (Madison, 1979).

23. Wei Juxian, 'Zhongguo minzu qiantu zhi shi de kaocha (Study on the future of the Chinese race), *Qiantu* 1: 10 (1933), 7.
24. Lin Yan, *Zhongguo minzu de youlai* (Origins of the Chinese race) (Shanghai, 1947), 27.
25. Gu Shoubai, *Renleixue* (Anthropology) (Shanghai, 1924), 51.
26. Gong Tingzhang, *Renlei yu wenhua jinbu shi* (History of the progress of culture and mankind) (Shanghai, 1926), 54.
27. Ibid. 59.
28. On the traditional idea of 'peasant stupidity' in a Chinese society dominated by an elite of highly educated scholar-officials, see F. Dikötter, 'The limits of benevolence: Wang Shiduo (1802–1889) and the peasant population' (in preparation).
29. Chen Yinghuang, *Renleixue* (Anthropology) (Shanghai, 1918), 5.
30. F. Dikötter, 'Eugenics in Republican China', *Republican China*, 15: 1 (1989), 1–17.
31. Ubukata Naokichi, 'Chugoku ni okeru jinshu sabetsu no kinshi' (On the prohibition of racial discrimination in China), *Hikakuho kenkyu*, 6 (1953), 40–6.
32. See e.g. Zhou Jianren, *Lun youshengxue yu zhongzu qishi* (About eugenics and racial discrimination) (Peking, 1950).

Extract 41

IMMANUEL GEISS: *Pan-Africanism and European Imperialism*

1. This term was already in use in the United States during the nineteenth century, as an alternative to 'negro' and 'colored', which were thought to be discriminatory. In the present work it is used as a synonym for these terms. For a more detailed discussion of this point see I. Geiss, *Die Afro-Amerikaner* (Frankfurt, 1969), 19–21; also R. B. Moore, *The Name 'Negro': its Origin and its Evil Use* (New York, 1960).
2. Cf. also H. P. Marc, 'Pan-Africanism: a Dream Come True', *Foreign Affairs* (Apr. 1955), 445 ff.
3. The German term *Panafrikanisten* was coined by Strauch on an analogy with *Panslawisten* (Pan-Slavs).
4. The best of the recent works on decolonization include H. Grimal, *La Décolonisation, 1919–1963* (Paris, 1965); R. V. Albertini, *Dekolonisation: die Diskussion über Verwaltung und Zukunft der Kolonien, 1919–1960* (Cologne, Opladen, 1966).
5. For the origins of German conservatism, which was most strongly imbued by the idea of reverting to medieval values, cf. the first volume of the work by K. Epstein, *The Genesis of German Conservatism* (Princeton, 1966); the author's untimely death prevented him from completing the three volumes originally planned.
6. Cf. especially H. Kohn, *Die Slawen und der Westen: eine Geschichte der Panslawismus* (Vienna, 1956).
7. Cf. T. L. Hodgkin, *Nationalism in Colonial Africa* (London, 1956, 4th edn. 1962), 16 f.
8. K. Nkrumah, *Consciencism: Philosophy and Ideology for Decolonization and Development with Particular Reference to the African Revolution* (London, 1964).

Extract 42

LEON POLIAKOV: *The Aryan Myth and Biblical Universalism*

1. This was certainly the teaching of Hebraic anthropology. Contrary to a widely held belief, the exclusiveness of the Mosaic law was religious not racial. The barrier between the 'chosen people' and 'the nations' was intended to preserve the former's function as a priestly people.
2. We have done so in vol. II (*De Mahomet aux Marranes*) of my *Histoire de l'anti-sémitisme*.
3. The relevant passage from Linnaeus which we have not quoted so far runs as follows: 'It is said that Réaumur has fertilized a chicken with a rabbit. The eggs produced chicks which were like ordinary fowl except that instead of having feathers they were covered by white fur. The experiment is conclusive up to a point but we cannot draw general conclusions from such cases. Indeed the most appalling consequences might result from doing so. With regard to the human race one might be induced to think that Negroes have a rather peculiar origin but for my part I refuse to believe this.' *Metamorphosis Plantarum (*1755).
4. Cf. S. Freud, *'On Narcissism: an Introduction'* (1914), etc., and B. Grundberger, *Le narcissisme. Une étude psychoanalytique* (Paris 1971).
5. With reference to this aspect of the anti-religious polemic see vol. III (*De Voltaire à Wagner*) of my *Histoire de l'antisémitisme*.

Extract 43

LEO KUPER: *Genocide and the Plural Society*

1. In this discussion of relevant variables, I have been drawing on the work of R. A. Schermerhorn, *Comparative Ethnic Relations* (New York, 1970), ch. 4. See also M. G. Smith's analysis of different patterns in the Caribbean, 'Race and stratification in the Caribbean', in *Corporations and Society* (London, 1974), ch. 4, and my paper on *The Theory of the Plural Society, Race and Conquest* (UNESCO, forthcoming).
2. In *The Pity of it All* (Minneapolis, 1977), 247–75, I analyse the process of polarization in Algeria.
3. Ibid. 66–70.
4. Ibid. 70–3. In the account of these conflicts, I relied on the work of Yves Courrière, *Le Temps des léopards* (Paris, 1969), 179 ff.
5. *The Pity*..., 74–83, 128–45.
6. See M. G. Smith, 'Pluralism in Pre-Colonial African Societies', in L. Kuper and M. G. Smith (eds.), *Pluralism in Africa* (Berkeley, 1969). See also R. Lemarchand, 'Revolutionary phenomena in stratified societies', *Civilisations*, 18 (1968), 16–51.
7. I have analysed this genocide in *The Pity*..., 170–97. The major analysis of this conflict is provided by R. Lemarchand, *Rwanda and Burundi* (New York, 1970).
8. For accounts of this genocide and the background to it, see Lemarchand, *Rwanda and Burundi*, pt. 3; id. and D. Martin, *Selective Genocide in Burundi*, Minority Rights Group, Report no. 20 (London, 1974), 5–25; D. Martin, *Selective Genocide in Burundi—Part II*, Minority Rights Group, Report no. 20 (London, 1974), 29–34; J. Greenland, 'Ethnic discrimination in Rwanda and Burundi', in Foundation for

the Study of Plural Societies, *Case Studies on Human Rights and Fundamental Freedoms* (1975), iv. 97–133; and Kuper, *The Pity*. . . , 87–107, 197–208.

9. L. Collins and D. Lapierre, *Freedom at Midnight* (New York, 1975), 38–9.
10. Ibid. 41–2.
11. P. Moon, *Divide and Quit* (Berkeley, 1962), 29. The Jats were the predominant agricultural tribe in the Punjab prior to partition; there were Muslim, Hindu, and Sikh Jats (ibid. 30).
12. Collins and Lapierre, 284–50; Moon, 31.
13. Collins and Lapierre, 319–20, 340–1.
14. Ibid. 131–2.
15. Ibid. 225–6, 295, 252, 309, 251. I have been following closely the account of Collins and Lapierre.
16. A. Campbell-Johnson, *Mission with Mountbatten* (London, 1951), 184.
17. Collins and Lapierre, 356. See also 309–10 and 354–8, and the novel by Khushwant Singh, *Mano Majna* (1956), set in a Muslim and Sikh village in the remote reaches of the northern frontier.
18. Moon, 93–4.
19. Collins and Lapierre, 343.
20. Moon, 231–6.
21. Campbell-Johnson, 202.
22. Moon, 237.
23. Ibid. 9.
24. Comment of the former Viceroy, in Collins and Lapierre, 254.

Extract 44

HELEN FEIN: *The Armenian Genocide and the Holocaust*

1. H. Fein, *Accounting for Genocide: National Responses and Jewish Victimization During the Holocaust* (New York, 1979), ch. 1.
2. Ibid. 9.
3. R. C. Baum, *The Holocaust and the German Elite* (Totowa, NJ, 1981).
4. Cf. ibid. 45 and Fein, *Accounting for Genocide*, 8.
5. F. Mazian, *Why Genocide? The Armenian and Jewish Experiences in Perspective* (Ames, Iowa, 1990).
6. *Accounting for Genocide*.
7. L. Dawidowicz, 'Was the Holocaust Unique? Responses to Pierre Papazian', *Midstream* (Apr. 1984), 20; P. Papazian, 'Was the Holocaust Unique?', ibid. 19–25.
8. M. Weber, *From Max Weber*, trans. and ed. H. H. Gerth and C. W. Mills (New York, 1946), 120.
9. L. Dawidowicz, *The War Against the Jews 1939–1945* (New York, 1975).
10. R. Melson, 'Provocation or Nationalism', in R. Hovannisian (ed.), *The Armenian Genocide in Perspective* (New Brunswick, 1986); also in F. Chalk and K. Jonassohn (eds.), *The History and Sociology of Genocide* (New Haven, Conn., 1990).
11. Ibid. 68.
12. Ibid. 79–80.
13. Fein, *Accounting for Genocide*, pt. 3.
14. R. H. Dekmajian, 'Determinants of genocide', in Hovannisian, *The Armenian Genocide in Perspective*.

15. M. Kater, *The Nazi Party* (Cambridge, Mass., 1983); T. Childers, *The Nazi Voter* (Chapel Hill, NC, 1983); T. F. Abel, *Why Hitler Came to Power* (New York, 1938); P. Merkl, *Political Violence under the Swastika* (Princeton, 1975).

Extract 45

JOHN STONE: *Internal Colonialism*

1. S. Carmichael and C. V. Hamilton, *Black Power: The Politics of Liberation in America* (New York, 1967); R. Blauner, 'Internal colonialism and ghetto revolt', *Social Problems*, 16 (1969).
2. M. Hechter, *Internal Colonialism: The Celtic Fringe in British National Development, 1536–1966* (Routledge, 1975).
3. E. T. Zureik, *The Palestinians in Israel* (London, 1979).
4. N. I. and S. S. Fainstein, 'Dependency theory and the American urban district', paper presented to the International Political Science Association's round table on Politics and ethnicity, St Antony's College, Oxford, 26–8 March 1979.
5. B. B. Khleif, 'Ethnic awakening in the First World: the case of Wales', in G. Williams (ed.), *Social and Cultural Change in Contemporary Wales* (London, 1978).
6. W. R. Louis, *Imperialism at Bay* (Oxford, 1977), 570.
7. W. Connor, 'The politics of ethnonationalism', *Journal of international Affairs*, 27: 1 (1973).
8. Id., 'A nation is a nation, is a state, is an ethnic group, is a . . .', *Ethnic and Racial Studies*, 1: 4 (1978).
9. Id., 'Ethnonationalism in the First World', in M. J. Esman, *Ethnic Conflict in the Western World* (Ithaca and London, 1977); J. Stone, 'Anglo-American social science and the regional question', paper presented to the CNEI conference on Language and Culture in Regional Development, Maison des Sciences de l'Homme, Paris, 15 June 1977.
10. A. M. Greely, *Ethnicity in the United States* (New York, 1974), 11; Stone, *op. cit.*
11. A. Smith, 'Towards a theory of ethnic separatism', *Ethnic and Racial Studies*, 2: 1 (1979), 24.
12. A. Mughan, 'Modernisation, deprivation and the distribution of power resources', *New Community*, 5: 4 (1977), 396.
13. C. H. Enloe, 'Central governments' strategies for coping with separatist movements', in W. H. Morris-Jones (ed.), *The Politics of Separatism*, University of London Institute of Commonwealth Studies, Collected Seminar Papers, no. 19 (1976).
14. J. Stone and S. J. Mennell, *Toqueville on Democracy, Revolution and Society* (Chicago, 1980).
15. W. R. Beer, 'The social class of ethnic activists in contemporary France', in M. J. Esman (ed.), *Ethnic Conflict in the Western World* (Cornell, 1977).

Extract 47

DONALD HOROWITZ: *Symbolic Politics and Ethnic Status*

1. *Africa Report* (Apr. 1970), 10–11.
2. I witnessed the parliamentary debate on the National Anthem Bill in Kuala Lumpur in 1968.

3. Gusfield, *Symbolic Crusade: Status Politics and the American Temperance Movement* (Urbana: Univ. of Illinois Press, 1963).
4. Ibid. 68.
5. Ibid. 167.
6. Ibid. 180.
7. Anthony Parel, 'The Political Symbolism of the Cow in India', *Journal of Commonwealth Political Studies*, 7 (Nov. 1969), 179–203, at 188.
8. Harold D. Lasswell and Abraham Kaplan, *Power and Society: A Framework for Political Inquiry* (New Haven: Yale Univ. Press, 1950), 104; Victor Turner, 'Symbolic Studies', *Annual Review of Anthropology*, 4 (1975), 145–61, at 145, 158.
9. Opposition to a demand advanced in terms of universal principles 'proceeds by contraction of its symbols: the groups in whose name and for whose benefit the demand is made are alleged to be as narrow as possible, and the values demanded are formulated in specific and particular terms, dissociated from the general and universal perspectives under which they have been subsumed.' Lasswell and Kaplan, *Power and Society*, 107.
10. Gusfield, *Symbolic Crusade*, 17–18.
11. Hadley Cantril, *The Psychology of Social Movements* (2nd edn., New York: John Wiley 1963), 46.
12. Murray Edelman, *The Symbolic Uses of Politics* (Urbana: Univ. of Illinois Press, 1964), 167.
13. See e.g. Mary Fainsod Katzenstein, 'Origins of Nativism: The Emergence of Shiv Sena in Bombay', *Asian Survey*, 13 (Apr. 1973), 386–99 ('proper place'); *Sunday Statesman* (Calcutta), 9 July 1972 ('rightful place').
14. Gusfield, *Symbolic Crusade*, 172.
15. Sushil Kumar, 'Panorama of State Politics,' in Iqbal Narain (ed.), *State Politics in India* (Meerut: Meenakshi Prakashan, 1967), 41.
16. Editorial, *Statesman* (Calcutta), 26 Oct. 1972. See also Alfred G. Gerteiny, *Mauritania* (New York: Praeger, 1967), 151–2; Hugh Tinker, *India and Pakistan: A Political Analysis*, rev. edn. (New York: Praeger, 1968), 143.
17. Brian Weinstein, 'Language Strategists: Redefining Political Frontiers on the Basis of Linguistic Choices', *World Politics*, 31 (Apr. 1979), 345–64.
18. Robert N. Kearney, *Communalism and Language in the Politics of Ceylon* (Durham: Duke University Press, 1967), 73.
19. Donald Eugene Smith, *Religion and Politics in Burma* (Princeton: Princeton Univ. Press, 1966), ch. 7.
20. Leo Despres, *Cultural Pluralism and Nationalist Politics in British Guiana* (Chicago: Rand, McNally, 1967), 93.
21. See Robert B. Kaplan, 'Language and Science Policies of New Nations', *Science*, 221 (2 Sept. 1983), 913.

Extract 48

FLORENCIA E. MALLON: *Indigenous Peoples and the State in Latin America*

1. Marie-Chantal Barre, *Ideologías indigenistas y movimientos indios* (México, 1983); Guillermo Bonfil, 'Los pueblos indios, sus culturas y las políticas culturales', in Néstor García Canclini (ed.), *Políticas culturales en América Latina* (México, 1987);

Jesús Contreras (ed.), *La cara india, la cruz del 92: Identidad étnica y movimientos indios* (Madrid, 1988).

2. For the percentage of the Indian population see Barre, *Ideologías indigenistas*, 59; for the treatment of the Náhuatl group see Jane H. Hill, 'In Neca Gobierno de Puebla: Mexicano Penetrations of the Mexican State', in Greg Urban and Joel Sherzer (eds.), *Nation-States and Indians in Latin America* (Austin, 1991), 72–94; Judith Friedlander, *Being Indian in Hueyapan: A Study of Forced Identity in Contemporary Mexico* (New York, 1975).
3. Morelos is one of the most-studied regions of central Mexico. See, for example, Guillermo de la Peña, *Herederos de promesas: Agricultura, politica y ritual en los Altos de Morelos* (México, 1980); Arturo Warman, *. . . y venimos a contradecir. Los campesinos de Morelos y el estado nacional* (México, 1976); Horacio Crespo (ed.), *Morelos: Cinco siglos de Historia Regional* (México, 1984); John Womack Jr., *Zapata and the Mexican Revolution* (New York, 1968).
4. Indian population figures come from Barre, *Ideologías indigenistas*, 49. Concerning the process of *mestizaje* and ethnic relations, one of the classic original works is Fernando Fuenzalida *et al.*, *El indio y el poder en el Perú rural* (Lima, 1970). For an original and new perspective see Marisol de la Cadena, '"Las mujeres son más indias": Etnicidad y género en una comunidad del Cusco', *Revista Andina*, 9: 1 (July 1991), 7–29.
5. Representative examples of the literature from the 1960s and 1970s are: José Matos Mar *et al.*, *Dominación y cambios en el Perú rural* (Lima, 1969); François Bourricaud, *Power and Society in Contemporary Peru*, translated by Paul Stevenson (New York, 1970); Julio Cotler, *Clases, estado y nación en el Perú* (Lima, 1978); Robert G. Keith *et al.*, *La hacienda, la comunidad y el campesino en el Perú* (Lima, 1970); Giorgio Alberti and Rodrigo Sánchez, *Poder y conflicto social en el valle del Mantaro* (Lima, 1974).
6. Silvia Rivera Cusicanqui, *Oppressed But Not Defeated: Peasant Struggles Among the Aymara and the Quechwa in Bolivia, 1900–1980* (Geneva, 1987); René Zavaleta Mercado, *Lo nacional-popular en Bolivia* (México, 1986); Erick Langer, *Economic Change and Rural Resistance in Southern Bolivia, 1880–1930* (Stanford, 1989); Erick Langer, 'Rituals of Rebellion: The Chayanta Revolt of 1927', *Ethnohistory*, 37: 3 (1990), 227–53; Erick Langer, 'Persistencia y cambio en comunidades indígenas del sur boliviano en el siglo XIX', in Heraclio Bonilla (ed.), *Los Andes en la Encrucijada: Indios, Comunidades y Estado en el siglo XIX* (Quito, 1991), 133–68; Javier Izko, 'Fronteras étnicas en litigio. Los ayllus de Sakaka y Kirkyawi (Bolivia), siglos XVI–XX', in Bonilla (ed.), *Los Andes*, 63–132; Gustavo Rodríguez Ostria, *El socavón y el sindicato. Ensayos históricos sobre los trabajadores mineros, siglos XIX–XX* (La Paz, 1991); Gustavo Rodríguez Ostria, 'Entre reformas y contrarreformas: las comunidades indígenas en el Valle Bajo cochabambino (1825–1900)', in Bonilla (ed.), *Los Andes*, 277–334; Brooke Larson, *Colonialism and Agrarian Transformation in Bolivia: Cochabamba, 1550–1900* (Princeton, 1988); Tristan Platt, *Estado boliviano y ayllu andino: Tierra y tributo en el Norte de Potosí* (Lima, 1982).
7. The anthropological literature includes, Platt, *Estado boliviano*; Tristan Platt, 'The Andean Experience of Bolivian Liberalism, 1825–1900: Roots of Rebellion in 19th-Century Chayanta (Potosí)', in Steve J. Stern (ed.), *Resistance, Rebellion, and Consciousness in the Andean Peasant World, 18th to 20th Centuries* (Madison, 1987), 280–323; Olivia Harris, 'Complementarity and Conflict: An Andean View

of Women and Men', in J. S. LaFontaine (ed.), *Sex and Age as Principles of Social Differentiation* (London, 1978), 21–40; Olivia Harris, 'El parentesco y la economía vertical en el ayllu Laymi', *Avances*, 1 (1978); Olivia Harris, 'The Dead and the Devils Among the Bolivian Laymi', in Maurice Bloch and Jonathon Parry (eds.), *Death and the Regeneration of Life* (Cambridge, 1982); Thomas Abercrombie, 'To Be Indian, To Be Bolivian: "Ethnic" and "National" Discourses of Identity', in Urban and Sherzer (eds.), *Nation States and Indians*, 95–130; Thomas Abercrombie and Mary Dillon, 'The Destroying Christ: An Aymara Myth of Conquest', in Jonathan D. Hill (ed.), *Rethinking History and Myth: Indigenous South American Perspectives on the Past* (Urbana, 1988), 50–77; Roger Rasnake, 'Images of Resistance to Colonial Domination', in Hill (ed.), *Rethinking History and Myth*, 136–56; Roger Rasnake, *Domination and Cultural Resistance: Authority and Power Among an Andean People* (Durham, 1988).

8. For information on the COCEI see Campbell, 'Zapotec Ethnic Politics'; for the Yaqui see Hu-Dehart, 'Peasant Rebellion'. The link between the Indian problem and the land problem is made in José Carlos Mariátegui, *Siete ensayos de interpretación de la realidad peruana* (Lima, 1978). For the Andean utopia see, especially, Flores Galindo, *Buscando un Inca*. Concerning Katarismo, see Rivera Cusicanqui, *Oppressed But Not Defeated*; and Albó, 'From MNRistas to Kataristas to Katari'.

Extract 49

SELIG S. HARRISON: *Ethnicity and Politics in Pakistan: The Baluch Case*

1. For a detailed discussion of Baluch nationalism, past and present, see Selig S. Harrison, *In Afghanistan's Shadow: Baluch Nationalism and Soviet Temptations* (New York: Carnegie Endowment for International Peace, 1981).
2. For example, see Sardar Mohammed Khan Baluch, *History of the Baluch Race and Baluchistan*, rev. edn. (Quetta: Gosha-e-Adab, 1977), 5, 16–17; and Ma'an Shana al-Ajli Al-Hakkami, *Baluchistan Dival Al-'Arab* (Baluchistan: The Home of Arabs) (Bahrain, 1979).
3. J. H. Elfenbein, 'Baluchi', in *Encyclopaedia of Islam*, vol. 1: *A–B* (Leiden: E. J. Brill, 1960), 1006. See also J. H. Elfenbein, *The Baluchi Language: A Dialectology With Text*, vol. 27 (London: Royal Asiatic Society, Monographs, 1966), 41–5; and Richard N. Frye, 'Remarks on Baluchi History', *Central Asiatic Journal*, 6: 1 (1961), 49.
4. Elfenbein, *The Baluchi Language*, 3, 10.
5. M. Longworth Dames, *Popular Poetry of the Baloches*, vol. 2 (London: Royal Asiatic Society, 1907), 201. M. A. R. Barker and A. K. Mengal in *A Course in Baluchi*, vol. 2 (Montreal: Institute of Islamic Studies, McGill University, 1969), 1, describe the Baluchi alphabet. The author is indebted to Richard N. Frye for a clarification of the relationship between Baluchi and the Arabic alphabet.
6. Harrison, *In Afghanistan's Shadow*, 183–5.
7. For a differing interpretation of Baluch history, see Brian Spooner, 'Tribal Ideal and Political Reality in a Cultural Borderland: Ethnohistorical Problems in Baluchistan' (Paper presented at the Ethnohistory workshop, University of Pennsylvania, Philadelphia, 10 Apr. 1978), esp. 8, 15–16.
8. For a discussion of the continuing controversy over the size of the Baluch population in Pakistan and the population balance in the province of Baluchistan,

see Harrison, *In Afghanistan's Shadow*, 175–82, esp. 181. In recent decades Baluch preponderance in Baluchistan province has been threatened by a growing influx of Pashtuns and Punjabis, and ethnic tensions in the province have been aggravated by the influx of Pashtun refugees from Afghanistan since 1978.

9. See Harrison, *In Afghanistan's Shadow*, 40–91, for a discussion of Mengal, Marri, and the principal Baluch nationalist organizations.
10. This estimate refers to literacy in all languages among Baluch in Pakistan, Iran, and the Persian Gulf. Robert G. Wirsing found that the highest literacy rate in eight of the nine districts in Pakistani Baluchistan was 7.7%. 'South Asia: The Baluch Frontier Tribes of Pakistan', in *Protection of Ethnic Minorities: Comparative Perspectives*, ed. Robert G. Wirsing (New York: Pergamon, 1982), 18. Alvin Moore, South Asia specialist of the Library of Congress, estimated that there were 123,000 literates in Baluchi in 1981. 'Publishing in Pushto, Baluchi and Brahui, Part 2', in *South Asia: Library Notes and Queries* (Chicago: South Asia Reference Center, University of Chicago Library, March 1980), 3. The *Census of Pakistan: Population 1961*, vol. 2 (Karachi, West Pakistan: Ministry of Home and Kashmir Affairs, 1961), IV–94, reported 87,000 literates in Baluchistan province. The 1972 census did not contain comparable tables.
11. Philip Carl Salzman, 'The Proto-State in Iranian Baluchistan', in *Origins of the State: The Anthropology of Political Evolution*, ed. Ronald Cohen and Elman R. Service (Philadelphia: Institute for the Study of Human Issues, 1978), 125–40. See also Salzman, 'Continuity and Change in Baluchi Tribal Leadership', *International Journal of Middle Eastern Studies*, 4: 4 (1973), 428–39, and 'Adaptation and Political Organization in Iranian Baluchistan', *Ethnology*, 10: 4 (Oct. 1971), 433–44.
12. For an analysis of this climate two years before the secession of Bangladesh, see Selig S. Harrison, 'East Pakistanis Resent Army Takeover', a two-part series from Dacca, *Washington Post*, 30 Mar. and 1 Apr. 1969.
13. Baluch economic grievances and the economic viability of an independent Baluchistan are examined in my book, *In Afghanistan's Shadow*, 161–75.

Extract 51

DAVID BROWN: *Ethnicity, Nationalism and Democracy in South-East Asia*

1. Meinecke's *Kulturnation* was the cultural community which did not necessarily possess, but had the potential for, national consciousness; whereas the *Staatsnation* was the active consciousness of political community. Kohn's distinction was between a western version of nationalism as a subjective, rational, civic association; and an eastern European form of nationalism which was derived from the objective organic unity of the community. Friedrich Meinecke, *Cosmopolitanism and the National State* (New Jersey, Princeton University Press, 1970); Hans Kohn, *The Idea of Nationalism: A Study in its Origins and Background* (New York, Collier-Macmillan, 1967).

Extract 52

DENIZ KANDIYOTI: *Women, Ethnicity, and Nationalism*

1. For an excellent account of Orientalist depictions of women see S. Graham-Brown, *Images of Women* (London: Quartet Books, 1988).

2. S. Zubaida, 'Islam, Cultural Nationalism and the Left', *Review of Middle East Studies*, 4 (1988), 7.
3. E. Gellner, *Nations and Nationalism* (Oxford: Blackwell, 1983), 124.
4. The memoirs of the Turkish and Egyptian feminists Halide Edib and Huda Sharaawi confirm this view. A broader assessment of women's nationalist activities may be found in B. Baron, 'Women's Nationalist Rhetoric and Activities in Early Twentieth Century Egypt', in L. Anderson, *et al.* (eds.), *The Origins of Arab Nationalism* (New York: Columbia University Press, 1991).
5. A. Najmabadi, 'The Hazards of Modernity and Morality: Women, State and Ideology in Contemporary Iran', in D. Kandiyoti (ed.), *Women, Islam and the State* (London: Macmillan, 1991), 49.
6. Graham-Brown, *op. cit.*, 220.
7. I. C. Schick, 'Representing Middle Eastern Women: Feminism and Colonial Discourse', *Feminist Studies*, 16: 2 (1990), 369.
8. M. Hatem, 'The Politics of Sexuality and Gender in Segregated Patriarchal Systems: The Case of Eighteenth and Nineteenth Century Egypt', *Feminist Studies*, 12: 2 (1986), 250–73.
9. G. J. Massell, *The Surrogate Proletariat* (Princeton, NJ: Princeton University Press, 1974).
10. M. Molyneux, 'Women in Socialist Societies: Problems of Theory and Practice', in K. Young, *et al.* (eds.), *Of Marriage and the Market* (London: CSE Books, 1981), 167–202; and M. Molyneux, 'The Law, the State and Socialist Policies with Regard to Women: The Case of the People's Democratic Republic of Yemen, 1967–1990', in Kandiyoti (ed.), *Women, Islam and the State* 237–71.
11. P. Vieille, 'The State of the Periphery and its Heritage', *Economy and Society*, 17: 1 (1988), 66.
12. *Ibid.* 67.
13. *Ibid.*
14. This is the subject of an ongoing feminist debate. As key divergent texts, see J. Elshtain, *Public Man, Private Woman* (Princeton, NJ: Princeton University Press, 1981): and M. Barret and M. McIntosh, *The Anti-Social Family* (London: Verso, 1982).
15. B. Anderson, *Imagined Communities* (London: Verso, 1983), 131.
16. F. Anthias and N. Yuval-Davis (eds.), *Woman–Nation–State* (London, Macmillan, 1989), 1–15.
17. R. Mandel, 'Turkish Headscarves and the "Foreigner Problem": Constructing Difference Through Emblems of Identity', *New German Critique*, 46 (Winter 1989), 42.

Extract 53

MILTON J. ESMAN: *Diasporas and International Relations*

1. Though diasporas originate in migration, their termination is more problematical. When its members assimilate into their host society to the point that the group loses its coherence and its interest in its land of origin, or becomes estranged from its former homeland, they cease to function as a diaspora community.

2. I owe this term to Myron Wiener.
3. John Armstrong, 'Mobilized and Proletarian Diasporas', *American Political Science Review*, 70: 2 (June 1976), 393–408.

Extract 54

HAKAN WIBERG: *Self-Determination as an International Issue*

1. Dictionary of the *Academie francaise*, 1878; here cited after Rigo Sureda, p. 23.
2. A. Christescu: *The historical and current development of the right to self-determination on the basis of the Charter of the United Nations and other instruments adopted by United Nations organs, with particular reference to the promotion and protection of human rights and fundamental freedoms*, study prepared for the Economic and Social Council of the United Nations, E/CN 4/Sub2/404 (Vol. I), p. 141 f.
3. Here cited after Christescu, p. 142.
4. See Rigo Sureda, 103 ff.
5. e.g. K. P. Misra: 'Inter-State Imperialism: Pakistan', *Journal of Peace Research*, 1 (1972), 27 ff.
6. See I. Kendex's articles, 'Twenty-five years of local wars' and 'Wars of ten years, 1967–1976', in *Journal of Peace Research*, 1 (1971), 5 ff., and 3 (1978), 227 ff., respectively.
7. Rigo Sureda, esp. 220–1.
8. e.g. in several resolutions condemning displacement and deportation.
9. Nor, for that matter, have the attempts by some colonial powers to define colonies as 'overseas territories' been generally successful in avoiding having them defined as Non-Self-Governing Territories.
10. In fact, the General Assembly has gradually taken the stand that, under certain circumstances, the surrounding state has a right to retrocession of enclaves. See Rigo Sureda, 176.
11. See S. Marrero, 'Puerto Rico's Status Debate', in W. Phillips Davidson and L. Gordenker (eds.), *Resolving National Conflicts: The Role of Public Opinion Research* (New York: Praeger, 1980).
12. The term has been put in quotation marks, so as to avoid value connotations. In our opinion, value judgments on these issues have to be made case by case, hardly being generalizable.
13. It should be kept in mind that we have limited ourselves to one, 'positivist', way of interpretation, which, of course, is not the only one possible.
14. This matter is further complicated by there being divergent opinions as to whether Tibet was an independent state.
15. See e.g. A. Eide, 'International law, dominance and the use of force', *Journal of Peace Research*, 1 (1974), 1 ff.

Extract 55

SAMMY SMOOHA AND THEODOR HANF: *Conflict-Regulation in Deeply Divided Societies*

1. Portions of this section are adapted from T. Hanf, 'The prospects of accommodation in communal conflicts: a comparative study', in *Bildung in Sozioökonomischer*

Sicht, ed. Peter A. Doring, Horst Weishaupt and Manfred Weiss (Köln and Wien, 1989), 313–32.

2. L. Kuper and M. G. Smith, *Pluralism in Africa* (Berkeley and Los Angeles, 1969); R. A. Schermerhorn, *Comparative Ethnic Relations* (2nd edn., Chicago, 1978); P. van der Berghe, *The Ethnic Phenomenon* (New York, 1981); A. Smith, *The Ethnic Revival in the Modern World* (Cambridge, 1981); D. Horowitz, *Ethnic Groups in Conflict* (Berkeley and Los Angeles, 1985).
3. I. Lustick, 'Deeply divided societies: consociationalism versus control', *World Politics*, 31: 3 (Apr. 1979), 325–44. Contrasts in detail two models for achieving political stability in deeply divided societies—control versus consociationalism. He rightly views control as clearly not democratic. It seems, however, that ethnic democracy falls somewhere between these two models.
4. *Democracy in Plural Societies* (New Haven, Conn., 1977).
5. The term 'liberal democracy' refers to what is called 'majoritarian democracy' in the literature. The latter term is avoided here because it may be confused with 'ethnic democracy' which is also majoritarian.

Extract 56

JOHN MCGARRY AND BRENDAN O'LEARY: *Eliminating and Managing Ethnic Differences*

1. We use the term semi-secessionist movements to cover those seeking to leave one state to unite or re-unite with another. Strict secessionists seek to create an independent state, and are often wrongly called irredentist. It is states which seek to expand to complete their nation-stateness which are properly irredentist. Naturally irredentist states and semi-secessionist movements often go together (e.g. the Republic of Ireland and Irish nationalists in Northern Ireland).
2. Self-determination can in principle be exercised to agree to integration, assimilation or cantonisation (autonomy). However, full self-determination is often understood as isomorphic with secession.
3. However, Northern Ireland unionists are ambiguous about whether they believe the boundaries of the UK or of Northern Ireland should be the ultimate jurisdiction for constitutional decision-making.
4. I. Jennings, *The Approach to Self-Government* (Cambridge, 1956), 56.
5. H. Beran, 'A liberal theory of secession', *Political Studies* 32: 1 (1984) and *The Consent Theory of Political Obligation* (London, 1987).
6. A. Buchanan, *Secession: The Morality of Political Divorce from Fort Sumter to Lithuania and Quebec* (Oxford, 1991), 159–61.
7. The one liberal democracy to have granted the right of secession is the United Kingdom. In 1949 it granted the right of secession to the Northern Ireland parliament, and in 1985 it granted the right of the people of Northern Ireland to become part of the Republic of Ireland. However, this right, as Irish nationalist critics point out, was not one which the local majority of unionists were ever likely to choose.
8. G. D. Khoshla, *Stern Reckoning: A Survey of Events leading up to and Following the Partition of India* (New Delhi, 1950).

9. W. Connor, 'The politics of ethno-nationalism', *Journal of International Affairs* 27: 1 (1973), 1–21.
10. D. Horowitz, *Ethnic Groups in Conflict* (Berkeley and Los Angeles, 1985), 229 ff.
11. I. Lustick, 'Stability in deeply divided societies', *World Politics*, 31 (1979), 325–44, and 'Israeli state-building in the West Bank and Gaza Strip', *International Organization*, 41: 1 (1987), 151–71.
12. B. O'Leary and P. Arthur, 'Introduction', in J. McGarry and B. O'Leary (eds.), *The Future of Northern Ireland* (Oxford, 1990); B. O'Leary and J. McGarry, *The Politics of Antagonism: Understanding Northern Ireland* (London, 1993), chs. 3 and 4.
13. Co-opting elites as a technique for monopolising power should be distinguished from offering to share power—the former is characteristic of control, the latter of consociationalism. Some leaders of the ANC believe that the South African government is offering them the former under the guise of offering them the latter.
14. South Africa's government was fond of reminding the US and Canadian governments that their treatment of aboriginals is like apartheid—and many native and left-wing intellectuals agreed.
15. Lustick, 'Stability in deeply divided societies'.

Extract 57

RAY TARAS: *Post-Soviet Ethnic Conflict and International Politics*

1. For an overview, see Rodolfo Stavenhagen, 'Les conflits ethniques et leur impact sur la société internationale', in *Revue Internationale des Sciences Sociales*, 127 (Feb. 1991), 123–38.
2. Stephen Ryan, *Ethnic Conflict and International Relations* (Aldershot: Dartmouth Publishing, 1990), pp. x–xi.
3. Ryan, *Ethnic Conflict and International Relations*, 36.
4. Jacob Bercovitch, 'Third Parties in Conflict Management: The Structure and Conditions of Effective Mediation in International Relations', *International Journal*, 40: 4 (Autumn 1985), 736–7.
5. Walzer, *The Company of Critics: Social Criticism and Political Commitment in the Twentieth Century* (New York: Basic Books 1988), 227.
6. James N. Rosenau, *Turbulence in World Politics* (Princeton, NJ: Princeton University Press, 1990), 403.
7. *Ibid.* 135–6 n.
8. *Ibid.* 418.
9. James Mayall, *Nationalism and International Society* (Cambridge: Cambridge University Press, 1991), 50, 64.
10. Rosenau, *Turbulence in World Politics*, 435–6.
11. Francis Fukuyama, *The End of History and the Last Man* (New York: Free Press, 1992), 215, 272.

Extract 58

RAYMOND BRETON: *From Ethnic to Civic Nationalism: English Canada and Quebec*

1. The 'survivance' theme was also present in English-Canadian nationalism: 'while the theme of survival in English-Canadian history has several variations,

it is none the less as all-pervasive as it is in French Canadian history. Its variants include the struggle for survival against the pressure of the United States, the struggle of a colony to achieve nationhood, and, finally, the struggle to maintain unity', R. Cook, 'La Survivance, English-Canadian Style', in id., *The Maple Leaf Forever, essays on Nationalism and Politics in Canada* (Toronto, 1971), 162.

2. It is now necessary to begin to talk in terms to Quebec rather than French Canadian nationalism. Although the latter has not disappeared and may even gain strength in the future, Quebecois nationalism is clearly a distinct reality whose impact affects the great majority of French-Canadians, that is those who live in Quebec.
3. D. J. Lee, 'The evolution of nationalism in Quebec', in J. L. Elliott (ed.), *Two Nations, Many Cultures* (Scarborough, Ont., 1979), 61.
4. Personal communication to the author.
5. P. Cappon, 'Nationalism and inter-ethnic and linguistic conflict in Quebec', in L. Driedger (ed.), *The Canadian Ethnic Mosaic* (Toronto, 1978), 331.
6. Ibid. 333. See also id., *Conflit entre les Néo-Canadiens et les Francophones de Montréal* (Quebec, 1974).
7. Reference is made to the perceived threat to language and culture; but this does not mean that this threat was not related in peoples' minds to their economic and political condition.
8. M. Paillé, *Aspects démolinguistiques de l'Avenir de la Population du Québec* (Quebec, 1986), 36–7. Dr Camille Laurin, the chief architect of Law 101 when a minister in the Parti Quebecois government has been recently quoted as quite satisfied with the success of the legislation as far as education is concerned: 'Ce qui me réjouit le plus, nous a-t-il confié spontanément, c'est de voir que dans certaines de nos écoles françaises, 77% des écoliers sont des nouveaux arrivants.' Avant l'adoption de la Charte, rappelle-t-il, 85% des immigrants fréquentaient l'école anglaise. La vapeur a été renversée. J.-P. Proulx, 'Le Scandale est Terminé mais il Reste l'Affichage', Montreal: *Le Devoir* (22 Aug. 1987), 1.
9. 'Finally' in the sense that it is the last to be briefly presented here; not in the sense that all other relevant factors have been discussed.
10. For a study about changes in the meaning assigned to the label 'Quebecois', see D. M. Taylor and R. J. Sigal, 'Defining "Quebecois": The role of ethnic heritage, language, and political orientation', *Canadian Ethnic Studies*, 14 (1982), 59–70.
11. S. Dansereau, 'Ouvrir le Québec aux immigrants, à condition qu'ils parlent Français', Montreal: *Le Devoir* (12. Aug. 1987), 2.
12. L. Bissonette, 'Quebec faces a challenge of the cradle', Toronto: *The Globe and Mail* (25 July, 1987).
13. Ibid.
14. G. Gendron, 'L'immigration est une fausse solution', Montreal: *Le Devoir* (25 June, 1987), 11.
15. Dansereau, *op. cit.*
16. Father Harvey's article 'Nos Médias sans Immigrants' in *Relations*, July–Aug. 1987 (179–80) and the debate it generated is a good illustration of this preoccupation. It is also forcefully expressed by Gendron, *op. cit.*

Extract 59

ERIC HOBSBAWM: *Ethnic Nationalism in the Late Twentieth Century*

1. Quebec nationalism in the 1970s produced a large business exodus from Montreal, hitherto both the largest Canadian city and the centre of Canadian business, to the advantage of Toronto. 'The city is coming to grips with a more modest destiny as a regional center for Quebec and eastern Canada.' Even so, the notably smaller impact of minority languages on Montreal than on other cities, does not seem to have lessened linguistic militancy. In Toronto and Vancouver white Anglo Protestants no longer form the majority of the population, whereas in Montreal French Canadians form 66% of the population. Cf. Alan F. J. Artibise, 'Canada as an urban nation', *Daedalus*, 117: 4 (Fall 1988), 237–64.
2. Martin E. Marty, 'Fundamentalism as a social phenomenon', *Bulletin, The American Academy of Arts and Sciences*, 42: 2 (Nov. 1988), 15–29.
3. *Ibid*. 20–1.
4. It is not clear how far genuinely traditional Jewish religious orthodoxy, which is, of course, opposed to the establishment of a state for all the Jews in Israel before the return of the Messiah, has attenuated or dropped its opposition to Zionism. At all events Jewish settlers in the occupied territories, advertising the paraphernalia of religious practice, must not be automatically identified with the other (and probably growing) wing of Jewish fundamentalism which seeks to reimpose the full rigours of ritual on a secularized society.
5. From 1958 to 1974 the three main Belgian parties (in their Flemish versions) never totalled less than 81.2% of the vote in Flanders. See A. Zolberg in M. Esman (eds.), *Ethnic Conflict in the Western World* (Ithaca, 1977), 118.

Extract 61

ALBERTO MELUCCI: *The Post-Modern Revival of Ethnicity*

1. T. Parsons, 'Some theoretical considerations on the nature and trends of change of ethnicity', in N. Glazer and P. Moynihan (eds.), *Ethnicity, Theory and Experience* (Cambridge, Mass., 1975).
2. See e.g. A. Lijphart, 'Political theories and the explanation of conflict in the western world', in M. J. Esman (ed.), *Ethnic Conflict in the Western World* (Ithaca, 1977).
3. A. Melucci and M. Diani, *Nazioni senza stato: i movimenti etnico-nazionali nelle società occidentali contemporanee* (Torino, 1983).

Extract 62

KOSAKU YOSHINO: *Globalization and Ethno-Cultural Differences*

1. Nippon Steel Corporation, Personnel Development Office, *Nippon: The Land and Its People*, 2nd edn. (Gakuseisha: Tokyo, 1984).
2. Taiyō Kōbe Bank, *The Nipponjin/The Scrutable Japanese* (Gakuseisha: Tokyo, 1988).
3. Mitsubishi Corporation, *Japanese Business Glossary/Nihonjingo* (Tōyōkeizai Shinpōsha: Tokyo, 1983).
4. Ibid. 4.
5. Nippon Steel Human Resources Development Co., Ltd., *Talking about Japan/Nihhon o kataru* (ALC: Tokyo, 1987), 405.

6. Mitsubishi Corp., *op. cit.*, 6.
7. Nippon Steel Corporation, Personnel Development Office, *op. cit.*, 11.
8. Taiyō Kōbe Bank, *op. cit.*, 4.
9. Cultural relativism as an explicit anthropological perspective originates with Ruth Benedict—*Patterns of Culture* (Houghton Mifflin: Boston, 1934)—and Melville Herskovits—*Man and His Works* (Alfred A. Knopf: New York, 1947).
10. Nippon Steel Corporation, Personnel Development Office, *op. cit.*, 11–12.
11. First, defence of the values of the less developed world could result in justifying the technologically backward stage of ex-colonial countries. George Stocking summarises this position by stating that cultural relativism, which 'buttressed the attack against racialism [can] be perceived as a sort of neo-racialism justifying the backward techno-economic status of once colonized peoples' ('Afterward: a view from the center', *Ethnos*, 47 (1982), 176). Second, one of the arguments by anti-relativists holds that cultural relativism perpetuated a kind of 'inverted racism'. Spiro remarks that cultural relativism was used 'as a powerful tool of cultural criticism, with the consequent derogation of Western culture and of the mentality which it produced. Espousing the philosophy of primitivism . . . the image of primitive man was used . . . as a vehicle for the pursuit of personal utopian quests, and/or as a fulcrum to express personal discontent with Western man and Western society': 'Culture and human nature', in G. Spindler (ed.), *The Making of Psychological Anthropology* (University of California Press: Berkeley, 1978), 336.

Extract 63

JOHN HUTCHINSON: *Ethnicity and Multiculturalism in Immigrant Societies*

1. See C. Van Woodward, 'The ageing of America', *American Historical Review*, 83 (1977), 583–94.

Select Bibliography

I. DEFINITIONS OF ETHNICITY

BANKS, MARCUS (1996), *Ethnicity: Anthropological Constructions* (London: Routledge).

BURGESS, ELAINE (1978), 'The resurgence of ethnicity', *Ethnic and Racial Studies*, 1: 3, 265–85.

COHEN, RONALD (1978), 'Ethnicity: problem and focus in anthropology', in Bernard Siegal, Alan Beals, and Stephen Tyler (eds.), *Annual Review of Anthropology*, 7 (Palo Alto: Annual Reviews Inc.).

COLEMAN, JAMES S. (1958), *Nigeria, Background to Nationalism*, Appendix (Berkeley and Los Angeles: University of California Press).

CONNOR, WALKER (1978), 'A nation is a nation, is a state, is an ethnic group, is a . . .', *Ethnic and Racial Studies*, 1: 4, 378–400.

DE VOS, GEORGE and ROMANUCCI-ROSS, LOLA (eds.) (1974), *Ethnic Identity* (Chicago: Chicago University Press).

GLAZER, NATHAN and MOYNIHAN, DANIEL P. (eds.) (1975), *Ethnicity: Theory and Experience* (Cambridge, Mass.: Harvard University Press).

HANDELMAN, DON (1977), 'The organisation of ethnicity', *Ethnic Groups*, 1, 187–200.

HERAUD, GUY (1963), *L'Europe des Ethnies* (Paris: Presses d'Europe).

JENKINS, RICHARD (1986), 'Social-anthropological models of inter-ethnic relations', in Rex and Mason (1986).

JUST, ROGER (1989), 'The triumph of the *ethnos*', in Tonkin, McDonald, and Chapman (1989).

LAL, BARBARA BALLIS (1983), 'Perspectives on ethnicity: old wine in new bottles', *Ethnic and Racial Studies*, 6: 2, 154–73.

LIDDELL, H. G. and SCOTT, R. (eds.) (1869), *A Greek–English Lexicon*, 6th edn. (Oxford: Clarendon Press).

II. THEORIES OF ETHNICITY

ARMSTRONG, JOHN (1982), *Nations before Nationalism* (Chapel Hill: University of North Carolina Press).

BANTON, MICHAEL (1983), *Racial and Ethnic Competition* (Cambridge: Cambridge University Press).

BHABHA, HOMI (ed.) (1990), *Nation and Narration* (London and New York: Routledge).

BRASS, PAUL (ed.) (1985), *Ethnic Groups and the State* (London: Croom Helm).

BROMLEI, YURI (1984), *Theoretical Ethnography*, trans. V. Epstein and E. Khazanov (Moscow: General Editorial Board for Foreign Publications, Nauka Publishers).

COHEN, ANTHONY P. (1985), *The Symbolic Construction of Community* (London: Tavistock).

EPSTEIN, A. L. (1978), *Ethos and Identity* (London: Tavistock).

FRANCIS, EMERICH (1976), *Inter-Ethnic Relations, An Essay in Sociological Theory* (New York: Elsevier Scientific Publishing Company).

GEERTZ, CLIFFORD (1973), *The Interpretation of Cultures* (New York: Basic Books).

HOROWITZ, DONALD (1985), *Ethnic Groups in Conflict* (Berkeley and Los Angeles: University of California Press).

MCKAY, JAMES (1982), 'An exploratory synthesis of primordial and mobilisationist approaches to ethnic phenomena', *Ethnic and Racial Studies*, 5: 4, 394–420.

OKAMURA, J. Y. (1981), 'Situational ethnicity', *Ethnic and Racial Studies*, 4: 4, 452–63.

REYNOLDS, VERNON (1980), 'Sociobiology and the idea of primordial discrimination', *Ethnic and Racial Studies*, 3: 3, 303–15.

REX, JOHN and MASON, DAVID (eds.) (1986), *Theories of Race and Ethnic Relations* (Cambridge: Cambridge University Press).

ROTHSCHILD, JOSEPH (1981), *Ethnopolitics: A Conceptual Framework* (New York: Columbia University Press).

SCOTT, GEORGE (1990), 'A resynthesis of the primordial and circumstantial approaches to ethnic group solidarity: towards an explanatory model', *Ethnic and Racial Studies*, 13: 2, 148–71.

SMITH, ANTHONY D. (1986), *The Ethnic Origins of Nations* (Oxford: Blackwell).

—— (1984), 'Ethnic myths and ethnic revivals', *European Journal of Sociology*, 25, 283–305.

SHILS, EDWARD (1957), 'Primordial, personal, sacred and civil ties', *British Journal of Sociology*, 7, 113–45.

VAN DEN BERGHE, PIERRE (1979), *The Ethnic Phenomenon* (New York: Elsevier).

—— (1986), 'Ethnicity and the sociobiology debate', in Rex and Mason (1986).

WALLMANN, SANDRA (1986), 'Ethnicity and the boundary process in context', in Rex and Mason (1986).

III. ETHNICITY IN HISTORY

ALTY, J. H. (1982), 'Dorians and Ionians', *Journal of Hellenic Studies*, 102, 1–14.

BALSDON, J. V. P. (1979), *Romans and Aliens* (London: Duckworth).

CURTIN, PHILIP (1984), *Cross-cultural Trade in World History* (Cambridge: Cambridge University Press).

DIKÖTTER, FRANK (1992), *The Discourse of 'Race' in Modern China* (London: C. Hurst and Co.).

FONDATION HARDT (1962), *Grecs et Barbares*, Entretiens sur l'antiquité classique, 8 (Geneva).

GROSBY, STEVEN (1991), 'Religion and nationality in antiquity', *European Journal of Sociology*, 32, 229–65.

LAPIDUS, IRA (1988), *A History of Islamic Societies* (Cambridge: Cambridge University Press).

LEWIS, BERNARD (1970), *The Arabs in History*, 5th edn. (London: Hutchinson).

LLOBERA, JOSEP (1994), *The God of Modernity: The Development of Nationalism in Western Europe* (Oxford and Providence, RI: Berg).

MENDELS, DORON (1992), *The Rise and Fall of Jewish Nationalism* (New York: Doubleday).

OLIVER, ROLAND and ATMORE, ANTHONY (1981), *The African Middle Ages, 1400–1800* (Cambridge: Cambridge University Press).

PEARSON, RAYMOND (1983), *National Minorities in Eastern Europe, 1848–1945* (London: Macmillan).

PORTAL, ROGER (1969), *The Slavs, A Cultural, Historical Survey of the Slavonic Peoples*, trans. Patrick Evans (London: Weidenfeld and Nicolson).

REYNOLDS, SUSAN (1984), *Kingdoms and Communities in Medieval Europe, 900–1300* (Cambridge: Clarendon Press).

SETON-WATSON, HUGH (1977), *Nations and States* (London: Methuen).

SHERWIN-WHITE, A. N. (1952), *Racial Prejudice in Ancient Rome* (Oxford: Blackwell).

WISEMAN, D. J. (ed.) (1973), *Peoples of the Old Testament* (Oxford: Clarendon Press).

IV. ETHNICITY AND MODERNITY

AFSHAR, HALEH (1989), 'Women and reproduction in Iran', in Yuval-Davis and Anthias (1989).

ANTHIAS, FLOYA (1989), 'Women and nationalism in Cyprus', in Yuval-Davis and Anthias (1989).

ALBA, RICHARD (1990), *Ethnic Identity: The Transformation of White America* (New Haven and London: Yale University Press).

BONACICH, EDNA (1972), 'A theory of ethnic antagonism: the split labor market', *American Sociological Review*, 37, 547–59.

CASTLES, STEPHEN and KOSACK, URSULA (1973), *Immigrant Workers and Class Structure in Western Europe* (London: Oxford University Press, for the Institute of Race Relations).

COHEN, ABNER (ed.) (1974), *Urban Ethnicity* (London: Tavistock).

COHEN, ROBIN (1994), *Frontiers of Identity: The British and the Others* (London: Longman).

GANS, HERBERT (1994), 'Symbolic ethnicity and symbolic religiosity: towards a comparison of ethnic and religious acculturation', *Ethnic and Racial Studies*, 17: 4, 577–92.

GLAZER, NATHAN and MOYNIHAN, DANIEL P. (eds.) (1975), *Ethnicity: Theory and Experience* (Cambridge, Mass.: Harvard University Press).

HAMMAR, THOMAS (1990), *Democracy and the Nation-State: Aliens, Denizens, and Citizens in a World of International Migration* (Aldershot: Avebury).

HERZFELD, MICHAEL (1987), *Anthropology Through the Looking-Glass. Critical Ethnography in the Margins of Europe* (Cambridge: Cambridge University Press).

HUSBANDS, CHRISTOPHER (1991), 'The mainstream right and the politics of immigration in France: major developments in the 1980s', *Ethnic and Racial Studies*, 14: 2, 170–98

HUTNICK, NIMMI (1991), *Ethnic Minority Identity: A Social Psychological Perspective* (Oxford: Clarendon Press).

KARKLINS, RASMA (1986), *Ethnic Relations in the USSR: The Perspective from Below* (Boston: Unwin Hyman).

KEYES, CHARLES (ed.) (1981), *Ethnic Change* (Seattle: University of Washington Press).

MODOOD, TARIQ *et al.* (1994), *Changing Ethnic Identities* (London: Policy Studies Institute).

LIGHT, IVAN (1972), *Ethnic Enterprise in America* (Berkeley: University of California Press).

NAGATA, JUDITH (ed.) (1975), *Pluralism in Malaysia: Myth and Reality* (Leiden: Canadian Association for South Asian Studies, Brill).

PATTERSON, ORLANDO (1977), *Ethnic Chauvinism: The Reactionary Impulse* (New York: Stein and Day).

SMITH, ANTHONY D. (1981*a*), *The Ethnic Revival in the Modern World* (Cambridge: Cambridge University Press).

SOLLORS, WERNER (ed.) (1989), *The Invention of Ethnicity* (New York: Oxford University Press).

SOWELL, T. (1981), *Ethnic America* (New York: Basic Books).

STACK, J. F. (ed) (1986), *The Primordial Challenge: Ethnicity in the Contemporary World* (New York: Greenwood).

WALBY, SYLVIA (1992), 'Woman and the Nation', *International Journal of Comparative Sociology*, 33, 1–2 and 81–100.

WALLMANN, SANDRA (ed.) (1979), *Ethnicity at Work* (London: Macmillan).

YUVAL-DAVIS, NIRA and ANTHIAS, FLOYA (eds.) (1989), *Woman–Nation–State* (Basingstoke and London: Macmillan Press).

V. ETHNICITY, RELIGION, AND LANGUAGE

ARMSTRONG, JOHN (1976), 'Mobilised and proletarian diasporas', *American Political Science Review*, 70, 393–408.

BENNIGSEN, ALEXANDRE and WIMBUSH, S. ENDERS (1985), *Muslims of the Soviet Empire: A Guide* (London: C. Hurst).

BRASS, PAUL (1974), *Religion, Language and Politics in North India* (Cambridge: Cambridge University Press).

EDWARDS, JOHN (1995), *Multi-Lingualism* (Harmondsworth: Penguin Books).

FISHMAN, JOSHUA (ed.) (1968), *Language Problems in Developing Countries* (New York: John Wiley).

GRILLO, RALPH (1989), *Dominant Languages* (Cambridge: Cambridge University Press).

HAUGEN, EINAR (1966), 'Dialect, language, nation', *American Anthropologist*, 68: 4, 922–35.

JUERGENSMEYER, MARK (1993), *The New Cold War? Religious Nationalism Confronts the Secular State* (Berkeley and Los Angeles: University of California Press).

KAPFERER, BRUCE (1988), *Legends of People, Myths of State: Violence, Intolerance and Political Culture in Sri Lanka and Australia* (Washington DC: Smithsonian Institute Press).

PETROVICH, MICHAEL (1980), 'Religion and ethnicity in Eastern Europe', in Sugar (1980).

RAMET, PEDRO (ed.) (1989), *Religion and Nationalism in Soviet and East European Politics* (Durham, NC, and London: Duke University Press).

SMITH, DONALD E. (ed.) (1974), *Religion and Political Modernisation* (New Haven, Conn.: Yale University Press).

SUGAR, PETER (ed.) (1980), *Ethnic Diversity and Conflict in Eastern Europe* (Santa Barbara: ABC-Clio).

TAYLOR, DAVID and YAPP, MALCOLM (eds.) (1979), *Political Identity in South Asia* (London and Dublin: SOAS, Curzon Press).

VAN DER VEER, PETER (1994), *Religious Nationalism: Hindus and Muslims in India* (Berkeley: University of California Press).

WEBBER, JONATHAN (ed.) (1994), *Jewish Identities in the New Europe* (London and Washington: Littman Library of Jewish Civilisation).

VI. RACE AND ETHNICITY

ADAM, HERIBERT and GUILLOMEE, H. (eds.) (1979): *Ethnic Power Mobilised: Can South Africa Change?* (New Haven: Yale University Press).

BANTON, MICHAEL (1967), *Race Relations* (London: Tavistock).

DONALD, J. and RATTANSI, ALI (eds.) (1992), *Race, Culture and Difference* (London: Sage).

FANON, FRANTZ (1963), *The Wretched of the Earth* (New York: Grove Press).

FURNIVALL, J. S. (1948), *Colonial Policy and Practice: A Comparative Study of Burma and Netherlands India* (Cambridge: Cambridge University Press).

GILROY, PAUL (1987), *There Ain't no Black in the Union Jack* (London: Hutchinson).

HOROWITZ, DONALD (1991), *A Democratic South Africa: Constitutional Engineering in a Divided Society* (Berkeley and Los Angeles: University of California Press).

HUSBANDS, CHRISTOPHER (1991), 'The support for the *Front National*: analyses and findings', *Ethnic and Racial Studies*, 14: 3, 382–416.

MILES, ROBERT (ed.) (1993), *Migration in the New Europe, Ethnic and Racial Studies*, 16: 3 (special section).

MODOOD, TARIQ (1994), 'The end of hegemony: the concept of Blacks and British Asians', in J. Rex and B. Drury (eds.), *Ethnic Mobilisation in Multi-cultural Europe* (Aldershot: Avebury).

REX, JOHN (1986), *Race and Ethnicity* (Milton Keynes: Open University Press).

ROTBERG, ROBERT and MAZRUI, ALI (eds.) (1970), *Protest and Power in Black Africa* (New York: Oxford University Press).

SAID, EDWARD (1978), *Orientalism* (Harmondsworth: Peregrine).

WESTWOOD, SALLIE and PARMINDER, BHACHU (eds.) (1988), *Enterprising Women: Ethnicity, Economy and Gender Relations* (London: Routledge).

WERBNER, PNINA and MUHAMMAD, ANWAR (eds.) (1991), *Black and Ethnic Leaderships in Britain: The Cultural Dimensions of Political Action* (London: Routledge).

YUVAL-DAVIS, NIRA and STASIULIS, DAIVA (eds.) (1995), *Unsettling Settler Societies* (London: Sage).

VII. ETHNIC CONFLICT AND NATIONALISM

ASIWAJU, A. I. (ed.) (1985), *Partitioned Africans: Ethnic Relations across Africa's International Boundaries, 1884–1984* (London: C. Hurst and Co.).

BANUAZIZI, ALI and WEINER, MYRON (eds.) (1986), *The State, Religion and Ethnic Politics: Afghanistan, Iran and Pakistan* (Syracuse, NY: Syracuse University Press).

COHEN, LEONARD (1995), *Broken Bonds: Yugoslavia's Disintegration and Balkan Politics in Transition* (Boulder, Col.: Westview Press).

CROSS, MALCOLM (1978), 'Colonialism and ethnicity: a theory and comparative case study', *Ethnic and Racial Studies*, 1: 1, 37–59.

De Silva, K., Duke, P., Goldberg, E., and Katz, N. (eds.) (1988), *Ethnic Conflict in Buddhist Societies: Sri Lanka, Thailand and Burma* (London: Pinter).

Enloe, Cynthia, 'Ethnicity, bureaucracy and state-building in Africa and Latin America', *Ethnic and Racial Studies*, 1: 3 (1978), 336–51.

Entessar, Nader (1989), 'The Kurdish mosaic of discord', *Third World Quarterly*, 11: 4, 83–100 (and whole of this issue).

Esman, Milton (ed.) (1977), *Ethnic Conflict in the Western World* (Ithaca, NY: Cornell University Press).

Fox, Richard G. (1985), *Lions of the Punjab: Culture in the Making* (Berkeley and Los Angeles: University of California Press).

Gurr, Ted and Harff, Barbara (1994), *Ethnic Conflict in World Politics* (Boulder, Col.: Westview Press).

Hechter, Michael (1992), 'The dynamics of secession', *Acta Sociologica*, 35, 267–83.

Heraclides, Alexander (1992), *The Self-determination of Minorities in International Politics* (London: Frank Cass).

Lijphart, Arendt (1977), *Democracy in Plural Societies: A Comparative Exploration* (New Haven: Yale University Press).

Lustick, Ian (1993), *Unsettled States, Disputed Lands: Britain and Ireland, France and Algeria, Israel and the West Bank-Gaza* (Ithaca: Cornell University Press).

May, R. J. (ed.) (1982), *Micro-nationalist Movements in Papua New Guinea*, (Canberra: Australian National University).

Mayall, James (1990), *Nationalism and International Society* (Cambridge: Cambridge University Press).

Moynihan, Daniel P. (1993), *Pandaemonium: Ethnicity in International Politics* (Oxford: Oxford University Press).

Norbu, Dawa (1992), *Culture and the Politics of Third World Nationalism* (London: Routledge).

Olszak, Susan (1982), 'Ethnic mobilisation in Quebec', *Ethnic and Racial Studies*, 5: 3, 253–75.

Peel, J. D. Y. (1989), 'The cultural work of Yoruba ethnogenesis', in Tonkin, McDonald, and Chapman (1989).

Rothchild, Donald and Olorunsola, Victor (eds.) (1983), *State versus Ethnic Claims: African Policy Dilemmas* (Boulder, Col.: Westview Press).

Said, Abdul and Simmons, Luis (eds.) (1977), *Ethnicity in an International Context* (New Brunswick, NJ: Transaction Books).

Smith, Anthony D. (1981*b*), 'War and ethnicity: the role of warfare in the cohesion and self-image of ethnic groups', *Ethnic and Racial Studies* 4: 4, 375–97.

—— (1991), *National Identity* (Harmondsworth: Penguin).

Stone, John (ed.) (1979), *Internal Colonialism, Ethnic and Racial Studies*, 2: 3 (special issue).

Tagil, Sven (ed.) (1995), *Ethnicity and Nation-building in the Nordic World* (London: Hurst and Company).

Urban, Greg and Scherzer, Joel (eds.) (1991), *Nation-states and Indians in Latin America* (Austin: University of Texas Press).

Wallerstein, Immanuel (1960), 'Ethnicity and national integration in West Africa', *Cahiers d'Études Africaines*, 3, 129–38.

WEINER, MYRON (1978), *Sons of the Soil: Migration and Ethnic Conflict in India* (Princeton: Princeton University Press).

WILLIAMS, COLIN (ed.) (1982), *National Separatism* (Cardiff: University of Wales Press).

YOUNG, CRAWFORD (1976), *The Politics of Cultural Pluralism* (Madison: University of Wisconsin Press)

VIII. TRANSCENDING ETHNICITY?

BILLIG, MICHAEL (1995), *Banal Nationalism* (London: Sage).

GIDDENS, ANTHONY (1991), *The Consequences of Modernity* (Cambridge: Polity Press).

KYMLICKA, W. (1995), *Multicultural Citizenship* (Oxford: Clarendon Press).

LACZKO, LESLIE C. (1994), 'Canada's pluralism in comparative perspective', *Ethnic and Racial Studies*, 17: 1, 20–41.

MILLER, DAVID (1995), *On Nationality* (Oxford: Clarendon Press).

RICHMOND, ANTHONY (1984), 'Ethnic nationalism and postindustrialism', *Ethnic and Racial Studies*, 7, 1, 4–18.

SCHLESINGER, PHILIP (1994), 'Europe's contradictory communicative space', *Daedalus (Europe through a Glass Darkly)*, 123: 2, 25–52.

SMITH, ANTHONY D. (1995), *Nations and Nationalism in a Global Era* (Cambridge: Polity Press).

TAYLOR, CHARLES (1992), *Multiculturalism and 'The Politics of Recognition'*, ed. A. Gutmann (Princeton: Princeton University Press).

VIROLI, MAURIZIO (1995), *For Love of Country: An Essay on Patriotism and Nationalism* (Oxford: Clarendon Press).

Biographical Notes

ARMSTRONG, JOHN Emeritus Professor of Political Science at the University of Wisconsin, John Armstrong is one of the most eminent scholars of ethnicity and nationalism. He is highly regarded as a specialist of East European politics and is the author of the classic *Ukrainian Nationalism* (1963). His *magnum opus* in the field is his pioneering *Nations before Nationalism* (1982), in which his exhaustive researches into the many factors that combine to produce a sense of ethnic identity in pre-modern Islamic and Christian civilizations are brought together through a rich phenomenological analysis of myths, symbols, and codes.

BALIBAR, ÉTIENNE Professor of Philosophy at the University of Paris-I, his influential books include *Classes, Masses, Ideas* (1993), and *The Philosophy of Marx* (1995).

BANTON, MICHAEL Professor Emeritus of Sociology, University of Bristol, has applied rational choice conceptions to the study of ethnicity and race. Among his recent books are *Racial and Ethnic Competition* (1983), *Promoting Racial Harmony* (1985), *Racial Theories* (1987), *International Action Against Racial Discrimination* (1996), and *Ethnic and Racial Consciousness* (1997). He is currently Chairman of the United Nations Committee on the Elimination of Racial Discrimination.

BARTH, FREDRIK Professor of Anthropology at the University of Oslo, Fredrik Barth is one of the most influential and original anthropologists. His studies of the Swat Pathans, such as *Political Leadership among the Swat Pathans* (1959), marked a breakthrough in the understanding of ethnic organization, as did his introduction to the pioneering work *Ethnic Groups and Boundaries* (1969), which first formulated his symbolic boundary approach. His recent books include *Cosmologies in the Making* (1987) and *Balinese Worlds* (1993).

BARTLETT, ROBERT Professor of Medieval History at the University of St Andrews, Robert Bartlett is an innovative medieval historian whose books include *Trial by Fire and Water* (1986), *Medieval Frontier Societies* (1989, co-edited), and *The Making of Europe* (1993, awarded the Wolfson Literary Prize for History).

BELL, DANIEL Former Professor of Sociology at Harvard University, Daniel Bell is one of the most distinguished and pioneering sociologists of industrial society. He is the author of *The End of Ideology* (1959) and the two influential analyses, *The Coming of Post-Industrial Society* (1973) and *The Cultural Contradictions of Capitalism* (1976).

BRASS, PAUL Professor of Political Science and South Asian Studies at the University of Washington, Seattle, Paul Brass is one of the leading theoreticians of ethnic politics and a distinguished authority on Indian society and politics. His influential élite-competition approach is developed through such major works as *Language, Religion and Politics in North India* (1974), *The Politics of India since Independence*, 2nd ed. (1994), and *Ethnicity and Nationalism* (1991).

BRETON, RAYMOND Emeritus Professor of Sociology at the University of Toronto, Raymond Breton is one of the foremost authorities on Canadian ethnicity and politics.

His major books include *Ethnic Communities and the Personal Relations of Immigrants* (1961), *Cultural Boundaries and the Cohesion of Canada* (1980, co-authored with J. Reitz and V. Valentine), and *The Governance of Ethnic Communities: Political Structures and Processes in Canada* (1991).

BROWN, DAVID Senior Lecturer in Political Science at the National University of Singapore, David Brown has specialized in the politics of ethnicity in Africa and South-East Asia, on which he has written several articles. His major work is *The State and Ethnic Politics in Southeast Asia* (1994).

BRUBAKER, ROGERS Professor at the University of California, Los Angeles (UCLA), Rogers Brubaker is an authority on western European politics and citizenship. His major work is *Citizenship and Nationhood in France and Germany* (1992), but he has written widely on the ethnic dimension of citizenship struggles in the Soviet successor states.

CASTLES, STEPHEN Head of the Centre for Multi-cultural Studies at the University of Wollongong, Stephen Castles is an authority on immigrants in Western Europe. Among his major works are *Here for Good: Western Europe's New Ethnic Minorities* (1984) and *Immigrant Workers and Class Structure in Western Europe* (1973 and 1985, with Godula Kosack).

CHAPMAN, MALCOLM A researcher in Anthropology, Malcolm Chapman teaches at Bradford University and has written several books, including *The Gaelic Vision in Scottish Culture* (1978) and *The Celts: The Construction of a Myth* (1992). He has also co-edited *History and Ethnicity* (1989) and *Social and Biological Aspects of Ethnicity* (1993).

COHEN, ABNER Emeritus Professor of Anthropology at the School of Oriental and African Studies, Abner Cohen is a distinguished scholar of African ethnic politics, in which he pioneered a more instrumental approach. His major works include *Arab Border Villages in Israel* (1965), *Custom and Politics in Africa* (1969), *Urban Ethnicity* (ed., 1974), *Two-Dimensional Man* (1974), *The Politics of Elite Culture* (1981), and *Masquerade Politics* (1993).

CONNOR, WALKER Reitemeyer Professor of Political Science at Trinity College, Hartford, Conn., Walker Connor is best known for his seminal and provocative articles on ethnicity and nationalism, which are now collected in *Ethnonationalism: The Quest for Understanding* (1993). A leading exponent of the power of ethnicity in modern society, Connor is also the author of the highly praised *The National Question in Marxist-Leninist Theory and Strategy* (1984).

COPE, BILL Senior Research Fellow in the Centre for Workplace, Communication and Culture at the University of Technology, Sydney, Bill Cope has written three books, including *Social Literacy Project* (with Mary Kalantzis).

COUGHLAN, REED Professor of Sociology at Empire State Building, SUNV, Reed Coughlan has written several articles on ethnicity and the state, and ethnic conflict in Northern Ireland and Cyprus. His major book is *The Economic Dimensions of Ethnic Conflict* (1991, co-edited with S. W. R. de A. Samarasinghe).

DIKÖTTER, FRANK Welcome Research Fellow and Lecturer at the School of Oriental and African Studies, University of London, he has pioneered the study of racial and gender ideas in China, notably in his major work, *The Discourse of Race in Modern China* (1992). His most recent publication is *Sex, Culture and Society in Modern China* (1995).

EDWARDS, JOHN Professor of Psychology at St Francis Xavier University in Nova Scotia, John Edwards is an authority on the relations between language, ethnicity, and society. He has published widely on socio-linguistics and ethnicity, including such major works as *Language, Society and Identity* (1985) and *Multilingualism* (1994). He is also the editor of *The Journal of Multilingual and Multicultural Development*.

ELLER, JACK Jack Eller is Assistant Professor of Anthropology at the Teikyo Loretto Heights University, Denver.

ENLOE, CYNTHIA Professor of Political Science at Clark University, Cynthia Enloe is a leading scholar of the politics of ethnicity and gender. She has published extensively on ethnic politics in Asia and Africa, including such widely cited books as *Ethnic Conflict and Political Development* (1973), *Ethnicity: Foundations of State Power* (1979), *Ethnic Soldiers* (1980), and *Bananas, Beaches and Bases: Making Feminist Sense of International Politics* (1989).

ERIKSEN, THOMAS Associate Professor of Social Anthropology at the University of Oslo, Thomas Eriksen is a leading anthropological researcher of the politics of ethnic and language relations, particularly in Mauritius and the West Indies. He is the author of *Us and Them in Modern Societies: Ethnicity and Nationalism in Trinidad, Mauritius and Beyond* (1992) and the much-cited *Ethnicity and Nationalism* (1993).

ESMAN, MILTON John S. Knight Professor of International Studies Emeritus at Cornell University, Esman Knight was Director of the Centre for International Studies, 1969–83. An influential scholar of ethnic politics, he has edited *Ethnic Conflict in the Western World* (1977) and co-edited (with Itamar Rabinovich) *Ethnicity, Pluralism and the State in the Middle East* (1988). He is the author of the recent *Ethnic Politics* (1994).

FEIN, HELEN Professor in the Institute for the Study of Genocide in New York, Helen Fein is an authority on genocide and especially the Holocaust. She is the author of the much-acclaimed *Accounting for Genocide: National Responses and Jewish Victimization during the Holocaust* (1979) and *Genocide* (1993).

FINLEY, MOSES Sir Moses Finley, former Professor of Ancient History at the University of Cambridge, was one of the most eminent scholars of classical antiquity. He greatly developed the social and economic approach pioneered by Rostovtzeff, and his many works include *The World of Odysseus* (1954), *The Ancient Greeks* (1963), *Economy and Society in Ancient Greece* (1981), and *The Use and Abuse of History* (1986).

FISHMAN, JOSHUA Professor of Sociology and Sociolinguistics at Yeshiva University, Joshua Fishman is a leading scholar of socio-linguistics and an eminent analyst of ethnicity and language. His many works include *Language Problems of Developing Countries* (1968, edited), *Language and Nationalism* (1972), *The Sociology of Language* (1972), and *Language and Ethnicity in Minority Sociolinguistic Perspective* (1989).

GANS, HERBERT Robert S. Lynd Professor of Sociology at Columbia University, Herbert Gans is one of the leading scholars of contemporary ethnicity in the United States. His seminal articles on the decline of ethnicity and religiosity in the United States have provoked considerable debate about the future of ethnic ties in the modern world. His books include *The Urban Villagers: Group and Class in the Life of Italian Americans* (1962), *People, Plans and Policies* (1991), and *The War Against the Poor* (1995).

GEERTZ, CLIFFORD Professor of Anthropology at the University of Chicago, Clifford Geertz is one of the most distinguished exponents of cultural anthropology and has published important studies of culture and society in Indonesia and Morocco, notably *Person, Time and Conduct in Bali* (1966), *Islam Observed* (1968), *The Interpretation of Cultures* (1973), *Negara: The Theatre State in Nineteenth Century Bali* (1980), *Local Knowledge* (1983), and *Works and Lives* (1988); and he is the editor of *Old Societies and New States* (1963). His emphasis on the cultural 'givens' is the starting-point of the major debate between so-called 'primordialists' and 'instrumentalists'.

GEISS, IMMANUEL Professor of History at the University of Bremen, Immanuel Geiss is an expert on Germany and foreign policy. Among his books are *July 1914: The Outbreak of the First World War* (1967) and *German Foreign Policy, 1871–1914* (1976). He is also an authority on African and Black American culture and nationalism, on which his major work is *The PanAfrican Movement* (1974).

GLAZER, NATHAN Professor of Education and Social Structure at the University of Harvard, Nathan Glazer is one of the pioneers in the study of ethnicity in the United States. Together with Daniel Moynihan, he originated the long-running debate about the vitality and future of America's white ethnic communities. Among his many works are *Beyond the Melting Pot* (1963, with Daniel Moynihan), *Ethnicity; Theory and Experience* (1975, edited with Daniel Moynihan), and *Ethnic Dilemmas* (1983).

GROSBY, STEVEN Assistant Professor of Political Science at Villanova University, Steven Grosby is a noted expert on the history and sociology of ancient Israel, and an incisive analyst, in the tradition of Edward Shils and Clifford Geertz, of the fundamentals of ethnicity and nationality, on which he has published several major articles. He is also editor of *The Virtue of Civility: Selected Papers of Edward Shils on Liberalism, Tradition and Civility* (forthcoming).

HALL, STUART Professor of Sociology at the Open University, Stuart Hall is a leading exponent of the cultural analysis of race, ethnic, and class relations in the West. His influential works include *Policing the Crises: Mugging, the State and Law and Order* (1978, with others), the co-edited book *Culture, Media and Language* (1980), and the edited book *New Times* (1989).

HANF, THEODOR Professor of Sociology at the *Deutsche Institut für Internationale Pedagogische Forschung* at Frankfurt, Theodor Hanf specializes in the area of ethnic conflict and education. He has published several works, including *South Africa* (1981) and *Koexistenz im Krieg: Staatszerfall und Enstehung einer Nation im Libanon* (1990).

HARRISON, SELIG Senior Associate of the Carnegie Endowment for International Peace, Selig Harrison is a leading specialist of South Asian studies. He has served as the Senior Fellow in charge of Asian studies at the Brookings Institute and has written extensively on the ethnic problems in this area, including *India, the Most Dangerous Decades* (1960) and *In Afghanistan's Shadow: Baluch Nationalism and Soviet Temptations* (1981).

HECHTER, MICHAEL Professor of Sociology at the University of Arizona and Fellow of New College, Oxford, Michael Hechter is renowned for his influential theory of 'internal colonialism' (*Internal Colonialism*, 1975) which illuminated ethnic persistence and change in modern Western Europe. He has now become one of the leading exponents of the application of rational choice theory to society and ethnicity. His more recent work includes *Principles of Group Solidarity* (1987), *The Origins of Values* (1993, co-edited), and several important articles on individual strategies and ethnic solidarity.

HOBSBAWM, ERIC Emeritus Professor of History at Birkbeck College, University of London, Eric Hobsbawm is one of the most distinguished historians of nineteenth- and twentieth-century Europe. His many influential books include *Primitive Rebels* (1959), *The Age of Revolution* (1962), *The Age of Capital* (1975), *The Age of Empire* (1987), and *The Age of Extremes* (1994). In *The Invention of Tradition* (co-edited with Terence Ranger, 1983), Hobsbawm and his associates analysed the nation in terms of 'invented traditions' used to bind the newly enfranchised masses together, a theme which he elaborated in *Nations and Nationalism since 1780* (1990).

HOROWITZ, DONALD James B. Duke Professor of Law and Political Science at Duke University, Donald Horowitz is a distinguished political scientist, who has made a special study of ethnic politics in Africa and Asia. His authoritative books include *Coup Theories and Officers' Motives* (1980), *Ethnic Groups in Conflict* (1985), and *A Democratic South Africa? Constitutional Engineering in a Divided Society* (1991), as well as many important articles on ethnicity. His approach seeks a balance between the economic, political, and psychological factors at work in ethnic conflicts in Africa and Asia.

HUTCHINSON, JOHN Associate Professor in the Faculty of Humanities at Griffith University, John Hutchinson is a leading specialist in the study of modern European ethnicity and nationalism. His influential book *The Dynamics of Cultural Nationalism* (1987) demonstrates the importance of cultural nationalism as a separate type, and his more recent *Modern Nationalism* (1994) develops these issues in relation to recent projects of ethnic nationalism, fundamentalism, supra-nationalism, and multi-culturalism.

JAMES, WINSTON Formerly Director of Caribbean Studies at the University of North London, Winston James now teaches history at Columbia University. He is a leading specialist on Caribbean ethnicity and migration, and has written several influential works in this field, including *Holding Aloft the Banner of Ethiopia: Caribbean Radicalism in America, 1900–1932* (1996) and the co-edited book *Inside Babylon: The Caribbean Diaspora in Britain* (1993).

KALANTZIS, MARY Director of the Centre for Workplace, Communication and Culture, at the University of Technology, Sydney, Mary Kalantzis is a leading researcher on multi-culturalism in Australia, and has written several books, including *Cultures of Schooling: Pedagogies for Cultural Difference and Social Access* (1990).

KANDIYOTI, DENIZ Senior Lecturer in Social Sciences at Richmond College, Deniz Kandiyoti is a leading feminist scholar and researcher on issues of gender, religion, and ethnicity, notably in the Middle East. She is the author of *Women in Rural Production Systems: Problems and Policies*, and is the editor of *Women, Islam and the State* (1990).

KITROMILIDES, PASCHALIS Professor of Political Science at the University of Athens and Director of the Centre d'Études d'Asie Mineure, Paschalis Kitromilides is a leading specialist of Balkan ethnicity and nationalism. His works include *Small States in the Modern World* (1979), *Culture and Society in Contemporary Europe* (1981), and *The Enlightenment as Social Criticism: Iossipos Moisiodax and Greek Culture in the Eighteenth Century* (1992).

KREJČI, JAROSLAV Former Professor in the School of European Studies at Lancaster University and presently director of a research centre in Prague. He has written widely on problems of ethnicity in contemporary Europe and on socio-cultural diversity and change at large. His most influential works include *Ethnic and Political Nations in Europe* (1981, with Vítezslav Vělímský) and *Great Revolutions Compared* (1994).

KUPER, LEO Former Professor of Sociology and Director of the African Studies Centre at the University of California, Los Angeles (UCLA), Leo Kuper was a distinguished social analyst of genocide and of the politics of ethnically divided societies, notably in Africa. His major works include *Race, Class and Power* (1974), *The Pity of It All* (1977), and *Genocide* (1981). He also co-edited the pioneering work, *Pluralism in Africa* (1969, with M. G. Smith).

LANDAU, JACOB Professor of Political Science at the Hebrew University, Jerusalem, Jacob Landau is a leading scholar on ethnic politics and a specialist on ethnic and linguistic issues in the Middle East. His major works include *The Arabs in Israel: A Political Study* (1969), *Radical Politics in Modern Turkey* (1974), *Pan-Turkism in Turkey* (1981), and *The Politics of Pan-Islam: Ideology and Organisation* (1989).

LEHMANN, JEAN-PIERRE Former Director of the Centre of Japanese Studies at Stirling and Professor at the Euro-Asian Centre, INSEAD, Fontainebleau, Jean-Pierre Lehmann has specialized in the study of modern Japan. His main works include *The Image of Japan, 1850–1905: From Feudal Isolation to World Power* (1978) and *The Roots of Modern Japan* (1982).

MCDONALD, MARYON Lecturer in Social Anthropology at the University of Brunel, Maryon McDonald has specialized in the anthropology of ethnic and linguistic issues in modern Europe. Her major work is *'We are not French!' Language, Culture and Identity in Brittany* (1989), and she has co-edited the influential *History and Ethnicity* (1989).

MCGARRY, JOHN Associate Professor of Political Science at Kings College, London, Ontario, John McGarry has written widely on contemporary Irish Politics and ethnic conflict resolution, including *The Politics of Antagonism* (1993, co-authored with B. O'Leary) and *Explaining Northern Ireland* (co-authored with B. O'Leary). He has also edited (with B. O'Leary) *The Politics of Ethnic Conflict Regulation* (1993).

MCNEILL, WILLIAM H. Emeritus Professor of History at the University of Chicago, William McNeill is the leading world historian of his generation. He is a major innovator in the study of world-historical processes, making special investigations of military technology and the role of disease and demography in history. His most influential works include *The Rise of the West* (1963), *Europe's Steppe Frontier, 1500–1800* (1964), *Plagues and Peoples* (1976), *The Pursuit of Power* (1982), and *Polyethnicity and National Unity in World History* (1986).

MALLON, FLORENCIA Professor of History at the University of Wisconsin-Madison, Florencia Mallon is a leading specialist on the role of peasants and women in Latin America, and has written extensively on the role of subordinate groups in the transition to capitalism and in nation-state formation. Her major book is *Peasant and Nation: The Making of Postcolonial Mexico and Peru* (1995).

MELUCCI, ALBERTO Professor of Sociology at the University of Trento, and a practising psychotherapist in Milan, Alberto Melucci is a leading analyst of post-industrial society and its problems, and is the author of influential investigations of social and cultural networks, including such works as *Altri Codici* (1984) and *Corpi Estranei* (1988), as well as the pioneering *Nomads of the Present* (1989).

MORRISSEY, MICHAEL Associate Head of the Centre for Multi-cultural Studies at the University of Wollongong, Michael Morrissey has published extensively on the role of ethnicity and race in the labour process.

MOYNIHAN, DANIEL P. Former United Nations Ambassador and Professor of Education at Harvard University, Senator Daniel P. Moynihan is an influential scholar and policy-maker with a special interest in problems of ethnicity, notably in the United States. He co-authored *Beyond the Melting Pot* (1963) and co-edited *Ethnicity: Theory and Experience* (1975), both with Nathan Glazer; and has recently published his influential *Pandaemonium: Ethnicity in International Politics* (1993).

NASH, MANNING Professor of Anthropology at the University of Chicago, Manning Nash is a distinguished cultural anthropologist, whose many important books include *Machine Age Maya* (1958), *Unfinished Agenda: The Dynamics of Modernisation in Developing Nations* (1984), and *The Cauldron of Ethnicity in the Modern World* (1989).

O'LEARY, BRENDAN Professor of Political Science at the London School of Economics, O'Leary specializes in national and ethnic conflict-regulation, and is best known for his work on Northern Ireland. Major books include *The Asiatic Mode of Production* (1989), *Theories of the State* (1987, co-authored with P. Dunleavy), *The Politics of Antagonism* (1993, co-authored with John McGarry), *Northern Ireland: Sharing Authority* (1993), and *Explaining Northern Ireland* (1995, co-authored with John McGarry). He is presently writing a book on *National Self-Determination* for Oxford University Press.

POLIAKOV, LEON Former Maître de Recherche at the Centre de la Recherche Scientifique in Paris, Leon Poliakov was one of the leading authorities on the roots and history of anti-Semitism and the rise of racial and nationalist ideas in Europe. His detailed historical researches are embodied in such major works as *Diary of Hate* (1954), *The Aryan Myth* (1974), and his *magnum opus*, the four-volume *History of Anti-Semitism* (1957–85).

REX, JOHN Research Professor of Ethnic Relations at the University of Warwick, John Rex is a distinguished scholar of the social foundations of race and ethnic relations. He pioneered the application of social theory to the study of race relations with *Race Relations in Sociological Theory* (1970) and *Race, Colonialism and the City* (1974). He has subsequently extended his interests to problems of ethnicity and migration in Western Europe with works like *Race and Ethnicity* (1986) and *Ethnic Mobilisation in a Multicultural Europe* (1994, co-edited with B. Drury).

SCHERMERHORN, RICHARD Formerly Professor of Sociology at Case Western University, Richard Schermerhorn was one of the pioneers of the study of ethnic relations, particularly in the United States. He is the author of such major works as *These Our People, Minorities in American Culture* (1949), *Comparative Ethnic Relations* (1970), and *Ethnic Plurality in India* (1978).

SMITH, ANTHONY D. Professor of Sociology at the London School of Economics, Anthony Smith has specialized in the study of ethnicity and nationalism, notably the ethnic origins of nations. He has published well-known studies in the field, including *Theories of Nationalism* (1971/83), *Nationalism in the Twentieth Century* (1979), *The Ethnic Revival* (1981), *State and Nation in the Third World* (1983), *The Ethnic Origins of Nations* (1986), *National Identity* (1991), and *Nations and Nationalism in a Global Era* (1995).

SMITH, M. G. Professor of Anthropology at Yale University, Michael Smith is a distinguished scholar of race and ethnic relations, and one of the pioneers of the concept of the plural society. His work on West Indian and African societies has proved highly influential; his major works include *The Plural Society in the British West Indies* (1965), *Pluralism in Africa* (1969, co-edited with Leo Kuper), *Corporations and Society* (1974), and *Culture, Race and Class in the Commonwealth Caribbean* (1984).

SMOOHA, SAMMY Professor of Sociology in the University of Haifa, Sammy Smooha is a leading specialist in the study of ethnic problems in the Middle East and has made a distinguished contribution to the understanding of ethnic politics. Among his major publications are *Israel: Pluralism and Conflict* (1978) and *Arabs and Jews in Israel* (1989), as well as several important articles on issues of ethnic democracy.

STONE, JOHN Professor of Sociology at George Mason University, John Stone is an internationally respected scholar of race relations and a specialist on ethnic migration. His major works include *Colonist or Uitlander?* (1973), *Race, Ethnicity and Social Change* (1977, edited) and *Racial Conflict in Contemporary Society* (1985). For many years he was chief editor of the leading specialist journal *Ethnic and Racial Studies*, which he founded in 1978.

TARAS, RAY Professor in Political Science at Tulane University, New Orleans, Ray Taras has written widely on the former Soviet Union, including *Ideology in a Socialist State* (1984) and *The Road to Disillusion: From Critical Marxism to Post-Communism in Eastern Europe* (1992); as well as *Nations and Politics in the Soviet Successor States* (1993, co-edited with I. Bremmer).

TIBI, BASSAM Professor of Political Science at the University of Göttingen, Bassam Tibi is a leading scholar of Islam and nationalism in the Middle East and the author of numerous works, including *Arab Nationalism: A Critical Inquiry* (2nd edn., 1990), *The Crisis of Modern Islam* (1988), and *Conflict and War in the Middle East, 1967–1991* (1993).

TONKIN, ELISABETH Professor of Social Anthropology at the Queen's University, Belfast, Elisabeth Tonkin is the co-editor of the pioneering anthropological work

History and Ethnicity (1989), and author of *Narrating Our Pasts: The Social Construction of Oral History* (1992/5).

VAIL, LEROY Associate Professor of History at Harvard University, and Director of its Programme of South African studies, LeRoy Vail has written widely on the history, literature, and linguistics of East-Central Africa. With Landeg White he has written *Colonialism and Capitalism in Mozambique* (1981) and subsequently worked on the political role of African songs and poetry.

VAN DEN BERGHE, PIERRE Professor of Sociology at the University of Washington, Seattle, Pierre van den Berghe is a distinguished scholar of race and ethnicity and is well-known for his pioneering studies of race relations, notably *South Africa* (1965) and *Race and Racism* (1967). In the 1970s he embraced a sociobiological framework and published his major controversial exposition, *The Ethnic Phenomenon* (1979), claiming that ethnic and racial sentiments are extensions of kinship, and reflect the biology of nepotism.

VĚLÍMSKÝ, VÍTEZSLAV Vítězslav Vělímský works with an International Agency in Brussels and is the co-author (with Jaroslav Krejči) of *Ethnic and Political Nations* (1981).

WIBERG, HAKAN Professor of Sociology at Lund University and former Director of the Department of Peace and Conflict Research, Hakan Wiberg is the author of books on conflict theory and peace research, the Horn of Africa, and armament and security issues, including *Peace Research for the 1990s* (1993, co-edited with J. Balazs).

WEBER, MAX One of the founders of sociology, Max Weber is renowned for his breadth of scholarship and erudition. Throughout his work, Weber sought to combine an 'interpretive method' with a strong commitment to causal analysis and value neutrality. In *Economy and Society* he emphasized the role of cultural and political factors in shaping ethnic groups and nations, locating them within the wider context of his comparative research into the religious and economic origins of Western and other civilizations. Though he never wrote the promised book on the formation of national states, Weber adopted a 'political' approach to ethnicity that has proved highly influential.

YOSHINO, KOSAKU Associate Professor of Sociology at Tokyo University, Kosaku Yoshino is an expert on cultural nationalism and Japanese sociology. His major work is *Cultural Nationalism in Contemporary Japan: A Sociological Enquiry* (1992), which develops an anthropological approach to the consumption of nationalism. He has also published pioneering articles on globalization, ethnicity and the 'cross-cultural industry'.

ZENNER, WALTER Professor of Anthropology at the State University of New York at Albany, Walter Zenner has written extensively on trading 'middlemen' minorities and on the Jewish diaspora, notably in his major work, *Minorities in the Middle* (1991). He is the editor of *Persistence and Flexibility: Anthropological Perspectives on the American Jewish Experience* (1988) and *Urban Life: Readings in Urban Anthropology* (1996, co-edited with G. Gmelch), and *Jews among Muslims* (forthcoming, co-edited with S. Deshen).

Acknowledgements

Armstrong, John, *Nations before Nationalism* (Copyright © 1982 by the University of North Carolina Press. Used by permission of the publisher).

Balibar, Etienne, 'The Nation Form', in Etienne Balibar and Immanuel Wallerstein, *Race, Nation, Class* (Verso, London, 1991, Copyright © Editions la Découverte, Paris).

Banton, Michael, 'Modelling Ethnic and National Relations', *Ethnic and Racial Studies*, 17: 1 (Routledge, London, 1994).

Barth, Fredrik, *Ethnic Groups and Boundaries* (Little, Brown, and Co, Boston, Mass., 1969).

Bartlett, Robert, *The Making of Europe* (Penguin Books, Harmondsworth, 1994).

Bell, Daniel, 'Ethnicity and Social Change' in Nathan Glazer and Daniel P. Moynihan (eds.), *Ethnicity: Theory and Experience* (Harvard University Press, Cambridge, Mass., Copyright © 1975 by the President and Fellows of Harvard College).

Brass, Paul, *Ethnicity and Nationalism* (Copyright © 1991 Paul Brass, Sage Publications India Private Limited, New Delhi, 1991).

—— 'Introduction: The Politics of India since Independence', in *New Cambridge History of India*, iv. 1 (reprinted by permission of the author, Cambridge University Press, Cambridge, 1990).

Breton, Harry, 'From Ethnic to Civic Nationalism', *Ethnic and Racial Studies*, 11: 1 (Routledge, London, 1988).

Brown, David, *The State and Ethnic Politics in Southeast Asia* (Routledge, London, 1994).

Brubaker, Rogers, *Citizenship and Nationhood* (Harvard University Press, Cambridge, Mass., Copyright © 1992 by the President and Fellows of Harvard College).

Castles, Stephen, *et al.*, *Mistaken Identity* (Pluto Press, Sydney, 1992).

Cohen, Abner, *Custom and Politics in Urban Africa: A Study of Hausa Migrants in Yoruba Towns*, pp. 198–201 (Copyright © 1969 Abner Cohen, University of California Press, Berkeley, 1969).

Connor, Walker, *Ethno-nationalism: The Quest for Understanding* (Copyright © 1994 by Princeton University Press. Reprinted by permission of Princeton University Press).

Dikotter, Frank, 'Group Definition and the idea of Race in Modern China', *Ethnic and Racial Studies*, 13: 3 (Routledge, London, 1990).

Edwards, John, *Language, Society and Identity* (Blackwell Publishers, Oxford, 1993).

Eller, Jack and Coughlan, Reed, 'The Poverty of Primordialism: The Demystification of Ethnic Attachments', *Ethnic and Racial Studies*, 16: 2 (Routledge, London, 1993).

Enloe, Cynthia, 'Religion and Ethnicity', in P. Sugar (ed.), *Ethnic Diversity and Conflict in Eastern Europe* (ABC-CLIO, Santa Barbara, California, 1980).

—— *Ethnic Soldiers* (Penguin Books, Harmondsworth, 1980).

Eriksen, Thomas, *Ethnicity and Nationalism* (Pluto Press, London, 1993).

Esman, Milton, 'Diasporas and International Relations', in Gabi Sheffer (ed.), *Modern Diasporas in International Politics* (Croom Helm, London and Sydney, 1986).

FEIN, HELEN, *Genocide, A Sociological Perspective* (Sage Publications, London, 1993).

FINLEY, MOSES, *The Use and Abuse of Ancient History* (Hogarth Press, London, 1986, © Random House UK Ltd., London and Viking Publishers, New York).

FISHMAN, JOSHUA, 'Social Theory and Ethnography', in Peter Sugar (ed.), *Ethnic Diversity and Conflict in Eastern Europe* (ABC-CLIO, Santa Barbara, California 1980).

GANS, HERBERT, 'Symbolic Ethnicity: The Future of Ethnic Groups and cultures in America', *Ethnic and Racial Studies*, 2: 1 (Routledge, London, 1979).

GEERTZ, CLIFFORD, 'The Integrative Revolution', in C. Geertz (ed.), *Old Societies and New States* (Free Press, New York, 1963).

GEISS, IMMANUEL, *The Pan African Movement* (Methuen, London, 1974).

GLAZER, NATHAN and MOYNIHAN, DANIEL P. (eds.), *Beyond the Melting Pot* (The MIT Press, Cambridge, Mass., 1963).

GROSBY, STEVEN, 'The Verdict of History: The Inexpungeable Tie of Primordiality—A Response to Eller and Coughlan', *Ethnic and Racial Studies*, 17: 2 (Routledge, London, 1994).

HALL, STUART, 'The new ethnicities', in J. Donald and A. Rattansi (eds.), *Race, Culture and Difference* (Copyright © 1992 by permission of Sage Publications Ltd., London).

HARRISON, SELIG, 'Ethnicity and Political Stalemate', in Ali Banuazizi and Myron Weiner (eds.), *The State, Religion and Ethnic Politics: Afghanistan, Iran and Pakistan* (Syracuse University Press, New York, 1986).

HECHTER, MICHAEL, 'A Rational Choice Approach to Race and Ethnic Relations', in D. Mason and J. Rex (eds.), *Theories of Race and Ethnic Relations* (reprinted by permission of the author, Cambridge University Press, Cambridge, 1986).

HOESBAWM, ERIC, *Nations and Nationalism since 1780* (reprinted by permission of the author, Cambridge University Press, Cambridge, 1990).

HOROWITZ, DONALD, *Ethnic Groups in Conflict* (Copyright © 1985 The Regents of the University of California, University of California Press, Berkeley and Los Angeles, 1985).

HUTCHINSON, JOHN, *Modern Nationalism* (Fontana Press, London, 1994, © Harper Collins Publishers Limited).

JAMES, WINSTON, 'The Making of Black Identities', in Raphael Samuel, *Patriotism: The Making and Unmaking of British National Identity*, ii (Routledge, London, 1989).

KREJCI, YAROSLAV and VELIMSKY, VITESLAV, *Ethnic and Political Nations* (Croom Helm, London, 1981).

KUPER, LEO, *Genocide* (Penguin Books, Harmondsworth, 1981).

LANDAU, JACOB, 'Diaspora and Language' in G. Sheffer (ed.), *Modern Diasporas in International Politics* (Croom Helm, London, 1986).

LEHMANN, JEAN-PIERRE, *The Roots of Modern Japan* (Macmillan Press Ltd., London, 1982. Reprinted by permission of the Peters Fraser & Dunlop Group Ltd., London).

MCGARRY, JOHN and O'LEARY, BRENDAN, *The Politics of Ethnic Antagonism* (Routledge, London, 1993).

MCNEILL, WILLIAM H., *Polyethnicity and National Unity in World History* (University of Toronto Press Incorporated, Toronto, 1986).

MALLON, FLORENCIA, 'Indian Communities, Political Cultures and the State in Latin America, 1780–1990', *Journal of Latin American Studies*, 24 (reprinted by permission of the author, Cambridge University Press, Cambridge, 1992).

MELUCCI, ALBERTO, *Nomads of the Present* (Hutchinson, London, 1989, © Random House UK Ltd.).

NASH, MANNING, *The Cauldron of Ethnicity in the Modern World* (University of Chicago Press, Chicago and London, 1989).

PASCHALIS, KITROMEDES, 'Imagined Communities and the Origins of the National Question in the Balkans', *European History Quarterly*, 19: 2 (Sage Publications Ltd., London, 1989).

POLIAKOV, LEON, *The Aryan Myth* (Basic Books, New York, 1974).

REX, JOHN, 'Multiculturalism in Europe and America', *Nations and Nationalism*, 1: 2 (reprinted by permission of the author, Cambridge University Press, Cambridge, 1995).

SCHERMERHORN, RICHARD, *Comparative Ethnic Relations* (Random House Inc., New York, 1970).

SMITH, ANTHONY D., 'Chosen Peoples: Why Ethnic Groups Survive', *Ethnic and Racial Studies*, 15: 3 (Routledge, London, 1992).

SMITH, M. G., 'Institutional and Political Conditions of Pluralism', in Leo Kuper and M. G. Smith (eds.), *Pluralism in Africa* (Copyright © 1986 M. G. Smith, the University of California Press, Los Angeles, California, 1969).

SMOOHA, SAMMY and HANF, THEODOR, 'The Diverse Modes of Conflict-Regulation in Deeply Divided Societies', in A. D. Smith (ed.), *Ethnicity and Nationalism* (E. J. Brill, Leiden and New York, 1992).

STONE, JOHN, 'Internal Colonalism', *Ethnic and Racial Studies*, 2: 2 (Routledge, London, 1979).

TARAS, RAY, 'Conclusion: Making Sense of Matrioshka Nationalism', in Ian Bremmer and Ray Taras (eds.), *Nations and Politics in the Soviet Successor States* (reprinted by permission of the author, Cambridge University Press, Cambridge, 1993).

TIBI, BASSAM, 'The Simultaneity of the Unsimultaneous: Old Tribes and Imposed Nation-States in the Modern Middle East', in Philip Khoury and Joseph Kostiner (eds.), *Tribes and State Formation in the Middle East*, pp. 137–43 (Copyright © 1991 The Regents of the University of California, 1991).

TONKIN, ELISABETH, MACDONALD, MARYON, and CHAPMAN, MALCOLM (eds.), *History and Ethnicity* (Routledge, London, 1989).

VAIL, LEROY (ed.), *Creation of Tribalism in Southern Africa* (Copyright © 1988 LeRoy Vail, the University of California Press, Berkeley, California, 1993).

VAN DEN BERGHE, PIERRE, 'Does Race Matter?', *Nations and Nationalism*, 1: 3 (reprinted by permission of the author, Cambridge University Press, Cambridge, 1995).

WEBER, MAX, *Economy and Society* (2 vols.), translated/edited by Günther Roth and Claus Wittich, from vol. i, pp. 389–95 (Copyright © 1978 The Regents of the University of California, the University of California Press, Berkeley, California, 1978).

WIBERG, HAKAN, 'Self-determination as an international issue', in Ioann Lewis (ed.), *Nationalism and Self-determination in the Horn of Africa* (Ithaca Press [Garnet Publishing], London 1983).

YOSHINO, KOSAKU, *Cultural Nationalism in Contemporary Japan* (Routledge, London, 1992).

ZENNER, WALTER, *Minorities in the Middle* (reprinted by permission of the State University of New York Press, Albany, New York, 1991).

Index